# 50% OFF
## Online ParaPro Prep Course!

By Mometrix

Dear Customer,

We consider it an honor and a privilege that you chose our ParaPro Study Guide. As a way of showing our appreciation and to help us better serve you, we are offering **50% off our online ParaPro Assessment Course.** Many ParaPro courses are needlessly expensive and don't deliver enough value. With our course, you get access to the best ParaPro prep material at **half price.**

**We have structured our online course to perfectly complement your printed study guide.** The ParaPro Online Course contains **in-depth lessons** that cover all the most important topics, **200+ video reviews** that explain difficult concepts, over **350 practice questions** to ensure you feel prepared, and more than **650 digital flashcards**, so you can study while you're on the go.

### *Online ParaPro Prep Course*

**Topics Covered:**

- Reading
  - Theme and Plot
  - Elements of a Text
  - Main Idea and Supporting Details
- Writing
  - Foundations of Grammar
  - Structure and Purpose of a Sentence
  - Style and Form
- Mathematics
  - Numbers and Operations
  - Statistical Analysis
  - Systems of Equations

**Course Features:**

- ParaPro Study Guide
  - Get content that complements our best-selling study guide.
- Full-Length Practice Tests
  - With over 350 practice questions, you can test yourself again and again.
- Mobile Friendly
  - If you need to study on the go, the course is easily accessible from your mobile device.
- ParaPro Flashcards
  - Our course includes a flashcards mode with over 650 content cards for you to study.

To receive this discount, visit our website at mometrix.com/university/parapro or simply scan this QR code with your smartphone. At the checkout page, enter the discount code: **para50off**

If you have any questions or concerns, please contact us at support@mometrix.com.

Sincerely,

# **FREE** Study Skills Videos/DVD Offer

Dear Customer,

Thank you for your purchase from Mometrix! We consider it an honor and a privilege that you have purchased our product and we want to ensure your satisfaction.

As part of our ongoing effort to meet the needs of test takers, we have developed a set of Study Skills Videos that we would like to give you for <u>FREE</u>. These videos cover our *best practices* for getting ready for your exam, from how to use our study materials to how to best prepare for the day of the test.

All that we ask is that you email us with feedback that would describe your experience so far with our product. Good, bad, or indifferent, we want to know what you think!

To get your FREE Study Skills Videos, you can use the **QR code** below, or send us an **email** at <u>studyvideos@mometrix.com</u> with *FREE VIDEOS* in the subject line and the following information in the body of the email:

- The name of the product you purchased.
- Your product rating on a scale of 1-5, with 5 being the highest rating.
- Your feedback. It can be long, short, or anything in between. We just want to know your impressions and experience so far with our product. (Good feedback might include how our study material met your needs and ways we might be able to make it even better. You could highlight features that you found helpful or features that you think we should add.)

If you have any questions or concerns, please don't hesitate to contact me directly.

Thanks again!

Sincerely,

Jay Willis
Vice President
<u>jay.willis@mometrix.com</u>
1-800-673-8175

# ParaProfessional Study Guide 2023-2024

# 3 Full-Length Practice Tests

**ParaPro Assessment Secrets Test Prep with Step-by-Step Video Tutorials**

Copyright © 2022 by Mometrix Media LLC

All rights reserved. This product, or parts thereof, may not be reproduced, stored in a retrieval system, or transmitted in any form or by any means—electronic, mechanical, photocopy, recording, scanning, or other—except for brief quotations in critical reviews or articles, without the prior written permission of the publisher.

Written and edited by the Mometrix Teacher Certification Test Team

Printed in the United States of America

This paper meets the requirements of ANSI/NISO Z39.48-1992 (Permanence of Paper).

Mometrix offers volume discount pricing to institutions. For more information or a price quote, please contact our sales department at sales@mometrix.com or 888-248-1219.

Mometrix Media LLC is not affiliated with or endorsed by any official testing organization. All organizational and test names are trademarks of their respective owners.

Paperback
ISBN 13: 978-1-5167-2148-1
ISBN 10: 1-5167-2148-9

# DEAR FUTURE EXAM SUCCESS STORY

First of all, **THANK YOU** for purchasing Mometrix study materials!

Second, congratulations! You are one of the few determined test-takers who are committed to doing whatever it takes to excel on your exam. **You have come to the right place.** We developed these study materials with one goal in mind: to deliver you the information you need in a format that's concise and easy to use.

In addition to optimizing your guide for the content of the test, we've outlined our recommended steps for breaking down the preparation process into small, attainable goals so you can make sure you stay on track.

We've also analyzed the entire test-taking process, identifying the most common pitfalls and showing how you can overcome them and be ready for any curveball the test throws you.

Standardized testing is one of the biggest obstacles on your road to success, which only increases the importance of doing well in the high-pressure, high-stakes environment of test day. Your results on this test could have a significant impact on your future, and this guide provides the information and practical advice to help you achieve your full potential on test day.

### Your success is our success

**We would love to hear from you!** If you would like to share the story of your exam success or if you have any questions or comments in regard to our products, please contact us at **800-673-8175** or **support@mometrix.com**.

Thanks again for your business and we wish you continued success!

Sincerely,
The Mometrix Test Preparation Team

> **Need more help? Check out our flashcards at:**
> **http://MometrixFlashcards.com/ParaPro**

# TABLE OF CONTENTS

INTRODUCTION _____ 1

SECRET KEY #1 – PLAN BIG, STUDY SMALL _____ 2

SECRET KEY #2 – MAKE YOUR STUDYING COUNT _____ 3

SECRET KEY #3 – PRACTICE THE RIGHT WAY _____ 4

SECRET KEY #4 – PACE YOURSELF _____ 6

SECRET KEY #5 – HAVE A PLAN FOR GUESSING _____ 7

TEST-TAKING STRATEGIES _____ 10

READING _____ 15
  INFORMATIONAL TEXTS _____ 15
  PERSUASIVE TECHNIQUES _____ 21
  ARGUMENTS AND LOGICAL ERRORS _____ 27
  VOCABULARY AND WORD RELATIONSHIPS _____ 31
  FIGURATIVE LANGUAGE _____ 43
  READING COMPREHENSION _____ 48
  MAKING PREDICTIONS AND INFERENCES _____ 53
  INTERACTIONS WITH TEXTS _____ 57

WRITING _____ 62
  PARTS OF SPEECH _____ 62
  AGREEMENT AND SENTENCE STRUCTURE _____ 72
  PUNCTUATION _____ 93
  COMMON USAGE MISTAKES _____ 101
  THE WRITING PROCESS _____ 106
  OUTLINING AND ORGANIZING IDEAS _____ 109
  WRITING STYLE AND FORM _____ 117
  MODES OF WRITING _____ 122
  RESEARCH WRITING _____ 128
  INFORMATION SOURCES _____ 133

MATHEMATICS _____ 139
  NUMBERS _____ 139
  OPERATIONS _____ 143
  FACTORING _____ 149
  RATIONAL NUMBERS _____ 150
  PROPORTIONS AND RATIOS _____ 163
  EXPRESSIONS _____ 168
  EQUATIONS _____ 169
  BASIC FUNCTIONS _____ 177
  MEASUREMENT PRINCIPLES _____ 185
  UNITS OF MEASUREMENT _____ 188
  LINES AND PLANES _____ 192
  ANGLES _____ 194

TRANSFORMATIONS_____197
TWO-DIMENSIONAL SHAPES _____200
THREE-DIMENSIONAL SHAPES _____212
TRIANGLE CLASSIFICATION AND PROPERTIES _____217
DISPLAYING INFORMATION _____222
COLLEGE STATISTICS_____228

**CLASSROOM INSTRUCTION**_____**241**
DEVELOPMENTAL LITERACY _____241
PLANNING DEVELOPMENTALLY APPROPRIATE INSTRUCTION AND ASSESSMENT_____251
STUDENT DIVERSITY AND EQUITY _____259
MATERIALS AND RESOURCES _____265
CLASSROOM MANAGEMENT, ROUTINES, AND PROCEDURES_____268
BEHAVIOR MANAGEMENT _____279
INSTRUCTIONAL TECHNIQUES_____284
ASSESSMENT METHODOLOGY _____293
EFFECTIVE FEEDBACK AND RESPONSIVE TEACHING _____301
PROFESSIONAL INTERACTION AND COLLABORATION_____308
LEGAL AND ETHICAL ROLES AND RESPONSIBILITIES _____318

**PARAPROFESSIONAL PRACTICE TEST #1**_____**325**
READING _____325
MATHEMATICS _____334
WRITING _____340

**ANSWER KEY AND EXPLANATIONS** _____**347**
READING _____347
MATHEMATICS _____350
WRITING _____352

**PARAPROFESSIONAL PRACTICE TEST #2**_____**355**
READING _____355
MATHEMATICS _____364
WRITING _____370

**ANSWER KEY AND EXPLANATIONS** _____**376**
READING _____376
MATHEMATICS _____379
WRITING _____383

**PARAPROFESSIONAL PRACTICE TEST #3**_____**386**
READING _____386
MATHEMATICS _____395
WRITING _____401

**ANSWER KEY AND EXPLANATIONS** _____**406**
READING _____406
MATHEMATICS _____409
WRITING _____412

**HOW TO OVERCOME TEST ANXIETY** _____**415**
CAUSES OF TEST ANXIETY _____415
ELEMENTS OF TEST ANXIETY _____416

EFFECTS OF TEST ANXIETY _____ 416
PHYSICAL STEPS FOR BEATING TEST ANXIETY _____ 417
MENTAL STEPS FOR BEATING TEST ANXIETY _____ 418
STUDY STRATEGY _____ 419
TEST TIPS _____ 421
IMPORTANT QUALIFICATION _____ 422

**HOW TO OVERCOME YOUR FEAR OF MATH** _____ **423**
WHAT IS MATH ANXIETY? _____ 423
DEBUNKING MATH MYTHS _____ 426
TIPS AND STRATEGIES FOR OVERCOMING MATH ANXIETY _____ 427
REMEMBER, YOU CAN DO THIS! _____ 429

**TELL US YOUR STORY** _____ **430**

**ADDITIONAL BONUS MATERIAL** _____ **431**

# Introduction

**Thank you for purchasing this resource**! You have made the choice to prepare yourself for a test that could have a huge impact on your future, and this guide is designed to help you be fully ready for test day. Obviously, it's important to have a solid understanding of the test material, but you also need to be prepared for the unique environment and stressors of the test, so that you can perform to the best of your abilities.

For this purpose, the first section that appears in this guide is the **Secret Keys**. We've devoted countless hours to meticulously researching what works and what doesn't, and we've boiled down our findings to the five most impactful steps you can take to improve your performance on the test. We start at the beginning with study planning and move through the preparation process, all the way to the testing strategies that will help you get the most out of what you know when you're finally sitting in front of the test.

We recommend that you start preparing for your test as far in advance as possible. However, if you've bought this guide as a last-minute study resource and only have a few days before your test, we recommend that you skip over the first two Secret Keys since they address a long-term study plan.

If you struggle with **test anxiety**, we strongly encourage you to check out our recommendations for how you can overcome it. Test anxiety is a formidable foe, but it can be beaten, and we want to make sure you have the tools you need to defeat it.

Copyright © Mometrix Media. You have been licensed one copy of this document for personal use only. Any other reproduction or redistribution is strictly prohibited. All rights reserved. This content is provided for test preparation purposes only and does not imply an endorsement by Mometrix of any particular political, scientific, or religious point of view.

# Secret Key #1 – Plan Big, Study Small

There's a lot riding on your performance. If you want to ace this test, you're going to need to keep your skills sharp and the material fresh in your mind. You need a plan that lets you review everything you need to know while still fitting in your schedule. We'll break this strategy down into three categories.

## Information Organization

Start with the information you already have: the official test outline. From this, you can make a complete list of all the concepts you need to cover before the test. Organize these concepts into groups that can be studied together, and create a list of any related vocabulary you need to learn so you can brush up on any difficult terms. You'll want to keep this vocabulary list handy once you actually start studying since you may need to add to it along the way.

## Time Management

Once you have your set of study concepts, decide how to spread them out over the time you have left before the test. Break your study plan into small, clear goals so you have a manageable task for each day and know exactly what you're doing. Then just focus on one small step at a time. When you manage your time this way, you don't need to spend hours at a time studying. Studying a small block of content for a short period each day helps you retain information better and avoid stressing over how much you have left to do. You can relax knowing that you have a plan to cover everything in time. In order for this strategy to be effective though, you have to start studying early and stick to your schedule. Avoid the exhaustion and futility that comes from last-minute cramming!

## Study Environment

The environment you study in has a big impact on your learning. Studying in a coffee shop, while probably more enjoyable, is not likely to be as fruitful as studying in a quiet room. It's important to keep distractions to a minimum. You're only planning to study for a short block of time, so make the most of it. Don't pause to check your phone or get up to find a snack. It's also important to **avoid multitasking**. Research has consistently shown that multitasking will make your studying dramatically less effective. Your study area should also be comfortable and well-lit so you don't have the distraction of straining your eyes or sitting on an uncomfortable chair.

 The time of day you study is also important. You want to be rested and alert. Don't wait until just before bedtime. Study when you'll be most likely to comprehend and remember. Even better, if you know what time of day your test will be, set that time aside for study. That way your brain will be used to working on that subject at that specific time and you'll have a better chance of recalling information.

Finally, it can be helpful to team up with others who are studying for the same test. Your actual studying should be done in as isolated an environment as possible, but the work of organizing the information and setting up the study plan can be divided up. In between study sessions, you can discuss with your teammates the concepts that you're all studying and quiz each other on the details. Just be sure that your teammates are as serious about the test as you are. If you find that your study time is being replaced with social time, you might need to find a new team.

Copyright © Mometrix Media. You have been licensed one copy of this document for personal use only. Any other reproduction or redistribution is strictly prohibited. All rights reserved. This content is provided for test preparation purposes only and does not imply an endorsement by Mometrix of any particular political, scientific, or religious point of view.

# Secret Key #2 – Make Your Studying Count

You're devoting a lot of time and effort to preparing for this test, so you want to be absolutely certain it will pay off. This means doing more than just reading the content and hoping you can remember it on test day. It's important to make every minute of study count. There are two main areas you can focus on to make your studying count.

## Retention

It doesn't matter how much time you study if you can't remember the material. You need to make sure you are retaining the concepts. To check your retention of the information you're learning, try recalling it at later times with minimal prompting. Try carrying around flashcards and glance at one or two from time to time or ask a friend who's also studying for the test to quiz you.

To enhance your retention, look for ways to put the information into practice so that you can apply it rather than simply recalling it. If you're using the information in practical ways, it will be much easier to remember. Similarly, it helps to solidify a concept in your mind if you're not only reading it to yourself but also explaining it to someone else. Ask a friend to let you teach them about a concept you're a little shaky on (or speak aloud to an imaginary audience if necessary). As you try to summarize, define, give examples, and answer your friend's questions, you'll understand the concepts better and they will stay with you longer. Finally, step back for a big picture view and ask yourself how each piece of information fits with the whole subject. When you link the different concepts together and see them working together as a whole, it's easier to remember the individual components.

Finally, practice showing your work on any multi-step problems, even if you're just studying. Writing out each step you take to solve a problem will help solidify the process in your mind, and you'll be more likely to remember it during the test.

## Modality

*Modality* simply refers to the means or method by which you study. Choosing a study modality that fits your own individual learning style is crucial. No two people learn best in exactly the same way, so it's important to know your strengths and use them to your advantage.

For example, if you learn best by visualization, focus on visualizing a concept in your mind and draw an image or a diagram. Try color-coding your notes, illustrating them, or creating symbols that will trigger your mind to recall a learned concept. If you learn best by hearing or discussing information, find a study partner who learns the same way or read aloud to yourself. Think about how to put the information in your own words. Imagine that you are giving a lecture on the topic and record yourself so you can listen to it later.

For any learning style, flashcards can be helpful. Organize the information so you can take advantage of spare moments to review. Underline key words or phrases. Use different colors for different categories. Mnemonic devices (such as creating a short list in which every item starts with the same letter) can also help with retention. Find what works best for you and use it to store the information in your mind most effectively and easily.

3

Copyright © Mometrix Media. You have been licensed one copy of this document for personal use only. Any other reproduction or redistribution is strictly prohibited. All rights reserved.
This content is provided for test preparation purposes only and does not imply an endorsement by Mometrix of any particular political, scientific, or religious point of view.

# Secret Key #3 – Practice the Right Way

Your success on test day depends not only on how many hours you put into preparing, but also on whether you prepared the right way. It's good to check along the way to see if your studying is paying off. One of the most effective ways to do this is by taking practice tests to evaluate your progress. Practice tests are useful because they show exactly where you need to improve. Every time you take a practice test, pay special attention to these three groups of questions:

- The questions you got wrong
- The questions you had to guess on, even if you guessed right
- The questions you found difficult or slow to work through

This will show you exactly what your weak areas are, and where you need to devote more study time. Ask yourself why each of these questions gave you trouble. Was it because you didn't understand the material? Was it because you didn't remember the vocabulary? Do you need more repetitions on this type of question to build speed and confidence? Dig into those questions and figure out how you can strengthen your weak areas as you go back to review the material.

 Additionally, many practice tests have a section explaining the answer choices. It can be tempting to read the explanation and think that you now have a good understanding of the concept. However, an explanation likely only covers part of the question's broader context. Even if the explanation makes perfect sense, **go back and investigate** every concept related to the question until you're positive you have a thorough understanding.

As you go along, keep in mind that the practice test is just that: practice. Memorizing these questions and answers will not be very helpful on the actual test because it is unlikely to have any of the same exact questions. If you only know the right answers to the sample questions, you won't be prepared for the real thing. **Study the concepts** until you understand them fully, and then you'll be able to answer any question that shows up on the test.

It's important to wait on the practice tests until you're ready. If you take a test on your first day of study, you may be overwhelmed by the amount of material covered and how much you need to learn. Work up to it gradually.

On test day, you'll need to be prepared for answering questions, managing your time, and using the test-taking strategies you've learned. It's a lot to balance, like a mental marathon that will have a big impact on your future. Like training for a marathon, you'll need to start slowly and work your way up. When test day arrives, you'll be ready.

Start with the strategies you've read in the first two Secret Keys—plan your course and study in the way that works best for you. If you have time, consider using multiple study resources to get different approaches to the same concepts. It can be helpful to see difficult concepts from more than one angle. Then find a good source for practice tests. Many times, the test website will suggest potential study resources or provide sample tests.

Copyright © Mometrix Media. You have been licensed one copy of this document for personal use only. Any other reproduction or redistribution is strictly prohibited. All rights reserved. This content is provided for test preparation purposes only and does not imply an endorsement by Mometrix of any particular political, scientific, or religious point of view.

# Practice Test Strategy

If you're able to find at least three practice tests, we recommend this strategy:

## UNTIMED AND OPEN-BOOK PRACTICE

Take the first test with no time constraints and with your notes and study guide handy. Take your time and focus on applying the strategies you've learned.

## TIMED AND OPEN-BOOK PRACTICE

Take the second practice test open-book as well, but set a timer and practice pacing yourself to finish in time.

## TIMED AND CLOSED-BOOK PRACTICE

Take any other practice tests as if it were test day. Set a timer and put away your study materials. Sit at a table or desk in a quiet room, imagine yourself at the testing center, and answer questions as quickly and accurately as possible.

Keep repeating timed and closed-book tests on a regular basis until you run out of practice tests or it's time for the actual test. Your mind will be ready for the schedule and stress of test day, and you'll be able to focus on recalling the material you've learned.

Copyright © Mometrix Media. You have been licensed one copy of this document for personal use only. Any other reproduction or redistribution is strictly prohibited. All rights reserved. This content is provided for test preparation purposes only and does not imply an endorsement by Mometrix of any particular political, scientific, or religious point of view.

# Secret Key #4 – Pace Yourself

Once you're fully prepared for the material on the test, your biggest challenge on test day will be managing your time. Just knowing that the clock is ticking can make you panic even if you have plenty of time left. Work on pacing yourself so you can build confidence against the time constraints of the exam. Pacing is a difficult skill to master, especially in a high-pressure environment, so **practice is vital**.

Set time expectations for your pace based on how much time is available. For example, if a section has 60 questions and the time limit is 30 minutes, you know you have to average 30 seconds or less per question in order to answer them all. Although 30 seconds is the hard limit, set 25 seconds per question as your goal, so you reserve extra time to spend on harder questions. When you budget extra time for the harder questions, you no longer have any reason to stress when those questions take longer to answer.

Don't let this time expectation distract you from working through the test at a calm, steady pace, but keep it in mind so you don't spend too much time on any one question. Recognize that taking extra time on one question you don't understand may keep you from answering two that you do understand later in the test. If your time limit for a question is up and you're still not sure of the answer, mark it and move on, and come back to it later if the time and the test format allow. If the testing format doesn't allow you to return to earlier questions, just make an educated guess; then put it out of your mind and move on.

On the easier questions, be careful not to rush. It may seem wise to hurry through them so you have more time for the challenging ones, but it's not worth missing one if you know the concept and just didn't take the time to read the question fully. Work efficiently but make sure you understand the question and have looked at all of the answer choices, since more than one may seem right at first.

Even if you're paying attention to the time, you may find yourself a little behind at some point. You should speed up to get back on track, but do so wisely. Don't panic; just take a few seconds less on each question until you're caught up. Don't guess without thinking, but do look through the answer choices and eliminate any you know are wrong. If you can get down to two choices, it is often worthwhile to guess from those. Once you've chosen an answer, move on and don't dwell on any that you skipped or had to hurry through. If a question was taking too long, chances are it was one of the harder ones, so you weren't as likely to get it right anyway.

On the other hand, if you find yourself getting ahead of schedule, it may be beneficial to slow down a little. The more quickly you work, the more likely you are to make a careless mistake that will affect your score. You've budgeted time for each question, so don't be afraid to spend that time. Practice an efficient but careful pace to get the most out of the time you have.

Copyright © Mometrix Media. You have been licensed one copy of this document for personal use only. Any other reproduction or redistribution is strictly prohibited. All rights reserved.
This content is provided for test preparation purposes only and does not imply an endorsement by Mometrix of any particular political, scientific, or religious point of view.

# Secret Key #5 – Have a Plan for Guessing

When you're taking the test, you may find yourself stuck on a question. Some of the answer choices seem better than others, but you don't see the one answer choice that is obviously correct. What do you do?

The scenario described above is very common, yet most test takers have not effectively prepared for it. Developing and practicing a plan for guessing may be one of the single most effective uses of your time as you get ready for the exam.

In developing your plan for guessing, there are three questions to address:

- When should you start the guessing process?
- How should you narrow down the choices?
- Which answer should you choose?

## When to Start the Guessing Process

Unless your plan for guessing is to select C every time (which, despite its merits, is not what we recommend), you need to leave yourself enough time to apply your answer elimination strategies. Since you have a limited amount of time for each question, that means that if you're going to give yourself the best shot at guessing correctly, you have to decide quickly whether or not you will guess.

Of course, the best-case scenario is that you don't have to guess at all, so first, see if you can answer the question based on your knowledge of the subject and basic reasoning skills. Focus on the key words in the question and try to jog your memory of related topics. Give yourself a chance to bring the knowledge to mind, but once you realize that you don't have (or you can't access) the knowledge you need to answer the question, it's time to start the guessing process.

It's almost always better to start the guessing process too early than too late. It only takes a few seconds to remember something and answer the question from knowledge. Carefully eliminating wrong answer choices takes longer. Plus, going through the process of eliminating answer choices can actually help jog your memory.

**Summary**: Start the guessing process as soon as you decide that you can't answer the question based on your knowledge.

7

Copyright © Mometrix Media. You have been licensed one copy of this document for personal use only. Any other reproduction or redistribution is strictly prohibited. All rights reserved. This content is provided for test preparation purposes only and does not imply an endorsement by Mometrix of any particular political, scientific, or religious point of view.

# How to Narrow Down the Choices

The next chapter in this book (**Test-Taking Strategies**) includes a wide range of strategies for how to approach questions and how to look for answer choices to eliminate. You will definitely want to read those carefully, practice them, and figure out which ones work best for you. Here though, we're going to address a mindset rather than a particular strategy.

Your odds of guessing an answer correctly depend on how many options you are choosing from.

| Number of options left | 5 | 4 | 3 | 2 | 1 |
|---|---|---|---|---|---|
| Odds of guessing correctly | 20% | 25% | 33% | 50% | 100% |

You can see from this chart just how valuable it is to be able to eliminate incorrect answers and make an educated guess, but there are two things that many test takers do that cause them to miss out on the benefits of guessing:

- Accidentally eliminating the correct answer
- Selecting an answer based on an impression

We'll look at the first one here, and the second one in the next section.

To avoid accidentally eliminating the correct answer, we recommend a thought exercise called **the $5 challenge**. In this challenge, you only eliminate an answer choice from contention if you are willing to bet $5 on it being wrong. Why $5? Five dollars is a small but not insignificant amount of money. It's an amount you could afford to lose but wouldn't want to throw away. And while losing

$5 once might not hurt too much, doing it twenty times will set you back $100. In the same way, each small decision you make—eliminating a choice here, guessing on a question there—won't by itself impact your score very much, but when you put them all together, they can make a big difference. By holding each answer choice elimination decision to a higher standard, you can reduce the risk of accidentally eliminating the correct answer.

The $5 challenge can also be applied in a positive sense: If you are willing to bet $5 that an answer choice *is* correct, go ahead and mark it as correct.

**Summary**: Only eliminate an answer choice if you are willing to bet $5 that it is wrong.

Copyright © Mometrix Media. You have been licensed one copy of this document for personal use only. Any other reproduction or redistribution is strictly prohibited. All rights reserved.
This content is provided for test preparation purposes only and does not imply an endorsement by Mometrix of any particular political, scientific, or religious point of view.

# Which Answer to Choose

You're taking the test. You've run into a hard question and decided you'll have to guess. You've eliminated all the answer choices you're willing to bet $5 on. Now you have to pick an answer. Why do we even need to talk about this? Why can't you just pick whichever one you feel like when the time comes?

The answer to these questions is that if you don't come into the test with a plan, you'll rely on your impression to select an answer choice, and if you do that, you risk falling into a trap. The test writers know that everyone who takes their test will be guessing on some of the questions, so they intentionally write wrong answer choices to seem plausible. You still have to pick an answer though, and if the wrong answer choices are designed to look right, how can you ever be sure that you're not falling for their trap? The best solution we've found to this dilemma is to take the decision out of your hands entirely. Here is the process we recommend:

**Once you've eliminated any choices that you are confident (willing to bet $5) are wrong, select the first remaining choice as your answer.**

Whether you choose to select the first remaining choice, the second, or the last, the important thing is that you use some preselected standard. Using this approach guarantees that you will not be enticed into selecting an answer choice that looks right, because you are not basing your decision on how the answer choices look.

This is not meant to make you question your knowledge. Instead, it is to help you recognize the difference between your knowledge and your impressions. There's a huge difference between thinking an answer is right because of what you know, and thinking an answer is right because it looks or sounds like it should be right.

**Summary**: To ensure that your selection is appropriately random, make a predetermined selection from among all answer choices you have not eliminated.

Copyright © Mometrix Media. You have been licensed one copy of this document for personal use only. Any other reproduction or redistribution is strictly prohibited. All rights reserved.
This content is provided for test preparation purposes only and does not imply an endorsement by Mometrix of any particular political, scientific, or religious point of view.

# Test-Taking Strategies

This section contains a list of test-taking strategies that you may find helpful as you work through the test. By taking what you know and applying logical thought, you can maximize your chances of answering any question correctly!

It is very important to realize that every question is different and every person is different: no single strategy will work on every question, and no single strategy will work for every person. That's why we've included all of them here, so you can try them out and determine which ones work best for different types of questions and which ones work best for you.

## Question Strategies

### ☑ READ CAREFULLY

Read the question and the answer choices carefully. Don't miss the question because you misread the terms. You have plenty of time to read each question thoroughly and make sure you understand what is being asked. Yet a happy medium must be attained, so don't waste too much time. You must read carefully and efficiently.

### ☑ CONTEXTUAL CLUES

Look for contextual clues. If the question includes a word you are not familiar with, look at the immediate context for some indication of what the word might mean. Contextual clues can often give you all the information you need to decipher the meaning of an unfamiliar word. Even if you can't determine the meaning, you may be able to narrow down the possibilities enough to make a solid guess at the answer to the question.

### ☑ PREFIXES

If you're having trouble with a word in the question or answer choices, try dissecting it. Take advantage of every clue that the word might include. Prefixes can be a huge help. Usually, they allow you to determine a basic meaning. *Pre-* means before, *post-* means after, *pro-* is positive, *de-* is negative. From prefixes, you can get an idea of the general meaning of the word and try to put it into context.

### ☑ HEDGE WORDS

Watch out for critical hedge words, such as *likely, may, can, sometimes, often, almost, mostly, usually, generally, rarely,* and *sometimes*. Question writers insert these hedge phrases to cover every possibility. Often an answer choice will be wrong simply because it leaves no room for exception. Be on guard for answer choices that have definitive words such as *exactly* and *always*.

### ☑ SWITCHBACK WORDS

Stay alert for *switchbacks*. These are the words and phrases frequently used to alert you to shifts in thought. The most common switchback words are *but, although,* and *however*. Others include *nevertheless, on the other hand, even though, while, in spite of, despite,* and *regardless of*. Switchback words are important to catch because they can change the direction of the question or an answer choice.

10

Copyright © Mometrix Media. You have been licensed one copy of this document for personal use only. Any other reproduction or redistribution is strictly prohibited. All rights reserved.
This content is provided for test preparation purposes only and does not imply an endorsement by Mometrix of any particular political, scientific, or religious point of view.

## ⊘ FACE VALUE

When in doubt, use common sense. Accept the situation in the problem at face value. Don't read too much into it. These problems will not require you to make wild assumptions. If you have to go beyond creativity and warp time or space in order to have an answer choice fit the question, then you should move on and consider the other answer choices. These are normal problems rooted in reality. The applicable relationship or explanation may not be readily apparent, but it is there for you to figure out. Use your common sense to interpret anything that isn't clear.

# Answer Choice Strategies

## ⊘ ANSWER SELECTION

The most thorough way to pick an answer choice is to identify and eliminate wrong answers until only one is left, then confirm it is the correct answer. Sometimes an answer choice may immediately seem right, but be careful. The test writers will usually put more than one reasonable answer choice on each question, so take a second to read all of them and make sure that the other choices are not equally obvious. As long as you have time left, it is better to read every answer choice than to pick the first one that looks right without checking the others.

## ⊘ ANSWER CHOICE FAMILIES

An answer choice family consists of two (in rare cases, three) answer choices that are very similar in construction and cannot all be true at the same time. If you see two answer choices that are direct opposites or parallels, one of them is usually the correct answer. For instance, if one answer choice says that quantity $x$ increases and another either says that quantity $x$ decreases (opposite) or says that quantity $y$ increases (parallel), then those answer choices would fall into the same family. An answer choice that doesn't match the construction of the answer choice family is more likely to be incorrect. Most questions will not have answer choice families, but when they do appear, you should be prepared to recognize them.

## ⊘ ELIMINATE ANSWERS

Eliminate answer choices as soon as you realize they are wrong, but make sure you consider all possibilities. If you are eliminating answer choices and realize that the last one you are left with is also wrong, don't panic. Start over and consider each choice again. There may be something you missed the first time that you will realize on the second pass.

## ⊘ AVOID FACT TRAPS

Don't be distracted by an answer choice that is factually true but doesn't answer the question. You are looking for the choice that answers the question. Stay focused on what the question is asking for so you don't accidentally pick an answer that is true but incorrect. Always go back to the question and make sure the answer choice you've selected actually answers the question and is not merely a true statement.

## ⊘ EXTREME STATEMENTS

In general, you should avoid answers that put forth extreme actions as standard practice or proclaim controversial ideas as established fact. An answer choice that states the "process should be used in certain situations, if..." is much more likely to be correct than one that states the "process should be discontinued completely." The first is a calm rational statement and doesn't even make a definitive, uncompromising stance, using a hedge word *if* to provide wiggle room, whereas the second choice is far more extreme.

Copyright © Mometrix Media. You have been licensed one copy of this document for personal use only. Any other reproduction or redistribution is strictly prohibited. All rights reserved.
This content is provided for test preparation purposes only and does not imply an endorsement by Mometrix of any particular political, scientific, or religious point of view.

### ☑ Benchmark

As you read through the answer choices and you come across one that seems to answer the question well, mentally select that answer choice. This is not your final answer, but it's the one that will help you evaluate the other answer choices. The one that you selected is your benchmark or standard for judging each of the other answer choices. Every other answer choice must be compared to your benchmark. That choice is correct until proven otherwise by another answer choice beating it. If you find a better answer, then that one becomes your new benchmark. Once you've decided that no other choice answers the question as well as your benchmark, you have your final answer.

### ☑ Predict the Answer

Before you even start looking at the answer choices, it is often best to try to predict the answer. When you come up with the answer on your own, it is easier to avoid distractions and traps because you will know exactly what to look for. The right answer choice is unlikely to be word-for-word what you came up with, but it should be a close match. Even if you are confident that you have the right answer, you should still take the time to read each option before moving on.

## General Strategies

### ☑ Tough Questions

If you are stumped on a problem or it appears too hard or too difficult, don't waste time. Move on! Remember though, if you can quickly check for obviously incorrect answer choices, your chances of guessing correctly are greatly improved. Before you completely give up, at least try to knock out a couple of possible answers. Eliminate what you can and then guess at the remaining answer choices before moving on.

### ☑ Check Your Work

Since you will probably not know every term listed and the answer to every question, it is important that you get credit for the ones that you do know. Don't miss any questions through careless mistakes. If at all possible, try to take a second to look back over your answer selection and make sure you've selected the correct answer choice and haven't made a costly careless mistake (such as marking an answer choice that you didn't mean to mark). This quick double check should more than pay for itself in caught mistakes for the time it costs.

### ☑ Pace Yourself

It's easy to be overwhelmed when you're looking at a page full of questions; your mind is confused and full of random thoughts, and the clock is ticking down faster than you would like. Calm down and maintain the pace that you have set for yourself. Especially as you get down to the last few minutes of the test, don't let the small numbers on the clock make you panic. As long as you are on track by monitoring your pace, you are guaranteed to have time for each question.

### ☑ Don't Rush

It is very easy to make errors when you are in a hurry. Maintaining a fast pace in answering questions is pointless if it makes you miss questions that you would have gotten right otherwise. Test writers like to include distracting information and wrong answers that seem right. Taking a little extra time to avoid careless mistakes can make all the difference in your test score. Find a pace that allows you to be confident in the answers that you select.

Copyright © Mometrix Media. You have been licensed one copy of this document for personal use only. Any other reproduction or redistribution is strictly prohibited. All rights reserved.
This content is provided for test preparation purposes only and does not imply an endorsement by Mometrix of any particular political, scientific, or religious point of view.

## ⊘ KEEP MOVING

Panicking will not help you pass the test, so do your best to stay calm and keep moving. Taking deep breaths and going through the answer elimination steps you practiced can help to break through a stress barrier and keep your pace.

# Final Notes

The combination of a solid foundation of content knowledge and the confidence that comes from practicing your plan for applying that knowledge is the key to maximizing your performance on test day. As your foundation of content knowledge is built up and strengthened, you'll find that the strategies included in this chapter become more and more effective in helping you quickly sift through the distractions and traps of the test to isolate the correct answer.

Now that you're preparing to move forward into the test content chapters of this book, be sure to keep your goal in mind. As you read, think about how you will be able to apply this information on the test. If you've already seen sample questions for the test and you have an idea of the question format and style, try to come up with questions of your own that you can answer based on what you're reading. This will give you valuable practice applying your knowledge in the same ways you can expect to on test day.

**Good luck and good studying!**

Copyright © Mometrix Media. You have been licensed one copy of this document for personal use only. Any other reproduction or redistribution is strictly prohibited. All rights reserved.
This content is provided for test preparation purposes only and does not imply an endorsement by Mometrix of any particular political, scientific, or religious point of view.

Copyright © Mometrix Media. You have been licensed one copy of this document for personal use only. Any other reproduction or redistribution is strictly prohibited. All rights reserved.
This content is provided for test preparation purposes only and does not imply an endorsement by Mometrix of any particular political, scientific, or religious point of view.

# Reading

## Informational Texts

### TEXT FEATURES IN INFORMATIONAL TEXTS

The **title of a text** gives readers some idea of its content. The **table of contents** is a list near the beginning of a text, showing the book's sections and chapters and their coinciding page numbers. This gives readers an overview of the whole text and helps them find specific chapters easily. An **appendix**, at the back of the book or document, includes important information that is not present in the main text. Also at the back, an **index** lists the book's important topics alphabetically with their page numbers to help readers find them easily. **Glossaries**, usually found at the backs of books, list technical terms alphabetically with their definitions to aid vocabulary learning and comprehension. Boldface print is used to emphasize certain words, often identifying words included in the text's glossary where readers can look up their definitions. **Headings** separate sections of text and show the topic of each. **Subheadings** divide subject headings into smaller, more specific categories to help readers organize information. **Footnotes**, at the bottom of the page, give readers more information, such as citations or links. **Bullet points** list items separately, making facts and ideas easier to see and understand. A **sidebar** is a box of information to one side of the main text giving additional information, often on a more focused or in-depth example of a topic.

**Illustrations** and **photographs** are pictures that visually emphasize important points in text. The captions below the illustrations explain what those images show. Charts and tables are visual forms of information that make something easier to understand quickly. Diagrams are drawings that show relationships or explain a process. Graphs visually show the relationships among multiple sets of information plotted along vertical and horizontal axes. Maps show geographical information visually to help readers understand the relative locations of places covered in the text. Timelines are visual graphics that show historical events in chronological order to help readers see their sequence.

> **Review Video: Informative Text**
> Visit mometrix.com/academy and enter code: 924964

### LANGUAGE USE

#### LITERAL AND FIGURATIVE LANGUAGE

As in fictional literature, informational text also uses both **literal language**, which means just what it says, and **figurative language**, which imparts more than literal meaning. For example, an informational text author might use a simile or direct comparison, such as writing that a racehorse "ran like the wind." Informational text authors also use metaphors or implied comparisons, such as "the cloud of the Great Depression." Imagery may also appear in informational texts to increase the reader's understanding of ideas and concepts discussed in the text.

### EXPLICIT AND IMPLICIT INFORMATION

When informational text states something explicitly, the reader is told by the author exactly what is meant, which can include the author's interpretation or perspective of events. For example, a professor writes, "I have seen students go into an absolute panic just because they weren't able to complete the exam in the time they were allotted." This explicitly tells the reader that the students were afraid, and by using the words "just because," the writer indicates their fear was exaggerated out of proportion relative to what happened. However, another professor writes, "I have had

15

Copyright © Mometrix Media. You have been licensed one copy of this document for personal use only. Any other reproduction or redistribution is strictly prohibited. All rights reserved.
This content is provided for test preparation purposes only and does not imply an endorsement by Mometrix of any particular political, scientific, or religious point of view.

students come to me, their faces drained of all color, saying 'We weren't able to finish the exam.'" This is an example of implicit meaning: the second writer did not state explicitly that the students were panicked. Instead, he wrote a description of their faces being "drained of all color." From this description, the reader can infer that the students were so frightened that their faces paled.

> **Review Video: Explicit and Implicit Information**
> Visit mometrix.com/academy and enter code: 735771

## TECHNICAL LANGUAGE

Technical language is more impersonal than literary and vernacular language. Passive voice makes the tone impersonal. For example, instead of writing, "We found this a central component of protein metabolism," scientists write, "This was found a central component of protein metabolism." While science professors have traditionally instructed students to avoid active voice because it leads to first-person ("I" and "we") usage, science editors today find passive voice dull and weak. Many journal articles combine both. Tone in technical science writing should be detached, concise, and professional. While one may normally write, "This chemical has to be available for proteins to be digested," professionals write technically, "The presence of this chemical is required for the enzyme to break the covalent bonds of proteins." The use of technical language appeals to both technical and non-technical audiences by displaying the author or speaker's understanding of the subject and suggesting their credibility regarding the message they are communicating.

## TECHNICAL MATERIAL FOR NON-TECHNICAL READERS

Writing about **technical subjects** for **non-technical readers** differs from writing for colleagues because authors place more importance on delivering a critical message than on imparting the maximum technical content possible. Technical authors also must assume that non-technical audiences do not have the expertise to comprehend extremely scientific or technical messages, concepts, and terminology. They must resist the temptation to impress audiences with their scientific knowledge and expertise and remember that their primary purpose is to communicate a message that non-technical readers will understand, feel, and respond to. Non-technical and technical styles include similarities. Both should formally cite any references or other authors' work utilized in the text. Both must follow intellectual property and copyright regulations. This includes the author's protecting his or her own rights, or a public domain statement, as he or she chooses.

> **Review Video: Technical Passages**
> Visit mometrix.com/academy and enter code: 478923

## NON-TECHNICAL AUDIENCES

Writers of technical or scientific material may need to write for many non-technical audiences. Some readers have no technical or scientific background, and those who do may not be in the same field as the authors. Government and corporate policymakers and budget managers need technical information they can understand for decision-making. Citizens affected by technology or science are a different audience. Non-governmental organizations can encompass many of the preceding groups. Elementary and secondary school programs also need non-technical language for presenting technical subject matter. Additionally, technical authors will need to use non-technical language when collecting consumer responses to surveys, presenting scientific or para-scientific material to the public, writing about the history of science, and writing about science and technology in developing countries.

Copyright © Mometrix Media. You have been licensed one copy of this document for personal use only. Any other reproduction or redistribution is strictly prohibited. All rights reserved.
This content is provided for test preparation purposes only and does not imply an endorsement by Mometrix of any particular political, scientific, or religious point of view.

## USE OF EVERYDAY LANGUAGE

Authors of technical information sometimes must write using non-technical language that readers outside their disciplinary fields can comprehend. They should use not only non-technical terms, but also normal, everyday language to accommodate readers whose native language is different than the language the text is written in. For example, instead of writing that "eustatic changes like thermal expansion are causing hazardous conditions in the littoral zone," an author would do better to write that "a rising sea level is threatening the coast." When technical terms cannot be avoided, authors should also define or explain them using non-technical language. Although authors must cite references and acknowledge their use of others' work, they should avoid the kinds of references or citations that they would use in scientific journals—unless they reinforce author messages. They should not use endnotes, footnotes, or any other complicated referential techniques because non-technical journal publishers usually do not accept them. Including high-resolution illustrations, photos, maps, or satellite images and incorporating multimedia into digital publications will enhance non-technical writing about technical subjects. Technical authors may publish using non-technical language in e-journals, trade journals, specialty newsletters, and daily newspapers.

## MAKING INFERENCES ABOUT INFORMATIONAL TEXT

With informational text, reader comprehension depends not only on recalling important statements and details, but also on reader inferences based on examples and details. Readers add information from the text to what they already know to draw inferences about the text. These inferences help the readers to fill in the information that the text does not explicitly state, enabling them to understand the text better. When reading a nonfictional autobiography or biography, for example, the most appropriate inferences might concern the events in the book, the actions of the subject of the autobiography or biography, and the message the author means to convey. When reading a nonfictional expository (informational) text, the reader would best draw inferences about problems and their solutions, and causes and their effects. When reading a nonfictional persuasive text, the reader will want to infer ideas supporting the author's message and intent.

## STRUCTURES OR ORGANIZATIONAL PATTERNS IN INFORMATIONAL TEXTS

Informational text can be **descriptive**, appealing to the five senses and answering the questions what, who, when, where, and why. Another method of structuring informational text is sequence and order. **Chronological** texts relate events in the sequence that they occurred, from start to finish, while how-to texts organize information into a series of instructions in the sequence in which the steps should be followed. **Comparison-contrast** structures of informational text describe various ideas to their readers by pointing out how things or ideas are similar and how they are different. **Cause and effect** structures of informational text describe events that occurred and identify the causes or reasons that those events occurred. **Problem and solution** structures of informational texts introduce and describe problems and offer one or more solutions for each problem described.

## DETERMINING AN INFORMATIONAL AUTHOR'S PURPOSE

Informational authors' purposes are why they write texts. Readers must determine authors' motivations and goals. Readers gain greater insight into a text by considering the author's motivation. This develops critical reading skills. Readers perceive writing as a person's voice, not simply printed words. Uncovering author motivations and purposes empowers readers to know what to expect from the text, read for relevant details, evaluate authors and their work critically, and respond effectively to the motivations and persuasions of the text. The main idea of a text is what the reader is supposed to understand from reading it; the purpose of the text is why the

Copyright © Mometrix Media. You have been licensed one copy of this document for personal use only. Any other reproduction or redistribution is strictly prohibited. All rights reserved. This content is provided for test preparation purposes only and does not imply an endorsement by Mometrix of any particular political, scientific, or religious point of view.

author has written it and what the author wants readers to do with its information. Authors state some purposes clearly, while other purposes may be unstated but equally significant. When stated purposes contradict other parts of a text, the author may have a hidden agenda. Readers can better evaluate a text's effectiveness, whether they agree or disagree with it, and why they agree or disagree through identifying unstated author purposes.

## IDENTIFYING AUTHOR'S POINT OF VIEW OR PURPOSE

In some informational texts, readers find it easy to identify the author's point of view and purpose, such as when the author explicitly states his or her position and reason for writing. But other texts are more difficult, either because of the content or because the authors give neutral or balanced viewpoints. This is particularly true in scientific texts, in which authors may state the purpose of their research in the report, but never state their point of view except by interpreting evidence or data.

To analyze text and identify point of view or purpose, readers should ask themselves the following four questions:

1. With what main point or idea does this author want to persuade readers to agree?
2. How does this author's word choice affect the way that readers consider this subject?
3. How do this author's choices of examples and facts affect the way that readers consider this subject?
4. What is it that this author wants to accomplish by writing this text?

> **Review Video: Understanding the Author's Intent**
> Visit mometrix.com/academy and enter code: 511819

## EVALUATING ARGUMENTS MADE BY INFORMATIONAL TEXT WRITERS

When evaluating an informational text, the first step is to identify the argument's conclusion. Then identify the author's premises that support the conclusion. Try to paraphrase premises for clarification and make the conclusion and premises fit. List all premises first, sequentially numbered, then finish with the conclusion. Identify any premises or assumptions not stated by the author but required for the stated premises to support the conclusion. Read word assumptions sympathetically, as the author might. Evaluate whether premises reasonably support the conclusion. For inductive reasoning, the reader should ask if the premises are true, if they support the conclusion, and if so, how strongly. For deductive reasoning, the reader should ask if the argument is valid or invalid. If all premises are true, then the argument is valid unless the conclusion can be false. If it can, then the argument is invalid. An invalid argument can be made valid through alterations such as the addition of needed premises.

## USE OF RHETORIC IN INFORMATIONAL TEXTS

There are many ways authors can support their claims, arguments, beliefs, ideas, and reasons for writing in informational texts. For example, authors can appeal to readers' sense of **logic** by communicating their reasoning through a carefully sequenced series of logical steps to help "prove" the points made. Authors can appeal to readers' **emotions** by using descriptions and words that evoke feelings of sympathy, sadness, anger, righteous indignation, hope, happiness, or any other emotion to reinforce what they express and share with their audience. Authors may appeal to the **moral** or **ethical values** of readers by using words and descriptions that can convince readers that something is right or wrong. By relating personal anecdotes, authors can supply readers with more accessible, realistic examples of points they make, as well as appealing to their emotions. They can

18

Copyright © Mometrix Media. You have been licensed one copy of this document for personal use only. Any other reproduction or redistribution is strictly prohibited. All rights reserved. This content is provided for test preparation purposes only and does not imply an endorsement by Mometrix of any particular political, scientific, or religious point of view.

provide supporting evidence by reporting case studies. They can also illustrate their points by making analogies to which readers can better relate.

Copyright © Mometrix Media. You have been licensed one copy of this document for personal use only. Any other reproduction or redistribution is strictly prohibited. All rights reserved.
This content is provided for test preparation purposes only and does not imply an endorsement by Mometrix of any particular political, scientific, or religious point of view.

## CHAPTER QUIZ

**1. Which of the following is the first step in evaluating an informational text?**

    a. Read word assumptions sympathetically

    b. List all premises sequentially

    c. Determine if the premises are true

    d. Identify the argument's conclusion

**2. Which of the following is NOT considered a type of appeal for an author to use?**

    a. Logic

    b. Ethics

    c. Emotions

    d. Imagination

## CHAPTER QUIZ ANSWER KEY

**1. D:** When evaluating an informational text, the first step is to identify the argument's conclusion. After that comes identifying the author's premises that support the conclusion. The reader should try to paraphrase premises for clarification and make the conclusion and premises fit. List all premises first, sequentially numbered, then finish with the conclusion. Identify any premises or assumptions not stated by the author but required for the stated premises to support the conclusion. Read word assumptions sympathetically, as the author might. Evaluate whether premises reasonably support the conclusion. For inductive reasoning, the reader should ask if the premises are true, if they support the conclusion, and how strong that support is. For deductive reasoning, the reader should ask if the argument is valid or invalid. If all premises are true, then the argument is valid unless the conclusion can be false. If it can, then the argument is invalid. An invalid argument can be made valid through alterations such as the addition of needed premises.

**2. D:** There are many ways authors can support their claims, arguments, beliefs, ideas, and reasons for writing in informational texts. For example, authors can appeal to readers' sense of logic by communicating their reasoning through a carefully sequenced series of logical steps to support their positions. Authors can appeal to readers' emotions by using descriptions and words that evoke feelings of sympathy, sadness, anger, righteous indignation, hope, happiness, or any other emotion to reinforce what they express and share with their audience. Authors may appeal to the moral or ethical values of readers by using words and descriptions that can convince readers that something is right or wrong. By relating personal anecdotes, authors can appeal to readers' emotions and supply them with more accessible, realistic examples of points they make. They can provide supporting evidence by reporting case studies. They can also illustrate their points by making analogies to which readers can better relate.

Copyright © Mometrix Media. You have been licensed one copy of this document for personal use only. Any other reproduction or redistribution is strictly prohibited. All rights reserved. This content is provided for test preparation purposes only and does not imply an endorsement by Mometrix of any particular political, scientific, or religious point of view.

# Persuasive Techniques

## PERSUASIVE TECHNIQUES

To **appeal using reason**, writers present logical arguments, such as using "If... then... because" statements. To **appeal to emotions**, authors may ask readers how they would feel about something or to put themselves in another's place, present their argument as one that will make the audience feel good, or tell readers how they should feel. To **appeal to character**, **morality**, or **ethics**, authors present their points to readers as the right or most moral choices. Authors cite expert opinions to show readers that someone very knowledgeable about the subject or viewpoint agrees with the author's claims. **Testimonials**, usually via anecdotes or quotations regarding the author's subject, help build the audience's trust in an author's message through positive support from ordinary people. **Bandwagon appeals** claim that everybody else agrees with the author's argument and persuade readers to conform and agree, also. Authors **appeal to greed** by presenting their choice as cheaper, free, or more valuable for less cost. They **appeal to laziness** by presenting their views as more convenient, easy, or relaxing. Authors also anticipate potential objections and argue against them before audiences think of them, thereby depicting those objections as weak.

Authors can use **comparisons** like analogies, similes, and metaphors to persuade audiences. For example, a writer might represent excessive expenses as "hemorrhaging" money, which the author's recommended solution will stop. Authors can use negative word connotations to make some choices unappealing to readers, and positive word connotations to make others more appealing. Using **humor** can relax readers and garner their agreement. However, writers must take care: ridiculing opponents can be a successful strategy for appealing to readers who already agree with the author, but can backfire by angering other readers. **Rhetorical questions** need no answer, but create effect that can force agreement, such as asking the question, "Wouldn't you rather be paid more than less?" **Generalizations** persuade readers by being impossible to disagree with. Writers can easily make generalizations that appear to support their viewpoints, like saying, "We all want peace, not war" regarding more specific political arguments. **Transfer** and **association** persuade by example: if advertisements show attractive actors enjoying their products, audiences imagine they will experience the same. **Repetition** can also sometimes effectively persuade audiences.

> **Review Video: Using Rhetorical Strategies for Persuasion**
> Visit mometrix.com/academy and enter code: 302658

## CLASSICAL AUTHOR APPEALS

In his *On Rhetoric,* ancient Greek philosopher Aristotle defined three basic types of appeal used in writing, which he called *pathos, ethos,* and *logos.* **Pathos** means suffering or experience and refers to appeals to the emotions (the English word *pathetic* comes from this root). Writing that is meant to entertain audiences, by making them either happy, as with comedy, or sad, as with tragedy, uses *pathos.* Aristotle's *Poetics* states that evoking the emotions of terror and pity is one of the criteria for writing tragedy. **Ethos** means character and connotes ideology (the English word *ethics* comes from this root). Writing that appeals to credibility, based on academic, professional, or personal merit, uses *ethos.* **Logos** means "I say" and refers to a plea, opinion, expectation, word or speech, account, opinion, or reason (the English word *logic* comes from this root.) Aristotle used it to mean persuasion that appeals to the audience through reasoning and logic to influence their opinions.

## CRITICAL EVALUATION OF EFFECTIVENESS OF PERSUASIVE METHODS

First, readers should identify the author's **thesis**—what he or she argues for or against. They should consider the argument's content and the author's reason for presenting it. Does the author

21

Copyright © Mometrix Media. You have been licensed one copy of this document for personal use only. Any other reproduction or redistribution is strictly prohibited. All rights reserved. This content is provided for test preparation purposes only and does not imply an endorsement by Mometrix of any particular political, scientific, or religious point of view.

offer **solutions** to problems raised? If so, are they realistic? Note all central ideas and evidence supporting the author's thesis. Research any unfamiliar subjects or vocabulary. Readers should then outline or summarize the work in their own words. Identify which types of appeals the author uses. Readers should evaluate how well the author communicated meaning from the reader's perspective: Did they respond to emotional appeals with anger, concern, happiness, etc.? If so, why? Decide if the author's reasoning sufficed for changing the reader's mind. Determine whether the content and presentation were accurate, cohesive, and clear. Readers should also ask themselves whether they found the author believable or not, and why or why not.

## EVALUATING AN ARGUMENT

Argumentative and persuasive passages take a stand on a debatable issue, seek to explore all sides of the issue, and find the best possible solution. Argumentative and persuasive passages should not be combative or abusive. The word *argument* may remind you of two or more people shouting at each other and walking away in anger. However, an argumentative or persuasive passage should be a calm and reasonable presentation of an author's ideas for others to consider. When an author writes reasonable arguments, his or her goal is not to win or have the last word. Instead, authors want to reveal current understanding of the question at hand and suggest a solution to a problem. The purpose of argument and persuasion in a free society is to reach the best solution.

### EVIDENCE

The term **text evidence** refers to information that supports a main point or minor points and can help lead the reader to a conclusion about the text's credibility. Information used as text evidence is precise, descriptive, and factual. A main point is often followed by supporting details that provide evidence to back up a claim. For example, a passage may include the claim that winter occurs during opposite months in the Northern and Southern hemispheres. Text evidence for this claim may include examples of countries where winter occurs in opposite months. Stating that the tilt of the Earth as it rotates around the sun causes winter to occur at different times in separate hemispheres is another example of text evidence. Text evidence can come from common knowledge, but it is also valuable to include text evidence from credible, relevant outside sources.

> **Review Video: Textual Evidence**
> Visit mometrix.com/academy and enter code: 486236

Evidence that supports the thesis and additional arguments needs to be provided. Most arguments must be supported by facts or statistics. A fact is something that is known with certainty, has been verified by several independent individuals, and can be proven to be true. In addition to facts, examples and illustrations can support an argument by adding an emotional component. With this component, you persuade readers in ways that facts and statistics cannot. The emotional component is effective when used alongside objective information that can be confirmed.

### CREDIBILITY

The text used to support an argument can be the argument's downfall if the text is not credible. A text is **credible**, or believable, when its author is knowledgeable and objective, or unbiased. The author's motivations for writing the text play a critical role in determining the credibility of the text and must be evaluated when assessing that credibility. Reports written about the ozone layer by an environmental scientist and a hairdresser will have a different level of credibility.

> **Review Video: Author Credibility**
> Visit mometrix.com/academy and enter code: 827257

Copyright © Mometrix Media. You have been licensed one copy of this document for personal use only. Any other reproduction or redistribution is strictly prohibited. All rights reserved.
This content is provided for test preparation purposes only and does not imply an endorsement by Mometrix of any particular political, scientific, or religious point of view.

## APPEAL TO EMOTION

Sometimes, authors will appeal to the reader's emotion in an attempt to persuade or to distract the reader from the weakness of the argument. For instance, the author may try to inspire the pity of the reader by delivering a heart-rending story. An author also might use the bandwagon approach, in which he suggests that his opinion is correct because it is held by the majority. Some authors resort to name-calling, in which insults and harsh words are delivered to the opponent in an attempt to distract. In advertising, a common appeal is the celebrity testimonial, in which a famous person endorses a product. Of course, the fact that a famous person likes something should not really mean anything to the reader. These and other emotional appeals are usually evidence of poor reasoning and a weak argument.

> **Review Video: Emotional Language in Literature**
> Visit mometrix.com/academy and enter code: 759390

## COUNTER ARGUMENTS

When authors give both sides to the argument, they build trust with their readers. As a reader, you should start with an undecided or neutral position. If an author presents only his or her side to the argument, then they are not exhibiting credibility and are weakening their argument.

Building common ground with readers can be effective for persuading neutral, skeptical, or opposed readers. Sharing values with undecided readers can allow people to switch positions without giving up what they feel is important. People who may oppose a position need to feel that they can change their minds without betraying who they are as a person. This appeal to having an open mind can be a powerful tool in arguing a position without antagonizing other views. Objections can be countered on a point-by-point basis or in a summary paragraph. Be mindful of how an author points out flaws in counter arguments. If they are unfair to the other side of the argument, then you should lose trust with the author.

## RHETORICAL DEVICES

- An **anecdote** is a brief story authors may relate to their argument, which can illustrate their points in a more real and relatable way.
- **Aphorisms** concisely state common beliefs and may rhyme. For example, Benjamin Franklin's "Early to bed and early to rise / Makes a man healthy, wealthy, and wise" is an aphorism.
- **Allusions** refer to literary or historical figures to impart symbolism to a thing or person and to create reader resonance. In John Steinbeck's *Of Mice and Men,* protagonist George's last name is Milton. This alludes to John Milton, who wrote *Paradise Lost*, and symbolizes George's eventual loss of his dream.
- **Satire** exaggerates, ridicules, or pokes fun at human flaws or ideas, as in the works of Jonathan Swift and Mark Twain.
- A **parody** is a form of satire that imitates another work to ridicule its topic or style.
- A **paradox** is a statement that is true despite appearing contradictory.
- **Hyperbole** is overstatement using exaggerated language.
- An **oxymoron** combines seeming contradictions, such as "deafening silence."
- **Analogies** compare two things that share common elements.
- **Similes** (stated comparisons using the words *like* or *as*) and **metaphors** (stated comparisons that do not use *like* or *as*) are considered forms of analogy.
- When using logic to reason with audiences, **syllogism** refers either to deductive reasoning or a deceptive, very sophisticated, or subtle argument.

Copyright © Mometrix Media. You have been licensed one copy of this document for personal use only. Any other reproduction or redistribution is strictly prohibited. All rights reserved. This content is provided for test preparation purposes only and does not imply an endorsement by Mometrix of any particular political, scientific, or religious point of view.

- **Deductive reasoning** moves from general to specific, **inductive reasoning** from specific to general.
- **Diction** is author word choice that establishes tone and effect.
- **Understatement** achieves effects like contrast or irony by downplaying or describing something more subtly than warranted.
- **Chiasmus** uses parallel clauses, the second reversing the order of the first. Examples include T. S. Eliot's "Has the Church failed mankind, or has mankind failed the Church?" and John F. Kennedy's "Ask not what your country can do for you; ask what you can do for your country."
- **Anaphora** regularly repeats a word or phrase at the beginnings of consecutive clauses or phrases to add emphasis to an idea. A classic example of anaphora was Winston Churchill's emphasis of determination: "[W]e shall fight on the beaches, we shall fight on the landing grounds, we shall fight in the fields and in the streets, we shall fight in the hills; we shall never surrender..."

Copyright © Mometrix Media. You have been licensed one copy of this document for personal use only. Any other reproduction or redistribution is strictly prohibited. All rights reserved. This content is provided for test preparation purposes only and does not imply an endorsement by Mometrix of any particular political, scientific, or religious point of view.

## CHAPTER QUIZ

**1. Which of the following rhetorical devices exaggerates, ridicules, or pokes fun at human flaws or ideas?**

    a. Allusions
    b. Satire
    c. Parody
    d. Hyperbole

**2. An author arguing that his point is correct because everybody else already agrees with it is an example of which persuasive technique?**

    a. Appeal to laziness
    b. Bandwagon appeal
    c. Testimonials
    d. Generalizations

## CHAPTER QUIZ ANSWER KEY

**1. B:** Rhetorical devices:

- An anecdote is a brief story authors may relate to their argument, which can illustrate their points in a more real and relatable way.
- Aphorisms concisely state common beliefs and may rhyme. For example, Benjamin Franklin's "Early to bed and early to rise / Makes a man healthy, wealthy, and wise" is an aphorism.
- Allusions refer to literary or historical figures to impart symbolism to a thing or person and to create reader resonance. In John Steinbeck's *Of Mice and Men,* protagonist George's last name is Milton. This alludes to John Milton, who wrote *Paradise Lost,* and symbolizes George's eventual loss of his dream.
- Satire exaggerates, ridicules, or pokes fun at human flaws or ideas, as in the works of Jonathan Swift and Mark Twain.
- A parody is a form of satire that imitates another work to ridicule its topic or style.
- A paradox is a statement that is true despite appearing contradictory.
- Hyperbole is overstatement using exaggerated language.
- An oxymoron combines seeming contradictions, such as "deafening silence."
- Analogies compare two things that share common elements.
- Similes (stated comparisons using the words *like* or *as*) and metaphors (stated comparisons that do not use *like* or *as*) are considered forms of analogy.
- When using logic to reason with audiences, syllogism refers either to deductive reasoning or a deceptive, very sophisticated, or subtle argument.
- Deductive reasoning moves from general to specific, while inductive reasoning moves from specific to general.
- Diction is author word choice that establishes tone and effect.
- Understatement achieves effects like contrast or irony by downplaying or describing something more subtly than warranted.
- Chiasmus uses parallel clauses, with the second clause reversing the order of the first. Examples include T. S. Eliot's "Has the Church failed mankind, or has mankind failed the Church?" and John F. Kennedy's "Ask not what your country can do for you—ask what you can do for your country."

Copyright © Mometrix Media. You have been licensed one copy of this document for personal use only. Any other reproduction or redistribution is strictly prohibited. All rights reserved. This content is provided for test preparation purposes only and does not imply an endorsement by Mometrix of any particular political, scientific, or religious point of view.

- Anaphora regularly repeats a word or phrase at the beginnings of consecutive clauses or phrases to add emphasis to an idea. A classic example of anaphora was Winston Churchill's emphasis of determination: "[W]e shall fight on the beaches, we shall fight on the landing grounds, we shall fight in the fields and in the streets, we shall fight in the hills; we shall never surrender..."

**2. B:** Bandwagon appeals claim that everybody else agrees with the author's argument and thus try to persuade readers to conform and agree as well.

Copyright © Mometrix Media. You have been licensed one copy of this document for personal use only. Any other reproduction or redistribution is strictly prohibited. All rights reserved. This content is provided for test preparation purposes only and does not imply an endorsement by Mometrix of any particular political, scientific, or religious point of view.

# Arguments and Logical Errors

## AUTHOR'S ARGUMENT IN ARGUMENTATIVE WRITING

In argumentative writing, the argument is a belief, position, or opinion that the author wants to convince readers to believe as well. For the first step, readers should identify the **issue**. Some issues are controversial, meaning people disagree about them. Gun control, foreign policy, and the death penalty are all controversial issues. The next step is to determine the **author's position** on the issue. That position or viewpoint constitutes the author's argument. Readers should then identify the **author's assumptions**: things he or she accepts, believes, or takes for granted without needing proof. Inaccurate or illogical assumptions produce flawed arguments and can mislead readers. Readers should identify what kinds of **supporting evidence** the author offers, such as research results, personal observations or experiences, case studies, facts, examples, expert testimony and opinions, and comparisons. Readers should decide how relevant this support is to the argument.

> **Review Video: Argumentative Writing**
> Visit mometrix.com/academy and enter code: 561544

## EVALUATING AN AUTHOR'S ARGUMENT

The first three reader steps to **evaluate an author's argument** are to identify the **author's assumptions**, identify the **supporting evidence**, and decide **whether the evidence is relevant**. For example, if an author is not an expert on a particular topic, then that author's personal experience or opinion might not be relevant. The fourth step is to assess the **author's objectivity**. For example, consider whether the author introduces clear, understandable supporting evidence and facts to support the argument. The fifth step is evaluating whether the author's **argument is complete**. When authors give sufficient support for their arguments and also anticipate and respond effectively to opposing arguments or objections to their points, their arguments are complete. However, some authors omit information that could detract from their arguments. If instead they stated this information and refuted it, it would strengthen their arguments. The sixth step in evaluating an author's argumentative writing is to assess whether the **argument is valid**. Providing clear, logical reasoning makes an author's argument valid. Readers should ask themselves whether the author's points follow a sequence that makes sense, and whether each point leads to the next. The seventh step is to determine whether the author's **argument is credible**, meaning that it is convincing and believable. Arguments that are not valid are not credible, so step seven depends on step six. Readers should be mindful of their own biases as they evaluate and should not expect authors to conclusively prove their arguments, but rather to provide effective support and reason.

## EVALUATING AN AUTHOR'S METHOD OF APPEAL

To evaluate the effectiveness of an appeal, it is important to consider the author's purpose for writing. Any appeals an author uses in their argument must be relevant to the argument's goal. For example, a writer that argues for the reclassification of Pluto, but primarily uses appeals to emotion, will not have an effective argument. This writer should focus on using appeals to logic and support their argument with provable facts. While most arguments should include appeals to logic, emotion, and credibility, some arguments only call for one or two of these types of appeal. Evidence can support an appeal, but the evidence must be relevant to truly strengthen the appeal's effectiveness. If the writer arguing for Pluto's reclassification uses the reasons for Jupiter's classification as evidence, their argument would be weak. This information may seem relevant because it is related to the classification of planets. However, this classification is highly dependent on the size of the celestial object, and Jupiter is significantly bigger than Pluto. This use of evidence

Copyright © Mometrix Media. You have been licensed one copy of this document for personal use only. Any other reproduction or redistribution is strictly prohibited. All rights reserved.
This content is provided for test preparation purposes only and does not imply an endorsement by Mometrix of any particular political, scientific, or religious point of view.

is illogical and does not support the appeal. Even when appropriate evidence and appeals are used, appeals and arguments lose their effectiveness when they create logical fallacies.

## OPINIONS, FACTS, AND FALLACIES

Critical thinking skills are mastered through understanding various types of writing and the different purposes of authors can have for writing different passages. Every author writes for a purpose. When you understand their purpose and how they accomplish their goal, you will be able to analyze their writing and determine whether or not you agree with their conclusions.

Readers must always be aware of the difference between fact and opinion. A **fact** can be subjected to analysis and proven to be true. An **opinion**, on the other hand, is the author's personal thoughts or feelings and may not be altered by research or evidence. If the author writes that the distance from New York City to Boston is about two hundred miles, then he or she is stating a fact. If the author writes that New York City is too crowded, then he or she is giving an opinion because there is no objective standard for overpopulation. Opinions are often supported by facts. For instance, an author might use a comparison between the population density of New York City and that of other major American cities as evidence of an overcrowded population. An opinion supported by facts tends to be more convincing. On the other hand, when authors support their opinions with other opinions, readers should employ critical thinking and approach the argument with skepticism.

> **Review Video: Fact or Opinion**
> Visit mometrix.com/academy and enter code: 870899

### RELIABLE SOURCES

When you have an argumentative passage, you need to be sure that facts are presented to the reader from **reliable sources**. An opinion is what the author thinks about a given topic. An opinion is not common knowledge or proven by expert sources, instead the information is the personal beliefs and thoughts of the author. To distinguish between fact and opinion, a reader needs to consider the type of source that is presenting information, the information that backs-up a claim, and the author's motivation to have a certain point-of-view on a given topic. For example, if a panel of scientists has conducted multiple studies on the effectiveness of taking a certain vitamin, then the results are more likely to be factual than those of a company that is selling a vitamin and simply claims that taking the vitamin can produce positive effects. The company is motivated to sell their product, and the scientists are using the scientific method to prove a theory. Remember, if you find sentences that contain phrases such as "I think...", then the statement is an opinion.

### BIASES

In their attempts to persuade, writers often make mistakes in their thought processes and writing choices. These processes and choices are important to understand so you can make an informed decision about the author's credibility. Every author has a point of view, but authors demonstrate a **bias** when they ignore reasonable counterarguments or distort opposing viewpoints. A bias is evident whenever the author's claims are presented in a way that is unfair or inaccurate. Bias can be intentional or unintentional, but readers should be skeptical of the author's argument in either case. Remember that a biased author may still be correct. However, the author will be correct in spite of, not because of, his or her bias.

A **stereotype** is a bias applied specifically to a group of people or a place. Stereotyping is considered to be particularly abhorrent because it promotes negative, misleading generalizations

Copyright © Mometrix Media. You have been licensed one copy of this document for personal use only. Any other reproduction or redistribution is strictly prohibited. All rights reserved. This content is provided for test preparation purposes only and does not imply an endorsement by Mometrix of any particular political, scientific, or religious point of view.

about people. Readers should be very cautious of authors who use stereotypes in their writing. These faulty assumptions typically reveal the author's ignorance and lack of curiosity.

> **Review Video:** <u>Bias and Stereotype</u>
> Visit mometrix.com/academy and enter code: 644829

Copyright © Mometrix Media. You have been licensed one copy of this document for personal use only. Any other reproduction or redistribution is strictly prohibited. All rights reserved. This content is provided for test preparation purposes only and does not imply an endorsement by Mometrix of any particular political, scientific, or religious point of view.

## CHAPTER QUIZ

**1. Which of the following is NOT one of the first three steps of evaluating an author's argument?**

    a.  Identify the author's assumptions
    b.  Identify the supporting evidence
    c.  Evaluate if the author's argument is complete
    d.  Decide if the supporting evidence is relevant

## CHAPTER QUIZ ANSWER KEY

**1. C:** The first three reader steps to evaluate an author's argument are to identify the author's assumptions, identify the supporting evidence, and decide whether the evidence is relevant. For example, if an author is not an expert on a particular topic, then that author's personal experience or opinion might not be relevant. The fourth step is to assess the author's objectivity. For example, consider whether the author introduces clear, understandable supporting evidence and facts to support the argument. The fifth step is evaluating whether the author's argument is complete. When authors give sufficient support for their arguments and also anticipate and respond effectively to opposing arguments or objections to their points, their arguments are complete. However, some authors omit information that could detract from their arguments. If instead they stated this information and refuted it, it would likely strengthen their arguments. The sixth step in evaluating an author's argumentative writing is to assess whether the argument is valid. Providing clear, logical reasoning makes an author's argument valid. Readers should ask themselves whether the author's points follow a sequence that makes sense, and whether each point leads to the next. The seventh step is to determine whether the author's argument is credible, meaning that it is convincing and believable. Arguments that are not valid are not credible, so step seven depends on step six. Readers should be mindful of their own biases as they evaluate and should not expect authors to conclusively prove their arguments, but rather to provide effective support and reason.

Copyright © Mometrix Media. You have been licensed one copy of this document for personal use only. Any other reproduction or redistribution is strictly prohibited. All rights reserved. This content is provided for test preparation purposes only and does not imply an endorsement by Mometrix of any particular political, scientific, or religious point of view.

# Vocabulary and Word Relationships

## SYNONYMS AND ANTONYMS

When you understand how words relate to each other, you will discover more in a passage. This is explained by understanding **synonyms** (e.g., words that mean the same thing) and **antonyms** (e.g., words that mean the opposite of one another). As an example, *dry* and *arid* are synonyms, and *dry* and *wet* are antonyms.

There are many pairs of words in English that can be considered synonyms, despite having slightly different definitions. For instance, the words *friendly* and *collegial* can both be used to describe a warm interpersonal relationship, and one would be correct to call them synonyms. However, *collegial* (kin to *colleague*) is often used in reference to professional or academic relationships, and *friendly* has no such connotation.

If the difference between the two words is too great, then they should not be called synonyms. *Hot* and *warm* are not synonyms because their meanings are too distinct. A good way to determine whether two words are synonyms is to substitute one word for the other word and verify that the meaning of the sentence has not changed. Substituting *warm* for *hot* in a sentence would convey a different meaning. Although warm and hot may seem close in meaning, warm generally means that the temperature is moderate, and hot generally means that the temperature is excessively high.

Antonyms are words with opposite meanings. *Light* and *dark*, *up* and *down*, *right* and *left*, *good* and *bad*: these are all sets of antonyms. Be careful to distinguish between antonyms and pairs of words that are simply different. *Black* and *gray*, for instance, are not antonyms because gray is not the opposite of black. *Black* and *white*, on the other hand, are antonyms.

Not every word has an antonym. For instance, many nouns do not. What would be the antonym of *chair*? During your exam, the questions related to antonyms are more likely to concern adjectives. You will recall that adjectives are words that describe a noun. Some common adjectives include *purple*, *fast*, *skinny*, and *sweet*. From those four adjectives, *purple* is the item that lacks a group of obvious antonyms.

> **Review Video: What Are Synonyms and Antonyms?**
> Visit mometrix.com/academy and enter code: 105612

## AFFIXES

Affixes in the English language are morphemes that are added to words to create related but different words. Derivational affixes form new words based on and related to the original words. For example, the affix *–ness* added to the end of the adjective *happy* forms the noun *happiness*. Inflectional affixes form different grammatical versions of words. For example, the plural affix *–s* changes the singular noun *book* to the plural noun *books*, and the past tense affix *–ed* changes the present tense verb *look* to the past tense *looked.* Prefixes are affixes placed in front of words. For example, *heat* means to make hot; *preheat* means to heat in advance. Suffixes are affixes placed at the ends of words. The *happiness* example above contains the suffix *–ness.* Circumfixes add parts both before and after words, such as how *light* becomes *enlighten* with the prefix *en-* and the suffix *–en.* Interfixes create compound words via central affixes: *speed* and *meter* become *speedometer* via the interfix *–o–.*

> **Review Video: Affixes**
> Visit mometrix.com/academy and enter code: 782422

Copyright © Mometrix Media. You have been licensed one copy of this document for personal use only. Any other reproduction or redistribution is strictly prohibited. All rights reserved.
This content is provided for test preparation purposes only and does not imply an endorsement by Mometrix of any particular political, scientific, or religious point of view.

## WORD ROOTS, PREFIXES, AND SUFFIXES TO HELP DETERMINE MEANINGS OF WORDS

Many English words were formed from combining multiple sources. For example, the Latin *habēre* means "to have," and the prefixes *in-* and *im-* mean a lack or prevention of something, as in *insufficient* and *imperfect.* Latin combined *in-* with *habēre* to form *inhibēre,* whose past participle was *inhibitus.* This is the origin of the English word *inhibit,* meaning to prevent from having. Hence by knowing the meanings of both the prefix and the root, one can decipher the word meaning. In Greek, the root *enkephalo-* refers to the brain. Many medical terms are based on this root, such as encephalitis and hydrocephalus. Understanding the prefix and suffix meanings (*-itis* means inflammation; *hydro-* means water) allows a person to deduce that encephalitis refers to brain inflammation and hydrocephalus refers to water (or other fluid) in the brain.

> **Review Video: Determining Word Meanings**
> Visit mometrix.com/academy and enter code: 894894
>
> **Review Video: Root Words in English**
> Visit mometrix.com/academy and enter code: 896380

### PREFIXES

While knowing prefix meanings helps ESL and beginning readers learn new words, other readers take for granted the meanings of known words. However, prefix knowledge will also benefit them for determining meanings or definitions of unfamiliar words. For example, native English speakers and readers familiar with recipes know what *preheat* means. Knowing that *pre-* means in advance can also inform them that *presume* means to assume in advance, that *prejudice* means advance judgment, and that this understanding can be applied to many other words beginning with *pre-.* Knowing that the prefix *dis-* indicates opposition informs the meanings of words like *disbar, disagree, disestablish,* and many more. Knowing *dys-* means bad, impaired, abnormal, or difficult informs *dyslogistic, dysfunctional, dysphagia,* and *dysplasia.*

### SUFFIXES

In English, certain suffixes generally indicate both that a word is a noun, and that the noun represents a state of being or quality. For example, *-ness* is commonly used to change an adjective into its noun form, as with *happy* and *happiness, nice* and *niceness,* and so on. The suffix *–tion* is commonly used to transform a verb into its noun form, as with *converse* and *conversation or move* and *motion.* Thus, if readers are unfamiliar with the second form of a word, knowing the meaning of the transforming suffix can help them determine meaning.

### PREFIXES FOR NUMBERS

| Prefix | Definition | Examples |
|---|---|---|
| **bi-** | two | bisect, biennial |
| **mono-** | one, single | monogamy, monologue |
| **poly-** | many | polymorphous, polygamous |
| **semi-** | half, partly | semicircle, semicolon |
| **uni-** | one | uniform, unity |

Copyright © Mometrix Media. You have been licensed one copy of this document for personal use only. Any other reproduction or redistribution is strictly prohibited. All rights reserved. This content is provided for test preparation purposes only and does not imply an endorsement by Mometrix of any particular political, scientific, or religious point of view.

## PREFIXES FOR TIME, DIRECTION, AND SPACE

| Prefix | Definition | Examples |
|---|---|---|
| a- | in, on, of, up, to | abed, afoot |
| ab- | from, away, off | abdicate, abjure |
| ad- | to, toward | advance, adventure |
| ante- | before, previous | antecedent, antedate |
| anti- | against, opposing | antipathy, antidote |
| cata- | down, away, thoroughly | catastrophe, cataclysm |
| circum- | around | circumspect, circumference |
| com- | with, together, very | commotion, complicate |
| contra- | against, opposing | contradict, contravene |
| de- | from | depart |
| dia- | through, across, apart | diameter, diagnose |
| dis- | away, off, down, not | dissent, disappear |
| epi- | upon | epilogue |
| ex- | out | extract, excerpt |
| hypo- | under, beneath | hypodermic, hypothesis |
| inter- | among, between | intercede, interrupt |
| intra- | within | intramural, intrastate |
| ob- | against, opposing | objection |
| per- | through | perceive, permit |
| peri- | around | periscope, perimeter |
| post- | after, following | postpone, postscript |
| pre- | before, previous | prevent, preclude |
| pro- | forward, in place of | propel, pronoun |
| retro- | back, backward | retrospect, retrograde |
| sub- | under, beneath | subjugate, substitute |
| super- | above, extra | supersede, supernumerary |
| trans- | across, beyond, over | transact, transport |
| ultra- | beyond, excessively | ultramodern, ultrasonic |

## NEGATIVE PREFIXES

| Prefix | Definition | Examples |
|---|---|---|
| a- | without, lacking | atheist, agnostic |
| in- | not, opposing | incapable, ineligible |
| non- | not | nonentity, nonsense |
| un- | not, reverse of | unhappy, unlock |

33

Copyright © Mometrix Media. You have been licensed one copy of this document for personal use only. Any other reproduction or redistribution is strictly prohibited. All rights reserved.
This content is provided for test preparation purposes only and does not imply an endorsement by Mometrix of any particular political, scientific, or religious point of view.

## EXTRA PREFIXES

| Prefix | Definition | Examples |
|--------|-----------|----------|
| belli- | war, warlike | bellicose |
| bene- | well, good | benefit, benefactor |
| equi- | equal | equivalent, equilibrium |
| for- | away, off, from | forget, forswear |
| fore- | previous | foretell, forefathers |
| homo- | same, equal | homogenized, homonym |
| hyper- | excessive, over | hypercritical, hypertension |
| in- | in, into | intrude, invade |
| magn- | large | magnitude, magnify |
| mal- | bad, poorly, not | malfunction, malpractice |
| mis- | bad, poorly, not | misspell, misfire |
| mor- | death | mortality, mortuary |
| neo- | new | Neolithic, neoconservative |
| omni- | all, everywhere | omniscient, omnivore |
| ortho- | right, straight | orthogonal, orthodox |
| over- | above | overbearing, oversight |
| pan- | all, entire | panorama, pandemonium |
| para- | beside, beyond | parallel, paradox |
| phil- | love, like | philosophy, philanthropic |
| prim- | first, early | primitive, primary |
| re- | backward, again | revoke, recur |
| sym- | with, together | sympathy, symphony |
| vis- | to see | visage, visible |

Below is a list of common suffixes and their meanings:

## ADJECTIVE SUFFIXES

| Suffix | Definition | Examples |
|--------|-----------|----------|
| -able (-ible) | capable of being | toler*able*, ed*ible* |
| -esque | in the style of, like | picturesque, grotesque |
| -ful | filled with, marked by | thankful, zestful |
| -ific | make, cause | terrific, beatific |
| -ish | suggesting, like | churlish, childish |
| -less | lacking, without | hopeless, countless |
| -ous | marked by, given to | religious, riotous |

Copyright © Mometrix Media. You have been licensed one copy of this document for personal use only. Any other reproduction or redistribution is strictly prohibited. All rights reserved.
This content is provided for test preparation purposes only and does not imply an endorsement by Mometrix of any particular political, scientific, or religious point of view.

## NOUN SUFFIXES

| Suffix | Definition | Examples |
|---|---|---|
| -acy | state, condition | accuracy, privacy |
| -ance | act, condition, fact | acceptance, vigilance |
| -ard | one that does excessively | drunkard, sluggard |
| -ation | action, state, result | occupation, starvation |
| -dom | state, rank, condition | serfdom, wisdom |
| -er (-or) | office, action | teacher, elevator, honor |
| -ess | feminine | waitress, duchess |
| -hood | state, condition | manhood, statehood |
| -ion | action, result, state | union, fusion |
| -ism | act, manner, doctrine | barbarism, socialism |
| -ist | worker, follower | monopolist, socialist |
| -ity (-ty) | state, quality, condition | acidity, civility, twenty |
| -ment | result, action | Refreshment |
| -ness | quality, state | greatness, tallness |
| -ship | position | internship, statesmanship |
| -sion (-tion) | state, result | revision, expedition |
| -th | act, state, quality | warmth, width |
| -tude | quality, state, result | magnitude, fortitude |

## VERB SUFFIXES

| Suffix | Definition | Examples |
|---|---|---|
| -ate | having, showing | separate, desolate |
| -en | cause to be, become | deepen, strengthen |
| -fy | make, cause to have | glorify, fortify |
| -ize | cause to be, treat with | sterilize, mechanize |

## DENOTATIVE VS. CONNOTATIVE MEANING

The **denotative** meaning of a word is the literal meaning. The **connotative** meaning goes beyond the denotative meaning to include the emotional reaction that a word may invoke. The connotative meaning often takes the denotative meaning a step further due to associations the reader makes with the denotative meaning. Readers can differentiate between the denotative and connotative meanings by first recognizing how authors use each meaning. Most non-fiction, for example, is fact-based and authors do not use flowery, figurative language. The reader can assume that the writer is using the denotative meaning of words. In fiction, the author may use the connotative meaning. Readers can determine whether the author is using the denotative or connotative meaning of a word by implementing context clues.

> **Review Video: Connotation and Denotation**
> Visit mometrix.com/academy and enter code: 310092

## NUANCES OF WORD MEANING RELATIVE TO CONNOTATION, DENOTATION, DICTION, AND USAGE

A word's denotation is simply its objective dictionary definition. However, its connotation refers to the subjective associations, often emotional, that specific words evoke in listeners and readers. Two or more words can have the same dictionary meaning, but very different connotations. Writers use diction (word choice) to convey various nuances of thought and emotion by selecting synonyms for other words that best communicate the associations they want to trigger for readers. For example,

Copyright © Mometrix Media. You have been licensed one copy of this document for personal use only. Any other reproduction or redistribution is strictly prohibited. All rights reserved.
This content is provided for test preparation purposes only and does not imply an endorsement by Mometrix of any particular political, scientific, or religious point of view.

a car engine is naturally greasy; in this sense, "greasy" is a neutral term. But when a person's smile, appearance, or clothing is described as "greasy," it has a negative connotation. Some words have even gained additional or different meanings over time. For example, *awful* used to be used to describe things that evoked a sense of awe. When *awful* is separated into its root word, awe, and suffix, -ful, it can be understood to mean "full of awe." However, the word is now commonly used to describe things that evoke repulsion, terror, or another intense, negative reaction.

**Review Video: <u>Word Usage</u>**
Visit mometrix.com/academy and enter code: 197863

## CONTEXT CLUES

Readers of all levels will encounter words that they have either never seen or have encountered only on a limited basis. The best way to define a word in **context** is to look for nearby words that can assist in revealing the meaning of the word. For instance, unfamiliar nouns are often accompanied by examples that provide a definition. Consider the following sentence: *Dave arrived at the party in hilarious garb: a leopard-print shirt, buckskin trousers, and bright green sneakers.* If a reader was unfamiliar with the meaning of garb, he or she could read the examples (i.e., a leopard-print shirt, buckskin trousers, and high heels) and quickly determine that the word means *clothing*. Examples will not always be this obvious. Consider this sentence: *Parsley, lemon, and flowers were just a few of the items he used as garnishes.* Here, the word *garnishes* is exemplified by parsley, lemon, and flowers. Readers who have eaten in a variety of restaurants will probably be able to identify a garnish as something used to decorate a plate.

**Review Video: <u>Context Clues</u>**
Visit mometrix.com/academy and enter code: 613660

### USING CONTRAST IN CONTEXT CLUES

In addition to looking at the context of a passage, readers can use contrast to define an unfamiliar word in context. In many sentences, the author will not describe the unfamiliar word directly; instead, he or she will describe the opposite of the unfamiliar word. Thus, you are provided with some information that will bring you closer to defining the word. Consider the following example: *Despite his intelligence, Hector's low brow and bad posture made him look obtuse.* The author writes that Hector's appearance does not convey intelligence. Therefore, *obtuse* must mean unintelligent. Here is another example: *Despite the horrible weather, we were beatific about our trip to Alaska.* The word *despite* indicates that the speaker's feelings were at odds with the weather. Since the weather is described as *horrible*, then *beatific* must mean something positive.

### SUBSTITUTION TO FIND MEANING

In some cases, there will be very few contextual clues to help a reader define the meaning of an unfamiliar word. When this happens, one strategy that readers may employ is **substitution**. A good reader will brainstorm some possible synonyms for the given word, and he or she will substitute these words into the sentence. If the sentence and the surrounding passage continue to make sense, then the substitution has revealed at least some information about the unfamiliar word. Consider the sentence: *Frank's admonition rang in her ears as she climbed the mountain.* A reader unfamiliar with *admonition* might come up with some substitutions like *vow*, *promise*, *advice*, *complaint*, or *compliment*. All of these words make general sense of the sentence, though their meanings are diverse. However, this process has suggested that an admonition is some sort of message. The substitution strategy is rarely able to pinpoint a precise definition, but this process can be effective as a last resort.

Copyright © Mometrix Media. You have been licensed one copy of this document for personal use only. Any other reproduction or redistribution is strictly prohibited. All rights reserved.
This content is provided for test preparation purposes only and does not imply an endorsement by Mometrix of any particular political, scientific, or religious point of view.

Occasionally, you will be able to define an unfamiliar word by looking at the descriptive words in the context. Consider the following sentence: *Fred dragged the recalcitrant boy kicking and screaming up the stairs.* The words *dragged*, *kicking*, and *screaming* all suggest that the boy does not want to go up the stairs. The reader may assume that *recalcitrant* means something like unwilling or protesting. In this example, an unfamiliar adjective was identified.

Additionally, using description to define an unfamiliar noun is a common practice compared to unfamiliar adjectives, as in this sentence: *Don's wrinkled frown and constantly shaking fist identified him as a curmudgeon of the first order.* Don is described as having a *wrinkled frown and constantly shaking fist*, suggesting that a *curmudgeon* must be a grumpy person. Contrasts do not always provide detailed information about the unfamiliar word, but they at least give the reader some clues.

## WORDS WITH MULTIPLE MEANINGS

When a word has more than one meaning, readers can have difficulty determining how the word is being used in a given sentence. For instance, the verb *cleave*, can mean either *join* or *separate*. When readers come upon this word, they will have to select the definition that makes the most sense. Consider the following sentence: *Hermione's knife cleaved the bread cleanly.* Since a knife cannot join bread together, the word must indicate separation. A slightly more difficult example would be the sentence: *The birds cleaved to one another as they flew from the oak tree.* Immediately, the presence of the words *to one another* should suggest that in this sentence *cleave* is being used to mean *join*. Discovering the intent of a word with multiple meanings requires the same tricks as defining an unknown word: look for contextual clues and evaluate the substituted words.

## CONTEXT CLUES TO HELP DETERMINE MEANINGS OF WORDS

If readers simply bypass unknown words, they can reach unclear conclusions about what they read. However, looking for the definition of every unfamiliar word in the dictionary can slow their reading progress. Moreover, the dictionary may list multiple definitions for a word, so readers must search the word's context for meaning. Hence context is important to new vocabulary regardless of reader methods. Four types of context clues are examples, definitions, descriptive words, and opposites. Authors may use a certain word, and then follow it with several different examples of what it describes. Sometimes authors actually supply a definition of a word they use, which is especially true in informational and technical texts. Authors may use descriptive words that elaborate upon a vocabulary word they just used. Authors may also use opposites with negation that help define meaning.

## EXAMPLES AND DEFINITIONS

An author may use a word and then give examples that illustrate its meaning. Consider this text: "Teachers who do not know how to use sign language can help students who are deaf or hard of hearing understand certain instructions by using gestures instead, like pointing their fingers to indicate which direction to look or go; holding up a hand, palm outward, to indicate stopping; holding the hands flat, palms up, curling a finger toward oneself in a beckoning motion to indicate 'come here'; or curling all fingers toward oneself repeatedly to indicate 'come on', 'more', or 'continue.'" The author of this text has used the word "gestures" and then followed it with examples, so a reader unfamiliar with the word could deduce from the examples that "gestures" means "hand motions." Readers can find examples by looking for signal words "for example," "for instance," "like," "such as," and "e.g."

While readers sometimes have to look for definitions of unfamiliar words in a dictionary or do some work to determine a word's meaning from its surrounding context, at other times an author

Copyright © Mometrix Media. You have been licensed one copy of this document for personal use only. Any other reproduction or redistribution is strictly prohibited. All rights reserved.
This content is provided for test preparation purposes only and does not imply an endorsement by Mometrix of any particular political, scientific, or religious point of view.

may make it easier for readers by defining certain words. For example, an author may write, "The company did not have sufficient capital, that is, available money, to continue operations." The author defined "capital" as "available money," and heralded the definition with the phrase "that is." Another way that authors supply word definitions is with appositives. Rather than being introduced by a signal phrase like "that is," "namely," or "meaning," an appositive comes after the vocabulary word it defines and is enclosed within two commas. For example, an author may write, "The Indians introduced the Pilgrims to pemmican, cakes they made of lean meat dried and mixed with fat, which proved greatly beneficial to keep settlers from starving while trapping." In this example, the appositive phrase following "pemmican" and preceding "which" defines the word "pemmican."

## DESCRIPTIONS

When readers encounter a word they do not recognize in a text, the author may expand on that word to illustrate it better. While the author may do this to make the prose more picturesque and vivid, the reader can also take advantage of this description to provide context clues to the meaning of the unfamiliar word. For example, an author may write, "The man sitting next to me on the airplane was obese. His shirt stretched across his vast expanse of flesh, strained almost to bursting." The descriptive second sentence elaborates on and helps to define the previous sentence's word "obese" to mean extremely fat. A reader unfamiliar with the word "repugnant" can decipher its meaning through an author's accompanying description: "The way the child grimaced and shuddered as he swallowed the medicine showed that its taste was particularly repugnant."

## OPPOSITES

Text authors sometimes introduce a contrasting or opposing idea before or after a concept they present. They may do this to emphasize or heighten the idea they present by contrasting it with something that is the reverse. However, readers can also use these context clues to understand familiar words. For example, an author may write, "Our conversation was not cheery. We sat and talked very solemnly about his experience and a number of similar events." The reader who is not familiar with the word "solemnly" can deduce by the author's preceding use of "not cheery" that "solemn" means the opposite of cheery or happy, so it must mean serious or sad. Or if someone writes, "Don't condemn his entire project because you couldn't find anything good to say about it," readers unfamiliar with "condemn" can understand from the sentence structure that it means the opposite of saying anything good, so it must mean reject, dismiss, or disapprove. "Entire" adds another context clue, meaning total or complete rejection.

## SYNTAX TO DETERMINE PART OF SPEECH AND MEANINGS OF WORDS

Syntax refers to sentence structure and word order. Suppose that a reader encounters an unfamiliar word when reading a text. To illustrate, consider an invented word like "splunch." If this word is used in a sentence like "Please splunch that ball to me," the reader can assume from syntactic context that "splunch" is a verb. We would not use a noun, adjective, adverb, or preposition with the object "that ball," and the prepositional phrase "to me" further indicates "splunch" represents an action. However, in the sentence, "Please hand that splunch to me," the reader can assume that "splunch" is a noun. Demonstrative adjectives like "that" modify nouns. Also, we hand someone some*thing*—a thing being a noun; we do not hand someone a verb, adjective, or adverb. Some sentences contain further clues. For example, from the sentence, "The princess wore the glittering splunch on her head," the reader can deduce that it is a crown, tiara, or something similar from the syntactic context, without knowing the word.

## SYNTAX TO INDICATE DIFFERENT MEANINGS OF SIMILAR SENTENCES

The syntax, or structure, of a sentence affords grammatical cues that aid readers in comprehending the meanings of words, phrases, and sentences in the texts that they read. Seemingly minor

Copyright © Mometrix Media. You have been licensed one copy of this document for personal use only. Any other reproduction or redistribution is strictly prohibited. All rights reserved. This content is provided for test preparation purposes only and does not imply an endorsement by Mometrix of any particular political, scientific, or religious point of view.

differences in how the words or phrases in a sentence are ordered can make major differences in meaning. For example, two sentences can use exactly the same words but have different meanings based on the word order:

- "The man with a broken arm sat in a chair."
- "The man sat in a chair with a broken arm."

While both sentences indicate that a man sat in a chair, differing syntax indicates whether the man's or chair's arm was broken.

## DETERMINING MEANING OF PHRASES AND PARAGRAPHS

Like unknown words, the meanings of phrases, paragraphs, and entire works can also be difficult to discern. Each of these can be better understood with added context. However, for larger groups of words, more context is needed. Unclear phrases are similar to unclear words, and the same methods can be used to understand their meaning. However, it is also important to consider how the individual words in the phrase work together. Paragraphs are a bit more complicated. Just as words must be compared to other words in a sentence, paragraphs must be compared to other paragraphs in a composition or a section.

## DETERMINING MEANING IN VARIOUS TYPES OF COMPOSITIONS

To understand the meaning of an entire composition, the type of composition must be considered. **Expository writing** is generally organized so that each paragraph focuses on explaining one idea, or part of an idea, and its relevance. **Persuasive writing** uses paragraphs for different purposes to organize the parts of the argument. **Unclear paragraphs** must be read in the context of the paragraphs around them for their meaning to be fully understood. The meaning of full texts can also be unclear at times. The purpose of composition is also important for understanding the meaning of a text. To quickly understand the broad meaning of a text, look to the introductory and concluding paragraphs. Fictional texts are different. Some fictional works have implicit meanings, but some do not. The target audience must be considered for understanding texts that do have an implicit meaning, as most children's fiction will clearly state any lessons or morals. For other fiction, the application of literary theories and criticism may be helpful for understanding the text.

## ADDITIONAL RESOURCES FOR DETERMINING WORD MEANING AND USAGE

While these strategies are useful for determining the meaning of unknown words and phrases, sometimes additional resources are needed to properly use the terms in different contexts. Some words have multiple definitions, and some words are inappropriate in particular contexts or modes of writing. The following tools are helpful for understanding all meanings and proper uses for words and phrases.

- **Dictionaries** provide the meaning of a multitude of words in a language. Many dictionaries include additional information about each word, such as its etymology, its synonyms, or variations of the word.
- **Glossaries** are similar to dictionaries, as they provide the meanings of a variety of terms. However, while dictionaries typically feature an extensive list of words and comprise an entire publication, glossaries are often included at the end of a text and only include terms and definitions that are relevant to the text they follow.

Copyright © Mometrix Media. You have been licensed one copy of this document for personal use only. Any other reproduction or redistribution is strictly prohibited. All rights reserved. This content is provided for test preparation purposes only and does not imply an endorsement by Mometrix of any particular political, scientific, or religious point of view.

- **Spell Checkers** are used to detect spelling errors in typed text. Some spell checkers may also detect the misuse of plural or singular nouns, verb tenses, or capitalization. While spell checkers are a helpful tool, they are not always reliable or attuned to the author's intent, so it is important to review the spell checker's suggestions before accepting them.
- **Style Manuals** are guidelines on the preferred punctuation, format, and grammar usage according to different fields or organizations. For example, the Associated Press Stylebook is a style guide often used for media writing. The guidelines within a style guide are not always applicable across different contexts and usages, as the guidelines often cover grammatical or formatting situations that are not objectively correct or incorrect.

Copyright © Mometrix Media. You have been licensed one copy of this document for personal use only. Any other reproduction or redistribution is strictly prohibited. All rights reserved.
This content is provided for test preparation purposes only and does not imply an endorsement by Mometrix of any particular political, scientific, or religious point of view.

## CHAPTER QUIZ

**1. Which of the following affixes refers to the -o- in "speedometer"?**

    a.  Prefix
    b.  Suffix
    c.  Interfix
    d.  Circumfix

**2. Adding the suffix -*ness* to a word typically does which of the following?**

    a.  Changes a verb to a noun
    b.  Changes a verb to an adjective
    c.  Changes an adjective to a noun
    d.  Changes a noun to a verb

**3. Which of the following is NOT considered a common adjective suffix?**

    a.  *-acy*
    b.  *-able*
    c.  *-ish*
    d.  *-less*

**4. Which of the following defines the noun suffix -*ation*?**

    a.  Act, condition, fact
    b.  Action, state, result
    c.  Quality, state, result
    d.  State, rank, condition

## CHAPTER QUIZ ANSWER KEY

**1. C:** Prefixes are affixes placed in front of words. For example, *heat* means to make hot, while *preheat* means to heat in advance. Suffixes are affixes placed at the ends of words. The *happiness* example above contains the suffix *-ness*. Circumfixes add parts both before and after words, such as how *light* becomes *enlighten* with the prefix *en-* and the suffix *-en.* Interfixes create compound words via central affixes: *speed* and *meter* become *speedometer* via the interfix *-o-*.

**2. C:** In English, certain suffixes generally indicate both that a word is a noun, and that the noun represents a state of being or quality. For example, *-ness* is commonly used to change an adjective into its noun form, as with *happy* and *happiness, kind* and *kindness,* and so on.

Copyright © Mometrix Media. You have been licensed one copy of this document for personal use only. Any other reproduction or redistribution is strictly prohibited. All rights reserved.
This content is provided for test preparation purposes only and does not imply an endorsement by Mometrix of any particular political, scientific, or religious point of view.

### 3. A: Adjective suffixes:

| Suffix | Definition | Examples |
|---|---|---|
| *-able (-ible)* | capable of being | tolerable, edible |
| *-esque* | in the style of, like | picturesque, grotesque |
| *-ful* | filled with, marked by | thankful, zestful |
| *-ific* | make, cause | terrific, beatific |
| *-ish* | suggesting, like | churlish, childish |
| *-less* | lacking, without | hopeless, countless |
| *-ous* | marked by, given to | religious, riotous |

### 4. B: Noun suffixes:

| Suffix | Definition | Examples |
|---|---|---|
| *-acy* | state, condition | accuracy, privacy |
| *-ance* | act, condition, fact | acceptance, vigilance |
| *-ard* | one that does excessively | drunkard, sluggard |
| *-ation* | action, state, result | occupation, starvation |
| *-dom* | state, rank, condition | serfdom, wisdom |
| *-er (-or)* | office, action | teacher, elevator, honor |
| *-ess* | feminine | waitress, duchess |
| *-hood* | state, condition | manhood, statehood |
| *-ion* | action, result, state | union, fusion |
| *-ism* | act, manner, doctrine | barbarism, socialism |
| *-ist* | worker, follower | monopolist, socialist |
| *-ity (-ty)* | state, quality, condition | acidity, civility, twenty |
| *-ment* | result, action | refreshment |
| *-ness* | quality, state | greatness, tallness |
| *-ship* | position | internship, statesmanship |
| *-sion (-tion)* | state, result | revision, expedition |
| *-th* | act, state, quality | warmth, width |
| *-tude* | quality, state, result | magnitude, fortitude |

Copyright © Mometrix Media. You have been licensed one copy of this document for personal use only. Any other reproduction or redistribution is strictly prohibited. All rights reserved.
This content is provided for test preparation purposes only and does not imply an endorsement by Mometrix of any particular political, scientific, or religious point of view.

# Figurative Language

## LITERAL AND FIGURATIVE MEANING

When language is used **literally**, the words mean exactly what they say and nothing more. When language is used **figuratively**, the words mean something beyond their literal meaning. For example, "The weeping willow tree has long, trailing branches and leaves" is a literal description. But "The weeping willow tree looks as if it is bending over and crying" is a figurative description—specifically, a **simile** or stated comparison. Another figurative language form is **metaphor**, or an implied comparison. A good example is the metaphor of a city, state, or city-state as a ship, and its governance as sailing that ship. Ancient Greek lyrical poet Alcaeus is credited with first using this metaphor, and ancient Greek tragedian Aeschylus then used it in *Seven Against Thebes,* and then Plato used it in the *Republic.*

## FIGURES OF SPEECH

A **figure of speech** is a verbal expression whose meaning is figurative rather than literal. For example, the phrase "butterflies in the stomach" does not refer to actual butterflies in a person's stomach. It is a metaphor representing the fluttery feelings experienced when a person is nervous or excited—or when one "falls in love," which does not mean physically falling. "Hitting a sales target" does not mean physically hitting a target with arrows as in archery; it is a metaphor for meeting a sales quota. "Climbing the ladder of success" metaphorically likens advancing in one's career to ascending ladder rungs. Similes, such as "light as a feather" (meaning very light, not a feather's actual weight), and hyperbole, like "I'm starving/freezing/roasting," are also figures of speech. Figures of speech are often used and crafted for emphasis, freshness of expression, or clarity.

> **Review Video: Figures of Speech**
> Visit mometrix.com/academy and enter code: 111295

## FIGURATIVE LANGUAGE

**Figurative language** extends past the literal meanings of words. It offers readers new insight into the people, things, events, and subjects covered in a work of literature. Figurative language also enables readers to feel they are sharing the authors' experiences. It can stimulate the reader's senses, make comparisons that readers find intriguing or even startling, and enable readers to view the world in different ways. When looking for figurative language, it is important to consider the context of the sentence or situation. Phrases that appear out of place or make little sense when read literally are likely instances of figurative language. Once figurative language has been recognized, context is also important to determining the type of figurative language being used and its function. For example, when a comparison is being made, a metaphor or simile is likely being used. This means the comparison may emphasize or create irony through the things being compared. Seven specific types of figurative language include: alliteration, onomatopoeia, personification, imagery, similes, metaphors, and hyperbole.

> **Review Video: Figurative Language**
> Visit mometrix.com/academy and enter code: 584902

## ALLITERATION AND ONOMATOPOEIA

**Alliteration** describes a series of words beginning with the same sounds. **Onomatopoeia** uses words imitating the sounds of things they name or describe. For example, in his poem "Come Down, O Maid," Alfred Tennyson writes of "The moan of doves in immemorial elms, / And murmuring of

Copyright © Mometrix Media. You have been licensed one copy of this document for personal use only. Any other reproduction or redistribution is strictly prohibited. All rights reserved. This content is provided for test preparation purposes only and does not imply an endorsement by Mometrix of any particular political, scientific, or religious point of view.

innumerable bees." The word "moan" sounds like some sounds doves make, "murmuring" represents the sounds of bees buzzing. Onomatopoeia also includes words that are simply meant to represent sounds, such as "meow," "kaboom," and "whoosh."

**Review Video: Alliterations Are All Around**
Visit mometrix.com/academy and enter code: 462837

### PERSONIFICATION

Another type of figurative language is **personification**. This is describing a non-human thing, like an animal or an object, as if it were human. The general intent of personification is to describe things in a manner that will be comprehensible to readers. When an author states that a tree *groans* in the wind, he or she does not mean that the tree is emitting a low, pained sound from a mouth. Instead, the author means that the tree is making a noise similar to a human groan. Of course, this personification establishes a tone of sadness or suffering. A different tone would be established if the author said that the tree was *swaying* or *dancing*. Alfred Tennyson's poem "The Eagle" uses all of these types of figurative language: "He clasps the crag with crooked hands." Tennyson used alliteration, repeating /k/ and /kr/ sounds. These hard-sounding consonants reinforce the imagery, giving visual and tactile impressions of the eagle.

**Review Video: Personification**
Visit mometrix.com/academy and enter code: 260066

### SIMILES AND METAPHORS

**Similes** are stated comparisons using "like" or "as." Similes can be used to stimulate readers' imaginations and appeal to their senses. Because a simile includes *like* or *as,* the device creates more space between the description and the thing being described than a metaphor does. If an author says that *a house was like a shoebox*, then the tone is different than the author saying that the house *was* a shoebox. Authors will choose between a metaphor and a simile depending on their intended tone.

Similes also help compare fictional characters to well-known objects or experiences, so the reader can better relate to them. William Wordsworth's poem about "Daffodils" begins, "I wandered lonely as a cloud." This simile compares his loneliness to that of a cloud. It is also personification, giving a cloud the human quality loneliness. In his novel *Lord Jim* (1900), Joseph Conrad writes in Chapter 33, "I would have given anything for the power to soothe her frail soul, tormenting itself in its invincible ignorance like a small bird beating about the cruel wires of a cage." Conrad uses the word "like" to compare the girl's soul to a small bird. His description of the bird beating at the cage shows the similar helplessness of the girl's soul to gain freedom.

**Review Video: Similes**
Visit mometrix.com/academy and enter code: 642949

A **metaphor** is a type of figurative language in which the writer equates something with another thing that is not particularly similar, instead of using *like* or *as*. For instance, *the bird was an arrow arcing through the sky*. In this sentence, the arrow is serving as a metaphor for the bird. The point of a metaphor is to encourage the reader to consider the item being described in a *different way*. Let's continue with this metaphor for a flying bird. You are asked to envision the bird's flight as being similar to the arc of an arrow. So, you imagine the flight to be swift and bending. Metaphors are a way for the author to describe an item *without being direct and obvious*. This literary device is a lyrical and suggestive way of providing information. Note that the reference for a metaphor will not

44

Copyright © Mometrix Media. You have been licensed one copy of this document for personal use only. Any other reproduction or redistribution is strictly prohibited. All rights reserved.
This content is provided for test preparation purposes only and does not imply an endorsement by Mometrix of any particular political, scientific, or religious point of view.

always be mentioned explicitly by the author. Consider the following description of a forest in winter: *Swaying skeletons reached for the sky and groaned as the wind blew through them.* In this example, the author is using *skeletons* as a metaphor for leafless trees. This metaphor creates a spooky tone while inspiring the reader's imagination.

## LITERARY EXAMPLES OF METAPHOR

A **metaphor** is an implied comparison, i.e., it compares something to something else without using "like", "as", or other comparative words. For example, in "The Tyger" (1794), William Blake writes, "Tyger Tyger, burning bright, / In the forests of the night." Blake compares the tiger to a flame not by saying it is like a fire, but by simply describing it as "burning." Henry Wadsworth Longfellow's poem "O Ship of State" (1850) uses an extended metaphor by referring consistently throughout the entire poem to the state, union, or republic as a seagoing vessel, referring to its keel, mast, sail, rope, anchors, and to its braving waves, rocks, gale, tempest, and "false lights on the shore." Within the extended metaphor, Wordsworth uses a specific metaphor: "the anchors of thy hope!"

## TED HUGHES' ANIMAL METAPHORS

Ted Hughes frequently used animal metaphors in his poetry. In "The Thought Fox," a model of concise, structured beauty, Hughes characterizes the poet's creative process with succinct, striking imagery of an idea entering his head like a wild fox. Repeating "loneliness" in the first two stanzas emphasizes the poet's lonely work: "Something else is alive / Beside the clock's loneliness." He treats an idea's arrival as separate from himself. Three stanzas detail in vivid images a fox's approach from the outside winter forest at starless midnight—its nose, "Cold, delicately" touching twigs and leaves; "neat" paw prints in snow; "bold" body; brilliant green eyes; and self-contained, focused progress—"Till, with a sudden sharp hot stink of fox," he metaphorically depicts poetic inspiration as the fox's physical entry into "the dark hole of the head." Hughes ends by summarizing his vision of a poet as an interior, passive idea recipient, with the outside world unchanged: "The window is starless still; the clock ticks, / The page is printed."

> **Review Video: Metaphors in Writing**
> Visit mometrix.com/academy and enter code: 133295

## *HYPERBOLE*

Hyperbole is excessive exaggeration used for humor or emphasis rather than for literal meaning. For example, in *To Kill a Mockingbird*, Harper Lee wrote, "People moved slowly then. There was no hurry, for there was nowhere to go, nothing to buy and no money to buy it with, nothing to see outside the boundaries of Maycomb County." This was not literally true; Lee exaggerates the scarcity of these things for emphasis. In "Old Times on the Mississippi," Mark Twain wrote, "I... could have hung my hat on my eyes, they stuck out so far." This is not literal, but makes his description vivid and funny. In his poem "As I Walked Out One Evening", W. H. Auden wrote, "I'll love you, dear, I'll love you / Till China and Africa meet, / And the river jumps over the mountain / And the salmon sing in the street." He used things not literally possible to emphasize the duration of his love.

> **Review Video: Hyperbole and Understatement**
> Visit mometrix.com/academy and enter code: 308470

## LITERARY IRONY

In literature, irony demonstrates the opposite of what is said or done. The three types of irony are **verbal irony**, **situational irony**, and **dramatic irony**. Verbal irony uses words opposite to the meaning. Sarcasm may use verbal irony. One common example is describing something that is

Copyright © Mometrix Media. You have been licensed one copy of this document for personal use only. Any other reproduction or redistribution is strictly prohibited. All rights reserved.
This content is provided for test preparation purposes only and does not imply an endorsement by Mometrix of any particular political, scientific, or religious point of view.

confusing as "clear as mud." For example, in his 1986 movie *Hannah and Her Sisters,* author, director, and actor Woody Allen says to his character's date, "I had a great evening; it was like the Nuremburg Trials." Notice these employ similes. In situational irony, what happens contrasts with what was expected. O. Henry's short story *The Gift of the Magi* uses situational irony: a husband and wife each sacrifice their most prized possession to buy each other a Christmas present. The irony is that she sells her long hair to buy him a watch fob, while he sells his heirloom pocket-watch to buy her the jeweled combs for her hair she had long wanted; in the end, neither of them can use their gifts. In dramatic irony, narrative informs audiences of more than its characters know. For example, in *Romeo and Juliet,* the audience is made aware that Juliet is only asleep, while Romeo believes her to be dead, which then leads to Romeo's death.

> **Review Video: <u>What is the Definition of Irony?</u>**
> Visit mometrix.com/academy and enter code: 374204

## IDIOMS

Idioms create comparisons, and often take the form of similes or metaphors. Idioms are always phrases and are understood to have a meaning that is different from its individual words' literal meaning. For example, "break a leg" is a common idiom that is used to wish someone luck or tell them to perform well. Literally, the phrase "break a leg" means to injure a person's leg, but the phrase takes on a different meaning when used as an idiom. Another example is "call it a day," which means to temporarily stop working on a task, or find a stopping point, rather than literally referring to something as "a day." Many idioms are associated with a region or group. For example, an idiom commonly used in the American South is "'til the cows come home." This phrase is often used to indicate that something will take or may last for a very long time, but not that it will literally last until the cows return to where they reside.

Copyright © Mometrix Media. You have been licensed one copy of this document for personal use only. Any other reproduction or redistribution is strictly prohibited. All rights reserved. This content is provided for test preparation purposes only and does not imply an endorsement by Mometrix of any particular political, scientific, or religious point of view.

## CHAPTER QUIZ

**1. Who is credited with first using the metaphor of a city, state, or city-state as a ship?**

   a. Theseus
   b. Aeschylus
   c. Alcaeus
   d. Plato

**2. How many forms of irony are there?**

   a. Two
   b. Three
   c. Four
   d. Five

## CHAPTER QUIZ ANSWER KEY

**1. C:** Another figurative language form is metaphor, or an implied comparison. A good example is the metaphor of a city, state, or city-state as a ship, and its governance as sailing that ship. Ancient Greek lyrical poet Alcaeus is credited with first using this metaphor, followed by ancient Greek tragedian Aeschylus using it in *Seven Against Thebes,* and then Plato using it in the *Republic.*

**2. B:** In literature, irony demonstrates the opposite of what is said or done. The three types of irony are verbal irony, situational irony, and dramatic irony. Verbal irony uses words opposite to the meaning. Sarcasm may use verbal irony. One common example is describing something that is confusing as "clear as mud." In his 1986 movie *Hannah and Her Sisters,* author, director, and actor Woody Allen says to his character's date, "I had a great evening; it was like the Nuremburg Trials." Notice these employ similes. In situational irony, what happens contrasts with what was expected. O. Henry's short story *The Gift of the Magi* uses situational irony: a husband and wife each sacrifice their most prized possession to buy each other a Christmas present. The irony is that she sells her long hair to buy him a watch fob, while he sells his heirloom pocket-watch to buy her the jeweled combs for her hair she had long wanted; in the end, neither of them can use their gifts. In dramatic irony, narrative informs audiences of more than its characters know. For example, in *Romeo and Juliet,* the audience is made aware that Juliet is only asleep, while Romeo believes her to be dead, which then leads to Romeo's death.

Copyright © Mometrix Media. You have been licensed one copy of this document for personal use only. Any other reproduction or redistribution is strictly prohibited. All rights reserved. This content is provided for test preparation purposes only and does not imply an endorsement by Mometrix of any particular political, scientific, or religious point of view.

# Reading Comprehension

## UNDERSTANDING A PASSAGE

One of the most important skills in reading comprehension is the identification of **topics** and **main ideas**. There is a subtle difference between these two features. The topic is the subject of a text (i.e., what the text is all about). The main idea, on the other hand, is the most important point being made by the author. The topic is usually expressed in a few words at the most while the main idea often needs a full sentence to be completely defined. As an example, a short passage might be written on the topic of penguins, and the main idea could be written as *Penguins are different from other birds in many ways*. In most nonfiction writing, the topic and the main idea will be **stated directly** and often appear in a sentence at the very beginning or end of the text. When being tested on an understanding of the author's topic, you may be able to skim the passage for the general idea by reading only the first sentence of each paragraph. A body paragraph's first sentence is often—but not always—the main **topic sentence** which gives you a summary of the content in the paragraph.

However, there are cases in which the reader must figure out an **unstated** topic or main idea. In these instances, you must read every sentence of the text and try to come up with an overarching idea that is supported by each of those sentences.

Note: The main idea should not be confused with the thesis statement. While the main idea gives a brief, general summary of a text, the thesis statement provides a **specific perspective** on an issue that the author supports with evidence.

> **Review Video: Topics and Main Ideas**
> Visit mometrix.com/academy and enter code: 407801

**Supporting details** are smaller pieces of evidence that provide backing for the main point. In order to show that a main idea is correct or valid, an author must add details that prove their point. All texts contain details, but they are only classified as supporting details when they serve to reinforce some larger point. Supporting details are most commonly found in informative and persuasive texts. In some cases, they will be clearly indicated with terms like *for example* or *for instance*, or they will be enumerated with terms like *first*, *second*, and *last*. However, you need to be prepared for texts that do not contain those indicators. As a reader, you should consider whether the author's supporting details really back up his or her main point. Details can be factual and correct, yet they may not be **relevant** to the author's point. Conversely, details can be relevant, but be ineffective because they are based on opinion or assertions that cannot be proven.

> **Review Video: Supporting Details**
> Visit mometrix.com/academy and enter code: 396297

An example of a main idea is: *Giraffes live in the Serengeti of Africa*. A supporting detail about giraffes could be: *A giraffe in this region benefits from a long neck by reaching twigs and leaves on tall trees*. The main idea gives the general idea that the text is about giraffes. The supporting detail gives a specific fact about how the giraffes eat.

## ORGANIZATION OF THE TEXT

The way a text is organized can help readers understand the author's intent and his or her conclusions. There are various ways to organize a text, and each one has a purpose and use. Usually, authors will organize information logically in a passage so the reader can follow and locate the

Copyright © Mometrix Media. You have been licensed one copy of this document for personal use only. Any other reproduction or redistribution is strictly prohibited. All rights reserved. This content is provided for test preparation purposes only and does not imply an endorsement by Mometrix of any particular political, scientific, or religious point of view.

information within the text. However, since not all passages are written with the same logical structure, you need to be familiar with several different types of passage structure.

> **Review Video: <u>Organizational Methods to Structure Text</u>**
> Visit mometrix.com/academy and enter code: 606263
>
> **Review Video: <u>Sequence of Events in a Story</u>**
> Visit mometrix.com/academy and enter code: 807512

## CHRONOLOGICAL

When using **chronological** order, the author presents information in the order that it happened. For example, biographies are typically written in chronological order. The subject's birth and childhood are presented first, followed by their adult life, and lastly the events leading up to the person's death.

## CAUSE AND EFFECT

One of the most common text structures is **cause and effect**. A **cause** is an act or event that makes something happen, and an **effect** is the thing that happens as a result of the cause. A cause-and-effect relationship is not always explicit, but there are some terms in English that signal causes, such as *since*, *because*, and *due to*. Furthermore, terms that signal effects include *consequently, therefore, this leads to*. As an example, consider the sentence *Because the sky was clear, Ron did not bring an umbrella*. The cause is the clear sky, and the effect is that Ron did not bring an umbrella. However, readers may find that sometimes the cause-and-effect relationship will not be clearly noted. For instance, the sentence *He was late and missed the meeting* does not contain any signaling words, but the sentence still contains a cause (he was late) and an effect (he missed the meeting).

> **Review Video: <u>Cause and Effect</u>**
> Visit mometrix.com/academy and enter code: 868099

## MULTIPLE EFFECTS

Be aware of the possibility for a single cause to have **multiple effects.** (e.g., *Single cause*: Because you left your homework on the table, your dog engulfed the assignment. *Multiple effects*: As a result, you receive a failing grade, your parents do not allow you to go out with your friends, you miss out on the new movie, and one of your classmates spoils it for you before you have another chance to watch it).

## MULTIPLE CAUSES

Also, there is the possibility for a single effect to have **multiple causes.** (e.g., *Single effect*: Alan has a fever. *Multiple causes*: An unexpected cold front came through the area, and Alan forgot to take his multi-vitamin to avoid getting sick.) Additionally, an effect can in turn be the cause of another effect, in what is known as a cause-and-effect chain. (e.g., As a result of her disdain for procrastination, Lynn prepared for her exam. This led to her passing her test with high marks. Hence, her resume was accepted and her application was approved.)

## CAUSE AND EFFECT IN PERSUASIVE ESSAYS

**Persuasive essays**, in which an author tries to make a convincing argument and change the minds of readers, usually include cause-and-effect relationships. However, these relationships should not always be taken at face value. Frequently, an author will assume a cause or take an effect for granted. To read a persuasive essay effectively, readers need to judge the cause-and-effect relationships that the author is presenting. For instance, imagine an author wrote the following: *The*

49

Copyright © Mometrix Media. You have been licensed one copy of this document for personal use only. Any other reproduction or redistribution is strictly prohibited. All rights reserved. This content is provided for test preparation purposes only and does not imply an endorsement by Mometrix of any particular political, scientific, or religious point of view.

*parking deck has been unprofitable because people would prefer to ride their bikes.* The relationship is clear: the cause is that people prefer to ride their bikes, and the effect is that the parking deck has been unprofitable. However, readers should consider whether this argument is conclusive. Perhaps there are other reasons for the failure of the parking deck: a down economy, excessive fees, etc. Too often, authors present causal relationships as if they are fact rather than opinion. Readers should be on the alert for these dubious claims.

## PROBLEM-SOLUTION

Some nonfiction texts are organized to **present a problem** followed by a solution. For this type of text, the problem is often explained before the solution is offered. In some cases, as when the problem is well known, the solution may be introduced briefly at the beginning. Other passages may focus on the solution, and the problem will be referenced only occasionally. Some texts will outline multiple solutions to a problem, leaving readers to choose among them. If the author has an interest or an allegiance to one solution, he or she may fail to mention or describe accurately some of the other solutions. Readers should be careful of the author's agenda when reading a problem-solution text. Only by understanding the author's perspective and interests can one develop a proper judgment of the proposed solution.

## COMPARE AND CONTRAST

Many texts follow the **compare-and-contrast** model in which the similarities and differences between two ideas or things are explored. Analysis of the similarities between ideas is called **comparison**. In an ideal comparison, the author places ideas or things in an equivalent structure, i.e., the author presents the ideas in the same way. If an author wants to show the similarities between cricket and baseball, then he or she may do so by summarizing the equipment and rules for each game. Be mindful of the similarities as they appear in the passage and take note of any differences that are mentioned. Often, these small differences will only reinforce the more general similarity.

> **Review Video: Compare and Contrast Essays**
> Visit mometrix.com/academy and enter code: 798319

Thinking critically about ideas and conclusions can seem like a daunting task. One way to ease this task is to understand the basic elements of ideas and writing techniques. Looking at the ways different ideas relate to each other can be a good way for readers to begin their analysis. For instance, sometimes authors will write about two ideas that are in opposition to each other. Or, one author will provide his or her ideas on a topic, and another author may respond in opposition. The analysis of these opposing ideas is known as **contrast**. Contrast is often marred by the author's obvious partiality to one of the ideas. A discerning reader will be put off by an author who does not engage in a fair fight. In an analysis of opposing ideas, both ideas should be presented in clear and reasonable terms. If the author does prefer a side, you need to read carefully to determine the areas where the author shows or avoids this preference. In an analysis of opposing ideas, you should proceed through the passage by marking the major differences point by point with an eye that is looking for an explanation of each side's view. For instance, in an analysis of capitalism and communism, there is an importance in outlining each side's view on labor, markets, prices, personal responsibility, etc. Additionally, as you read through the passages, you should note whether the opposing views present each side in a similar manner.

## SEQUENCE

Readers must be able to identify a text's **sequence**, or the order in which things happen. Often, when the sequence is very important to the author, the text is indicated with signal words like *first,*

Copyright © Mometrix Media. You have been licensed one copy of this document for personal use only. Any other reproduction or redistribution is strictly prohibited. All rights reserved. This content is provided for test preparation purposes only and does not imply an endorsement by Mometrix of any particular political, scientific, or religious point of view.

*then*, *next*, and *last*. However, a sequence can be merely implied and must be noted by the reader. Consider the sentence *He walked through the garden and gave water and fertilizer to the plants*. Clearly, the man did not walk through the garden before he collected water and fertilizer for the plants. So, the implied sequence is that he first collected water, then he collected fertilizer, next he walked through the garden, and last he gave water or fertilizer as necessary to the plants. Texts do not always proceed in an orderly sequence from first to last. Sometimes they begin at the end and start over at the beginning. As a reader, you can enhance your understanding of the passage by taking brief notes to clarify the sequence.

## MAKING CONNECTIONS TO ENHANCE COMPREHENSION

Reading involves thinking. For good comprehension, readers make **text-to-self**, **text-to-text**, and **text-to-world connections**. Making connections helps readers understand text better and predict what might occur next based on what they already know, such as how characters in the story feel or what happened in another text. Text-to-self connections with the reader's life and experiences make literature more personally relevant and meaningful to readers. Readers can make connections before, during, and after reading—including whenever the text reminds them of something similar they have encountered in life or other texts. The genre, setting, characters, plot elements, literary structure and devices, and themes an author uses allow a reader to make connections to other works of literature or to people and events in their own lives. Venn diagrams and other graphic organizers help visualize connections. Readers can also make double-entry notes: key content, ideas, events, words, and quotations on one side, and the connections with these on the other.

## SUMMARIZING LITERATURE TO SUPPORT COMPREHENSION

When reading literature, especially demanding works, **summarizing** helps readers identify important information and organize it in their minds. They can also identify themes, problems, and solutions, and can sequence the story. Readers can summarize before, during, and after they read. They should use their own words, as they do when describing a personal event or giving directions. Previewing a text's organization before reading by examining the book cover, table of contents, and illustrations also aids summarizing. Making notes of key words and ideas in a graphic organizer while reading can benefit readers in the same way. Graphic organizers are another useful method; readers skim the text to determine main ideas and then narrow the list with the aid of the organizer. Unimportant details should be omitted in summaries. Summaries can be organized using description, problem-solution, comparison-contrast, sequence, main ideas, or cause-and-effect.

> **Review Video: Summarizing Text**
> Visit mometrix.com/academy and enter code: 172903

## PARAPHRASING

**Paraphrasing** is another method that the reader can use to aid in comprehension. When paraphrasing, one puts what they have read into their own words by rephrasing what the author has written, or one "translates" all of what the author shared into their own words by including as many details as they can.

Copyright © Mometrix Media. You have been licensed one copy of this document for personal use only. Any other reproduction or redistribution is strictly prohibited. All rights reserved. This content is provided for test preparation purposes only and does not imply an endorsement by Mometrix of any particular political, scientific, or religious point of view.

## CHAPTER QUIZ

**1. All of the following are used for good comprehension, EXCEPT:**

    a.  Text-to-self connections.

    b.  Text-to-others connections.

    c.  Text-to-text connections.

    d.  Text-to-world connections.

**2. All of the following are terms in English that signal causes, EXCEPT:**

    a.  Because.

    b.  Due to.

    c.  Since.

    d.  Therefore.

## CHAPTER QUIZ ANSWER KEY

**1. B:** Reading involves thinking. For good comprehension, readers make text-to-self, text-to-text, and text-to-world connections. Making connections helps readers understand text better and predict what might occur next based on what they already know, such as how characters in the story feel or what happened in another text. Text-to-self connections with the reader's life and experiences make literature more personally relevant and meaningful to readers. Readers can make connections before, during, and after reading—including whenever the text reminds them of something similar they have encountered in life or other texts. The genre, setting, characters, plot elements, themes, and literary structure and devices an author uses allow a reader to make connections to other works of literature or to people and events in their own lives. Venn diagrams and other graphic organizers help visualize connections. Readers can also make double-entry notes: key content, ideas, events, words, and quotations on one side, and the connections with these on the other.

**2. D:** One of the most common text structures is cause and effect. A cause is an act or event that makes something happen, and an effect is the thing that happens as a result of the cause. A cause-and-effect relationship is not always explicit, but there are some terms in English that signal causes, such as *since, because,* and *due to.* Furthermore, terms that signal effects include *consequently, therefore,* and *this leads to.* As an example, consider the sentence, "Because the sky was clear, Ron did not bring an umbrella." The cause is the clear sky, and the effect is that Ron did not bring an umbrella. However, readers may find that sometimes the cause-and-effect relationship will not be clearly noted. For instance, the sentence, "He was late and missed the meeting," does not contain any signaling words, but the sentence still contains a cause ("he was late") and an effect ("he missed the meeting").

Copyright © Mometrix Media. You have been licensed one copy of this document for personal use only. Any other reproduction or redistribution is strictly prohibited. All rights reserved. This content is provided for test preparation purposes only and does not imply an endorsement by Mometrix of any particular political, scientific, or religious point of view.

# Making Predictions and Inferences

## MAKING PREDICTIONS

When we read literature, **making predictions** about what will happen in the writing reinforces our purpose for reading and prepares us mentally. A **prediction** is a guess about what will happen next. Readers constantly make predictions based on what they have read and what they already know. We can make predictions before we begin reading and during our reading. Consider the following sentence: *Staring at the computer screen in shock, Kim blindly reached over for the brimming glass of water on the shelf to her side.* The sentence suggests that Kim is distracted, and that she is not looking at the glass that she is going to pick up. So, a reader might predict that Kim is going to knock over the glass. Of course, not every prediction will be accurate: perhaps Kim will pick the glass up cleanly. Nevertheless, the author has certainly created the expectation that the water might be spilled.

As we read on, we can test the accuracy of our predictions, revise them in light of additional reading, and confirm or refute our predictions. Predictions are always subject to revision as the reader acquires more information. A reader can make predictions by observing the title and illustrations; noting the structure, characters, and subject; drawing on existing knowledge relative to the subject; and asking "why" and "who" questions. Connecting reading to what we already know enables us to learn new information and construct meaning. For example, before third-graders read a book about Johnny Appleseed, they may start a KWL chart—a list of what they *Know*, what they *Want* to know or learn, and what they have *Learned* after reading. Activating existing background knowledge and thinking about the text before reading improves comprehension.

> **Review Video: Predictive Reading**
> Visit mometrix.com/academy and enter code: 437248

***Test-taking tip***: To respond to questions requiring future predictions, your answers should be based on evidence of past or present behavior and events.

## EVALUATING PREDICTIONS

When making predictions, readers should be able to explain how they developed their prediction. One way readers can defend their thought process is by citing textual evidence. Textual evidence to evaluate reader predictions about literature includes specific synopses of the work, paraphrases of the work or parts of it, and direct quotations from the work. These references to the text must support the prediction by indicating, clearly or unclearly, what will happen later in the story. A text may provide these indications through literary devices such as foreshadowing. Foreshadowing is anything in a text that gives the reader a hint about what is to come by emphasizing the likelihood of an event or development. Foreshadowing can occur through descriptions, exposition, and dialogue. Foreshadowing in dialogue usually occurs when a character gives a warning or expresses a strong feeling that a certain event will occur. Foreshadowing can also occur through irony. However, unlike other forms of foreshadowing, the events that seem the most likely are the opposite of what actually happens. Instances of foreshadowing and irony can be summarized, paraphrased, or quoted to defend a reader's prediction.

> **Review Video: Textual Evidence for Predictions**
> Visit mometrix.com/academy and enter code: 261070

Copyright © Mometrix Media. You have been licensed one copy of this document for personal use only. Any other reproduction or redistribution is strictly prohibited. All rights reserved. This content is provided for test preparation purposes only and does not imply an endorsement by Mometrix of any particular political, scientific, or religious point of view.

## DRAWING CONCLUSIONS FROM INFERENCES

Inferences about literary text are logical conclusions that readers make based on their observations and previous knowledge. An inference is based on both what is found in a passage or a story and what is known from personal experience. For instance, a story may say that a character is frightened and can hear howling in the distance. Based on both what is in the text and personal knowledge, it is a logical conclusion that the character is frightened because he hears the sound of wolves. A good inference is supported by the information in a passage.

### IMPLICIT AND EXPLICIT INFORMATION

By inferring, readers construct meanings from text that are personally relevant. By combining their own schemas or concepts and their background information pertinent to the text with what they read, readers interpret it according to both what the author has conveyed and their own unique perspectives. Inferences are different from **explicit information**, which is clearly stated in a passage. Authors do not always explicitly spell out every meaning in what they write; many meanings are implicit. Through inference, readers can comprehend implied meanings in the text, and also derive personal significance from it, making the text meaningful and memorable to them. Inference is a natural process in everyday life. When readers infer, they can draw conclusions about what the author is saying, predict what may reasonably follow, amend these predictions as they continue to read, interpret the import of themes, and analyze the characters' feelings and motivations through their actions.

### EXAMPLE OF DRAWING CONCLUSIONS FROM INFERENCES

*Read the excerpt and decide why Jana finally relaxed.*

> Jana loved her job, but the work was very demanding. She had trouble relaxing. She called a friend, but she still thought about work. She ordered a pizza, but eating it did not help. Then, her kitten jumped on her lap and began to purr. Jana leaned back and began to hum a little tune. She felt better.

You can draw the conclusion that Jana relaxed because her kitten jumped on her lap. The kitten purred, and Jana leaned back and hummed a tune. Then she felt better. The excerpt does not explicitly say that this is the reason why she was able to relax. The text leaves the matter unclear, but the reader can infer or make a "best guess" that this is the reason she is relaxing. This is a logical conclusion based on the information in the passage. It is the best conclusion a reader can make based on the information he or she has read. Inferences are based on the information in a passage, but they are not directly stated in the passage.

***Test-taking tip***: While being tested on your ability to make correct inferences, you must look for **contextual clues**. An answer can be true, but not the best or most correct answer. The contextual clues will help you find the answer that is the **best answer** out of the given choices. Be careful in your reading to understand the context in which a phrase is stated. When asked for the implied meaning of a statement made in the passage, you should immediately locate the statement and read the **context** in which the statement was made. Also, look for an answer choice that has a similar phrase to the statement in question.

> **Review Video: Inference**
> Visit mometrix.com/academy and enter code: 379203
>
> **Review Video: How to Support a Conclusion**
> Visit mometrix.com/academy and enter code: 281653

Copyright © Mometrix Media. You have been licensed one copy of this document for personal use only. Any other reproduction or redistribution is strictly prohibited. All rights reserved. This content is provided for test preparation purposes only and does not imply an endorsement by Mometrix of any particular political, scientific, or religious point of view.

Copyright © Mometrix Media. You have been licensed one copy of this document for personal use only. Any other reproduction or redistribution is strictly prohibited. All rights reserved. This content is provided for test preparation purposes only and does not imply an endorsement by Mometrix of any particular political, scientific, or religious point of view.

## CHAPTER QUIZ

**1. Which of the following describes logical conclusions that readers make based on their observations and previous knowledge?**

- a. Imperatives
- b. Interrogatives
- c. Inferences
- d. Predictions

## CHAPTER QUIZ ANSWER KEY

**1. C:** Inferences about literary text are logical conclusions that readers make based on their observations and previous knowledge. An inference is based on both what is found in a passage or a story and what is known from personal experience. For instance, a story may say that a character is frightened and can hear howling in the distance. Based on both what is in the text and personal knowledge, it is a logical conclusion that the character is frightened because they hear the sound of wolves. A good inference is supported by the information in a passage.

Copyright © Mometrix Media. You have been licensed one copy of this document for personal use only. Any other reproduction or redistribution is strictly prohibited. All rights reserved.
This content is provided for test preparation purposes only and does not imply an endorsement by Mometrix of any particular political, scientific, or religious point of view.

# Interactions with Texts

## PURPOSES FOR WRITING

In order to be an effective reader, one must pay attention to the author's **position** and **purpose**. Even those texts that seem objective and impartial, like textbooks, have a position and bias. Readers need to take these positions into account when considering the author's message. When an author uses emotional language or clearly favors one side of an argument, his or her position is clear. However, the author's position may be evident not only in what he or she writes, but also in what he or she doesn't write. In a normal setting, a reader would want to review some other texts on the same topic in order to develop a view of the author's position. If this was not possible, then you would want to at least acquire some background about the author. However, since you are in the middle of an exam and the only source of information is the text, you should look for language and argumentation that seems to indicate a particular stance on the subject.

> **Review Video: Author's Position**
> Visit mometrix.com/academy and enter code: 827954

Usually, identifying the author's **purpose** is easier than identifying his or her position. In most cases, the author has no interest in hiding his or her purpose. A text that is meant to entertain, for instance, should be written to please the reader. Most narratives, or stories, are written to entertain, though they may also inform or persuade. Informative texts are easy to identify, while the most difficult purpose of a text to identify is persuasion because the author has an interest in making this purpose hard to detect. When a reader discovers that the author is trying to persuade, he or she should be skeptical of the argument. For this reason, persuasive texts often try to establish an entertaining tone and hope to amuse the reader into agreement. On the other hand, an informative tone may be implemented to create an appearance of authority and objectivity.

An author's purpose is evident often in the organization of the text (e.g., section headings in bold font points to an informative text). However, you may not have such organization available to you in your exam. Instead, if the author makes his or her main idea clear from the beginning, then the likely purpose of the text is to inform. If the author begins by making a claim and provides various arguments to support that claim, then the purpose is probably to persuade. If the author tells a story or wants to gain the reader's attention more than to push a particular point or deliver information, then his or her purpose is most likely to entertain. As a reader, you must judge authors on how well they accomplish their purpose. In other words, you need to consider the type of passage (e.g., technical, persuasive, etc.) that the author has written and if the author has followed the requirements of the passage type.

## MAKING LOGICAL CONCLUSIONS ABOUT A PASSAGE

A reader should always be drawing conclusions from the text. Sometimes conclusions are **implied** from written information, and other times the information is **stated directly** within the passage. One should always aim to draw conclusions from information stated within a passage, rather than to draw them from mere implications. At times an author may provide some information and then describe a counterargument. Readers should be alert for direct statements that are subsequently rejected or weakened by the author. Furthermore, you should always read through the entire passage before drawing conclusions. Many readers are trained to expect the author's conclusions at either the beginning or the end of the passage, but many texts do not adhere to this format.

Drawing conclusions from information implied within a passage requires confidence on the part of the reader. **Implications** are things that the author does not state directly, but readers can assume

57

Copyright © Mometrix Media. You have been licensed one copy of this document for personal use only. Any other reproduction or redistribution is strictly prohibited. All rights reserved.
This content is provided for test preparation purposes only and does not imply an endorsement by Mometrix of any particular political, scientific, or religious point of view.

based on what the author does say. Consider the following passage: *I stepped outside and opened my umbrella. By the time I got to work, the cuffs of my pants were soaked.* The author never states that it is raining, but this fact is clearly implied. Conclusions based on implication must be well supported by the text. In order to draw a solid conclusion, readers should have **multiple pieces of evidence**. If readers have only one piece, they must be assured that there is no other possible explanation than their conclusion. A good reader will be able to draw many conclusions from information implied by the text, which will be a great help on the exam.

## DRAWING CONCLUSIONS

A common type of inference that a reader has to make is **drawing a conclusion**. The reader makes this conclusion based on the information provided within a text. Certain facts are included to help a reader come to a specific conclusion. For example, a story may open with a man trudging through the snow on a cold winter day, dragging a sled behind him. The reader can logically **infer** from the setting of the story that the man is wearing heavy winter clothes in order to stay warm. Information is implied based on the setting of a story, which is why **setting** is an important element of the text. If the same man in the example was trudging down a beach on a hot summer day, dragging a surf board behind him, the reader would assume that the man is not wearing heavy clothes. The reader makes inferences based on their own experiences and the information presented to them in the story.

*Test-taking tip*: When asked to identify a conclusion that may be drawn, look for critical "hedge" phrases, such as *likely, may, can*, and *will often*, among many others. When you are being tested on this knowledge, remember the question that writers insert into these hedge phrases to cover every possibility. Often an answer will be wrong simply because there is no room for exception. Extreme positive or negative answers (such as always or never) are usually not correct. When answering these questions, the reader **should not** use any outside knowledge that is not gathered directly or reasonably inferred from the passage. Correct answers can be derived straight from the passage.

### EXAMPLE

Read the following sentence from *Little Women* by Louisa May Alcott and draw a conclusion based upon the information presented:

> *You know the reason Mother proposed not having any presents this Christmas was because it is going to be a hard winter for everyone; and she thinks we ought not to spend money for pleasure, when our men are suffering so in the army.*

Based on the information in the sentence, the reader can conclude, or **infer**, that the men are away at war while the women are still at home. The pronoun *our* gives a clue to the reader that the character is speaking about men she knows. In addition, the reader can assume that the character is speaking to a brother or sister, since the term "Mother" is used by the character while speaking to another person. The reader can also come to the conclusion that the characters celebrate Christmas, since it is mentioned in the **context** of the sentence. In the sentence, the mother is presented as an unselfish character who is opinionated and thinks about the wellbeing of other people.

Copyright © Mometrix Media. You have been licensed one copy of this document for personal use only. Any other reproduction or redistribution is strictly prohibited. All rights reserved.
This content is provided for test preparation purposes only and does not imply an endorsement by Mometrix of any particular political, scientific, or religious point of view.

## COMPARING TWO STORIES

When presented with two different stories, there will be **similarities** and **differences** between the two. A reader needs to make a list, or other graphic organizer, of the points presented in each story. Once the reader has written down the main point and supporting points for each story, the two sets of ideas can be compared. The reader can then present each idea and show how it is the same or different in the other story. This is called **comparing and contrasting ideas**.

The reader can compare ideas by stating, for example: "In Story 1, the author believes that humankind will one day land on Mars, whereas in Story 2, the author believes that Mars is too far away for humans to ever step foot on." Note that the two viewpoints are different in each story that the reader is comparing. A reader may state that: "Both stories discussed the likelihood of humankind landing on Mars." This statement shows how the viewpoint presented in both stories is based on the same topic, rather than how each viewpoint is different. The reader will complete a comparison of two stories with a conclusion.

> **Review Video: <u>Comparing Two Stories</u>**
> Visit mometrix.com/academy and enter code: 833765

## OUTLINING A PASSAGE

As an aid to drawing conclusions, **outlining** the information contained in the passage should be a familiar skill to readers. An effective outline will reveal the structure of the passage and will lead to solid conclusions. An effective outline will have a title that refers to the basic subject of the text, though the title does not need to restate the main idea. In most outlines, the main idea will be the first major section. Each major idea in the passage will be established as the head of a category. For instance, the most common outline format calls for the main ideas of the passage to be indicated with Roman numerals. In an effective outline of this kind, each of the main ideas will be represented by a Roman numeral and none of the Roman numerals will designate minor details or secondary ideas. Moreover, all supporting ideas and details should be placed in the appropriate place on the outline. An outline does not need to include every detail listed in the text, but it should feature all of those that are central to the argument or message. Each of these details should be listed under the corresponding main idea.

> **Review Video: <u>Outlining</u>**
> Visit mometrix.com/academy and enter code: 584445

## USING GRAPHIC ORGANIZERS

Ideas from a text can also be organized using **graphic organizers**. A graphic organizer is a way to simplify information and take key points from the text. A graphic organizer such as a timeline may have an event listed for a corresponding date on the timeline, while an outline may have an event listed under a key point that occurs in the text. Each reader needs to create the type of graphic organizer that works the best for him or her in terms of being able to recall information from a story. Examples include a spider-map, which takes a main idea from the story and places it in a bubble with supporting points branching off the main idea. An outline is useful for diagramming the main and supporting points of the entire story, and a Venn diagram compares and contrasts characteristics of two or more ideas.

> **Review Video: <u>Graphic Organizers</u>**
> Visit mometrix.com/academy and enter code: 665513

Copyright © Mometrix Media. You have been licensed one copy of this document for personal use only. Any other reproduction or redistribution is strictly prohibited. All rights reserved. This content is provided for test preparation purposes only and does not imply an endorsement by Mometrix of any particular political, scientific, or religious point of view.

## SUMMARIZING

A helpful tool is the ability to **summarize** the information that you have read in a paragraph or passage format. This process is similar to creating an effective outline. First, a summary should accurately define the main idea of the passage, though the summary does not need to explain this main idea in exhaustive detail. The summary should continue by laying out the most important supporting details or arguments from the passage. All of the significant supporting details should be included, and none of the details included should be irrelevant or insignificant. Also, the summary should accurately report all of these details. Too often, the desire for brevity in a summary leads to the sacrifice of clarity or accuracy. Summaries are often difficult to read because they omit all of the graceful language, digressions, and asides that distinguish great writing. However, an effective summary should communicate the same overall message as the original text.

## EVALUATING A PASSAGE

It is important to understand the logical conclusion of the ideas presented in an informational text. **Identifying a logical conclusion** can help you determine whether you agree with the writer or not. Coming to this conclusion is much like making an inference: the approach requires you to combine the information given by the text with what you already know and make a logical conclusion. If the author intended for the reader to draw a certain conclusion, then you can expect the author's argumentation and detail to be leading in that direction.

One way to approach the task of drawing conclusions is to make brief **notes** of all the points made by the author. When the notes are arranged on paper, they may clarify the logical conclusion. Another way to approach conclusions is to consider whether the reasoning of the author raises any pertinent questions. Sometimes you will be able to draw several conclusions from a passage. On occasion these will be conclusions that were never imagined by the author. Therefore, be aware that these conclusions must be **supported directly by the text**.

## EVALUATION OF SUMMARIES

A summary of a literary passage is a condensation in the reader's own words of the passage's main points. Several guidelines can be used in evaluating a summary. The summary should be complete yet concise. It should be accurate, balanced, fair, neutral, and objective, excluding the reader's own opinions or reactions. It should reflect in similar proportion how much each point summarized was covered in the original passage. Summary writers should include tags of attribution, like "Macaulay argues that" to reference the original author whose ideas are represented in the summary. Summary writers should not overuse quotations; they should only quote central concepts or phrases they cannot precisely convey in words other than those of the original author. Another aspect of evaluating a summary is considering whether it can stand alone as a coherent, unified composition. In addition, evaluation of a summary should include whether its writer has cited the original source of the passage they have summarized so that readers can find it.

Copyright © Mometrix Media. You have been licensed one copy of this document for personal use only. Any other reproduction or redistribution is strictly prohibited. All rights reserved.
This content is provided for test preparation purposes only and does not imply an endorsement by Mometrix of any particular political, scientific, or religious point of view.

## CHAPTER QUIZ

**1. Which of the following is most important when drawing conclusions from a text?**
- a. The conclusions make sense to others.
- b. The conclusions are supported directly by the text.
- c. The conclusions agree with previous convictions.
- d. The conclusions align with the author's purpose for writing the text.

**2. All of the following are true about summaries, EXCEPT:**
- a. They should focus on the main point of the text rather than proportional to how much each point was covered in the passage.
- b. They should be accurate, balanced, fair, neutral, and objective.
- c. They should be complete and concise.
- d. They should only quote central concepts or phrases that cannot be precisely conveyed in words other than those of the original author.

## CHAPTER QUIZ ANSWER KEY

**1. B:** It is important to understand the logical conclusion of the ideas presented in an informational text. Identifying a logical conclusion can help readers determine whether they agree with the writer or not. Coming to this conclusion is much like making an inference: the approach requires readers to combine the information given by the text with what they already know and make a logical conclusion. If the author intended for the reader to draw a certain conclusion, then readers can expect the author's argumentation and detail to be leading in that direction. Sometimes a reader will be able to draw several conclusions from a passage. On occasion these will be conclusions that were never imagined by the author. Therefore, be aware that these conclusions must be supported directly by the text.

**2. A:** A summary of a literary passage is a condensation in the reader's own words of the passage's main points. Several guidelines can be used in evaluating a summary. The summary should be complete yet concise. It should be accurate, balanced, fair, neutral, and objective, excluding the reader's own opinions or reactions. It should reflect in similar proportion how much each point summarized was covered in the original passage. Summary writers should include tags of attribution, like "Macaulay argues that" to reference the original author whose ideas are represented in the summary. Summary writers should not overuse quotations, but only quote central concepts or phrases they cannot precisely convey in words other than those of the original author. Another aspect of evaluating a summary is considering whether it can stand alone as a coherent, unified composition. In addition, evaluation of a summary should include whether its writer has cited the original source of the passage they have summarized so that readers can find it.

61

Copyright © Mometrix Media. You have been licensed one copy of this document for personal use only. Any other reproduction or redistribution is strictly prohibited. All rights reserved.
This content is provided for test preparation purposes only and does not imply an endorsement by Mometrix of any particular political, scientific, or religious point of view.

# Writing

## Parts of Speech

### THE EIGHT PARTS OF SPEECH

#### NOUNS

When you talk about a person, place, thing, or idea, you are talking about a **noun**. The two main types of nouns are **common** and **proper** nouns. Also, nouns can be abstract (i.e., general) or concrete (i.e., specific).

#### COMMON NOUNS

**Common nouns** are generic names for people, places, and things. Common nouns are not usually capitalized.

Examples of common nouns:

> *People*: boy, girl, worker, manager

> *Places*: school, bank, library, home

> *Things*: dog, cat, truck, car

#### PROPER NOUNS

**Proper nouns** name specific people, places, or things. All proper nouns are capitalized.

Examples of proper nouns:

> *People*: Abraham Lincoln, George Washington, Martin Luther King, Jr.

> *Places*: Los Angeles, California; New York; Asia

> *Things*: Statue of Liberty, Earth, Lincoln Memorial

Note: When referring to the planet that we live on, capitalize *Earth*. When referring to the dirt, rocks, or land, lowercase *earth*.

#### GENERAL AND SPECIFIC NOUNS

**General nouns** are the names of conditions or ideas. **Specific nouns** name people, places, and things that are understood by using your senses.

General nouns:

> *Condition*: beauty, strength

> *Idea*: truth, peace

Copyright © Mometrix Media. You have been licensed one copy of this document for personal use only. Any other reproduction or redistribution is strictly prohibited. All rights reserved.
This content is provided for test preparation purposes only and does not imply an endorsement by Mometrix of any particular political, scientific, or religious point of view.

Specific nouns:

*People*: baby, friend, father

*Places*: town, park, city hall

*Things*: rainbow, cough, apple, silk, gasoline

## COLLECTIVE NOUNS

**Collective nouns** are the names for a group of people, places, or things that may act as a whole. The following are examples of collective nouns: *class, company, dozen, group, herd, team,* and *public*. Collective nouns usually require an article, which denotes the noun as being a single unit. For instance, a choir is a group of singers. Even though there are many singers in a choir, the word choir is grammatically treated as a single unit. If we refer to the members of the group, and not the group itself, it is no longer a collective noun.

Incorrect: The *choir are* going to compete nationally this year.

Correct: The *choir is* going to compete nationally this year.

Incorrect: The *members* of the choir *is* competing nationally this year.

Correct: The *members* of the choir *are* competing nationally this year.

## PRONOUNS

Pronouns are words that are used to stand in for nouns. A pronoun may be classified as personal, intensive, relative, interrogative, demonstrative, indefinite, and reciprocal.

**Personal**: *Nominative* is the case for nouns and pronouns that are the subject of a sentence. *Objective* is the case for nouns and pronouns that are an object in a sentence. *Possessive* is the case for nouns and pronouns that show possession or ownership.

*Singular*

|  | Nominative | Objective | Possessive |
|---|---|---|---|
| **First Person** | I | me | my, mine |
| **Second Person** | you | you | your, yours |
| **Third Person** | he, she, it | him, her, it | his, her, hers, its |

*Plural*

|  | Nominative | Objective | Possessive |
|---|---|---|---|
| **First Person** | we | us | our, ours |
| **Second Person** | you | you | your, yours |
| **Third Person** | they | them | their, theirs |

**Intensive**: I myself, you yourself, he himself, she herself, the (thing) itself, we ourselves, you yourselves, they themselves

**Relative**: which, who, whom, whose

**Interrogative**: what, which, who, whom, whose

Copyright © Mometrix Media. You have been licensed one copy of this document for personal use only. Any other reproduction or redistribution is strictly prohibited. All rights reserved. This content is provided for test preparation purposes only and does not imply an endorsement by Mometrix of any particular political, scientific, or religious point of view.

**Demonstrative**: this, that, these, those

**Indefinite**: all, any, each, everyone, either/neither, one, some, several

**Reciprocal**: each other, one another

---

**Review Video: <u>Nouns and Pronouns</u>**
Visit mometrix.com/academy and enter code: 312073

---

## VERBS

If you want to write a sentence, then you need a verb. Without a verb, you have no sentence. The verb of a sentence indicates action or being. In other words, the verb shows something's action or state of being or the action that has been done to something.

### TRANSITIVE AND INTRANSITIVE VERBS

A **transitive verb** is a verb whose action (e.g., drive, run, jump) indicates a receiver (e.g., car, dog, kangaroo). **Intransitive verbs** do not indicate a receiver of an action. In other words, the action of the verb does not point to a subject or object.

    **Transitive**: He plays the piano. | The piano was played by him.

    **Intransitive**: He plays. | John plays well.

A dictionary will tell you whether a verb is transitive or intransitive. Some verbs can be transitive and intransitive.

### ACTION VERBS AND LINKING VERBS

**Action verbs** show what the subject is doing. In other words, an action verb shows action. Unlike most types of words, a single action verb, in the right context, can be an entire sentence. **Linking verbs** link the subject of a sentence to a noun or pronoun, or they link a subject with an adjective. You always need a verb if you want a complete sentence. However, linking verbs on their own cannot be a complete sentence.

Common linking verbs include *appear, be, become, feel, grow, look, seem, smell, sound,* and *taste.* However, any verb that shows a condition and connects to a noun, pronoun, or adjective that describes the subject of a sentence is a linking verb.

**Action**: He sings. | Run! | Go! | I talk with him every day. | She reads.

**Linking**:

    Incorrect: I am.

    Correct: I am John. | The roses smell lovely. | I feel tired.

Note: Some verbs are followed by words that look like prepositions, but they are a part of the verb and a part of the verb's meaning. These are known as phrasal verbs, and examples include *call off, look up,* and *drop off.*

---

**Review Video: <u>Action Verbs and Linking Verbs</u>**
Visit mometrix.com/academy and enter code: 743142

---

Copyright © Mometrix Media. You have been licensed one copy of this document for personal use only. Any other reproduction or redistribution is strictly prohibited. All rights reserved.
This content is provided for test preparation purposes only and does not imply an endorsement by Mometrix of any particular political, scientific, or religious point of view.

## VOICE

Transitive verbs come in active or passive **voice**. If something does an action or is acted upon, then you will know whether a verb is active or passive. When the subject of the sentence is doing the action, the verb is in **active voice**. When the subject is acted upon, the verb is in **passive voice**.

**Active**: Jon drew the picture. (The subject *Jon* is doing the action of *drawing a picture*.)

**Passive**: The picture is drawn by Jon. (The subject *picture* is receiving the action from Jon.)

## VERB TENSES

A verb **tense** shows the different form of a verb to point to the time of an action. The present and past tense are indicated by the verb's form. An action in the present, *I talk*, can change form for the past: *I talked*. However, for the other tenses, an auxiliary (i.e., helping) verb is needed to show the change in form. These helping verbs include *am, are, is | have, has, had | was, were, will* (or *shall*).

| | |
|---|---|
| Present: I talk | Present perfect: I have talked |
| Past: I talked | Past perfect: I had talked |
| Future: I will talk | Future perfect: I will have talked |

**Present**: The action happens at the current time.

Example: He *walks* to the store every morning.

To show that something is happening right now, use the progressive present tense: I *am walking*.

**Past**: The action happened in the past.

Example: He *walked* to the store an hour ago.

**Future**: The action is going to happen later.

Example: I *will walk* to the store tomorrow.

**Present perfect**: The action started in the past and continues into the present or took place previously at an unspecified time

Example: I *have walked* to the store three times today.

**Past perfect**: The second action happened in the past. The first action came before the second.

Example: Before I walked to the store (Action 2), I *had walked* to the library (Action 1).

**Future perfect**: An action that uses the past and the future. In other words, the action is complete before a future moment.

Example: When she comes for the supplies (future moment), I *will have walked* to the store (action completed before the future moment).

> **Review Video: Present Perfect, Past Perfect, and Future Perfect Verb Tenses**
> Visit mometrix.com/academy and enter code: 269472

Copyright © Mometrix Media. You have been licensed one copy of this document for personal use only. Any other reproduction or redistribution is strictly prohibited. All rights reserved. This content is provided for test preparation purposes only and does not imply an endorsement by Mometrix of any particular political, scientific, or religious point of view.

## CONJUGATING VERBS

When you need to change the form of a verb, you are **conjugating** a verb. The key forms of a verb are singular, present tense (dream); singular, past tense (dreamed); and the past participle (have dreamed). Note: the past participle needs a helping verb to make a verb tense. For example, I *have dreamed* of this day. The following tables demonstrate some of the different ways to conjugate a verb:

*Singular*

| Tense | First Person | Second Person | Third Person |
|---|---|---|---|
| Present | I dream | You dream | He, she, it dreams |
| Past | I dreamed | You dreamed | He, she, it dreamed |
| Past Participle | I have dreamed | You have dreamed | He, she, it has dreamed |

*Plural*

| Tense | First Person | Second Person | Third Person |
|---|---|---|---|
| Present | We dream | You dream | They dream |
| Past | We dreamed | You dreamed | They dreamed |
| Past Participle | We have dreamed | You have dreamed | They have dreamed |

## MOOD

There are three **moods** in English: the indicative, the imperative, and the subjunctive.

The **indicative mood** is used for facts, opinions, and questions.

Fact: You can do this.

Opinion: I think that you can do this.

Question: Do you know that you can do this?

The **imperative** is used for orders or requests.

Order: You are going to do this!

Request: Will you do this for me?

The **subjunctive mood** is for wishes and statements that go against fact.

Wish: I wish that I were famous.

Statement against fact: If I were you, I would do this. (This goes against fact because I am not you. You have the chance to do this, and I do not have the chance.)

Copyright © Mometrix Media. You have been licensed one copy of this document for personal use only. Any other reproduction or redistribution is strictly prohibited. All rights reserved.
This content is provided for test preparation purposes only and does not imply an endorsement by Mometrix of any particular political, scientific, or religious point of view.

## ADJECTIVES

An **adjective** is a word that is used to modify a noun or pronoun. An adjective answers a question: *Which one? What kind?* or *How many?* Usually, adjectives come before the words that they modify, but they may also come after a linking verb.

Which one? The *third* suit is my favorite.

What kind? This suit is *navy blue*.

How many? I am going to buy *four* pairs of socks to match the suit.

> **Review Video: Descriptive Text**
> Visit mometrix.com/academy and enter code: 174903

## ARTICLES

**Articles** are adjectives that are used to distinguish nouns as definite or indefinite. **Definite** nouns are preceded by the article *the* and indicate a specific person, place, thing, or idea. **Indefinite** nouns are preceded by *a* or *an* and do not indicate a specific person, place, thing, or idea. *A*, *an*, and *the* are the only articles. Note: *An* comes before words that start with a vowel sound. For example, "Are you going to get an **u**mbrella?"

**Definite**: I lost *the* bottle that belongs to me.

**Indefinite**: Does anyone have *a* bottle to share?

> **Review Video: Function of Articles**
> Visit mometrix.com/academy and enter code: 449383

## COMPARISON WITH ADJECTIVES

Some adjectives are relative and other adjectives are absolute. Adjectives that are **relative** can show the comparison between things. **Absolute** adjectives can also show comparison, but they do so in a different way. Let's say that you are reading two books. You think that one book is perfect, and the other book is not exactly perfect. It is not possible for one book to be more perfect than the other. Either you think that the book is perfect, or you think that the book is imperfect. In this case, perfect and imperfect are absolute adjectives.

Relative adjectives will show the different **degrees** of something or someone to something else or someone else. The three degrees of adjectives include positive, comparative, and superlative.

The **positive** degree is the normal form of an adjective.

Example: This work is *difficult.* | She is *smart.*

The **comparative** degree compares one person or thing to another person or thing.

Example: This work is *more difficult* than your work. | She is *smarter* than me.

**67**

Copyright © Mometrix Media. You have been licensed one copy of this document for personal use only. Any other reproduction or redistribution is strictly prohibited. All rights reserved.
This content is provided for test preparation purposes only and does not imply an endorsement by Mometrix of any particular political, scientific, or religious point of view.

The **superlative** degree compares more than two people or things.

Example: This is the *most difficult* work of my life. | She is the *smartest* lady in school.

> **Review Video: Adjectives**
> Visit mometrix.com/academy and enter code: 470154

### ADVERBS

An **adverb** is a word that is used to **modify** a verb, adjective, or another adverb. Usually, adverbs answer one of these questions: *When? Where? How?* and *Why?* The negatives *not* and *never* are considered adverbs. Adverbs that modify adjectives or other adverbs **strengthen** or **weaken** the words that they modify.

Examples:

He walks *quickly* through the crowd.

The water flows *smoothly* on the rocks.

Note: Adverbs are usually indicated by the morpheme *-ly*, which has been added to the root word. For instance, *quick* can be made into an adverb by adding *-ly* to construct *quickly*. Some words that end in *-ly* do not follow this rule and can behave as other parts of speech. Examples of adjectives ending in *-ly* include: *early, friendly, holy, lonely, silly*, and *ugly*. To know if a word that ends in *-ly* is an adjective or adverb, check your dictionary. Also, while many adverbs end in *-ly*, you need to remember that not all adverbs end in *-ly*.

Examples:

He is *never* angry.

You walked *across* the bridge.

> **Review Video: What is an Adverb?**
> Visit mometrix.com/academy and enter code: 713951
>
> **Review Video: Adverbs that Modify Adjectives**
> Visit mometrix.com/academy and enter code: 122570

### COMPARISON WITH ADVERBS

The rules for comparing adverbs are the same as the rules for adjectives.

The **positive** degree is the standard form of an adverb.

Example: He arrives *soon*. | She speaks *softly* to her friends.

The **comparative** degree compares one person or thing to another person or thing.

Example: He arrives *sooner* than Sarah. | She speaks *more softly* than him.

The **superlative** degree compares more than two people or things.

Copyright © Mometrix Media. You have been licensed one copy of this document for personal use only. Any other reproduction or redistribution is strictly prohibited. All rights reserved.
This content is provided for test preparation purposes only and does not imply an endorsement by Mometrix of any particular political, scientific, or religious point of view.

Example: He arrives *soonest* of the group. | She speaks the *most softly* of any of her friends.

## PREPOSITIONS

A **preposition** is a word placed before a noun or pronoun that shows the relationship between an object and another word in the sentence.

*Common prepositions*:

| | | | | |
|---|---|---|---|---|
| about | before | during | on | under |
| after | beneath | for | over | until |
| against | between | from | past | up |
| among | beyond | in | through | with |
| around | by | of | to | within |
| at | down | off | toward | without |

Examples:

The napkin is *in* the drawer.

The Earth rotates *around* the Sun.

The needle is *beneath* the haystack.

Can you find "me" *among* the words?

> **Review Video: Prepositions**
> Visit mometrix.com/academy and enter code: 946763

## CONJUNCTIONS

**Conjunctions** join words, phrases, or clauses and they show the connection between the joined pieces. **Coordinating conjunctions** connect equal parts of sentences. **Correlative conjunctions** show the connection between pairs. **Subordinating conjunctions** join subordinate (i.e., dependent) clauses with independent clauses.

### COORDINATING CONJUNCTIONS

The **coordinating conjunctions** include: *and, but, yet, or, nor, for,* and *so*

Examples:

The rock was small, *but* it was heavy.

She drove in the night, *and* he drove in the day.

Copyright © Mometrix Media. You have been licensed one copy of this document for personal use only. Any other reproduction or redistribution is strictly prohibited. All rights reserved. This content is provided for test preparation purposes only and does not imply an endorsement by Mometrix of any particular political, scientific, or religious point of view.

### CORRELATIVE CONJUNCTIONS

The **correlative conjunctions** are: *either…or | neither…nor | not only…but also*

Examples:

*Either* you are coming *or* you are staying.

He *not only* ran three miles *but also* swam 200 yards.

> **Review Video: Coordinating and Correlative Conjunctions**
> Visit mometrix.com/academy and enter code: 390329
>
> **Review Video: Adverb Equal Comparisons**
> Visit mometrix.com/academy and enter code: 231291

### SUBORDINATING CONJUNCTIONS

Common **subordinating conjunctions** include:

| | | |
|---|---|---|
| after | since | whenever |
| although | so that | where |
| because | unless | wherever |
| before | until | whether |
| in order that | when | while |

Examples:

I am hungry *because* I did not eat breakfast.

He went home *when* everyone left.

> **Review Video: Subordinating Conjunctions**
> Visit mometrix.com/academy and enter code: 958913

### INTERJECTIONS

**Interjections** are words of exclamation (i.e., audible expression of great feeling) that are used alone or as a part of a sentence. Often, they are used at the beginning of a sentence for an introduction. Sometimes, they can be used in the middle of a sentence to show a change in thought or attitude.

Common Interjections: Hey! | Oh, | Ouch! | Please! | Wow!

Copyright © Mometrix Media. You have been licensed one copy of this document for personal use only. Any other reproduction or redistribution is strictly prohibited. All rights reserved. This content is provided for test preparation purposes only and does not imply an endorsement by Mometrix of any particular political, scientific, or religious point of view.

## CHAPTER QUIZ

**1. Which of the following is NOT considered a type of mood?**

    a. Indicative
    b. Imperative
    c. Subjunctive
    d. Conjunctive

**2. How many different degrees of relative adjectives are there?**

    a. Two
    b. Three
    c. Four
    d. Five

**3. In general, adverbs may modify all of the following, EXCEPT:**

    a. Another adverb.
    b. Adjectives.
    c. Proper nouns.
    d. Verbs.

## CHAPTER QUIZ ANSWER KEY

**1. D:** There are three moods in English: the indicative, the imperative, and the subjunctive.

**2. B:** Relative adjectives will show the different degrees of something or someone to something else or someone else. The three degrees of adjectives include positive, comparative, and superlative.

**3. C:** An adverb is a word that is used to modify a verb, adjective, or another adverb. Usually, adverbs answer one of the questions: *When? Where? How?* and *Why?* The negatives *not* and *never* are considered adverbs. Adverbs that modify adjectives or other adverbs strengthen or weaken the words that they modify.

Copyright © Mometrix Media. You have been licensed one copy of this document for personal use only. Any other reproduction or redistribution is strictly prohibited. All rights reserved.
This content is provided for test preparation purposes only and does not imply an endorsement by Mometrix of any particular political, scientific, or religious point of view.

# Agreement and Sentence Structure

## SUBJECTS AND PREDICATES

### SUBJECTS

The **subject** of a sentence names who or what the sentence is about. The subject may be directly stated in a sentence, or the subject may be the implied *you*. The **complete subject** includes the simple subject and all of its modifiers. To find the complete subject, ask *Who* or *What* and insert the verb to complete the question. The answer, including any modifiers (adjectives, prepositional phrases, etc.), is the complete subject. To find the **simple subject**, remove all of the modifiers in the complete subject. Being able to locate the subject of a sentence helps with many problems, such as those involving sentence fragments and subject-verb agreement.

Examples:

> **Review Video: Subjects in English**
> Visit mometrix.com/academy and enter code: 444771

In **imperative** sentences, the verb's subject is understood (e.g., [You] Run to the store), but is not actually present in the sentence. Normally, the subject comes before the verb. However, the subject comes after the verb in sentences that begin with *There are* or *There was*.

Direct:

| John knows the way to the park. | Who knows the way to the park? | John |
| The cookies need ten more minutes. | What needs ten minutes? | The cookies |
| By five o'clock, Bill will need to leave. | Who needs to leave? | Bill |
| There are five letters on the table for him. | What is on the table? | Five letters |
| There were coffee and doughnuts in the house. | What was in the house? | Coffee and doughnuts |

Implied:

| Go to the post office for me. | Who is going to the post office? | You |
| Come and sit with me, please? | Who needs to come and sit? | You |

### PREDICATES

In a sentence, you always have a predicate and a subject. The subject tells what the sentence is about, and the **predicate** explains or describes the subject.

72

Copyright © Mometrix Media. You have been licensed one copy of this document for personal use only. Any other reproduction or redistribution is strictly prohibited. All rights reserved.
This content is provided for test preparation purposes only and does not imply an endorsement by Mometrix of any particular political, scientific, or religious point of view.

Think about the sentence *He sings*. In this sentence, we have a subject (He) and a predicate (sings). This is all that is needed for a sentence to be complete. Most sentences contain more information, but if this is all the information that you are given, then you have a complete sentence.

Now, let's look at another sentence: *John and Jane sing on Tuesday nights at the dance hall.*

subject          predicate
John and Jane  sing on Tuesday nights at the dance hall.

## SUBJECT-VERB AGREEMENT

Verbs **agree** with their subjects in number. In other words, singular subjects need singular verbs. Plural subjects need plural verbs. **Singular** is for **one** person, place, or thing. **Plural** is for **more than one** person, place, or thing. Subjects and verbs must also share the same point of view, as in first, second, or third person. The present tense ending -*s* is used on a verb if its subject is third person singular; otherwise, the verb's ending is not modified.

> **Review Video: Subject-Verb Agreement**
> Visit mometrix.com/academy and enter code: 479190

### NUMBER AGREEMENT EXAMPLES:

singular  singular
subject   verb
Single Subject and Verb: Dan  calls  home.

Dan is one person. So, the singular verb *calls* is needed.

plural   plural
subject  verb
Plural Subject and Verb: Dan and Bob  call  home.

More than one person needs the plural verb *call*.

### PERSON AGREEMENT EXAMPLES:

First Person: I *am* walking.

Second Person: You *are* walking.

Third Person: He *is* walking.

## COMPLICATIONS WITH SUBJECT-VERB AGREEMENT
### WORDS BETWEEN SUBJECT AND VERB

Words that come between the simple subject and the verb have no bearing on subject-verb agreement.

Examples:

singular          singular
subject           verb
The joy of my life returns home tonight.

The phrase *of my life* does not influence the verb *returns*.

Copyright © Mometrix Media. You have been licensed one copy of this document for personal use only. Any other reproduction or redistribution is strictly prohibited. All rights reserved. This content is provided for test preparation purposes only and does not imply an endorsement by Mometrix of any particular political, scientific, or religious point of view.

singular
subject

singular
verb

The question that still remains unanswered is "Who are you?"

Don't let the phrase "*that still remains...*" trouble you. The subject *question* goes with *is*.

## COMPOUND SUBJECTS

A compound subject is formed when two or more nouns joined by *and*, *or*, or *nor* jointly act as the subject of the sentence.

### JOINED BY AND

When a compound subject is joined by *and*, it is treated as a plural subject and requires a plural verb.

Examples:

plural
subject

plural
verb

You and Jon are invited to come to my house.

plural
subject

plural
verb

The pencil and paper belong to me.

### JOINED BY OR/NOR

For a compound subject joined by *or* or *nor*, the verb must agree in number with the part of the subject that is closest to the verb (italicized in the examples below).

Examples:

subject   verb

Today or *tomorrow* is the day.

subject   verb

Stan or *Phil* wants to read the book.

subject   verb

Neither the pen nor the *book* is on the desk.

subject   verb

Either the blanket or *pillows* arrive this afternoon.

## INDEFINITE PRONOUNS AS SUBJECT

An indefinite pronoun is a pronoun that does not refer to a specific noun. Different indefinite pronouns may only function as a singular noun, only function as a plural noun, or change depending on how they are used.

Copyright © Mometrix Media. You have been licensed one copy of this document for personal use only. Any other reproduction or redistribution is strictly prohibited. All rights reserved.
This content is provided for test preparation purposes only and does not imply an endorsement by Mometrix of any particular political, scientific, or religious point of view.

## ALWAYS SINGULAR

Pronouns such as *each*, *either*, *everybody*, *anybody*, *somebody*, and *nobody* are always singular.

Examples:

<table>
<tr><td>singular<br>subject</td><td></td><td>singular<br>verb</td><td></td></tr>
</table>

Each of the runners has a different bib number.

Is either of you ready for the game?

Note: The words *each* and *either* can also be used as adjectives (e.g., *each* person is unique). When one of these adjectives modifies the subject of a sentence, it is always a singular subject.

Everybody grows a day older every day.

Anybody is welcome to bring a tent.

## ALWAYS PLURAL

Pronouns such as *both*, *several*, and *many* are always plural.

Examples:

Both of the siblings were too tired to argue.

Many have tried, but none have succeeded.

## DEPEND ON CONTEXT

Pronouns such as *some*, *any*, *all*, *none*, *more*, and *most* can be either singular or plural depending on what they are representing in the context of the sentence.

Examples:

All of my dog's food was still there in his bowl.

By the end of the night, all of my guests were already excited about coming to my next party.

Copyright © Mometrix Media. You have been licensed one copy of this document for personal use only. Any other reproduction or redistribution is strictly prohibited. All rights reserved.
This content is provided for test preparation purposes only and does not imply an endorsement by Mometrix of any particular political, scientific, or religious point of view.

## *OTHER CASES INVOLVING PLURAL OR IRREGULAR FORM*

Some nouns are **singular in meaning but plural in form**: news, mathematics, physics, and economics.

> The *news is* coming on now.

> *Mathematics is* my favorite class.

Some nouns are plural in form and meaning, and have **no singular equivalent**: scissors and pants.

> Do these *pants come* with a shirt?

> The *scissors are* for my project.

Mathematical operations are **irregular** in their construction, but are normally considered to be **singular in meaning**.

> *One plus one is* two.

> *Three times three is* nine.

Note: Look to your **dictionary** for help when you aren't sure whether a noun with a plural form has a singular or plural meaning.

## COMPLEMENTS

A complement is a noun, pronoun, or adjective that is used to give more information about the subject or verb in the sentence.

## DIRECT OBJECTS

A direct object is a noun or pronoun that takes or receives the **action** of a verb. (Remember: a complete sentence does not need a direct object, so not all sentences will have them. A sentence needs only a subject and a verb.) When you are looking for a direct object, find the verb and ask *who* or *what*.

Examples:

> I took *the blanket.*

> Jane read *books.*

## INDIRECT OBJECTS

An indirect object is a word or group of words that show how an action had an **influence** on someone or something. If there is an indirect object in a sentence, then you always have a direct object in the sentence. When you are looking for the indirect object, find the verb and ask *to/for whom or what.*

Copyright © Mometrix Media. You have been licensed one copy of this document for personal use only. Any other reproduction or redistribution is strictly prohibited. All rights reserved.
This content is provided for test preparation purposes only and does not imply an endorsement by Mometrix of any particular political, scientific, or religious point of view.

Examples:

indirect object · direct object

We taught the old dog a new trick.

indirect object · direct object

I gave them a math lesson.

> **Review Video: Direct and Indirect Objects**
> Visit mometrix.com/academy and enter code: 817385

### PREDICATE NOMINATIVES AND PREDICATE ADJECTIVES

As we looked at previously, verbs may be classified as either action verbs or linking verbs. A linking verb is so named because it links the subject to words in the predicate that describe or define the subject. These words are called predicate nominatives (if nouns or pronouns) or predicate adjectives (if adjectives).

Examples:

subject · predicate nominative

My father is a lawyer.

subject · predicate adjective

Your mother is patient.

### PRONOUN USAGE

The **antecedent** is the noun that has been replaced by a pronoun. A pronoun and its antecedent **agree** when they have the same number (singular or plural) and gender (male, female, or neutral).

Examples:

antecedent · pronoun

**Singular agreement**: John came into town, and he played for us.

antecedent · pronoun

**Plural agreement**: John and Rick came into town, and they played for us.

To determine which is the correct pronoun to use in a compound subject or object, try each pronoun **alone** in place of the compound in the sentence. Your knowledge of pronouns will tell you which one is correct.

Example:

Bob and (I, me) will be going.

Test: (1) *I will be going* or (2) *Me will be going*. The second choice cannot be correct because *me* cannot be used as the subject of a sentence. Instead, *me* is used as an object.

**Answer**: Bob and I will be going.

Copyright © Mometrix Media. You have been licensed one copy of this document for personal use only. Any other reproduction or redistribution is strictly prohibited. All rights reserved. This content is provided for test preparation purposes only and does not imply an endorsement by Mometrix of any particular political, scientific, or religious point of view.

When a pronoun is used with a noun immediately following (as in "we boys"), try the sentence **without the added noun**.

Example:

(We/Us) boys played football last year.

Test: (1) *We played football last ye*ar or (2) *Us played football last year*. Again, the second choice cannot be correct because *us* cannot be used as a subject of a sentence. Instead, *us* is used as an object.

**Answer**: We boys played football last year.

---

**Review Video: Pronoun Usage**
Visit mometrix.com/academy and enter code: 666500

**Review Video: What is Pronoun-Antecedent Agreement?**
Visit mometrix.com/academy and enter code: 919704

---

A pronoun should point clearly to the **antecedent**. Here is how a pronoun reference can be unhelpful if it is puzzling or not directly stated.

             antecedent                      pronoun
**Unhelpful**: Ron and Jim went to the store, and he bought soda.

Who bought soda? Ron or Jim?

          antecedent                 pronoun
**Helpful**: Jim went to the store, and he bought soda.

The sentence is clear. Jim bought the soda.

Some pronouns change their form by their placement in a sentence. A pronoun that is a **subject** in a sentence comes in the **subjective case**. Pronouns that serve as **objects** appear in the **objective case**. Finally, the pronouns that are used as **possessives** appear in the **possessive case**.

Examples:

**Subjective case**: *He* is coming to the show.

The pronoun *He* is the subject of the sentence.

**Objective case**: Josh drove *him* to the airport.

The pronoun *him* is the object of the sentence.

**Possessive case**: The flowers are *mine*.

The pronoun *mine* shows ownership of the flowers.

The word *who* is a subjective-case pronoun that can be used as a **subject**. The word *whom* is an objective-case pronoun that can be used as an **object**. The words *who* and *whom* are common in subordinate clauses or in questions.

Copyright © Mometrix Media. You have been licensed one copy of this document for personal use only. Any other reproduction or redistribution is strictly prohibited. All rights reserved.
This content is provided for test preparation purposes only and does not imply an endorsement by Mometrix of any particular political, scientific, or religious point of view.

Examples:

He knows $\overbrace{\text{who}}^{\text{subject}}$ $\overbrace{\text{wants}}^{\text{verb}}$ to come.

He knows the man $\overbrace{\text{whom}}^{\text{object}}$ we $\overbrace{\text{want}}^{\text{verb}}$ at the party.

## CLAUSES

A clause is a group of words that contains both a subject and a predicate (verb). There are two types of clauses: independent and dependent. An **independent clause** contains a complete thought, while a **dependent (or subordinate) clause** does not. A dependent clause includes a subject and a verb, and may also contain objects or complements, but it cannot stand as a complete thought without being joined to an independent clause. Dependent clauses function within sentences as adjectives, adverbs, or nouns.

Example:

$\overbrace{\text{I am running}}^{\substack{\text{independent}\\\text{clause}}}$ $\overbrace{\text{because I want to stay in shape.}}^{\substack{\text{dependent}\\\text{clause}}}$

The clause *I am running* is an independent clause: it has a subject and a verb, and it gives a complete thought. The clause *because I want to stay in shape* is a dependent clause: it has a subject and a verb, but it does not express a complete thought. It adds detail to the independent clause to which it is attached.

---

**Review Video: What is a Clause?**
Visit mometrix.com/academy and enter code: 940170

**Review Video: Independent and Dependent Clauses**
Visit mometrix.com/academy and enter code: 556903

---

### TYPES OF DEPENDENT CLAUSES
#### ADJECTIVE CLAUSES

An **adjective clause** is a dependent clause that modifies a noun or a pronoun. Adjective clauses begin with a relative pronoun (*who, whose, whom, which,* and *that*) or a relative adverb (*where, when,* and *why*).

Also, adjective clauses come after the noun that the clause needs to explain or rename. This is done to have a clear connection to the independent clause.

Examples:

$\overbrace{\text{I learned the reason}}^{\substack{\text{independent}\\\text{clause}}}$ $\overbrace{\text{why I won the award.}}^{\substack{\text{adjective}\\\text{clause}}}$

$\overbrace{\text{This is the place}}^{\substack{\text{independent}\\\text{clause}}}$ $\overbrace{\text{where I started my first job.}}^{\substack{\text{adjective}\\\text{clause}}}$

An adjective clause can be an essential or nonessential clause. An essential clause is very important to the sentence. **Essential clauses** explain or define a person or thing. **Nonessential clauses** give

79

Copyright © Mometrix Media. You have been licensed one copy of this document for personal use only. Any other reproduction or redistribution is strictly prohibited. All rights reserved. This content is provided for test preparation purposes only and does not imply an endorsement by Mometrix of any particular political, scientific, or religious point of view.

more information about a person or thing but are not necessary to define them. Nonessential clauses are set off with commas while essential clauses are not.

Examples:

essential
clause

A person who works hard at first can often rest later in life.

nonessential
clause

Neil Armstrong, who walked on the moon, is my hero.

> **Review Video: Adjective Clauses and Phrases**
> Visit mometrix.com/academy and enter code: 520888

## ADVERB CLAUSES

An **adverb clause** is a dependent clause that modifies a verb, adjective, or adverb. In sentences with multiple dependent clauses, adverb clauses are usually placed immediately before or after the independent clause. An adverb clause is introduced with words such as *after, although, as, before, because, if, since, so, unless, when, where,* and *while.*

Examples:

adverb
clause

When you walked outside, I called the manager.

adverb
clause

I will go with you unless you want to stay.

## NOUN CLAUSES

A **noun clause** is a dependent clause that can be used as a subject, object, or complement. Noun clauses begin with words such as *how, that, what, whether, which, who,* and *why.* These words can also come with an adjective clause. Unless the noun clause is being used as the subject of the sentence, it should come after the verb of the independent clause.

Examples:

noun
clause

The real mystery is how you avoided serious injury.

noun
clause

What you learn from each other depends on your honesty with others.

## SUBORDINATION

When two related ideas are not of equal importance, the ideal way to combine them is to make the more important idea an independent clause and the less important idea a dependent or subordinate clause. This is called **subordination**.

Copyright © Mometrix Media. You have been licensed one copy of this document for personal use only. Any other reproduction or redistribution is strictly prohibited. All rights reserved. This content is provided for test preparation purposes only and does not imply an endorsement by Mometrix of any particular political, scientific, or religious point of view.

Example:

> **Separate ideas**: The team had a perfect regular season. The team lost the championship.
>
> **Subordinated**: Despite having a perfect regular season, *the team lost the championship*.

## PHRASES

A phrase is a group of words that functions as a single part of speech, usually a noun, adjective, or adverb. A **phrase** is not a complete thought, but it adds detail or explanation to a sentence, or renames something within the sentence.

### PREPOSITIONAL PHRASES

One of the most common types of phrases is the prepositional phrase. A **prepositional phrase** begins with a preposition and ends with a noun or pronoun that is the object of the preposition. Normally, the prepositional phrase functions as an **adjective** or an **adverb** within the sentence.

Examples:

The picnic is on the blanket.

I am sick with a fever today.

Among the many flowers, John found a four-leaf clover.

### VERBAL PHRASES

A **verbal** is a word or phrase that is formed from a verb but does not function as a verb. Depending on its particular form, it may be used as a noun, adjective, or adverb. A verbal does **not** replace a verb in a sentence.

Examples:

Correct: Walk a mile daily.

This is a complete sentence with the implied subject *you*.

Incorrect: To walk a mile.

This is not a sentence since there is no functional verb.

There are three types of verbal: **participles**, **gerunds**, and **infinitives**. Each type of verbal has a corresponding **phrase** that consists of the verbal itself along with any complements or modifiers.

Copyright © Mometrix Media. You have been licensed one copy of this document for personal use only. Any other reproduction or redistribution is strictly prohibited. All rights reserved. This content is provided for test preparation purposes only and does not imply an endorsement by Mometrix of any particular political, scientific, or religious point of view.

## PARTICIPLES

A **participle** is a type of verbal that always functions as an adjective. The present participle always ends with -*ing*. Past participles end with -*d, -ed, -n,* or -*t.*

Examples:

|  | present | past |
| verb | participle | participle |
| dance | dancing | danced |

**Participial phrases** most often come right before or right after the noun or pronoun that they modify.

Examples:

participial
phrase

Shipwrecked on an island, the boys started to fish for food.

participial
phrase

Having been seated for five hours, we got out of the car to stretch our legs.

participial
phrase

Praised for their work, the group accepted the first-place trophy.

## GERUNDS

A **gerund** is a type of verbal that always functions as a **noun**. Like present participles, gerunds always end with -*ing*, but they can be easily distinguished from one another by the part of speech they represent (participles always function as adjectives). Since a gerund or gerund phrase always functions as a noun, it can be used as the subject of a sentence, the predicate nominative, or the object of a verb or preposition.

Examples:

gerund

We want to be known for teaching the poor.

object of preposition

gerund

Coaching this team is the best job of my life.

subject

gerund

We like practicing our songs in the basement.

object of verb

## INFINITIVES

An **infinitive** is a type of verbal that can function as a noun, an adjective, or an adverb. An infinitive is made of the word *to* and the basic form of the verb. As with all other types of verbal phrases, an infinitive phrase includes the verbal itself and all of its complements or modifiers.

Copyright © Mometrix Media. You have been licensed one copy of this document for personal use only. Any other reproduction or redistribution is strictly prohibited. All rights reserved.
This content is provided for test preparation purposes only and does not imply an endorsement by Mometrix of any particular political, scientific, or religious point of view.

Examples:

infinitive
To join the team is my goal in life.
noun

infinitive
The animals have enough food to eat for the night.
adjective

infinitive
People lift weights to exercise their muscles.
adverb

> **Review Video: Gerunds, Infinitives, and Participles**
> Visit mometrix.com/academy and enter code: 634263

## APPOSITIVE PHRASES

An **appositive** is a word or phrase that is used to explain or rename nouns or pronouns. Noun phrases, gerund phrases, and infinitive phrases can all be used as appositives.

Examples:

appositive
Terriers, hunters at heart, have been dressed up to look like lap dogs.

The noun phrase *hunters at heart* renames the noun *terriers*.

appositive
His plan, to save and invest his money, was proven as a safe approach.

The infinitive phrase explains what the plan is.

Appositive phrases can be **essential** or **nonessential**. An appositive phrase is essential if the person, place, or thing being described or renamed is too general for its meaning to be understood without the appositive.

Examples:

essential
Two of America's Founding Fathers, George Washington and Thomas Jefferson, served as presidents.

nonessential
George Washington and Thomas Jefferson, two Founding Fathers, served as presidents.

## ABSOLUTE PHRASES

An absolute phrase is a phrase that consists of **a noun followed by a participle**. An absolute phrase provides **context** to what is being described in the sentence, but it does not modify or explain any particular word; it is essentially independent.

Copyright © Mometrix Media. You have been licensed one copy of this document for personal use only. Any other reproduction or redistribution is strictly prohibited. All rights reserved. This content is provided for test preparation purposes only and does not imply an endorsement by Mometrix of any particular political, scientific, or religious point of view.

Examples:

## PARALLELISM

When multiple items or ideas are presented in a sentence in series, such as in a list, the items or ideas must be stated in grammatically equivalent ways. In other words, if one idea is stated in gerund form, the second cannot be stated in infinitive form. For example, to write, *I enjoy reading and to study* would be incorrect. An infinitive and a gerund are not equivalent. Instead, you should write *I enjoy reading and studying*. In lists of more than two, all items must be parallel.

Example:

**Incorrect**: He stopped at the office, grocery store, and the pharmacy before heading home.

The first and third items in the list of places include the article *the*, so the second item needs it as well.

**Correct**: He stopped at the office, *the* grocery store, and the pharmacy before heading home.

Example:

**Incorrect**: While vacationing in Europe, she went biking, skiing, and climbed mountains.

The first and second items in the list are gerunds, so the third item must be as well.

**Correct**: While vacationing in Europe, she went biking, skiing, and *mountain climbing*.

> **Review Video: Parallel Construction**
> Visit mometrix.com/academy and enter code: 831988

## SENTENCE PURPOSE

There are four types of sentences: declarative, imperative, interrogative, and exclamatory.

A **declarative** sentence states a fact and ends with a period.

*The football game starts at seven o'clock.*

An **imperative** sentence tells someone to do something and generally ends with a period. An urgent command might end with an exclamation point instead.

*Don't forget to buy your ticket.*

An **interrogative** sentence asks a question and ends with a question mark.

*Are you going to the game on Friday?*

Copyright © Mometrix Media. You have been licensed one copy of this document for personal use only. Any other reproduction or redistribution is strictly prohibited. All rights reserved.
This content is provided for test preparation purposes only and does not imply an endorsement by Mometrix of any particular political, scientific, or religious point of view.

An **exclamatory** sentence shows strong emotion and ends with an exclamation point.

*I can't believe we won the game!*

> **Review Video: <u>Functions of a Sentence</u>**
> Visit mometrix.com/academy and enter code: 475974

## SENTENCE STRUCTURE

Sentences are classified by structure based on the type and number of clauses present. The four classifications of sentence structure are the following:

**Simple**: A simple sentence has one independent clause with no dependent clauses. A simple sentence may have **compound elements** (i.e., compound subject or verb).

Examples:

single subject   single verb
Judy watered the lawn.

compound subject   single verb
Judy and Alan watered the lawn.

single subject   compound verb   compound verb
Judy watered the lawn and pulled weeds.

compound subject   compound verb   compound verb
Judy and Alan watered the lawn and pulled weeds.

**Compound**: A compound sentence has two or more independent clauses with no dependent clauses. Usually, the independent clauses are joined with a comma and a coordinating conjunction or with a semicolon.

Examples:

independent clause   independent clause
The time has come, and we are ready.

independent clause   independent clause
I woke up at dawn; the sun was just coming up.

**Complex**: A complex sentence has one independent clause and at least one dependent clause.

Examples:

dependent clause   independent clause
Although he had the flu, Harry went to work.

independent clause   dependent clause
Marcia got married, after she finished college.

Copyright © Mometrix Media. You have been licensed one copy of this document for personal use only. Any other reproduction or redistribution is strictly prohibited. All rights reserved.
This content is provided for test preparation purposes only and does not imply an endorsement by Mometrix of any particular political, scientific, or religious point of view.

**Compound-Complex**: A compound-complex sentence has at least two independent clauses and at least one dependent clause.

Examples:

| independent clause | dependent clause | independent clause |

John is my friend who went to India, and he brought back souvenirs.

| independent clause | independent clause | dependent clause |

You may not realize this, but we heard the music that you played last night.

> **Review Video: Sentence Structure**
> Visit mometrix.com/academy and enter code: 700478

**Sentence variety** is important to consider when writing an essay or speech. A variety of sentence lengths and types creates rhythm, makes a passage more engaging, and gives writers an opportunity to demonstrate their writing style. Writing that uses the same length or type of sentence without variation can be boring or difficult to read. To evaluate a passage for effective sentence variety, it is helpful to note whether the passage contains diverse sentence structures and lengths. It is also important to pay attention to the way each sentence starts and avoid beginning with the same words or phrases.

## SENTENCE FRAGMENTS

Recall that a group of words must contain at least one **independent clause** in order to be considered a sentence. If it doesn't contain even one independent clause, it is called a **sentence fragment**.

The appropriate process for **repairing** a sentence fragment depends on what type of fragment it is. If the fragment is a dependent clause, it can sometimes be as simple as removing a subordinating word (e.g., when, because, if) from the beginning of the fragment. Alternatively, a dependent clause can be incorporated into a closely related neighboring sentence. If the fragment is missing some required part, like a subject or a verb, the fix might be as simple as adding the missing part.

Examples:

**Fragment**: Because he wanted to sail the Mediterranean.

**Removed subordinating word**: He wanted to sail the Mediterranean.

**Combined with another sentence**: Because he wanted to sail the Mediterranean, he booked a Greek island cruise.

## RUN-ON SENTENCES

Run-on sentences consist of multiple independent clauses that have not been joined together properly. Run-on sentences can be corrected in several different ways:

**Join clauses properly**: This can be done with a comma and coordinating conjunction, with a semicolon, or with a colon or dash if the second clause is explaining something in the first.

Copyright © Mometrix Media. You have been licensed one copy of this document for personal use only. Any other reproduction or redistribution is strictly prohibited. All rights reserved. This content is provided for test preparation purposes only and does not imply an endorsement by Mometrix of any particular political, scientific, or religious point of view.

Example:

**Incorrect**: I went on the trip, we visited lots of castles.

**Corrected**: I went on the trip, and we visited lots of castles.

**Split into separate sentences**: This correction is most effective when the independent clauses are very long or when they are not closely related.

Example:

**Incorrect**: The drive to New York takes ten hours, my uncle lives in Boston.

**Corrected**: The drive to New York takes ten hours. My uncle lives in Boston.

**Make one clause dependent**: This is the easiest way to make the sentence correct and more interesting at the same time. It's often as simple as adding a subordinating word between the two clauses or before the first clause.

Example:

**Incorrect**: I finally made it to the store and I bought some eggs.

**Corrected**: When I finally made it to the store, I bought some eggs.

**Reduce to one clause with a compound verb**: If both clauses have the same subject, remove the subject from the second clause, and you now have just one clause with a compound verb.

Example:

**Incorrect**: The drive to New York takes ten hours, it makes me very tired.

**Corrected**: The drive to New York takes ten hours and makes me very tired.

Note: While these are the simplest ways to correct a run-on sentence, often the best way is to completely reorganize the thoughts in the sentence and rewrite it.

> **Review Video: Fragments and Run-on Sentences**
> Visit mometrix.com/academy and enter code: 541989

Copyright © Mometrix Media. You have been licensed one copy of this document for personal use only. Any other reproduction or redistribution is strictly prohibited. All rights reserved.
This content is provided for test preparation purposes only and does not imply an endorsement by Mometrix of any particular political, scientific, or religious point of view.

## DANGLING AND MISPLACED MODIFIERS

### DANGLING MODIFIERS

A dangling modifier is a dependent clause or verbal phrase that does not have a clear logical connection to a word in the sentence.

Example:

dangling
modifier

**Incorrect**: Reading each magazine article, the stories caught my attention.

The word *stories* cannot be modified by *Reading each magazine article*. People can read, but stories cannot read. Therefore, the subject of the sentence must be a person.

dependent
clause

**Corrected**: Reading each magazine article, I was entertained by the stories.

Example:

dangling
modifier

**Incorrect**: Ever since childhood, my grandparents have visited me for Christmas.

The speaker in this sentence can't have been visited by her grandparents when *they* were children, since she wouldn't have been born yet. Either the modifier should be clarified or the sentence should be rearranged to specify whose childhood is being referenced.

dependent
clause

**Clarified**: Ever since I was a child, my grandparents have visited for Christmas.

dependent
clause

**Rearranged**: I have enjoyed my grandparents visiting for Christmas, ever since childhood.

### MISPLACED MODIFIERS

Because modifiers are grammatically versatile, they can be put in many different places within the structure of a sentence. The danger of this versatility is that a modifier can accidentally be placed where it is modifying the wrong word or where it is not clear which word it is modifying.

Example:

modifier

**Incorrect**: She read the book to a crowd that was filled with beautiful pictures.

The book was filled with beautiful pictures, not the crowd.

modifier

**Corrected**: She read the book that was filled with beautiful pictures to a crowd.

Copyright © Mometrix Media. You have been licensed one copy of this document for personal use only. Any other reproduction or redistribution is strictly prohibited. All rights reserved. This content is provided for test preparation purposes only and does not imply an endorsement by Mometrix of any particular political, scientific, or religious point of view.

Example:

modifier

**Ambiguous**: Derek saw a bus nearly hit a man on his way to work.

Was Derek on his way to work or was the other man?

modifier

**Derek**: On his way to work, Derek saw a bus nearly hit a man.

modifier

**The other man**: Derek saw a bus nearly hit a man who was on his way to work.

## *SPLIT INFINITIVES*

A split infinitive occurs when a modifying word comes between the word *to* and the verb that pairs with *to*.

Example: To *clearly* explain vs. *To explain* clearly | To *softly* sing vs. *To sing* softly

Though considered improper by some, split infinitives may provide better clarity and simplicity in some cases than the alternatives. As such, avoiding them should not be considered a universal rule.

## DOUBLE NEGATIVES

Standard English allows **two negatives** only when a **positive** meaning is intended. For example, *The team was not displeased with their performance.* Double negatives to emphasize negation are not used in standard English.

**Negative modifiers** (e.g., never, no, and not) should not be paired with other negative modifiers or negative words (e.g., none, nobody, nothing, or neither). The modifiers *hardly, barely*, and *scarcely* are also considered negatives in standard English, so they should not be used with other negatives.

Copyright © Mometrix Media. You have been licensed one copy of this document for personal use only. Any other reproduction or redistribution is strictly prohibited. All rights reserved.
This content is provided for test preparation purposes only and does not imply an endorsement by Mometrix of any particular political, scientific, or religious point of view.

## CHAPTER QUIZ

**1. Which of the following is an imperative statement?**

    a. John knows the way to the park.
    b. There are five letters on the table for him.
    c. Go to the post office for me.
    d. The cookies need to cook for a few more minutes.

**2. Which of the following is NOT a word used to combine nouns to make a compound subject?**

    a. Or
    b. Nor
    c. And
    d. Also

**3. Which of the following is always singular?**

    a. Each
    b. Both
    c. Several
    d. Many

**4. Identify the indirect object of the following sentence: "We taught the old dog a new trick."**

    a. We
    b. Taught
    c. The old dog
    d. A new trick

**5. Identify the infinitive of the following sentence: "The animals have enough food to eat for the night."**

    a. The animals
    b. Have enough food
    c. To eat
    d. For the night

**6. How many types of sentences are there?**

    a. Three
    b. Four
    c. Five
    d. Six

**7. Which of the following sentences correctly expresses the idea of parallelism?**

    a. He stopped at the office, grocery store, and the pharmacy before heading home.
    b. While vacationing in Europe, she went biking, skiing, and climbed mountains.
    c. The crowd jumped and cheered, roared and hollered, and whistled as the game concluded.
    d. The flurry of blows left him staggered, discombobulated, and overwhelmed before falling.

Copyright © Mometrix Media. You have been licensed one copy of this document for personal use only. Any other reproduction or redistribution is strictly prohibited. All rights reserved.
This content is provided for test preparation purposes only and does not imply an endorsement by Mometrix of any particular political, scientific, or religious point of view.

**8. Identify the phrase, "The music paused," in the following sample sentence:**

"The music paused, she continued to dance through the crowd."

a. Subordinate phrase
b. Essential appositive
c. Nonessential appositive
d. Absolute phrase

## CHAPTER QUIZ ANSWER KEY

**1. C:** In an imperative sentence, the verb's subject is understood without actually appearing or being named in the sentence itself. For example, in the imperative sentence, "Run to the store," the subject is the person being told to run.

**2. D:** A compound subject is formed when two or more nouns joined by *and*, *or*, or *nor* jointly act as the subject of the sentence.

**3. A:** Pronouns such as *each*, *either*, *everybody*, *anybody*, *somebody*, and *nobody* are always singular.

**4. C:** An indirect object is a word or group of words that show how an action had an influence on someone or something. If there is an indirect object in a sentence, then there will always be a direct object in the sentence. When looking for the indirect object, find the verb and ask *to*, *for whom*, or *what*.

indirect    direct
object     object
We taught the old dog a new trick.

**5. C:** An infinitive is a type of verbal that can function as a noun, an adjective, or an adverb. An infinitive is made of the word *to* and the basic form of the verb. As with all other types of verbal phrases, an infinitive phrase includes the verbal itself and all of its complements or modifiers.

infinitive
The animals have enough food to eat for the night.
adjective

**6. B:** There are four types of sentences: declarative, imperative, interrogative, and exclamatory.

**7. D:** When multiple items or ideas are presented in a sentence in series, such as in a list, the items or ideas must be stated in grammatically equivalent ways. In other words, if one idea is stated in gerund form, the second cannot be stated in infinitive form. For example, writing "I enjoy *reading* and *to study*" would be incorrect. An infinitive and a gerund are not equivalent. Instead, the sentence should be, "I enjoy *reading* and *studying*." In lists of more than two, all items must be parallel.

Copyright © Mometrix Media. You have been licensed one copy of this document for personal use only. Any other reproduction or redistribution is strictly prohibited. All rights reserved. This content is provided for test preparation purposes only and does not imply an endorsement by Mometrix of any particular political, scientific, or religious point of view.

Example:

Incorrect: He stopped at the office, grocery store, and the pharmacy before heading home.

(The first and third items in the list of places include the article *the*, so the second item needs it as well.)

Correct: He stopped at the office, *the* grocery store, and the pharmacy before heading home.

**8. D:** An absolute phrase is a phrase that consists of a noun followed by a participle. An absolute phrase provides context to what is being described in the sentence, but it does not modify or explain any particular word; it is essentially independent.

noun     participle

The music paused, she continued to dance through the crowd.

absolute
phrase

Copyright © Mometrix Media. You have been licensed one copy of this document for personal use only. Any other reproduction or redistribution is strictly prohibited. All rights reserved.
This content is provided for test preparation purposes only and does not imply an endorsement by Mometrix of any particular political, scientific, or religious point of view.

# Punctuation

## END PUNCTUATION

### PERIODS

Use a period to end all sentences except direct questions and exclamations. Periods are also used for abbreviations.

Examples: 3 p.m. | 2 a.m. | Mr. Jones | Mrs. Stevens | Dr. Smith | Bill, Jr. | Pennsylvania Ave.

Note: An abbreviation is a shortened form of a word or phrase.

### QUESTION MARKS

Question marks should be used following a **direct question**. A polite request can be followed by a period instead of a question mark.

**Direct Question**: What is for lunch today? | How are you? | Why is that the answer?

**Polite Requests**: Can you please send me the item tomorrow. | Will you please walk with me on the track.

> **Review Video: Question Marks**
> Visit mometrix.com/academy and enter code: 118471

### EXCLAMATION MARKS

Exclamation marks are used after a word group or sentence that shows much feeling or has special importance. Exclamation marks should not be overused. They are saved for proper **exclamatory interjections**.

Example: We're going to the finals! | You have a beautiful car! | "That's crazy!" she yelled.

> **Review Video: Exclamation Points**
> Visit mometrix.com/academy and enter code: 199367

## COMMAS

The comma is a punctuation mark that can help you understand connections in a sentence. Not every sentence needs a comma. However, if a sentence needs a comma, you need to put it in the

Copyright © Mometrix Media. You have been licensed one copy of this document for personal use only. Any other reproduction or redistribution is strictly prohibited. All rights reserved.
This content is provided for test preparation purposes only and does not imply an endorsement by Mometrix of any particular political, scientific, or religious point of view.

right place. A comma in the wrong place (or an absent comma) will make a sentence's meaning unclear. These are some of the rules for commas:

| Use Case | Example |
| --- | --- |
| Before a **coordinating conjunction** joining independent clauses | Bob caught three fish, and I caught two fish. |
| After an **introductory phrase** | After the final out, we went to a restaurant to celebrate. |
| After an **adverbial clause** | Studying the stars, I was awed by the beauty of the sky. |
| Between **items in a series** | I will bring the turkey, the pie, and the coffee. |
| For **interjections** | Wow, you know how to play this game. |
| After *yes* and *no* responses | No, I cannot come tomorrow. |
| Separate **nonessential modifiers** | John Frank, who coaches the team, was promoted today. |
| Separate **nonessential appositives** | Thomas Edison, an American inventor, was born in Ohio. |
| Separate **nouns of direct address** | You, John, are my only hope in this moment. |
| Separate **interrogative tags** | This is the last time, correct? |
| Separate **contrasts** | You are my friend, not my enemy. |
| Writing **dates** | July 4, 1776, is an important date to remember. |
| Writing **addresses** | He is meeting me at 456 Delaware Avenue, Washington, D.C., tomorrow morning. |
| Writing **geographical names** | Paris, France, is my favorite city. |
| Writing **titles** | John Smith, PhD, will be visiting your class today. |
| Separate **expressions like** *he said* | "You can start," she said, "with an apology." |

Also, you can use a comma **between coordinate adjectives** not joined with *and*. However, not all adjectives are coordinate (i.e., equal or parallel).

**Incorrect**: The kind, brown dog followed me home.

**Correct**: The kind, loyal dog followed me home.

There are two simple ways to know if your adjectives are coordinate. One, you can join the adjectives with *and*: *The kind and loyal dog*. Two, you can change the order of the adjectives: *The loyal, kind dog*.

| Review Video: **When to Use a Comma** |
| --- |
| Visit mometrix.com/academy and enter code: 786797 |

## SEMICOLONS

The semicolon is used to connect major sentence pieces of equal value. Some rules for semicolons include:

| Use Case | Example |
| --- | --- |
| Between closely connected independent clauses **not connected with a coordinating conjunction** | You are right; we should go with your plan. |
| Between independent clauses **linked with a transitional word** | I think that we can agree on this; however, I am not sure about my friends. |
| Between items in a **series that has internal punctuation** | I have visited New York, New York; Augusta, Maine; and Baltimore, Maryland. |

| Review Video: **How to Use Semicolons** |
| --- |
| Visit mometrix.com/academy and enter code: 370605 |

Copyright © Mometrix Media. You have been licensed one copy of this document for personal use only. Any other reproduction or redistribution is strictly prohibited. All rights reserved. This content is provided for test preparation purposes only and does not imply an endorsement by Mometrix of any particular political, scientific, or religious point of view.

## COLONS

The colon is used to call attention to the words that follow it. A colon must come after a **complete independent clause**. The rules for colons are as follows:

| Use Case | Example |
| --- | --- |
| After an independent clause to **make a list** | I want to learn many languages: Spanish, German, and Italian. |
| For **explanations** | There is one thing that stands out on your resume: responsibility. |
| To give a **quote** | He started with an idea: "We are able to do more than we imagine." |
| After the **greeting in a formal letter** | To Whom It May Concern: |
| Show **hours and minutes** | It is 3:14 p.m. |
| Separate a **title and subtitle** | The essay is titled "America: A Short Introduction to a Modern Country." |

> **Review Video: Colons**
> Visit mometrix.com/academy and enter code: 868673

## PARENTHESES

Parentheses are used for additional information. Also, they can be used to put labels for letters or numbers in a series. Parentheses should be not be used very often. If they are overused, parentheses can be a distraction instead of a help.

Examples:

> **Extra Information**: The rattlesnake (see Image 2) is a dangerous snake of North and South America.

> **Series**: Include in the email (1) your name, (2) your address, and (3) your question for the author.

> **Review Video: Parentheses**
> Visit mometrix.com/academy and enter code: 947743

## QUOTATION MARKS

Use quotation marks to close off **direct quotations** of a person's spoken or written words. Do not use quotation marks around indirect quotations. An indirect quotation gives someone's message without using the person's exact words. Use **single quotation marks** to close off a quotation inside a quotation.

> **Direct Quote**: Nancy said, "I am waiting for Henry to arrive."

> **Indirect Quote**: Henry said that he is going to be late to the meeting.

> **Quote inside a Quote**: The teacher asked, "Has everyone read 'The Gift of the Magi'?"

Quotation marks should be used around the titles of **short works**: newspaper and magazine articles, poems, short stories, songs, television episodes, radio programs, and subdivisions of books or websites.

Copyright © Mometrix Media. You have been licensed one copy of this document for personal use only. Any other reproduction or redistribution is strictly prohibited. All rights reserved. This content is provided for test preparation purposes only and does not imply an endorsement by Mometrix of any particular political, scientific, or religious point of view.

Examples:

"Rip Van Winkle" (short story by Washington Irving)

"O Captain! My Captain!" (poem by Walt Whitman)

Although it is not standard usage, quotation marks are sometimes used to highlight **irony** or the use of words to mean something other than their dictionary definition. This type of usage should be employed sparingly, if at all.

Examples:

| The boss warned Frank that he was walking on "thin ice." | Frank is not walking on real ice. Instead, he is being warned to avoid mistakes. |
|---|---|
| The teacher thanked the young man for his "honesty." | The quotation marks around *honesty* show that the teacher does not believe the young man's explanation. |

> **Review Video: Quotation Marks**
> Visit mometrix.com/academy and enter code: 884918

Periods and commas are put **inside** quotation marks. Colons and semicolons are put **outside** the quotation marks. Question marks and exclamation points are placed inside quotation marks when they are part of a quote. When the question or exclamation mark goes with the whole sentence, the mark is left outside of the quotation marks.

Examples:

| Period and comma | We read "The Gift of the Magi," "The Skylight Room," and "The Cactus." |
|---|---|
| Semicolon | They watched "The Nutcracker"; then, they went home. |
| Exclamation mark that is a part of a quote | The crowd cheered, "Victory!" |
| Question mark that goes with the whole sentence | Is your favorite short story "The Tell-Tale Heart"? |

## APOSTROPHES

An apostrophe is used to show **possession** or the **deletion of letters in contractions**. An apostrophe is not needed with the possessive pronouns *his, hers, its, ours, theirs, whose*, and *yours*.

**Singular Nouns**: David's car | a book's theme | my brother's board game

**Plural Nouns that end with -s**: the scissors' handle | boys' basketball

**Plural Nouns that end without -s**: Men's department | the people's adventure

> **Review Video: When to Use an Apostrophe**
> Visit mometrix.com/academy and enter code: 213068
>
> **Review Video: Punctuation Errors in Possessive Pronouns**
> Visit mometrix.com/academy and enter code: 221438

Copyright © Mometrix Media. You have been licensed one copy of this document for personal use only. Any other reproduction or redistribution is strictly prohibited. All rights reserved. This content is provided for test preparation purposes only and does not imply an endorsement by Mometrix of any particular political, scientific, or religious point of view.

## HYPHENS

Hyphens are used to **separate compound words**. Use hyphens in the following cases:

| Use Case | Example |
|---|---|
| **Compound numbers** from 21 to 99 when written out in words | This team needs twenty-five points to win the game. |
| **Written-out fractions** that are used as adjectives | The recipe says that we need a three-fourths cup of butter. |
| Compound adjectives that come before a noun | The well-fed dog took a nap. |
| **Unusual compound words** that would be hard to read or easily confused with other words | This is the best anti-itch cream on the market. |

Note: This is not a complete set of the rules for hyphens. A dictionary is the best tool for knowing if a compound word needs a hyphen.

> **Review Video: Hyphens**
> Visit mometrix.com/academy and enter code: 981632

## DASHES

Dashes are used to show a **break** or a **change in thought** in a sentence or to act as parentheses in a sentence. When typing, use two hyphens to make a dash. Do not put a space before or after the dash. The following are the functions of dashes:

| Use Case | Example |
|---|---|
| Set off parenthetical statements or an **appositive with internal punctuation** | The three trees—oak, pine, and magnolia—are coming on a truck tomorrow. |
| Show a **break or change in tone or thought** | The first question—how silly of me—does not have a correct answer. |

## ELLIPSIS MARKS

The ellipsis mark has **three** periods (…) to show when **words have been removed** from a quotation. If a **full sentence or more** is removed from a quoted passage, you need to use **four** periods to show the removed text and the end punctuation mark. The ellipsis mark should not be used at the beginning of a quotation. The ellipsis mark should also not be used at the end of a quotation unless some words have been deleted from the end of the final sentence.

Example:

"Then he picked up the groceries…paid for them…later he went home."

Copyright © Mometrix Media. You have been licensed one copy of this document for personal use only. Any other reproduction or redistribution is strictly prohibited. All rights reserved.
This content is provided for test preparation purposes only and does not imply an endorsement by Mometrix of any particular political, scientific, or religious point of view.

## BRACKETS

There are two main reasons to use brackets:

| Use Case | Example |
|---|---|
| Placing **parentheses inside of parentheses** | The hero of this story, Paul Revere (a silversmith and industrialist [see Ch. 4]), rode through towns of Massachusetts to warn of advancing British troops. |
| Adding **clarification or detail to a quotation** that is not part of the quotation | The father explained, "My children are planning to attend my alma mater [State University]." |

| **Review Video: <u>Brackets</u>** |
|:---:|
| Visit mometrix.com/academy and enter code: 727546 |

Copyright © Mometrix Media. You have been licensed one copy of this document for personal use only. Any other reproduction or redistribution is strictly prohibited. All rights reserved.
This content is provided for test preparation purposes only and does not imply an endorsement by Mometrix of any particular political, scientific, or religious point of view.

## CHAPTER QUIZ

**1. Which of the following correctly implements the use of parentheses?**

 a. The rattlesnake (see Image 2) is a dangerous snake of North and South America.
 b. The rattlesnake see (Image 2) is a dangerous snake of North and South America.
 c. The rattlesnake see Image (2) is a dangerous snake of North and South America.
 d. The rattlesnake (see Image) (2) is a dangerous snake of North and South America.

**2. Which of the following correctly describes the placement of punctuation in reference to quotations?**

 a. Periods and commas are put outside quotation marks; colons and semicolons go inside.
 b. Periods and colons are put outside quotation marks; commas and semicolons go inside.
 c. Periods and commas are put inside quotation marks; colons and semicolons go outside.
 d. Periods and colons are put inside quotation marks; commas and semicolons go outside.

**3. Which of the following correctly implements the use of commas?**

 a. He is meeting me at, 456 Delaware Avenue, Washington, D.C., tomorrow morning.
 b. He is meeting me at 456 Delaware Avenue, Washington, D.C., tomorrow morning.
 c. He is meeting me at 456 Delaware Avenue Washington, D.C. tomorrow morning.
 d. He is meeting me at 456 Delaware Avenue, Washington, D.C. tomorrow morning.

## CHAPTER QUIZ ANSWER KEY

**1. A:** Parentheses are used for additional information. Also, they can be used to put labels for letters or numbers in a series. Parentheses should be not be used very often because their overuse can become a distraction.

**2. C:** Periods and commas are put inside quotation marks, while colons and semicolons are put outside quotation marks. Question marks and exclamation points are placed inside quotation marks when they are part of a quote. When the question mark or exclamation point is not part of a quoted section but instead part of an entire sentence, then it is left outside of the quotation marks.

Copyright © Mometrix Media. You have been licensed one copy of this document for personal use only. Any other reproduction or redistribution is strictly prohibited. All rights reserved.
This content is provided for test preparation purposes only and does not imply an endorsement by Mometrix of any particular political, scientific, or religious point of view.

**3. B:** These are some of the rules for commas:

| Use Case | Example |
|---|---|
| Before a **coordinating conjunction** joining independent clauses | Bob caught three fish, and I caught two fish. |
| After an **introductory phrase** | After the final out, we went to a restaurant to celebrate. |
| After an **adverbial clause** | Studying the stars, I was awed by the beauty of the sky. |
| Between **items in a series** | I will bring the turkey, the pie, and the coffee. |
| For **interjections** | Wow, you know how to play this game. |
| After *yes* and *no* responses | No, I cannot come tomorrow. |
| Separate **nonessential modifiers** | John Frank, who coaches the team, was promoted today. |
| Separate **nonessential appositives** | Thomas Edison, an American inventor, was born in Ohio. |
| Separate **nouns of direct address** | You, John, are my only hope in this moment. |
| Separate **interrogative tags** | This is the last time, correct? |
| Separate **contrasts** | You are my friend, not my enemy. |
| Writing **dates** | July 4, 1776, is an important date to remember. |
| Writing **addresses** | He is meeting me at 456 Delaware Avenue, Washington, D.C., tomorrow morning. |
| Writing **geographical names** | Paris, France, is my favorite city. |
| Writing **titles** | John Smith, PhD, will be visiting your class today. |
| Separate **expressions like "he said"** | "You can start," she said, "with an apology." |

Copyright © Mometrix Media. You have been licensed one copy of this document for personal use only. Any other reproduction or redistribution is strictly prohibited. All rights reserved. This content is provided for test preparation purposes only and does not imply an endorsement by Mometrix of any particular political, scientific, or religious point of view.

# Common Usage Mistakes

## WORD CONFUSION

### WHICH, THAT, AND WHO

The words *which*, *that*, and *who* can act as **relative pronouns** to help clarify or describe a noun.

*Which* is used for things only.

> Example: Andrew's car, *which is old and rusty*, broke down last week.

*That* is used for people or things. *That* is usually informal when used to describe people.

> Example: Is this the only book *that Louis L'Amour wrote?*

> Example: Is Louis L'Amour the author *that wrote Western novels?*

*Who* is used for people or for animals that have an identity or personality.

> Example: Mozart was the composer *who wrote those operas.*

> Example: John's dog, *who is called Max*, is large and fierce.

### HOMOPHONES

**Homophones** are words that sound alike (or similar) but have different **spellings** and **definitions**. A homophone is a type of **homonym**, which is a pair or group of words that are pronounced or spelled the same, but do not mean the same thing.

### TO, TOO, AND TWO

*To* can be an adverb or a preposition for showing direction, purpose, and relationship. See your dictionary for the many other ways to use *to* in a sentence.

> Examples: I went to the store. | I want to go with you.

*Too* is an adverb that means *also, as well, very,* or *in excess.*

> Examples: I can walk a mile too. | You have eaten too much.

*Two* is a number.

> Example: You have two minutes left.

### THERE, THEIR, AND THEY'RE

*There* can be an adjective, adverb, or pronoun. Often, *there* is used to show a place or to start a sentence.

> Examples: I went there yesterday. | There is something in his pocket.

*Their* is a pronoun that is used to show ownership.

> Examples: He is their father. | This is their fourth apology this week.

*They're* is a contraction of *they are.*

> Example: Did you know that they're in town?

Copyright © Mometrix Media. You have been licensed one copy of this document for personal use only. Any other reproduction or redistribution is strictly prohibited. All rights reserved. This content is provided for test preparation purposes only and does not imply an endorsement by Mometrix of any particular political, scientific, or religious point of view.

### KNEW AND NEW

*Knew* is the past tense of *know*.

> Example: I knew the answer.

*New* is an adjective that means something is current, has not been used, or is modern.

> Example: This is my new phone.

### THEN AND THAN

*Then* is an adverb that indicates sequence or order:

> Example: I'm going to run to the library and then come home.

*Than* is special-purpose word used only for comparisons:

> Example: Susie likes chips more than candy.

### ITS AND IT'S

*Its* is a pronoun that shows ownership.

> Example: The guitar is in its case.

*It's* is a contraction of *it is*.

> Example: It's an honor and a privilege to meet you.

Note: The *h* in honor is silent, so *honor* starts with the vowel sound *o*, which must have the article *an*.

### YOUR AND YOU'RE

*Your* is a pronoun that shows ownership.

> Example: This is your moment to shine.

*You're* is a contraction of *you are*.

> Example: Yes, you're correct.

### SAW AND SEEN

*Saw* is the past-tense form of *see*.

> Example: I saw a turtle on my walk this morning.

*Seen* is the past participle of *see*.

> Example: I have seen this movie before.

### AFFECT AND EFFECT

There are two main reasons that *affect* and *effect* are so often confused: 1) both words can be used as either a noun or a verb, and 2) unlike most homophones, their usage and meanings are closely related to each other. Here is a quick rundown of the four usage options:

Copyright © Mometrix Media. You have been licensed one copy of this document for personal use only. Any other reproduction or redistribution is strictly prohibited. All rights reserved.
This content is provided for test preparation purposes only and does not imply an endorsement by Mometrix of any particular political, scientific, or religious point of view.

**Affect (n)**: feeling, emotion, or mood that is displayed

Example: The patient had a flat *affect*. (i.e., his face showed little or no emotion)

**Affect (v)**: to alter, to change, to influence

Example: The sunshine *affects* the plant's growth.

**Effect (n)**: a result, a consequence

Example: What *effect* will this weather have on our schedule?

**Effect (v)**: to bring about, to cause to be

Example: These new rules will *effect* order in the office.

The noun form of *affect* is rarely used outside of technical medical descriptions, so if a noun form is needed on the test, you can safely select *effect*. The verb form of *effect* is not as rare as the noun form of *affect*, but it's still not all that likely to show up on your test. If you need a verb and you can't decide which to use based on the definitions, choosing *affect* is your best bet.

## HOMOGRAPHS

**Homographs** are words that share the same spelling, but have different meanings and sometimes different pronunciations. To figure out which meaning is being used, you should be looking for context clues. The context clues give hints to the meaning of the word. For example, the word *spot* has many meanings. It can mean "a place" or "a stain or blot." In the sentence "After my lunch, I saw a spot on my shirt," the word *spot* means "a stain or blot." The context clues of "After my lunch" and "on my shirt" guide you to this decision. A homograph is another type of homonym.

### BANK

(noun): an establishment where money is held for savings or lending

(verb): to collect or pile up

### CONTENT

(noun): the topics that will be addressed within a book

(adjective): pleased or satisfied

(verb): to make someone pleased or satisfied

### FINE

(noun): an amount of money that acts a penalty for an offense

(adjective): very small or thin

(adverb): in an acceptable way

(verb): to make someone pay money as a punishment

### INCENSE

(noun): a material that is burned in religious settings and makes a pleasant aroma

(verb): to frustrate or anger

Copyright © Mometrix Media. You have been licensed one copy of this document for personal use only. Any other reproduction or redistribution is strictly prohibited. All rights reserved.
This content is provided for test preparation purposes only and does not imply an endorsement by Mometrix of any particular political, scientific, or religious point of view.

### LEAD
(noun): the first or highest position

(noun): a heavy metallic element

(verb): to direct a person or group of followers

(adjective): containing lead

### OBJECT
(noun): a lifeless item that can be held and observed

(verb): to disagree

### PRODUCE
(noun): fruits and vegetables

(verb): to make or create something

### REFUSE
(noun): garbage or debris that has been thrown away

(verb): to not allow

### SUBJECT
(noun): an area of study

(verb): to force or subdue

### TEAR
(noun): a fluid secreted by the eyes

(verb): to separate or pull apart

Copyright © Mometrix Media. You have been licensed one copy of this document for personal use only. Any other reproduction or redistribution is strictly prohibited. All rights reserved. This content is provided for test preparation purposes only and does not imply an endorsement by Mometrix of any particular political, scientific, or religious point of view.

## CHAPTER QUIZ

**1. Which of the following correctly implements the word "affect"?**

  a. These new rules will affect order in the office.
  b. What affect will this weather have on our schedule?
  c. The patient had a flat affect during her examination.
  d. His narcissism had a detrimental affect on everyone around him.

**2. "Affect" and "effect" would be considered which of the following?**

  a. Homographs
  b. Synonyms
  c. Antonyms
  d. Homophones

## CHAPTER QUIZ ANSWER KEY

**1. C:** There are two main reasons that *affect* and *effect* are so often confused: 1) both words can be used as either a noun or a verb; and 2) unlike most homophones, their usage and meanings are closely related to each other. Here is a quick rundown of the four usage options:

**Affect (n)**: feeling, emotion, or mood that is displayed

> Example: The patient had a flat *affect* (i.e., his face showed little or no emotion).

**Affect (v)**: to alter, to change, to influence

> Example: The sunshine *affects* the plant's growth.

**Effect (n)**: a result, a consequence

> Example: What *effect* will this weather have on our schedule?

**Effect (v)**: to bring about, to cause to be

> Example: These new rules will *effect* order in the office.

The noun form of *affect* is rarely used outside of technical medical descriptions, so if a noun form is needed on the test, *effect* is a safe selection. The verb form of *effect* is not as rare as the noun form of *affect*, but it's still not likely to show up on a test. If a verb is needed and the definitions aren't enough of an indicator for which one to use, choosing *affect* is the safest option.

**2. D:** Homophones are words that sound alike (or similar) but have different spellings and definitions. A homophone is a type of homonym, which is a pair or group of words that are pronounced or spelled the same, but do not mean the same thing.

Copyright © Mometrix Media. You have been licensed one copy of this document for personal use only. Any other reproduction or redistribution is strictly prohibited. All rights reserved.
This content is provided for test preparation purposes only and does not imply an endorsement by Mometrix of any particular political, scientific, or religious point of view.

# The Writing Process

## BRAINSTORMING

Brainstorming is a technique that is used to find a creative approach to a subject. This can be accomplished by simple **free-association** with a topic. For example, with paper and pen, write every thought that you have about the topic in a word or phrase. This is done without critical thinking. You should put everything that comes to your mind about the topic on your scratch paper. Then, you need to read the list over a few times. Next, look for patterns, repetitions, and clusters of ideas. This allows a variety of fresh ideas to come as you think about the topic.

## FREE WRITING

Free writing is a more structured form of brainstorming. The method involves taking a limited amount of time (e.g., 2 to 3 minutes) to write everything that comes to mind about the topic in complete sentences. When time expires, review everything that has been written down. Many of your sentences may make little or no sense, but the insights and observations that can come from free writing make this method a valuable approach. Usually, free writing results in a fuller expression of ideas than brainstorming because thoughts and associations are written in complete sentences. However, both techniques can be used to complement each other.

## PLANNING

Planning is the process of organizing a piece of writing before composing a draft. Planning can include creating an outline or a graphic organizer, such as a Venn diagram, a spider-map, or a flowchart. These methods should help the writer identify their topic, main ideas, and the general organization of the composition. Preliminary research can also take place during this stage. Planning helps writers organize all of their ideas and decide if they have enough material to begin their first draft. However, writers should remember that the decisions they make during this step will likely change later in the process, so their plan does not have to be perfect.

## DRAFTING

Writers may then use their plan, outline, or graphic organizer to compose their first draft. They may write subsequent drafts to improve their writing. Writing multiple drafts can help writers consider different ways to communicate their ideas and address errors that may be difficult to correct without rewriting a section or the whole composition. Most writers will vary in how many drafts they choose to write, as there is no "right" number of drafts. Writing drafts also takes away the pressure to write perfectly on the first try, as writers can improve with each draft they write.

## REVISING, EDITING, AND PROOFREADING

Once a writer completes a draft, they can move on to the revising, editing, and proofreading steps to improve their draft. These steps begin with making broad changes that may apply to large sections of a composition and then making small, specific corrections. **Revising** is the first and broadest of these steps. Revising involves ensuring that the composition addresses an appropriate audience, includes all necessary material, maintains focus throughout, and is organized logically. Revising may occur after the first draft to ensure that the following drafts improve upon errors from the first draft. Some revision should occur between each draft to avoid repeating these errors. The **editing** phase of writing is narrower than the revising phase. Editing a composition should include steps such as improving transitions between paragraphs, ensuring each paragraph is on topic, and improving the flow of the text. The editing phase may also include correcting grammatical errors that cannot be fixed without significantly altering the text. **Proofreading** involves fixing misspelled words, typos, other grammatical errors, and any remaining surface-level flaws in the composition.

Copyright © Mometrix Media. You have been licensed one copy of this document for personal use only. Any other reproduction or redistribution is strictly prohibited. All rights reserved. This content is provided for test preparation purposes only and does not imply an endorsement by Mometrix of any particular political, scientific, or religious point of view.

## RECURSIVE WRITING PROCESS

However you approach writing, you may find comfort in knowing that the revision process can occur in any order. The **recursive writing process** is not as difficult as the phrase may make it seem. Simply put, the recursive writing process means that you may need to revisit steps after completing other steps. It also implies that the steps are not required to take place in any certain order. Indeed, you may find that planning, drafting, and revising can all take place at about the same time. The writing process involves moving back and forth between planning, drafting, and revising, followed by more planning, more drafting, and more revising until the writing is satisfactory.

> **Review Video: Recursive Writing Process**
> Visit mometrix.com/academy and enter code: 951611

## TECHNOLOGY IN THE WRITING PROCESS

Modern technology has yielded several tools that can be used to make the writing process more convenient and organized. Word processors and online tools, such as databases and plagiarism detectors, allow much of the writing process to be completed in one place, using one device.

### TECHNOLOGY FOR PLANNING AND DRAFTING

For the planning and drafting stages of the writing process, word processors are a helpful tool. These programs also feature formatting tools, allowing users to create their own planning tools or create digital outlines that can be easily converted into sentences, paragraphs, or an entire essay draft. Online databases and references also complement the planning process by providing convenient access to information and sources for research. Word processors also allow users to keep up with their work and update it more easily than if they wrote their work by hand. Online word processors often allow users to collaborate, making group assignments more convenient. These programs also allow users to include illustrations or other supplemental media in their compositions.

### TECHNOLOGY FOR REVISING, EDITING, AND PROOFREADING

Word processors also benefit the revising, editing, and proofreading stages of the writing process. Most of these programs indicate errors in spelling and grammar, allowing users to catch minor errors and correct them quickly. There are also websites designed to help writers by analyzing text for deeper errors, such as poor sentence structure, inappropriate complexity, lack of sentence variety, and style issues. These websites can help users fix errors they may not know to look for or may have simply missed. As writers finish these steps, they may benefit from checking their work for any plagiarism. There are several websites and programs that compare text to other documents and publications across the internet and detect any similarities within the text. These websites show the source of the similar information, so users know whether or not they referenced the source and unintentionally plagiarized its contents.

### TECHNOLOGY FOR PUBLISHING

Technology also makes managing written work more convenient. Digitally storing documents keeps everything in one place and is easy to reference. Digital storage also makes sharing work easier, as documents can be attached to an email or stored online. This also allows writers to publish their work easily, as they can electronically submit it to other publications or freely post it to a personal blog, profile, or website.

Copyright © Mometrix Media. You have been licensed one copy of this document for personal use only. Any other reproduction or redistribution is strictly prohibited. All rights reserved. This content is provided for test preparation purposes only and does not imply an endorsement by Mometrix of any particular political, scientific, or religious point of view.

## CHAPTER QUIZ

**1. Which of the following is a more structured form of brainstorming?**

- a. Free writing
- b. Planning
- c. Drafting
- d. Proofreading

## CHAPTER QUIZ ANSWER KEY

**1. A:** Free writing is a more structured form of brainstorming. The method involves taking a limited amount of time (e.g., two to three minutes) to write everything that comes to mind about the topic in complete sentences. When time expires, review everything that has been written down. Many of the sentences may make little or no sense, but the insights and observations that can come from free writing make this method a valuable approach. Usually, free writing results in a fuller expression of ideas than brainstorming because thoughts and associations are written in complete sentences. However, both techniques can be used to complement each other.

Copyright © Mometrix Media. You have been licensed one copy of this document for personal use only. Any other reproduction or redistribution is strictly prohibited. All rights reserved.
This content is provided for test preparation purposes only and does not imply an endorsement by Mometrix of any particular political, scientific, or religious point of view.

# Outlining and Organizing Ideas

## MAIN IDEAS, SUPPORTING DETAILS, AND OUTLINING A TOPIC

A writer often begins the first paragraph of a paper by stating the **main idea** or point, also known as the **topic sentence**. The rest of the paragraph supplies particular details that develop and support the main point. One way to visualize the relationship between the main point and supporting information is by considering a table: the tabletop is the main point, and each of the table's legs is a supporting detail or group of details. Both professional authors and students can benefit from planning their writing by first making an outline of the topic. Outlines facilitate quick identification of the main point and supporting details without having to wade through the additional language that will exist in the fully developed essay, article, or paper. Outlining can also help readers to analyze a piece of existing writing for the same reason. The outline first summarizes the main idea in one sentence. Then, below that, it summarizes the supporting details in a numbered list. Writing the paper then consists of filling in the outline with detail, writing a paragraph for each supporting point, and adding an introduction and conclusion.

## INTRODUCTION

The purpose of the introduction is to capture the reader's attention and announce the essay's main idea. Normally, the introduction contains 50-80 words, or 3-5 sentences. An introduction can begin with an interesting quote, a question, or a strong opinion—something that will **engage** the reader's interest and prompt them to keep reading. If you are writing your essay to a specific prompt, your introduction should include a **restatement or summarization** of the prompt so that the reader will have some context for your essay. Finally, your introduction should briefly state your **thesis or main idea**: the primary thing you hope to communicate to the reader through your essay. Don't try to include all of the details and nuances of your thesis, or all of your reasons for it, in the introduction. That's what the rest of the essay is for!

> **Review Video: Introduction**
> Visit mometrix.com/academy and enter code: 961328

## THESIS STATEMENT

The thesis is the main idea of the essay. A temporary thesis, or working thesis, should be established early in the writing process because it will serve to keep the writer focused as ideas develop. This temporary thesis is subject to change as you continue to write.

The temporary thesis has two parts: a **topic** (i.e., the focus of your essay based on the prompt) and a **comment**. The comment makes an important point about the topic. A temporary thesis should be interesting and specific. Also, you need to limit the topic to a manageable scope. These three questions are useful tools to measure the effectiveness of any temporary thesis:

- Does the focus of my essay have enough interest to hold an audience?
- Is the focus of my essay specific enough to generate interest?
- Is the focus of my essay manageable for the time limit? Too broad? Too narrow?

The thesis should be a generalization rather than a fact because the thesis prepares readers for facts and details that support the thesis. The process of bringing the thesis into sharp focus may

Copyright © Mometrix Media. You have been licensed one copy of this document for personal use only. Any other reproduction or redistribution is strictly prohibited. All rights reserved.
This content is provided for test preparation purposes only and does not imply an endorsement by Mometrix of any particular political, scientific, or religious point of view.

help in outlining major sections of the work. Once the thesis and introduction are complete, you can address the body of the work.

> **Review Video: Thesis Statements**
> Visit mometrix.com/academy and enter code: 691033

## SUPPORTING THE THESIS

Throughout your essay, the thesis should be **explained clearly and supported** adequately by additional arguments. The thesis sentence needs to contain a clear statement of the purpose of your essay and a comment about the thesis. With the thesis statement, you have an opportunity to state what is noteworthy of this particular treatment of the prompt. Each sentence and paragraph should build on and support the thesis.

When you respond to the prompt, use parts of the passage to support your argument or defend your position. Using supporting evidence from the passage strengths your argument because readers can see your attention to the entire passage and your response to the details and facts within the passage. You can use facts, details, statistics, and direct quotations from the passage to uphold your position. Be sure to point out which information comes from the original passage and base your argument around that evidence.

## BODY

In an essay's introduction, the writer establishes the thesis and may indicate how the rest of the piece will be structured. In the body of the piece, the writer **elaborates** upon, **illustrates**, and **explains** the **thesis statement**. How writers arrange supporting details and their choices of paragraph types are development techniques. Writers may give examples of the concept introduced in the thesis statement. If the subject includes a cause-and-effect relationship, the author may explain its causality. A writer will explain or analyze the main idea of the piece throughout the body, often by presenting arguments for the veracity or credibility of the thesis statement. Writers may use development to define or clarify ambiguous terms. Paragraphs within the body may be organized using natural sequences, like space and time. Writers may employ **inductive reasoning**, using multiple details to establish a generalization or causal relationship, or **deductive reasoning**, proving a generalized hypothesis or proposition through a specific example or case.

> **Review Video: Drafting Body Paragraphs**
> Visit mometrix.com/academy and enter code: 724590

## PARAGRAPHS

After the introduction of a passage, a series of body paragraphs will carry a message through to the conclusion. Each paragraph should be **unified around a main point**. Normally, a good topic sentence summarizes the paragraph's main point. A topic sentence is a general sentence that gives an introduction to the paragraph.

The sentences that follow support the topic sentence. However, though it is usually the first sentence, the topic sentence can come as the final sentence to the paragraph if the earlier sentences give a clear explanation of the paragraph's topic. This allows the topic sentence to function as a concluding sentence. Overall, the paragraphs need to stay true to the main point. This means that any unnecessary sentences that do not advance the main point should be removed.

The main point of a paragraph requires adequate development (i.e., a substantial paragraph that covers the main point). A paragraph of two or three sentences does not cover a main point. This is

Copyright © Mometrix Media. You have been licensed one copy of this document for personal use only. Any other reproduction or redistribution is strictly prohibited. All rights reserved.
This content is provided for test preparation purposes only and does not imply an endorsement by Mometrix of any particular political, scientific, or religious point of view.

especially true when the main point of the paragraph gives strong support to the argument of the thesis. An occasional short paragraph is fine as a transitional device. However, a well-developed argument will have paragraphs with more than a few sentences.

## METHODS OF DEVELOPING PARAGRAPHS

Common methods of adding substance to paragraphs include examples, illustrations, analogies, and cause and effect.

- **Examples** are supporting details to the main idea of a paragraph or a passage. When authors write about something that their audience may not understand, they can provide an example to show their point. When authors write about something that is not easily accepted, they can give examples to prove their point.
- **Illustrations** are extended examples that require several sentences. Well-selected illustrations can be a great way for authors to develop a point that may not be familiar to their audience.
- **Analogies** make comparisons between items that appear to have nothing in common. Analogies are employed by writers to provoke fresh thoughts about a subject. These comparisons may be used to explain the unfamiliar, to clarify an abstract point, or to argue a point. Although analogies are effective literary devices, they should be used carefully in arguments. Two things may be alike in some respects but completely different in others.
- **Cause and effect** is an excellent device to explain the connection between an action or situation and a particular result. One way that authors can use cause and effect is to state the effect in the topic sentence of a paragraph and add the causes in the body of the paragraph. This method can give an author's paragraphs structure, which always strengthens writing.

## TYPES OF PARAGRAPHS

A **paragraph of narration** tells a story or a part of a story. Normally, the sentences are arranged in chronological order (i.e., the order that the events happened). However, flashbacks (i.e., an anecdote from an earlier time) can be included.

A **descriptive paragraph** makes a verbal portrait of a person, place, or thing. When specific details are used that appeal to one or more of the senses (i.e., sight, sound, smell, taste, and touch), authors give readers a sense of being present in the moment.

A **process paragraph** is related to time order (i.e., First, you open the bottle. Second, you pour the liquid, etc.). Usually, this describes a process or teaches readers how to perform a process.

**Comparing two things** draws attention to their similarities and indicates a number of differences. When authors contrast, they focus only on differences. Both comparing and contrasting may be done point-by-point, noting both the similarities and differences of each point, or in sequential paragraphs, where you discuss all the similarities and then all the differences, or vice versa.

Copyright © Mometrix Media. You have been licensed one copy of this document for personal use only. Any other reproduction or redistribution is strictly prohibited. All rights reserved. This content is provided for test preparation purposes only and does not imply an endorsement by Mometrix of any particular political, scientific, or religious point of view.

## BREAKING TEXT INTO PARAGRAPHS

For most forms of writing, you will need to use multiple paragraphs. As such, determining when to start a new paragraph is very important. Reasons for starting a new paragraph include:

- To mark off the introduction and concluding paragraphs
- To signal a shift to a new idea or topic
- To indicate an important shift in time or place
- To explain a point in additional detail
- To highlight a comparison, contrast, or cause and effect relationship

## PARAGRAPH LENGTH

Most readers find that their comfort level for a paragraph is between 100 and 200 words. Shorter paragraphs cause too much starting and stopping and give a choppy effect. Paragraphs that are too long often test the attention span of readers. Two notable exceptions to this rule exist. In scientific or scholarly papers, longer paragraphs suggest seriousness and depth. In journalistic writing, constraints are placed on paragraph size by the narrow columns in a newspaper format.

The first and last paragraphs of a text will usually be the introduction and conclusion. These special-purpose paragraphs are likely to be shorter than paragraphs in the body of the work. Paragraphs in the body of the essay follow the subject's outline (e.g., one paragraph per point in short essays and a group of paragraphs per point in longer works). Some ideas require more development than others, so it is good for a writer to remain flexible. A paragraph of excessive length may be divided, and shorter ones may be combined.

## COHERENT PARAGRAPHS

A smooth flow of sentences and paragraphs without gaps, shifts, or bumps will lead to paragraph **coherence**. Ties between old and new information can be smoothed using several methods:

- **Linking ideas clearly**, from the topic sentence to the body of the paragraph, is essential for a smooth transition. The topic sentence states the main point, and this should be followed by specific details, examples, and illustrations that support the topic sentence. The support may be direct or indirect. In **indirect support**, the illustrations and examples may support a sentence that in turn supports the topic directly.
- The **repetition of key words** adds coherence to a paragraph. To avoid dull language, variations of the key words may be used.
- **Parallel structures** are often used within sentences to emphasize the similarity of ideas and connect sentences giving similar information.
- Maintaining a **consistent verb tense** throughout the paragraph helps. Shifting tenses affects the smooth flow of words and can disrupt the coherence of the paragraph.

> **Review Video: How to Write a Good Paragraph**
> Visit mometrix.com/academy and enter code: 682127

## SEQUENCE WORDS AND PHRASES

When a paragraph opens with the topic sentence, the second sentence may begin with a phrase like *first of all*, introducing the first supporting detail or example. The writer may introduce the second supporting item with words or phrases like *also*, *in addition*, and *besides*. The writer might introduce succeeding pieces of support with wording like, *another thing*, *moreover*, *furthermore*, or *not only that, but*. The writer may introduce the last piece of support with *lastly*, *finally*, or *last but not least*. Writers get off the point by presenting off-target items not supporting the main point. For

Copyright © Mometrix Media. You have been licensed one copy of this document for personal use only. Any other reproduction or redistribution is strictly prohibited. All rights reserved.
This content is provided for test preparation purposes only and does not imply an endorsement by Mometrix of any particular political, scientific, or religious point of view.

example, a main point *my dog is not smart* is supported by the statement, *he's six years old and still doesn't answer to his name.* But *he cries when I leave for school* is not supportive, as it does not indicate lack of intelligence. Writers stay on point by presenting only supportive statements that are directly relevant to and illustrative of their main point.

> **Review Video: Sequence**
> Visit mometrix.com/academy and enter code: 489027

## TRANSITIONS

Transitions between sentences and paragraphs guide readers from idea to idea and indicate relationships between sentences and paragraphs. Writers should be judicious in their use of transitions, inserting them sparingly. They should also be selected to fit the author's purpose— transitions can indicate time, comparison, and conclusion, among other purposes. Tone is also important to consider when using transitional phrases, varying the tone for different audiences. For example, in a scholarly essay, *in summary* would be preferable to the more informal *in short*.

When working with transitional words and phrases, writers usually find a natural flow that indicates when a transition is needed. In reading a draft of the text, it should become apparent where the flow is disrupted. At this point, the writer can add transitional elements during the revision process. Revising can also afford an opportunity to delete transitional devices that seem heavy handed or unnecessary.

> **Review Video: Transitions in Writing**
> Visit mometrix.com/academy and enter code: 233246

Copyright © Mometrix Media. You have been licensed one copy of this document for personal use only. Any other reproduction or redistribution is strictly prohibited. All rights reserved. This content is provided for test preparation purposes only and does not imply an endorsement by Mometrix of any particular political, scientific, or religious point of view.

## TYPES OF TRANSITIONAL WORDS

| | |
|---|---|
| **Time** | Afterward, immediately, earlier, meanwhile, recently, lately, now, since, soon, when, then, until, before, etc. |
| **Sequence** | too, first, second, further, moreover, also, again, and, next, still, besides, finally |
| **Comparison** | similarly, in the same way, likewise, also, again, once more |
| **Contrasting** | but, although, despite, however, instead, nevertheless, on the one hand... on the other hand, regardless, yet, in contrast. |
| **Cause and Effect** | because, consequently, thus, therefore, then, to this end, since, so, as a result, if... then, accordingly |
| **Examples** | for example, for instance, such as, to illustrate, indeed, in fact, specifically |
| **Place** | near, far, here, there, to the left/right, next to, above, below, beyond, opposite, beside |
| **Concession** | granted that, naturally, of course, it may appear, although it is true that |
| **Repetition, Summary, or Conclusion** | as mentioned earlier, as noted, in other words, in short, on the whole, to summarize, therefore, as a result, to conclude, in conclusion |
| **Addition** | and, also, furthermore, moreover |
| **Generalization** | in broad terms, broadly speaking, in general |

**Review Video: Transitional Words and Phrases**
Visit mometrix.com/academy and enter code: 197796

**Review Video: Transitions**
Visit mometrix.com/academy and enter code: 707563

**Review Video: How to Effectively Connect Sentences**
Visit mometrix.com/academy and enter code: 948325

## CONCLUSION

Two important principles to consider when writing a conclusion are strength and closure. A strong conclusion gives the reader a sense that the author's main points are meaningful and important, and that the supporting facts and arguments are convincing, solid, and well developed. When a conclusion achieves closure, it gives the impression that the writer has stated all necessary information and points and completed the work, rather than simply stopping after a specified length. Some things to avoid when writing concluding paragraphs include:

- Introducing a completely new idea
- Beginning with obvious or unoriginal phrases like "In conclusion" or "To summarize"
- Apologizing for one's opinions or writing
- Repeating the thesis word for word rather than rephrasing it
- Believing that the conclusion must always summarize the piece

**Review Video: Drafting Conclusions**
Visit mometrix.com/academy and enter code: 209408

Copyright © Mometrix Media. You have been licensed one copy of this document for personal use only. Any other reproduction or redistribution is strictly prohibited. All rights reserved.
This content is provided for test preparation purposes only and does not imply an endorsement by Mometrix of any particular political, scientific, or religious point of view.

## CHAPTER QUIZ

**1. Which of the following is considered the main idea of an essay?**

 a. Topic
 b. Body
 c. Theme
 d. Thesis

**2. Which of the following are supporting details to the main idea of a paragraph or a passage?**

 a. Analogies
 b. Examples
 c. Cause and effect
 d. Transitions

**3. Which of the following is NOT a transitional word or phrase in the concession category?**

 a. Granted that
 b. Naturally
 c. Broadly speaking
 d. It may appear

## CHAPTER QUIZ ANSWER KEY

**1. D:** The thesis is the main idea of an essay. A temporary thesis, or working thesis, should be established early in the writing process because it will serve to keep the writer focused as ideas develop. This temporary thesis is subject to change as writing continues. The thesis should be a generalization rather than a fact because the thesis prepares readers for facts and details that support the thesis. The process of bringing the thesis into sharp focus may help in outlining major sections of the work. Once the thesis and introduction are complete, the body of the work can be addressed.

**2. B:** Examples are supporting details to the main idea of a paragraph or a passage. When authors write about something that their audience may not understand or that is not easily accepted, they can provide an example to show their point.

**3. C:** Types of transitional words

| Time | Afterward, immediately, earlier, meanwhile, recently, lately, now, since, soon, when, then, until, before, etc. |
|---|---|
| Sequence | Too, first, second, further, moreover, also, again, and, next, still, besides, finally |
| Comparison | Similarly, in the same way, likewise, also, again, once more |
| Contrasting | But, although, despite, however, instead, nevertheless, on the one hand… on the other hand, regardless, yet, in contrast. |
| Cause and effect | Because, consequently, thus, therefore, then, to this end, since, so, as a result, if… then, accordingly |
| Examples | For example, for instance, such as, to illustrate, indeed, in fact, specifically |
| Place | Near, far, here, there, to the left/right, next to, above, below, beyond, opposite, beside |
| Concession | Granted that, naturally, of course, it may appear, although it is true that |

Copyright © Mometrix Media. You have been licensed one copy of this document for personal use only. Any other reproduction or redistribution is strictly prohibited. All rights reserved.
This content is provided for test preparation purposes only and does not imply an endorsement by Mometrix of any particular political, scientific, or religious point of view.

| Repetition, summary, or conclusion | As mentioned earlier, as noted, in other words, in short, on the whole, to summarize, therefore, as a result, to conclude, in conclusion |
|---|---|
| Addition | And, also, furthermore, moreover |
| Generalization | In broad terms, broadly speaking, in general |

Copyright © Mometrix Media. You have been licensed one copy of this document for personal use only. Any other reproduction or redistribution is strictly prohibited. All rights reserved.
This content is provided for test preparation purposes only and does not imply an endorsement by Mometrix of any particular political, scientific, or religious point of view.

# Writing Style and Form

## WRITING STYLE AND LINGUISTIC FORM

**Linguistic form** encodes the literal meanings of words and sentences. It comes from the phonological, morphological, syntactic, and semantic parts of a language. **Writing style** consists of different ways of encoding the meaning and indicating figurative and stylistic meanings. An author's writing style can also be referred to as his or her **voice**.

Writers' stylistic choices accomplish three basic effects on their audiences:

- They **communicate meanings** beyond linguistically dictated meanings,
- They communicate the **author's attitude**, such as persuasive or argumentative effects accomplished through style, and
- They communicate or **express feelings**.

Within style, component areas include:

- Narrative structure
- Viewpoint
- Focus
- Sound patterns
- Meter and rhythm
- Lexical and syntactic repetition and parallelism
- Writing genre
- Representational, realistic, and mimetic effects
- Representation of thought and speech
- Meta-representation (representing representation)
- Irony
- Metaphor and other indirect meanings
- Representation and use of historical and dialectal variations
- Gender-specific and other group-specific speech styles, both real and fictitious
- Analysis of the processes for inferring meaning from writing

## LEVEL OF FORMALITY

The relationship between writer and reader is important in choosing a **level of formality** as most writing requires some degree of formality. **Formal writing** is for addressing a superior in a school or work environment. Business letters, textbooks, and newspapers use a moderate to high level of formality. **Informal writing** is appropriate for private letters, personal emails, and business correspondence between close associates.

For your exam, you will want to be aware of informal and formal writing. One way that this can be accomplished is to watch for shifts in point of view in the essay. For example, unless writers are using a personal example, they will rarely refer to themselves (e.g., "*I* think that *my* point is very clear.") to avoid being informal when they need to be formal.

Also, be mindful of an author who addresses his or her audience **directly** in their writing (e.g., "Readers, *like you*, will understand this argument.") as this can be a sign of informal writing. Good writers understand the need to be consistent with their level of formality. Shifts in levels of formality or point of view can confuse readers and cause them to discount the message.

Copyright © Mometrix Media. You have been licensed one copy of this document for personal use only. Any other reproduction or redistribution is strictly prohibited. All rights reserved.
This content is provided for test preparation purposes only and does not imply an endorsement by Mometrix of any particular political, scientific, or religious point of view.

## CLICHÉS

Clichés are phrases that have been **overused** to the point that the phrase has no importance or has lost the original meaning. These phrases have no originality and add very little to a passage. Therefore, most writers will avoid the use of clichés. Another option is to make changes to a cliché so that it is not predictable and empty of meaning.

Examples:

When life gives you lemons, make lemonade.

Every cloud has a silver lining.

## JARGON

Jargon is **specialized vocabulary** that is used among members of a certain trade or profession. Since jargon is understood by only a small audience, writers will use jargon in passages that will only be read by a specialized audience. For example, medical jargon should be used in a medical journal but not in a New York Times article. Jargon includes exaggerated language that tries to impress rather than inform. Sentences filled with jargon are not precise and are difficult to understand.

Examples:

"He is going to *toenail* these frames for us." (Toenail is construction jargon for nailing at an angle.)

"They brought in a *kip* of material today." (Kip refers to 1000 pounds in architecture and engineering.)

## SLANG

Slang is an **informal** and sometimes private language that is understood by some individuals. Slang terms have some usefulness, but they can have a small audience. So, most formal writing will not include this kind of language.

Examples:

"Yes, the event was a blast!" (In this sentence, *blast* means that the event was a great experience.)

"That attempt was an epic fail." (By *epic fail*, the speaker means that his or her attempt was not a success.)

## COLLOQUIALISM

A colloquialism is a word or phrase that is found in informal writing. Unlike slang, **colloquial language** will be familiar to a greater range of people. However, colloquialisms are still considered inappropriate for formal writing. Colloquial language can include some slang, but these are limited to contractions for the most part.

Examples:

"Can *y'all* come back another time?" (Y'all is a contraction of "you all.")

Copyright © Mometrix Media. You have been licensed one copy of this document for personal use only. Any other reproduction or redistribution is strictly prohibited. All rights reserved. This content is provided for test preparation purposes only and does not imply an endorsement by Mometrix of any particular political, scientific, or religious point of view.

"Will you stop him from building this *castle in the air*?" (A "castle in the air" is an improbable or unlikely event.)

## ACADEMIC LANGUAGE

In educational settings, students are often expected to use academic language in their schoolwork. Academic language is also commonly found in dissertations and theses, texts published by academic journals, and other forms of academic research. Academic language conventions may vary between fields, but general academic language is free of slang, regional terminology, and noticeable grammatical errors. Specific terms may also be used in academic language, and it is important to understand their proper usage. A writer's command of academic language impacts their ability to communicate in an academic or professional context. While it is acceptable to use colloquialisms, slang, improper grammar, or other forms of informal speech in social settings or at home, it is inappropriate to practice non-academic language in academic contexts.

## TONE

Tone may be defined as the writer's **attitude** toward the topic, and to the audience. This attitude is reflected in the language used in the writing. The tone of a work should be **appropriate to the topic** and to the intended audience. While it may be fine to use slang or jargon in some pieces, other texts should not contain such terms. Tone can range from humorous to serious and any level in between. It may be more or less formal, depending on the purpose of the writing and its intended audience. All these nuances in tone can flavor the entire writing and should be kept in mind as the work evolves.

## WORD SELECTION

A writer's choice of words is a signature of their style. Careful thought about the use of words can improve a piece of writing. A passage can be an exciting piece to read when attention is given to the use of vivid or specific nouns rather than general ones.

Example:

General: His kindness will never be forgotten.

Specific: His thoughtful gifts and bear hugs will never be forgotten.

Attention should also be given to the kind of verbs that are used in sentences. Active verbs (e.g., run, swim) are about an action. Whenever possible, an **active verb should replace a linking verb** to provide clear examples for arguments and to strengthen a passage overall. When using an active verb, one should be sure that the verb is used in the active voice instead of the passive voice. Verbs are in the active voice when the subject is the one doing the action. A verb is in the passive voice when the subject is the recipient of an action.

Example:

Passive: The winners were called to the stage by the judges.

Active: The judges called the winners to the stage.

## CONCISENESS

**Conciseness** is writing that communicates a message in the fewest words possible. Writing concisely is valuable because short, uncluttered messages allow the reader to understand the author's message more easily and efficiently. Planning is important in writing concise messages. If

119

Copyright © Mometrix Media. You have been licensed one copy of this document for personal use only. Any other reproduction or redistribution is strictly prohibited. All rights reserved. This content is provided for test preparation purposes only and does not imply an endorsement by Mometrix of any particular political, scientific, or religious point of view.

you have in mind what you need to write beforehand, it will be easier to make a message short and to the point. Do not state the obvious.

Revising is also important. After the message is written, make sure you have effective, pithy sentences that efficiently get your point across. When reviewing the information, imagine a conversation taking place, and concise writing will likely result.

## APPROPRIATE KINDS OF WRITING FOR DIFFERENT TASKS, PURPOSES, AND AUDIENCES

When preparing to write a composition, consider the audience and purpose to choose the best type of writing. Three common types of writing are persuasive, expository, and narrative. **Persuasive**, or argumentative writing, is used to convince the audience to take action or agree with the author's claims. **Expository** writing is meant to inform the audience of the author's observations or research on a topic. **Narrative** writing is used to tell the audience a story and often allows more room for creativity. While task, purpose, and audience inform a writer's mode of writing, these factors also impact elements such as tone, vocabulary, and formality.

For example, students who are writing to persuade their parents to grant them some additional privilege, such as permission for a more independent activity, should use more sophisticated vocabulary and diction that sounds more mature and serious to appeal to the parental audience. However, students who are writing for younger children should use simpler vocabulary and sentence structure, as well as choose words that are more vivid and entertaining. They should treat their topics more lightly, and include humor when appropriate. Students who are writing for their classmates may use language that is more informal, as well as age-appropriate.

> **Review Video: <u>Writing Purpose and Audience</u>**
> Visit mometrix.com/academy and enter code: 146627

Copyright © Mometrix Media. You have been licensed one copy of this document for personal use only. Any other reproduction or redistribution is strictly prohibited. All rights reserved.
This content is provided for test preparation purposes only and does not imply an endorsement by Mometrix of any particular political, scientific, or religious point of view.

## CHAPTER QUIZ

**1. Which of the following would NOT be considered formal writing?**

    a. Private letters
    b. Business letters
    c. Textbooks
    d. Newspapers

**2. Which of the following sentences contains a verb in the passive voice?**

    a. The judges called the winners to the stage for their awards.
    b. Each applicant must fill out all of the forms required.
    c. He raced through the copse of trees with the grace of a deer.
    d. I was told that there would be food available at the party.

## CHAPTER QUIZ ANSWER KEY

**1. A:** The relationship between writer and reader is important in choosing a level of formality because most writing requires some degree of formality. Formal writing is for addressing a superior in a school or work environment. Business letters, textbooks, and newspapers use a moderate to high level of formality. Informal writing is appropriate for private letters, personal emails, and business correspondence between close associates.

**2. D:** Attention should also be given to the kind of verbs that are used in sentences. Active verbs (e.g., run, swim) are about an action. Whenever possible, an active verb should replace a linking verb to provide clear examples for arguments and to strengthen a passage overall. When using an active verb, one should be sure that the verb is used in the active voice instead of the passive voice. Verbs are in the active voice when the subject is the one doing the action. A verb is in the passive voice when the subject is the recipient of an action.

Copyright © Mometrix Media. You have been licensed one copy of this document for personal use only. Any other reproduction or redistribution is strictly prohibited. All rights reserved. This content is provided for test preparation purposes only and does not imply an endorsement by Mometrix of any particular political, scientific, or religious point of view.

# Modes of Writing

## ESSAYS

Essays usually focus on one topic, subject, or goal. There are several types of essays, including informative, persuasive, and narrative. An essay's structure and level of formality depend on the type of essay and its goal. While narrative essays typically do not include outside sources, other types of essays often require some research and the integration of primary and secondary sources.

The basic format of an essay typically has three major parts: the introduction, the body, and the conclusion. The body is further divided into the writer's main points. Short and simple essays may have three main points, while essays covering broader ranges and going into more depth can have almost any number of main points, depending on length.

An essay's introduction should answer three questions:

1. What is the **subject** of the essay?

   If a student writes an essay about a book, the answer would include the title and author of the book and any additional information needed—such as the subject or argument of the book.

2. How does the essay **address** the subject?

   To answer this, the writer identifies the essay's organization by briefly summarizing main points and the evidence supporting them.

3. What will the essay **prove**?

   This is the thesis statement, usually the opening paragraph's last sentence, clearly stating the writer's message.

The body elaborates on all the main points related to the thesis, introducing one main point at a time, and includes supporting evidence with each main point. Each body paragraph should state the point in a topic sentence, which is usually the first sentence in the paragraph. The paragraph should then explain the point's meaning, support it with quotations or other evidence, and then explain how this point and the evidence are related to the thesis. The writer should then repeat this procedure in a new paragraph for each additional main point.

The conclusion reiterates the content of the introduction, including the thesis, to remind the reader of the essay's main argument or subject. The essay writer may also summarize the highlights of the argument or description contained in the body of the essay, following the same sequence originally used in the body. For example, a conclusion might look like: Point 1 + Point 2 + Point 3 = Thesis, or Point 1 → Point 2 → Point 3 → Thesis Proof. Good organization makes essays easier for writers to compose and provides a guide for readers to follow. Well-organized essays hold attention better and are more likely to get readers to accept their theses as valid.

## INFORMATIVE VS. PERSUASIVE WRITING

**Informative** writing, also called explanatory or expository writing, begins with the basis that something is true or factual, while **persuasive** writing strives to prove something that may or may not be true or factual. Whereas argumentative text is written to **persuade** readers to agree with the author's position, informative text merely **provides information and insight** to readers. Informative writing concentrates on **informing** readers about why or how something is as it is. This can include offering new information, explaining how a process works, and developing a

Copyright © Mometrix Media. You have been licensed one copy of this document for personal use only. Any other reproduction or redistribution is strictly prohibited. All rights reserved. This content is provided for test preparation purposes only and does not imply an endorsement by Mometrix of any particular political, scientific, or religious point of view.

concept for readers. To accomplish these objectives, the essay may name and distinguish various things within a category, provide definitions, provide details about the parts of something, explain a particular function or behavior, and give readers explanations for why a fact, object, event, or process exists or occurs.

## NARRATIVE WRITING

Put simply, **narrative** writing tells a story. The most common examples of literary narratives are novels. Non-fictional biographies, autobiographies, memoirs, and histories are also narratives. Narratives should tell stories in such a way that the readers learn something or gain insight or understanding. Students can write more interesting narratives by describing events or experiences that were meaningful to them. Narratives should start with the story's actions or events, rather than long descriptions or introductions. Students should ensure that there is a point to each story by describing what they learned from the experience they narrate. To write an effective description, students should include sensory details, asking themselves what they saw, heard, felt or touched, smelled, and tasted during the experiences they describe. In narrative writing, the details should be **concrete** rather than **abstract**. Using concrete details enables readers to imagine everything that the writer describes.

> **Review Video: Narratives**
> Visit mometrix.com/academy and enter code: 280100

### SENSORY DETAILS

Students need to use vivid descriptions when writing descriptive essays. Narratives should also include descriptions of characters, things, and events. Students should remember to describe not only the visual detail of what someone or something looks like, but details from other senses, as well. For example, they can contrast the feeling of a sea breeze to that of a mountain breeze, describe how they think something inedible would taste, and compare sounds they hear in the same location at different times of day and night. Readers have trouble visualizing images or imagining sensory impressions and feelings from abstract descriptions, so concrete descriptions make these more real.

### CONCRETE VS. ABSTRACT DESCRIPTIONS IN NARRATIVE

**Concrete language** provides information that readers can grasp and may empathize with, while **abstract language**, which is more general, can leave readers feeling disconnected, empty, or even confused. "It was a lovely day" is abstract, but "The sun shone brightly, the sky was blue, the air felt warm, and a gentle breeze wafted across my skin" is concrete. "Ms. Couch was a good teacher" uses abstract language, giving only a general idea of the writer's opinion. But "Ms. Couch is excellent at helping us take our ideas and turn them into good essays and stories" uses concrete language, giving more specific examples of what makes Ms. Couch a good teacher. "I like writing poems but not essays" gives readers a general idea that the student prefers one genre over another, but not why. But when reading, "I like writing short poems with rhythm and rhyme, but I hate writing five-page essays that go on and on about the same ideas," readers understand that the student prefers the brevity, rhyme, and meter of short poetry over the length and redundancy of longer prose.

### AUTOBIOGRAPHICAL NARRATIVES

**Autobiographical narratives** are narratives written by an author about an event or period in their life. Autobiographical narratives are written from one person's perspective, in first person, and often include the author's thoughts and feelings alongside their description of the event or period. Structure, style, or theme varies between different autobiographical narratives, since each narrative is personal and specific to its author and his or her experience.

Copyright © Mometrix Media. You have been licensed one copy of this document for personal use only. Any other reproduction or redistribution is strictly prohibited. All rights reserved. This content is provided for test preparation purposes only and does not imply an endorsement by Mometrix of any particular political, scientific, or religious point of view.

## REFLECTIVE ESSAY

A less common type of essay is the reflective essay. **Reflective essays** allow the author to reflect, or think back, on an experience and analyze what they recall. They should consider what they learned from the experience, what they could have done differently, what would have helped them during the experience, or anything else that they have realized from looking back on the experience. Reflection essays incorporate both objective reflection on one's own actions and subjective explanation of thoughts and feelings. These essays can be written for a number of experiences in a formal or informal context.

## JOURNALS AND DIARIES

A **journal** is a personal account of events, experiences, feelings, and thoughts. Many people write journals to express their feelings and thoughts or to help them process experiences they have had. Since journals are **private documents** not meant to be shared with others, writers may not be concerned with grammar, spelling, or other mechanics. However, authors may write journals that they expect or hope to publish someday; in this case, they not only express their thoughts and feelings and process their experiences, but they also attend to their craft in writing them. Some authors compose journals to record a particular time period or a series of related events, such as a cancer diagnosis, treatment, surviving the disease, and how these experiences have changed or affected them. Other experiences someone might include in a journal are recovering from addiction, journeys of spiritual exploration and discovery, time spent in another country, or anything else someone wants to personally document. Journaling can also be therapeutic, as some people use journals to work through feelings of grief over loss or to wrestle with big decisions.

### EXAMPLES OF DIARIES IN LITERATURE

*The Diary of a Young Girl* by Dutch Jew Anne Frank (1947) contains her life-affirming, nonfictional diary entries from 1942-1944 while her family hid in an attic from World War II's genocidal Nazis. *Go Ask Alice* (1971) by Beatrice Sparks is a cautionary, fictional novel in the form of diary entries by Alice, an unhappy, rebellious teen who takes LSD, runs away from home and lives with hippies, and eventually returns home. Frank's writing reveals an intelligent, sensitive, insightful girl, raised by intellectual European parents—a girl who believes in the goodness of human nature despite surrounding atrocities. Alice, influenced by early 1970s counterculture, becomes less optimistic. However, similarities can be found between them: Frank dies in a Nazi concentration camp while the fictitious Alice dies from a drug overdose. Both young women are also unable to escape their surroundings. Additionally, adolescent searches for personal identity are evident in both books.

> **Review Video: Journals, Diaries, Letters, and Blogs**
> Visit mometrix.com/academy and enter code: 432845

## LETTERS

**Letters** are messages written to other people. In addition to letters written between individuals, some writers compose letters to the editors of newspapers, magazines, and other publications, while some write "Open Letters" to be published and read by the general public. Open letters, while intended for everyone to read, may also identify a group of people or a single person whom the letter directly addresses. In everyday use, the most-used forms are business letters and personal or friendly letters. Both kinds share common elements: business or personal letterhead stationery; the writer's return address at the top; the addressee's address next; a salutation, such as "Dear [name]" or some similar opening greeting, followed by a colon in business letters or a comma in personal letters; the body of the letter, with paragraphs as indicated; and a closing, like "Sincerely/Cordially/Best regards/etc." or "Love," in intimate personal letters.

Copyright © Mometrix Media. You have been licensed one copy of this document for personal use only. Any other reproduction or redistribution is strictly prohibited. All rights reserved. This content is provided for test preparation purposes only and does not imply an endorsement by Mometrix of any particular political, scientific, or religious point of view.

## EARLY LETTERS

The Greek word for "letter" is *epistolē*, which became the English word "epistle." The earliest letters were called epistles, including the New Testament's epistles from the apostles to the Christians. In ancient Egypt, the writing curriculum in scribal schools included the epistolary genre. Epistolary novels frame a story in the form of letters. Examples of noteworthy epistolary novels include:

- *Pamela* (1740), by 18th-century English novelist Samuel Richardson
- *Shamela* (1741), Henry Fielding's satire of *Pamela* that mocked epistolary writing.
- *Lettres persanes* (1721) by French author Montesquieu
- *The Sorrows of Young Werther* (1774) by German author Johann Wolfgang von Goethe
- *The History of Emily Montague* (1769), the first Canadian novel, by Frances Brooke
- *Dracula* (1897) by Bram Stoker
- *Frankenstein* (1818) by Mary Shelley
- *The Color Purple* (1982) by Alice Walker

## BLOGS

The word "blog" is derived from "weblog" and refers to writing done exclusively on the internet. Readers of reputable newspapers expect quality content and layouts that enable easy reading. These expectations also apply to blogs. For example, readers can easily move visually from line to line when columns are narrow, while overly wide columns cause readers to lose their places. Blogs must also be posted with layouts enabling online readers to follow them easily. However, because the way people read on computer, tablet, and smartphone screens differs from how they read print on paper, formatting and writing blog content is more complex than writing newspaper articles. Two major principles are the bases for blog-writing rules: The first is while readers of print articles skim to estimate their length, online they must scroll down to scan; therefore, blog layouts need more subheadings, graphics, and other indications of what information follows. The second is onscreen reading can be harder on the eyes than reading printed paper, so legibility is crucial in blogs.

## RULES AND RATIONALES FOR WRITING BLOGS

1. Format all posts for smooth page layout and easy scanning.
2. Column width should not be too wide, as larger lines of text can be difficult to read
3. Headings and subheadings separate text visually, enable scanning or skimming, and encourage continued reading.
4. Bullet-pointed or numbered lists enable quick information location and scanning.
5. Punctuation is critical, so beginners should use shorter sentences until confident in their knowledge of punctuation rules.
6. Blog paragraphs should be far shorter—two to six sentences each—than paragraphs written on paper to enable "chunking" because reading onscreen is more difficult.
7. Sans-serif fonts are usually clearer than serif fonts, and larger font sizes are better.
8. Highlight important material and draw attention with **boldface**, but avoid overuse. Avoid hard-to-read *italics* and ALL CAPITALS.
9. Include enough blank spaces: overly busy blogs tire eyes and brains. Images not only break up text but also emphasize and enhance text and can attract initial reader attention.
10. Use background colors judiciously to avoid distracting the eye or making it difficult to read.
11. Be consistent throughout posts, since people read them in different orders.
12. Tell a story with a beginning, middle, and end.

Copyright © Mometrix Media. You have been licensed one copy of this document for personal use only. Any other reproduction or redistribution is strictly prohibited. All rights reserved. This content is provided for test preparation purposes only and does not imply an endorsement by Mometrix of any particular political, scientific, or religious point of view.

## SPECIALIZED MODES OF WRITING

### EDITORIALS

Editorials are articles in newspapers, magazines, and other serial publications. Editorials express an opinion or belief belonging to the majority of the publication's leadership. This opinion or belief generally refers to a specific issue, topic, or event. These articles are authored by a member, or a small number of members, of the publication's leadership and are often written to affect their readers, such as persuading them to adopt a stance or take a particular action.

### RESUMES

Resumes are brief, but formal, documents that outline an individual's experience in a certain area. Resumes are most often used for job applications. Such resumes will list the applicant's work experience, certification, and achievements or qualifications related to the position. Resumes should only include the most pertinent information. They should also use strategic formatting to highlight the applicant's most impressive experiences and achievements, to ensure the document can be read quickly and easily, and to eliminate both visual clutter and excessive negative space.

### REPORTS

Reports summarize the results of research, new methodology, or other developments in an academic or professional context. Reports often include details about methodology and outside influences and factors. However, a report should focus primarily on the results of the research or development. Reports are objective and deliver information efficiently, sacrificing style for clear and effective communication.

### MEMORANDA

A memorandum, also called a memo, is a formal method of communication used in professional settings. Memoranda are printed documents that include a heading listing the sender and their job title, the recipient and their job title, the date, and a specific subject line. Memoranda often include an introductory section explaining the reason and context for the memorandum. Next, a memorandum includes a section with details relevant to the topic. Finally, the memorandum will conclude with a paragraph that politely and clearly defines the sender's expectations of the recipient.

Copyright © Mometrix Media. You have been licensed one copy of this document for personal use only. Any other reproduction or redistribution is strictly prohibited. All rights reserved. This content is provided for test preparation purposes only and does not imply an endorsement by Mometrix of any particular political, scientific, or religious point of view.

## CHAPTER QUIZ

**1. The Greek word *epistolē* means:**

    a. Pistol.
    b. Epistaxis.
    c. Essay.
    d. Letter.

**2. What are the two major principles used to create an orderly blog?**

    a. The content must be interesting with various fonts and color combinations, and it should take less than 10 minutes to read in its entirety.
    b. Blog layouts need more subheadings, graphics, and other indications of what information follows, and the content must be interesting with various fonts and color combinations.
    c. Legibility is crucial because onscreen reading is hard on the eyes, and it should take less than 10 minutes to read in its entirety.
    d. Blog layouts need more subheadings, graphics, and other indications of what information follows, and legibility is crucial because onscreen reading is hard on the eyes.

## CHAPTER QUIZ ANSWER KEY

**1. D:** The Greek word for "letter" is *epistolē*, which became the English word "epistle." The earliest letters were called epistles, including the New Testament's epistles from the apostles to the Christians. In ancient Egypt, the writing curriculum in scribal schools included the epistolary genre. Epistolary novels frame a story in the form of letters.

**2. D:** There are two major principles that form the basis for blog-writing rules. The first is that while readers of print can skim articles to estimate their length, they must scroll down to scan something published online, meaning that blog layouts need more subheadings, graphics, and other indications of what information follows. The second principle is that onscreen reading can be harder on the eyes than reading printed paper, so legibility is crucial in blogs.

Copyright © Mometrix Media. You have been licensed one copy of this document for personal use only. Any other reproduction or redistribution is strictly prohibited. All rights reserved.
This content is provided for test preparation purposes only and does not imply an endorsement by Mometrix of any particular political, scientific, or religious point of view.

# Research Writing

## RESEARCH WRITING

Writing for research is essentially writing to answer a question or a problem about a particular **research topic**. A **problem statement** is written to clearly define the problem with a topic before asking about how to solve the problem. A **research question** serves to ask what can be done to address the problem. Before a researcher should try to solve a problem, the researcher should spend significant time performing a **literature review** to find out what has already been learned about the topic and if there are already solutions in place. The literature review can help to re-evaluate the research question as well. If the question has not been thoroughly answered, then it is proper to do broader research to learn about the topic and build up the body of literature. If the literature review provides plenty of background, but no practical solutions to the problem, then the research question should be targeted at solving a problem more directly. After the research has been performed, a **thesis** can act as a proposal for a solution or as a recommendation to future researchers to continue to learn more about the topic. The thesis should then be supported by significant contributing evidence to help support the proposed solution.

## EXAMPLE OF RESEARCH WRITING ELEMENTS

| Topic | The general idea the research is about. This is usually broader than the problem itself.<br>Example: Clean Water |
|---|---|
| Problem Statement | A problem statement is a brief, clear description of a problem with the topic.<br>Example: Not all villages in third-world countries have ready access to clean water. |
| Research Question | A research question asks a specific question about what needs to be learned or done about the problem statement.<br>Example: What can local governments do to improve access to clean water? |
| Literature Review | A review of the body of literature by the researcher to show what is already known about the topic and the problem. If the literature review shows that the research question has already been thoroughly answered, the researcher should consider changing problem statements to something that has not been solved. |
| Thesis | A brief proposal of a solution to a problem. Theses do not include their own support, but are supported by later evidence.<br>Example: Local governments can improve access to clean water by installing sealed rain-water collection units. |
| Body Paragraphs | Paragraphs focused on the primary supporting evidence for the main idea of the thesis. There are usually three body paragraphs, but there can be more if needed. |
| Conclusion | A final wrap-up of the research project. The conclusion should reiterate the problem, question, thesis, and briefly mention how the main evidences support the thesis. |

## THE RESEARCH PROCESS

Researchers should prepare some information before gathering sources. Researchers who have chosen a **research question** should choose key words or names that pertain to their question. They should also identify what type of information and sources they are looking for. Researchers should consider whether secondary or primary sources will be most appropriate for their research project. As researchers find credible and appropriate sources, they should be prepared to adjust the scope of their research question or topic in response to the information and insights they gather.

Copyright © Mometrix Media. You have been licensed one copy of this document for personal use only. Any other reproduction or redistribution is strictly prohibited. All rights reserved. This content is provided for test preparation purposes only and does not imply an endorsement by Mometrix of any particular political, scientific, or religious point of view.

## USING SOURCES AND SYNTHESIZING INFORMATION

As researchers find potential sources for their research project, it is important to keep a **record** of the material they find and note how each source may impact their work. When taking these notes, researchers should keep their research question or outline in mind and consider how their chosen references would complement their discussion. **Literature reviews** and **annotated bibliographies** are helpful tools for evaluating sources, as they require the researcher to consider the qualities and offerings of the sources they choose to use. These tools also help researchers synthesize the information they find.

## SYNTHESIZING INFORMATION

**Synthesizing information** requires the researcher to integrate sources and their own thoughts by quoting, paraphrasing, or summarizing outside information in their research project. Synthesizing information indicates that the research complements the writer's claims, ensures that the ideas in the composition flow logically, and makes including small details and quotes easier. Paraphrasing is one of the simplest ways to integrate a source. **Paraphrasing** allows the writer to support their ideas with research while presenting the information in their own words, rather than using the source's original wording. Paraphrasing also allows the writer to reference the source's main ideas instead of specific details. While paraphrasing does not require the writer to quote the source, it still entails a direct reference to the source, meaning that any paraphrased material still requires a citation.

## CITING SOURCES

While researchers should combine research with their own ideas, the information and ideas that come from outside sources should be attributed to the author of the source. When conducting research, it is helpful to record the publication information for each source so that **citations** can be easily added within the composition. Keeping a close record of the source of each idea in a composition or project is helpful for avoiding plagiarism, as both direct and indirect references require documentation.

## PLAGIARISM

Understanding what is considered to be plagiarism is important to preventing unintentional plagiarism. Using another person's work in any way without proper attribution is **plagiarism**. However, it is easy to mistakenly commit plagiarism by improperly citing a source or creating a citation that is not intended for the way the source was used. Even when an honest attempt to attribute information is made, small errors can still result in plagiarized content. For this reason, it is important to create citations carefully and review citations before submitting or publishing research. It is also possible to plagiarize one's own work. This occurs when a writer has published work with one title and purpose and then attempts to publish it again as new material under a new title or purpose.

## LITERATURE REVIEW

One of the two main parts of a literature review is searching through existing literature. The other is actually writing the review. Researchers must take care not to get lost in the information and inhibit progress toward their research goal. A good precaution is to write out the research question and keep it nearby. It is also wise to make a search plan and establish a time limit in advance. Finding a seemingly endless number of references indicates a need to revisit the research question because the topic is too broad. Finding too little material means that the research topic is too narrow. With new or cutting-edge research, one may find that nobody has investigated this particular question. This requires systematic searching, using abstracts in periodicals for an

Copyright © Mometrix Media. You have been licensed one copy of this document for personal use only. Any other reproduction or redistribution is strictly prohibited. All rights reserved. This content is provided for test preparation purposes only and does not imply an endorsement by Mometrix of any particular political, scientific, or religious point of view.

overview of available literature, research papers or other specific sources to explore its reference, and references in books and other sources.

When searching published literature on a research topic, one must take thorough notes. It is common to find a reference that could be useful later in the research project, but is not needed yet. In situations like this, it is helpful to make a note of the reference so it will be easy to find later. These notes can be grouped in a word processing document, which also allows for easy compiling of links and quotes from internet research. Researchers should explore the internet regularly, view resources for their research often, learn how to use resources correctly and efficiently, experiment with resources available within the disciplines, open and examine databases, become familiar with reference desk materials, find publications with abstracts of articles and books on one's topic, use papers' references to locate the most useful journals and important authors, identify keywords for refining and narrowing database searches, and peruse library catalogues online for available sources—all while taking notes.

As one searches for references, one will gradually develop an overview of the body of literature available for his or her subject. This signals the time to prepare for writing the literature review. The researcher should assemble his or her notes along with copies of all the journal articles and all the books he or she has acquired. Then one should write the research question again at the top of a page and list below it all of the author names and keywords discovered while searching. It is also helpful to observe whether any groups or pairs of these stand out. These activities are parts of structuring one's literature review—the first step for writing a thesis, dissertation, or research paper. Writers should rewrite their work as necessary rather than expecting to write only one draft. However, stopping to edit along the way can distract from the momentum of writing the first draft. If the writer is dissatisfied with a certain part of the draft, it may be better to skip to a later portion of the paper and revisit the problem section at another time.

### BODY AND CONCLUSION IN LITERATURE REVIEW

The first step of a literature review paper is to create a rough draft. The next step is to edit: rewrite for clarity, eliminate unnecessary verbiage, and change terminology that could confuse readers. After editing, a writer should ask others to read and give feedback. Additionally, the writer should read the paper aloud to hear how it sounds, editing as needed. Throughout a literature review, the writer should not only summarize and comment on each source reviewed, but should also relate these findings to the original research question. The writer should explicitly state in the conclusion how the research question and pertinent literature interaction is developed throughout the body, reflecting on insights gained through the process.

### SUMMARIES AND ABSTRACTS

When preparing to submit or otherwise publish research, it may be necessary to compose a summary or abstract to accompany the research composition.

A summary is a brief description of the contents of a longer work that provides an overview of the work and may include its most important details. One common type of summary is an abstract. Abstracts are specialized summaries that are most commonly used in the context of research. Abstracts may include details such as the purpose for the research, the researcher's methodology, and the most significant results of the research. Abstracts sometimes include sections and headings, where most summaries are limited to one or a few paragraphs with no special groupings.

Copyright © Mometrix Media. You have been licensed one copy of this document for personal use only. Any other reproduction or redistribution is strictly prohibited. All rights reserved. This content is provided for test preparation purposes only and does not imply an endorsement by Mometrix of any particular political, scientific, or religious point of view.

## EDITING AND REVISING

After composing a rough draft of a research paper, the writer should **edit** it. The purpose of the paper is to communicate the answer to one's research question in an efficient and effective manner. The writing should be as **concise** and **clear** as possible, and the style should also be consistent. Editing is often easier to do after writing the first draft rather than during it, as taking time between writing and editing allows writers to be more objective. If the paper includes an abstract and an introduction, the writer should compose these after writing the rest, when he or she will have a better grasp of the theme and arguments. Not all readers understand technical terminology or long words, so writers should use these sparingly. Finally, writers should consult a writing and style guide to address any industry- or institution-specific issues that may arise as they edit.

> **Review Video: Revising and Editing**
> Visit mometrix.com/academy and enter code: 674181

Copyright © Mometrix Media. You have been licensed one copy of this document for personal use only. Any other reproduction or redistribution is strictly prohibited. All rights reserved.
This content is provided for test preparation purposes only and does not imply an endorsement by Mometrix of any particular political, scientific, or religious point of view.

## CHAPTER QUIZ

### 1. Which of the following correctly matches the term with its definition?

   a. Topic: A brief, clear description of a problem with the topic.
   b. Research question: A general idea of what the research is about.
   c. Thesis: A brief proposal of a solution to a problem.
   d. Literature review: A final wrap-up of the research project.

### 2. All of the following are true about paraphrasing, EXCEPT:

   a. Paraphrasing allows the writer to support their ideas with research while presenting the information in their own words.
   b. Paraphrasing allows the writer to reference the source's main ideas instead of specific details.
   c. Paraphrasing does not require the writer to quote the source.
   d. Paraphrasing does not require a citation for any paraphrased material.

## CHAPTER QUIZ ANSWER KEY

**1. C:** Example of research writing elements

| Topic | The general idea the research is about. This is usually broader than the problem itself. Example: Clean water |
|---|---|
| Problem statement | A brief, clear description of a problem with the topic. Example: Not all villages in third-world countries have ready access to clean water. |
| Research question | A specific question about what needs to be learned or done about the problem statement. Example: What can local governments do to improve access to clean water? |
| Literature review | A review of the body of literature by the researcher to show what is already known about the topic and the problem. If the literature review shows that the research question has already been thoroughly answered, the researcher should consider changing problem statements to something that has not been solved. |
| Thesis | A brief proposal of a solution to a problem. Theses do not include their own support, but are supported by later evidence. Example: Local governments can improve access to clean water by installing sealed rainwater collection units. |
| Body paragraphs | Paragraphs focused on the primary supporting evidence for the main idea of the thesis. There are usually three body paragraphs, but there can be more if needed. |
| Conclusion | A final wrap-up of the research project. The conclusion should reiterate the problem, question, thesis, and briefly mention how the main evidences support the thesis. |

**2. D:** Paraphrasing allows the writer to support their ideas with research while presenting the information in their own words rather than using the source's original wording. Paraphrasing also allows the writer to reference the source's main ideas instead of specific details. While paraphrasing does not require the writer to quote the source, it still entails a direct reference to the source, meaning that any paraphrased material still requires a citation.

Copyright © Mometrix Media. You have been licensed one copy of this document for personal use only. Any other reproduction or redistribution is strictly prohibited. All rights reserved. This content is provided for test preparation purposes only and does not imply an endorsement by Mometrix of any particular political, scientific, or religious point of view.

# Information Sources

## PRIMARY SOURCES

In literature review, one may examine both primary and secondary sources. Primary sources contain original information that was witnessed, gathered, or otherwise produced by the source's author. **Primary sources** can include firsthand accounts, found in sources such as books, autobiographies, transcripts, speeches, videos, photos, and personal journals or diaries. Primary sources may also include records of information, such as government documents, or personally-conducted research in sources like reports and essays. They may be found in academic books, journals and other periodicals, and authoritative databases. Using primary sources allows researchers to develop their own conclusions about the subject. Primary sources are also reliable for finding information about a person or their personal accounts and experiences. Primary sources such as photos, videos, audio recordings, transcripts, and government documents are often reliable, as they are usually objective and can be used to confirm information from other sources.

## SECONDARY SOURCES

Secondary sources are sources that reference information originally provided by another source. The original source may be cited, quoted, paraphrased, or described in a secondary source. **Secondary sources** may be articles, essays, videos, or books found in periodicals, magazines, newspapers, films, databases, or websites. A secondary source can be used to reference another researcher's analysis or conclusion from a primary source. This information can inform the researcher of the existing discussions regarding their subject. These types of sources may also support the researcher's claims by providing a credible argument that contributes to the researcher's argument. Secondary sources may also highlight connections between primary sources or criticize both primary and other secondary sources. These types of secondary sources are valuable because they provide information and conclusions the researcher may not have considered or found, otherwise.

> **Review Video: Primary and Secondary Sources**
> Visit mometrix.com/academy and enter code: 383328

## TYPES OF SOURCES

- **Textbooks** are specialized materials that are designed to thoroughly instruct readers on a particular topic. Textbooks often include features such as a table of contents, visuals, an index, a glossary, headings, and practice questions and exercises.
- **Newspapers** are collections of several written pieces and are primarily used to distribute news stories to their audience. In addition to news articles, newspapers may also include advertisements or pieces meant to entertain their audience, such as comic strips, columns, and letters from readers. Newspapers are written for a variety of audiences, as they are published on both the local and national levels.
- **Manuals** are instructional documents that accompany a product or explain an important procedure. Manuals include a table of contents, guidelines, and instructional content. Instructional manuals often include information about safe practices, risks, and product warranty. The instructions in manuals are often presented as step-by-step instructions, as they are meant to help users properly use a product or complete a task.

Copyright © Mometrix Media. You have been licensed one copy of this document for personal use only. Any other reproduction or redistribution is strictly prohibited. All rights reserved. This content is provided for test preparation purposes only and does not imply an endorsement by Mometrix of any particular political, scientific, or religious point of view.

- **Electronic texts** are written documents that are read digitally and are primarily accessed online or through a network. Many electronic texts have characteristics similar to printed texts, such as a table of contents, publication information, a main text, and supplemental materials. However, electronic texts are more interactive and can be navigated more quickly. Electronic texts can also provide more accessibility, as they can be easily resized or narrated by text-to-speech software.

## FINDING SOURCES

Finding sources for a research project may be intimidating or difficult. There are numerous sources available, and several research tools to help researchers find them. Starting with one of these tools can help narrow down the number of sources a researcher is working with at one time.

- **Libraries** house independent, printed publications that are organized by subject. This makes finding sources easy, since researchers can visit sections with sources relevant to their topic and immediately see what sources are available. Many libraries also offer printed journals and collections that include sources related to a common subject or written by the same author.
- **Databases** offer digital access to sources from a wide variety of libraries and online containers. To use a database, users search for keywords related to their topic or the type of source they want to use. The database then lists results related to or featuring those key words. Users can narrow their results using filters that will limit their results based on factors such as publication year, source type, or whether the sources are peer-reviewed. Database search results also list individual articles and methods of accessing the article directly. While databases help users find sources, they do not guarantee users access to each source.
- **Academic Journals** are collections of articles that cover a particular topic or fit within a certain category. These journals are often offered both online and in print. Academic journals typically contain peer-reviewed works or works that have undergone another type of reviewing process.

## CREDIBILITY

There are innumerable primary and secondary sources available in print and online. However, not every published or posted source is appropriate for a research project. When finding sources, the researcher must know how to evaluate each source for credibility and relevance. Not only must the sources be reliable and relevant to the research subject, but they must also be appropriate and help form an answer to the research question. As researchers progress in their research and composition, the relevance of each source will become clear. Appropriate sources will contribute valuable information and arguments to the researcher's own thoughts and conclusions, providing useful evidence to bolster the researcher's claims. The researcher has the freedom to choose which sources they reference or even change their research topic and question in response to the sources they find. However, the researcher should not use unreliable sources, and determining a source's credibility is not always easy.

### CONSIDERATIONS FOR EVALUATING THE CREDIBILITY OF A SOURCE
- The author and their purpose for writing the source
- The author's qualifications to write on the topic
- Whether the source is peer-reviewed or included in a scholarly publication
- The publisher
- The target audience

Copyright © Mometrix Media. You have been licensed one copy of this document for personal use only. Any other reproduction or redistribution is strictly prohibited. All rights reserved. This content is provided for test preparation purposes only and does not imply an endorsement by Mometrix of any particular political, scientific, or religious point of view.

- The jargon or dialect the source is written in (e.g., academic, technical)
- The presence of bias or manipulation of information
- The date of publication
- The author's use of other sources to support their claims
- Whether any outside sources are cited appropriately in the source
- The accuracy of information presented

## AUTHOR'S PURPOSE AND CREDIBILITY

Knowing who wrote a source and why they wrote it is important to determine whether a source is appropriate for a research project. The author should be qualified to write on the subject of the material. Their purpose may be to inform their audience of information, to present and defend an analysis, or even to criticize a work or other argument. The researcher must decide whether the author's purpose makes the source appropriate to use. The source's container and publisher are important to note because they indicate the source's reputability and whether other qualified individuals have reviewed the information in the source. Credible secondary sources should also reference other sources, primary or secondary, that support or inform the source's content. Evaluating the accuracy of the information or the presence of bias in a source will require careful reading and critical thinking on the part of the researcher. However, a source with excellent credentials may still contain pieces of inaccurate information or bias, so it is the researcher's responsibility to be careful in their use of each source.

## INTEGRATING REFERENCES AND QUOTATIONS

In research papers, one can include studies whose conclusions agree with one's position (Reed 284; Becker and Fagen 93), as well as studies that disagree (Limbaugh 442, Beck 69) by including parenthetical citations as demonstrated in this sentence. Quotations should be selective: writers should compose an original sentence and incorporate only a few words from a research source. If students cannot use more original words than quotation, they are likely padding their compositions. However, including quotations appropriately increases the credibility of the writer and their argument.

## PROPERLY INTEGRATING QUOTATIONS

When using sources in a research paper, it is important to integrate information so that the flow of the composition is not interrupted as the two compositions are combined. When quoting outside sources, it is necessary to lead into the quote and ensure that the whole sentence is logical, is grammatically correct, and flows well. Below is an example of an incorrectly integrated quote.

> During the Industrial Revolution, many unions organized labor strikes "child labor, unregulated working conditions, and excessive working hours" in America.

Below is the same sentence with a properly integrated quote.

> During the Industrial Revolution, many unions organized labor strikes to protest the presence of "child labor, unregulated working conditions, and excessive working hours" in America.

In the first example, the connection between "strikes" and the quoted list is unclear. In the second example, the phrase "to protest the presence of" link the ideas together and successfully creates a suitable place for the quotation.

When quoting sources, writers should work quotations and references seamlessly into their sentences instead of interrupting the flow of their own argument to summarize a source.

Copyright © Mometrix Media. You have been licensed one copy of this document for personal use only. Any other reproduction or redistribution is strictly prohibited. All rights reserved. This content is provided for test preparation purposes only and does not imply an endorsement by Mometrix of any particular political, scientific, or religious point of view.

Summarizing others' content is often a ploy to bolster word counts. Writing that analyzes the content, evaluates it, and synthesizes material from various sources demonstrates critical thinking skills and is thus more valuable.

## PROPERLY INCORPORATING OUTSIDE SOURCES

Writers do better to include short quotations rather than long. For example, quoting six to eight long passages in a 10-page paper is excessive. It is also better to avoid wording like "This quotation shows," "As you can see from this quotation," or "It talks about." These are amateur, feeble efforts to interact with other authors' ideas. Also, writing about sources and quotations wastes words that should be used to develop one's own ideas. Quotations should be used to stimulate discussion rather than taking its place. Ending a paragraph, section, or paper with a quotation is not incorrect per se, but using it to prove a point, without including anything more in one's own words regarding the point or subject, suggests a lack of critical thinking about the topic and consideration of multiple alternatives. It can also be a tactic to dissuade readers from challenging one's propositions. Writers should include references and quotations that challenge as well as support their thesis statements. Presenting evidence on both sides of an issue makes it easier for reasonably skeptical readers to agree with a writer's viewpoint.

## CITING SOURCES

Formal research writers must **cite all sources used**—books, articles, interviews, conversations, and anything else that contributed to the research. One reason is to **avoid plagiarism** and give others credit for their ideas. Another reason is to help readers find the sources consulted in the research and access more information about the subject for further reading and research. Additionally, citing sources helps to make a paper academically authoritative. To prepare, research writers should keep a running list of sources consulted, in an electronic file or on file cards. For every source used, the writer needs specific information. For books, a writer needs to record the author's and editor's names, book title, publication date, city, and publisher name. For articles, one needs the author's name, article title, journal (or magazine or newspaper) name, volume and issue number, publication date, and page numbers. For electronic resources, a writer will need the author's name, article information plus the URL, database name, name of the database's publisher, and the date of access.

## COMMON REFERENCE STYLES

Three common reference styles are **MLA** (Modern Language Association), **APA** (American Psychological Association), and **Turabian** (created by author Kate Turabian, also known as the Chicago Manual of Style). Each style formats citation information differently. Professors and instructors often specify that students use one of these. Generally, APA style is used in psychology and sociology papers, and MLA style is used in English literature papers and similar scholarly projects. To understand how these styles differ, consider an imaginary article cited in each of these styles. This article is titled "Ten Things You Won't Believe Dragons Do," written by author Andra Gaines, included in the journal *Studies in Fantasy Fiction*, and published by Quest for Knowledge Publishing.

### *MLA:*

Gaines, Andra. "Ten Things You Won't Believe Dragons Do." Studies in Fantasy Fiction, vol. 3, no. 8, Quest for Knowledge Publishing, 21 Aug. 2019.

### *APA:*

Gaines, A. (2019). Ten Things You Won't Believe Dragons Do. *Studies in Fantasy Fiction, 3(8)*, 42-65.

Copyright © Mometrix Media. You have been licensed one copy of this document for personal use only. Any other reproduction or redistribution is strictly prohibited. All rights reserved.
This content is provided for test preparation purposes only and does not imply an endorsement by Mometrix of any particular political, scientific, or religious point of view.

*Chicago:*

Gaines, Andra. "Ten Things You Won't Believe Dragons Do," *Studies in Fantasy Fiction* 3, no. 8 (2019): 42-65.

Within each of these styles, citations, though they vary according to the type of source and how its used, generally follow a structure and format similar to those above. For example, citations for whole books will probably not include a container title or a volume number, but will otherwise look very similar.

> **Review Video: Citing Sources**
> Visit mometrix.com/academy and enter code: 993637

Copyright © Mometrix Media. You have been licensed one copy of this document for personal use only. Any other reproduction or redistribution is strictly prohibited. All rights reserved. This content is provided for test preparation purposes only and does not imply an endorsement by Mometrix of any particular political, scientific, or religious point of view.

## CHAPTER QUIZ

### 1. Which of the following citations follows the Turabian format?

    a. Gaines, Andra. "Ten Things You Won't Believe Dragons Do". *Studies in Fantasy Fiction*, vol. 3, no. 8, Quest for Knowledge Publishing, 21 Aug. 2019.

    b. Gaines, Andra. "Ten Things You Won't Believe Dragons Do," *Studies in Fantasy Fiction* 3, no. 8 (2019): 42-65.

    c. Gaines, A. (2019). Ten Things You Won't Believe Dragons Do. *Studies in Fantasy Fiction*, *3(8)*, 42-65.

    d. Gaines, Andra. (2019). "Ten Things You Won't Believe Dragons Do," *Studies in Fantasy Fiction*, *3(8)*, 42-65.

### 2. While writing a research paper, a student cites a study on the subject from three years prior. What type of source is the student's research paper?

    a. Primary

    b. Secondary

    c. Tertiary

    d. Quaternary

## CHAPTER QUIZ ANSWER KEY

**1. B:** Three common reference styles are MLA (Modern Language Association), APA (American Psychological Association), and Turabian (created by author Kate Turabian, also known as the Chicago Manual of Style). Each style formats citation information differently.

**MLA**:

Gaines, Andra. "Ten Things You Won't Believe Dragons Do." *Studies in Fantasy Fiction*, vol. 3, no. 8, Quest for Knowledge Publishing, 21 Aug. 2019.

**APA**:

Gaines, A. (2019). Ten Things You Won't Believe Dragons Do. *Studies in Fantasy Fiction*, *3(8)*, 42-65.

**Chicago**:

Gaines, Andra. "Ten Things You Won't Believe Dragons Do," *Studies in Fantasy Fiction* 3, no. 8 (2019): 42-65.

**2. B:** Secondary sources are sources that reference information originally provided by another source. The original source may be cited, quoted, paraphrased, or described in a secondary source. A secondary source can be used to reference another researcher's analysis or conclusion from a primary source. This information can inform the researcher of the existing discussions regarding their subject. These types of sources may also support the researcher's claims by providing a credible argument that contributes to the researcher's argument. Secondary sources may also highlight connections between primary sources or criticize both primary and other secondary sources. These types of secondary sources are valuable because they provide information and conclusions that the researcher may not have considered or found otherwise.

Copyright © Mometrix Media. You have been licensed one copy of this document for personal use only. Any other reproduction or redistribution is strictly prohibited. All rights reserved. This content is provided for test preparation purposes only and does not imply an endorsement by Mometrix of any particular political, scientific, or religious point of view.

# Mathematics

## Numbers

### CLASSIFICATIONS OF NUMBERS

**Numbers** are the basic building blocks of mathematics. Specific features of numbers are identified by the following terms:

**Integer** – any positive or negative whole number, including zero. Integers do not include fractions $\left(\frac{1}{3}\right)$, decimals (0.56), or mixed numbers $\left(7\frac{3}{4}\right)$.

**Prime number** – any whole number greater than 1 that has only two factors, itself and 1; that is, a number that can be divided evenly only by 1 and itself.

**Composite number** – any whole number greater than 1 that has more than two different factors; in other words, any whole number that is not a prime number. For example: The composite number 8 has the factors of 1, 2, 4, and 8.

**Even number** – any integer that can be divided by 2 without leaving a remainder. For example: 2, 4, 6, 8, and so on.

**Odd number** – any integer that cannot be divided evenly by 2. For example: 3, 5, 7, 9, and so on.

**Decimal number** – any number that uses a decimal point to show the part of the number that is less than one. Example: 1.234.

**Decimal point** – a symbol used to separate the ones place from the tenths place in decimals or dollars from cents in currency.

**Decimal place** – the position of a number to the right of the decimal point. In the decimal 0.123, the 1 is in the first place to the right of the decimal point, indicating tenths; the 2 is in the second place, indicating hundredths; and the 3 is in the third place, indicating thousandths.

The **decimal**, or base 10, system is a number system that uses ten different digits (0, 1, 2, 3, 4, 5, 6, 7, 8, 9). An example of a number system that uses something other than ten digits is the **binary**, or base 2, number system, used by computers, which uses only the numbers 0 and 1. It is thought that the decimal system originated because people had only their 10 fingers for counting.

**Rational numbers** include all integers, decimals, and fractions. Any terminating or repeating decimal number is a rational number.

**Irrational numbers** cannot be written as fractions or decimals because the number of decimal places is infinite and there is no recurring pattern of digits within the number. For example, pi ($\pi$) begins with 3.141592 and continues without terminating or repeating, so pi is an irrational number.

139

Copyright © Mometrix Media. You have been licensed one copy of this document for personal use only. Any other reproduction or redistribution is strictly prohibited. All rights reserved. This content is provided for test preparation purposes only and does not imply an endorsement by Mometrix of any particular political, scientific, or religious point of view.

**Real numbers** are the set of all rational and irrational numbers.

**Review Video: <u>Numbers and Their Classifications</u>**
Visit mometrix.com/academy and enter code: 461071

**Review Video: <u>Prime and Composite Numbers</u>**
Visit mometrix.com/academy and enter code: 565581

## THE NUMBER LINE

A number line is a graph to see the distance between numbers. Basically, this graph shows the relationship between numbers. So a number line may have a point for zero and may show negative numbers on the left side of the line. Any positive numbers are placed on the right side of the line. For example, consider the points labeled on the following number line:

We can use the dashed lines on the number line to identify each point. Each dashed line between two whole numbers is $\frac{1}{4}$. The line halfway between two numbers is $\frac{1}{2}$.

**Review Video: <u>The Number Line</u>**
Visit mometrix.com/academy and enter code: 816439

## NUMBERS IN WORD FORM AND PLACE VALUE

When writing numbers out in word form or translating word form to numbers, it is essential to understand how a place value system works. In the decimal or base-10 system, each digit of a number represents how many of the corresponding place value—a specific factor of 10—are contained in the number being represented. To make reading numbers easier, every three digits to the left of the decimal place is preceded by a comma. The following table demonstrates some of the place values:

| Power of 10 | $10^3$ | $10^2$ | $10^1$ | $10^0$ | $10^{-1}$ | $10^{-2}$ | $10^{-3}$ |
|---|---|---|---|---|---|---|---|
| Value | 1,000 | 100 | 10 | 1 | 0.1 | 0.01 | 0.001 |
| Place | thousands | hundreds | tens | ones | tenths | hundredths | thousandths |

Copyright © Mometrix Media. You have been licensed one copy of this document for personal use only. Any other reproduction or redistribution is strictly prohibited. All rights reserved.
This content is provided for test preparation purposes only and does not imply an endorsement by Mometrix of any particular political, scientific, or religious point of view.

For example, consider the number 4,546.09, which can be separated into each place value like this:

4: thousands
5: hundreds
4: tens
6: ones
0: tenths
9: hundredths

This number in word form would be *four thousand five hundred forty-six and nine hundredths.*

> **Review Video: Place Value**
> Visit mometrix.com/academy and enter code: 205433

## ABSOLUTE VALUE

A precursor to working with negative numbers is understanding what **absolute values** are. A number's absolute value is simply the distance away from zero a number is on the number line. The absolute value of a number is always positive and is written $|x|$. For example, the absolute value of 3, written as $|3|$, is 3 because the distance between 0 and 3 on a number line is three units. Likewise, the absolute value of –3, written as $|-3|$, is 3 because the distance between 0 and –3 on a number line is three units. So $|3| = |-3|$.

> **Review Video: Absolute Value**
> Visit mometrix.com/academy and enter code: 314669

## PRACTICE

**P1**. Write the place value of each digit in 14,059.826

**P2**. Write out each of the following in words:

   **(a)** 29
   **(b)** 478
   **(c)** 98,542
   **(d)** 0.06
   **(e)** 13.113

**P3**. Write each of the following in numbers:

   **(a)** nine thousand four hundred thirty-five
   **(b)** three hundred two thousand eight hundred seventy-six
   **(c)** nine hundred one thousandths
   **(d)** nineteen thousandths
   **(e)** seven thousand one hundred forty-two and eighty-five hundredths

Copyright © Mometrix Media. You have been licensed one copy of this document for personal use only. Any other reproduction or redistribution is strictly prohibited. All rights reserved.
This content is provided for test preparation purposes only and does not imply an endorsement by Mometrix of any particular political, scientific, or religious point of view.

## Practice Solutions

**P1**. The place value for each digit would be as follows:

| Digit | Place Value |
|---|---|
| 1 | ten-thousands |
| 4 | thousands |
| 0 | hundreds |
| 5 | tens |
| 9 | ones |
| 8 | tenths |
| 2 | hundredths |
| 6 | thousandths |

**P2.** Each written out in words would be:

**(a)** twenty-nine
**(b)** four hundred seventy-eight
**(c)** ninety-eight thousand five hundred forty-two
**(d)** six hundredths
**(e)** thirteen and one hundred thirteen thousandths

**P3.** Each in numeric form would be:

**(a)** 9,435
**(b)** 302876
**(c)** 0.901
**(d)** 0.019
**(e)** 7,142.85

Copyright © Mometrix Media. You have been licensed one copy of this document for personal use only. Any other reproduction or redistribution is strictly prohibited. All rights reserved.
This content is provided for test preparation purposes only and does not imply an endorsement by Mometrix of any particular political, scientific, or religious point of view.

## Operations

### OPERATIONS

An **operation** is simply a mathematical process that takes some value(s) as input(s) and produces an output. Elementary operations are often written in the following form: *value operation value.* For instance, in the expression $1 + 2$ the values are 1 and 2 and the operation is addition. Performing the operation gives the output of 3. In this way we can say that $1 + 2$ and 3 are equal, or $1 + 2 = 3$.

### ADDITION

**Addition** increases the value of one quantity by the value of another quantity (both called **addends**). Example: $2 + 4 = 6$ or $8 + 9 = 17$. The result is called the **sum**. With addition, the order does not matter, $4 + 2 = 2 + 4$.

When adding signed numbers, if the signs are the same simply add the absolute values of the addends and apply the original sign to the sum. For example, $(+4) + (+8) = +12$ and $(-4) + (-8) = -12$. When the original signs are different, take the absolute values of the addends and subtract the smaller value from the larger value, then apply the original sign of the larger value to the difference. Example: $(+4) + (-8) = -4$ and $(-4) + (+8) = +4$.

### SUBTRACTION

**Subtraction** is the opposite operation to addition; it decreases the value of one quantity (the **minuend**) by the value of another quantity (the **subtrahend**). For example, $6 - 4 = 2$ or $17 - 8 = 9$. The result is called the **difference**. Note that with subtraction, the order does matter, $6 - 4 \neq 4 - 6$.

For subtracting signed numbers, change the sign of the subtrahend and then follow the same rules used for addition. Example: $(+4) - (+8) = (+4) + (-8) = -4$

### MULTIPLICATION

**Multiplication** can be thought of as repeated addition. One number (the **multiplier**) indicates how many times to add the other number (the **multiplicand**) to itself. Example: $3 \times 2 = 2 + 2 + 2 = 6$. With multiplication, the order does not matter, $2 \times 3 = 3 \times 2$ or $3 + 3 = 2 + 2 + 2$, either way the result (the **product**) is the same.

If the signs are the same, the product is positive when multiplying signed numbers. Example: $(+4) \times (+8) = +32$ and $(-4) \times (-8) = +32$. If the signs are opposite, the product is negative. Example: $(+4) \times (-8) = -32$ and $(-4) \times (+8) = -32$. When more than two factors are multiplied together, the sign of the product is determined by how many negative factors are present. If there are an odd number of negative factors then the product is negative, whereas an even number of negative factors indicates a positive product. Example: $(+4) \times (-8) \times (-2) = +64$ and $(-4) \times (-8) \times (-2) = -64$.

### DIVISION

**Division** is the opposite operation to multiplication; one number (the **divisor**) tells us how many parts to divide the other number (the **dividend**) into. The result of division is called the **quotient**. Example: $20 \div 4 = 5$. If 20 is split into 4 equal parts, each part is 5. With division, the order of the numbers does matter, $20 \div 4 \neq 4 \div 20$.

Copyright © Mometrix Media. You have been licensed one copy of this document for personal use only. Any other reproduction or redistribution is strictly prohibited. All rights reserved. This content is provided for test preparation purposes only and does not imply an endorsement by Mometrix of any particular political, scientific, or religious point of view.

The rules for dividing signed numbers are similar to multiplying signed numbers. If the dividend and divisor have the same sign, the quotient is positive. If the dividend and divisor have opposite signs, the quotient is negative. Example: $(-4) \div (+8) = -0.5$.

**Review Video: Mathematical Operations**
Visit mometrix.com/academy and enter code: 208095

## PARENTHESES

**Parentheses** are used to designate which operations should be done first when there are multiple operations. Example: $4 - (2 + 1) = 1$; the parentheses tell us that we must add 2 and 1, and then subtract the sum from 4, rather than subtracting 2 from 4 and then adding 1 (this would give us an answer of 3).

**Review Video: Mathematical Parentheses**
Visit mometrix.com/academy and enter code: 978600

## EXPONENTS

An **exponent** is a superscript number placed next to another number at the top right. It indicates how many times the base number is to be multiplied by itself. Exponents provide a shorthand way to write what would be a longer mathematical expression, Example: $2^4 = 2 \times 2 \times 2 \times 2$. A number with an exponent of 2 is said to be "squared," while a number with an exponent of 3 is said to be "cubed." The value of a number raised to an exponent is called its power. So $8^4$ is read as "8 to the 4th power," or "8 raised to the power of 4."

The properties of exponents are as follows:

| Property | Description |
|---|---|
| $a^1 = a$ | Any number to the power of 1 is equal to itself |
| $1^n = 1$ | The number 1 raised to any power is equal to 1 |
| $a^0 = 1$ | Any number raised to the power of 0 is equal to 1 |
| $a^n \times a^m = a^{n+m}$ | Add exponents to multiply powers of the same base number |
| $a^n \div a^m = a^{n-m}$ | Subtract exponents to divide powers of the same base number |
| $(a^n)^m = a^{n \times m}$ | When a power is raised to a power, the exponents are multiplied |
| $(a \times b)^n = a^n \times b^n$ $(a \div b)^n = a^n \div b^n$ | Multiplication and division operations inside parentheses can be raised to a power. This is the same as each term being raised to that power. |
| $a^{-n} = \dfrac{1}{a^n}$ | A negative exponent is the same as the reciprocal of a positive exponent |

Note that exponents do not have to be integers. Fractional or decimal exponents follow all the rules above as well. Example: $5^{\frac{1}{4}} \times 5^{\frac{3}{4}} = 5^{\frac{1}{4}+\frac{3}{4}} = 5^1 = 5$.

**Review Video: Introduction to Exponents**
Visit mometrix.com/academy and enter code: 600998

**Review Video: Properties of Exponents**
Visit mometrix.com/academy and enter code: 532558

Copyright © Mometrix Media. You have been licensed one copy of this document for personal use only. Any other reproduction or redistribution is strictly prohibited. All rights reserved. This content is provided for test preparation purposes only and does not imply an endorsement by Mometrix of any particular political, scientific, or religious point of view.

## ROOTS

A **root**, such as a square root, is another way of writing a fractional exponent. Instead of using a superscript, roots use the radical symbol ($\sqrt{\phantom{x}}$) to indicate the operation. A radical will have a number underneath the bar, and may sometimes have a number in the upper left: $\sqrt[n]{a}$, read as "the $n^{th}$ root of $a$." The relationship between radical notation and exponent notation can be described by this equation:

$$\sqrt[n]{a} = a^{\frac{1}{n}}$$

The two special cases of $n = 2$ and $n = 3$ are called square roots and cube roots. If there is no number to the upper left, the radical is understood to be a square root ($n = 2$). Nearly all of the roots you encounter will be square roots. A square root is the same as a number raised to the one-half power. When we say that $a$ is the square root of $b$ ($a = \sqrt{b}$), we mean that $a$ multiplied by itself equals $b$: ($a \times a = b$).

A **perfect square** is a number that has an integer for its square root. There are 10 perfect squares from 1 to 100: 1, 4, 9, 16, 25, 36, 49, 64, 81, 100 (the squares of integers 1 through 10).

> **Review Video: <u>Roots</u>**
> Visit mometrix.com/academy and enter code: 795655
>
> **Review Video: <u>Square Root and Perfect Squares</u>**
> Visit mometrix.com/academy and enter code: 648063

## ORDER OF OPERATIONS

The **order of operations** is a set of rules that dictates the order in which we must perform each operation in an expression so that we will evaluate it accurately. If we have an expression that includes multiple different operations, the order of operations tells us which operations to do first. The most common mnemonic for the order of operations is **PEMDAS**, or "Please Excuse My Dear Aunt Sally." PEMDAS stands for parentheses, exponents, multiplication, division, addition, and subtraction. It is important to understand that multiplication and division have equal precedence, as do addition and subtraction, so those pairs of operations are simply worked from left to right in order.

For example, evaluating the expression $5 + 20 \div 4 \times (2 + 3)^2 - 6$ using the correct order of operations would be done like this:

- **P:** Perform the operations inside the parentheses: $(2 + 3) = 5$
- **E:** Simplify the exponents: $(5)^2 = 5 \times 5 = 25$
  - The equation now looks like this: $5 + 20 \div 4 \times 25 - 6$
- **MD:** Perform multiplication and division from left to right: $20 \div 4 = 5$; then $5 \times 25 = 125$
  - The equation now looks like this: $5 + 125 - 6$
- **AS:** Perform addition and subtraction from left to right: $5 + 125 = 130$; then $130 - 6 = 124$

> **Review Video: <u>Order of Operations</u>**
> Visit mometrix.com/academy and enter code: 259675

Copyright © Mometrix Media. You have been licensed one copy of this document for personal use only. Any other reproduction or redistribution is strictly prohibited. All rights reserved. This content is provided for test preparation purposes only and does not imply an endorsement by Mometrix of any particular political, scientific, or religious point of view.

## SUBTRACTION WITH REGROUPING

A great way to make use of some of the features built into the decimal system would be regrouping when attempting longform subtraction operations. When subtracting within a place value, sometimes the minuend is smaller than the subtrahend, **regrouping** enables you to 'borrow' a unit from a place value to the left in order to get a positive difference. For example, consider subtracting 189 from 525 with regrouping.

> **Review Video: Subtracting Large Numbers**
> Visit mometrix.com/academy and enter code: 603350

First, set up the subtraction problem in vertical form:

$$
\begin{array}{r}
525 \\
-\ 189 \\
\hline
\end{array}
$$

Notice that the numbers in the ones and tens columns of 525 are smaller than the numbers in the ones and tens columns of 189. This means you will need to use regrouping to perform subtraction:

$$
\begin{array}{ccc}
5 & 2 & 5 \\
-\quad 1 & 8 & 9 \\
\hline
\end{array}
$$

To subtract 9 from 5 in the ones column you will need to borrow from the 2 in the tens columns:

$$
\begin{array}{ccc}
5 & 1 & 15 \\
-\quad 1 & 8 & 9 \\
\hline
 & & 6
\end{array}
$$

Next, to subtract 8 from 1 in the tens column you will need to borrow from the 5 in the hundreds column:

$$
\begin{array}{ccc}
4 & 11 & 15 \\
-\quad 1 & 8 & 9 \\
\hline
 & 3 & 6
\end{array}
$$

Last, subtract the 1 from the 4 in the hundreds column:

$$
\begin{array}{ccc}
4 & 11 & 15 \\
-\quad 1 & 8 & 9 \\
\hline
3 & 3 & 6
\end{array}
$$

## WORD PROBLEMS AND MATHEMATICAL SYMBOLS

When working on word problems, you must be able to translate verbal expressions or "math words" into math symbols. This chart contains several "math words" and their appropriate symbols:

| Phrase | Symbol |
|---|---|
| equal, is, was, will be, has, costs, gets to, is the same as, becomes | = |
| times, of, multiplied by, product of, twice, doubles, halves, triples | × |
| divided by, per, ratio of/to, out of | ÷ |
| plus, added to, sum, combined, and, more than, totals of | + |
| subtracted from, less than, decreased by, minus, difference between | − |
| what, how much, original value, how many, a number, a variable | $x, n,$ etc. |

Copyright © Mometrix Media. You have been licensed one copy of this document for personal use only. Any other reproduction or redistribution is strictly prohibited. All rights reserved.
This content is provided for test preparation purposes only and does not imply an endorsement by Mometrix of any particular political, scientific, or religious point of view.

## EXAMPLES OF TRANSLATED MATHEMATICAL PHRASES

- The phrase four more than twice a number can be written algebraically as $2x + 4$.
- The phrase half a number decreased by six can be written algebraically as $\frac{1}{2}x - 6$.
- The phrase the sum of a number and the product of five and that number can be written algebraically as $x + 5x$.
- You may see a test question that says, "Olivia is constructing a bookcase from seven boards. Two of them are for vertical supports and five are for shelves. The height of the bookcase is twice the width of the bookcase. If the seven boards total 36 feet in length, what will be the height of Olivia's bookcase?" You would need to make a sketch and then create the equation to determine the width of the shelves. The height can be represented as double the width. (If $x$ represents the width of the shelves in feet, then the height of the bookcase is $2x$. Since the seven boards total 36 feet, $2x + 2x + x + x + x + x + x = 36$ or $9x = 36$; $x = 4$. The height is twice the width, or 8 feet.)

## PRACTICE

**P1.** Demonstrate how to subtract 477 from 620 using regrouping.

**P2.** Simplify the following expressions with exponents:

(a) $37^0$
(b) $1^{30}$
(c) $2^3 \times 2^4 \times 2^x$
(d) $(3^x)^3$
(e) $(12 \div 3)^2$

## Practice Solutions

**P1.** First, set up the subtraction problem in vertical form:

$$\begin{array}{ccc} 6 & 2 & 0 \\ - \quad 4 & 7 & 7 \\ \hline \end{array}$$

To subtract 7 from 0 in the ones column you will need to borrow from the 2 in the tens column:

$$\begin{array}{ccc} 6 & 1 & 10 \\ - \quad 4 & 7 & 7 \\ \hline & & 3 \end{array}$$

Next, to subtract 7 from the 1 that's still in the tens column you will need to borrow from the 6 in the hundreds column:

$$\begin{array}{ccc} 5 & 11 & 10 \\ - \quad 4 & 7 & 7 \\ \hline & 4 & 3 \end{array}$$

Lastly, subtract 4 from the 5 remaining in the hundreds column:

$$\begin{array}{ccc} 5 & 11 & 10 \\ - \quad 4 & 7 & 7 \\ \hline 1 & 4 & 3 \end{array}$$

Copyright © Mometrix Media. You have been licensed one copy of this document for personal use only. Any other reproduction or redistribution is strictly prohibited. All rights reserved. This content is provided for test preparation purposes only and does not imply an endorsement by Mometrix of any particular political, scientific, or religious point of view.

**P2**. Using the properties of exponents and the proper order of operations:

**(a)** Any number raised to the power of 0 is equal to 1: $37^0 = 1$
**(b)** The number 1 raised to any power is equal to 1: $1^{30} = 1$
**(c)** Add exponents to multiply powers of the same base: $2^3 \times 2^4 \times 2^x = 2^{(3+4+x)} = 2^{(7+x)}$
**(d)** When a power is raised to a power, the exponents are multiplied: $(3^x)^3 = 3^{3x}$
**(e)** Perform the operation inside the parentheses first: $(12 \div 3)^2 = 4^2 = 16$

Copyright © Mometrix Media. You have been licensed one copy of this document for personal use only. Any other reproduction or redistribution is strictly prohibited. All rights reserved.
This content is provided for test preparation purposes only and does not imply an endorsement by Mometrix of any particular political, scientific, or religious point of view.

# Factoring

## FACTORS AND GREATEST COMMON FACTOR

Factors are numbers that are multiplied together to obtain a **product**. For example, in the equation $2 \times 3 = 6$, the numbers 2 and 3 are factors. A **prime number** has only two factors (1 and itself), but other numbers can have many factors.

A **common factor** is a number that divides exactly into two or more other numbers. For example, the factors of 12 are 1, 2, 3, 4, 6, and 12, while the factors of 15 are 1, 3, 5, and 15. The common factors of 12 and 15 are 1 and 3.

A **prime factor** is also a prime number. Therefore, the prime factors of 12 are 2 and 3. For 15, the prime factors are 3 and 5.

The **greatest common factor (GCF)** is the largest number that is a factor of two or more numbers. For example, the factors of 15 are 1, 3, 5, and 15; the factors of 35 are 1, 5, 7, and 35. Therefore, the greatest common factor of 15 and 35 is 5.

> **Review Video: Factors**
> Visit mometrix.com/academy and enter code: 920086
>
> **Review Video: Prime Numbers and Factorization**
> Visit mometrix.com/academy and enter code: 760669
>
> **Review Video: GCF and LCM**
> Visit mometrix.com/academy and enter code: 838699

## MULTIPLES AND LEAST COMMON MULTIPLE

Often listed out in multiplication tables, **multiples** are integer increments of a given factor. In other words, dividing a multiple by the factor will result in an integer. For example, the multiples of 7 include: $1 \times 7 = 7, 2 \times 7 = 14, 3 \times 7 = 21, 4 \times 7 = 28, 5 \times 7 = 35$. Dividing 7, 14, 21, 28, or 35 by 7 will result in the integers 1, 2, 3, 4, and 5, respectively.

The least common multiple (**LCM**) is the smallest number that is a multiple of two or more numbers. For example, the multiples of 3 include 3, 6, 9, 12, 15, etc.; the multiples of 5 include 5, 10, 15, 20, etc. Therefore, the least common multiple of 3 and 5 is 15.

> **Review Video: Multiples**
> Visit mometrix.com/academy and enter code: 626738

Copyright © Mometrix Media. You have been licensed one copy of this document for personal use only. Any other reproduction or redistribution is strictly prohibited. All rights reserved.
This content is provided for test preparation purposes only and does not imply an endorsement by Mometrix of any particular political, scientific, or religious point of view.

# Rational Numbers

## FRACTIONS

A **fraction** is a number that is expressed as one integer written above another integer, with a dividing line between them $\left(\frac{x}{y}\right)$. It represents the **quotient** of the two numbers "$x$ divided by $y$." It can also be thought of as $x$ out of $y$ equal parts.

The top number of a fraction is called the **numerator**, and it represents the number of parts under consideration. The 1 in $\frac{1}{4}$ means that 1 part out of the whole is being considered in the calculation. The bottom number of a fraction is called the **denominator**, and it represents the total number of equal parts. The 4 in $\frac{1}{4}$ means that the whole consists of 4 equal parts. A fraction cannot have a denominator of zero; this is referred to as "*undefined*."

Fractions can be manipulated, without changing the value of the fraction, by multiplying or dividing (but not adding or subtracting) both the numerator and denominator by the same number. If you divide both numbers by a common factor, you are **reducing** or simplifying the fraction. Two fractions that have the same value but are expressed differently are known as **equivalent fractions**. For example, $\frac{2}{10}, \frac{3}{15}, \frac{4}{20}$, and $\frac{5}{25}$ are all equivalent fractions. They can also all be reduced or simplified to $\frac{1}{5}$.

When two fractions are manipulated so that they have the same denominator, this is known as finding a **common denominator**. The number chosen to be that common denominator should be the least common multiple of the two original denominators. Example: $\frac{3}{4}$ and $\frac{5}{6}$; the least common multiple of 4 and 6 is 12. Manipulating to achieve the common denominator: $\frac{3}{4} = \frac{9}{12}; \frac{5}{6} = \frac{10}{12}$.

## *PROPER FRACTIONS AND MIXED NUMBERS*

A fraction whose denominator is greater than its numerator is known as a **proper fraction**, while a fraction whose numerator is greater than its denominator is known as an **improper fraction**. Proper fractions have values *less than one* and improper fractions have values *greater than one*.

A **mixed number** is a number that contains both an integer and a fraction. Any improper fraction can be rewritten as a mixed number. Example: $\frac{8}{3} = \frac{6}{3} + \frac{2}{3} = 2 + \frac{2}{3} = 2\frac{2}{3}$. Similarly, any mixed number can be rewritten as an improper fraction. Example: $1\frac{3}{5} = 1 + \frac{3}{5} = \frac{5}{5} + \frac{3}{5} = \frac{8}{5}$.

---

**Review Video: <u>Improper Fractions and Mixed Numbers</u>**
Visit mometrix.com/academy and enter code: 211077

**Review Video: <u>Overview of Fractions</u>**
Visit mometrix.com/academy and enter code: 262335

---

Copyright © Mometrix Media. You have been licensed one copy of this document for personal use only. Any other reproduction or redistribution is strictly prohibited. All rights reserved. This content is provided for test preparation purposes only and does not imply an endorsement by Mometrix of any particular political, scientific, or religious point of view.

## ADDING AND SUBTRACTING FRACTIONS

If two fractions have a common denominator, they can be added or subtracted simply by adding or subtracting the two numerators and retaining the same denominator. If the two fractions do not already have the same denominator, one or both of them must be manipulated to achieve a common denominator before they can be added or subtracted. Example: $\frac{1}{2} + \frac{1}{4} = \frac{2}{4} + \frac{1}{4} = \frac{3}{4}$.

> **Review Video: Adding and Subtracting Fractions**
> Visit mometrix.com/academy and enter code: 378080

## MULTIPLYING FRACTIONS

Two fractions can be multiplied by multiplying the two numerators to find the new numerator and the two denominators to find the new denominator. Example: $\frac{1}{3} \times \frac{2}{3} = \frac{1 \times 2}{3 \times 3} = \frac{2}{9}$.

## DIVIDING FRACTIONS

Two fractions can be divided by flipping the numerator and denominator of the second fraction and then proceeding as though it were a multiplication problem. Example: $\frac{2}{3} \div \frac{3}{4} = \frac{2}{3} \times \frac{4}{3} = \frac{8}{9}$.

> **Review Video: Multiplying and Dividing Fractions**
> Visit mometrix.com/academy and enter code: 473632

## MULTIPLYING A MIXED NUMBER BY A WHOLE NUMBER OR A DECIMAL

When multiplying a mixed number by something, it is usually best to convert it to an improper fraction first. Additionally, if the multiplicand is a decimal, it is most often simplest to convert it to a fraction. For instance, to multiply $4\frac{3}{8}$ by 3.5, begin by rewriting each quantity as a whole number plus a proper fraction. Remember, a mixed number is a fraction added to a whole number and a decimal is a representation of the sum of fractions, specifically tenths, hundredths, thousandths, and so on:

$$4\frac{3}{8} \times 3.5 = \left(4 + \frac{3}{8}\right) \times \left(3 + \frac{1}{2}\right)$$

Next, the quantities being added need to be expressed with the same denominator. This is achieved by multiplying and dividing the whole number by the denominator of the fraction. Recall that a whole number is equivalent to that number divided by 1:

$$= \left(\frac{4}{1} \times \frac{8}{8} + \frac{3}{8}\right) \times \left(\frac{3}{1} \times \frac{2}{2} + \frac{1}{2}\right)$$

When multiplying fractions, remember to multiply the numerators and denominators separately:

$$= \left(\frac{4 \times 8}{1 \times 8} + \frac{3}{8}\right) \times \left(\frac{3 \times 2}{1 \times 2} + \frac{1}{2}\right)$$
$$= \left(\frac{32}{8} + \frac{3}{8}\right) \times \left(\frac{6}{2} + \frac{1}{2}\right)$$

Now that the fractions have the same denominators, they can be added:

$$= \frac{35}{8} \times \frac{7}{2}$$

Copyright © Mometrix Media. You have been licensed one copy of this document for personal use only. Any other reproduction or redistribution is strictly prohibited. All rights reserved. This content is provided for test preparation purposes only and does not imply an endorsement by Mometrix of any particular political, scientific, or religious point of view.

Finally, perform the last multiplication and then simplify:

$$= \frac{35 \times 7}{8 \times 2} = \frac{245}{16} = \frac{240}{16} + \frac{5}{16} = 15\frac{5}{16}$$

## DECIMALS

Decimals are one way to represent parts of a whole. Using the place value system, each digit to the right of a decimal point denotes the number of units of a corresponding *negative* power of ten. For example, consider the decimal 0.24. We can use a model to represent the decimal. Since a dime is worth one-tenth of a dollar and a penny is worth one-hundredth of a dollar, one possible model to represent this fraction is to have 2 dimes representing the 2 in the tenths place and 4 pennies representing the 4 in the hundredths place:

To write the decimal as a fraction, put the decimal in the numerator with 1 in the denominator. Multiply the numerator and denominator by tens until there are no more decimal places. Then simplify the fraction to lowest terms. For example, converting 0.24 to a fraction:

$$0.24 = \frac{0.24}{1} = \frac{0.24 \times 100}{1 \times 100} = \frac{24}{100} = \frac{6}{25}$$

> **Review Video: Decimals**
> Visit mometrix.com/academy and enter code: 837268

### OPERATIONS WITH DECIMALS
#### ADDING AND SUBTRACTING DECIMALS

When adding and subtracting decimals, the decimal points must always be aligned. Adding decimals is just like adding regular whole numbers. Example: $4.5 + 2.0 = 6.5$.

If the problem-solver does not properly align the decimal points, an incorrect answer of 4.7 may result. An easy way to add decimals is to align all of the decimal points in a vertical column visually. This will allow you to see exactly where the decimal should be placed in the final answer. Begin adding from right to left. Add each column in turn, making sure to carry the number to the left if a column adds up to more than 9. The same rules apply to the subtraction of decimals.

> **Review Video: Adding and Subtracting Decimals**
> Visit mometrix.com/academy and enter code: 381101

#### MULTIPLYING DECIMALS

A simple multiplication problem has two components: a **multiplicand** and a **multiplier**. When multiplying decimals, work as though the numbers were whole rather than decimals. Once the final product is calculated, count the number of places to the right of the decimal in both the multiplicand and the multiplier. Then, count that number of places from the right of the product and place the decimal in that position.

Copyright © Mometrix Media. You have been licensed one copy of this document for personal use only. Any other reproduction or redistribution is strictly prohibited. All rights reserved. This content is provided for test preparation purposes only and does not imply an endorsement by Mometrix of any particular political, scientific, or religious point of view.

For example, 12.3 × 2.56 has a total of three places to the right of the respective decimals. Multiply 123 × 256 to get 31,488. Now, beginning on the right, count three places to the left and insert the decimal. The final product will be 31.488.

---
**Review Video: How to Multiply Decimals**
Visit mometrix.com/academy and enter code: 731574

---

## DIVIDING DECIMALS

Every division problem has a **divisor** and a **dividend**. The dividend is the number that is being divided. In the problem 14 ÷ 7, 14 is the dividend and 7 is the divisor. In a division problem with decimals, the divisor must be converted into a whole number. Begin by moving the decimal in the divisor to the right until a whole number is created. Next, move the decimal in the dividend the same number of spaces to the right. For example, 4.9 into 24.5 would become 49 into 245. The decimal was moved one space to the right to create a whole number in the divisor, and then the same was done for the dividend. Once the whole numbers are created, the problem is carried out normally: 245 ÷ 49 = 5.

---
**Review Video: How to Divide Decimals**
Visit mometrix.com/academy and enter code: 560690

**Review Video: Dividing Decimals by Whole Numbers**
Visit mometrix.com/academy and enter code: 535669

---

## PERCENTAGES

**Percentages** can be thought of as fractions that are based on a whole of 100; that is, one whole is equal to 100%. The word **percent** means "per hundred." Percentage problems are often presented in three main ways:

- Find what percentage of some number another number is.
  - Example: What percentage of 40 is 8?
- Find what number is some percentage of a given number.
  - Example: What number is 20% of 40?
- Find what number another number is a given percentage of.
  - Example: What number is 8 20% of?

There are three components in each of these cases: a **whole** ($W$), a **part** ($P$), and a **percentage** (%). These are related by the equation: $P = W \times \%$. This can easily be rearranged into other forms that may suit different questions better: $\% = \frac{P}{W}$ and $W = \frac{P}{\%}$. Percentage problems are often also word problems. As such, a large part of solving them is figuring out which quantities are what. For example, consider the following word problem:

*In a school cafeteria, 7 students choose pizza, 9 choose hamburgers, and 4 choose tacos. What percentage of student choose tacos?*

To find the whole, you must first add all of the parts: $7 + 9 + 4 = 20$. The percentage can then be found by dividing the part by the whole $\left(\% = \frac{P}{W}\right): \frac{4}{20} = \frac{20}{100} = 20\%$.

---
**Review Video: Computation with Percentages**
Visit mometrix.com/academy and enter code: 693099

---

Copyright © Mometrix Media. You have been licensed one copy of this document for personal use only. Any other reproduction or redistribution is strictly prohibited. All rights reserved. This content is provided for test preparation purposes only and does not imply an endorsement by Mometrix of any particular political, scientific, or religious point of view.

## CONVERTING BETWEEN PERCENTAGES, FRACTIONS, AND DECIMALS

Converting decimals to percentages and percentages to decimals is as simple as moving the decimal point. To *convert from a decimal to a percentage*, move the decimal point **two places to the right**. To *convert from a percentage to a decimal*, move it **two places to the left**. It may be helpful to remember that the percentage number will always be larger than the equivalent decimal number. Example:

$$0.23 = 23\% \quad 5.34 = 534\% \quad 0.007 = 0.7\%$$
$$700\% = 7.00 \quad 86\% = 0.86 \quad 0.15\% = 0.0015$$

To convert a fraction to a decimal, simply divide the numerator by the denominator in the fraction. To convert a decimal to a fraction, put the decimal in the numerator with 1 in the denominator. Multiply the numerator and denominator by tens until there are no more decimal places. Then simplify the fraction to lowest terms. For example, converting 0.24 to a fraction:

$$0.24 = \frac{0.24}{1} = \frac{0.24 \times 100}{1 \times 100} = \frac{24}{100} = \frac{6}{25}$$

Fractions can be converted to a percentage by finding equivalent fractions with a denominator of 100. Example:

$$\frac{7}{10} = \frac{70}{100} = 70\% \quad \frac{1}{4} = \frac{25}{100} = 25\%$$

To convert a percentage to a fraction, divide the percentage number by 100 and reduce the fraction to its simplest possible terms. Example:

$$60\% = \frac{60}{100} = \frac{3}{5} \quad 96\% = \frac{96}{100} = \frac{24}{25}$$

> **Review Video: <u>Converting Decimals, Improper Fractions, and Mixed Numbers</u>**
> Visit mometrix.com/academy and enter code: 696924
>
> **Review Video: <u>Converting Fractions to Percentages and Decimals</u>**
> Visit mometrix.com/academy and enter code: 306233
>
> **Review Video: <u>Converting Percentages to Decimals and Fractions</u>**
> Visit mometrix.com/academy and enter code: 287297
>
> **Review Video: <u>Converting Decimals to Fractions and Percentages</u>**
> Visit mometrix.com/academy and enter code: 986765

## RATIONAL NUMBERS

The term **rational** means that the number can be expressed as a ratio or fraction. That is, a number, $r$, is rational if and only if it can be represented by a fraction $\frac{a}{b}$ where $a$ and $b$ are integers and $b$ does not equal 0. The set of rational numbers includes integers and decimals. If there is no finite

Copyright © Mometrix Media. You have been licensed one copy of this document for personal use only. Any other reproduction or redistribution is strictly prohibited. All rights reserved.
This content is provided for test preparation purposes only and does not imply an endorsement by Mometrix of any particular political, scientific, or religious point of view.

way to represent a value with a fraction of integers, then the number is **irrational**. Common examples of irrational numbers include: $\sqrt{5}$, $\left(1 + \sqrt{2}\right)$, and $\pi$.

| **Review Video: <u>Rational and Irrational Numbers</u>** |
|:---:|
| Visit mometrix.com/academy and enter code: 280645 |

Copyright © Mometrix Media. You have been licensed one copy of this document for personal use only. Any other reproduction or redistribution is strictly prohibited. All rights reserved.
This content is provided for test preparation purposes only and does not imply an endorsement by Mometrix of any particular political, scientific, or religious point of view.

## PRACTICE

**P1.** What is 30% of 120?

**P2.** What is 150% of 20?

**P3.** What is 14.5% of 96?

**P4.** Simplify the following expressions:

(a) $\frac{2}{5} \div \frac{4}{7}$

(b) $\frac{7}{8} - \frac{8}{16}$

(c) $\frac{1}{2} + \left(3\left(\frac{3}{4}\right) - 2\right) + 4$

(d) $0.22 + 0.5 - (5.5 + 3.3 \div 3)$

(e) $\frac{3}{2} + (4(0.5) - 0.75) + 2$

**P5.** Convert the following to a fraction and to a decimal: **(a)** 15%; **(b)** 24.36%

**P6.** Convert the following to a decimal and to a percentage. **(a)** $\frac{4}{5}$; **(b)** $3\frac{2}{5}$

**P7.** A woman's age is thirteen more than half of 60. How old is the woman?

**P8.** A patient was given pain medicine at a dosage of 0.22 grams. The patient's dosage was then increased to 0.80 grams. By how much was the patient's dosage increased?

**P9.** At a hotel, $\frac{3}{4}$ of the 100 rooms are occupied today. Yesterday, $\frac{4}{5}$ of the 100 rooms were occupied. On which day were more of the rooms occupied and by how much more?

**P10.** At a school, 40% of the teachers teach English. If 20 teachers teach English, how many teachers work at the school?

**P11.** A patient was given blood pressure medicine at a dosage of 2 grams. The patient's dosage was then decreased to 0.45 grams. By how much was the patient's dosage decreased?

**P12.** Two weeks ago, $\frac{2}{3}$ of the 60 customers at a skate shop were male. Last week, $\frac{3}{6}$ of the 80 customers were male. During which week were there more male customers?

**P13.** Jane ate lunch at a local restaurant. She ordered a $4.99 appetizer, a $12.50 entrée, and a $1.25 soda. If she wants to tip her server 20%, how much money will she spend in all?

**P14.** According to a survey, about 82% of engineers were highly satisfied with their job. If 145 engineers were surveyed, how many reported that they were highly satisfied?

**P15.** A patient was given 40 mg of a certain medicine. Later, the patient's dosage was increased to 45 mg. What was the percent increase in his medication?

**P16.** Order the following rational numbers from least to greatest: 0.55, 17%, $\sqrt{25}$, $\frac{64}{4}$, $\frac{25}{50}$, 3.

**P17.** Order the following rational numbers from greatest to least: 0.3, 27%, $\sqrt{100}$, $\frac{72}{9}$, $\frac{1}{9}$, 4.5

Copyright © Mometrix Media. You have been licensed one copy of this document for personal use only. Any other reproduction or redistribution is strictly prohibited. All rights reserved.
This content is provided for test preparation purposes only and does not imply an endorsement by Mometrix of any particular political, scientific, or religious point of view.

**P18.** Perform the following multiplication. Write each answer as a mixed number.

(a) $\left(1\frac{11}{16}\right) \times 4$

(b) $\left(12\frac{1}{3}\right) \times 1.1$

(c) $3.71 \times \left(6\frac{1}{5}\right)$

**P19.** Suppose you are making doughnuts and you want to triple the recipe you have. If the following list is the original amounts for the ingredients, what would be the amounts for the tripled recipe?

| | | | | | |
|---|---|---|---|---|---|
| $1\frac{3}{4}$ | cup | Flour | $1\frac{1}{2}$ | Tbsp | Butter |
| $1\frac{1}{4}$ | tsp | Baking powder | 2 | large | Eggs |
| $\frac{3}{4}$ | tsp | Salt | $\frac{3}{4}$ | tsp | Vanilla extract |
| $\frac{3}{8}$ | cup | Sugar | $\frac{3}{8}$ | cup | Sour cream |

## PRACTICE SOLUTIONS

**P1.** The word *of* indicates multiplication, so 30% of 120 is found by multiplying 120 by 30%. Change 30% to a decimal, then multiply: $120 \times 0.3 = 36$

**P2.** The word *of* indicates multiplication, so 150% of 20 is found by multiplying 20 by 150%. Change 150% to a decimal, then multiply: $20 \times 1.5 = 30$

**P3.** Change 14.5% to a decimal before multiplying. $0.145 \times 96 = 13.92$.

**P4.** Follow the order of operations and utilize properties of fractions to solve each:

(a) Rewrite the problem as a multiplication problem: $\frac{2}{5} \times \frac{7}{4} = \frac{2\times7}{5\times4} = \frac{14}{20}$. Make sure the fraction is reduced to lowest terms. Both 14 and 20 can be divided by 2.

$$\frac{14}{20} = \frac{14\div2}{20\div2} = \frac{7}{10}$$

(b) The denominators of $\frac{7}{8}$ and $\frac{8}{16}$ are 8 and 16, respectively. The lowest common denominator of 8 and 16 is 16 because 16 is the least common multiple of 8 and 16. Convert the first fraction to its equivalent with the newly found common denominator of 16: $\frac{7\times2}{8\times2} = \frac{14}{16}$. Now that the fractions have the same denominator, you can subtract them.

$$\frac{14}{16} - \frac{8}{16} = \frac{6}{16} = \frac{3}{8}$$

157

Copyright © Mometrix Media. You have been licensed one copy of this document for personal use only. Any other reproduction or redistribution is strictly prohibited. All rights reserved. This content is provided for test preparation purposes only and does not imply an endorsement by Mometrix of any particular political, scientific, or religious point of view.

**(c)** When simplifying expressions, first perform operations within groups. Within the set of parentheses are multiplication and subtraction operations. Perform the multiplication first to get $\frac{1}{2} + \left(\frac{9}{4} - 2\right) + 4$. Then, subtract two to obtain $\frac{1}{2} + \frac{1}{4} + 4$. Finally, perform addition from left to right:

$$\frac{1}{2} + \frac{1}{4} + 4 = \frac{2}{4} + \frac{1}{4} + \frac{16}{4} = \frac{19}{4} = 4\frac{3}{4}$$

**(d)** First, evaluate the terms in the parentheses $(5.5 + 3.3 \div 3)$ using order of operations. $3.3 \div 3 = 1.1$, and $5.5 + 1.1 = 6.6$. Next, rewrite the problem: $0.22 + 0.5 - 6.6$. Finally, add and subtract from left to right: $0.22 + 0.5 = 0.72$; $0.72 - 6.6 = -5.88$. The answer is $-5.88$.

**(e)** First, simplify within the parentheses, then change the fraction to a decimal and perform addition from left to right:

$$\frac{3}{2} + (2 - 0.75) + 2 =$$

$$\frac{3}{2} + 1.25 + 2 =$$

$$1.5 + 1.25 + 2 = 4.75$$

**P5. (a)** 15% can be written as $\frac{15}{100}$. Both 15 and 100 can be divided by 5: $\frac{15 \div 5}{100 \div 5} = \frac{3}{20}$

When converting from a percentage to a decimal, drop the percent sign and move the decimal point two places to the left: $15\% = 0.15$

**(b)** 24.36% written as a fraction is $\frac{24.36}{100}$, or $\frac{2436}{10,000}$, which reduces to $\frac{609}{2500}$. 24.36% written as a decimal is 0.2436. Recall that dividing by 100 moves the decimal two places to the left.

**P6. (a)** Recall that in the decimal system the first decimal place is one tenth: $\frac{4 \times 2}{5 \times 2} = \frac{8}{10} = 0.8$

Percent means "per hundred." $\frac{4 \times 20}{5 \times 20} = \frac{80}{100} = 80\%$

**(b)** The mixed number $3\frac{2}{5}$ has a whole number and a fractional part. The fractional part $\frac{2}{5}$ can be written as a decimal by dividing 5 into 2, which gives 0.4. Adding the whole to the part gives 3.4.

To find the equivalent percentage, multiply the decimal by 100. $3.4(100) = 340\%$. Notice that this percentage is greater than 100%. This makes sense because the original mixed number $3\frac{2}{5}$ is greater than 1.

**P7.** "More than" indicates addition, and "of" indicates multiplication. The expression can be written as $\frac{1}{2}(60) + 13$. So, the woman's age is equal to $\frac{1}{2}(60) + 13 = 30 + 13 = 43$. The woman is 43 years old.

**P8.** The first step is to determine what operation (addition, subtraction, multiplication, or division) the problem requires. Notice the keywords and phrases "by how much" and "increased."

Copyright © Mometrix Media. You have been licensed one copy of this document for personal use only. Any other reproduction or redistribution is strictly prohibited. All rights reserved.
This content is provided for test preparation purposes only and does not imply an endorsement by Mometrix of any particular political, scientific, or religious point of view.

"Increased" means that you go from a smaller amount to a larger amount. This change can be found by subtracting the smaller amount from the larger amount: 0.80 grams– 0.22 grams = 0.58 grams.

Remember to line up the decimal when subtracting:

$$
\begin{array}{r}
0.80 \\
-\ \ 0.22 \\
\hline
0.58
\end{array}
$$

**P9.** First, find the number of rooms occupied each day. To do so, multiply the fraction of rooms occupied by the number of rooms available:

$$\text{Number occupied} = \text{Fraction occupied} \times \text{Total number}$$

$$\text{Number of rooms occupied today} = \frac{3}{4} \times 100 = 75$$

$$\text{Number of rooms occupied} = \frac{4}{5} \times 100 = 80$$

The difference in the number of rooms occupied is: $80 - 75 = 5$ rooms

**P10.** To answer this problem, first think about the number of teachers that work at the school. Will it be more or less than the number of teachers who work in a specific department such as English? More teachers work at the school, so the number you find to answer this question will be greater than 20.

40% of the teachers are English teachers. "Of" indicates multiplication, and words like "is" and "are" indicate equivalence. Translating the problem into a mathematical sentence gives $40\% \times t = 20$, where $t$ represents the total number of teachers. Solving for $t$ gives $t = \frac{20}{40\%} = \frac{20}{0.40} = 50$. Fifty teachers work at the school.

**P11.** The decrease is represented by the difference between the two amounts:

$$2 \text{ grams} - 0.45 \text{ grams} = 1.55 \text{ grams}.$$

Remember to line up the decimal point before subtracting.

$$
\begin{array}{r}
2.00 \\
-\ \ 0.45 \\
\hline
1.55
\end{array}
$$

**P12.** First, you need to find the number of male customers that were in the skate shop each week. You are given this amount in terms of fractions. To find the actual number of male customers, multiply the fraction of male customers by the number of customers in the store.

$$\text{Actual number of male customers} = \text{fraction of male customers} \times \text{total customers}$$

$$\text{Number of male customers two weeks ago} = \frac{2}{3} \times 60 = \frac{120}{3} = 40$$

$$\text{Number of male customers last week} = \frac{3}{6} \times 80 = \frac{1}{2} \times 80 = \frac{80}{2} = 40$$

The number of male customers was the same both weeks.

Copyright © Mometrix Media. You have been licensed one copy of this document for personal use only. Any other reproduction or redistribution is strictly prohibited. All rights reserved. This content is provided for test preparation purposes only and does not imply an endorsement by Mometrix of any particular political, scientific, or religious point of view.

**P13.** To find total amount, first find the sum of the items she ordered from the menu and then add 20% of this sum to the total.

$$\$4.99 + \$12.50 + \$1.25 = \$18.74$$

$$\$18.74 \times 20\% = (0.20)(\$18.74) = \$3.748 \approx \$3.75$$

$$\text{Total} = \$18.74 + \$3.75 = \$22.49$$

**P14.** 82% of 145 is 0.82 $\times$ 145 = 118.9. Because you can't have 0.9 of a person, we must round up to say that 119 engineers reported that they were highly satisfied with their jobs.

**P15.** To find the percent increase, first compare the original and increased amounts. The original amount was 40 mg, and the increased amount is 45 mg, so the dosage of medication was increased by 5 mg (45− 40 = 5). Note, however, that the question asks not by how much the dosage increased but by what percentage it increased.

$$\text{Percent increase} = \frac{\text{new amount} - \text{original amount}}{\text{original amount}} \times 100\%$$

$$= \frac{45 \text{ mg} - 40 \text{ mg}}{40 \text{ mg}} \times 100\% = \frac{5}{40} \times 100\% = 0.125 \times 100\% = 12.5\%$$

**P16.** Recall that the term rational simply means that the number can be expressed as a ratio or fraction. Notice that each of the numbers in the problem can be written as a decimal or integer:

$$17\% = 0.1717$$
$$\sqrt{25} = 5$$
$$\frac{64}{4} = 16$$
$$\frac{25}{50} = \frac{1}{2} = 0.5$$

So, the answer is 17%, $\frac{25}{50}$, 0.55, 3, $\sqrt{25}$, $\frac{64}{4}$.

**P17.** Converting all the numbers to integers and decimals makes it easier to compare the values:

$$27\% = 0.27$$
$$\sqrt{100} = 10$$
$$\frac{72}{9} = 8$$
$$\frac{1}{9} \approx 0.11$$

So, the answer is $\sqrt{100}$, $\frac{72}{9}$, 4.5, 0.3, 27%, $\frac{1}{9}$.

> **Review Video: Ordering Rational Numbers**
> Visit mometrix.com/academy and enter code: 419578

Copyright © Mometrix Media. You have been licensed one copy of this document for personal use only. Any other reproduction or redistribution is strictly prohibited. All rights reserved.
This content is provided for test preparation purposes only and does not imply an endorsement by Mometrix of any particular political, scientific, or religious point of view.

**P18.** For each, convert improper fractions, adjust to a common denominator, perform the operations, and then simplify:

**(a)** Sometimes, you can skip converting the denominator and just distribute the multiplication.

$$\left(1\frac{11}{16}\right) \times 4 = \left(1 + \frac{11}{16}\right) \times 4$$
$$= 1 \times 4 + \frac{11}{16} \times 4$$
$$= 4 + \frac{11}{16} \times \frac{4}{1}$$
$$= 4 + \frac{44}{16} = 4 + \frac{11}{4} = 4 + 2\frac{3}{4} = 6\frac{3}{4}$$

**(b)**

$$\left(12\frac{1}{3}\right) \times 1.1 = \left(12 + \frac{1}{3}\right) \times \left(1 + \frac{1}{10}\right)$$
$$= \left(\frac{12}{1} \times \frac{3}{3} + \frac{1}{3}\right) \times \left(\frac{10}{10} + \frac{1}{10}\right)$$
$$= \left(\frac{36}{3} + \frac{1}{3}\right) \times \frac{11}{10}$$
$$= \frac{37}{3} \times \frac{11}{10}$$
$$= \frac{407}{30} = \frac{390}{30} + \frac{17}{30} = 13\frac{17}{30}$$

**(c)**

$$3.71 \times \left(6\frac{1}{5}\right) = \left(3 + \frac{71}{100}\right) \times \left(6 + \frac{1}{5}\right)$$
$$= \left(\frac{300}{100} + \frac{71}{100}\right) \times \left(\frac{6}{1} \times \frac{5}{5} + \frac{1}{5}\right)$$
$$= \frac{371}{100} \times \left(\frac{30}{5} + \frac{1}{5}\right)$$
$$= \frac{371}{100} \times \frac{31}{5}$$
$$= \frac{11501}{500} = \frac{11500}{500} + \frac{1}{500} = 23\frac{1}{500}$$

Copyright © Mometrix Media. You have been licensed one copy of this document for personal use only. Any other reproduction or redistribution is strictly prohibited. All rights reserved.
This content is provided for test preparation purposes only and does not imply an endorsement by Mometrix of any particular political, scientific, or religious point of view.

**P19.** Fortunately, some of the amounts are duplicated, so we do not need to convert every amount.

$$1\frac{3}{4} \times 3 = (1 \times 3) + \left(\frac{3}{4} \times 3\right)$$
$$= 3 + \frac{9}{4}$$
$$= 3 + 2\frac{1}{4}$$
$$= 5\frac{1}{4}$$

$$1\frac{1}{4} \times 3 = (1 \times 3) + \left(\frac{1}{4} \times 3\right)$$
$$= 3 + \frac{3}{4}$$
$$= 3\frac{3}{4}$$

$$\frac{3}{4} \times 3 = \frac{3}{4} \times 3$$
$$= \frac{9}{4}$$
$$= 2\frac{1}{4}$$

$$\frac{3}{8} \times 3 = \frac{3}{8} \times 3$$
$$= \frac{9}{8}$$
$$= 1\frac{1}{8}$$

$$1\frac{1}{2} \times 3 = 1 \times 3 + \frac{1}{2} \times 3$$
$$= 3 + \frac{3}{2}$$
$$= 3 + 1\frac{1}{2}$$
$$= 4\frac{1}{2}$$

$$2 \times 3 = 6$$

So, the result for the triple recipe is:

| | | | | | |
|---|---|---|---|---|---|
| $5\frac{1}{4}$ | cup | Flour | $4\frac{1}{2}$ | Tbsp | Butter |
| $3\frac{3}{4}$ | tsp | Baking powder | 6 | large | Eggs |
| $2\frac{1}{4}$ | tsp | Salt | $2\frac{1}{4}$ | tsp | Vanilla extract |
| $1\frac{1}{8}$ | cup | Sugar | $1\frac{1}{8}$ | cup | Sour cream |

Copyright © Mometrix Media. You have been licensed one copy of this document for personal use only. Any other reproduction or redistribution is strictly prohibited. All rights reserved.
This content is provided for test preparation purposes only and does not imply an endorsement by Mometrix of any particular political, scientific, or religious point of view.

# Proportions and Ratios

## PROPORTIONS

A proportion is a relationship between two quantities that dictates how one changes when the other changes. A **direct proportion** describes a relationship in which a quantity increases by a set amount for every increase in the other quantity, or decreases by that same amount for every decrease in the other quantity. Example: Assuming a constant driving speed, the time required for a car trip increases as the distance of the trip increases. The distance to be traveled and the time required to travel are directly proportional.

An **inverse proportion** is a relationship in which an increase in one quantity is accompanied by a decrease in the other, or vice versa. Example: the time required for a car trip decreases as the speed increases and increases as the speed decreases, so the time required is inversely proportional to the speed of the car.

> **Review Video: Proportions**
> Visit mometrix.com/academy and enter code: 505355

## RATIOS

A **ratio** is a comparison of two quantities in a particular order. Example: If there are 14 computers in a lab, and the class has 20 students, there is a student to computer ratio of 20 to 14, commonly written as 20: 14. Ratios are normally reduced to their smallest whole number representation, so 20: 14 would be reduced to 10: 7 by dividing both sides by 2.

> **Review Video: Ratios**
> Visit mometrix.com/academy and enter code: 996914

## CONSTANT OF PROPORTIONALITY

When two quantities have a proportional relationship, there exists a **constant of proportionality** between the quantities. The product of this constant and one of the quantities is equal to the other quantity. For example, if one lemon costs $0.25, two lemons cost $0.50, and three lemons cost $0.75, there is a proportional relationship between the total cost of lemons and the number of lemons purchased. The constant of proportionality is the **unit price**, namely $0.25/lemon. Notice that the total price of lemons, $t$, can be found by multiplying the unit price of lemons, $p$, and the number of lemons, $n$: $t = pn$.

## WORK/UNIT RATE

**Unit rate** expresses a quantity of one thing in terms of one unit of another. For example, if you travel 30 miles every two hours, a unit rate expresses this comparison in terms of one hour: in one hour you travel 15 miles, so your unit rate is 15 miles per hour. Other examples are how much one ounce of food costs (price per ounce) or figuring out how much one egg costs out of the dozen (price per 1 egg, instead of price per 12 eggs). The denominator of a unit rate is always 1. Unit rates are used to compare different situations to solve problems. For example, to make sure you get the best deal when deciding which kind of soda to buy, you can find the unit rate of each. If soda #1 costs $1.50 for a 1-liter bottle, and soda #2 costs $2.75 for a 2-liter bottle, it would be a better deal to buy soda #2, because its unit rate is only $1.375 per 1-liter, which is cheaper than soda #1. Unit rates can also help determine the length of time a given event will take. For example, if you can

163

Copyright © Mometrix Media. You have been licensed one copy of this document for personal use only. Any other reproduction or redistribution is strictly prohibited. All rights reserved. This content is provided for test preparation purposes only and does not imply an endorsement by Mometrix of any particular political, scientific, or religious point of view.

paint 2 rooms in 4.5 hours, you can determine how long it will take you to paint 5 rooms by solving for the unit rate per room and then multiplying that by 5.

**Review Video: Rates and Unit Rates**
Visit mometrix.com/academy and enter code: 185363

## SLOPE

On a graph with two points, $(x_1, y_1)$ and $(x_2, y_2)$, the **slope** is found with the formula $m = \frac{y_2 - y_1}{x_2 - x_1}$; where $x_1 \neq x_2$ and $m$ stands for slope. If the value of the slope is **positive**, the line has an *upward direction* from left to right. If the value of the slope is **negative**, the line has a *downward direction* from left to right. Consider the following example:

A new book goes on sale in bookstores and online stores. In the first month, 5,000 copies of the book are sold. Over time, the book continues to grow in popularity. The data for the number of copies sold is in the table below.

| # of Months on Sale | 1 | 2 | 3 | 4 | 5 |
|---|---|---|---|---|---|
| # of Copies Sold (In Thousands) | 5 | 10 | 15 | 20 | 25 |

So, the number of copies that are sold and the time that the book is on sale is a proportional relationship. In this example, an equation can be used to show the data: $y = 5x$, where $x$ is the number of months that the book is on sale. Also, $y$ is the number of copies sold. So, the slope of the corresponding line is $\frac{\text{rise}}{\text{run}} = \frac{5}{1} = 5$.

**Review Video: Finding the Slope of a Line**
Visit mometrix.com/academy and enter code: 766664

## FINDING AN UNKNOWN IN EQUIVALENT EXPRESSIONS

It is often necessary to apply information given about a rate or proportion to a new scenario. For example, if you know that Jedha can run a marathon (26.2 miles) in 3 hours, how long would it take her to run 10 miles at the same pace? Start by setting up equivalent expressions:

$$\frac{26.2 \text{ mi}}{3 \text{ hr}} = \frac{10 \text{ mi}}{x \text{ hr}}$$

Now, cross multiply and solve for $x$:

$$26.2x = 30$$
$$x = \frac{30}{26.2} = \frac{15}{13.1}$$
$$x \approx 1.15 \text{ hrs } or \text{ 1 hr 9 min}$$

So, at this pace, Jedha could run 10 miles in about 1.15 hours or about 1 hour and 9 minutes.

**Review Video: Cross Multiply Fractions**
Visit mometrix.com/academy and enter code: 893904

Copyright © Mometrix Media. You have been licensed one copy of this document for personal use only. Any other reproduction or redistribution is strictly prohibited. All rights reserved.
This content is provided for test preparation purposes only and does not imply an endorsement by Mometrix of any particular political, scientific, or religious point of view.

## PRACTICE

**P1.** Solve the following for $x$.

(a) $\frac{45}{12} = \frac{15}{x}$

(b) $\frac{0.50}{2} = \frac{1.50}{x}$

(c) $\frac{40}{8} = \frac{x}{24}$

**P2.** At a school, for every 20 female students there are 15 male students. This same student ratio happens to exist at another school. If there are 100 female students at the second school, how many male students are there?

**P3.** In a hospital emergency room, there are 4 nurses for every 12 patients. What is the ratio of nurses to patients? If the nurse-to-patient ratio remains constant, how many nurses must be present to care for 24 patients?

**P4.** In a bank, the banker-to-customer ratio is $1:2$. If seven bankers are on duty, how many customers are currently in the bank?

**P5.** Janice made $40 during the first 5 hours she spent babysitting. She will continue to earn money at this rate until she finishes babysitting in 3 more hours. Find how much money Janice earns per hour and the total she earned babysitting.

**P6.** The McDonalds are taking a family road trip, driving 300 miles to their cabin. It took them 2 hours to drive the first 120 miles. They will drive at the same speed all the way to their cabin. Find the speed at which the McDonalds are driving and how much longer it will take them to get to their cabin.

**P7.** It takes Andy 10 minutes to read 6 pages of his book. He has already read 150 pages in his book that is 210 pages long. Find how long it takes Andy to read 1 page and also find how long it will take him to finish his book if he continues to read at the same speed.

## PRACTICE SOLUTIONS

**P1.** Cross multiply, then solve for $x$:

(a)

$$45x = 12 \times 15$$
$$45x = 180$$
$$x = \frac{180}{45} = 4$$

(b)

$$0.5x = 1.5 \times 2$$
$$0.5x = 3$$
$$x = \frac{3}{0.5} = 6$$

Copyright © Mometrix Media. You have been licensed one copy of this document for personal use only. Any other reproduction or redistribution is strictly prohibited. All rights reserved. This content is provided for test preparation purposes only and does not imply an endorsement by Mometrix of any particular political, scientific, or religious point of view.

**(c)**

$$8x = 40 \times 24$$
$$8x = 960$$
$$x = \frac{960}{8} = 120$$

**P2.** One way to find the number of male students is to set up and solve a proportion.

$$\frac{\text{number of female students}}{\text{number of male students}} = \frac{20}{15} = \frac{100}{\text{number of male students}}$$

Represent the unknown number of male students as the variable $x$: $\frac{20}{15} = \frac{100}{x}$

Cross multiply and then solve for $x$:

$$20x = 15 \times 100$$
$$x = \frac{1500}{20}$$
$$x = 75$$

**P3.** The ratio of nurses to patients can be written as 4 to 12, 4 : 12, or $\frac{4}{12}$. Because four and twelve have a common factor of four, the ratio should be reduced to 1 : 3, which means that there is one nurse present for every three patients. If this ratio remains constant, there must be eight nurses present to care for 24 patients.

**P4.** Use proportional reasoning or set up a proportion to solve. Because there are twice as many customers as bankers, there must be fourteen customers when seven bankers are on duty. Setting up and solving a proportion gives the same result:

$$\frac{\text{number of bankers}}{\text{number of customers}} = \frac{1}{2} = \frac{7}{\text{number of customers}}$$

Represent the unknown number of customers as the variable $x$: $\frac{1}{2} = \frac{7}{x}$.

To solve for $x$, cross multiply: $1 \times x = 7 \times 2$, so $x = 14$.

**P5.** Janice earns \$8 per hour. This can be found by taking her initial amount earned, \$40, and dividing it by the number of hours worked, 5. Since $\frac{40}{5} = 8$, Janice makes \$8 in one hour. This can also be found by finding the unit rate, money earned per hour: $\frac{40}{5} = \frac{x}{1}$. Since cross multiplying yields $5x = 40$, and division by 5 shows that $x = 8$, Janice earns \$8 per hour.

Janice will earn \$64 babysitting in her 8 total hours (adding the first 5 hours to the remaining 3 gives the 8-hour total). Since Janice earns \$8 per hour and she worked 8 hours, $\frac{\$8}{\text{hr}} \times 8 \text{ hrs} = \$64$. This can also be found by setting up a proportion comparing money earned to babysitting hours. Since she earns \$40 for 5 hours and since the rate is constant, she will earn a proportional amount in 8 hours: $\frac{40}{5} = \frac{x}{8}$. Cross multiplying will yield $5x = 320$, and division by 5 shows that $x = 64$.

Copyright © Mometrix Media. You have been licensed one copy of this document for personal use only. Any other reproduction or redistribution is strictly prohibited. All rights reserved.
This content is provided for test preparation purposes only and does not imply an endorsement by Mometrix of any particular political, scientific, or religious point of view.

**P6.** The McDonalds are driving 60 miles per hour. This can be found by setting up a proportion to find the unit rate, the number of miles they drive per one hour: $\frac{120}{2} = \frac{x}{1}$. Cross multiplying yields $2x = 120$ and division by 2 shows that $x = 60$.

Since the McDonalds will drive this same speed for the remaining miles, it will take them another 3 hours to get to their cabin. This can be found by first finding how many miles the McDonalds have left to drive, which is $300-120 = 180$. The McDonalds are driving at 60 miles per hour, so a proportion can be set up to determine how many hours it will take them to drive 180 miles: $\frac{180}{x} = \frac{60}{1}$. Cross multiplying yields $60x = 180$, and division by 60 shows that $x = 3$. This can also be found by using the formula $D = r \times t$ (or distance = rate × time), where $180 = 60 \times t$, and division by 60 shows that $t = 3$.

**P7.** It takes Andy 10 minutes to read 6 pages, $\frac{10}{6} = 1\frac{2}{3}$ minutes, which is 1 minute and 40 seconds.

Next, determine how many pages Andy has left to read, $210 - 150 = 60$. Since it is now known that it takes him $1\frac{2}{3}$ minutes to read each page, that rate must be multiplied by however many pages he has left to read (60) to find the time he'll need: $60 \times 1\frac{2}{3} = 100$, so it will take him 100 minutes, or 1 hour and 40 minutes, to read the rest of his book.

Copyright © Mometrix Media. You have been licensed one copy of this document for personal use only. Any other reproduction or redistribution is strictly prohibited. All rights reserved.
This content is provided for test preparation purposes only and does not imply an endorsement by Mometrix of any particular political, scientific, or religious point of view.

# Expressions

## TERMS AND COEFFICIENTS

**Mathematical expressions** consist of a combination of one or more values arranged in terms that are added together. As such, an expression could be just a single number, including zero. A **variable term** is the product of a real number, also called a **coefficient**, and one or more variables, each of which may be raised to an exponent. Expressions may also include numbers without a variable, called **constants** or **constant terms**. The expression $6s^2$, for example, is a single term where the coefficient is the real number 6 and the variable term is $s^2$. Note that if a term is written as simply a variable to some exponent, like $t^2$, then the coefficient is 1, because $t^2 = 1t^2$.

## LINEAR EXPRESSIONS

A **single variable linear expression** is the sum of a single variable term, where the variable has no exponent, and a constant, which may be zero. For instance, the expression $2w + 7$ has $2w$ as the variable term and 7 as the constant term. It is important to realize that terms are separated by addition or subtraction. Since an expression is a sum of terms, expressions such as $5x - 3$ can be written as $5x + (-3)$ to emphasize that the constant term is negative. A real-world example of a single variable linear expression is the perimeter of a square, four times the side length, often expressed: $4s$.

In general, a **linear expression** is the sum of any number of variable terms so long as none of the variables have an exponent. For example, $3m + 8n - \frac{1}{4}p + 5.5q - 1$ is a linear expression, but $3y^3$ is not. In the same way, the expression for the perimeter of a general triangle, the sum of the side lengths $(a + b + c)$ is considered to be linear, but the expression for the area of a square, the side length squared $(s^2)$is not.

Copyright © Mometrix Media. You have been licensed one copy of this document for personal use only. Any other reproduction or redistribution is strictly prohibited. All rights reserved. This content is provided for test preparation purposes only and does not imply an endorsement by Mometrix of any particular political, scientific, or religious point of view.

# Equations

## LINEAR EQUATIONS

Equations that can be written as $ax + b = 0$, where $a \neq 0$, are referred to as **one variable linear equations**. A solution to such an equation is called a **root**. In the case where we have the equation $5x + 10 = 0$, if we solve for $x$ we get a solution of $x = -2$. In other words, the root of the equation is –2. This is found by first subtracting 10 from both sides, which gives $5x = -10$. Next, simply divide both sides by the coefficient of the variable, in this case 5, to get $x = -2$. This can be checked by plugging –2 back into the original equation $(5)(-2) + 10 = -10 + 10 = 0$.

The **solution set** is the set of all solutions of an equation. In our example, the solution set would simply be –2. If there were more solutions (there usually are in multivariable equations) then they would also be included in the solution set. When an equation has no true solutions, it is referred to as an **empty set**. Equations with identical solution sets are **equivalent equations**. An **identity** is a term whose value or determinant is equal to 1.

Linear equations can be written many ways. Below is a list of some forms linear equations can take:

- **Standard Form**: $Ax + By = C$; the slope is $\frac{-A}{B}$ and the $y$-intercept is $\frac{C}{B}$
- **Slope Intercept Form**: $y = mx + b$, where $m$ is the slope and $b$ is the $y$-intercept
- **Point-Slope Form**: $y - y_1 = m(x - x_1)$, where $m$ is the slope and $(x_1, y_1)$ is a point on the line
- **Two-Point Form**: $\frac{y - y_1}{x - x_1} = \frac{y_2 - y_1}{x_2 - x_1}$, where $(x_1, y_1)$ and $(x_2, y_2)$ are two points on the given line
- **Intercept Form**: $\frac{x}{x_1} + \frac{y}{y_1} = 1$, where $(x_1, 0)$ is the point at which a line intersects the $x$-axis, and $(0, y_1)$ is the point at which the same line intersects the $y$-axis

> **Review Video: Slope-Intercept and Point-Slope Forms**
> Visit mometrix.com/academy and enter code: 113216
>
> **Review Video: Linear Equations Basics**
> Visit mometrix.com/academy and enter code: 793005

## SOLVING ONE-VARIABLE LINEAR EQUATIONS

Multiply all terms by the lowest common denominator to eliminate any fractions. Look for addition or subtraction to undo so you can isolate the variable on one side of the equal sign. Divide both sides by the coefficient of the variable. When you have a value for the variable, substitute this value into the original equation to make sure you have a true equation. Consider the following example:

Kim's savings are represented by the table below. Represent her savings, using an equation.

| X (Months) | Y (Total Savings) |
|------------|-------------------|
| 2          | $1,300            |
| 5          | $2,050            |
| 9          | $3,050            |
| 11         | $3,550            |
| 16         | $4,800            |

169

Copyright © Mometrix Media. You have been licensed one copy of this document for personal use only. Any other reproduction or redistribution is strictly prohibited. All rights reserved. This content is provided for test preparation purposes only and does not imply an endorsement by Mometrix of any particular political, scientific, or religious point of view.

The table shows a function with a constant rate of change, or slope, of 250. Given the points on the table, the slopes can be calculated as $\frac{(2,050-1300)}{(5-2)}$, $\frac{(3,050-2,050)}{(9-5)}$, $\frac{(3,550-3,050)}{(11-9)}$, and $\frac{(4,800-3,550)}{(16-11)}$, each of which equals 250. Thus, the table shows a constant rate of change, indicating a linear function. The slope-intercept form of a linear equation is written as $y = mx + b$, where $m$ represents the slope and $b$ represents the $y$-intercept. Substituting the slope into this form gives $y = 250x + b$. Substituting corresponding $x$- and $y$-values from any point into this equation will give the $y$-intercept, or $b$. Using the point, $(2, 1,300)$, gives $1,300 = 250(2) + b$, which simplifies as $b = 800$. Thus, her savings may be represented by the equation, $y = 250x + 800$.

## RULES FOR MANIPULATING EQUATIONS

### LIKE TERMS

**Like terms** are terms in an equation that have the same variable, regardless of whether or not they also have the same coefficient. This includes terms that *lack* a variable; all constants (i.e., numbers without variables) are considered like terms. If the equation involves terms with a variable raised to different powers, the like terms are those that have the variable raised to the same power.

For example, consider the equation $x^2 + 3x + 2 = 2x^2 + x - 7 + 2x$. In this equation, 2 and –7 are like terms; they are both constants. $3x$, $x$, and $2x$ are like terms, they all include the variable $x$ raised to the first power. $x^2$ and $2x^2$ are like terms, they both include the variable $x$, raised to the second power. $2x$ and $2x^2$ are not like terms; although they both involve the variable $x$, the variable is not raised to the same power in both terms. The fact that they have the same coefficient, 2, is not relevant.

> **Review Video: Rules for Manipulating Equations**
> Visit mometrix.com/academy and enter code: 838871

### CARRYING OUT THE SAME OPERATION ON BOTH SIDES OF AN EQUATION

When solving an equation, the general procedure is to carry out a series of operations on both sides of an equation, choosing operations that will tend to simplify the equation when doing so. The reason why the same operation must be carried out on both sides of the equation is because that leaves the meaning of the equation unchanged, and yields a result that is equivalent to the original equation. This would not be the case if we carried out an operation on one side of an equation and not the other. Consider what an equation means: it is a statement that two values or expressions are equal. If we carry out the same operation on both sides of the equation—add 3 to both sides, for example—then the two sides of the equation are changed in the same way, and so remain equal. If we do that to only one side of the equation—add 3 to one side but not the other—then that wouldn't be true; if we change one side of the equation but not the other then the two sides are no longer equal.

### ADVANTAGE OF COMBINING LIKE TERMS

**Combining like terms** refers to adding or subtracting like terms—terms with the same variable— and therefore reducing sets of like terms to a single term. The main advantage of doing this is that it simplifies the equation. Often, combining like terms can be done as the first step in solving an equation, though it can also be done later, such as after distributing terms in a product.

For example, consider the equation $2(x + 3) + 3(2 + x + 3) = -4$. The 2 and the 3 in the second set of parentheses are like terms, and we can combine them, yielding $2(x + 3) + 3(x + 5) = -4$.

Copyright © Mometrix Media. You have been licensed one copy of this document for personal use only. Any other reproduction or redistribution is strictly prohibited. All rights reserved. This content is provided for test preparation purposes only and does not imply an endorsement by Mometrix of any particular political, scientific, or religious point of view.

Now we can carry out the multiplications implied by the parentheses, distributing the outer 2 and 3 accordingly: $2x + 6 + 3x + 15 = -4$. The $2x$ and the $3x$ are like terms, and we can add them together: $5x + 6 + 15 = -4$. Now, the constants 6, 15, and –4 are also like terms, and we can combine them as well: subtracting 6 and 15 from both sides of the equation, we get $5x = -4 - 6 - 15$, or $5x = -25$, which simplifies further to $x = -5$.

> **Review Video: <u>Solving Equations by Combining Like Terms</u>**
> Visit mometrix.com/academy and enter code: 668506

## CANCELING TERMS ON OPPOSITE SIDES OF AN EQUATION

Two terms on opposite sides of an equation can be canceled if and only if they *exactly* match each other. They must have the same variable raised to the same power and the same coefficient. For example, in the equation $3x + 2x^2 + 6 = 2x^2 - 6$, $2x^2$ appears on both sides of the equation and can be canceled, leaving $3x + 6 = -6$. The 6 on each side of the equation *cannot* be canceled, because it is added on one side of the equation and subtracted on the other. While they cannot be canceled, however, the 6 and –6 are like terms and can be combined, yielding $3x = -12$, which simplifies further to $x = -4$.

It's also important to note that the terms to be canceled must be independent terms and cannot be part of a larger term. For example, consider the equation $2(x + 6) = 3(x + 4) + 1$. We cannot cancel the $x$'s, because even though they match each other they are part of the larger terms $2(x + 6)$ and $3(x + 4)$. We must first distribute the 2 and 3, yielding $2x + 12 = 3x + 12 + 1$. Now we see that the terms with the $x$'s do not match, but the 12s do, and can be canceled, leaving $2x = 3x + 1$, which simplifies to $x = -1$.

## PROCESS FOR MANIPULATING EQUATIONS
### ISOLATING VARIABLES

To **isolate a variable** means to manipulate the equation so that the variable appears by itself on one side of the equation, and does not appear at all on the other side. Generally, an equation or inequality is considered to be solved once the variable is isolated and the other side of the equation or inequality is simplified as much as possible. In the case of a two-variable equation or inequality, only one variable needs to be isolated; it will not usually be possible to simultaneously isolate both variables.

For a linear equation—an equation in which the variable only appears raised to the first power— isolating a variable can be done by first moving all the terms with the variable to one side of the equation and all other terms to the other side. (*Moving* a term really means adding the inverse of the term to both sides; when a term is *moved* to the other side of the equation its sign is flipped.) Then combine like terms on each side. Finally, divide both sides by the coefficient of the variable, if applicable. The steps need not necessarily be done in this order, but this order will always work.

> **Review Video: <u>Solving One-Step Equations</u>**
> Visit mometrix.com/academy and enter code: 777004

## EQUATIONS WITH MORE THAN ONE SOLUTION

Some types of non-linear equations, such as equations involving squares of variables, may have more than one solution. For example, the equation $x^2 = 4$ has two solutions: 2 and –2. Equations with absolute values can also have multiple solutions: $|x| = 1$ has the solutions $x = 1$ and $x = -1$.

Copyright © Mometrix Media. You have been licensed one copy of this document for personal use only. Any other reproduction or redistribution is strictly prohibited. All rights reserved.
This content is provided for test preparation purposes only and does not imply an endorsement by Mometrix of any particular political, scientific, or religious point of view.

It is also possible for a linear equation to have more than one solution, but only if the equation is true regardless of the value of the variable. In this case, the equation is considered to have infinitely many solutions, because any possible value of the variable is a solution. We know a linear equation has infinitely many solutions if when we combine like terms the variables cancel, leaving a true statement. For example, consider the equation $2(3x + 5) = x + 5(x + 2)$. Distributing, we get $6x + 10 = x + 5x + 10$; combining like terms gives $6x + 10 = 6x + 10$, and the $6x$-terms cancel to leave $10 = 10$. This is clearly true, so the original equation is true for any value of $x$. We could also have canceled the 10s leaving $0 = 0$, but again this is clearly true—in general if both sides of the equation match exactly, it has infinitely many solutions.

## EQUATIONS WITH NO SOLUTION

Some types of non-linear equations, such as equations involving squares of variables, may have no solution. For example, the equation $x^2 = -2$ has no solutions in the real numbers, because the square of any real number must be positive. Similarly, $|x| = -1$ has no solution, because the absolute value of a number is always positive.

It is also possible for an equation to have no solution even if does not involve any powers greater than one, absolute values, or other special functions. For example, the equation $2(x + 3) + x = 3x$ has no solution. We can see that if we try to solve it: first we distribute, leaving $2x + 6 + x = 3x$. But now if we try to combine all the terms with the variable, we find that they cancel: we have $3x$ on the left and $3x$ on the right, canceling to leave us with $6 = 0$. This is clearly false. In general, whenever the variable terms in an equation cancel leaving different constants on both sides, it means that the equation has no solution. (If we are left with the *same* constant on both sides, the equation has infinitely many solutions instead.)

## FEATURES OF EQUATIONS THAT REQUIRE SPECIAL TREATMENT
### LINEAR EQUATIONS

A linear equation is an equation in which variables only appear by themselves: not multiplied together, not with exponents other than one, and not inside absolute value signs or any other functions. For example, the equation $x + 1 - 3x = 5 - x$ is a linear equation; while $x$ appears multiple times, it never appears with an exponent other than one, or inside any function. The two-variable equation $2x - 3y = 5 + 2x$ is also a linear equation. In contrast, the equation $x^2 - 5 = 3x$ is *not* a linear equation, because it involves the term $x^2$. $\sqrt{x} = 5$ is not a linear equation, because it involves a square root. $(x - 1)^2 = 4$ is not a linear equation because even though there's no exponent on the $x$ directly, it appears as part of an expression that is squared. The two-variable equation $x + xy - y = 5$ is not a linear equation because it includes the term $xy$, where two variables are multiplied together.

Linear equations can always be solved (or shown to have no solution) by combining like terms and performing simple operations on both sides of the equation. Some non-linear equations can be solved by similar methods, but others may require more advanced methods of solution, if they can be solved analytically at all.

### SOLVING EQUATIONS INVOLVING ROOTS

In an equation involving roots, the first step is to isolate the term with the root, if possible, and then raise both sides of the equation to the appropriate power to eliminate it. Consider an example equation, $2\sqrt{x + 1} - 1 = 3$. In this case, begin by adding 1 to both sides, yielding $2\sqrt{x + 1} = 4$, and then dividing both sides by 2, yielding $\sqrt{x + 1} = 2$. Now square both sides, yielding $x + 1 = 4$. Finally, subtracting 1 from both sides yields $x = 3$.

Copyright © Mometrix Media. You have been licensed one copy of this document for personal use only. Any other reproduction or redistribution is strictly prohibited. All rights reserved. This content is provided for test preparation purposes only and does not imply an endorsement by Mometrix of any particular political, scientific, or religious point of view.

Squaring both sides of an equation may, however, yield a spurious solution—a solution to the squared equation that is *not* a solution of the original equation. It's therefore necessary to plug the solution back into the original equation to make sure it works. In this case, it does: $2\sqrt{3+1} - 1 = 2\sqrt{4} - 1 = 2(2) - 1 = 4 - 1 = 3$.

The same procedure applies for other roots as well. For example, given the equation $3 + \sqrt[3]{2x} = 5$, we can first subtract 3 from both sides, yielding $\sqrt[3]{2x} = 2$ and isolating the root. Raising both sides to the third power yields $2x = 2^3$; i.e., $2x = 8$. We can now divide both sides by 2 to get $x = 4$.

> **Review Video: Solving Equations Involving Roots**
> Visit mometrix.com/academy and enter code: 297670

## SOLVING EQUATIONS WITH EXPONENTS

To solve an equation involving an exponent, the first step is to isolate the variable with the exponent. We can then take the appropriate root of both sides to eliminate the exponent. For instance, for the equation $2x^3 + 17 = 5x^3 - 7$, we can subtract $5x^3$ from both sides to get $-3x^3 + 17 = -7$, and then subtract 17 from both sides to get $-3x^3 = -24$. Finally, we can divide both sides by –3 to get $x^3 = 8$. Finally, we can take the cube root of both sides to get $x = \sqrt[3]{8} = 2$.

One important but often overlooked point is that equations with an exponent greater than 1 may have more than one answer. The solution to $x^2 = 9$ isn't simply $x = 3$; it's $x = \pm 3$ (that is, $x = 3$ or $x = -3$). For a slightly more complicated example, consider the equation $(x - 1)^2 - 1 = 3$. Adding 1 to both sides yields $(x - 1)^2 = 4$; taking the square root of both sides yields $x - 1 = 2$. We can then add 1 to both sides to get $x = 3$. However, there's a second solution. We also have the possibility that $x - 1 = -2$, in which case $x = -1$. Both $x = 3$ and $x = -1$ are valid solutions, as can be verified by substituting them both into the original equation.

> **Review Video: Solving Equations with Exponents**
> Visit mometrix.com/academy and enter code: 514557

## SOLVING EQUATIONS WITH ABSOLUTE VALUES

When solving an equation with an absolute value, the first step is to isolate the absolute value term. We then consider two possibilities: when the expression inside the absolute value is positive or when it is negative. In the former case, the expression in the absolute value equals the expression on the other side of the equation; in the latter, it equals the additive inverse of that expression—the expression times negative one. We consider each case separately and finally check for spurious solutions.

For instance, consider solving $|2x - 1| + x = 5$ for $x$. We can first isolate the absolute value by moving the $x$ to the other side: $|2x - 1| = -x + 5$. Now, we have two possibilities. First, that $2x - 1$ is positive, and hence $2x - 1 = -x + 5$. Rearranging and combining like terms yields $3x = 6$, and hence $x = 2$. The other possibility is that $2x - 1$ is negative, and hence $2x - 1 = -(-x + 5) = x - 5$. In this case, rearranging and combining like terms yields $x = -4$. Substituting $x = 2$ and $x = -4$ back into the original equation, we see that they are both valid solutions.

Note that the absolute value of a sum or difference applies to the sum or difference as a whole, not to the individual terms; in general, $|2x - 1|$ is not equal to $|2x + 1|$ or to $|2x| - 1$.

Copyright © Mometrix Media. You have been licensed one copy of this document for personal use only. Any other reproduction or redistribution is strictly prohibited. All rights reserved. This content is provided for test preparation purposes only and does not imply an endorsement by Mometrix of any particular political, scientific, or religious point of view.

### SPURIOUS SOLUTIONS

A **spurious solution** may arise when we square both sides of an equation as a step in solving it or under certain other operations on the equation. It is a solution to the squared or otherwise modified equation that is *not* a solution of the original equation. To identify a spurious solution, it's useful when you solve an equation involving roots or absolute values to plug the solution back into the original equation to make sure it's valid.

### CHOOSING WHICH VARIABLE TO ISOLATE IN TWO-VARIABLE EQUATIONS

Similar to methods for a one-variable equation, solving a two-variable equation involves isolating a variable: manipulating the equation so that a variable appears by itself on one side of the equation, and not at all on the other side. However, in a two-variable equation, you will usually only be able to isolate one of the variables; the other variable may appear on the other side along with constant terms, or with exponents or other functions.

Often one variable will be much more easily isolated than the other, and therefore that's the variable you should choose. If one variable appears with various exponents, and the other is only raised to the first power, the latter variable is the one to isolate: given the equation $a^2 + 2b = a^3 + b + 3$, the $b$ only appears to the first power, whereas $a$ appears squared and cubed, so $b$ is the variable that can be solved for: combining like terms and isolating the $b$ on the left side of the equation, we get $b = a^3 - a^2 + 3$. If both variables are equally easy to isolate, then it's best to isolate the independent variable, if one is defined; if the two variables are $x$ and $y$, the convention is that $y$ is the independent variable.

## PRACTICE

**P1.** Seeing the equation $2x + 4 = 4x + 7$, a student divides the first terms on each side by 2, yielding $x + 4 = 2x + 7$, and then combines like terms to get $x = -3$. However, this is incorrect, as can be seen by substituting –3 into the original equation. Explain what is wrong with the student's reasoning.

**P2.** Describe the steps necessary to solve the equation $2x + 1 - x = 4 + 3x + 7$.

**P3.** Describe the steps necessary to solve the equation $2(x + 5) = 7(4 - x)$.

**P4.** Find all real solutions to the equation $1 - \sqrt{x} = 2$.

**P5.** Find all real solutions to the equation $|x + 1| = 2x + 5$.

**P6.** Solve for $x$: $-x + 2\sqrt{x + 5} + 1 = 3$.

**P7.** Ray earns $10 an hour at his job. Write an equation for his earnings as a function of time spent working. Determine how long Ray has to work in order to earn $360.

**P8.** Simplify the following: $3x + 2 + 2y = 5y - 7 + |2x - 1|$

## PRACTICE SOLUTIONS

**P1.** As stated, it's easy to verify that the student's solution is incorrect: $2(-3) + 4 = -2$ and $4(-3) + 7 = -5$; clearly $-2 \neq -5$. The mistake was in the first step, which illustrates a common type of error in solving equations. The student tried to simplify the two variable terms by dividing them by 2. However, it's not valid to multiply or divide only one term on each side of an equation by a number; when multiplying or dividing, the operation must be applied to *every* term in the

Copyright © Mometrix Media. You have been licensed one copy of this document for personal use only. Any other reproduction or redistribution is strictly prohibited. All rights reserved. This content is provided for test preparation purposes only and does not imply an endorsement by Mometrix of any particular political, scientific, or religious point of view.

equation. So, dividing by 2 would yield not $x + 4 = 2x + 7$, but $x + 2 = 2x + \frac{7}{2}$. While this is now valid, that fraction is inconvenient to work with, so this may not be the best first step in solving the equation. Rather, it may have been better to first combine like terms. Subtracting $4x$ from both sides yields $-2x + 4 = 7$; subtracting 4 from both sides yields $-2x = 3$; *now* we can divide both sides by –2 to get $x = -\frac{3}{2}$.

**P2.** Our ultimate goal is to isolate the variable, $x$. To that end we first move all the terms containing $x$ to the left side of the equation, and all the constant terms to the right side. Note that when we move a term to the other side of the equation its sign changes. We are therefore now left with $2x - x - 3x = 4 + 7 - 1$.

Next, we combine the like terms on each side of the equation, adding and subtracting the terms as appropriate. This leaves us with $-2x = 10$.

At this point, we're almost done; all that remains is to divide both sides by $-2$ to leave the $x$ by itself. We now have our solution, $x = -5$. We can verify that this is a correct solution by substituting it back into the original equation.

**P3.** Generally, in equations that have a sum or difference of terms multiplied by another value or expression, the first step is to multiply those terms, distributing as necessary: $2(x + 5) = 2(x) + 2(5) = 2x + 10$, and $7(4 - x) = 7(4) - 7(x) = 28 - 7x$. So, the equation becomes $2x + 10 = 28 - 7x$. We can now add $7x$ to both sides to eliminate the variable from the right-hand side: $9x + 10 = 28$. Similarly, we can subtract 10 from both sides to move all the constants to the right: $9x = 18$. Finally, we can divide both sides by 9, yielding the final answer, $x = 2$.

**P4.** It's not hard to isolate the root: subtract one from both sides, yielding $-\sqrt{x} = 1$. Finally, multiply both sides by –1, yielding $\sqrt{x} = -1$. Squaring both sides of the equation yields $x = 1$. However, if we plug this back into the original equation, we get $1 - \sqrt{1} = 2$, which is false. Therefore $x = 1$ is a spurious solution, and the equation has no real solutions.

**P5.** This equation has two possibilities: $x + 1 = 2x + 5$, which simplifies to $x = -4$; or $x + 1 = -(2x + 5) = -2x - 5$, which simplifies to $x = -2$. However, if we try substituting both values back into the original equation, we see that only $x = -2$ yields a true statement. $x = -4$ is a spurious solution; $x = -2$ is the only valid solution to the equation.

**P6.** Start by isolating the term with the root. We can do that by moving the $-x$ and the 1 to the other side, yielding $2\sqrt{x + 5} = 3 + x - 1$, or $2\sqrt{x + 5} = x + 2$. Dividing both sides of the equation by 2 would give us a fractional term that could be messy to deal with, so we won't do that for now. Instead, we square both sides of the equation; note that on the left-hand side the 2 is outside the square root sign, so we have to square it. As a result, we get $4(x + 5) = (x + 2)^2$. Expanding both sides gives us $4x + 20 = x^2 + 4x + 4$. In this case, we see that we have $4x$ on both sides, so we can cancel the $4x$ (which is what allows us to solve this equation despite the different powers of $x$). We now have $20 = x^2 + 4$, or $x^2 = 16$. Since the variable is raised to an even power, we need to take the positive and negative roots, so $x = \pm 4$: that is, $x = 4$ or $x = -4$. Substituting both values into the original equation, we see that $x = 4$ satisfies the equation but $x = -4$ does not; hence $x = -4$ is a spurious solution, and the only solution to the equation is $x = 4$.

**P7.** The number of dollars that Ray earns is dependent on the number of hours he works, so earnings will be represented by the dependent variable $y$ and hours worked will be represented by

Copyright © Mometrix Media. You have been licensed one copy of this document for personal use only. Any other reproduction or redistribution is strictly prohibited. All rights reserved.
This content is provided for test preparation purposes only and does not imply an endorsement by Mometrix of any particular political, scientific, or religious point of view.

the independent variable $x$. He earns 10 dollars per hour worked, so his earnings can be calculated as $y = 10x$. To calculate the number of hours Ray must work in order to earn \$360, plug in 360 for $y$ and solve for $x$:

$$360 = 10x$$

$$x = \frac{360}{10} = 36$$

**P8.** To simplify this equation, we must isolate one of its variables on one side of the equation. In this case, the $x$ appears under an absolute value sign, which makes it difficult to isolate. The $y$, on the other hand, only appears without an exponent—the equation is linear in $y$. We will therefore choose to isolate the $y$. The first step, then, is to move all the terms with $y$ to the left side of the equation, which we can do by subtracting $5y$ from both sides:

$$3x + 2 - 3y = -7 + |2x - 1|$$

We can then move all the terms that do *not* include $y$ to the right side of the equation, by subtracting $3x$ and 2 from both sides of the equation:

$$-3y = -3x - 9 + |2x - 1|$$

Finally, we can isolate the $y$ by dividing both sides by –3.

$$y = x + 3 - \frac{1}{3}|2x - 1|$$

This is as far as we can simplify the equation; we cannot combine the terms inside and outside the absolute value sign. We can therefore consider the equation to be solved.

Copyright © Mometrix Media. You have been licensed one copy of this document for personal use only. Any other reproduction or redistribution is strictly prohibited. All rights reserved. This content is provided for test preparation purposes only and does not imply an endorsement by Mometrix of any particular political, scientific, or religious point of view.

# Basic Functions

## FUNCTION AND RELATION

When expressing functional relationships, the **variables** $x$ and $y$ are typically used. These values are often written as the **coordinates** $(x, y)$. The $x$-value is the independent variable and the $y$-value is the dependent variable. A **relation** is a set of data in which there is not a unique $y$-value for each $x$-value in the dataset. This means that there can be two of the same $x$-values assigned to different $y$-values. A relation is simply a relationship between the $x$- and $y$-values in each coordinate but does not apply to the relationship between the values of $x$ and $y$ in the data set. A **function** is a relation where one quantity depends on the other. For example, the amount of money that you make depends on the number of hours that you work. In a function, each $x$-value in the data set has one unique $y$-value because the $y$-value depends on the $x$-value.

## FUNCTIONS

A function has exactly one value of **output variable** (dependent variable) for each value of the **input variable** (independent variable). The set of all values for the input variable (here assumed to be $x$) is the domain of the function, and the set of all corresponding values of the output variable (here assumed to be $y$) is the range of the function. When looking at a graph of an equation, the easiest way to determine if the equation is a function or not is to conduct the vertical line test. If a vertical line drawn through any value of $x$ crosses the graph in more than one place, the equation is not a function.

## DETERMINING A FUNCTION

You can determine whether an equation is a **function** by substituting different values into the equation for $x$. You can display and organize these numbers in a data table. A **data table** contains the values for $x$ and $y$, which you can also list as coordinates. In order for a function to exist, the table cannot contain any repeating $x$-values that correspond with different $y$-values. If each $x$-coordinate has a unique $y$-coordinate, the table contains a function. However, there can be repeating $y$-values that correspond with different $x$-values. An example of this is when the function contains an exponent. Example: if $x^2 = y$, $2^2 = 4$, and $(-2)^2 = 4$.

> **Review Video: Definition of a Function**
> Visit mometrix.com/academy and enter code: 784611

### FINDING THE DOMAIN AND RANGE OF A FUNCTION

The **domain** of a function $f(x)$ is the set of all input values for which the function is defined. The **range** of a function $f(x)$ is the set of all possible output values of the function—that is, of every possible value of $f(x)$, for any value of $x$ in the function's domain. For a function expressed in a table, every input-output pair is given explicitly. To find the domain, we just list all the $x$-values and to find the range, we just list all the values of $f(x)$. Consider the following example:

| $x$ | −1 | 4 | 2 | 1 | 0 | 3 | 8 | 6 |
|---|---|---|---|---|---|---|---|---|
| $f(x)$ | 3 | 0 | 3 | −1 | −1 | 2 | 4 | 6 |

In this case, the domain would be $\{-1, 4, 2, 1, 0, 3, 8, 6\}$ or, putting them in ascending order, $\{-1, 0, 1, 2, 3, 4, 6, 8\}$. (Putting the values in ascending order isn't strictly necessary, but generally makes the set easier to read.) The range would be $\{3, 0, 3, -1, -1, 2, 4, 6\}$. Note that some of these values appear more than once. This is entirely permissible for a function; while each value of $x$ must be matched to a unique value of $f(x)$, the converse is not true. We don't need to list each value

Copyright © Mometrix Media. You have been licensed one copy of this document for personal use only. Any other reproduction or redistribution is strictly prohibited. All rights reserved. This content is provided for test preparation purposes only and does not imply an endorsement by Mometrix of any particular political, scientific, or religious point of view.

more than once, so eliminating duplicates, the range is $\{3, 0, -1, 2, 4, 6\}$, or, putting them in ascending order, $\{-1, 0, 2, 3, 4, 6\}$.

Note that by definition of a function, no input value can be matched to more than one output value. It is good to double-check to make sure that the data given follows this and is therefore actually a function.

**Review Video: Domain and Range**
Visit mometrix.com/academy and enter code: 778133

**Review Video: Domain and Range of Quadratic Functions**
Visit mometrix.com/academy and enter code: 331768

## WRITING A FUNCTION RULE USING A TABLE

If given a set of data, place the corresponding $x$- and $y$-values into a table and analyze the relationship between them. Consider what you can do to each $x$-value to obtain the corresponding $y$-value. Try adding or subtracting different numbers to and from $x$ and then try multiplying or dividing different numbers to and from $x$. If none of these **operations** give you the $y$-value, try combining the operations. Once you find a rule that works for one pair, make sure to try it with each additional set of ordered pairs in the table. If the same operation or combination of operations satisfies each set of coordinates, then the table contains a function. The rule is then used to write the equation of the function in "$y =$" form.

### DIRECT AND INVERSE VARIATIONS OF VARIABLES

Variables that vary directly are those that either both increase at the same rate or both decrease at the same rate. For example, in the functions $y = kx$ or $y = kx^n$, where $k$ and $n$ are positive, the value of $y$ increases as the value of $x$ increases and decreases as the value of $x$ decreases.

Variables that vary inversely are those where one increases while the other decreases. For example, in the functions $y = \frac{k}{x}$ or $y = \frac{k}{x^n}$ where $k$ and $n$ are positive, the value of $y$ increases as the value of $x$ decreases and decreases as the value of $x$ increases.

In both cases, $k$ is the constant of variation.

## PROPERTIES OF FUNCTIONS

There are many different ways to classify functions based on their structure or behavior. Important features of functions include:

- **End behavior**: the behavior of the function at extreme values ($f(x)$ as $x \to \pm\infty$)
- **$y$-intercept**: the value of the function at $f(0)$
- **Roots**: the values of $x$ where the function equals zero ($f(x) = 0$)
- **Extrema**: minimum or maximum values of the function or where the function changes direction ($f(x) \geq k$ or $f(x) \leq k$)

Copyright © Mometrix Media. You have been licensed one copy of this document for personal use only. Any other reproduction or redistribution is strictly prohibited. All rights reserved.
This content is provided for test preparation purposes only and does not imply an endorsement by Mometrix of any particular political, scientific, or religious point of view.

## CLASSIFICATION OF FUNCTIONS

An **invertible function** is defined as a function, $f(x)$, for which there is another function, $f^{-1}(x)$, such that $f^{-1}(f(x)) = x$. For example, if $f(x) = 3x - 2$ the inverse function, $f^{-1}(x)$, can be found:

$$x = 3(f^{-1}(x)) - 2$$
$$\frac{x+2}{3} = f^{-1}(x)$$

$$f^{-1}(f(x)) = \frac{3x - 2 + 2}{3}$$
$$= \frac{3x}{3}$$
$$= x$$

Note that $f^{-1}(x)$ is a valid function over all values of $x$.

In a **one-to-one function**, each value of $x$ has exactly one value for $y$ on the coordinate plane (this is the definition of a function) and each value of $y$ has exactly one value for $x$. While the vertical line test will determine if a graph is that of a function, the horizontal line test will determine if a function is a one-to-one function. If a horizontal line drawn at any value of $y$ intersects the graph in more than one place, the graph is not that of a one-to-one function. Do not make the mistake of using the horizontal line test exclusively in determining if a graph is that of a one-to-one function. A one-to-one function must pass both the vertical line test and the horizontal line test. As such, one-to-one functions are invertible functions.

A **many-to-one function** is a function whereby the relation is a function, but the inverse of the function is not a function. In other words, each element in the domain is mapped to one and only one element in the range. However, one or more elements in the range may be mapped to the same element in the domain. A graph of a many-to-one function would pass the vertical line test, but not the horizontal line test. This is why many-to-one functions are not invertible.

A **monotone function** is a function whose graph either constantly increases or constantly decreases. Examples include the functions $f(x) = x$, $f(x) = -x$, or $f(x) = x^3$.

An **even function** has a graph that is symmetric with respect to the y-axis and satisfies the equation $f(x) = f(-x)$. Examples include the functions $f(x) = x^2$ and $f(x) = ax^n$, where $a$ is any real number and $n$ is a positive even integer.

An **odd function** has a graph that is symmetric with respect to the origin and satisfies the equation $f(x) = -f(-x)$. Examples include the functions $f(x) = x^3$ and $f(x) = ax^n$, where $a$ is any real number and $n$ is a positive odd integer.

> **Review Video: <u>Even and Odd Functions</u>**
> Visit mometrix.com/academy and enter code: 278985

**Constant functions** are given by the equation $f(x) = b$, where $b$ is a real number. There is no independent variable present in the equation, so the function has a constant value for all $x$. The graph of a constant function is a horizontal line of slope 0 that is positioned $b$ units from the $x$-axis. If $b$ is positive, the line is above the $x$-axis; if $b$ is negative, the line is below the $x$-axis.

**Identity functions** are identified by the equation $f(x) = x$, where every value of the function is equal to its corresponding value of $x$. The only zero is the point $(0,0)$. The graph is a line with a slope of 1.

Copyright © Mometrix Media. You have been licensed one copy of this document for personal use only. Any other reproduction or redistribution is strictly prohibited. All rights reserved. This content is provided for test preparation purposes only and does not imply an endorsement by Mometrix of any particular political, scientific, or religious point of view.

In **linear functions**, the value of the function changes in direct proportion to $x$. The rate of change, represented by the slope on its graph, is constant throughout. The standard form of a linear equation is $ax + cy = d$, where $a, c,$ and $d$ are real numbers. As a function, this equation is commonly in the form $y = mx + b$ or $f(x) = mx + b$ where $m = -\frac{a}{c}$ and $b = \frac{d}{c}$. This is known as the slope-intercept form, because the coefficients give the slope of the graphed function $(m)$ and its $y$-intercept $(b)$. Solve the equation $mx + b = 0$ for $x$ to get $x = -\frac{b}{m}$, which is the only zero of the function. The domain and range are both the set of all real numbers.

> **Review Video: Linear Functions**
> Visit mometrix.com/academy and enter code: 699478

**Algebraic functions** are those that exclusively use polynomials and roots. These would include polynomial functions, rational functions, square root functions, and all combinations of these functions, such as polynomials as the radicand. These combinations may be joined by addition, subtraction, multiplication, or division, but may not include variables as exponents.

## ABSOLUTE VALUE FUNCTIONS

An **absolute value function** is in the format $f(x) = |ax + b|$. Like other functions, the domain is the set of all real numbers. However, because absolute value indicates positive numbers, the range is limited to positive real numbers. To find the zero of an absolute value function, set the portion inside the absolute value sign equal to zero and solve for $x$. An absolute value function is also known as a piecewise function because it must be solved in pieces—one for if the value inside the absolute value sign is positive, and one for if the value is negative. The function can be expressed as

$$f(x) = \begin{cases} ax + b & \text{if } ax + b \geq 0 \\ -(ax + b) & \text{if } ax + b < 0 \end{cases}$$

This will allow for an accurate statement of the range. The graph of an example absolute value function, $f(x) = |2x - 1|$, is below:

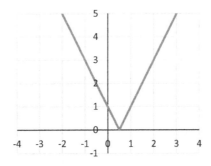

## PIECEWISE FUNCTIONS

A **piecewise function** is a function that has different definitions on two or more different intervals. The following, for instance, is one example of a piecewise-defined function:

$$f(x) = \begin{cases} x^2, & x < 0 \\ x, & 0 \leq x \leq 2 \\ (x - 2)^2, & x > 2 \end{cases}$$

Copyright © Mometrix Media. You have been licensed one copy of this document for personal use only. Any other reproduction or redistribution is strictly prohibited. All rights reserved. This content is provided for test preparation purposes only and does not imply an endorsement by Mometrix of any particular political, scientific, or religious point of view.

To graph this function, you would simply graph each part separately in the appropriate domain. The final graph would look like this:

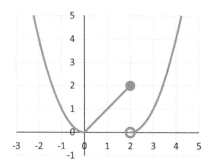

Note the filled and hollow dots at the discontinuity at $x = 2$. This is important to show which side of the graph that point corresponds to. Because $f(x) = x$ on the closed interval $0 \leq x \leq 2$, $f(2) = 2$. The point $(2, 2)$ is therefore marked with a filled circle, and the point $(2,0)$, which is the endpoint of the rightmost $(x - 2)^2$ part of the graph but *not actually part of the function*, is marked with a hollow dot to indicate this.

> **Review Video: Piecewise Functions**
> Visit mometrix.com/academy and enter code: 707921

## QUADRATIC FUNCTIONS

A **quadratic function** is a function in the form $y = ax^2 + bx + c$, where $a$ does not equal 0. While a linear function forms a line, a quadratic function forms a **parabola**, which is a u-shaped figure that either opens upward or downward. A parabola that opens upward is said to be a **positive quadratic function,** and a parabola that opens downward is said to be a **negative quadratic function**. The shape of a parabola can differ, depending on the values of $a$, $b$, and $c$. All parabolas contain a **vertex**, which is the highest possible point, the **maximum**, or the lowest possible point, the **minimum**. This is the point where the graph begins moving in the opposite direction. A quadratic function can have zero, one, or two solutions, and therefore zero, one, or two $x$-intercepts. Recall that the $x$-intercepts are referred to as the zeros, or roots, of a function. A quadratic function will have only one $y$-intercept. Understanding the basic components of a quadratic function can give you an idea of the shape of its graph.

Example graph of a positive quadratic function, $x^2 + 2x - 3$:

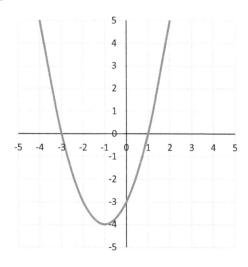

Copyright © Mometrix Media. You have been licensed one copy of this document for personal use only. Any other reproduction or redistribution is strictly prohibited. All rights reserved. This content is provided for test preparation purposes only and does not imply an endorsement by Mometrix of any particular political, scientific, or religious point of view.

## POLYNOMIAL FUNCTIONS

A **polynomial function** is a function with multiple terms and multiple powers of $x$, such as:

$$f(x) = a_n x^n + a_{n-1} x^{n-1} + a_{n-2} x^{n-2} + \cdots + a_1 x + a_0$$

where $n$ is a non-negative integer that is the highest exponent in the polynomial and $a_n \neq 0$. The domain of a polynomial function is the set of all real numbers. If the greatest exponent in the polynomial is even, the polynomial is said to be of even degree and the range is the set of real numbers that satisfy the function. If the greatest exponent in the polynomial is odd, the polynomial is said to be odd and the range, like the domain, is the set of all real numbers.

## RATIONAL FUNCTIONS

A **rational function** is a function that can be constructed as a ratio of two polynomial expressions: $f(x) = \frac{p(x)}{q(x)}$, where $p(x)$ and $q(x)$ are both polynomial expressions and $q(x) \neq 0$. The domain is the set of all real numbers, except any values for which $q(x) = 0$. The range is the set of real numbers that satisfies the function when the domain is applied. When you graph a rational function, you will have vertical asymptotes wherever $q(x) = 0$. If the polynomial in the numerator is of lesser degree than the polynomial in the denominator, the $x$-axis will also be a horizontal asymptote. If the numerator and denominator have equal degrees, there will be a horizontal asymptote not on the $x$-axis. If the degree of the numerator is exactly one greater than the degree of the denominator, the graph will have an oblique, or diagonal, asymptote. The asymptote will be along the line $y = \frac{p_n}{q_{n-1}} x + \frac{p_{n-1}}{q_{n-1}}$, where $p_n$ and $q_{n-1}$ are the coefficients of the highest degree terms in their respective polynomials.

## SQUARE ROOT FUNCTIONS

A **square root function** is a function that contains a radical and is in the format $f(x) = \sqrt{ax + b}$. The domain is the set of all real numbers that yields a positive radicand or a radicand equal to zero. Because square root values are assumed to be positive unless otherwise identified, the range is all real numbers from zero to infinity. To find the zero of a square root function, set the radicand equal to zero and solve for $x$. The graph of a square root function is always to the right of the zero and always above the $x$-axis.

Example graph of a square root function, $f(x) = \sqrt{2x + 1}$:

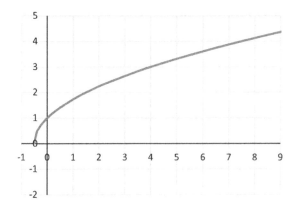

Copyright © Mometrix Media. You have been licensed one copy of this document for personal use only. Any other reproduction or redistribution is strictly prohibited. All rights reserved. This content is provided for test preparation purposes only and does not imply an endorsement by Mometrix of any particular political, scientific, or religious point of view.

## PRACTICE

**P1.** Martin needs a 20% medicine solution. The pharmacy has a 5% solution and a 30% solution. He needs 50 mL of the solution. If the pharmacist must mix the two solutions, how many milliliters of 5% solution and 30% solution should be used?

**P2.** Describe two different strategies for solving the following problem:

Kevin can mow the yard in 4 hours. Mandy can mow the same yard in 5 hours. If they work together, how long will it take them to mow the yard?

**P3.** A car, traveling at 65 miles per hour, leaves Flagstaff and heads east on I-40. Another car, traveling at 75 miles per hour, leaves Flagstaff 2 hours later, from the same starting point and also heads east on I-40. Determine how many hours it will take the second car to catch the first car by:

**(a)** Using a table.

**(b)** Using algebra.

## PRACTICE SOLUTIONS

**P1.** To solve this problem, a table may be created to represent the variables, percentages, and total amount of solution. Such a table is shown below:

|  | mL solution | % medicine | Total mL medicine |
|---|---|---|---|
| **5% solution** | $x$ | 0.05 | $0.05x$ |
| **30% solution** | $y$ | 0.30 | $0.30y$ |
| **Mixture** | $x + y = 50$ | 0.20 | $(0.20)(50) = 10$ |

The variable $x$ may be rewritten as $50 - y$, so the equation $0.05(50 - y) + 0.30y = 10$ may be written and solved for $y$. Doing so gives $y = 30$. So, 30 mL of 30% solution are needed. Evaluating the expression, $50 - y$ for an $x$-value of 20, shows that 20 mL of 5% solution are needed.

**P2.** Two possible strategies both involve the use of rational equations to solve. The first strategy involves representing the fractional part of the yard mowed by each person in one hour and setting this sum equal to the ratio of 1 to the total time needed. The appropriate equation is $\frac{1}{4} + \frac{1}{5} = \frac{1}{t}$, which simplifies as $\frac{9}{20} = \frac{1}{t}$, and finally as $t = \frac{20}{9}$. So, the time it will take them to mow the yard, when working together, is a little more than 2.2 hours.

A second strategy involves representing the time needed for each person as two fractions and setting the sum equal to 1 (representing 1 yard). The appropriate equation is $\frac{t}{4} + \frac{t}{5} = 1$, which simplifies as $\frac{9t}{20} = 1$, and finally as $t = \frac{20}{9}$. This strategy also shows the total time to be a little more than 2.2 hours.

Copyright © Mometrix Media. You have been licensed one copy of this document for personal use only. Any other reproduction or redistribution is strictly prohibited. All rights reserved. This content is provided for test preparation purposes only and does not imply an endorsement by Mometrix of any particular political, scientific, or religious point of view.

**P3. (a)** One strategy might involve creating a table of values for the number of hours and distances for each car. The table may be examined to find the same distance traveled and the corresponding number of hours taken. Such a table is shown below:

| Car A | | Car B | |
|---|---|---|---|
| *x* (hours) | *y* (distance) | *x* (hours) | *y* (distance) |
| 0 | 0 | 0 | |
| 1 | 65 | 1 | |
| 2 | 130 | 2 | 0 |
| 3 | 195 | 3 | 75 |
| 4 | 260 | 4 | 150 |
| 5 | 325 | 5 | 225 |
| 6 | 390 | 6 | 300 |
| 7 | 455 | 7 | 375 |
| 8 | 520 | 8 | 450 |
| 9 | 585 | 9 | 525 |
| 10 | 650 | 10 | 600 |
| 11 | 715 | 11 | 675 |
| 12 | 780 | 12 | 750 |
| 13 | 845 | 13 | 825 |
| 14 | 910 | 14 | 900 |
| 15 | 975 | 15 | 975 |

The table shows that after 15 hours, the distance traveled is the same. Thus, the second car catches up with the first car after a distance of 975 miles and 15 hours.

**(b)** A second strategy might involve setting up and solving an algebraic equation. This situation may be modeled as $65x = 75(x - 2)$. This equation sets the distances traveled by each car equal to one another. Solving for $x$ gives $x = 15$. Thus, once again, the second car will catch up with the first car after 15 hours.

Copyright © Mometrix Media. You have been licensed one copy of this document for personal use only. Any other reproduction or redistribution is strictly prohibited. All rights reserved.
This content is provided for test preparation purposes only and does not imply an endorsement by Mometrix of any particular political, scientific, or religious point of view.

# Measurement Principles

## PRECISION, ACCURACY, AND ERROR

**Precision**: How reliable and repeatable a measurement is. The more consistent the data is with repeated testing, the more precise it is. For example, hitting a target consistently in the same spot, which may or may not be the center of the target, is precision.

**Accuracy**: How close the data is to the correct data. For example, hitting a target consistently in the center area of the target, whether or not the hits are all in the same spot, is accuracy.

Note: it is possible for data to be precise without being accurate. If a scale is off balance, the data will be precise, but will not be accurate. For data to have precision and accuracy, it must be repeatable and correct.

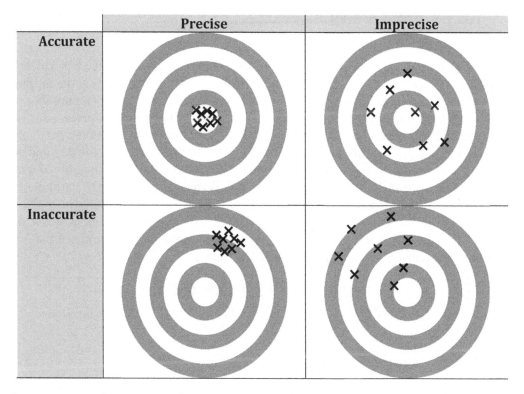

**Approximate error**: The amount of error in a physical measurement. Approximate error is often reported as the measurement, followed by the $\pm$ symbol and the amount of the approximate error.

**Maximum possible error**: Half the magnitude of the smallest unit used in the measurement. For example, if the unit of measurement is 1 centimeter, the maximum possible error is $\frac{1}{2}$ cm, written as $\pm 0.5$ cm following the measurement. It is important to apply significant figures in reporting maximum possible error. Do not make the answer appear more accurate than the least accurate of your measurements.

---

**Review Video: Precision, Accuracy, and Error**
Visit mometrix.com/academy and enter code: 520377

---

Copyright © Mometrix Media. You have been licensed one copy of this document for personal use only. Any other reproduction or redistribution is strictly prohibited. All rights reserved.
This content is provided for test preparation purposes only and does not imply an endorsement by Mometrix of any particular political, scientific, or religious point of view.

## ROUNDING AND ESTIMATION

**Rounding** is reducing the digits in a number while still trying to keep the value similar. The result will be less accurate but in a simpler form and easier to use. Whole numbers can be rounded to the nearest ten, hundred, or thousand.

When you are asked to estimate the solution to a problem, you will need to provide only an approximate figure or **estimation** for your answer. In this situation, you will need to round each number in the calculation to the level indicated (nearest hundred, nearest thousand, etc.) or to a level that makes sense for the numbers involved. When estimating a sum **all numbers must be rounded to the same level**. You cannot round one number to the nearest thousand while rounding another to the nearest hundred.

> **Review Video: Rounding and Estimation**
> Visit mometrix.com/academy and enter code: 126243

## SCIENTIFIC NOTATION

Scientific notation is a way of writing large numbers in a shorter form. The form $a \times 10^n$ is used in scientific notation, where $a$ is greater than or equal to 1 but less than 10, and $n$ is the number of places the decimal must move to get from the original number to $a$. Example: The number 230,400,000 is cumbersome to write. To write the value in scientific notation, place a decimal point between the first and second numbers, and include all digits through the last non-zero digit ($a = 2.304$). To find the appropriate power of 10, count the number of places the decimal point had to move ($n = 8$). The number is positive if the decimal moved to the left, and negative if it moved to the right. We can then write 230,400,000 as $2.304 \times 10^8$. If we look instead at the number 0.00002304, we have the same value for $a$, but this time the decimal moved 5 places to the right ($n = -5$). Thus, 0.00002304 can be written as $2.304 \times 10^{-5}$. Using this notation makes it simple to compare very large or very small numbers. By comparing exponents, it is easy to see that $3.28 \times 10^4$ is smaller than $1.51 \times 10^5$, because 4 is less than 5.

> **Review Video: Scientific Notation**
> Visit mometrix.com/academy and enter code: 976454

## PRACTICE

**P1.** Round each number to the indicated degree:

  **(a)** Round to the nearest ten: 11; 47; 118

  **(b)** Round to the nearest hundred: 78; 980; 248

  **(c)** Round each number to the nearest thousand: 302; 1,274; 3,756

**P2.** Estimate the solution to 345,932 + 96,369 by rounding each number to the nearest ten thousand.

**P3.** A runner's heart beats 422 times over the course of six minutes. About how many times did the runner's heart beat during each minute?

Copyright © Mometrix Media. You have been licensed one copy of this document for personal use only. Any other reproduction or redistribution is strictly prohibited. All rights reserved.
This content is provided for test preparation purposes only and does not imply an endorsement by Mometrix of any particular political, scientific, or religious point of view.

## PRACTICE SOLUTIONS

**P1. (a)** When rounding to the nearest ten, anything ending in 5 or greater rounds up. So, 11 rounds to 10, 47 rounds to 50, and 118 rounds to 120.

**(b)** When rounding to the nearest hundred, anything ending in 50 or greater rounds up. So, 78 rounds to 100, 980 rounds to 1000, and 248 rounds to 200.

**(c)** When rounding to the nearest thousand, anything ending in 500 or greater rounds up. So, 302 rounds to 0, 1,274 rounds to 1,000, and 3,756 rounds to 4,000.

**P2.** Start by rounding each number to the nearest ten thousand: 345,932 becomes 350,000, and 96,369 becomes 100,000. Then, add the rounded numbers: $350,000 + 100,000 = 450,000$. So, the answer is approximately 450,000. The exact answer would be $345,932 + 96,369 = 442,301$. So, the estimate of 450,000 is a similar value to the exact answer.

**P3.** "About how many" indicates that you need to estimate the solution. In this case, look at the numbers you are given. 422 can be rounded down to 420, which is easily divisible by 6. A good estimate is $420 \div 6 = 70$ beats per minute. More accurately, the patient's heart rate was just over 70 beats per minute since his heart actually beat a little more than 420 times in six minutes.

Copyright © Mometrix Media. You have been licensed one copy of this document for personal use only. Any other reproduction or redistribution is strictly prohibited. All rights reserved.
This content is provided for test preparation purposes only and does not imply an endorsement by Mometrix of any particular political, scientific, or religious point of view.

# Units of Measurement

## METRIC MEASUREMENT PREFIXES

| Giga- | One billion | 1 *giga*watt is one billion watts |
|-------|-------------|-----------------------------------|
| Mega- | One million | 1 *mega*hertz is one million hertz |
| Kilo- | One thousand | 1 *kilo*gram is one thousand grams |
| Deci- | One-tenth | 1 *deci*meter is one-tenth of a meter |
| Centi- | One-hundredth | 1 *centi*meter is one-hundredth of a meter |
| Milli- | One-thousandth | 1 *milli*liter is one-thousandth of a liter |
| Micro- | One-millionth | 1 *micro*gram is one-millionth of a gram |

> **Review Video: <u>Metric System Conversion - How the Metric System Works</u>**
> Visit mometrix.com/academy and enter code: 163709

## MEASUREMENT CONVERSION

When converting between units, the goal is to maintain the same meaning but change the way it is displayed. In order to go from a larger unit to a smaller unit, multiply the number of the known amount by the equivalent amount. When going from a smaller unit to a larger unit, divide the number of the known amount by the equivalent amount.

For complicated conversions, it may be helpful to set up conversion fractions. In these fractions, one fraction is the **conversion factor**. The other fraction has the unknown amount in the numerator. So, the known value is placed in the denominator. Sometimes, the second fraction has the known value from the problem in the numerator and the unknown in the denominator. Multiply the two fractions to get the converted measurement. Note that since the numerator and the denominator of the factor are equivalent, the value of the fraction is 1. That is why we can say that the result in the new units is equal to the result in the old units even though they have different numbers.

It can often be necessary to chain known conversion factors together. As an example, consider converting 512 square inches to square meters. We know that there are 2.54 centimeters in an inch and 100 centimeters in a meter, and we know we will need to square each of these factors to achieve the conversion we are looking for.

$$\frac{512 \text{ in}^2}{1} \times \left(\frac{2.54 \text{ cm}}{1 \text{ in}}\right)^2 \times \left(\frac{1 \text{ m}}{100 \text{ cm}}\right)^2 = \frac{512 \text{ in}^2}{1} \times \left(\frac{6.4516 \text{ cm}^2}{1 \text{ in}^2}\right) \times \left(\frac{1 \text{ m}^2}{10{,}000 \text{ cm}^2}\right) = 0.330 \text{ m}^2$$

> **Review Video: <u>Measurement Conversions</u>**
> Visit mometrix.com/academy and enter code: 316703

Copyright © Mometrix Media. You have been licensed one copy of this document for personal use only. Any other reproduction or redistribution is strictly prohibited. All rights reserved. This content is provided for test preparation purposes only and does not imply an endorsement by Mometrix of any particular political, scientific, or religious point of view.

## COMMON UNITS AND EQUIVALENTS

### METRIC EQUIVALENTS

| | |
|---|---|
| 1000 μg (microgram) | 1 mg |
| 1000 mg (milligram) | 1 g |
| 1000 g (gram) | 1 kg |
| 1000 kg (kilogram) | 1 metric ton |
| 1000 mL (milliliter) | 1 L |
| 1000 μm (micrometer) | 1 mm |
| 1000 mm (millimeter) | 1 m |
| 100 cm (centimeter) | 1 m |
| 1000 m (meter) | 1 km |

> **Review Video: Metric System Conversions**
> Visit mometrix.com/academy and enter code: 163709

### DISTANCE AND AREA MEASUREMENT

| Unit | Abbreviation | US equivalent | Metric equivalent |
|---|---|---|---|
| Inch | in | 1 inch | 2.54 centimeters |
| Foot | ft | 12 inches | 0.305 meters |
| Yard | yd | 3 feet | 0.914 meters |
| Mile | mi | 5280 feet | 1.609 kilometers |
| Acre | ac | 4840 square yards | 0.405 hectares |
| Square Mile | sq. mi. or mi.$^2$ | 640 acres | 2.590 square kilometers |

### CAPACITY MEASUREMENTS

| Unit | Abbreviation | US equivalent | Metric equivalent |
|---|---|---|---|
| Fluid Ounce | fl oz | 8 fluid drams | 29.573 milliliters |
| Cup | c | 8 fluid ounces | 0.237 liter |
| Pint | pt. | 16 fluid ounces | 0.473 liter |
| Quart | qt. | 2 pints | 0.946 liter |
| Gallon | gal. | 4 quarts | 3.785 liters |
| Teaspoon | t or tsp. | 1 fluid dram | 5 milliliters |
| Tablespoon | T or tbsp. | 4 fluid drams | 15 or 16 milliliters |
| Cubic Centimeter | cc or cm$^3$ | 0.271 drams | 1 milliliter |

### WEIGHT MEASUREMENTS

| Unit | Abbreviation | US equivalent | Metric equivalent |
|---|---|---|---|
| Ounce | oz | 16 drams | 28.35 grams |
| Pound | lb | 16 ounces | 453.6 grams |
| Ton | tn. | 2,000 pounds | 907.2 kilograms |

## VOLUME AND WEIGHT MEASUREMENT CLARIFICATIONS

Always be careful when using ounces and fluid ounces. They are not equivalent.

| | |
|---|---|
| 1 pint = 16 fluid ounces | 1 fluid ounce ≠ 1 ounce |
| 1 pound = 16 ounces | 1 pint ≠ 1 pound |

Copyright © Mometrix Media. You have been licensed one copy of this document for personal use only. Any other reproduction or redistribution is strictly prohibited. All rights reserved.
This content is provided for test preparation purposes only and does not imply an endorsement by Mometrix of any particular political, scientific, or religious point of view.

Having one pint of something does not mean you have one pound of it. In the same way, just because something weighs one pound does not mean that its volume is one pint.

In the United States, the word "ton" by itself refers to a short ton or a net ton. Do not confuse this with a long ton (also called a gross ton) or a metric ton (also spelled *tonne*), which have different measurement equivalents.

$$1 \text{ US ton} = 2000 \text{ pounds} \qquad \neq \qquad 1 \text{ metric ton} = 1000 \text{ kilograms}$$

## PRACTICE

**P1.** Perform the following conversions:

   **(a)** 1.4 meters to centimeters

   **(b)** 218 centimeters to meters

   **(c)** 42 inches to feet

   **(d)** 15 kilograms to pounds

   **(e)** 80 ounces to pounds

   **(f)** 2 miles to kilometers

   **(g)** 5 feet to centimeters

   **(h)** 15.14 liters to gallons

   **(i)** 8 quarts to liters

   **(j)** 13.2 pounds to grams

## PRACTICE SOLUTIONS

**P1. (a)** $\frac{100 \text{ cm}}{1 \text{ m}} = \frac{x \text{ cm}}{1.4 \text{ m}}$ Cross multiply to get $x = 140$

   **(b)** $\frac{100 \text{ cm}}{1 \text{ m}} = \frac{218 \text{ cm}}{x \text{ m}}$ Cross multiply to get $100x = 218$, or $x = 2.18$

   **(c)** $\frac{12 \text{ in}}{1 \text{ ft}} = \frac{42 \text{ in}}{x \text{ ft}}$ Cross multiply to get $12x = 42$, or $x = 3.5$

   **(d)** 15 kilograms $\times \frac{2.2 \text{ pounds}}{1 \text{ kilogram}} = 33$ pounds

   **(e)** 80 ounces $\times \frac{1 \text{ pound}}{16 \text{ ounces}} = 5$ pounds

   **(f)** 2 miles $\times \frac{1.609 \text{ kilometers}}{1 \text{ mile}} = 3.218$ kilometers

   **(g)** 5 feet $\times \frac{12 \text{ inches}}{1 \text{ foot}} \times \frac{2.54 \text{ centimeters}}{1 \text{ inch}} = 152.4$ centimeters

   **(h)** 15.14 liters $\times \frac{1 \text{ gallon}}{3.785 \text{ liters}} = 4$ gallons

Copyright © Mometrix Media. You have been licensed one copy of this document for personal use only. Any other reproduction or redistribution is strictly prohibited. All rights reserved. This content is provided for test preparation purposes only and does not imply an endorsement by Mometrix of any particular political, scientific, or religious point of view.

**(i)** 8 quarts $\times \dfrac{1 \text{ gallon}}{4 \text{ quarts}} \times \dfrac{3.785 \text{ liters}}{1 \text{ gallon}} = 7.57$ liters

**(j)** 13.2 pounds $\times \dfrac{1 \text{ kilogram}}{2.2 \text{ pounds}} \times \dfrac{1,000 \text{ grams}}{1 \text{ kilogram}} = 6,000$ grams

Copyright © Mometrix Media. You have been licensed one copy of this document for personal use only. Any other reproduction or redistribution is strictly prohibited. All rights reserved.
This content is provided for test preparation purposes only and does not imply an endorsement by Mometrix of any particular political, scientific, or religious point of view.

# Lines and Planes

## POINTS AND LINES

A **point** is a fixed location in space, has no size or dimensions, and is commonly represented by a dot. A **line** is a set of points that extends infinitely in two opposite directions. It has length, but no width or depth. A line can be defined by any two distinct points that it contains. A **line segment** is a portion of a line that has definite endpoints. A **ray** is a portion of a line that extends from a single point on that line in one direction along the line. It has a definite beginning, but no ending.

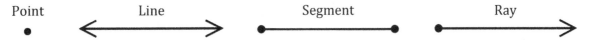

## INTERACTIONS BETWEEN LINES

**Intersecting lines** are lines that have exactly one point in common. **Concurrent lines** are multiple lines that intersect at a single point. **Perpendicular lines** are lines that intersect at right angles. They are represented by the symbol ⊥. The shortest distance from a line to a point not on the line is a perpendicular segment from the point to the line. **Parallel lines** are lines in the same plane that have no points in common and never meet. It is possible for lines to be in different planes, have no points in common, and never meet, but they are not parallel because they are in different planes.

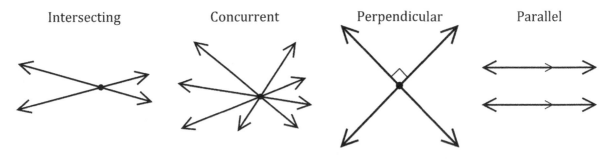

> **Review Video: Parallel and Perpendicular Lines**
> Visit mometrix.com/academy and enter code: 815923

A **transversal** is a line that intersects at least two other lines, which may or may not be parallel to one another. A transversal that intersects parallel lines is a common occurrence in geometry. A **bisector** is a line or line segment that divides another line segment into two equal lengths. A **perpendicular bisector** of a line segment is composed of points that are equidistant from the endpoints of the segment it is dividing.

The **projection of a point on a line** is the point at which a perpendicular line drawn from the given point to the given line intersects the line. This is also the shortest distance from the given point to

Copyright © Mometrix Media. You have been licensed one copy of this document for personal use only. Any other reproduction or redistribution is strictly prohibited. All rights reserved.
This content is provided for test preparation purposes only and does not imply an endorsement by Mometrix of any particular political, scientific, or religious point of view.

the line. The **projection of a segment on a line** is a segment whose endpoints are the points formed when perpendicular lines are drawn from the endpoints of the given segment to the given line. This is similar to the length a diagonal line appears to be when viewed from above.

Projection of a point on a line

Projection of a segment on a line

## PLANES

A **plane** is a two-dimensional flat surface defined by three non-collinear points. A plane extends an infinite distance in all directions in those two dimensions. It contains an infinite number of points, parallel lines and segments, intersecting lines and segments, as well as parallel or intersecting rays. A plane will never contain a three-dimensional figure or skew lines, which are lines that don't intersect and are not parallel. Two given planes are either parallel or they intersect at a line. A plane may intersect a circular conic surface to form **conic sections**, such as a parabola, hyperbola, circle or ellipse.

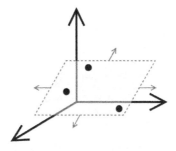

| Review Video: **Lines and Planes** |
| :---: |
| Visit mometrix.com/academy and enter code: 554267 |

Copyright © Mometrix Media. You have been licensed one copy of this document for personal use only. Any other reproduction or redistribution is strictly prohibited. All rights reserved.
This content is provided for test preparation purposes only and does not imply an endorsement by Mometrix of any particular political, scientific, or religious point of view.

# Angles

## ANGLES AND VERTICES

An **angle** is formed when two lines or line segments meet at a common point. It may be a common starting point for a pair of segments or rays, or it may be the intersection of lines. Angles are represented by the symbol ∠.

The **vertex** is the point at which two segments or rays meet to form an angle. If the angle is formed by intersecting rays, lines, and/or line segments, the vertex is the point at which four angles are formed. The pairs of angles opposite one another are called vertical angles, and their measures are equal.

- An **acute** angle is an angle with a degree measure less than 90°.
- A **right** angle is an angle with a degree measure of exactly 90°.
- An **obtuse** angle is an angle with a degree measure greater than 90° but less than 180°.
- A **straight angle** is an angle with a degree measure of exactly 180°. This is also a semicircle.
- A **reflex angle** is an angle with a degree measure greater than 180° but less than 360°.

A **full angle** is an angle with a degree measure of exactly 360°. This is also a circle.

> **Review Video: <u>Angles</u>**
> Visit mometrix.com/academy and enter code: 264624

## RELATIONSHIPS BETWEEN ANGLES

Two angles whose sum is exactly 90° are said to be **complementary**. The two angles may or may not be adjacent. In a right triangle, the two acute angles are complementary.

Two angles whose sum is exactly 180° are said to be **supplementary**. The two angles may or may not be adjacent. Two intersecting lines always form two pairs of supplementary angles. Adjacent supplementary angles will always form a straight line.

Two angles that have the same vertex and share a side are said to be **adjacent**. Vertical angles are not adjacent because they share a vertex but no common side.

**Adjacent**
**Share vertex and side**

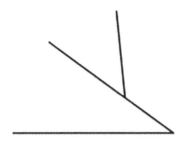

**Not adjacent**
**Share part of a side, but not vertex**

When two parallel lines are cut by a transversal, the angles that are between the two parallel lines are **interior angles**. In the diagram below, angles 3, 4, 5, and 6 are interior angles.

When two parallel lines are cut by a transversal, the angles that are outside the parallel lines are **exterior angles**. In the diagram below, angles 1, 2, 7, and 8 are exterior angles.

Copyright © Mometrix Media. You have been licensed one copy of this document for personal use only. Any other reproduction or redistribution is strictly prohibited. All rights reserved.
This content is provided for test preparation purposes only and does not imply an endorsement by Mometrix of any particular political, scientific, or religious point of view.

When two parallel lines are cut by a transversal, the angles that are in the same position relative to the transversal and a parallel line are **corresponding angles**. The diagram below has four pairs of corresponding angles: angles 1 and 5, angles 2 and 6, angles 3 and 7, and angles 4 and 8. Corresponding angles formed by parallel lines are congruent.

When two parallel lines are cut by a transversal, the two interior angles that are on opposite sides of the transversal are called **alternate interior angles**. In the diagram below, there are two pairs of alternate interior angles: angles 3 and 6, and angles 4 and 5. Alternate interior angles formed by parallel lines are congruent.

When two parallel lines are cut by a transversal, the two exterior angles that are on opposite sides of the transversal are called **alternate exterior angles**.

In the diagram below, there are two pairs of alternate exterior angles: angles 1 and 8, and angles 2 and 7. Alternate exterior angles formed by parallel lines are congruent.

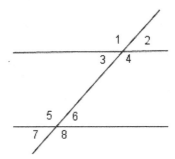

When two lines intersect, four angles are formed. The non-adjacent angles at this vertex are called vertical angles. Vertical angles are congruent. In the diagram, $\angle ABD \cong \angle CBE$ and $\angle ABC \cong \angle DBE$.

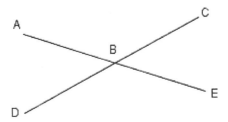

Copyright © Mometrix Media. You have been licensed one copy of this document for personal use only. Any other reproduction or redistribution is strictly prohibited. All rights reserved.
This content is provided for test preparation purposes only and does not imply an endorsement by Mometrix of any particular political, scientific, or religious point of view.

## PRACTICE

**P1.** Find the measure of angles $\angle a$, $\angle b$, and $\angle c$ based on the figure with two parallel lines, two perpendicular lines and one transversal:

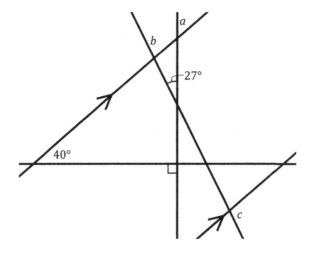

## PRACTICE SOLUTIONS

**P1. (a)** The vertical angle paired with $\angle a$ is part of a right triangle with the 40° angle. Thus the measure can be found:

$$90° = 40° + a$$
$$a = 50°$$

**(b)** The triangle formed by the supplementary angle to $\angle b$ is part of a triangle with the vertical angle paired with $\angle a$ and the given angle of 27°. Since $\angle a = 50°$:

$$180° = (180° - b) + 50° + 27°$$
$$103° = 180° - b$$
$$-77° = -b$$
$$77° = b$$

**(c)** As they are part of a transversal crossing parallel lines, angles $\angle b$ and $\angle c$ are supplementary. Thus $\angle c = 103°$.

Copyright © Mometrix Media. You have been licensed one copy of this document for personal use only. Any other reproduction or redistribution is strictly prohibited. All rights reserved.
This content is provided for test preparation purposes only and does not imply an endorsement by Mometrix of any particular political, scientific, or religious point of view.

# Transformations

## ROTATION

A **rotation** is a transformation that turns a figure around a point called the **center of rotation**, which can lie anywhere in the plane. If a line is drawn from a point on a figure to the center of rotation, and another line is drawn from the center to the rotated image of that point, the angle between the two lines is the **angle of rotation**. The vertex of the angle of rotation is the center of rotation.

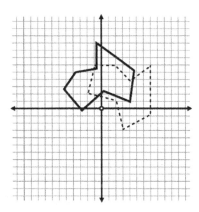

> **Review Video: Rotation**
> Visit mometrix.com/academy and enter code: 602600

## TRANSLATION AND DILATION

A **translation** is a transformation which slides a figure from one position in the plane to another position in the plane. The original figure and the translated figure have the same size, shape, and orientation. A **dilation** is a transformation which proportionally stretches or shrinks a figure by a **scale factor**. The dilated image is the same shape and orientation as the original image but a different size. A polygon and its dilated image are similar.

Translation

Dilation

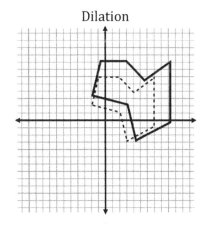

> **Review Video: Translation**
> Visit mometrix.com/academy and enter code: 718628
>
> **Review Video: Dilation**
> Visit mometrix.com/academy and enter code: 471630

Copyright © Mometrix Media. You have been licensed one copy of this document for personal use only. Any other reproduction or redistribution is strictly prohibited. All rights reserved. This content is provided for test preparation purposes only and does not imply an endorsement by Mometrix of any particular political, scientific, or religious point of view.

A **reflection of a figure over a line** (a "flip") creates a congruent image that is the same distance from the line as the original figure but on the opposite side. The **line of reflection** is the perpendicular bisector of any line segment drawn from a point on the original figure to its reflected image (unless the point and its reflected image happen to be the same point, which happens when a figure is reflected over one of its own sides). A **reflection of a figure over a point** (an inversion) in two dimensions is the same as the rotation of the figure 180° about that point. The image of the figure is congruent to the original figure. The **point of reflection** is the midpoint of a line segment which connects a point in the figure to its image (unless the point and its reflected image happen to be the same point, which happens when a figure is reflected in one of its own points).

Reflection of a figure over a line

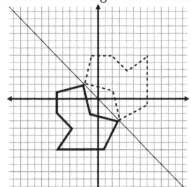

Reflection of a figure over a point

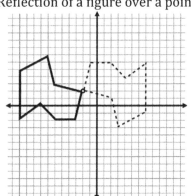

| Review Video: **Reflection** |
| :---: |
| Visit mometrix.com/academy and enter code: 955068 |

## PRACTICE

**P1.** Use the coordinate plane to reflect the figure below across the *y*-axis.

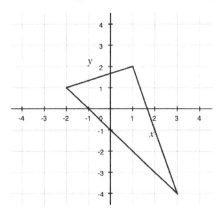

Copyright © Mometrix Media. You have been licensed one copy of this document for personal use only. Any other reproduction or redistribution is strictly prohibited. All rights reserved.
This content is provided for test preparation purposes only and does not imply an endorsement by Mometrix of any particular political, scientific, or religious point of view.

**P2.** Use the coordinate plane to enlarge the figure below by a factor of 2.

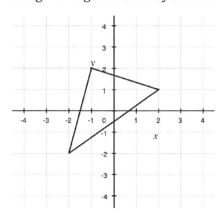

## PRACTICE SOLUTIONS

**P1.** To reflect the image across the $y$-axis, replace each $x$-coordinate of the points that are the vertex of the triangle, $x$, with its negative, $-x$.

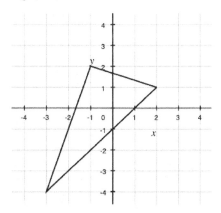

**P2.** An enlargement can be found by multiplying each coordinate of the coordinate pairs located at the triangle's vertices by 2. The original coordinates were $(-1, 2), (2, 1), (-2, -2)$, so the new coordinates are $(-2, 4), (4, 2), (-4, -4)$:

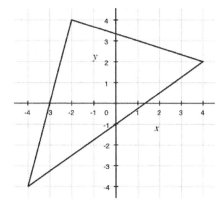

Copyright © Mometrix Media. You have been licensed one copy of this document for personal use only. Any other reproduction or redistribution is strictly prohibited. All rights reserved.
This content is provided for test preparation purposes only and does not imply an endorsement by Mometrix of any particular political, scientific, or religious point of view.

# Two-Dimensional Shapes

## POLYGONS

A **polygon** is a closed, two-dimensional figure with three or more straight line segments called **sides**. The point at which two sides of a polygon intersect is called the **vertex**. In a polygon, the number of sides is always equal to the number of vertices. A polygon with all sides congruent and all angles equal is called a **regular polygon**. Common polygons are:

Triangle = 3 sides
Quadrilateral = 4 sides
Pentagon = 5 sides
Hexagon = 6 sides
Heptagon = 7 sides
Octagon = 8 sides
Nonagon = 9 sides
Decagon = 10 sides
Dodecagon = 12 sides

More generally, an $n$-gon is a polygon that has $n$ angles and $n$ sides.

**Review Video: Intro to Polygons**
Visit mometrix.com/academy and enter code: 271869

The sum of the interior angles of an $n$-sided polygon is $(n - 2) \times 180°$. For example, in a triangle $n = 3$. So the sum of the interior angles is $(3 - 2) \times 180° = 180°$. In a quadrilateral, $n = 4$, and the sum of the angles is $(4 - 2) \times 180° = 360°$.

**Review Video: Sum of Interior Angles**
Visit mometrix.com/academy and enter code: 984991

## APOTHEM AND RADIUS

A line segment from the center of a polygon that is perpendicular to a side of the polygon is called the **apothem**. A line segment from the center of a polygon to a vertex of the polygon is called a **radius**. In a regular polygon, the apothem can be used to find the area of the polygon using the formula $A = \frac{1}{2}ap$, where $a$ is the apothem, and $p$ is the perimeter.

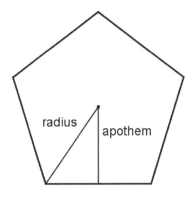

Copyright © Mometrix Media. You have been licensed one copy of this document for personal use only. Any other reproduction or redistribution is strictly prohibited. All rights reserved. This content is provided for test preparation purposes only and does not imply an endorsement by Mometrix of any particular political, scientific, or religious point of view.

A **diagonal** is a line segment that joins two non-adjacent vertices of a polygon. The number of diagonals a polygon has can be found by using the formula:

$$\text{number of diagonals} = \frac{n(n-3)}{2}$$

Note that $n$ is the number of sides in the polygon. This formula works for all polygons, not just regular polygons.

## CONVEX AND CONCAVE POLYGONS

A **convex polygon** is a polygon whose diagonals all lie within the interior of the polygon. A **concave polygon** is a polygon with a least one diagonal that is outside the polygon. In the diagram below, quadrilateral $ABCD$ is concave because diagonal $\overline{AC}$ lies outside the polygon and quadrilateral $EFGH$ is convex because both diagonals lie inside the polygon.

Concave

Convex
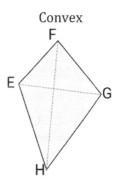

## CONGRUENCE AND SIMILARITY

Congruent figures are geometric figures that have the same size and shape. All corresponding angles are equal, and all corresponding sides are equal. Congruence is indicated by the symbol $\cong$.

Congruent polygons

Copyright © Mometrix Media. You have been licensed one copy of this document for personal use only. Any other reproduction or redistribution is strictly prohibited. All rights reserved.
This content is provided for test preparation purposes only and does not imply an endorsement by Mometrix of any particular political, scientific, or religious point of view.

Similar figures are geometric figures that have the same shape, but do not necessarily have the same size. All corresponding angles are equal, and all corresponding sides are proportional, but they do not have to be equal. It is indicated by the symbol ~.

Similar polygons

Note that all congruent figures are also similar, but not all similar figures are congruent.

**Review Video: What is a Congruent Shape?**
Visit mometrix.com/academy and enter code: 492281

## LINE OF SYMMETRY

A line that divides a figure or object into congruent parts is called a **line of symmetry**. An object may have no lines of symmetry, one line of symmetry, or multiple (i.e., more than one) lines of symmetry.

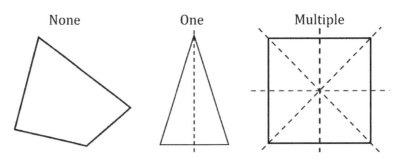

None            One            Multiple

**Review Video: Symmetry**
Visit mometrix.com/academy and enter code: 528106

Copyright © Mometrix Media. You have been licensed one copy of this document for personal use only. Any other reproduction or redistribution is strictly prohibited. All rights reserved.
This content is provided for test preparation purposes only and does not imply an endorsement by Mometrix of any particular political, scientific, or religious point of view.

## TRIANGLES

A triangle is a three-sided figure with the sum of its interior angles being 180°. The **perimeter of any triangle** is found by summing the three side lengths; $P = a + b + c$. For an equilateral triangle, this is the same as $P = 3a$, where $a$ is any side length, since all three sides are the same length.

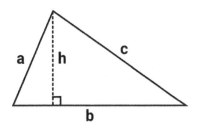

**Review Video: Proof that a Triangle is 180 Degrees**
Visit mometrix.com/academy and enter code: 687591

**Review Video: Area and Perimeter of a Triangle**
Visit mometrix.com/academy and enter code: 853779

The **area of any triangle** can be found by taking half the product of one side length referred to as the base, often given the variable $b$ and the perpendicular distance from that side to the opposite vertex called the altitude or height and given the variable $h$. In equation form that is $A = \frac{1}{2}bh$. Another formula that works for any triangle is $A = \sqrt{s(s-a)(s-b)(s-c)}$, where $s$ is the semiperimeter: $\frac{a+b+c}{2}$, and $a$, $b$, and $c$ are the lengths of the three sides. Special cases include isosceles triangles, $A = \frac{1}{2}b\sqrt{a^2 - \frac{b^2}{4}}$, where $b$ is the unique side and $a$ is the length of one of the two congruent sides, and equilateral triangles, $A = \frac{\sqrt{3}}{4}a^2$, where $a$ is the length of a side.

**Review Video: Area of Any Triangle**
Visit mometrix.com/academy and enter code: 138510

### PARTS OF A TRIANGLE

An **altitude** of a triangle is a line segment drawn from one vertex perpendicular to the opposite side. In the diagram that follows, $\overline{BE}$, $\overline{AD}$, and $\overline{CF}$ are altitudes. The length of an altitude is also called the height of the triangle. The three altitudes in a triangle are always concurrent. The point of concurrency of the altitudes of a triangle, $O$, is called the **orthocenter**. Note that in an obtuse triangle, the orthocenter will be outside the triangle, and in a right triangle, the orthocenter is the vertex of the right angle.

A **median** of a triangle is a line segment drawn from one vertex to the midpoint of the opposite side. In the diagram that follows, $\overline{BH}$, $\overline{AG}$, and $\overline{CI}$ are medians. This is not the same as the altitude, except the altitude to the base of an isosceles triangle and all three altitudes of an equilateral triangle. The point of concurrency of the medians of a triangle, $T$, is called the **centroid**. This is the same point as the orthocenter only in an equilateral triangle. Unlike the orthocenter, the centroid is always inside the triangle. The centroid can also be considered the exact center of the triangle. Any

Copyright © Mometrix Media. You have been licensed one copy of this document for personal use only. Any other reproduction or redistribution is strictly prohibited. All rights reserved.
This content is provided for test preparation purposes only and does not imply an endorsement by Mometrix of any particular political, scientific, or religious point of view.

shape triangle can be perfectly balanced on a tip placed at the centroid. The centroid is also the point that is two-thirds the distance from the vertex to the opposite side.

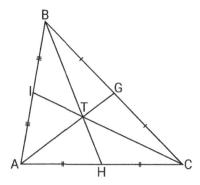

**Review Video: Centroid, Incenter, Circumcenter, and Orthocenter**
Visit mometrix.com/academy and enter code: 598260

## QUADRILATERALS

A **quadrilateral** is a closed two-dimensional geometric figure that has four straight sides. The sum of the interior angles of any quadrilateral is 360°.

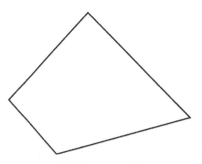

**Review Video: Diagonals of Parallelograms, Rectangles, and Rhombi**
Visit mometrix.com/academy and enter code: 320040

## KITE

A **kite** is a quadrilateral with two pairs of adjacent sides that are congruent. A result of this is perpendicular diagonals. A kite can be concave or convex and has one line of symmetry.

Copyright © Mometrix Media. You have been licensed one copy of this document for personal use only. Any other reproduction or redistribution is strictly prohibited. All rights reserved. This content is provided for test preparation purposes only and does not imply an endorsement by Mometrix of any particular political, scientific, or religious point of view.

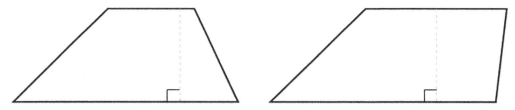

## TRAPEZOID

**Trapezoid**: A trapezoid is defined as a quadrilateral that has at least one pair of parallel sides. There are no rules for the second pair of sides. So, there are no rules for the diagonals and no lines of symmetry for a trapezoid.

The **area of a trapezoid** is found by the formula $A = \frac{1}{2}h(b_1 + b_2)$, where $h$ is the height (segment joining and perpendicular to the parallel bases), and $b_1$ and $b_2$ are the two parallel sides (bases). Do not use one of the other two sides as the height unless that side is also perpendicular to the parallel bases.

The **perimeter of a trapezoid** is found by the formula $P = a + b_1 + c + b_2$, where $a$, $b_1$, $c$, and $b_2$ are the four sides of the trapezoid.

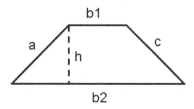

> **Review Video: Area and Perimeter of a Trapezoid**
> Visit mometrix.com/academy and enter code: 587523

**Isosceles trapezoid**: A trapezoid with equal base angles. This gives rise to other properties including: the two nonparallel sides have the same length, the two non-base angles are also equal, and there is one line of symmetry through the midpoints of the parallel sides.

## PARALLELOGRAM

A **parallelogram** is a quadrilateral that has two pairs of opposite parallel sides. As such it is a special type of trapezoid. The sides that are parallel are also congruent. The opposite interior angles are always congruent, and the consecutive interior angles are supplementary. The diagonals of a parallelogram divide each other. Each diagonal divides the parallelogram into two congruent

205

Copyright © Mometrix Media. You have been licensed one copy of this document for personal use only. Any other reproduction or redistribution is strictly prohibited. All rights reserved. This content is provided for test preparation purposes only and does not imply an endorsement by Mometrix of any particular political, scientific, or religious point of view.

triangles. A parallelogram has no line of symmetry, but does have 180-degree rotational symmetry about the midpoint.

The **area of a parallelogram** is found by the formula $A = bh$, where $b$ is the length of the base, and $h$ is the height. Note that the base and height correspond to the length and width in a rectangle, so this formula would apply to rectangles as well. Do not confuse the height of a parallelogram with the length of the second side. The two are only the same measure in the case of a rectangle.

The **perimeter of a parallelogram** is found by the formula $P = 2a + 2b$ or $P = 2(a + b)$, where $a$ and $b$ are the lengths of the two sides.

| Review Video: **How to Find the Area and Perimeter of a Parallelogram** |
| :---: |
| Visit mometrix.com/academy and enter code: 718313 |

## RECTANGLE

A **rectangle** is a quadrilateral with four right angles. All rectangles are parallelograms and trapezoids, but not all parallelograms or trapezoids are rectangles. The diagonals of a rectangle are congruent. Rectangles have two lines of symmetry (through each pair of opposing midpoints) and 180-degree rotational symmetry about the midpoint.

The **area of a rectangle** is found by the formula $A = lw$, where $A$ is the area of the rectangle, $l$ is the length (usually considered to be the longer side) and $w$ is the width (usually considered to be the shorter side). The numbers for $l$ and $w$ are interchangeable.

The **perimeter of a rectangle** is found by the formula $P = 2l + 2w$ or $P = 2(l + w)$, where $l$ is the length, and $w$ is the width. It may be easier to add the length and width first and then double the result, as in the second formula.

## RHOMBUS

A **rhombus** is a quadrilateral with four congruent sides. All rhombuses are parallelograms and kites; thus, they inherit all the properties of both types of quadrilaterals. The diagonals of a rhombus are perpendicular to each other. Rhombi have two lines of symmetry (along each of the

Copyright © Mometrix Media. You have been licensed one copy of this document for personal use only. Any other reproduction or redistribution is strictly prohibited. All rights reserved.
This content is provided for test preparation purposes only and does not imply an endorsement by Mometrix of any particular political, scientific, or religious point of view.

diagonals) and 180° rotational symmetry. The **area of a rhombus** is half the product of the diagonals: $A = \frac{d_1 d_2}{2}$ and the perimeter of a rhombus is: $P = 2\sqrt{(d_1)^2 + (d_2)^2}$ .

## SQUARE

A **square** is a quadrilateral with four right angles and four congruent sides. Squares satisfy the criteria of all other types of quadrilaterals. The diagonals of a square are congruent and perpendicular to each other. Squares have four lines of symmetry (through each pair of opposing midpoints and along each of the diagonals) as well as 90° rotational symmetry about the midpoint.

The **area of a square** is found by using the formula $A = s^2$, where $s$ is the length of one side. The **perimeter of a square** is found by using the formula $P = 4s$, where $s$ is the length of one side. Because all four sides are equal in a square, it is faster to multiply the length of one side by 4 than to add the same number four times. You could use the formulas for rectangles and get the same answer.

Copyright © Mometrix Media. You have been licensed one copy of this document for personal use only. Any other reproduction or redistribution is strictly prohibited. All rights reserved.
This content is provided for test preparation purposes only and does not imply an endorsement by Mometrix of any particular political, scientific, or religious point of view.

### HIERARCHY OF QUADRILATERALS

The hierarchy of quadrilaterals is as follows:

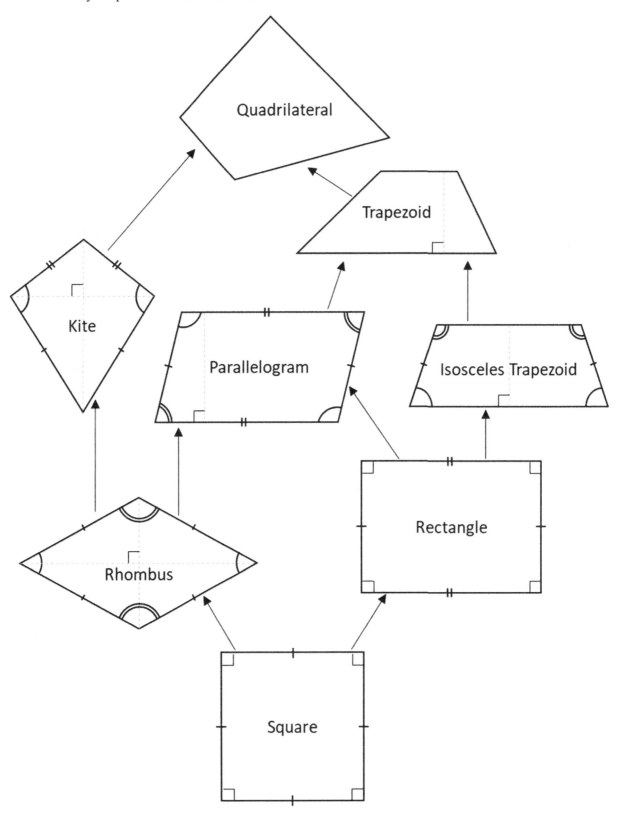

Copyright © Mometrix Media. You have been licensed one copy of this document for personal use only. Any other reproduction or redistribution is strictly prohibited. All rights reserved.
This content is provided for test preparation purposes only and does not imply an endorsement by Mometrix of any particular political, scientific, or religious point of view.

## CIRCLES

The **center** of a circle is the single point from which every point on the circle is **equidistant**. The **radius** is a line segment that joins the center of the circle and any one point on the circle. All radii of a circle are equal. Circles that have the same center but not the same length of radii are **concentric**. The **diameter** is a line segment that passes through the center of the circle and has both endpoints on the circle. The length of the diameter is exactly twice the length of the radius. Point $O$ in the diagram below is the center of the circle, segments $\overline{OX}$, $\overline{OY}$, and $\overline{OZ}$ are radii; and segment $\overline{XZ}$ is a diameter.

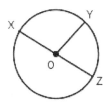

| Review Video: <u>Points of a Circle</u> |
| --- |
| Visit mometrix.com/academy and enter code: 420746 |
| |
| Review Video: <u>The Diameter, Radius, and Circumference of Circles</u> |
| Visit mometrix.com/academy and enter code: 448988 |

The **area of a circle** is found by the formula $A = \pi r^2$, where $r$ is the length of the radius. If the diameter of the circle is given, remember to divide it in half to get the length of the radius before proceeding.

The **circumference** of a circle is found by the formula $C = 2\pi r$, where $r$ is the radius. Again, remember to convert the diameter if you are given that measure rather than the radius.

| Review Video: <u>Area and Circumference of a Circle</u> |
| --- |
| Visit mometrix.com/academy and enter code: 243015 |

### INSCRIBED AND CIRCUMSCRIBED FIGURES

These terms can both be used to describe a given arrangement of figures, depending on perspective. If each of the vertices of figure A lie on figure B, then it can be said that figure A is **inscribed** in figure B, but it can also be said that figure B is **circumscribed** about figure A. The following table and examples help to illustrate the concept. Note that the figures cannot both be circles, as they would be completely overlapping and neither would be inscribed or circumscribed.

| Given | Description | Equivalent Description | Figures |
| --- | --- | --- | --- |
| Each of the sides of a pentagon is tangent to a circle | The circle is inscribed in the pentagon | The pentagon is circumscribed about the circle | |
| Each of the vertices of a pentagon lie on a circle | The pentagon is inscribed in the circle | The circle is circumscribed about the pentagon | |

Copyright © Mometrix Media. You have been licensed one copy of this document for personal use only. Any other reproduction or redistribution is strictly prohibited. All rights reserved.
This content is provided for test preparation purposes only and does not imply an endorsement by Mometrix of any particular political, scientific, or religious point of view.

## PRACTICE

**P1.** Find the area and perimeter of the following quadrilaterals:

**(a)** A square with side length 2.5 cm.

**(b)** A parallelogram with height 3 m, base 4 m, and other side 6 m.

**(c)** A rhombus with diagonals 15 in and 20 in.

**P2.** Calculate the area of a triangle with side lengths of 7 ft, 8 ft, and 9 ft.

**P3.** Square $ABCD$ is inscribed in a circle with radius 20 m. What is the area of the part of the circle outside of the square?

## PRACTICE SOLUTIONS

**P1. (a)** $A = s^2 = (2.5 \text{ cm})^2 = 6.25 \text{ cm}^2; P = 4s = 4 \times 2.5 \text{ cm} = 10 \text{ cm}$

**(b)** $A = bh = (3 \text{ m})(4 \text{ m}) = 12 \text{ m}^2; P = 2a + 2b = 2 \times 6 \text{ m} + 2 \times 4 \text{ m} = 20 \text{ m}$

**(c)** $A = \frac{d_1 d_2}{2} = \frac{(15 \text{ in})(20 \text{ in})}{2} = 150 \text{ in}^2;$
$P = 2\sqrt{(d_1)^2 + (d_2)^2} = 2\sqrt{(15 \text{ in})^2 + (20 \text{ in})^2} = 2\sqrt{625 \text{ in}^2} = 50 \text{ in}$

**P2.** Given only side lengths, we can use the semi perimeter to the find the area based on the formula, $A = \sqrt{s(s-a)(s-b)(s-c)}$, where $s$ is the semiperimeter, $\frac{a+b+c}{2} = \frac{7+8+9}{2} = 12$ ft:

$$A = \sqrt{12(12-7)(12-8)(12-9)}$$
$$= \sqrt{(12)(5)(4)(3)}$$
$$= 12\sqrt{5} \text{ ft}^2$$

**P3.** Begin by drawing a diagram of the situation, where we want to find the shaded area:

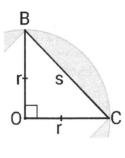

Copyright © Mometrix Media. You have been licensed one copy of this document for personal use only. Any other reproduction or redistribution is strictly prohibited. All rights reserved.
This content is provided for test preparation purposes only and does not imply an endorsement by Mometrix of any particular political, scientific, or religious point of view.

The area of the square is $s^2$, so the area we want to find is: $\pi r^2 - s^2$. Since the inscribed figure is a square, the triangle $BCO$ is a 45-45-90 right triangle. Now we can find $s^2 = r^2 + r^2 = 2r^2$. So the shaded area is:

$$
\begin{aligned}
A &= \pi r^2 - s^2 \\
&= \pi r^2 - 2r^2 \\
&= (\pi - 2)r^2 \\
&= (\pi - 2) \times 400 \\
&\approx 456.6 \text{ m}^2
\end{aligned}
$$

Copyright © Mometrix Media. You have been licensed one copy of this document for personal use only. Any other reproduction or redistribution is strictly prohibited. All rights reserved.
This content is provided for test preparation purposes only and does not imply an endorsement by Mometrix of any particular political, scientific, or religious point of view.

# Three-Dimensional Shapes

## SOLIDS

The **surface area of a solid object** is the area of all sides or exterior surfaces. For objects such as prisms and pyramids, a further distinction is made between base surface area ($B$) and lateral surface area ($LA$). For a prism, the total surface area ($SA$) is $SA = LA + 2B$. For a pyramid or cone, the total surface area is $SA = LA + B$.

The **surface area of a sphere** can be found by the formula $A = 4\pi r^2$, where $r$ is the radius. The volume is given by the formula $V = \frac{4}{3}\pi r^3$, where $r$ is the radius. Both quantities are generally given in terms of $\pi$.

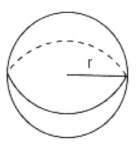

**Review Video: Volume and Surface Area of a Sphere**
Visit mometrix.com/academy and enter code: 786928

The **volume of any prism** is found by the formula $V = Bh$, where $B$ is the area of the base, and $h$ is the height (perpendicular distance between the bases). The surface area of any prism is the sum of the areas of both bases and all sides. It can be calculated as $SA = 2B + Ph$, where $P$ is the perimeter of the base.

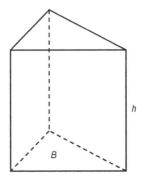

**Review Video: Volume and Surface Area of a Prism**
Visit mometrix.com/academy and enter code: 420158

Copyright © Mometrix Media. You have been licensed one copy of this document for personal use only. Any other reproduction or redistribution is strictly prohibited. All rights reserved. This content is provided for test preparation purposes only and does not imply an endorsement by Mometrix of any particular political, scientific, or religious point of view.

For a **rectangular prism**, the volume can be found by the formula $V = lwh$, where $V$ is the volume, $l$ is the length, $w$ is the width, and $h$ is the height. The surface area can be calculated as $SA = 2lw + 2hl + 2wh$ or $SA = 2(lw + hl + wh)$.

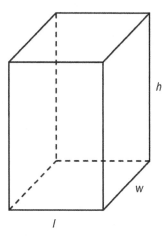

**Review Video: <u>Volume and Surface Area of a Rectangular Prism</u>**
Visit mometrix.com/academy and enter code: 282814

The **volume of a cube** can be found by the formula $V = s^3$, where $s$ is the length of a side. The surface area of a cube is calculated as $SA = 6s^2$, where $SA$ is the total surface area and $s$ is the length of a side. These formulas are the same as the ones used for the volume and surface area of a rectangular prism, but simplified since all three quantities (length, width, and height) are the same.

**Review Video: <u>Volume and Surface Area of a Cube</u>**
Visit mometrix.com/academy and enter code: 664455

The **volume of a cylinder** can be calculated by the formula $V = \pi r^2 h$, where $r$ is the radius, and $h$ is the height. The surface area of a cylinder can be found by the formula $SA = 2\pi r^2 + 2\pi rh$. The

Copyright © Mometrix Media. You have been licensed one copy of this document for personal use only. Any other reproduction or redistribution is strictly prohibited. All rights reserved.
This content is provided for test preparation purposes only and does not imply an endorsement by Mometrix of any particular political, scientific, or religious point of view.

first term is the base area multiplied by two, and the second term is the perimeter of the base multiplied by the height.

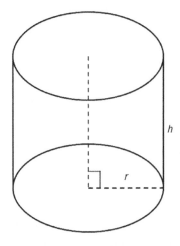

**Review Video: Finding the Volume and Surface Area of a Right Circular Cylinder**
Visit mometrix.com/academy and enter code: 226463

The **volume of a pyramid** is found by the formula $V = \frac{1}{3}Bh$, where $B$ is the area of the base, and $h$ is the height (perpendicular distance from the vertex to the base). Notice this formula is the same as $\frac{1}{3}$ times the volume of a prism. Like a prism, the base of a pyramid can be any shape.

Finding the **surface area of a pyramid** is not as simple as the other shapes we've looked at thus far. If the pyramid is a right pyramid, meaning the base is a regular polygon and the vertex is directly over the center of that polygon, the surface area can be calculated as $SA = B + \frac{1}{2}Ph_s$, where $P$ is the perimeter of the base, and $h_s$ is the slant height (distance from the vertex to the midpoint of one side of the base). If the pyramid is irregular, the area of each triangle side must be calculated individually and then summed, along with the base.

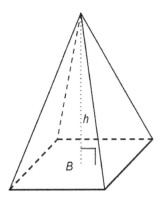

**Review Video: Finding the Volume and Surface Area of a Pyramid**
Visit mometrix.com/academy and enter code: 621932

214

Copyright © Mometrix Media. You have been licensed one copy of this document for personal use only. Any other reproduction or redistribution is strictly prohibited. All rights reserved.
This content is provided for test preparation purposes only and does not imply an endorsement by Mometrix of any particular political, scientific, or religious point of view.

The **volume of a cone** is found by the formula $V = \frac{1}{3}\pi r^2 h$, where $r$ is the radius, and $h$ is the height. Notice this is the same as $\frac{1}{3}$ times the volume of a cylinder. The surface area can be calculated as $SA = \pi r^2 + \pi rs$, where $s$ is the slant height. The slant height can be calculated using the Pythagorean theorem to be $\sqrt{r^2 + h^2}$, so the surface area formula can also be written as $SA = \pi r^2 + \pi r\sqrt{r^2 + h^2}$.

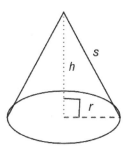

> **Review Video: <u>Volume and Surface Area of a Right Circular Cone</u>**
> Visit mometrix.com/academy and enter code: 573574

## PRACTICE

**P1.** Find the surface area and volume of the following solids:

(a) A cylinder with radius 5 m and height 0.5 m.

(b) A trapezoidal prism with base area of 254 mm², base perimeter 74 mm, and height 10 mm.

(c) A half sphere (radius 5 yds) on the base of an inverted cone with the same radius and a height of 7 yds.

## PRACTICE SOLUTIONS

**P1. (a)** $SA = 2\pi r^2 + 2\pi rh = 2\pi(5\text{ m})^2 + 2\pi(5\text{ m})(0.5\text{ m}) = 55\pi\text{ m}^2 \approx 172.79\text{ m}^2$;
$V = \pi r^2 h = \pi(5\text{ m})^2(0.5\text{ m}) = 12.5\pi\text{ m}^3 \approx 39.27\text{ m}^3$

**(b)** $SA = 2B + Ph = 2(254\text{ mm}^2) + (74\text{ mm})(10\text{ mm}) = 1{,}248\text{ mm}^2$;
$V = Bh = (254\text{ mm}^2)(10\text{ mm}) = 2{,}540\text{ mm}^3$

Copyright © Mometrix Media. You have been licensed one copy of this document for personal use only. Any other reproduction or redistribution is strictly prohibited. All rights reserved.
This content is provided for test preparation purposes only and does not imply an endorsement by Mometrix of any particular political, scientific, or religious point of view.

(c) We can find $s$, the slant height using the Pythagorean theorem, and since this solid is made of parts of simple solids, we can combine the formulas to find surface area and volume:

$$s = \sqrt{r^2 + h^2} = \sqrt{(5 \text{ yd})^2 + (7 \text{ yd})^2} = \sqrt{74} \text{ yd}$$

$$SA_{Total} = \frac{\left(SA_{sphere}\right)}{2} + SA_{cone} - SA_{base}$$

$$= \frac{4\pi r^2}{2} + \left(\pi r s + \pi r^2\right) - \pi r^2$$

$$= 2\pi(5 \text{ yd})^2 + \pi(5 \text{ yd})\left(\sqrt{74} \text{ yd}\right)$$

$$= 5\pi\left(10 + \sqrt{74}\right) \text{ yd}^2$$

$$\approx 292.20 \text{ yd}^2$$

$$V_{Total} = \frac{\left(V_{sphere}\right)}{2} + V_{cone}$$

$$= \frac{\frac{4}{3}\pi r^3}{2} + \frac{1}{3}\pi r^2 h$$

$$= \frac{2}{3}\pi(5 \text{ yd})^3 + \frac{1}{3}\pi(5 \text{ yd})^2(7 \text{ yd})$$

$$= \frac{5^2 \times \pi}{3}(10 + 7) \text{ yd}^3$$

$$\approx 445.06 \text{ yd}^3$$

Copyright © Mometrix Media. You have been licensed one copy of this document for personal use only. Any other reproduction or redistribution is strictly prohibited. All rights reserved.
This content is provided for test preparation purposes only and does not imply an endorsement by Mometrix of any particular political, scientific, or religious point of view.

# Triangle Classification and Properties

## CLASSIFICATIONS OF TRIANGLES

A **scalene triangle** is a triangle with no congruent sides. A scalene triangle will also have three angles of different measures. The angle with the largest measure is opposite the longest side, and the angle with the smallest measure is opposite the shortest side. An **acute triangle** is a triangle whose three angles are all less than 90°. If two of the angles are equal, the acute triangle is also an **isosceles triangle**. An isosceles triangle will also have two congruent angles opposite the two congruent sides. If the three angles are all equal, the acute triangle is also an **equilateral triangle**. An equilateral triangle will also have three congruent angles, each 60°. All equilateral triangles are also acute triangles. An **obtuse triangle** is a triangle with exactly one angle greater than 90°. The other two angles may or may not be equal. If the two remaining angles are equal, the obtuse triangle is also an isosceles triangle. A **right triangle** is a triangle with exactly one angle equal to 90°. All right triangles follow the Pythagorean theorem. A right triangle can never be acute or obtuse.

Copyright © Mometrix Media. You have been licensed one copy of this document for personal use only. Any other reproduction or redistribution is strictly prohibited. All rights reserved. This content is provided for test preparation purposes only and does not imply an endorsement by Mometrix of any particular political, scientific, or religious point of view.

The table below illustrates how each descriptor places a different restriction on the triangle:

| Sides \ Angles | Acute: All angles < 90° | Obtuse: One angle > 90° | Right: One angle = 90° |
|---|---|---|---|
| **Scalene: No equal side lengths** | | | |
| | $90° > \angle a > \angle b > \angle c$ <br> $x > y > z$ | $\angle a > 90° > \angle b > \angle c$ <br> $x > y > z$ | $90° = \angle a > \angle b > \angle c$ <br> $x > y > z$ |
| **Isosceles: Two equal side lengths** | | | |
| | $90° > \angle a, \angle b, or \angle c$ <br> $\angle b = \angle c, \qquad y = z$ | $\angle a > 90° > \angle b = \angle c$ <br> $x > y = z$ | $\angle a = 90°$ <br> $\angle b = \angle c = 45°$ <br> $x > y = z$ |
| **Equilateral: Three equal side lengths** | | | |
| | $60° = \angle a = \angle b = \angle c$ <br> $x = y = z$ | | |

**Review Video: <u>Introduction to Types of Triangles</u>**
Visit mometrix.com/academy and enter code: 511711

## SIMILARITY AND CONGRUENCE RULES

**Similar triangles** are triangles whose corresponding angles are equal and whose corresponding sides are proportional. Represented by AAA. Similar triangles whose corresponding sides are congruent are also congruent triangles.

Triangles can be shown to be **congruent** in 5 ways:

- **SSS**: Three sides of one triangle are congruent to the three corresponding sides of the second triangle.
- **SAS**: Two sides and the included angle (the angle formed by those two sides) of one triangle are congruent to the corresponding two sides and included angle of the second triangle.
- **ASA**: Two angles and the included side (the side that joins the two angles) of one triangle are congruent to the corresponding two angles and included side of the second triangle.

Copyright © Mometrix Media. You have been licensed one copy of this document for personal use only. Any other reproduction or redistribution is strictly prohibited. All rights reserved. This content is provided for test preparation purposes only and does not imply an endorsement by Mometrix of any particular political, scientific, or religious point of view.

- **AAS**: Two angles and a non-included side of one triangle are congruent to the corresponding two angles and non-included side of the second triangle.
- **HL**: The hypotenuse and leg of one right triangle are congruent to the corresponding hypotenuse and leg of the second right triangle.

> **Review Video: Similar Triangles**
> Visit mometrix.com/academy and enter code: 398538

## GENERAL RULES FOR TRIANGLES

The **triangle inequality theorem** states that the sum of the measures of any two sides of a triangle is always greater than the measure of the third side. If the sum of the measures of two sides were equal to the third side, a triangle would be impossible because the two sides would lie flat across the third side and there would be no vertex. If the sum of the measures of two of the sides was less than the third side, a closed figure would be impossible because the two shortest sides would never meet. In other words, for a triangle with sides lengths $A$, $B$, and $C$: $A + B > C$, $B + C > A$, and $A + C > B$.

The sum of the measures of the interior angles of a triangle is always 180°. Therefore, a triangle can never have more than one angle greater than or equal to 90°.

In any triangle, the angles opposite congruent sides are congruent, and the sides opposite congruent angles are congruent. The largest angle is always opposite the longest side, and the smallest angle is always opposite the shortest side.

The line segment that joins the midpoints of any two sides of a triangle is always parallel to the third side and exactly half the length of the third side.

> **Review Video: General Rules (Triangle Inequality Theorem)**
> Visit mometrix.com/academy and enter code: 166488

Copyright © Mometrix Media. You have been licensed one copy of this document for personal use only. Any other reproduction or redistribution is strictly prohibited. All rights reserved.
This content is provided for test preparation purposes only and does not imply an endorsement by Mometrix of any particular political, scientific, or religious point of view.

## PRACTICE

**P1.** Given the following pairs of triangles, determine whether they are similar, congruent, or neither (note that the figures are not drawn to scale):

(a).

(b).

(c).

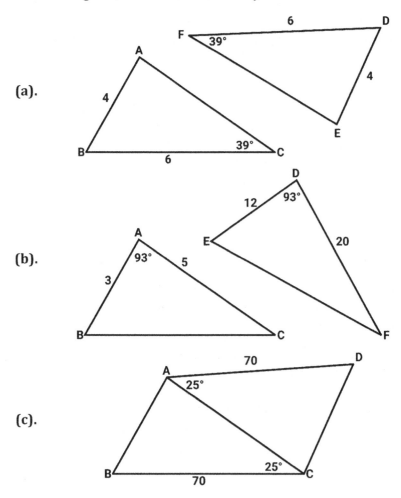

## PRACTICE SOLUTIONS

**P1. (a).** Neither: We are given that two sides lengths and an angle are equal, however, the angle given is not between the given side lengths. That means there are two possible triangles that could satisfy the given measurements. Thus, we cannot be certain of congruence:

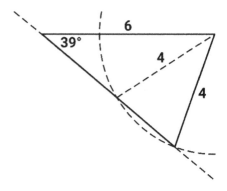

Copyright © Mometrix Media. You have been licensed one copy of this document for personal use only. Any other reproduction or redistribution is strictly prohibited. All rights reserved. This content is provided for test preparation purposes only and does not imply an endorsement by Mometrix of any particular political, scientific, or religious point of view.

**(b)** Similar: Since we are given a side-angle-side of each triangle and the side lengths given are scaled evenly $\left(\frac{3}{5} \times \frac{4}{4} = \frac{12}{20}\right)$ and the angles are equal. Thus, $\triangle ABC \sim \triangle DEF$. If the side lengths were equal, then they would be congruent.

**(c)** Congruent: Even though we aren't given a measurement for the shared side of the figure, since it is shared it is equal. So, this is a case of SAS. Thus, $\triangle ABC \cong \triangle CDA$.

Copyright © Mometrix Media. You have been licensed one copy of this document for personal use only. Any other reproduction or redistribution is strictly prohibited. All rights reserved.
This content is provided for test preparation purposes only and does not imply an endorsement by Mometrix of any particular political, scientific, or religious point of view.

# Displaying Information

## FREQUENCY TABLES

**Frequency tables** show how frequently each unique value appears in a set. A **relative frequency table** is one that shows the proportions of each unique value compared to the entire set. Relative frequencies are given as percentages; however, the total percent for a relative frequency table will not necessarily equal 100 percent due to rounding. An example of a frequency table with relative frequencies is below.

| Favorite Color | Frequency | Relative Frequency |
|---|---|---|
| Blue | 4 | 13% |
| Red | 7 | 22% |
| Green | 3 | 9% |
| Purple | 6 | 19% |
| Cyan | 12 | 38% |

> **Review Video: Data Interpretation of Graphs**
> Visit mometrix.com/academy and enter code: 200439

## CIRCLE GRAPHS

**Circle graphs**, also known as *pie charts*, provide a visual depiction of the relationship of each type of data compared to the whole set of data. The circle graph is divided into sections by drawing radii to create central angles whose percentage of the circle is equal to the individual data's percentage of the whole set. Each 1% of data is equal to 3.6° in the circle graph. Therefore, data represented by a 90° section of the circle graph makes up 25% of the whole. When complete, a circle graph often looks like a pie cut into uneven wedges. The pie chart below shows the data from the frequency table referenced earlier where people were asked their favorite color.

### Favorite Color

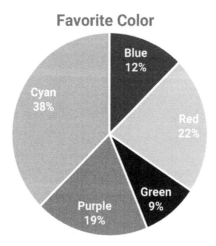

## PICTOGRAPHS

A **pictograph** is a graph, generally in the horizontal orientation, that uses pictures or symbols to represent the data. Each pictograph must have a key that defines the picture or symbol and gives the quantity each picture or symbol represents. Pictures or symbols on a pictograph are not always shown as whole elements. In this case, the fraction of the picture or symbol shown represents the same fraction of the quantity a whole picture or symbol stands for. For example, a row with $3\frac{1}{2}$ ears

Copyright © Mometrix Media. You have been licensed one copy of this document for personal use only. Any other reproduction or redistribution is strictly prohibited. All rights reserved.
This content is provided for test preparation purposes only and does not imply an endorsement by Mometrix of any particular political, scientific, or religious point of view.

of corn, where each ear of corn represents 100 stalks of corn in a field, would equal $3\frac{1}{2} \times 100 = 350$ stalks of corn in the field.

**Review Video: Pictographs**
Visit mometrix.com/academy and enter code: 147860

## LINE GRAPHS

**Line graphs** have one or more lines of varying styles (solid or broken) to show the different values for a set of data. The individual data are represented as ordered pairs, much like on a Cartesian plane. In this case, the $x$- and $y$-axes are defined in terms of their units, such as dollars or time. The individual plotted points are joined by line segments to show whether the value of the data is increasing (line sloping upward), decreasing (line sloping downward), or staying the same (horizontal line). Multiple sets of data can be graphed on the same line graph to give an easy visual comparison. An example of this would be graphing achievement test scores for different groups of students over the same time period to see which group had the greatest increase or decrease in performance from year to year (as shown below).

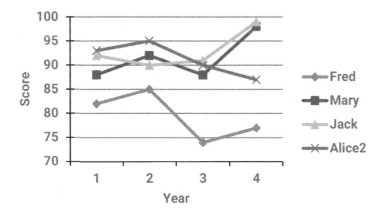

**Review Video: How to Create a Line Graph**
Visit mometrix.com/academy and enter code: 480147

## LINE PLOTS

A **line plot**, also known as a *dot plot*, has plotted points that are not connected by line segments. In this graph, the horizontal axis lists the different possible values for the data, and the vertical axis lists the number of times the individual value occurs. A single dot is graphed for each value to show the number of times it occurs. This graph is more closely related to a bar graph than a line graph. Do not connect the dots in a line plot or it will misrepresent the data.

**Review Video: Line Plot**
Visit mometrix.com/academy and enter code: 754610

## STEM AND LEAF PLOTS

A **stem and leaf plot** is useful for depicting groups of data that fall into a range of values. Each piece of data is separated into two parts: the first, or left, part is called the stem; the second, or right, part is called the leaf. Each stem is listed in a column from smallest to largest. Each leaf that has the common stem is listed in that stem's row from smallest to largest. For example, in a set of two-digit

Copyright © Mometrix Media. You have been licensed one copy of this document for personal use only. Any other reproduction or redistribution is strictly prohibited. All rights reserved.
This content is provided for test preparation purposes only and does not imply an endorsement by Mometrix of any particular political, scientific, or religious point of view.

numbers, the digit in the tens place is the stem, and the digit in the ones place is the leaf. With a stem and leaf plot, you can easily see which subset of numbers (10s, 20s, 30s, etc.) is the largest. This information is also readily available by looking at a histogram, but a stem and leaf plot also allows you to look closer and see exactly which values fall in that range. Using all of the test scores from above, we can assemble a stem and leaf plot like the one below.

**Test Scores**

| 7 | 4 | 8 | | | | | | |
|---|---|---|---|---|---|---|---|---|
| 8 | 2 | 5 | 7 | 8 | 8 | | | |
| 9 | 0 | 0 | 1 | 2 | 2 | 3 | 5 | 8 | 9 |

> **Review Video: Stem and Leaf Plots**
> Visit mometrix.com/academy and enter code: 302339

## BAR GRAPHS

A **bar graph** is one of the few graphs that can be drawn correctly in two different configurations – both horizontally and vertically. A bar graph is similar to a line plot in the way the data is organized on the graph. Both axes must have their categories defined for the graph to be useful. Rather than placing a single dot to mark the point of the data's value, a bar, or thick line, is drawn from zero to the exact value of the data, whether it is a number, percentage, or other numerical value. Longer bar lengths correspond to greater data values. To read a bar graph, read the labels for the axes to find the units being reported. Then, look where the bars end in relation to the scale given on the corresponding axis and determine the associated value.

The bar chart below represents the responses from our favorite-color survey.

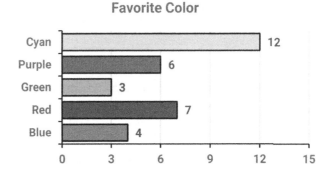

## HISTOGRAMS

At first glance, a **histogram** looks like a vertical bar graph. The difference is that a bar graph has a separate bar for each piece of data and a histogram has one continuous bar for each *range* of data. For example, a histogram may have one bar for the range 0–9, one bar for 10–19, etc. While a bar graph has numerical values on one axis, a histogram has numerical values on both axes. Each range is of equal size, and they are ordered left to right from lowest to highest. The height of each column on a histogram represents the number of data values within that range. Like a stem and leaf plot, a

Copyright © Mometrix Media. You have been licensed one copy of this document for personal use only. Any other reproduction or redistribution is strictly prohibited. All rights reserved. This content is provided for test preparation purposes only and does not imply an endorsement by Mometrix of any particular political, scientific, or religious point of view.

histogram makes it easy to glance at the graph and quickly determine which range has the greatest quantity of values. A simple example of a histogram is below.

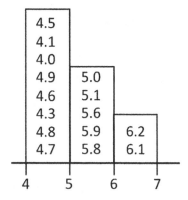

## BIVARIATE DATA

**Bivariate data** is simply data from two different variables. (The prefix *bi-* means *two*.) In a *scatter plot*, each value in the set of data is plotted on a grid similar to a Cartesian plane, where each axis represents one of the two variables. By looking at the pattern formed by the points on the grid, you can often determine whether or not there is a relationship between the two variables, and what that relationship is, if it exists. The variables may be directly proportionate, inversely proportionate, or show no proportion at all. It may also be possible to determine if the data is linear, and if so, to find an equation to relate the two variables. The following scatter plot shows the relationship between preference for brand "A" and the age of the consumers surveyed.

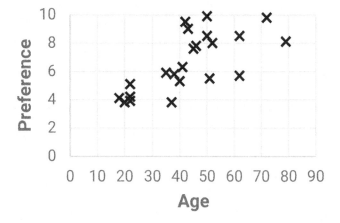

Copyright © Mometrix Media. You have been licensed one copy of this document for personal use only. Any other reproduction or redistribution is strictly prohibited. All rights reserved.
This content is provided for test preparation purposes only and does not imply an endorsement by Mometrix of any particular political, scientific, or religious point of view.

## SCATTER PLOTS

**Scatter plots** are also useful in determining the type of function represented by the data and finding the simple regression. Linear scatter plots may be positive or negative. Nonlinear scatter plots are generally exponential or quadratic. Below are some common types of scatter plots:

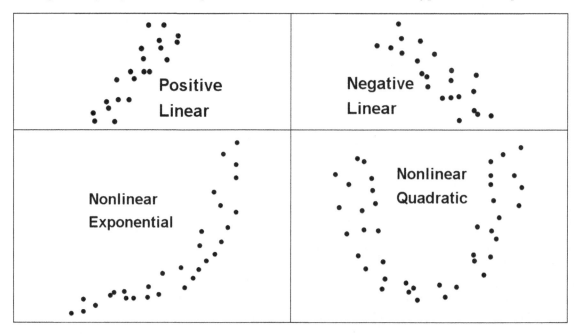

**Review Video: What is a Scatter Plot?**
Visit mometrix.com/academy and enter code: 596526

## 5-NUMBER SUMMARY

The **5-number summary** of a set of data gives a very informative picture of the set. The five numbers in the summary include the minimum value, maximum value, and the three quartiles. This information gives the reader the range and median of the set, as well as an indication of how the data is spread about the median.

## BOX AND WHISKER PLOTS

A **box-and-whiskers plot** is a graphical representation of the 5-number summary. To draw a box-and-whiskers plot, plot the points of the 5-number summary on a number line. Draw a box whose ends are through the points for the first and third quartiles. Draw a vertical line in the box through

Copyright © Mometrix Media. You have been licensed one copy of this document for personal use only. Any other reproduction or redistribution is strictly prohibited. All rights reserved.
This content is provided for test preparation purposes only and does not imply an endorsement by Mometrix of any particular political, scientific, or religious point of view.

the median to divide the box in half. Draw a line segment from the first quartile point to the minimum value, and from the third quartile point to the maximum value.

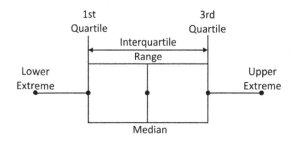

> **Review Video: Box and Whisker Plots**
> Visit mometrix.com/academy and enter code: 810817

## 68-95-99.7 RULE

The **68–95–99.7 rule** describes how a normal distribution of data should appear when compared to the mean. This is also a description of a normal bell curve. According to this rule, 68 percent of the data values in a normally distributed set should fall within one standard deviation of the mean (34 percent above and 34 percent below the mean), 95 percent of the data values should fall within two standard deviations of the mean (47.5 percent above and 47.5 percent below the mean), and 99.7 percent of the data values should fall within three standard deviations of the mean, again, equally distributed on either side of the mean. This means that only 0.3 percent of all data values should fall more than three standard deviations from the mean. On the graph below, the normal curve is centered on the $y$-axis. The $x$-axis labels are how many standard deviations away from the center you are. Therefore, it is easy to see how the 68-95-99.7 rule can apply.

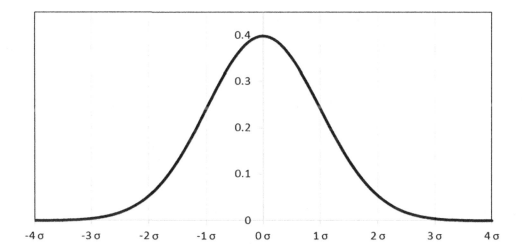

Copyright © Mometrix Media. You have been licensed one copy of this document for personal use only. Any other reproduction or redistribution is strictly prohibited. All rights reserved.
This content is provided for test preparation purposes only and does not imply an endorsement by Mometrix of any particular political, scientific, or religious point of view.

# College Statistics

## FREQUENCY DISTRIBUTIONS

A **frequency distribution** sorts data to give a clear visual representation of the distribution. Numbers are grouped with like numbers (for instance, all numbers in their twenties may be grouped together) to measure the frequency.

### EXAMPLE

We can sort the following set of numbers into a frequency distribution based on the value of the tens place: 20, 12, 37, 18, 21, 19, 32, 21, 16, and 14. To do this, we group them into sets by first digit and create a table. This can include just category and frequency, but can also include relative frequency or percentage:

| Category | Frequency | Relative Frequency | Percentage |
|----------|-----------|--------------------|------------|
| Tens | 5 | 0.5 | 50% |
| Twenties | 3 | 0.3 | 30% |
| Thirties | 2 | 0.2 | 20% |

We can see that there is a higher concentration of numbers in the tens than any other group. This means that the data will likely be skewed right, with the mean greater than the median.

## HISTOGRAMS

A **histogram** is similar to a frequency distribution, providing a visual of the data. Each category is represented by a vertical bar, showing which categories have the most (or least) data.

> **Review Video: Data Interpretation of Graphs**
> Visit mometrix.com/academy and enter code: 200439

### EXAMPLE

Given the following set of data, we can sort it into categories based on the value of their hundred's place: 332, 489, 550, 301, 299, 506, 420, 319, 370, 406, 520, 389, 340. This gives us 1 value in the 200s, 6 values in the 300s, 3 values in the 400s, and 3 values in the 500s. So we can create a histogram:

## BOX PLOTS

A **box plot** gives a visual depiction of data, dividing it into its quartiles to show distribution. The minimum, lower quartile ($Q_1$), median, upper quartile ($Q_3$), and maximum are labeled.

> **Review Video: Box Plot**
> Visit mometrix.com/academy and enter code: 810817

Copyright © Mometrix Media. You have been licensed one copy of this document for personal use only. Any other reproduction or redistribution is strictly prohibited. All rights reserved. This content is provided for test preparation purposes only and does not imply an endorsement by Mometrix of any particular political, scientific, or religious point of view.

## EXAMPLE

Given the following data (32, 28, 29, 26, 35, 27, 30, 31, 27, 32), we first sort it into numerical order: 26, 27, 27, 28, 29, 30, 31, 32, 32, 35. We can then find the median. Since there are ten values, we take the average of the 5th and 6th values to get 29.5. We find the lower quartile by taking the median of the data smaller than the median. Since there are five values, we take the 3rd value, which is 27. We find the upper quartile by taking the median of the data larger than the overall median, which is 32. Finally, we note our minimum and maximum, which are simply the smallest and largest values in the set: 26 and 35, respectively. Now we can create our box plot:

This plot is fairly "long" on the right whisker, showing one or more unusually high values (but not quite outliers). The other quartiles are similar in length, showing a fairly even distribution of data.

## CUMULATIVE FREQUENCY DISTRIBUTIONS

A **cumulative frequency distribution**, rather than showing the amount in each category, shows the *cumulative* amount. In other words, the amount for each new category is added to each of the previous amounts to show the cumulative sum. This is helpful when the goal is to compare not single groups against each other, but to look at several groups as a sample. For instance, in a cumulative frequency distribution based on employees' salaries, a person could immediately see how many employees make at or below a certain amount per year.

## EXAMPLE

A teacher could create a cumulative frequency distribution out of the following test grades: 89, 76, 74, 92, 83, 86, 90, 87, 85, 82, 95, 68, 97, 94, 86, 82, 89, 81, 78, 82. The grades could be divided into groups and placed in a table, adding on each new group to the previous to find the cumulative frequency:

| Limits | Frequency | Cumulative frequency |
|--------|-----------|----------------------|
| 0–75   | 2         | 2                    |
| 76–80  | 2         | 4                    |
| 81–85  | 6         | 10                   |
| 86–90  | 6         | 16                   |
| 91–95  | 3         | 19                   |
| 96–100 | 1         | 20                   |

Now the teacher can easily see, for instance, that 10 of the 20 students are scoring at 85 or below.

## MEASURES OF CENTRAL TENDENCY

The measures of central tendency refer to mean, median, mode, and range, which describe the basic shape of a set of numbers. Each can be useful in different scenarios.

Copyright © Mometrix Media. You have been licensed one copy of this document for personal use only. Any other reproduction or redistribution is strictly prohibited. All rights reserved. This content is provided for test preparation purposes only and does not imply an endorsement by Mometrix of any particular political, scientific, or religious point of view.

## MEAN

The **mean**, or average, is a good way to get an overall idea of the data set, particularly if the numbers are close together. It is found by adding all numbers of a set together and dividing by the number of values in the set.

To find the average of the following set of quiz grades (98, 91, 76, 84, 89, 74, 92, 86, 88, 80), we add all the numbers together and divide by how many there are:

$$\frac{98 + 91 + 76 + 84 + 89 + 74 + 92 + 86 + 88 + 80}{10} = 85.8$$

## MEDIAN

The **median** is the middle value of a set when it is arranged in numerical order. If there are an even number of values, the median can be found by taking the average of the two middle values. The median is a useful measurement to use instead of the mean if there are outliers that would skew the mean.

To find the median of the following set of data (13, 32, 27, 23, 18, 31, 23, 25, 28, 19), we first rearrange the numbers in numerical order: 13, 18, 19, 23, 23, 25, 27, 28, 31, 32. This is an even number of values (10), so we take the average of the 5th and 6th values:

$$\frac{23 + 25}{2} = 24$$

## MODE

The **mode** of a data set is the value (or values) that occurs most often. It can be used as a measure of central tendency in nominal data.

In the following set of data (13, 21, 17, 8, 21, 18, 19, 20, 21, 18), two numbers appear multiple times. While 18 appears twice, 21 appears three times, so 21 is the mode.

> **Review Video: Mean, Median, and Mode**
> Visit mometrix.com/academy and enter code: 286207

## RANGE

The **range** refers to the difference between the highest and lowest values of a data set and is found by subtracting the lowest value from the highest.

> **Review Video: Statistical Range**
> Visit mometrix.com/academy and enter code: 778541

To find the range in the following set of data (31, 17, 42, 21, 38, 16, 41, 19), we subtract the lowest value (16) from the highest (42): $42 - 16 = 26$.

## INTERQUARTILE RANGE

The **interquartile range, or IQR**, is the difference between the upper and lower quartiles. It measures how the data is dispersed: a high IQR means that the data is more spread out, while a low IQR means that the data is clustered more tightly around the median. To find the IQR, subtract the lower quartile value ($Q_1$) from the upper quartile value ($Q_3$).

Copyright © Mometrix Media. You have been licensed one copy of this document for personal use only. Any other reproduction or redistribution is strictly prohibited. All rights reserved.
This content is provided for test preparation purposes only and does not imply an endorsement by Mometrix of any particular political, scientific, or religious point of view.

## EXAMPLE

To find the upper and lower quartiles, we first find the median and then take the median of all values above it and all values below it. In the following data set (16, 18, 13, 24, 16, 51, 32, 21, 27, 39), we first rearrange the values in numerical order: 13, 16, 16, 18, 21, 24, 27, 32, 39, 51. There are 10 values, so the median is the average of the 5th and 6th: $\frac{21+24}{2} = \frac{45}{2} = 22.5$. We do not actually need this value to find the upper and lower quartiles. We look at the set of numbers below the median: 13, 16, 16, 18, 21. There are five values, so the 3rd is the median (16), or the value of the lower quartile ($Q_1$). Then we look at the numbers above the median: 24, 27, 32, 39, 51. Again there are five values, so the 3rd is the median (32), or the value of the upper quartile ($Q_3$). We find the IQR by subtracting $Q_1$ from $Q_3$: $32 - 16 = 16$.

## STANDARD DEVIATION

The **standard deviation** ($\sigma$) of a data set measures variation, or how spread out the values are. To calculate it, first find the mean of the data set. Then find the difference of each value and the mean and square the differences. Find the **variance** ($\sigma^2$) by adding each of these squared differences together and dividing by one less than the number of values. Finally, take the root of the variance and you have the standard deviation.

> **Review Video: Standard Deviation**
> Visit mometrix.com/academy and enter code: 419469

## EXAMPLE

For the following data set (4, 8, 2, 7, 11, 13, 6, 5, 7), we first find the mean:

$$\frac{4+8+2+7+11+13+6+5+7}{9} = 7$$

Then we find the difference of each value and the mean, square and add them, and divide by one less than the number of data points:

$$\sigma^2 = \frac{(7-4)^2 + (7-8)^2 + (7-2)^2 + (7-7)^2 + (7-11)^2 + (7-13)^2 + (7-6)^2 + (7-5)^2 + (7-7)^2}{9-1}$$
$$= \frac{9 + 1 + 25 + 0 + 16 + 36 + 1 + 4 + 0}{8}$$
$$= \frac{92}{8}$$
$$= 11.5$$

So the variance is 11.5, and we take the root to find the standard deviation: $\sigma = \sqrt{11.5} \approx 3.39$.

## EXPECTED VALUE

The **expected value** is the return that can be expected for a certain action. For example, if you flip a coin four times you can expect to get heads twice since the probability for each flip is $\frac{1}{2}$. Expected

Copyright © Mometrix Media. You have been licensed one copy of this document for personal use only. Any other reproduction or redistribution is strictly prohibited. All rights reserved. This content is provided for test preparation purposes only and does not imply an endorsement by Mometrix of any particular political, scientific, or religious point of view.

value is calculated by multiplying the probability of the event by the number of times the event occurs.

### EXAMPLE

To find the expected value of rolling a six-sided die one time, we calculate the potential outcomes and their likelihood. There is a $\frac{1}{6}$ chance of rolling a 1, a $\frac{1}{6}$ chance of rolling a 2, and so on. So the expected value is found by multiplying each outcome by $\frac{1}{6}$ and adding them together:

$$\frac{1}{6} \times 1 + \frac{1}{6} \times 2 + \frac{1}{6} \times 3 + \frac{1}{6} \times 4 + \frac{1}{6} \times 5 + \frac{1}{6} \times 6 = \frac{1+2+3+4+5+6}{6} = \frac{21}{6} = 3.5$$

## NORMAL DISTRIBUTIONS

If a distribution is **normal**, this means that the variables are mostly symmetrical about the mean. Approximately half of the values are below the mean and half are above. Most values are clustered closely about the mean, with approximately 68% within one standard deviation, 95% within two standard deviations, and 99.7% within three standard deviations. Anything beyond this is an **outlier**.

### EXAMPLE

If the height of freshman women at a university is normally distributed with a mean of 66" and a standard deviation of 1.5", we can calculate the percentage of women in various height brackets. Since the standard deviation is 1.5" and 68% of values in a normal distribution fall within one distribution, we can say that approximately 68% of the freshman women are between 64.5" and 67.5", 95% are between 63" and 69", and 99.7% within 61.5" and 70.5". Anyone shorter than 61.5" or taller than 70.5" is an outlier.

## UNIFORM DISTRIBUTIONS

In a **uniform distribution**, every outcome is equally likely. For instance, in flipping a fair coin or rolling a die, each outcome is as likely as any of the others. A random generator is another example, since each number within the parameters has an equal chance of being selected.

### EXAMPLE

Suppose a collection of songs has a range of anywhere from 4 to 11 notes, inclusive, and they are distributed uniformly. We could find the probability that a given song has six or fewer notes. There are eight possibilities (from 4 to 11) and three of them have six or fewer notes (4, 5, 6). So the probability is $\frac{3}{8}$ or 0.375.

## BINOMIAL DISTRIBUTIONS

A binomial distribution has two possible outcomes, like flipping a coin or a true/false quiz. It is typically used on a series of trials (like flipping a coin 50 times). None of the trials impact the others, so the probability of success or failure is the same on each, but the number of trials can affect overall probability. For example, flipping a coin 20 times gives a much higher probability of getting at least one heads than flipping it once, even though the probability for each individual flip is the same. The formula for **binomial distribution** is $P_x = \binom{n}{x} p^x q^{n-x}$, where $P$ is the probability, $n$ is the number of trials, $x$ is the number of times of the desired outcome, $p$ is the probability of success on any trial, and $q$ is the probability of failure on any trial.

Copyright © Mometrix Media. You have been licensed one copy of this document for personal use only. Any other reproduction or redistribution is strictly prohibited. All rights reserved. This content is provided for test preparation purposes only and does not imply an endorsement by Mometrix of any particular political, scientific, or religious point of view.

## EXAMPLE

Suppose a jar has 20 marbles, 10 red and 10 blue. If Lea draws a marble 10 times, replacing it after each draw, there is a 50% chance on each draw of getting red, and a 50% chance of getting blue, so this is a binomial distribution. The probability of getting three reds can be calculated:

$$P_3 = \binom{10}{3}\left(\frac{1}{2}\right)^3\left(\frac{1}{2}\right)^7 = \frac{10!}{3!\,7!}(0.5)^3(0.5)^7 = \frac{10 \times 9 \times 8 \times 7 \times 6 \times 5 \times 4 \times 3 \times 2 \times 1}{7 \times 6 \times 5 \times 4 \times 3 \times 2 \times 1 \times 3 \times 2 \times 1}\left(\frac{1}{2}\right)^{10} = \frac{15}{128}$$

## SAMPLE MEAN

A **sample mean** is the mean (average) of a specific set of data taken as a sample from a much larger population. It is often the most manageable way to assess central tendency and other measures for groups that would be impractical or impossible to survey completely. It is calculated like a normal mean: adding all values from the sample and dividing by the total number of values in the sample.

## EXAMPLE

Suppose a scientist has 15 different experimental results. He decides to take a sample of five to calculate a sample mean of the weights by taking every 3rd value. If his individual results weigh 1.2, 0.9, 1.1, 0.8, 1.3, 1.0, 0.6, 1.2, 0.7, 0.8, 0.9, 0.9, 1.3, 0.8, and 0.6 grams, we select every third value, add them together, and divide by 5:

$$\frac{1.1 + 1.0 + 0.7 + 0.9 + 0.6}{5} = \frac{4.3}{5} = 0.86$$

## SAMPLE PROPORTION

The sample proportion is a proportion calculated from a specific sample of a population. For many occasions the full population may be difficult or impossible to calculate, so a sample is taken to provide a more manageable amount of data but still give a good representation of the whole population. The sample proportion is calculated by dividing the number of desired or measured outcomes by the total sample size.

## EXAMPLE

At an ice cream stand, 100 customers purchase ice cream between 1:00pm and 2:00pm. Out of these, 32 choose chocolate ice cream. Our sample size is 100, because it is a sample of the total ice cream purchases for the day, and the sample proportion of those who chose chocolate is $\frac{32}{100} = 0.32$, or 32%.

## CONFIDENCE INTERVALS FOR A SINGLE POPULATION MEAN

A **confidence interval** is calculated to measure how a sample compares to the full population. An upper and lower value are calculated to state that the population mean can be assumed to be within these values with a certain level of confidence (often 95%, but other percentages can also be used). The first step is to find the mean and standard deviation (also called the **error bound**) of the sample. The error bound is both added and subtracted from the mean to find the confidence interval.

## EXAMPLE

If a sample has a mean of 0.72 and an error bound of 0.03, we can calculate the confidence interval by simply subtracting and then adding the error bound from the sample mean. Since $0.72 - 0.03 = 0.69$ and $0.72 + 0.03 = 0.75$, the confidence interval is [0.69, 0.75]. In other words, there is a 95% probability that the true mean of the population lies between 0.69 and 0.75.

Copyright © Mometrix Media. You have been licensed one copy of this document for personal use only. Any other reproduction or redistribution is strictly prohibited. All rights reserved. This content is provided for test preparation purposes only and does not imply an endorsement by Mometrix of any particular political, scientific, or religious point of view.

## CONFIDENCE INTERVAL FOR PROPORTIONS

Confidence intervals for proportions are used in instances with two possible outcomes. For instance, if a store took a sample of 100 customers and found that 72 of them made a purchase before leaving, we could find that the sample proportion of customers who make a purchase is $\frac{72}{100}$ or 0.72. This can then be used to calculate the confidence interval by both adding and subtracting the margin of error. There are multiple levels that can be found, but the standard is 95%.

### EXAMPLE

Val sells 150 donuts and notes that 45 of them were chocolate glazed. Given that the margin of error is 0.073, we can calculate the confidence interval. First, we find that the sample proportion is: $\frac{45}{150} = \frac{3}{10} = 0.3$. So the confidence level is: $0.3 \pm 0.073$. So we both add to and subtract the margin of error from the sample proportion to find the bounds of the confidence interval: $[0.227, 0.373]$, or $[22.7\%, 37.3\%]$. In other words, Val can say with 95% confidence that, based on the sample, between 22.7% and 37.3% of her customers purchase chocolate glazed donuts. Note that the confidence interval will become smaller as the sample size grows, because it becomes more and more likely to be true to the whole population.

## HYPOTHESIS TESTS FOR SINGLE POPULATION MEANS

A **hypothesis test** can be conducted on a random sample of a population, using a smaller amount of data to test a hypothesis about the entire population. For example, if a company claims that each bag of candy it produces contains, on average, 25 pieces, we could test this hypothesis by taking a sample of the total bags of candy produced and seeing how the mean of this sample compares to the hypothesis. To find whether the difference in a sample mean and the purported population mean is within reason, we run a **$t$-test**. The value of $t$ is a way of comparing two means to see how different they are. This could be a sample mean compared to the supposed population mean. From this $t$-value, we can find the $p$-value in a table to find the exact probability, but we can often get an idea of it simply from the $t$-value.

### EXAMPLE

A store claims that it averages 520 sales per day. Jon obtains records from the past 50 days and finds that the average number of sales is 505, with a standard deviation of 15. To see if the store's claim is likely true, he runs a $t$-test and discovers that $t = -7.07$. This means that the sample data is 7 standard deviations below the claimed value. It is highly unlikely that the claim is true if the sample is this far off.

## HYPOTHESIS TESTS FOR PROPORTION CLAIMS

A hypothesis test can also be conducted to test a proportion claim. For example, if someone wanted to test the claim that a flipped coin lands on heads exactly half the time, he or she could create a sample, flipping a coin a number of times and calculating the proportion. From this, one can calculate the **$p$-value**. This is the probability that the sample results differ from the claim by mere chance. A small $p$-value means that it is more unlikely that the original claim is true, since the sample is significantly different. A large $p$-value means it is difficult to disprove or reject the original claim, which is more likely to be true. The $p$-value is compared to the level of significance ($\alpha$), which is the probability that the original claim could be true but still rejected due to a faulty sample. This is typically set at 5%, or 0.05, but can be other percentages as well. If the $p$-value is less than the level of significance, this means it is statistically significant: the original claim (also called the null hypothesis) can be rejected. A $p$-value greater than or equal to the level of significance means that the null hypothesis cannot be rejected: the sample data is not significantly different.

Copyright © Mometrix Media. You have been licensed one copy of this document for personal use only. Any other reproduction or redistribution is strictly prohibited. All rights reserved.
This content is provided for test preparation purposes only and does not imply an endorsement by Mometrix of any particular political, scientific, or religious point of view.

## EXAMPLE

Suppose a store claimed that 75% of its clientele were women (so the null hypothesis is that the proportion of female clients is 0.75). To test that claim, a sample of 2,000 customers is taken, and a sample proportion is calculated, along with the $p$-value. If the level of significance is 5% and $p = 0.039$, we can conclude that the sample data is statistically significant and reject the null hypothesis. In other words, we can say with 95% certainty that women do NOT make up 75% of the store's clientele.

## CORRELATION COEFFICIENTS

A **correlation coefficient** describes the relationship between data. The value can be anywhere between –1 and 1, where –1 is a strong negative correlation (meaning that as one value increases, the other decreases proportionally), 1 is a strong positive correlation (both values increase proportionally), and 0 means no relationship between the values.

## EXAMPLE

Zac calculated the correlation coefficient between the number of rainy days in a month and the number of times he had to mow. If he found a correlation coefficient of 0.89, this shows a strong positive correlation between the rainy days and the number of times Zac had to mow. In other words, the rain and growth of the grass appear to be closely linked in a positive way: as one value increases, the other increases proportionally.

## REGRESSION EQUATIONS

A **regression equation** is used to find the relationship (if any) between sets of data. Given several plot points, one can draw a regression line, or line of best fit, through the points to approximate the best representation of the points. This line can give a good idea of how the data is progressing. Regression is not always linear. It can also be exponential, etc.

## EXAMPLE

In the scatter plot below, we can create a line of best fit by choosing two points that seem to best represent the graph. For example, we may choose (2,5) and (6,9). Note that these are not actual data points, but good "average" points that a line of best fit may go through. We calculate the slope: $m = \frac{9-5}{6-2} = \frac{4}{4} = 1$. Then we plug one of the points into the formula $y = mx + b$, where $m = 1$, to find the $y$-intercept: $5 = 1(2) + b$, so $b = 3$. So our line of best fit is $y = x + 3$. From this we can make predictions about how the data will behave outside of this portion of the graph.

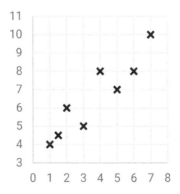

235

Copyright © Mometrix Media. You have been licensed one copy of this document for personal use only. Any other reproduction or redistribution is strictly prohibited. All rights reserved.
This content is provided for test preparation purposes only and does not imply an endorsement by Mometrix of any particular political, scientific, or religious point of view.

## PRACTICE

**P1.** Sort the following data into a frequency distribution based on the value of the tens place: 42, 18, 16, 33, 47, 24, 48, 34, 42, 24, 44, 38, 14, 22, 46, 40, 15, 42, 27, 28.

**P2.** Create a histogram with the following salaries: $108,000, $86,000, $82,500, $72,000, $81,250, $101,750, $88,950, $76,000.

**P3.** Interpret the box plot below (define the quartiles and what this tells us about the data):

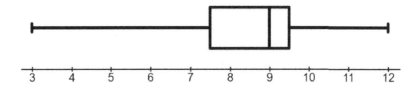

**P4.** To better understand students and their families, a school tracks how many children are in each family. A small sample is listed below. Create a cumulative frequency table and use it to find the percent of families who have three or more children. 3, 1, 2, 2, 1, 4, 1, 5, 2, 1, 1, 6, 3, 2, 1, 4, 2, 2, 1, 2, 1, 3, 2, 1, 3.

**P5.** Given the following selling prices for homes recently sold in a given area ($312,500, $289,750, $189,900, $246,800, and $308,500), what is the average home cost in that area?

**P6.** Find the median test score of the following results: 99, 82, 73, 82, 78, 82, 94, 91, 90, 88, 89.

**P7.** Find the mode(s) of the following data set: 3, 19, 8, 16, 19, 18, 4, 12, 6, 21, 17, 8.

**P8.** At ABC Industries, the CEO makes $348,000/year, project managers make $86,000/year, technicians make $57,500/year, and the quality control head makes $91,000/year. Part-time interns make $17.50/hr. What is the range of annual salaries?

**P9.** Find the IQR of the following data set: 33, 38, 41, 63, 21, 41, 57, 34, 52.

**P10.** Leah counts the number of candies in seven bags of chocolates and finds that there are 32, 34, 31, 35, 29, 31, and 32 pieces. What is the standard deviation?

**P11.** Lucas plays a game rolling a die. If he gets 1, 2, 3, or 4 he earns $3 but if he gets 5 or 6 he loses $5. What is the expected value?

**P12.** At a doctor's office, the heart rate of patients is normally distributed. The average is 75 beats per minute, and 68% of patients have heart rates between 68 and 82 bpm. Based on this, 99.7% of patients fall into what range?

**P13.** A random number generator chooses numbers between 1 and 10, inclusive. What is the probability of getting a multiple of 3?

**P14.** Levi flips a fair coin 10 times. What is the probability that he gets heads at least once?

**P15.** The heights of the students in Ms. Reyes' class are as follows (in inches): 60, 55, 57, 59, 62, 60, 49, 62, 53, 55, 55, 60, 61, 57, 60, 58, 59, 54, 61, 53, 52, 60, and 59. She chooses to use the first 8 values as a sample. Find the sample mean.

Copyright © Mometrix Media. You have been licensed one copy of this document for personal use only. Any other reproduction or redistribution is strictly prohibited. All rights reserved.
This content is provided for test preparation purposes only and does not imply an endorsement by Mometrix of any particular political, scientific, or religious point of view.

**P16.** A gym employee notes that during his four-hour shift, 250 people come in. Of these, 64 stay less than 30 minutes, 102 stay between 30 minutes and an hour, and 84 stay longer than an hour. Find the sample proportion of patrons who stay longer than an hour.

**P17.** A sample of students have an average height of 161 centimeters. If the standard deviation is 3.5 centimeters, what is the confidence interval?

**P18.** A survey of 1,200 fifth graders found that 684 preferred soccer to basketball. If the margin of error is 0.028, calculate the confidence interval.

**P19.** A waitress says that her average customer tips $5. A sample of her last 100 tips shows an average of $5.08 and a standard deviation of $0.85. Can it be concluded that her average tip is $5, if the $t$-value is 0.94?

**P20.** A candy company claims that half of its candy-covered chocolates are red. In a study, 1,000 bags are opened and it is calculated that the $p$-value is 0.015. If $\alpha = 0.01$, what can be concluded?

**P21.** A study shows a correlation coefficient of –0.18 between an endangered species population and a new plant that was introduced in the species' grazing area. What can be concluded?

**P22.** From the scatter plot below, what is a possible slope of the line of best fit?

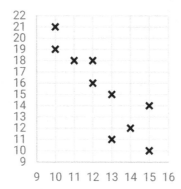

Copyright © Mometrix Media. You have been licensed one copy of this document for personal use only. Any other reproduction or redistribution is strictly prohibited. All rights reserved. This content is provided for test preparation purposes only and does not imply an endorsement by Mometrix of any particular political, scientific, or religious point of view.

## PRACTICE SOLUTIONS

**P1.** We sort the data into 10s, 20s, 30s, and 40s and create a table:

| Category | Frequency | Relative Frequency | Percentage |
|---|---|---|---|
| Tens | 4 | 0.2 | 20% |
| Twenties | 5 | 0.25 | 25% |
| Thirties | 3 | 0.15 | 15% |
| Forties | 8 | 0.4 | 40% |

We can see that there is a disproportionately large amount of data in the 40s, so a graph of the data will likely be skewed left, with the median greater than the mean.

**P2.** We can rearrange the salaries in order to find that there are 2 values in the 70,000s, 4 values in the 80,000s, 0 values in the 90,000s, and 2 values in the 100,000s. So we can create a histogram:

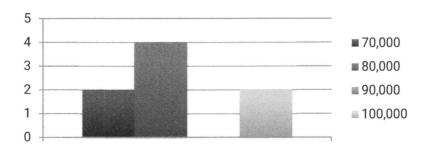

**P3.** We can see that the minimum is 3, the lower quartile is 7.5, the median is 9, the upper quartile is 9.5, and the maximum is 12. The long whisker on the left shows that there are one or more unusually low values. The uneven length of the sections shows that the data is not distributed evenly: there are multiple values between 9 and 10, but the values are more spread out between 3 and 7, for instance.

**P4.** We create a table to show the frequency. Although we could sort bottom to top as usual and subtract anything below 3, it is easier to sort top to bottom instead:

| Limits | Frequency | Cumulative frequency |
|---|---|---|
| 6 | 1 | 1 |
| 5 | 1 | 2 |
| 4 | 2 | 4 |
| 3 | 4 | 8 |
| 2 | 8 | 16 |
| 1 | 9 | 25 |

The cumulative frequency for 3 or more is 8, so 8 out of 25, or 32%, of the families in the sample have three or more children.

**P5.** There are five values, so we add them together and divide by 5:

$$\frac{\$312{,}500 + \$289{,}750 + \$189{,}900 + \$246{,}800 + \$308{,}500}{5} = \$269{,}490$$

**P6.** We rearrange the numbers in numerical order: 73, 78, 82, 82, 82, 88, 89, 90, 91, 94, 99. There are eleven values, so we take the 6th value: 88.

Copyright © Mometrix Media. You have been licensed one copy of this document for personal use only. Any other reproduction or redistribution is strictly prohibited. All rights reserved.
This content is provided for test preparation purposes only and does not imply an endorsement by Mometrix of any particular political, scientific, or religious point of view.

**P7.** The numbers 8 and 19 each appear twice, so they are both modes of the set.

**P8.** The annual salaries include all but the interns (as they have an hourly salary). The highest salary is \$348,000 and the lowest is \$57,500. Subtracting these yields \$348,000 − \$57,500 = \$290,500.

**P9.** We rearrange the values in numerical order: 21, 33, 34, 38, 41, 41, 52, 57, 63. There are nine values, so the 5th is the median (41). We then look at the numbers below the median: 21, 33, 34, 38. There are four values so the median is the average of the 2nd and 3rd: $\frac{33+34}{2} = 33.5$, which gives us the value of our lower quartile ($Q_1$). Now we look at the numbers above the median: 41, 52, 57, 63. We again take the average of the 2nd and 3rd values: $\frac{52+57}{2} = 54.5$, which is the value of our upper quartile ($Q_3$). Subtracting $Q_1$ from $Q_3$ yields: $54.5 − 33.5 = 21$.

**P10.** We first take the mean: $\frac{32+34+31+35+29+31+32}{7} = 32$. Now we find the difference of each value and the mean, square the difference, and add them all together. Then we divide by $7 − 1 = 6$:

$$
\begin{aligned}
\sigma^2 &= \frac{(32-32)^2 + (32-34)^2 + (32-31)^2 + (32-35)^2 + (32-29)^2 + (32-31)^2 + (32-32)^2}{6} \\
&= \frac{0 + 4 + 1 + 9 + 9 + 1 + 0}{6} \\
&= 4
\end{aligned}
$$

Finally, we take the square root: $\sigma = \sqrt{4} = 2$.

**P11.** We calculate the chance for each value: $\frac{4}{6}$, or $\frac{2}{3}$, chance of earning \$3 and $\frac{2}{6}$, or $\frac{1}{3}$, chance of losing \$5 (aka earning –\$5). We multiply the chance by the earning and add the two values together: $\frac{2}{3}(3) + \frac{1}{3}(-5) = 2 - \frac{5}{3} = \frac{1}{3}$. So the expected value is $\frac{1}{3}$ of a dollar, or approximately 33 cents.

**P12.** We know that 68% of the data in a normal distribution falls within one standard deviation of the mean, so we calculate that one standard deviation is 7, since 68 is 7 less than 75 and 82 is 7 more than 75. Three standard deviations include 99.7% of the data, so we find three standard deviations ($3 \times 7 = 21$) on each side of 75 by subtracting 21 from 75 and adding 21 to 75. So 99.7% of patients have heart rates between 54 and 96 bpm.

**P13.** There are three possible multiples of 3 (3, 6, 9) and ten numbers total. Since each are equally likely, the probability is $\frac{3}{10}$ or 0.3.

**P14.** If Levi gets heads at least once, that means he may get heads 1, 2, 3, 4, 5, 6, 7, 8, 9, or 10 times. However, he cannot get zero heads. One possible way to solve is to find the probability of getting each number of heads. But that would take a very long time, so the easiest way to solve is to find the probability of NOT getting one of those numbers: i.e., the probability of zero heads, or ten tails. Since all probabilities of an event add up to 1, we can then subtract our answer from 1 to find the probability of getting heads at least once: $P_0 = \binom{10}{0}\left(\frac{1}{2}\right)^0 \left(\frac{1}{2}\right)^{10} = \frac{10!}{10!}\left(\frac{1}{2}\right)^{10} = \frac{1}{1,024}$. So if the probability of zero heads (10 tails) is $\frac{1}{1,024}$, then the probability of getting any number of heads is $1 - \frac{1}{1,024} = \frac{1,023}{1,024}$.

Copyright © Mometrix Media. You have been licensed one copy of this document for personal use only. Any other reproduction or redistribution is strictly prohibited. All rights reserved. This content is provided for test preparation purposes only and does not imply an endorsement by Mometrix of any particular political, scientific, or religious point of view.

**P15.** We add the first 8 values together and divide by 8: $\frac{60+55+57+59+62+60+49+62}{8} = \frac{464}{8} = 58$ inches.

**P16.** There are 84 people who stay longer than an hour, out of a sample size of 250. We divide to calculate the sample proportion: $\frac{84}{250} = 0.336$, or 33.6%.

**P17.** We both subtract and add 3.5 cm from the mean: $161 - 3.5 = 157.5$, $161 + 3.5 = 164.5$. So the confidence interval is [157.5, 164.5].

**P18.** We first calculate the sample proportion: $\frac{684}{1,200} = 0.57$. Then we calculate the confidence interval: $0.57 \pm 0.028$. So the confidence interval is [0.542, 0.598], or [54.2%, 59.8%]. So we can say with 95% confidence that the number of fifth graders in the entire population who prefer soccer to basketball is between 54.2% and 59.8%.

**P19.** A $t$-value of 0.94 means that the sample data is within one standard deviation of the claim, meaning her claim is plausible.

**P20.** The $p$-value is greater than the level of significance, so the null hypothesis cannot be rejected. In other words, the results of the study are not significantly different enough from the claim to doubt it.

**P21.** The correlation coefficient is a negative number close to zero. This means there is a slight negative correlation, so possibly the new plant may have a small negative impact on the endangered species. But it is a very weak correlation, indicating that there is likely little to no relationship between the two variables.

**P22.** We can choose any two points that approximate a line of best fit. There are a variety of possibilities, but the slope between any two good points should be similar. Let us choose (11,20) and (14,13). The slope is $\frac{13-20}{14-11} = -\frac{7}{3}$.

Copyright © Mometrix Media. You have been licensed one copy of this document for personal use only. Any other reproduction or redistribution is strictly prohibited. All rights reserved.
This content is provided for test preparation purposes only and does not imply an endorsement by Mometrix of any particular political, scientific, or religious point of view.

# Classroom Instruction

## Developmental Literacy

### LITERACY

Literacy is commonly understood as the **ability to read and write**. UNESCO, the United Nations Educational, Scientific, and Cultural Organization, has further defined literacy as the "ability to identify, understand, interpret, create, communicate, compute, and use printed and written materials associated with varying contexts." Under the UNESCO definition, understanding cultural, political, and historical contexts of communities falls under the definition of literacy. While **reading literacy** may be gauged simply by the ability to read a newspaper, **writing literacy** includes spelling, grammar, and sentence structure. To be literate in a foreign language, one would also need to be able to understand a language by listening and be able to speak the language. Some argue that visual representation and numeracy should be included in the requirements one must meet to be considered literate. **Computer literacy** refers to one's ability to utilize the basic functions of computers and other technologies. Subsets of reading literacy include phonological awareness, decoding, comprehension, and vocabulary.

### PHONOLOGICAL AWARENESS

A subskill of literacy, phonological awareness is the ability to perceive sound structures in a spoken word, such as syllables and the individual phonemes within syllables. **Phonemes** are the sounds represented by the letters in the alphabet. The ability to separate, blend, and manipulate sounds is critical to developing reading and spelling skills. Phonological awareness is concerned with not only syllables, but also **onset sounds** (the initial sound in a word, such as /k/ in 'cat') and **rime** (the sounds that follow the onset in a word, such as /at/ in 'cat'). Phonological awareness is an auditory skill that does not necessarily involve print. It should be developed before the student has learned letter to sound correspondences. A student's phonological awareness is an indicator of future reading success.

### COMMUNICATION DEVELOPMENT NORMALLY OCCURRING WITHIN A CHILD'S FIRST FIVE YEARS OF LIFE

Language and communication development depend strongly on the language a child develops within the first five years of life. During this time, three developmental periods are observed. At birth, the first period begins. This period is characterized by infant crying and gazing. Babies communicate their sensations and emotions through these behaviors, so they are expressive; however, they are not yet intentional. They indirectly indicate their needs through expressing how they feel, and when these needs are met, these communicative behaviors are reinforced. These expressions and reinforcement are the foundations for the later development of intentional communication. This becomes possible in the second developmental period, between 6 and 18 months. At this time, infants become able to coordinate their attention visually with other people relative to things and events, enabling purposeful communication with adults. During the third developmental period, from 18 months on, children come to use language as their main way of communicating and learning. Preschoolers can carry on conversations, exercise self-control through language use, and conduct verbal negotiations.

### MILESTONES OF NORMAL LANGUAGE DEVELOPMENT BY THE 2 YEARS OLD

By the time most children reach the age of 2 years, they have acquired a vocabulary of about 150 to 300 words. They can name various familiar objects found in their environments. They are able to

241

Copyright © Mometrix Media. You have been licensed one copy of this document for personal use only. Any other reproduction or redistribution is strictly prohibited. All rights reserved.
This content is provided for test preparation purposes only and does not imply an endorsement by Mometrix of any particular political, scientific, or religious point of view.

use at least two prepositions in their speech (e.g., *in*, *on*, and/or *under*). Two-year-olds typically combine the words they know into short sentences. These sentences tend to be mostly noun-verb or verb-noun combinations (e.g., "Daddy work," "Watch this"). They may also include verb-preposition combinations (e.g., "Go out," "Come in"). By the age of 2 years, children use pronouns, such as *I*, *me*, and *you*. They typically can use at least two such pronouns correctly. A normally developing 2-year-old will respond to some commands, directions, or questions, such as "Show me your eyes" or "Where are your ears?"

## SALIENT GENERAL ASPECTS OF HUMAN LANGUAGE ABILITIES FROM BEFORE BIRTH TO 5 YEARS OF AGE

Language and communication abilities are integral parts of human life that are central to learning, successful school performance, successful social interactions, and successful living. Human language ability begins before birth: the developing fetus can hear not only internal maternal sounds, but also the mother's voice, others' voices, and other sounds outside the womb. Humans have a natural sensitivity to human sounds and languages from before they are born until they are about 4½ years old. These years are critical for developing language and communication. Babies and young children are predisposed to greater sensitivity to human sounds than other sounds, orienting them toward the language spoken around them. Children absorb their environmental language completely, including vocal tones, syntax, usage, and emphasis. This linguistic absorption occurs very rapidly. Children's first 2½ years particularly involve amazing abilities to learn language, including grammatical expression.

### 6 MONTHS, 12 MONTHS, AND 18 MONTHS

Individual differences dictate a broad range of language development that is still normal. However, parents observing noticeably delayed language development in their children should consult professionals. Typically, babies respond to hearing their names by 6 months of age, turn their heads and eyes toward the sources of human voices they hear, and respond accordingly to friendly and angry tones of voice. By the age of 12 months, toddlers can usually understand and follow simple directions, especially when these are accompanied by physical and/or vocal cues. They can intentionally use one or more words with the correct meaning. By the age of 18 months, a normally developing child usually has acquired a vocabulary of roughly 5 to 20 words. Eighteen-month-old children use nouns in their speech most of the time. They are very likely to repeat certain words and/or phrases over and over. At this age, children typically are able to follow simple verbal commands without needing as many visual or auditory cues as at 12 months.

### THREE YEARS

By the time they are 3 years old, most normally developing children have acquired vocabularies of between 900 and 1,000 words. Typically, they correctly use the pronouns *I*, *me*, and *you*. They use more verbs more frequently. They apply past tenses to some verbs and plurals to some nouns. 3-year-olds usually can use at least three prepositions; the most common are *in*, *on*, and *under*. The normally developing 3-year-old knows the major body parts and can name them. 3-year-olds typically use 3-word sentences with ease. Normally, parents should find approximately 75 to 100 percent of what a 3-year-old says to be intelligible, while strangers should find between 50 and 75 percent of a 3-year-old's speech intelligible. Children this age comprehend most simple questions about their activities and environments and can answer questions about what they should do when they are thirsty, hungry, sleepy, hot, or cold. They can tell about their experiences in ways that adults can generally follow. By the age of 3 years, children should also be able to tell others their name, age, and sex.

Copyright © Mometrix Media. You have been licensed one copy of this document for personal use only. Any other reproduction or redistribution is strictly prohibited. All rights reserved. This content is provided for test preparation purposes only and does not imply an endorsement by Mometrix of any particular political, scientific, or religious point of view.

## FOUR YEARS

When normally developing children are 4 years old, most know the names of animals familiar to them. They can use at least four prepositions in their speech (e.g., *in, on, under, to, from,* etc.). They can name familiar objects in pictures, and they know and can identify one color or more. Usually, they are able to repeat four-syllable words they hear. They verbalize as they engage in their activities, which Vygotsky dubbed "private speech." Private speech helps young children think through what they are doing, solve problems, make decisions, and reinforce the correct sequences in multistep activities. When presented with contrasting items, 4-year-olds can understand comparative concepts like bigger and smaller. At this age, they are able to comply with simple commands without the target stimuli being in their sight (e.g., "Put those clothes in the hamper" [upstairs]). Four-year-old children will also frequently repeat speech sounds, syllables, words, and phrases, similar to 18-month-olds' repetitions but at higher linguistic and developmental levels.

## FIVE YEARS

Once most children have reached the age of 5 years, their speech has expanded from the emphasis of younger children on nouns, verbs, and a few prepositions, and is now characterized by many more descriptive words, including adjectives and adverbs. Five-year-olds understand common antonyms, such as big/little, heavy/light, long/short, and hot/cold. They can now repeat longer sentences they hear, up to about 9 words. When given three consecutive, uninterrupted commands, the typical 5-year-old can follow these without forgetting one or two. At age 5, most children have learned simple concepts of time like today, yesterday, and tomorrow; day, morning, afternoon, and night; and before, after, and later. Five-year-olds typically speak in relatively long sentences and normally should be incorporating some compound sentences (with more than one independent clause) and complex sentences (with one or more independent and dependent clauses). Five-year-old children's speech is also grammatically correct most of the time.

## ACTIVITIES THAT TEACH PHONOLOGICAL AWARENESS

Classroom activities that teach phonological awareness include language play and exposure to a variety of sounds and the contexts of sounds. Activities that teach phonological awareness include:

- Clapping to the sounds of individual words, names, or all words in a sentence
- Practicing saying blended phonemes
- Singing songs that involve phoneme replacement (e.g., The Name Game)
- Reading poems, songs, and nursery rhymes out loud
- Reading patterned and predictable texts out loud
- Listening to environmental sounds or following verbal directions
- Playing games with rhyming chants or fingerplays
- Reading alliterative texts out loud
- Grouping objects by beginning sounds
- Reordering words in a well-known sentence or making silly phrases by deleting words from a well-known sentence (perhaps from a favorite storybook)

## TEACHING OF READING THROUGH PHONICS

**Phonics** is the process of learning to read by learning how spoken language is represented by letters. Students learn to read phonetically by sounding out the **phonemes** in words and then blending them together to produce the correct sounds in words. In other words, the student connects speech sounds with letters or groups of letters and blends the sounds together to determine the pronunciation of an unknown word. Phonics is a method commonly used to teach **decoding and reading**, but it has been challenged by other methods, such as the whole language

Copyright © Mometrix Media. You have been licensed one copy of this document for personal use only. Any other reproduction or redistribution is strictly prohibited. All rights reserved. This content is provided for test preparation purposes only and does not imply an endorsement by Mometrix of any particular political, scientific, or religious point of view.

approach. Despite the complexity of pronunciation and combined sounds in the English language, phonics is a highly effective way to teach reading. Being able to read or pronounce a word does not mean the student comprehends the meaning of the word, but context aids comprehension. When phonics is used as a foundation for decoding, children eventually learn to recognize words automatically and advance to decoding multisyllable words with practice.

## ALPHABETIC PRINCIPLE AND ALPHABET WRITING SYSTEMS

The **alphabetic principle** refers to the use of letters and combinations of letters to represent speech sounds. The way letters are combined and pronounced is guided by a system of rules that establishes relationships between written and spoken words and their letter symbols. Alphabet writing systems are common around the world. Some are **phonological** in that each letter stands for an individual sound and words are spelled just as they sound. However, keep in mind that there are other writing systems as well, such as the Chinese **logographic** system and the Japanese **syllabic** system.

## FACTS CHILDREN SHOULD KNOW ABOUT LETTERS

To be appropriately prepared to learn to read and write, a child should learn:

- That each letter is **distinct** in appearance
- What **direction and shape** must be used to write each letter
- That each letter has a **name**, which can be associated with the shape of a letter
- That there are **26** letters in the English alphabet, and letters are grouped in a certain order
- That letters represent **sounds of speech**
- That **words** are composed of letters and have meaning
- That one must be able to **correspond** letters and sounds to read

## DEVELOPMENT OF LANGUAGE SKILLS

Children learn language through interacting with others, by experiencing language in daily and relevant context, and through understanding that speaking and listening are necessary for effective communication. Teachers can promote **language development** by intensifying the opportunities a child has to experience and understand language.

Teachers can assist language development by:

- Modeling enriched vocabulary and teaching new words
- Using questions and examples to extend a child's descriptive language skills
- Providing ample response time to encourage children to practice speech
- Asking for clarification to provide students with the opportunity to develop communication skills
- Promoting conversations among children
- Providing feedback to let children know they have been heard and understood, and providing further explanation when needed

## RELATIONSHIP BETWEEN ORAL AND WRITTEN LANGUAGE DEVELOPMENT

Oral and written language development occur simultaneously. The acquisition of skills in one area supports the acquisition of skills in the other. However, oral language is not a prerequisite to written language. An immature form of oral language development is babbling, and an immature form of written language development is scribbling. **Oral language development** does not occur naturally, but does occur in a social context. This means it is best to include children in conversations rather than simply talk at them. **Written language development** can occur without

Copyright © Mometrix Media. You have been licensed one copy of this document for personal use only. Any other reproduction or redistribution is strictly prohibited. All rights reserved. This content is provided for test preparation purposes only and does not imply an endorsement by Mometrix of any particular political, scientific, or religious point of view.

direct instruction. In fact, reading and writing do not necessarily need to be taught through formal lessons if the child is exposed to a print-rich environment. A teacher can assist a child's language development by building on what the child already knows, discussing relevant and meaningful events and experiences, teaching vocabulary and literacy skills, and providing opportunities to acquire more complex language.

## PRINT-RICH ENVIRONMENT

A teacher can provide a **print-rich environment** in the classroom in a number of ways. These include:

- **Displaying** the following in the classroom:
  - Children's names in print or cursive
  - Children's written work
  - Newspapers and magazines
  - Instructional charts
  - Written schedules
  - Signs and labels
  - Printed songs, poems, and rhymes
- Using **graphic organizers** such as KWL charts or story road maps to:
  - Remind students about what was read and discussed
  - Expand on the lesson topic or theme
  - Show the relationships among books, ideas, and words
- Using **big books** to:
  - Point out features of print, such as specific letters and punctuation
  - Track print from right to left
  - Emphasize the concept of words and the fact that they are used to communicate

## BENEFITS OF PRINT AND BOOK AWARENESS

**Print and book awareness** helps a child understand:

- That there is a **connection** between print and messages contained on signs, labels, and other print forms in the child's environment
- That reading and writing are ways to obtain information and communicate ideas
- That **print** written in English runs from left to right and from top to bottom
- That a book has **parts**, such as a title, a cover, a title page, and a table of contents
- That a book has an **author** and contains a **story**
- That **illustrations** can carry meaning
- That **letters and words** are different
- That **words and sentences** are separated by spaces and punctuation
- That different **text forms** are used for different functions
- That print represents **spoken language**
- How to **hold** a book

## DECODING

Decoding is the method or strategy used to make sense of printed words and figure out how to correctly pronounce them. In order to **decode**, a student needs to know the relationships between letters and sounds, including letter patterns; that words are constructed from phonemes and phoneme blends; and that a printed word represents a word that can be spoken. This knowledge

Copyright © Mometrix Media. You have been licensed one copy of this document for personal use only. Any other reproduction or redistribution is strictly prohibited. All rights reserved.
This content is provided for test preparation purposes only and does not imply an endorsement by Mometrix of any particular political, scientific, or religious point of view.

will help the student recognize familiar words and make informed guesses about the pronunciation of unfamiliar words. Decoding is not the same as comprehension. It does not require an understanding of the meaning of a word, only a knowledge of how to recognize and pronounce it. Decoding can also refer to the skills a student uses to determine the meaning of a **sentence**. These skills include applying knowledge of vocabulary, sentence structure, and context.

## ROLE OF FLUENCY IN LITERACY DEVELOPMENT

**Fluency** is the goal of literacy development. It is the ability to read accurately and quickly. Evidence of fluency includes the ability to recognize words automatically and group words for comprehension. At this point, the student no longer needs to decode words except for complex, unfamiliar ones. He or she is able to move to the next level and understand the **meaning** of a text. The student should be able to self-check for comprehension and should feel comfortable expressing ideas in writing. Teachers can help students build fluency by continuing to provide:

- Reading experiences and discussions about text that gradually increase in level of difficulty
- Reading practice, both silently and out loud
- Word analysis practice
- Instruction on reading comprehension strategies
- Opportunities to express responses to readings through writing

> **Review Video: Fluency**
> Visit mometrix.com/academy and enter code: 531179

## ROLE OF VOCABULARY IN LITERACY DEVELOPMENT

When students do not know the meaning of words in a text, their comprehension is limited. As a result, the text becomes boring or confusing. The larger a student's **vocabulary** is, the better their reading comprehension will be. A larger vocabulary is also associated with an enhanced ability to **communicate** in speech and writing. It is the teacher's role to help students develop a good working vocabulary. Students learn most of the words they use and understand by listening to the world around them (adults, other students, media, etc.) They also learn from their reading experiences, which include being read to and reading independently. Carefully designed activities can also stimulate vocabulary growth, and should emphasize useful words that students see frequently, important words necessary for understanding text, and difficult words and phrases, such as idioms or words with more than one meaning.

## TEACHING TECHNIQUES PROMOTING VOCABULARY DEVELOPMENT

A student's **vocabulary** can be developed by:

- Calling upon a student's **prior knowledge** and making comparisons to that knowledge
- **Defining** a word and providing multiple examples of the use of the word in context
- Showing a student how to use **context clues** to discover the meaning of a word
- Providing instruction on **prefixes**, **roots**, and **suffixes** to help students break a word into its parts and decipher its meaning
- Showing students how to use a **dictionary and a thesaurus**
- Asking students to **practice** new vocabulary by using the words in their own writing
- Providing a **print-rich environment** with a word wall
- Studying a group of words related to a **single subject**, such as farm words, transportation words, etc. so that concept development is enhanced

Copyright © Mometrix Media. You have been licensed one copy of this document for personal use only. Any other reproduction or redistribution is strictly prohibited. All rights reserved.
This content is provided for test preparation purposes only and does not imply an endorsement by Mometrix of any particular political, scientific, or religious point of view.

## Affixes, Prefixes, and Root Words

**Affixes** are syllables attached to the beginning or end of a word to make a derivative or inflectional form of a word. Both prefixes and suffixes are affixes. A **prefix** is a syllable that appears at the beginning of a word that creates a specific meaning in combination with the root or base word. For example, the prefix *mis* means wrong. When combined with the root word *spelling*, the word *misspelling* is created, which means wrong spelling. A **root word** is the base of a word to which affixes can be added. For example, the prefix *in-* or *pre-* can be added to the latin root word *vent* to create *invent* or *prevent*, respectively. The suffix *-er* can be added to the root word *manage* to create *manager*, which means one who manages. The suffix *-able*, meaning capable of, can be added to *manage* to create *managable*, which means capable of being managed.

## Suffixes

A **suffix** is a syllable that appears at the end of a word that creates a specific meaning in combination with the root or base word. There are three types of suffixes:

- **Noun suffixes**—Noun suffixes can change a verb or adjective to a noun. They can denote the act of, state of, quality of, or result of something. For example, *-ment* added to *argue* becomes *argument*, which can be understood as the act the act of resulting state from arguing or the reasons given to prove an idea. Noun suffixes can also denote the doer, or one who acts. For example, *-eer* added to *auction* becomes *auctioneer*, meaning one who auctions. Other examples include *-hood*, *-ness*, *-tion*, *-ship*, and *-ism*.
- **Verb suffixes**—These change other words to verbs and denote to make or to perform the act of. For example, *-en* added to *soft* makes *soften*, which means to make soft. Other verb suffixes are *-ate* (perpetuate), *-fy* (dignify), and *-ize* (sterilize).
- **Adjectival suffixes**—These suffixes change other words to adjectives and include suffixes such as *-ful*, which means full of. When added to *care*, the word *careful* is formed, which means full of care. Other examples are *-ish* and *-less*.

## Strategies to Improve Reading Comprehension

Teachers can model the strategies students can use on their own to better comprehend a text through a read-aloud. First, the teacher should do a walk-through of the story **illustrations** and ask, "What's happening here?" The teacher should then ask students to **predict** what the story will be about based on what they have seen. As the book is read, the teacher should ask open-ended questions such as, "Why do you think the character did this?" and "How do you think the character feels?" The teacher should also ask students if they can **relate** to the story or have background knowledge of something similar. After the reading, the teacher should ask the students to **retell** the story in their own words to check for comprehension. Possible methods of retelling include performing a puppet show or summarizing the story to a partner.

## Role of Prior Knowledge in Determining Appropriate Literacy Education

Even preschool children have some literacy skills, and the extent and type of these skills have implications for instructional approaches. **Comprehension** results from relating two or more pieces of information. One piece comes from the text, and another piece might come from **prior knowledge** (something from a student's long-term memory). For a child, that prior knowledge comes from being read to at home; taking part in other literacy experiences, such as playing computer or word games; being exposed to a print-rich environment at home; and observing parents' reading habits. Children who have had **extensive literacy experience** are better prepared to further develop their literacy skills in school than children who have not been read to, have few books or magazines in their homes, are seldom exposed to high-level oral or written language activities, and seldom witness adults engaged in reading and writing. Children with a scant literacy

Copyright © Mometrix Media. You have been licensed one copy of this document for personal use only. Any other reproduction or redistribution is strictly prohibited. All rights reserved. This content is provided for test preparation purposes only and does not imply an endorsement by Mometrix of any particular political, scientific, or religious point of view.

background are at a disadvantage. The teacher must not make any assumptions about their prior knowledge, and should use intense, targeted instruction. Otherwise, the student may have trouble improving their reading comprehension.

Copyright © Mometrix Media. You have been licensed one copy of this document for personal use only. Any other reproduction or redistribution is strictly prohibited. All rights reserved.
This content is provided for test preparation purposes only and does not imply an endorsement by Mometrix of any particular political, scientific, or religious point of view.

## CHAPTER QUIZ

### 1. Chinese uses which type of writing system?

    a. Alphabetic
    b. Syllabic
    c. Logographic
    d. Featural

### 2. Which of the following is an adjectival suffix?

    a. *-ish*
    b. *-eer*
    c. *-ize*
    d. *-fy*

### 3. Which of the following further defines literacy as the "ability to identify, understand, interpret, create, communicate, compute, and use printed and written materials associated with varying contexts"?

    a. W.H.O.
    b. N.A.E.D.U.
    c. U.N.E.S.C.O.
    d. D.O.E.

## CHAPTER QUIZ ANSWER KEY

**1. C:** The alphabetic principle refers to the use of letters and combinations of letters to represent speech sounds. The way letters are combined and pronounced is guided by a system of rules that establishes relationships between written and spoken words and their letter symbols. Alphabet writing systems are common around the world. Some are phonological, meaning that each letter stands for an individual sound and words are spelled just as they sound. However, it is important to note that there are other writing systems as well, such as the Chinese logographic system and the Japanese syllabic system.

**2. A:** A suffix is a syllable that appears at the end of a word and creates a specific meaning in combination with the root or base word. There are three types of suffixes:

- Noun suffixes can change a verb or adjective to a noun. They can denote the act of, state of, quality of, or result of something. For example, *-ment* added to *argue* becomes *argument*, which can be understood as the resulting state from arguing or the reasons given to prove an idea. Noun suffixes can also denote the doer, or one who acts. For example, *-eer* added to *auction* becomes *auctioneer*, meaning one who auctions. Other examples include *-hood*, *-ness*, *-tion*, *-ship*, and *-ism*.
- Verb suffixes change other words to verbs and denote to make or to perform the act of. For example, *-en* added to *soft* makes *soften*, which means to make soft. Other verb suffixes are *-ate* (perpetuate), *-fy* (dignify), and *-ize* (sterilize).
- Adjectival suffixes change other words to adjectives and include suffixes such as *-ful*, which means full of. When added to *care*, the word *careful* is formed, which means full of care. Other examples are *-ish* and *-less*.

**3. C:** UNESCO, the United Nations Educational, Scientific, and Cultural Organization, has further defined literacy as the "ability to identify, understand, interpret, create, communicate, compute, and use printed and written materials associated with varying contexts." Under the UNESCO definition,

Copyright © Mometrix Media. You have been licensed one copy of this document for personal use only. Any other reproduction or redistribution is strictly prohibited. All rights reserved. This content is provided for test preparation purposes only and does not imply an endorsement by Mometrix of any particular political, scientific, or religious point of view.

understanding cultural, political, and historical contexts of communities falls under the definition of literacy.

Copyright © Mometrix Media. You have been licensed one copy of this document for personal use only. Any other reproduction or redistribution is strictly prohibited. All rights reserved. This content is provided for test preparation purposes only and does not imply an endorsement by Mometrix of any particular political, scientific, or religious point of view.

# Planning Developmentally Appropriate Instruction and Assessment

## DEVELOPMENTALLY APPROPRIATE PRACTICE

Developmentally Appropriate Practice **(DAP)** is an approach to teaching grounded in theories of child development. It is derived from the belief that children are naturally curious to learn, and when provided a stimulating environment, are encouraged to take initiative in their own learning. This approach allows for a great deal of choice in learning experiences. The teacher's role is to facilitate active learning by creating developmentally appropriate activities based on the awareness of similarities between children in various developmental stages and the knowledge that each child develops at their own rate. With this knowledge, the teacher can then adjust the curriculum, activities, and assessments to fit the needs of individual students based on an awareness of age, cultural, social, and individual expectations.

## USING KNOWLEDGE OF COGNITIVE CHANGES TO CREATE INSTRUCTION

A developmentally responsive teacher understands that the needs of students change as they mature through the stages of cognitive development. Furthermore, an effective teacher uses this knowledge to plan instruction that coincides with each developmental level. The early childhood teacher understands the needs and abilities of preoperational children, and designs instruction that focuses on interacting with the world around them through hands-on activities and pretend play. Such activities foster exploration of the environment, roles, and connections. Developmentally responsive elementary school teachers are aware of the logical thinking patterns that occur during the concrete operational stage. Thus, they create instruction that allows children to interact with tangible materials to help them draw logical conclusions about their environment and understand abstract ideas. As children reach adolescence, a developmentally responsive teacher understands the increased ability to think abstractly, hypothetically, and reflectively in the formal operational stage. They use this knowledge to create instruction that encourages discussion, debate, creative problem solving, and opportunities to develop opinions, beliefs, and values.

## APPROPRIATE INSTRUCTIONAL ACTIVITIES

The following are some examples of appropriate instructional activities for early childhood, middle-level, and high school students:

- **Early childhood:** Activities that allow for exploration, play, and movement while teaching young children to function and cooperate in a group setting are most valuable in early childhood classrooms. **Movement activities** such as dancing, jumping rope, using outdoor play equipment, as well as structured and unstructured play, are beneficial in developing gross motor skills and teaching young children to properly interact with others. **Whole-group** activities such as circle time, class songs, and read-aloud sessions are also valuable in teaching young children appropriate communication skills within a group. **Thematic learning stations**, such as a science center, dramatic play area, library corner, block area, art center, and technology center, allow young children to explore their own interests on a variety of topics while developing creative and imaginative skills. **Sensory play** stations that include such items as a sand box or water table, are beneficial in further developing motor skills and allowing young children to explore and experiment with a variety of textures. Young children also require opportunities for quiet activities, such as naptime, self-selected reading, or meditation throughout the day in order to process information, reflect, and rest after active movement.

Copyright © Mometrix Media. You have been licensed one copy of this document for personal use only. Any other reproduction or redistribution is strictly prohibited. All rights reserved. This content is provided for test preparation purposes only and does not imply an endorsement by Mometrix of any particular political, scientific, or religious point of view.

- **Middle-level**: Students at this age are best supported by the implementation of **hands-on** learning activities that develop **logical reasoning** and **collaboration** skills. Collaborative activities such as science experiments, mathematical word problems, the use of manipulatives, and projects that allow opportunities for building, creating, disassembling, and exploring, are beneficial in facilitating such a learning experience. Social and emotional learning activities are also important in developing middle school students' skills in these domains. Incorporating such activities as class meetings, community building activities, and self-reflection activities, are valuable methods for teaching social and emotional skills. In addition, cooperative learning opportunities should be implemented frequently across subject areas to further develop students' ability to work productively with others. Examples include literacy circles, creating teams for class review games, or group presentations.

- **High School:** Instructional activities for high school students should be designed to foster the development of **abstract** and **hypothetical** thinking abilities while preparing them to become productive members of society as they enter adulthood. Activities such as debates, class discussions, and mock trials are beneficial in providing high school students the opportunity to employ abstract reasoning, consider solutions to hypothetical situations, and develop empathy for opposing viewpoints. Assignments that require students to engage in the research process are valuable opportunities for developing higher-order thinking skills, as they encourage students to analyze, compare, and interpret information, as well as seek evidence to support their claims. In addition, incorporating activities that benefit the community, such as fundraisers or food and clothing drives, are beneficial in teaching high school students the importance of positively contributing to society.

## EFFECTIVE AND DEVELOPMENTALLY APPROPRIATE LEARNING EXPERIENCES AND ASSESSMENTS

Effective developmentally appropriate instruction requires careful consideration when planning to ensure that students' individual needs across domains are supported to facilitate growth and a positive learning experience. The teacher must consider the developmental stage of their students based upon their age group, as well as students' individual differences. With this knowledge in mind, teachers must ensure that they provide an inclusive learning environment that fosters growth and development by creating challenging, yet attainable activities based on students' needs. Likewise, teachers must evaluate whether learning experiences and assessments are age, developmentally, and culturally appropriate while ensuring that they are tailored to students' unique learning differences. Learning experiences must provide opportunities for hands-on, cooperative, and self-directed learning, exploration, and participation to allow students to interact with their environment and build experiences. Additionally, lessons and activities should be flexible in nature to allow for inquiry and build upon students' prior experiences. Effective developmentally appropriate assessments are aimed at monitoring student progress and allow for flexibility based on students' learning differences. They should be intended to provide feedback to the teacher on how to better adapt instruction to meet students' individual needs and foster developmental growth.

## FACILITATING DEVELOPMENT OF LIFE SKILLS AND ATTITUDES IN MIDDLE SCHOOL-AGE CHILDREN

Middle school-age children are at a pivotal development point in which they experience rapid and profound change. In this transition, they often demonstrate characteristics of younger and older children and are therefore at a critical stage for developing the beliefs, attitudes, and habits that will be the foundation for their future. Teachers must understand the implications of these changes and design instruction that addresses students' learning needs and facilitates the development of such

Copyright © Mometrix Media. You have been licensed one copy of this document for personal use only. Any other reproduction or redistribution is strictly prohibited. All rights reserved.
This content is provided for test preparation purposes only and does not imply an endorsement by Mometrix of any particular political, scientific, or religious point of view.

important life skills as working and getting along with others, appreciating diversity, and committing to continued schooling. Cooperative learning and team building strategies instill the importance of working together positively to problem solve, building on one another's strengths, and valuing other's perspectives. These strategies also teach students to appreciate diversity through encouraging them to work with peers with different backgrounds and experiences. Additionally, teachers can teach students to embrace diversity through creating a culturally responsive classroom environment that models acceptance and incorporates elements of students' differences into instruction to demonstrate the value of diverse perspectives. Teachers promote positive attitudes toward academics that encourage a commitment to continued schooling by teaching organization, time management, and goal-setting skills that instill a growth mindset and provide a foundation for success.

## IMPACT OF STUDENT CHARACTERISTICS ON TEACHING AND LEARNING
### YOUNG CHILDREN

The developmental level of young children is characterized by defining attributes that impact teaching and learning, and for which several considerations must be made to design and implement effective instruction. As the attention span of young children is limited, the teacher must think about how to effectively act as a facilitator for learning more often than directly instructing students. **Direct instruction** must be delivered in small, manageable chunks to accommodate students' attention spans and ensure they retain and understand new concepts. Thus, the teacher must evaluate which elements of the curriculum require structured learning, while allowing for flexibility within instruction to accommodate student inquiry. Young children also need frequent **movement**, **physical activity**, and **social interaction**, as they learn and build experiences concretely through moving, playing, interacting with, and exploring their environment. To create a learning environment that accommodates these characteristics, the teacher must consider the physical arrangement of the classroom, and whether it adequately allows for movement. Additionally, teachers must incorporate **structured** and **unstructured activities** that foster and promote exploration, inquiry, play, cooperative learning, and hands-on interactions with the learning environment. With these considerations in mind, the teacher enhances students' learning experience by tailoring instruction to their developmental characteristics.

### MIDDLE SCHOOL AGED CHILDREN

As middle school-age children transition from childhood to adolescence, they experience vast changes across all developmental domains. Consequently, they exhibit characteristics that affect teaching and learning that require careful consideration when adapting instruction to their unique learning needs. While these students require increasing independence as they mature, they still need a structured, predictable environment to ease the transition into high school. The teacher must create a balance between fostering independence and growth while providing a schedule and routine. Opportunities for self-directed learning and student choice, as well as strategies for self-assessment and reflection foster autonomy and self-responsibility over learning while the teacher facilitates and monitors progress. Strategies to teach effective organizational and time management skills further promote independence and prepare students for success upon entering high school. As middle school-age students develop, the importance of peers becomes increasingly prevalent as they begin to search for their identity and shape their own values and beliefs. Teachers must ensure to provide opportunities for cooperative and small group learning to facilitate students' social development while considering the importance of promoting positive peer relationships at this impressionable developmental level.

Copyright © Mometrix Media. You have been licensed one copy of this document for personal use only. Any other reproduction or redistribution is strictly prohibited. All rights reserved. This content is provided for test preparation purposes only and does not imply an endorsement by Mometrix of any particular political, scientific, or religious point of view.

## ADOLESCENT CHILDREN

The developmental changes that occur in adolescence result in distinct characteristics as students in this age group transition into young adulthood. During this stage, students are discovering their identities, values, and beliefs and begin to explore long-term career and life choices. As they navigate their development and shape the person they will become, social relationships come to be increasingly important. Teachers must consider the impact of these characteristics when developing instruction to effectively address the unique needs of this age group and establish foundational attitudes, habits, and skills necessary for success in life. Effective instruction encourages adolescents to consider different perspectives, morals, and values to broaden their worldview and foster the development of their own beliefs. Lessons and activities should allow for exploration of personal interests, skills, and abilities as students shape their personalities and begin to consider long-term life goals. Moreover, the teacher should incorporate strategies that assist adolescents in goal setting to successfully foster a growth mindset and provide a foundation for success. Additionally, as socialization is highly influential at this stage, teachers must consider the importance of incorporating cooperative learning strategies and opportunities for socialization within instruction to encourage healthy peer relationships and foster positive identity development.

## INTERCONNECTION OF DEVELOPMENTAL DOMAINS

Developmental domains are deeply interconnected. If one area of a child's development is negatively impacted, it is likely to pose negative consequences on other developmental areas. Proper physical development is key to developing cognitively, socially, and emotionally in that physical development allows children to acquire the necessary gross and fine motor skills to explore and experiment with the world around them, as well as interact with others. Physical development includes development of the brain, and factors such as poor nutrition, sleep, or prenatal exposure to drugs potentially hinder brain development. Consequentially, this may result in cognitive delays, and ultimately lead to social or emotional developmental delays through negatively impacting the child's ability to interact with others, build relationships, emotionally regulate, or communicate effectively.

## CHARACTERISTICS OF THE DEVELOPMENTAL PLAY STAGES

As children develop, so do their styles of play. Developmental play stages are divided into five primary phases: **solitary play** (Birth-2 years), **onlooker play** (2 years), **parallel play** (2-3 years), **associative play** (3-4 years) and **cooperative play** (4 years and beyond). During the **solitary play** stage, children play alone and are uninterested in playing with others, or what other children around them are doing. When they reach the **onlooker play** stage, children will watch other children play, but will not actively engage in playing with others. In **parallel play**, children do not play with one another, but will often play next to each other and will use similar materials. They may be curious about what other children are doing, and may copy them, but will not directly play with them. Children begin to intentionally play with others in the **associative play** stage, but the play is unorganized and still largely individual in its goals. In **cooperative play**, children begin to intentionally play and share materials in organized groups, and often have a common purpose or goal when playing.

## PURPOSES AND BENEFITS OF PLAY IN EARLY CHILDHOOD EDUCATION

Purposeful play is an integral part of learning and development in the early childhood classroom. Its purpose is to aid and allow children to incorporate all aspects of development and thus provides cognitive, social, emotional, and physical benefits. Purposeful play deepens children's understanding of new concepts through allowing them to explore and experiment in the world

Copyright © Mometrix Media. You have been licensed one copy of this document for personal use only. Any other reproduction or redistribution is strictly prohibited. All rights reserved. This content is provided for test preparation purposes only and does not imply an endorsement by Mometrix of any particular political, scientific, or religious point of view.

around them using imagination and creativity. Integrating purposeful play into the early childhood classroom is further beneficial in that it allows children to construct and build on knowledge through experiences and helps develop divergent and convergent thinking. The socialization children get from play strengthens their language skills through speaking to one another, using new vocabulary, and listening to others. Purposeful play strengthens physical-motor development in that it calls for children to move their bodies in games, running, jumping, etc. Play is necessary for building important emotional and social skills that are necessary for being a successful member of society later in life.

## FACTORS TO CONSIDER WHEN SELECTING MATERIALS FOR LEARNING AND PLAY

To plan meaningful, integrated, and active learning and play experiences, the teacher must have a deep understanding of both the developmental stage of the students and an understanding of students' individual needs. With this knowledge in mind, there are several factors that the teacher must consider when choosing materials that support active learning and play experiences, and ultimately, the development of the whole child. Materials should be adaptable in use to facilitate development in multiple areas. Versatility is also important in fostering imagination and creativity. The teacher must consider how the chosen materials will support understanding of concepts covered in instruction, as well as how they will support conceptual, perceptual, and language development. Furthermore, the teacher must ensure that materials are age-appropriate, stimulating, and encourage active participation both independently and cooperatively.

## EQUALITY VS. EQUITY

**Equality** refers to providing everyone with the same resources when working toward a goal, regardless of the unique needs or situation of the individual. **Equity** means considering an individual's needs and circumstances to provide the proper supports that allow them a fair opportunity to achieve a common goal. In the classroom, creating an equitable environment requires the consideration of students' individual learning styles, needs, and personal situations, and using this knowledge to instill necessary supports to help each student achieve the same objectives relative to their peers. Equity in the classroom is especially important for closing the achievement gap, particularly in low socioeconomic areas, because many of these students come from disadvantaged situations and need additional help to gain a fair opportunity for academic success.

## SUPPORTS UTILIZED TO PROVIDE AN EQUITABLE LEARNING ENVIRONMENT

The nature of academic, physical, and behavioral supports depends largely on the needs of the individual student. However, some common supports are effective in addressing an array of needs to facilitate an equitable learning environment. Students with **learning disabilities** may benefit from such academic supports as preferential seating near the front of the room and minimized distractions to enhance focus. Modified test questions or alternate assignments, graphic organizers, scaffolded texts, extra copies of class notes, and individualized instruction as necessary are also valuable in enhancing focus, preventing overwhelm, and ensuring learning activities are aligned with students' capabilities. Students with **physical disabilities** may require wheelchair access, a sign language interpreter or scribe, braille text, enlarged fonts, or the use of technology devices to aid in reading and writing. Common **behavioral supports** in the classroom include opportunities for frequent breaks or movement as needed, a daily check-in with a caseworker or other dedicated staff member, or a behavior chart to allow students to self-monitor.

## CHARACTERISTICS OF A DEVELOPMENTALLY RESPONSIVE CLASSROOM

A developmentally responsive classroom is one in which the teacher understands the cognitive, physical, social, and emotional developmental stages of students while recognizing nuances and

Copyright © Mometrix Media. You have been licensed one copy of this document for personal use only. Any other reproduction or redistribution is strictly prohibited. All rights reserved. This content is provided for test preparation purposes only and does not imply an endorsement by Mometrix of any particular political, scientific, or religious point of view.

individual developmental differences within these stages. The teacher understands that developmental domains are interconnected, and effectively responds to unique developmental differences by designing a learner-centered curriculum and classroom environment that caters to each students' abilities, needs, and developmental levels to develop the whole child. The developmentally responsive classroom is engaging, supportive, and provides challenging learning opportunities based on individual learner abilities. There are several factors the teacher must consider in the developmentally responsive classroom when planning an appropriate, engaging, and challenging learning experience. The teacher must have a deep understanding of which teaching strategies will most effectively appeal to students of varying developmental levels and be prepared to teach content in multiple ways. Furthermore, the teacher must consider how to plan and organize activities, lessons, breaks, and the overall classroom environment. This would include considering how to arrange the classroom, which activity areas to include, spacing, and classroom equipment. The developmentally responsive classroom should promote positivity and productivity through creating a supportive yet challenging learning atmosphere that welcomes and respects differences, thus encouraging students' curiosity and excitement for learning.

## ESTABLISHING HIGH ACADEMIC EXPECTATIONS

In any classroom, establishing high academic standards is imperative for motivating and empowering students to succeed. By communicating high expectations clearly and frequently, the teacher demonstrates belief that each student can overcome obstacles and excel academically, thus inspiring student engagement, curiosity for learning, and an overall positive and productive learning environment. To create an environment of high academic standards, the teachers' expectations must be apparent in instruction. The teacher must provide lessons and activities that are rigorous but not so challenging that students are unable to complete them without assistance, as this would disempower and disengage students from learning. The teacher must set achievable learning goals based on knowledge of student abilities and encourage self-reflection. Additionally, the teacher must utilize knowledge of students' individual needs to instill necessary supports to help students in achieving tasks and create an equitable environment for learning. This will ultimately empower students to overcome obstacles and motivate them for academic success.

Copyright © Mometrix Media. You have been licensed one copy of this document for personal use only. Any other reproduction or redistribution is strictly prohibited. All rights reserved.
This content is provided for test preparation purposes only and does not imply an endorsement by Mometrix of any particular political, scientific, or religious point of view.

## CHAPTER QUIZ

**1. From which of the following beliefs is developmentally appropriate practice derived?**

a. Children are naturally curious to learn and should be encouraged to take initiative in their own learning.

b. Given a stimulating enough environment, with a teacher that is committed enough, any child is capable of learning.

c. Because each child develops at their own rate, the teacher should ensure that the lesson is always geared toward the child having the most difficulty, so that everybody learns at the same pace.

d. Children require and desire structured environments that are free from distraction in order to be taught sufficiently.

**2. List the developmental play stages from earliest to latest.**

a. Onlooker, solitary, parallel, associative, cooperative

b. Parallel, onlooker, solitary, associative, cooperative

c. Solitary, onlooker, parallel, associative, cooperative

d. Solitary, parallel, onlooker, associative, cooperative

**3. Which of the following is a developmentally appropriate activity for a middle-level child?**

a. Whole-group activities

b. Thematic learning stations

c. Collaborative activities

d. Sensory play stations

**4. Which of the following is correct about direct instruction for young children?**

a. It should be given as a single large block to maximize the amount of information given.

b. It should be geared toward the lowest-performing student so that everyone can understand it.

c. It should be explained broadly, with time scheduled after to test how well it is understood.

d. It should be delivered in small, manageable chunks to accommodate students' attention spans.

## CHAPTER QUIZ ANSWER KEY

**1. A:** Developmentally appropriate practice (DAP) is a teaching approach grounded in theories of child development. It is derived from the belief that children are naturally curious to learn, and when provided a stimulating environment, should be encouraged to take initiative in their own learning. This approach allows for a great deal of choice in learning experiences. The teacher's role is to facilitate active learning by creating developmentally appropriate activities. These activities are based on the awareness of similarities between children in various developmental stages and the knowledge that each child develops at their own rate.

**2. C:** As children develop, so do their styles of play. Developmental play stages are divided into five primary phases: solitary play (birth-2 years), onlooker play (2 years), parallel play (2-3 years), associative play (3-4 years), and cooperative play (4 years and beyond).

**3. C:** Students at this age are best supported by the implementation of hands-on learning activities that develop logical reasoning and collaboration skills. Collaborative activities such as science experiments, mathematical word problems, the use of manipulatives, and projects that allow opportunities for building, creating, disassembling, and exploring, are beneficial in facilitating such a learning experience.

Copyright © Mometrix Media. You have been licensed one copy of this document for personal use only. Any other reproduction or redistribution is strictly prohibited. All rights reserved. This content is provided for test preparation purposes only and does not imply an endorsement by Mometrix of any particular political, scientific, or religious point of view.

**4. D:** Direct instruction must be delivered in small, manageable chunks to accommodate students' attention spans and ensure they retain and understand new concepts. Thus, the teacher must evaluate which elements of the curriculum require structured learning, while allowing for flexibility within instruction to accommodate student inquiry.

Copyright © Mometrix Media. You have been licensed one copy of this document for personal use only. Any other reproduction or redistribution is strictly prohibited. All rights reserved.
This content is provided for test preparation purposes only and does not imply an endorsement by Mometrix of any particular political, scientific, or religious point of view.

# Student Diversity and Equity

## IMPLICATIONS FOR TEACHING, LEARNING, AND ASSESSMENT IN DIVERSE CLASSROOMS

In any classroom, a teacher will encounter a wide range of variances among individual students that inevitably will influence teaching, learning, and assessment. Diversities in ethnicity, gender, language background, and learning exceptionality will likely exist simultaneously in a single classroom. Educators must be prepared to teach to these diversities while concurrently teaching students the value and importance of diversity. The curriculum and classroom environment must be adjusted to meet individual student needs and create an **inclusive**, **respectful**, and **equitable** environment that welcomes differences and allows for success in learning. This begins with the teacher developing an understanding of the unique diversities that exist within their students and using this knowledge to **differentiate** curriculum, materials, activities, and assessments in such a way that students of all needs, interests, backgrounds, and abilities feel encouraged and included. Furthermore, the teacher must understand how to instill appropriate supports to accommodate the diverse needs of students, as well as how to modify the classroom environment in such a way that is reflective of the diversity of the students.

## CONSIDERATIONS FOR TEACHING IN DIVERSE CLASSROOMS
### ETHNICALLY-DIVERSE CLASSROOMS

As society becomes increasingly diverse, teachers will certainly encounter classrooms with students of multiple ethnicities. Thus, to create an accepting and respectful classroom environment that allows for success in learning for all students, there are several factors to consider. Teachers must educate themselves on the various ethnicities within their classroom. This includes being mindful of **social norms, values, beliefs, traditions,** and **lifestyles** of different ethnic groups, and learning to communicate with students and families in a respectful, culturally sensitive manner. Additionally, the teacher must make a conscious effort to incorporate aspects of each ethnicity into the curriculum, activities, and classroom environment to create an inclusive atmosphere that teaches the acceptance, respect for, and celebration of differences. Teachers must be **culturally competent** and ensure that all materials are accurate, relevant, authentic, and portray the different ethnicities within the classroom in a respectful, unbiased manner. Furthermore, teachers must consider how their own ethnicity impacts their teaching style and interactions with students, how they may be perceived by other ethnic groups, and how to respond in a manner that fosters respect and inclusivity.

### GENDER-DIVERSE CLASSROOMS

When approaching a gender-diverse classroom, teachers need to consider their perceptions, interactions with, and expectations of different genders, as well as how the classroom environment and materials portray gender differences. Teachers must work to eliminate possible stereotypical beliefs so all students feel respected, accepted, and encouraged to participate. Furthermore, teachers must consider how their behavior acts as a model for how students perceive gender roles and should act in a way that eliminates gender divisiveness. Teachers should use gender-neutral language when addressing students and ensure that all students receive equal attention. Teachers must maintain equal academic and behavioral expectations between genders and be sure to equally praise and discipline students so that neither gender feels superior or inferior to another. Regarding curriculum and classroom materials, teachers must ensure that the classroom environment encourages equal participation in, access to, and choice of all activities and procedures. Activities and materials should provide equal opportunities and foster collaboration between genders. Furthermore, teachers must ensure that curriculum materials avoid gender stereotypes, and highlight each gender equally in order to create an accepting and respectful

Copyright © Mometrix Media. You have been licensed one copy of this document for personal use only. Any other reproduction or redistribution is strictly prohibited. All rights reserved. This content is provided for test preparation purposes only and does not imply an endorsement by Mometrix of any particular political, scientific, or religious point of view.

learning environment that provides equal opportunities for students of all genders to develop their individual identities and abilities.

## LINGUISTICALLY DIVERSE CLASSROOMS

In a **linguistically diverse** classroom, teachers must consider how to effectively demonstrate value for students' native languages while simultaneously supporting the development of necessary language skills to thrive in the school setting. By accepting and encouraging students to use their native languages, teachers can establish an inclusive learning environment that celebrates linguistic differences, and therefore, encourages students to want to build upon their language skills. Through this, teachers create an equitable learning environment that allows for academic success. To develop English language skills, the teacher must first consider each students' language ability and level of exposure to English prior to entering the classroom, as well as the level of language learning support each student has at home. Teachers can then implement effective instructional strategies and supports to modify curriculum in a way that addresses students' language needs. Teachers must also consider the implications of the classroom environment on language acquisition. By creating an atmosphere that encourages language acquisition through **literacy-rich resources** and **cooperative learning**, teachers promote the use of language skills and ultimately provide opportunities for success for all students.

## LINGUISTIC SUPPORTS AND INSTRUCTIONAL STRATEGIES PROMOTING ENGLISH LANGUAGE PROFICIENCY

Incorporating a variety of linguistic aids and instructional strategies is beneficial in supporting ELL students of varying levels of English language proficiency. **Visual representations** to accompany instruction, such as posters, charts, pictures, slide shows, videos, tables, or anchor charts, are valuable in providing clarification and reference while promoting vocabulary acquisition. When delivering instruction, **body language** such as hand gestures, eye contact, and movement to mimic verbal directions and explanations can provide clarification to enhance understanding. These students may also require **translation devices** for clarification, an interpreter to help with understanding instructions and new concepts, alternate assignments with simplified language, or **individualized instruction** from an ESL teacher. Frequently checking for understanding and providing clarification as necessary throughout instruction are necessary to ensuring ELL students understand learning materials, instructions, and assessments. In addition, creating a print and literacy-rich environment by including word walls for new vocabulary, reading materials that vary in complexity, labels, and opportunities for speaking, reading, and writing within instruction are valuable in promoting English language acquisition.

## LEARNING DISABILITIES AND OTHER EXCEPTIONALITIES

In a classroom where learning disabilities and exceptionalities are present, teachers must consider accommodations for students of various learning needs while fostering an atmosphere of respect and acceptance. Teachers must understand the individual learning needs of each student and differentiate instruction accordingly to create an equitable and inclusive learning atmosphere. For **learning disabled** students, teachers must consider accommodations that allow for inclusion in all areas of curriculum and instruction. Such considerations may include extended work time, individualized instruction, and cooperative learning activities to ensure that learning disabled students are provided the necessary supports to achieve academic success. For students with other exceptionalities, such as **gifted and talented** students, teachers need to consider ways to provide challenging and stimulating opportunities for expansion and enrichment of curriculum. Furthermore, the teacher must be aware of their own interactions with students in order to demonstrate and encourage respect and acceptance among students. By providing supports for individual student success, teachers can effectively highlight students' strengths and therefore, teach students to accept and celebrate differences in learning abilities.

Copyright © Mometrix Media. You have been licensed one copy of this document for personal use only. Any other reproduction or redistribution is strictly prohibited. All rights reserved. This content is provided for test preparation purposes only and does not imply an endorsement by Mometrix of any particular political, scientific, or religious point of view.

## GOALS OF TEACHING DIVERSITY IN THE CLASSROOM

Teaching diversity in the classroom aims to establish a welcoming and inclusive classroom environment that encourages academic achievement and whole-child development. Diversity education works to develop students' understanding, acceptance, and respect for others' perspectives while instilling the concept that people are ultimately more alike than different, and that diversities should be celebrated. Teaching the importance of differences creates a positive, inclusive classroom atmosphere in which all students feel respected, safe, and valued by their teacher and peers. Such an environment promotes academic achievement among students in that it encourages participation in learning and builds the self-esteem necessary for positive growth and development. Furthermore, teaching diversity has a significant role in **whole-child development** in that it instills the ability to understand and respect multiple frames of reference, thus increasing their ability to problem solve, cooperate with others, and develop a broader global perspective. Additionally, it allows for the development of cultural competency and ultimately creates accepting and respectful contributors to society.

## RECOGNIZING AND ELIMINATING PERSONAL BIASES

Personal biases are often subtle and unconscious, yet it is essential that teachers work to recognize and eliminate them to create an accepting and respectful classroom environment. Personal biases may negatively impact teaching style, interactions with students, and ultimately, student learning and self-esteem. In eliminating personal bias, teachers ensure that they establish an inclusive classroom environment where each student is treated fairly. Furthermore, students' beliefs toward diversity are influenced by the attitudes and behaviors modeled by their teacher, and therefore, eradicating personal bias is vital in positively influencing students to accept and respect differences. To eliminate personal bias, teachers must **reflect** on their own culture's attitudes toward diversity, as well as how these attitudes influence their interactions toward other groups, and work to make positive changes. Teachers must **educate** themselves on the diversities among their students and work to deepen their understanding of different groups through **communicating** with families, **integrating** themselves into students' communities, and participating in **professional development** that focuses on **cultural competency** and the importance of teaching diversity. Through making positive changes against personal biases, teachers foster a classroom environment that promotes diversity and empowers all students to be successful.

## IMPACT OF DIVERSE CULTURAL CLIMATE IN THE CLASSROOM

Creating a diverse cultural climate in the classroom results in an empowering and engaging learning environment that facilitates academic success. An atmosphere that respects and accepts differences fosters a sense of inclusivity and welcoming among teachers and students, which allows students to feel comfortable with differences, safe in their own identities, and consequently, comfortable to engage in learning. This fosters a positive attitude toward learning that promotes academic achievement. Additionally, when students accept one another's differences in a diverse cultural climate, they are better able to work together and adopt creative problem-solving solutions through others' perspectives, which results in success in learning. Furthermore, a successfully diverse cultural climate reflects the diversity of the students within it, which ultimately creates a more engaging and relevant academic environment that sparks motivation and curiosity toward learning. Learning environments that reflect students' diversity create a sense of unity and belonging in the classroom and positively contribute to success in learning through building students' self-esteem and self-concept to empower them in believing they can achieve academic success.

Copyright © Mometrix Media. You have been licensed one copy of this document for personal use only. Any other reproduction or redistribution is strictly prohibited. All rights reserved. This content is provided for test preparation purposes only and does not imply an endorsement by Mometrix of any particular political, scientific, or religious point of view.

## AUTHENTIC CLASSROOM MATERIALS

**Authentic classroom materials** are artifacts from various cultures, events, or periods of time. These items enhance the relevancy of instruction by promoting students' real-world connection to learning and may also be used to incorporate students' backgrounds and experiences into the classroom to increase engagement. Such materials include magazines, newspapers, advertisements, restaurant menus, and recipes. In addition, resources such as video clips, films, television shows, documentaries, news segments, and music serve as authentic media sources to incorporate into instruction. Original works or documents, including art pieces, literature, poetry, maps, or historical records, are also valuable authentic resources for providing students with a real-world learning experience.

### LOCATING AND IMPLEMENTING

**Authentic classroom materials** and resources are integral in creating a classroom environment that fosters engaging, relevant, and positive learning experiences. Teachers must work to develop an understanding of the diversities among their students and use this knowledge to locate and implement authentic classroom materials into daily instruction. In doing so, teachers create a positive learning environment that accepts and respects differences through incorporating **relevant** and **familiar** materials that make students from all backgrounds feel valued and included in instruction. When students can see aspects of their culture reflected in authentic learning materials, they can make **personal connections** between what they are learning and their own lives, and learning becomes more valuable, engaging, and relevant, thereby promoting success in learning.

## INCORPORATING DIVERSITY EDUCATION INTO THE CLASSROOM

Incorporating diversity into the classroom maximizes student opportunities for academic success through creating a welcoming, empowering, and inclusive atmosphere. Teachers can implement multiple strategies to incorporate **diversity education** into the curriculum both as its own unit and woven into content instruction once they develop an understanding of the diversities among their own students. Through **building relationships** with students, teachers can use their knowledge of students' lives to incorporate aspects of their backgrounds into the curriculum by creating specific **cultural lessons** on food, music, language, art, and history. Additionally, **cultural comparison** studies are an effective method of teaching students the value of diversity, as well as highlighting the fact that people from different backgrounds often have more similarities than differences. Teachers can further implement diversity education by encouraging students to participate in learning through having them share elements of their culture and background with the class through activities such as show and tell or hosting family nights. Furthermore, integrating **cooperative learning** activities into instruction allow and encourage students from different backgrounds to work together and gain an understanding of the perspectives and backgrounds of others.

## INCORPORATING DIVERSITY IN THE ENTIRE CLASSROOM ENVIRONMENT

Incorporating diversity into the curriculum is vital for teaching the value and importance of differences and for contributing to a respectful and accepting environment. Additionally, it is imperative that diversity education extend from the curriculum to the entire classroom environment to maximize student growth and opportunity to reach potential. When students learn in an atmosphere that celebrates diversity and identifies strengths in differences, they feel a sense of belonging and confidence that encourages them to engage in learning, thus maximizing the potential for academic success. Teachers can effectively integrate diversity into the classroom environment through making authentic cultural materials such as texts, music, and art readily

Copyright © Mometrix Media. You have been licensed one copy of this document for personal use only. Any other reproduction or redistribution is strictly prohibited. All rights reserved. This content is provided for test preparation purposes only and does not imply an endorsement by Mometrix of any particular political, scientific, or religious point of view.

accessible for students. Additionally, providing several opportunities for students to collaborate and socialize in a natural setting allows them to gain an understanding and respect for their peers' backgrounds. By encouraging students to share aspects of their own lives and backgrounds with the class through cultural activities, teachers facilitate a diverse climate that celebrates differences.

## UNDERSTANDING STUDENTS' DIVERSE BACKGROUNDS AND NEEDS
### *SELF-EDUCATION*

Educating oneself on students' diverse backgrounds and needs enhances one's overall understanding of their students and creates a culturally sensitive, accepting classroom environment tailored to students' individual needs. There are several avenues through which teachers should educate themselves in an effort to build an accepting and respectful classroom climate. Communication is key for learning about diversities; thus, it is important for teachers to foster and maintain positive communications with students' families to deepen understanding of cultures, beliefs, lifestyles, and needs that exist within their classroom. This could include learning some language of students with different cultural backgrounds, attending family nights at school, or participating in social events within their students' communities to integrate themselves into the culture. Furthermore, teachers can learn more about their students' backgrounds and needs through gaining an understanding of student differences, incorporating these diversities into the curriculum, and encouraging students to participate in learning by sharing aspects of their lives with the class.

### *TEACHING, LEARNING, AND CLASSROOM CLIMATE BENEFITS*

A deep understanding of students' diverse backgrounds and needs provides multiple benefits for teaching, learning, and overall classroom climate. Knowledge of students' diversities allows teachers to understand the individual needs and abilities of their students, and tailor instruction accordingly to maximize student development and achievement. Additionally, it allows teachers to know which authentic materials to incorporate in lessons and instructions to best create an engaging, relevant, and respectful learning experience that fosters student interest in learning and promotes success. Furthermore, by enhancing understanding of students' diverse backgrounds and needs, teachers consequently begin to model an attitude of inclusivity, acceptance, and respect for differences, which is then reflected by students and achieves a positive, welcoming classroom climate that promotes diversity.

Copyright © Mometrix Media. You have been licensed one copy of this document for personal use only. Any other reproduction or redistribution is strictly prohibited. All rights reserved. This content is provided for test preparation purposes only and does not imply an endorsement by Mometrix of any particular political, scientific, or religious point of view.

## CHAPTER QUIZ

**1. Which of the following is NOT conducive to promoting English-language acquisition?**
   a. Providing reading materials of minimal complexity
   b. Frequently checking for understanding and providing clarification as necessary
   c. Implementing visual representations to accompany instruction
   d. Creating a print- and literacy-rich environment

**2. All of the following are ways for a teacher to eliminate personal bias EXCEPT:**
   a. Reflecting on their own culture's attitudes toward diversity and the influence this has on interactions with other groups
   b. Recognizing any dominant majorities within the classroom and giving them extra attention
   c. Integrating themselves into students' communities
   d. Participating in professional development that focuses on cultural competency

**3. Teachers may use artifacts from various cultures, events, or periods of time that are integral in creating a classroom environment that fosters positive learning experiences. What are these artifacts called?**
   a. Appropriate classroom materials
   b. Historically significant school supplies
   c. Authentic classroom materials
   d. Diversity education school supplies

## CHAPTER QUIZ ANSWER KEY

**1. A:** Frequently checking for understanding, and providing clarification as necessary throughout instruction, are necessary to ensure that ELL students understand learning materials, instructions, and assessments. In addition, it is valuable in promoting English-language acquisition to create a print- and literacy-rich environment by including word walls for new vocabulary, reading materials that vary in complexity, labels, and opportunities for speaking, reading, and writing.

**2. B:** To eliminate personal bias, teachers must reflect on their own culture's attitudes toward diversity, as well as how these attitudes influence their interactions toward other groups, and they must work to make positive changes. Teachers must educate themselves on the diversities among their students and work to deepen their understanding of different groups by communicating with families, integrating themselves into students' communities, and participating in professional development that focuses on cultural competency and the importance of teaching diversity. Through making positive changes against personal biases, teachers foster a classroom environment that promotes diversity and empowers all students to be successful.

**3. C:** Authentic classroom materials are artifacts from various cultures, events, or periods of time. These items enhance the relevance of instruction by promoting students' real-world connection to learning, and may also be used to incorporate students' backgrounds and experiences into the classroom to increase engagement. Such materials include magazines, newspapers, advertisements, restaurant menus, and recipes.

Copyright © Mometrix Media. You have been licensed one copy of this document for personal use only. Any other reproduction or redistribution is strictly prohibited. All rights reserved. This content is provided for test preparation purposes only and does not imply an endorsement by Mometrix of any particular political, scientific, or religious point of view.

# Materials and Resources

## MATERIALS AND RESOURCES THAT ENHANCE STUDENT LEARNING AND ENGAGEMENT

### INSTRUCTIONAL MATERIALS AND RESOURCES

The careful selection of instructional materials and resources for lesson plans is an integral component of enhancing student engagement and the overall learning experience. Lesson materials should be relevant to students' interests so as to facilitate personal connections to learning and ultimately, deepen understanding. In building positive relationships with students by educating themselves on students' backgrounds and interests, teachers can effectively locate and implement varied instructional materials and resources that are relevant to students and foster motivation for learning. Additionally, interactive materials, such as manipulatives or other hands-on learning resources, enhance learning and engagement through encouraging participation. Similarly, cooperative learning materials encourage student participation, and therefore, engagement, through fostering collaboration. Teachers can also enhance learning experiences through incorporating authentic materials that are relevant to instruction such as maps, brochures, historical documents, or similar materials that enhance student engagement and learning.

### TECHNOLOGICAL RESOURCES

Technology is integrated in nearly every aspect of life as a tool to enhance and assist in daily activities. This notion also applies in the classroom, as technological resources are an excellent method of increasing student engagement and interest, supporting students in their individual learning needs, and ultimately, enhancing learning. The use of computers, tablets, smartphones, and other technological resources serve to improve understanding of classroom instruction, foster relevancy and personal connections, and scaffold instruction to address diverse learning styles and needs. Additionally, teachers have myriad digital resources available in the form of interactive websites, videos clips, and apps that can be implemented to enrich lessons and increase development across all subject areas. Often, these resources accommodate students' individual learning needs through providing increasingly challenging activities based on individual skill level, and therefore, the teacher can utilize these resources to tailor instruction to address individual student needs. Technological resources can also add authenticity to learning experiences, making them more engaging and enhancing student learning. Virtual field trips or science experiments can provide real-world connections to instruction by recreating authentic learning experiences without students having to leave the classroom.

### COMMUNITY RESOURCES

Community resources are beneficial in enriching instruction to foster engagement and enhance student learning. They provide students the opportunity to connect and apply what they learn in the classroom with the real world. This ultimately makes learning more authentic, as students are able to see the relevancy of what they are learning, and therefore, enhances learning by making it more engaging. Through field trips, teachers can incorporate community resources such as museums, art exhibits, science centers, and even local areas such as parks or historical sites into curriculum to accompany material learned in class. Additionally, if access to field trips is limited, teachers can take advantage of community outreach programs that bring learning experiences to classrooms. Reaching out to members of the community that are relevant to topics being covered in class, such as scientists or local historians, can be beneficial in allowing students to understand how what they are learning is applicable outside of the classroom. Locating and implementing community resources enhances student learning and engagement through making learning authentic, relevant, and applicable in the real world.

Copyright © Mometrix Media. You have been licensed one copy of this document for personal use only. Any other reproduction or redistribution is strictly prohibited. All rights reserved. This content is provided for test preparation purposes only and does not imply an endorsement by Mometrix of any particular political, scientific, or religious point of view.

## DEVELOPMENTALLY APPROPRIATE MATERIALS AND RESOURCES

To create engaging and effective learning experiences, instructional materials and resources must be developmentally appropriate. Teachers must have a solid understanding of the general cognitive, physical, social, and emotional developmental levels of their students, as well as individual differences in skills and abilities to properly select developmentally appropriate materials. The age and developmental level appropriateness of instructional resources can be determined by considering the material's size, height, and level of difficulty for students. Whether materials accommodate individual differences in skill level, ability, or interest can be determined by their versatility. If a resource can be used in multiple ways, it will appeal to a variety of learning needs and interests and support development across domains. Developmentally appropriate materials are reflective and considerate of students' diversities. Teachers can determine this by using their knowledge of students' backgrounds to select materials that incorporate and are sensitive to their students' cultural differences to support development by fostering personal connections to learning.

Copyright © Mometrix Media. You have been licensed one copy of this document for personal use only. Any other reproduction or redistribution is strictly prohibited. All rights reserved. This content is provided for test preparation purposes only and does not imply an endorsement by Mometrix of any particular political, scientific, or religious point of view.

## CHAPTER QUIZ

**1. What are the purpose of manipulatives?**

- a. To enhance learning and engagement through hands-on participation
- b. To foster collaboration through cooperative activity
- c. To accommodate individual learning needs through increasingly challenging activities
- d. To make learning more authentic as students apply what they learn in the classroom to the real world

## CHAPTER QUIZ ANSWER KEY

**1. A:** Additionally, interactive materials—such as manipulatives or other hands-on learning resources—enhance learning and engagement through encouraging participation.

Copyright © Mometrix Media. You have been licensed one copy of this document for personal use only. Any other reproduction or redistribution is strictly prohibited. All rights reserved.
This content is provided for test preparation purposes only and does not imply an endorsement by Mometrix of any particular political, scientific, or religious point of view.

# Classroom Management, Routines, and Procedures

## CLASSROOM ROUTINES AND PROCEDURES

### INFLUENCE ON CLASSROOM CLIMATE, PRODUCTIVITY, STUDENT BEHAVIOR, AND LEARNING

A well-managed classroom focused on productivity, positive behavior, and success in learning relies on the effectiveness and consistency of **routines** and **procedures** instilled for daily activities. By implementing these at the beginning of the school year and continuously reinforcing them throughout, the teacher establishes an orderly, efficient classroom that facilitates students' ability to productively engage in learning. Classroom management, and therefore, student behavior and productivity, is enhanced by structured routines and procedures, as students that are clear on expectations are more inclined to follow them. Such structure provides students with a sense of predictability and security in their environment that contributes to their willingness to participate in learning. Routines and procedures simplify daily tasks and allow for smooth transitions between activities. This minimizes opportunities for student distraction or disruption, thus promoting positive behavior, increasing instructional time, and enhancing students' ability to focus on learning in an orderly, productive classroom climate.

> **Review Video: Classroom Management - Rhythms of Teaching**
> Visit mometrix.com/academy and enter code: 809399

### CONSIDERATIONS REGARDING AGE-APPROPRIATENESS TO ENSURE EFFECTIVENESS

Classroom procedures and routines must reflect the characteristics and capabilities of the students' **age group**. It is important that the teacher understand and apply their knowledge of students' **developmental levels** across domains when considering which routines and procedures to establish in their classroom. In doing so, the teacher ensures that expectations are age-appropriate, realistic, and effective in creating an orderly, productive environment. Procedures and routines must always be clear, succinct, and limited in number to avoid overwhelming students. However, in communicating them, the teacher must use comprehensible language relative to students' age-group. The nature of learning must be considered when determining age-appropriate routines and procedures. For young children, procedures for cleaning up toys after playtime is appropriate, whereas procedures for turning in homework and taking assessments applies to older students. The degree to which students are expected to perform routines and procedures independently must also be considered and reflective of their capabilities. Young children may need a great deal of assistance, whereas older students can perform certain tasks independently. Consequences for not following expectations must be appropriate to students' age group. Losing free play time may be appropriate for young children, whereas parent communication may be effective for older students.

### EXAMPLES OF AGE-APPROPRIATE ROUTINES AND PROCEDURES

**Young children:** Young children can reasonably be expected to perform **basic daily routines** independently, although they likely will need frequent reminders. Daily procedures may include having young children hang up their coats, put away lunchboxes, and unpack their backpacks at the beginning of the day as they prepare to begin morning work. Similarly, young children can be expected to independently follow end-of-day procedures and routines, such as packing up their backpacks, cleaning up learning materials, and lining up at the door for dismissal. Young children should be able to follow simple behavioral procedures as well, such as keeping hands to themselves, responding to attention signals from the teacher, and cleaning up learning materials before transitioning between activities. Young children also benefit from being assigned classroom "jobs," such as line leader, paper collector, or teacher assistant, as these routines instill a sense of accountability and self-responsibility.

Copyright © Mometrix Media. You have been licensed one copy of this document for personal use only. Any other reproduction or redistribution is strictly prohibited. All rights reserved.
This content is provided for test preparation purposes only and does not imply an endorsement by Mometrix of any particular political, scientific, or religious point of view.

**Middle-level:** Middle-level students can be expected to follow a variety of routines and procedures with **increasing levels of independence**. These students can reasonably be expected to enter the classroom on time and prepared with necessary learning materials. In addition, middle-level students can be held responsible for independently turning in homework according to the procedures for doing so and beginning their morning work. Middle-level students should be able to follow procedures for accessing learning materials, transitioning to cooperative learning activities, cleaning up their own materials before moving to a new activity, and non-instructional tasks, such as sharpening pencils, using the restroom, or throwing away trash with minimal reminders from the teacher.

**High school:** Routines and procedures in the high school classroom should **reflect** students' level of **maturity and increasing capabilities for independence** as they approach adulthood. These students can reasonably be expected to independently come to class on time, prepared, and follow procedures for turning in homework and beginning morning work. In addition, high school students can be expected to follow procedures for direct instruction, cooperative learning activities, and independently transitioning between activities. High school students can be held to a greater degree of accountability regarding grading procedures, tardiness and attendance, and procedures for turning in late assignments.

## FACILITATING AN ORGANIZED, PRODUCTIVE ENVIRONMENT THAT MAXIMIZES STUDENT LEARNING

Clear routines and procedures for daily classroom activities are necessary to create an organized, productive environment that maximizes student learning. In order to be effective, routines and procedures must be reflective of the teacher's **instructional** and **classroom management** style, explicitly stated, and consistently reinforced. This ensures expectations are relevant, realistic, and that students are continuously aware of them as they engage in learning. Procedures for entering and exiting the classroom, as well as how students will begin and end their day, establish a structured, **predictable** routine that enhances focus on instruction. Smooth **transition procedures** maintain order and enhance efficiency when moving between activities, as they eliminate idle time, minimize student distraction, and allow for increased time dedicated to productive teaching and learning. Such transition procedures include how and when to access and clean up materials, move from independent to collaborative group work, or move between learning stations. The teacher must also consider procedures for performing non-instructional activities, such as sharpening pencils or going to the restroom, as these further avoid disruptions to instructional time. Procedures and routines establish organization and efficiency in the classroom by simplifying tasks to allow for increased productive instructional time and enhanced student learning.

Procedures and routines are necessary for establishing a well-managed and productive classroom environment. While the specifics of routines may vary depending upon the teacher's classroom management style and students' learning needs, many common procedures and routines share similar guidelines.

- **Entering the classroom/morning routine:** A procedure for the beginning of class ensures that students enter the room in an orderly manner with a clear understanding of what is expected of them. This routine should include entering the room quietly, unpacking necessary items for class, turning in homework, and working on an opening activity while the teacher takes attendance.

Copyright © Mometrix Media. You have been licensed one copy of this document for personal use only. Any other reproduction or redistribution is strictly prohibited. All rights reserved.
This content is provided for test preparation purposes only and does not imply an endorsement by Mometrix of any particular political, scientific, or religious point of view.

- **Leaving the classroom/packing up routine:** A procedure for packing up and leaving the classroom at the end of class or the school day ensures that students have all of their necessary materials, leave the room clean and organized, and exit in an orderly manner. Such a routine may include cleaning up learning materials, putting away assignments or papers, straightening desks, throwing away trash, packing up backpacks, and lining up by the door prior to dismissal. Students may be assigned specific jobs for cleaning up and organizing the room.

- **Turning in work:** Procedures for turning in classwork and homework allow for smoother transitions between activities and limit interruptions to instruction. This should occur at a specific time during the class period and can include designating a "turn in" box in the classroom for students to hand in assignments, or having students pass their papers to the front in a specific order. A student may be designated to collect papers at the end of an activity as well.

- **Using the restroom:** Restroom procedures limit student distraction and interruptions to instruction. Restroom breaks should generally not occur during direct instruction, and students should be permitted to go one at a time to avoid misbehavior. Students should be given a restroom pass, sign out before leaving the room, and sign back in upon returning to ensure that the teacher is always aware of students' whereabouts. Specific hand signals in which students can silently request permission to use the restroom are beneficial in further minimizing disruptions.

- **Transitions between activities:** Procedures for transitions allow for an orderly learning environment in that they indicate to students when and how to move between activities in the classroom. These procedures should include an attention signal and a clear explanation of the steps for transitioning, such as cleaning up materials from the previous activity, and a signal to indicate when students are permitted to move. Students should be expected to transition between activities quickly, quietly, and without disruption.

- **Non-instructional tasks:** Procedures for non-instructional tasks limit interruptions to instructional time for more focused learning. Activities such as getting a tissue, sharpening pencils, and throwing away trash should occur during specific times when the teacher is not directly instructing and should be done quietly and without disruption.

- **Managing student behavior:** Clear procedures for misbehavior establish a predictable, orderly learning environment. These procedures should be explicit, consistent, and follow a logical sequence. They may include a verbal warning, seating change, loss of privileges, or communication with home.

- **Accessing and using materials, supplies, and technology:** Procedures for these activities are beneficial in limiting disruption, maintaining organization, and avoiding interruptions to instruction. Such procedures indicate when and how to access and use materials, supplies, and technology in a respectful and orderly manner. The teacher should clearly communicate expectations for access and use, as well as utilize a specific signal to indicate when students are permitted to move. These procedures should also include methods for proper cleanup at the end of the activity.

- **Finishing work early:** A procedure for finishing work early minimizes idle time and limits student disruption. Students that finish early may be permitted to work on other assignments or read quietly, or the teacher can dedicate an area of the room for extra practice and review activities for students to work on if they finish early. The teacher may also permit early finishers to assist other students in applicable learning situations.

Copyright © Mometrix Media. You have been licensed one copy of this document for personal use only. Any other reproduction or redistribution is strictly prohibited. All rights reserved.
This content is provided for test preparation purposes only and does not imply an endorsement by Mometrix of any particular political, scientific, or religious point of view.

- **Emergency drills:** Procedures for emergency drills ensure that students know how to complete them in a safe, orderly manner. When the drill begins, students should immediately stop what they are doing, leave all materials on their desks, and line up by the door in an organized fashion. Students should exit the room with the teacher and move quickly and quietly through the hallways to the designated drill location. For emergency drills that occur inside the classroom, students should move quickly and quietly to a previously designated location within the room and remain there until the drill is over.
- **Attention signal:** A dedicated signal to capture students' attention indicates that they need to stop what they are doing, focus, and listen quietly to the teacher for further information or instructions. This signal could be in the form of a hand signal, call and response, phrase, or sound and should be used consistently.
- **Direct instruction:** A procedure for direct instruction is beneficial in maintaining students' focus on learning. This should include steps for active listening, including sitting up straight, facing the teacher, maintaining eye contact, and refraining from distracting neighboring classmates. Students should have clear steps regarding how to ask questions, such as raising their hand or utilizing color-coded cards to indicate levels of understanding, and how to take notes, when applicable.
- **Independent work:** An independent work procedure limits distractions and promotes students' ability to focus. This should include communicating expectations for quiet time during this period, including refraining from talking to neighboring peers, working at and remaining in assigned seats, and engaging in the proper procedure if a student finishes early. If a student needs assistance, he or she can indicate it by raising a hand, or utilizing a dedicated signal to request help, such as color-coded cards.
- **Collaborative work:** A procedure for collaborative work indicates to students how to move from independent to group activities. This includes moving to a group setting without disruption, maintaining a normal volume, communicating respectfully, and cleaning up materials when finished before moving back to assigned seats in an orderly manner.

## DEVELOPMENTAL CHARACTERISTICS OF YOUNG CHILDREN IN RELATION TO INTERACTIONS WITH OTHERS

Designing group activities that align with young children's ability to collaborate while supporting social development requires a realistic understanding of their capacity to do so. This entails understanding the **developmental characteristics** of young children at varying stages, including how the nature of their interactions with others evolves. Young children learn by exploring and interacting with their environment, so they need ample opportunities for play and active movement to do so. However, the teacher must recognize that the way young children play and collaborate develops over time. Young children typically exhibit little interest in actively playing with others until approximately age four. Until then, they progress through stages of solitary play, observing their peers, playing independently alongside others, and eventually, loosely interacting, perhaps with the same toys, while still primarily engaging in independent play. During these stages, it is important that the teacher foster **collaboration** by providing multiple opportunities for play as well as learning materials that encourage **cooperation** and **sharing**. The teacher must, however, maintain the understanding that these children have yet to develop the capacity to intentionally work with others. Once this ability is developed, the teacher can integrate coordinated group activities that encourage collaboration toward a common goal.

## CONSIDERATIONS WHEN DESIGNING GROUP ACTIVITIES FOR YOUNG CHILDREN

For young children, thoughtfully designed group activities are integral in promoting development across domains. These opportunities facilitate social and emotional development by encouraging

Copyright © Mometrix Media. You have been licensed one copy of this document for personal use only. Any other reproduction or redistribution is strictly prohibited. All rights reserved. This content is provided for test preparation purposes only and does not imply an endorsement by Mometrix of any particular political, scientific, or religious point of view.

collaboration and positive communication, as well as physical and cognitive growth as children play, explore, and interact with others in the learning environment. It is therefore important that the teacher carefully consider the particulars of group activities when planning to ensure maximized learning and development. The teacher must consider the **developmental characteristics** of their students' age group, including their capacity to collaborate with others. This enables the teacher to plan group activities that align with students' abilities while promoting collaboration and development. All **learning materials** must be carefully selected to encourage collaboration, sharing, and the development of positive social skills at a developmentally appropriate level. The teacher must also consider **desired learning outcomes** and the nature of the learning taking place to determine whether group activities should be structured or unstructured. Unstructured play is valuable in allowing students to develop their social and emotional skills in a natural setting, whereas structured, teacher-led group activities allow for more focused learning. Desired outcomes also determine the size of groups for the activity to best promote collaboration and learning.

## GROUP ACTIVITIES THAT REFLECT AND DEVELOP YOUNG CHILDREN'S ABILITY TO COLLABORATE

Young children benefit from a variety of **whole-class** and **small-group** activities designed to reflect and develop their collaborative skills. When the teacher incorporates group activities to encourage cooperation, sharing, and positive interactions, young children gain important social and emotional skills necessary for development across domains. Whole-group activities such as **circle time** provide young children with the opportunity to interact with others, express ideas, and ask questions in a developmentally appropriate setting. This activity develops important collaborative skills, such as taking turns, active listening, and respectful communication. Other **whole-group activities**, such as reading aloud, group songs, dances, games, or class nature walks, are effective in teaching young children how to productively contribute to and function in a group setting. **Small-group activities** can be incorporated throughout all aspects of structured and unstructured learning to develop young children's collaborative skills. Learning centers, such as a science area, pretend play area, or building block center, provide materials that encourage collaboration while allowing students to interact with others according to their abilities in a student-led setting. Problem-solving activities, such as puzzles, games, age-appropriate science experiments, or scavenger hunts, are effective in teaching young children how to work together toward a common goal.

## ORGANIZING AND MANAGING GROUP ACTIVITIES TO PROMOTE COLLABORATIVE SKILLS AND INDIVIDUAL ACCOUNTABILITY

Well-planned group activities are beneficial in developing students' collaborative skills and sense of individual accountability. Such group activities are well-organized, effectively managed, and intentionally structured with a **clear goal** or problem that must be solved while allowing room for creativity to enhance the collaborative process. When designing these activities, the teacher must incorporate enough **significant components** to ensure all students within the group can productively contribute. If the assignment is too simple, students can easily complete it on their own, whereas a multifaceted activity instills a sense of interdependence within the group that fosters the development of collaborative skills. To promote individual accountability, **meaningful roles** and responsibilities should be assigned to each group member because when students feel others are relying on their contributions to complete a task, they develop a sense of ownership that motivates active participation. To further develop collaborative skills and individual accountability, students should be graded both as a **whole-group** and **individually**. This encourages group cooperation while ensuring that students' individual contributions are recognized. Including **self-**

Copyright © Mometrix Media. You have been licensed one copy of this document for personal use only. Any other reproduction or redistribution is strictly prohibited. All rights reserved.
This content is provided for test preparation purposes only and does not imply an endorsement by Mometrix of any particular political, scientific, or religious point of view.

**assessments** at the end of group activities is beneficial in allowing students to reflect on the quality of their contributions to the group and ways they could improve their collaborative skills.

Thoughtful consideration of how to best organize and manage collaborative activities helps establish an environment that supports students in learning to work together productively and assume responsible roles within a group. When planning group activities, the teacher must consider the **desired learning outcomes** and the **nature of the task** to determine whether there are enough significant components that would benefit from collaboration. **Group size** must also be considered to most effectively foster collaboration and individual accountability when assuming responsible roles. Groups with too few students may be inadequate for addressing all the components of a complex task, whereas grouping too many students together limits productive collaboration and makes it difficult for each member to assume a significant, responsible role. The teacher must be selective regarding which students are grouped together to best facilitate productive collaboration. This includes determining which students will work well together, as well as grouping students that may need support with others that can provide scaffolding. It is also important to consider how **responsibilities** will be divided to ensure each member is given a significant role that allows them to contribute productively to the group, as well how their contributions will be monitored and **assessed**.

## IDEAL SCHEDULE FOR YOUNG CHILDREN

An ideal schedule for young children reflects their developmental characteristics and capabilities to maximize their learning. A **predictable** routine is necessary for young children to feel secure in their learning environment, and therefore, each day should follow a similar schedule while allowing room for **flexibility** if an activity takes longer than expected. Each day should begin with a clear routine, such as unpacking, a "warm-up" activity, and a class meeting to allow students to share thoughts, ask questions, and allow the teacher to discuss what will occur that day. This establishes a positive tone for the day while focusing the attention on learning. Similarly, the end of the day should have a specific routine, such as cleaning up materials and packing up for dismissal. Young children learn best by physically interacting with and exploring their environment. As such, each day should include large blocks of time for **active movement** throughout the day in the form of play, projects, and learning centers. Periods of **rest** must follow such activities, as this enables young children to process and internalize what they learned. **Direct instruction** should occur before active movement periods and last approximately 15-20 minutes to sustain engagement and attention on learning.

| Example Daily Schedule for the Early Childhood Education Classroom | |
|---|---|
| 8:00-8:30 | Welcome, unpack, morning work |
| 8:30-8:45 | Circle time, review class calendar |
| 8:45-9:30 | Literacy/Language Arts |
| 9:30-10:15 | Learning Stations |
| 10:15-11:00 | Math |
| 11:00-11:30 | Music/Dance/Movement |
| 11:30-12:15 | Lunch |
| 12:15-1:00 | Recess/Unstructured play |
| 1:00-1:20 | Rest/Quiet time |
| 1:20-2:00 | Science |
| 2:00-2:45 | Creative Arts |
| 2:45-3:15 | Daily reflection, pack up, dismissal |

Copyright © Mometrix Media. You have been licensed one copy of this document for personal use only. Any other reproduction or redistribution is strictly prohibited. All rights reserved.
This content is provided for test preparation purposes only and does not imply an endorsement by Mometrix of any particular political, scientific, or religious point of view.

Some examples of restful and active movement activities for young children are discussed below:

- **Restful:** Incorporating restful activities into the early childhood classroom are beneficial in helping young children process and retain new concepts and providing them the opportunity to unwind after active movement activities. Examples of such activities include nap time, class meditation, self-reflection activities, independent art projects, or self-selected reading time. Teachers can also read aloud to students or play an audiobook during these periods.
- **Active:** Providing young children with multiple opportunities for active movement throughout the day is beneficial in promoting the development of gross motor skills, connections to learning, and the ability to function in a group setting. Active movement opportunities should include whole-class, small group, and independent activities. Examples include class dances, songs, or games, nature walks, or total participation activities such as gallery walks or four corners. Physical education activities, such as jump rope, tag, sports, or using playground equipment are also beneficial. Young children should also be provided with ample time for both structured and unstructured play throughout the day.

## BALANCING RESTFUL AND ACTIVE MOVEMENT ACTIVITIES

A schedule that balances **rest** and **active movement** is necessary for positive cognitive, physical, emotional, and social development in young children. Connecting learning to active movement strengthens students' understanding of new concepts, as it allows them to physically explore and interact with their environment, experiment with new ideas, and gain new experiences for healthy **cognitive development**. In addition, incorporating active movement encourages the use of **gross motor skills** and provides students with the space to physically express themselves in an appropriate setting, thus promoting physical and emotional development. Active movement also encourages the development of positive **interpersonal skills** as young children interact and explore with one another. Restful periods are equally as important to young children's development. Incorporating rest after a period of active movement further strengthens young children's connection to learning by providing them the opportunity to reflect, process, and internalize new information.

## PROVIDING LARGE BLOCKS OF TIME FOR PLAY, PROJECTS, AND LEARNING CENTERS

Providing young children with ample time for play, projects, and learning centers throughout the school day is integral to fostering their development across domains. Young children learn most effectively through active movement as they physically interact with their environment, and incorporating large blocks of time for such activities allows them to do so. Significant time dedicated to active play, projects, and learning centers on a variety of topics allows young children to explore and experiment with the world around them, test new ideas, draw conclusions, and acquire new knowledge. This supports healthy **physical** and **cognitive development**, as it provides young children the opportunity to engage in learning across subject areas while connecting it to active movement for strengthened understanding. In addition, allowing large blocks of time for these activities is necessary for **social** and **emotional development**, as it provides young children the space to interact with one another and develop important skills such as cooperation, sharing, conflict resolution, and emotional self-regulation. Dedicating large blocks of time to play, projects, and learning centers establishes a student-led, hands-on learning environment that is reflective of the developmental characteristics and needs of young children.

Copyright © Mometrix Media. You have been licensed one copy of this document for personal use only. Any other reproduction or redistribution is strictly prohibited. All rights reserved. This content is provided for test preparation purposes only and does not imply an endorsement by Mometrix of any particular political, scientific, or religious point of view.

## Noninstructional Duties and Instructional Activities Maximizing Efficiency

Many non-instructional duties, such as taking attendance, grading papers, and facilitating communication, can be coordinated with instructional activities when effective **routines** and **procedures** are instilled to accomplish them. This enhances overall efficiency in the classroom, as time is not lost on completing administrative tasks, allowing more dedicated time to instruction for maximized student learning. Taking attendance, for example, can be incorporated into students' morning work routine, as they can mark their own presence as part of the procedure for entering the classroom and beginning the day. Grading and communication with colleagues or families can take place during independent work, assessments, or recreational time. The teacher can also observe, monitor, and assess students' progress as they engage in learning. Student **self-correction** in lieu of formal grading can be beneficial in allowing students to reflect on their performance, seek areas for improvement, and strengthen their understanding, while integrating grading as an instructional activity. In addition, a variety of **digital resources** are available that allow for immediate student feedback and communication with families throughout instruction. In utilizing such resources, the teacher can efficiently coordinate administrative duties with instructional activities to maximize time for student learning.

## Effective Time Management

Practicing effective time management is beneficial in establishing an efficient, orderly classroom environment focused on productivity and maximizing student learning. By instilling specific **procedures** for managing daily routines such as transitioning, accessing materials and supplies, and using technology, the teacher can ensure that these tasks are completed in a timely manner while minimizing time lost on non-instructional activities and student distraction. This allows more time to be focused on instruction and student learning. To achieve this, procedures for such tasks must be **explicit** and consistently reinforced. Prior to transitioning between activities, accessing materials, or using technology, the teacher must provide a clear, detailed explanation of each step of the procedure, as well as expectations for how students will complete it. Modeling the procedure is beneficial in providing a visual example to ensure student understanding. In order to be effective, each procedure must include a specific **signal** to indicate when students can begin, and the teacher must consistently monitor to ensure students are completing the task correctly. When students have a clear understanding on how to accomplish daily activities, they can do so quickly, effectively, and without disruption. This increases overall efficiency in the classroom and maximizes time dedicated to student learning.

## Using Technology to Perform Administrative Tasks

Technology resources are widely available to assist teachers in accomplishing a variety of administrative tasks, and therefore, are highly beneficial in establishing a **well-managed**, **organized**, and **productive** learning environment. Completing such tasks as taking attendance, maintaining gradebooks, or facilitating communication through technology allows the teacher to do so more **efficiently**. This allows for more time dedicated to productive teaching and learning, as well as smoother transitions between activities, as time is not lost on completing such duties. Increased efficiency in completing administrative duties is beneficial in sustaining students' attention, engagement, and productivity in learning, as it minimizes idle time that could lead to distraction or disruption. In addition, utilizing technology to perform administrative duties enhances overall organization, as all tasks performed digitally can be stored in a single area on the device used for easy access and recall of information. Through email, digital apps, or class websites, the teacher can efficiently communicate with colleagues and students' families to update them regarding important events, assignments, and individual progress. This creates a sense of

Copyright © Mometrix Media. You have been licensed one copy of this document for personal use only. Any other reproduction or redistribution is strictly prohibited. All rights reserved. This content is provided for test preparation purposes only and does not imply an endorsement by Mometrix of any particular political, scientific, or religious point of view.

connectedness between the teacher and community that contributes to a positive, productive classroom climate.

## VOLUNTEERS AND PARAPROFESSIONALS

### ENHANCING AND ENRICHING INSTRUCTION

**Paraprofessionals** and **volunteers** are highly valuable in enhancing and enriching the overall learning experience, as their efforts contribute to an organized, positive, and productive classroom environment. These aides collaborate with the teacher throughout planning and instruction to implement best practices in meeting students' learning needs. Paraprofessionals and volunteers can lead small groups of students as they engage in instruction for a more focused, **student-centered** learning experience. They can also provide additional support to struggling students while the teacher engages in whole-class instruction. Specifically, paraprofessionals are typically licensed in the educational field and are qualified to provide **individual accommodations** to students with individual learning needs to create an inclusive learning environment. In addition, working with paraprofessionals and volunteers is beneficial in creating an efficient, organized classroom that enhances student learning, as they can assist with **non-instructional duties** that allow for smooth transitions during instruction, such as preparing learning materials, handing back papers, or grading assignments. **Classroom management** is also enhanced when paraprofessionals and volunteers are present, as they can assist in reinforcing expectations and monitoring behavior to ensure all students are positively and productively engaging in learning.

### MONITORING THEIR PERFORMANCE IN THE CLASSROOM

Paraprofessionals and volunteers are invaluable resources for creating a positive, productive classroom environment. However, to ensure the contributions of these aides are consistently beneficial in meeting students' needs and maximizing learning, it is important to continuously monitor their performance in the classroom. Paraprofessionals and volunteers are typically interviewed by administration prior to entering the classroom to determine whether their qualifications are aligned with meeting students' needs to enhance instruction. The administration is also often responsible for monitoring their performance throughout the school year. Specifically, paraprofessionals are licensed in the field of education, and therefore, are often formally evaluated against specific **performance measurement tools**. **Observations** by administration can either be scheduled or conducted as an informal "walk-through" to assess how the paraprofessional or volunteer interacts with the teacher and students and their effectiveness in contributing to a productive learning environment. The teacher can also monitor the performance of volunteers and paraprofessionals in their classroom. By analyzing **students' progress** when working with these aides and eliciting **feedback** from students, the teacher can determine their effectiveness in enhancing the learning experience. Frequently communicating with paraprofessionals and volunteers provides valuable insight regarding whether they contribute to a positive classroom climate focused on student learning.

Copyright © Mometrix Media. You have been licensed one copy of this document for personal use only. Any other reproduction or redistribution is strictly prohibited. All rights reserved. This content is provided for test preparation purposes only and does not imply an endorsement by Mometrix of any particular political, scientific, or religious point of view.

## Chapter Quiz

**1. Effective and consistent implementation of routines and procedures directly affects all of the following EXCEPT:**

    a. Student behavior and productivity
    b. Students' sense of predictability and security
    c. Simplifying daily tasks
    d. Student achievement

**2. Which of the following is true concerning age-appropriate routines for young children?**

    a. Young children cannot reasonably be expected to perform basic daily routines independently.
    b. Young children benefit from being assigned classroom leadership roles.
    c. Young children can reasonably be expected to independently turn in work.
    d. Young children can reasonably be expected to follow procedures for accessing learning materials.

**3. Which of the following is most important for teachers to consider when designing effective group activities?**

    a. The specific age of each child
    b. The developmental characteristics of each child
    c. The types of toys each child likes
    d. The types of activities that garner each child's attention

**4. What activities are most appropriate for whole-group learning?**

    a. Puzzles and blocks
    b. Pretend play
    c. Science experiments
    d. Reading aloud and nature walks

**5. What is the most important reason to build rest periods into routines?**

    a. To give the teacher a chance to recuperate
    b. To allow the children time to collaborate and socialize
    c. To help children process and internalize what they have learned
    d. To focus on getting quiet before returning to regular direct instruction

**6. Active movement is useful for all of the following EXCEPT:**

    a. Developing fine motor skills
    b. Allowing children to physically interact with their environment
    c. Developing interpersonal skills
    d. Strengthening understanding of new concepts

## Chapter Quiz Answer Key

**1. D:** A well-managed classroom, focused on productivity, positive behavior, and success in learning, relies on the effectiveness and consistency of routines and procedures instilled for daily activities. By implementing these at the beginning of the school year and continuously reinforcing them throughout, the teacher establishes an orderly, efficient classroom that facilitates students' ability to productively engage in learning. Classroom management—and therefore, student behavior and productivity—is enhanced by structured routines and procedures, because students who are clear on expectations are more inclined to follow them. Such structure provides students

Copyright © Mometrix Media. You have been licensed one copy of this document for personal use only. Any other reproduction or redistribution is strictly prohibited. All rights reserved. This content is provided for test preparation purposes only and does not imply an endorsement by Mometrix of any particular political, scientific, or religious point of view.

with a sense of predictability and security in their environment that contributes to their willingness to participate in learning.

**2. B:** Young children can reasonably be expected to perform basic daily routines independently, although they likely will need frequent reminders. Daily procedures may include having young children hang up their coats, put away lunchboxes, and unpack their backpacks at the beginning of the day as they prepare to begin morning work. Similarly, young children can be expected to independently follow end-of-day procedures and routines, such as packing up their backpacks, cleaning up learning materials, and lining up at the door for dismissal. Young children should be able to follow simple behavioral procedures as well, such as keeping hands to themselves, responding to attention signals from the teacher, and cleaning up learning materials before transitioning between activities. Young children also benefit from being assigned classroom "jobs," such as line leader, paper collector, or teacher assistant, as these routines instill a sense of accountability and self-responsibility. Middle-level students can be held responsible for independently turning in homework and accessing learning materials.

**3. B:** Designing group activities that support social development and align with young children's ability to collaborate requires a realistic understanding of their capacity to do so. This entails understanding the developmental characteristics of young children at varying stages, including how the nature of their interactions with others evolves.

**4. D:** When the teacher incorporates group activities to encourage cooperation, sharing, and positive interactions, young children gain important social and emotional skills necessary for development across domains. Whole-group activities such as circle time let young children interact with others, express ideas, and ask questions in a developmentally appropriate setting. These activities develop important collaborative skills, such as taking turns, active listening, and respectful communication. Other whole-group activities, such as reading aloud, group songs, dances, games, or class nature walks, are effective in teaching young children how to productively contribute to and function in a group setting.

**5. C:** Young children learn best by physically interacting with and exploring their environment. Therefore, each day should include large blocks of time for active movement throughout the day in the form of play, projects, and learning centers. Periods of rest must follow such activities, as this enables young children to process and internalize what they learned. Direct instruction should occur before active movement periods and last approximately 15-20 minutes to sustain engagement and attention on learning.

**6. A:** Connecting learning to active movement strengthens students' understanding of new concepts, as it allows them to physically explore and interact with their environment, experiment with new ideas, and gain new experiences for healthy cognitive development. In addition, incorporating active movement encourages the use of gross motor skills and provides students with the space to physically express themselves in an appropriate setting, thus promoting physical and emotional development. Active movement also encourages the development of positive interpersonal skills as young children interact and explore with one another.

Copyright © Mometrix Media. You have been licensed one copy of this document for personal use only. Any other reproduction or redistribution is strictly prohibited. All rights reserved. This content is provided for test preparation purposes only and does not imply an endorsement by Mometrix of any particular political, scientific, or religious point of view.

# Behavior Management

## MANAGING AND MONITORING STUDENT BEHAVIOR

### BEHAVIORISM AND CONDITIONING

The theoretical school of **behaviorism** was established by John B. Watson and further developed by Ivan Pavlov and B.F. Skinner. Behaviorism emphasizes the role of environmental and experiential learning in the behavior of animals and humans. Simply put, if a person experiences a desirable result from a particular behavior, that person is more likely to perform the behavior in pursuit of the result. Likewise, undesirable results cause a person to avoid performing an associated behavior. This process of **reinforcing** or rewarding good behaviors and **punishing** unwanted behaviors is known as conditioning. Behaviorists use the terms positive and negative to refer to the mode of conditioning. The term **positive** refers to an added stimulus, such as giving a child a treat as positive reinforcement or giving added homework as positive punishment. **Negative**, on the other hand refers to removing a stimulus, such as taking recess away as a negative punishment, or taking away extra classwork as negative reinforcement for students performing their homework independently. In the classroom, the teacher has the opportunity to help students learn to meet specific behavioral expectations. The tools of behaviorism may be carefully employed in the classrooms through positive and negative punishments and rewards. Classroom rules and expectations should be made clear as soon as possible and reinforced through verbal praise, prizes, or special privileges. Likewise, negative behaviors should be discouraged through verbal warnings, loss of privileges, and communication with the family or administrators when necessary.

### CHOICE THEORY

Choice theory, developed by **William Glasser**, states that behavior is chosen, either consciously or unconsciously, to meet the **five basic needs** of survival, love and belonging, power, freedom, and fun. Rather than implement positive and negative reinforcements to drive behavior, the teacher must aim to teach students self-responsibility for their actions. This includes encouraging students to reflect and consider the reasons for their actions and attempt to rectify any misbehavior. This method relies on the notion that if students understand how their desire to meet certain needs impacts their actions, they are more likely to engage in positive behavior. In the classroom, the teacher focuses on meeting students' **five basic needs** to encourage positive behavior by creating a classroom climate that emphasizes **communication, relationship building**, and **self-reflection**. This includes establishing positive relationships with students, holding class discussions, and teaching conflict resolution skills to create a safe, welcoming learning environment. Instructional activities are tailored to individual needs, and students have a great deal of choice in their own learning with the intention of promoting positive behavior by meeting their needs for power and freedom.

### ASSERTIVE DISCIPLINE THEORY

The **Assertive Discipline theory** was developed by **Lee** and **Marlene Canter**. This theory states that the teacher is in charge of **instruction, the classroom**, and **students' behavior**. The expectation is that the teacher establishes clear behavioral standards that protect their right to teach and students' right to learn without distraction or disruption. Negative consequences for unwanted behavior are instilled to deter students from deviating from behavioral expectations. This theory argues that if teachers are viewed as firm and consistent, students will have a greater respect for them and ultimately engage in positive behavior. In the classroom, the teacher is in control of **establishing** and **consistently reinforcing** standards for student behavior. This establishes a sense of predictability, as students are clear on what is expected of them as they engage in learning. Students are expected to comply with the teacher's expectations, and a system

Copyright © Mometrix Media. You have been licensed one copy of this document for personal use only. Any other reproduction or redistribution is strictly prohibited. All rights reserved. This content is provided for test preparation purposes only and does not imply an endorsement by Mometrix of any particular political, scientific, or religious point of view.

of **negative consequences** are in place to discourage unwanted behavior. Positive behavior is rewarded to further reinforce desired behavior. The teacher in this classroom believes that creating such an environment enhances students' ability to focus on learning without disruption.

## STUDENT-DIRECTED LEARNING THEORY

The **Student-Directed Learning theory**, or the idea of the **Democratic Classroom**, was founded by **Alfie Kohn** and emphasizes the importance of **student choice** and **classroom community** in influencing behavior. This includes having students contribute to the development of behavioral expectations, as this helps students understand their purpose while instilling a sense of ownership and accountability. Instructional activities are tailored to accommodate students' individual interests and natural curiosity while emphasizing cooperation to foster an engaging learning environment that promotes positive behavior. This theory focuses on eliciting students' intrinsic motivation to engage in positive behavior, rather than relying on positive and negative reinforcements. In the classroom, students primarily direct their own learning based upon their **natural curiosity** while the teacher acts as a **facilitator**. Students contribute to the development of behavioral expectations that are instilled to promote respect and focus on learning. **Active engagement**, **cooperation**, and **collaborative learning** are emphasized over direct instruction. Students may be engaging in differing activities simultaneously as the teacher moves around the classroom to monitor progress and assist as necessary.

## SOCIAL LEARNING THEORY

The **Social Learning theory**, developed by **Albert Bandura**, asserts that one's **environment** and the **people** within it heavily influence behavior. As humans are social creatures, they learn a great deal by **observing** and **imitating** one another. This theory is also rooted in the importance of **self-efficacy** in achieving desired behavior, as students must be motivated and confident that they can effectively imitate what they observe. In the classroom, the teacher establishes behavioral expectations and focuses on **modeling** positive behaviors, attitudes, and interactions with the intention of encouraging students to do the same. The teacher recognizes and praises positive behavior from students to elicit the same behavior from others. The teacher also emphasizes a growth mindset in the classroom to promote students' sense of self-efficacy.

## BEHAVIOR STANDARDS AND EXPECTATIONS FOR STUDENTS AT DEVELOPMENTAL LEVELS

Behavioral standards that emphasize respect for oneself, others, and property are necessary in creating a safe, positive, and productive learning environment for students of all ages. However, as students at varying developmental levels differ in their capabilities across domains, behavioral expectations must be **realistic**, **applicable**, and reflect an **awareness** of these **differences** while encouraging growth. Young children, for example, are learning to interact with others and function in a group setting. Behavioral expectations must be attuned to this understanding while promoting the development of positive interpersonal skills. Young children also require ample opportunities for active movement and cannot reasonably be expected to sit still for long periods of time. Middle level students are at a unique transitional period in their development and often exhibit characteristics of both young children and adolescents. Behavioral standards for these students must recognize the significant social, emotional, cognitive, and physical changes occurring at this stage by emphasizing self-control, emotional regulation, and positive interactions. As older students prepare for adulthood, they can generally be expected to conduct themselves with a degree of maturity and responsibility in a variety of settings. Appropriate behavioral standards for these students emphasize self-responsibility, respectful interactions, and independently completing necessary tasks.

Copyright © Mometrix Media. You have been licensed one copy of this document for personal use only. Any other reproduction or redistribution is strictly prohibited. All rights reserved. This content is provided for test preparation purposes only and does not imply an endorsement by Mometrix of any particular political, scientific, or religious point of view.

## EFFECTIVE MANAGEMENT OF STUDENT BEHAVIOR
### MANAGEMENT PROCEDURES AND SIGNIFICANCE IN POSITIVE, PRODUCTIVE, AND ORGANIZED LEARNING ENVIRONMENT

Promoting **appropriate behavior** and **ethical work habits** while taking specific measures to **manage student behavior** creates a safe, organized, and productive classroom. Such an environment is beneficial for students' motivation, engagement, and ability to focus on learning. This is achieved by communicating and consistently reinforcing **high**, yet **realistic behavioral expectations** for all students. This, when combined with **relationship building** strategies, establishes a positive rapport between the teacher and students that encourages appropriate behavior and ethical work habits. Students are more inclined to adhere to expectations for behavior and work habits when their relationship with the teacher is founded on mutual understanding and respect. In addition, students that feel they are a part of developing academic and behavioral expectations feel a greater sense of **ownership** and responsibility to follow them, and, therefore, it is beneficial to include students in this process. Encouraging students to **self-monitor** their behavior and utilize conflict resolution strategies furthers this sense of accountability, as it prompts students to positively manage their own actions and work habits. Misbehavior must be addressed appropriately and in a timely manner, and consequences must follow a logical sequence, such as a verbal warning, followed by loss of privileges or communication with family.

### STRATEGIES

Proactively implementing effective behavior management strategies is beneficial to establishing and maintaining a positive, productive learning environment. The **physical environment** should be arranged in such a way that facilitates ease of movement while limiting the amount of free space that could encourage student disruption. Planning for **smooth transitions** from one activity to the next further discourages behavioral disruptions. Desks should be arranged so that students can easily view the teacher, projector, chalkboard, or other information pertinent to learning. Expectations for behavior, procedures, and routines, including consequences, should be predictable, consistent, succinct, and visible at all times. Allowing students to participate in the development of classroom procedures and routines is valuable in providing students with a sense of personal accountability that increases the likelihood that they will follow them. Students also often respond well to incentives for modeling appropriate behavior, such as a **PBIS reward system**, verbal praise, or a positive phone call home. Nonverbal strategies are valuable in subtly managing student behavior throughout instruction, such as hand gestures, proximity, or eye contact. Misbehavior should be addressed discreetly and privately so as to avoid embarrassing the student or encouraging further disruption.

### IMPORTANCE OF CONSISTENCY

Standards for behavior must be enforced consistently in order to establish a well-managed classroom in which students can focus on learning. This includes communicating **clear expectations**, holding all students equally accountable with specific **positive and negative consequences**, and **following through** on implementing them. In doing so, the teacher ensures that students are always aware of the behavior expected from them, and what will happen if they do not adhere to the standards. When students are clear regarding behavioral expectations and assured that they will be enforced, they are more inclined to demonstrate appropriate conduct. This creates a predictable, secure environment that promotes student motivation, engagement, and focused productivity in learning. Consistently enforcing behavior standards gives the teacher a sense of credibility among students, and therefore, students are more likely to respect and adhere to these expectations. In addition, holding all students to the same high behavioral standards contributes to a positive classroom climate in which all students feel they are treated fairly.

Copyright © Mometrix Media. You have been licensed one copy of this document for personal use only. Any other reproduction or redistribution is strictly prohibited. All rights reserved. This content is provided for test preparation purposes only and does not imply an endorsement by Mometrix of any particular political, scientific, or religious point of view.

Copyright © Mometrix Media. You have been licensed one copy of this document for personal use only. Any other reproduction or redistribution is strictly prohibited. All rights reserved.
This content is provided for test preparation purposes only and does not imply an endorsement by Mometrix of any particular political, scientific, or religious point of view.

## CHAPTER QUIZ

**1. Which of the following is NOT one of the five basic needs according to Glasser's choice theory?**

a. Love and belonging
b. Freedom
c. Fun
d. Meaning

**2. Who is the founder of the concept of the democratic classroom, or student-directed learning theory?**

a. Albert Bandura
b. Marlene Canter
c. B. F. Skinner
d. Alfie Kohn

## CHAPTER QUIZ ANSWER KEY

**1. D:** Choice theory, developed by William Glasser, states that behavior is chosen, either consciously or unconsciously, to meet the five basic needs: survival, love and belonging, power, freedom, and fun.

**2. D:** The student-directed learning theory, or the idea of the democratic classroom, was founded by Alfie Kohn and emphasizes the importance of student choice and classroom community in influencing behavior. This includes having students contribute to the development of behavioral expectations, because such contribution helps students understand their purpose while instilling a sense of ownership and accountability. Instructional activities are tailored to accommodate students' individual interests and natural curiosity while emphasizing cooperation to foster an engaging learning environment that promotes positive behavior. This theory focuses on eliciting students' intrinsic motivation to engage in positive behavior, rather than relying on positive and negative reinforcements.

Copyright © Mometrix Media. You have been licensed one copy of this document for personal use only. Any other reproduction or redistribution is strictly prohibited. All rights reserved. This content is provided for test preparation purposes only and does not imply an endorsement by Mometrix of any particular political, scientific, or religious point of view.

# Instructional Techniques

### IMPLEMENTING MULTIPLE INSTRUCTIONAL TECHNIQUES TO MAXIMIZE STUDENT LEARNING

Incorporating multiple instructional techniques into the classroom maximizes student learning by enhancing intellectual involvement and overall engagement. When instructional material is presented through a variety of means, it facilitates an **active learning** environment in which students' interest is captured and they are motivated to participate in learning. Varying teaching strategies stimulates engagement and fosters achievement by encouraging students to actively participate in their own learning and implement critical thinking skills to consider information more deeply. Students' understanding is strengthened when content is presented in different ways through various instructional techniques by providing them with multiple frames of reference for making connections and internalizing new concepts. In addition, utilizing multiple instructional techniques allows the teacher to effectively **differentiate instruction** to access multiple learning styles and address individual student needs to ensure understanding and enhance the overall learning process.

### INSTRUCTIONAL STRATEGIES TO DIFFERENTIATE INSTRUCTION

Implementing a variety of strategies for differentiation helps to ensure that instruction appeals to students' varying learning styles and needs. By incorporating **multiple modalities** into direct instruction, such as visual representations, written directions, video or audio clips, songs, graphs, or mnemonic devices, teachers can differentiate the presentation of new concepts and information. Using strategies to differentiate instructional activities is also beneficial in diversifying the learning experience. By providing opportunities for **independent, collaborative**, and **hands-on** learning, teachers can ensure that learning is accessible and engaging to all students. In addition, learning activities should allow for a degree of flexibility in order to appeal to students' varying needs and preferences. Activities such as task cards, educational technology resources, and learning stations provide this **flexibility** and allow for a student-directed experience in which they can choose to learn in the way that best suits their needs. Similarly, assigning open-ended projects as summative assessments allows for a degree of **student-choice**, thus differentiating the method in which students demonstrate their understanding.

### VARYING THE TEACHER AND STUDENT ROLES IN THE INSTRUCTIONAL PROCESS

Varying the roles of the teacher and students as an instructional technique is beneficial in creating an engaging, dynamic classroom environment that maximizes learning. When different roles are implemented, instruction is diversified, thus stimulating student interest and engagement. In addition, certain teacher and student roles are most applicable and effective in specific learning situations. When teachers acknowledge this and understand when to adopt and assign particular roles, they can effectively deliver instruction in a way that deepens student understanding and fosters success in learning. In presenting new content, directions, or modeling new skills for example, the roles of **lecturer** and student **observer** are effective. In hands-on learning situations, students can take on the role of **active participant** while the teacher acts as a **facilitator** to create a student-centered and engaging learning environment in which students are given ownership over their own learning. Such variation enhances intellectual involvement by promoting critical thinking and problem-solving skills through self-directed learning. Skillfully assigning different roles throughout the learning process also allows the teacher to effectively address students' individual learning needs and preferences to promote engagement and enhance the learning experience.

### FOSTERING INTELLECTUAL INVOLVEMENT AND ENGAGEMENT

Effective instruction includes a variety of strategies for fostering intellectual involvement and engagement to promote academic success. Presenting instruction using various approaches

Copyright © Mometrix Media. You have been licensed one copy of this document for personal use only. Any other reproduction or redistribution is strictly prohibited. All rights reserved. This content is provided for test preparation purposes only and does not imply an endorsement by Mometrix of any particular political, scientific, or religious point of view.

provides multiple avenues for learning new content, thus ensuring and strengthening student understanding to facilitate achievement. In addition, diversifying instructional strategies creates variety in the classroom that effectively stimulates students' interest and motivation to engage in learning. Such strategies as **cooperative learning**, **discussion**, and **self-directed opportunities** encourage active student participation that enhances intellectual involvement by allowing students to build on background knowledge, deepen understanding by exploring others' perspectives, and take ownership over their own learning. This ultimately increases student engagement and motivation for success in learning. Similarly, incorporating **inquiry**, **problem-solving**, and **project-based** strategies promote curiosity in learning, creativity, and the development of critical thinking skills that stimulate intellectual participation and engagement to create a productive learning environment. Implementing **digital resources** and media throughout instruction is integral in enhancing academic success by making learning relevant, interesting, and differentiated to accommodate various learning needs. At the end of a lesson or activity, allowing students the opportunity to reflect is a valuable strategy in increasing intellectual involvement, retainment, and academic success by facilitating personal connections with learning to build understanding.

## ACTIVELY ENGAGING STUDENTS BY INCORPORATING DISCUSSION INTO INSTRUCTION

Classroom discussion is a valuable instructional technique in engaging students throughout the learning process. When the teacher skillfully poses higher-level questions in discussions, they establish an active learning environment in which students are encouraged and motivated to participate, thus enhancing overall engagement. Effective discussions prompt students to become **intellectually invested** in instruction by promoting the use of **critical** and **higher-order thinking** skills to consider information more deeply and devise creative solutions to problems. In addition, discussions stimulate engagement by providing students the opportunity to express their own thoughts and reasoning regarding a given topic to establish a sense of ownership over their learning. Furthermore, discussions foster a collaborative learning environment that actively engages students by prompting them to understand others' perspectives, consider alternative approaches, and build on one another's experiences to make deeper connections to learning.

## PROMOTING STUDENT INQUIRY

The promotion of inquiry is a valuable instructional technique in enhancing student engagement and intellectual involvement. In an **inquiry-based** learning environment, students are encouraged to explore instructional material and devise their own conclusions or solutions to problems. This increases the effectiveness of the learning process by providing students with a sense of agency over their own learning. In addition, implementing this strategy fosters curiosity, self-motivation, and active participation, as it allows for hands-on, **student-led** learning that increases overall engagement. Incorporating inquiry into the classroom stimulates critical and higher-order thinking skills as students construct their own understanding by interacting with learning materials, analyzing their findings, and synthesizing their learning to create new conclusions, results, and responses. To effectively incorporate inquiry int the learning process, the teacher must provide several opportunities for self-directed and project-based learning, as well as student choice, to stimulate curiosity. Questions must be open-ended, and students must be encouraged to hypothesize, predict, and experiment in their learning. The teacher must be flexible in instruction to allow space and opportunity for exploration and allow time for reflection and extended learning opportunities to facilitate further inquiry.

## INCORPORATING PROBLEM-SOLVING INTO INSTRUCTION

Providing opportunities for creative problem solving within instruction effectively creates an engaging and successful learning experience. Students become more **intellectually involved** when encouraged to actively participate in learning and utilize **critical thinking skills** to test hypotheses,

Copyright © Mometrix Media. You have been licensed one copy of this document for personal use only. Any other reproduction or redistribution is strictly prohibited. All rights reserved. This content is provided for test preparation purposes only and does not imply an endorsement by Mometrix of any particular political, scientific, or religious point of view.

analyze results, and devise creative solutions to problems. This hands-on, **student-directed** approach promotes success in learning by allowing students to interact with learning materials as they seek answers to complex ideas and problems in an engaging environment. Problem-solving enables students to make deeper connections to their learning to enhance understanding, as this strategy prompts them to employ and develop background knowledge. In addition, problem-solving activities allow for collaborative learning in which students can actively engage with peers to build on one another's knowledge and experience, thus enhancing successful learning.

## RELATIONSHIP BETWEEN INTELLECTUAL INVOLVEMENT, ACTIVE STUDENT ENGAGEMENT, AND SUCCESS IN LEARNING

A productive learning environment is comprised of intellectually involved students that are actively engaged in successful learning. A strong correlation exists between **intellectual involvement**, **active student engagement**, and **success in learning**, and each component is necessary for effective instruction. Effective instruction consists of challenging students based on their abilities and teaching them to think deeply about new ideas and concepts. This ultimately encourages students' intellectual involvement, as it prompts them to utilize their critical thinking skills to build on their background knowledge, consider alternative perspectives, and synthesize their learning to devise creative solutions. When students are intellectually involved in instruction, they become more personally invested and engaged, as learning becomes relevant, interesting, and challenging. Engaged students are active participants in their learning, thus enhancing their overall productivity and academic success.

## EFFECTIVELY STRUCTURING LESSONS

When developing instruction, it is imperative that the teacher is knowledgeable on how to effectively structure lessons to maximize student engagement and success. Each lesson must include a clear **objective** and explicitly state the process for achieving it. To initiate engagement, effective lessons begin with an **opening**, or "warm-up," activity to introduce a new topic, diagnose student understanding, and activate prior knowledge. Instruction of new material must be delivered through a variety of teaching strategies that are consciously tailored to students' individual learning needs to enhance participation and ensure comprehension. Direct instruction should be followed by **active learning** activities with clear directions and procedures to allow students to practice new concepts and skills. Throughout a successful lesson, the teacher checks frequently for understanding and comprehension by conducting a variety of **formative assessments** and adjusts instruction as necessary. Including **closure** activities is essential to successful learning, as it gives students the opportunity to reflect, process information, make connections, and demonstrate comprehension. In structuring lessons effectively according to students' learning needs, the teacher establishes a focused and engaging learning environment that promotes academic success.

### Example of a Daily Lesson Plan Structure

## FLEXIBLE INSTRUCTIONAL GROUPINGS

**Flexible instructional groupings** provide the teacher and students with a versatile, engaging environment for successful learning. Skillfully grouping students allows for productive, cooperative learning opportunities in which individual strengths are enhanced and necessary support is provided, thus enhancing motivation and engagement. When working in groups, students'

Copyright © Mometrix Media. You have been licensed one copy of this document for personal use only. Any other reproduction or redistribution is strictly prohibited. All rights reserved. This content is provided for test preparation purposes only and does not imply an endorsement by Mometrix of any particular political, scientific, or religious point of view.

understanding of instruction is strengthened, as they are able to learn and build upon one another's background knowledge, perspectives, and abilities. Instructional groups can include students of the **same** or **varied abilities** depending on the learning objective and task to increase productivity and provide scaffolding as necessary for support. This strategy is effective in enabling the teacher to **differentiate** instruction and adjust groups as needed to accommodate varying learning styles, abilities, and interests to maximize engagement and success in learning.

## EFFECTIVE PACING OF LESSONS AND IMPORTANCE OF FLEXIBILITY TO STUDENTS' NEEDS

Effective pacing is imperative to focused and engaging instruction. The teacher must be conscientious of the pace of their instruction and ensure that it is reflective of their student's learning needs and sustains their attention. Instruction that is delivered too quickly results in confusion and discouragement, whereas if instruction is too slow, students will lose interest and become disengaged. A well-paced lesson states clear learning goals and objectives while clearly outlining the means to achieve them to elicit student motivation. The teacher must consider the most **efficient** and **engaging** instructional strategies for presenting new material to establish a steady pace and maintain it by incorporating smooth **transitions** from one activity to the next. It is important that the teacher is conscious of the rate of instruction throughout all stages of learning while maintaining **flexibility** in pacing in order to be responsive to their students. As individual students have different learning needs and processing times, they may require a faster or slower rate of instruction to understand new concepts and remain engaged in learning. Frequent checks for understanding and reflection activities are essential strategies in determining if the pace of instruction must be adjusted to accommodate students' needs.

## CONNECTING CONTENT TO STUDENTS' PRIOR KNOWLEDGE AND EXPERIENCES

When the teacher implements effective instructional strategies for connecting content to students' prior knowledge and experiences, it enhances the relevancy of learning and fosters deeper connections that strengthen understanding. To achieve this, the teacher must educate themselves on students' backgrounds, experiences, communities, and interests to determine what is important and interesting to them. With this knowledge in mind, the teacher can successfully locate and implement **authentic materials** into instruction to enhance relevancy. Additionally, encouraging students to bring materials to class that reflect their backgrounds and including these materials in instruction makes learning relevant by allowing students to make **personal connections** to content. Instructional strategies such as brainstorming, KWL charts, prereading, and anticipation guides allow the teacher to determine what students know prior to learning a new concept, thus enabling them to connect content to students' background knowledge in a relevant way. Incorporating digital resources further enhances relevancy in learning in that the teacher can locate videos or audio clips that relate to instruction and reflect students' background experiences and interests. Using digital resources to introduce a new concept is a valuable strategy in developing students' **schema** on a topic to build prior knowledge and make learning meaningful by fostering connections.

### MAKING LEARNING RELEVANT AND MEANINGFUL

For learning to be relevant and meaningful, it is essential that the teacher present content in a way that connects with students' **prior knowledge** and experiences. When students are able to apply new ideas and information to what they already know through effective instructional techniques, it facilitates strong **personal connections** that make learning relevant and meaningful. In addition, personal connections and **relevancy** are strengthened when the teacher consciously incorporates materials to reflect students' individual backgrounds and experiences in instruction. Linking content to students' background experiences enables them to relate instruction to real-world situations, thus establishing a sense of purpose for learning by making it applicable to their lives.

Copyright © Mometrix Media. You have been licensed one copy of this document for personal use only. Any other reproduction or redistribution is strictly prohibited. All rights reserved. This content is provided for test preparation purposes only and does not imply an endorsement by Mometrix of any particular political, scientific, or religious point of view.

Intentionally connecting content with students' prior knowledge and experiences enhances the effectiveness of the instructional process and fosters positive attitudes toward learning.

## ENHANCING STUDENT ENGAGEMENT AND SUCCESS IN LEARNING

Engaging instruction employs a variety of instructional strategies and materials to create a relevant, meaningful, and successful learning experience. Effective content establishes a clear and applicable purpose for instruction that increases student participation in the learning process. Presenting relevant and meaningful content enhances understanding and engagement by enabling students to create real-world, **personal connections** to learning based upon their own backgrounds and experiences. In addition, when instruction is tailored to reflect students' unique interests and preferences, content becomes more appealing and students' willingness to learn is enhanced. When students can perceive content through their own frames of reference with instructional materials that reflect their unique differences, they are able to effectively internalize and relate information to their lives, thus increasing engagement. Engaged learning ultimately facilitates academic success in that when students are motivated to learn, they demonstrate positive attitudes toward learning and are more likely to actively participate.

## EVALUATING ACTIVITIES AND MATERIALS TO MEET INDIVIDUAL CHARACTERISTICS AND LEARNING NEEDS

The careful selection of instructional activities and materials is integral to accommodating students' varying characteristics and needs to foster success in learning. When evaluating the appropriateness of activities and materials, several considerations must be made. The teacher must consider whether activities and materials align with state and district **academic standards**, as well as their quality and effectiveness in supporting students' unique differences as they achieve learning goals and objectives. All materials and activities must be **developmentally appropriate** across domains, yet adaptable to individual students' learning needs. In addition, they must be challenging, yet feasible for student achievement relative to students' grade level and abilities to promote engagement and the development of critical and **higher-order thinking** skills. The teacher must evaluate activities and materials for versatility to allow for student choice and differentiation in order to address varying characteristics and needs. The teacher must also ensure that activities and materials are accurate, **culturally sensitive**, and reflective of students' diversities to foster an inclusive learning environment that promotes engagement.

## INSTRUCTIONAL RESOURCES AND TECHNOLOGIES

The implementation of varied instructional resources and technologies is highly valuable in supporting student engagement and achievement. Effective use of resources and technologies requires the teacher to evaluate their appropriateness in addressing students' individual characteristics and learning needs for academic success. The teacher must be attuned to students' unique differences in order to seek high quality technologies and resources that address their students' needs to support and enhance the achievement of learning goals and objectives. Technologies and resources must be **accurate, comprehensible**, and easily **accessible** to students, as well as **relevant** to the curriculum and the development of particular skills. The teacher must also consider the grade-level and **developmental appropriateness** of technologies and resources, as well as their adaptability to allow for differentiation. Effective technologies and resources are interactive, engaging, and multifaceted to allow for varying levels of complexity based on students' abilities. This allows the teacher to provide appropriate challenges while diversifying instruction to appeal to varied characteristics and learning needs, thus fostering an engaging environment that supports success in learning for all students.

Copyright © Mometrix Media. You have been licensed one copy of this document for personal use only. Any other reproduction or redistribution is strictly prohibited. All rights reserved. This content is provided for test preparation purposes only and does not imply an endorsement by Mometrix of any particular political, scientific, or religious point of view.

## ADAPTING ACTIVITIES AND MATERIALS TO MEET INDIVIDUAL CHARACTERISTICS AND NEEDS

In effective instruction, activities and materials are adapted to accommodate students' individual characteristics and needs. The teacher must be attuned to students' unique differences and understand how to adjust activities and materials accordingly to facilitate academic success and growth. To achieve this, the teacher must incorporate a **variety** of activities and materials that appeal to all styles of learners. Activities and materials should provide **student choice** for engagement in learning and demonstration of understanding. By differentiating instruction, the teacher can effectively scaffold activities and materials to provide supports as necessary, as well as include extensions or alternate activities for enrichment. **Chunking** instruction, allowing extra time as necessary, and accompanying activities and materials with aids such as graphic organizers, visual representations, and anticipation guides further differentiates learning to accommodate students' learning characteristics and needs. Conducting **formative assessments** provides the teacher with valuable feedback regarding student understanding and engagement, thus allowing them to modify and adjust the complexity of activities and materials as necessary to adapt to varied characteristics and learning differences.

### INSTRUCTIONAL RESOURCES AND TECHNOLOGIES

When the teacher understands students' individual characteristics and needs, they can adapt instructional resources and technologies accordingly to maximize learning. To do so effectively, the teacher must incorporate a diverse array of **multifaceted** resources and technologies that support and enhance learning through a variety of methods. This ensures that varying learning needs are met, as students of all learning styles are provided with several avenues for building and strengthening understanding. Additionally, the teacher can adapt resources and technologies to accommodate individual students by **varying the complexity** to provide challenges, support, and opportunities for enrichment based on ability level. Supplementing technologies and resources with **scaffolds**, such as extra time, visual representations, or opportunities for collaborative learning, further enables the teacher to adapt to individual learning needs. When effectively implemented and adapted to students' characteristics and needs, instructional technologies and resources serve as valuable tools for differentiating curriculum to enhance the learning experience.

## SIGNIFICANCE OF EVALUATION OF INSTRUCTION IN FACILITATING SUCCESS IN LEARNING

Evaluating the appropriateness of instructional materials, activities, resources, and technologies is integral to establishing a successful learning environment. Doing so provides students with high-quality and inclusive instruction by ensuring **clarity**, **accuracy**, **relevancy**, and **reflection** of student diversities. By determining whether these components of instruction meet varying characteristics and learning needs, the teacher can deliver **student-centered** instruction, that is challenging based on individual ability, to promote development and academic success. This process also allows the teacher to effectively **differentiate** instruction to provide necessary personalized support for success in achieving learning targets, as well as create engaging learning opportunities tailored to students' unique differences and interests. Effectively determining the appropriateness of activities, materials, resources, and technologies in meeting students' learning needs ultimately maximizes academic achievement and fosters positive attitudes toward learning that establish a foundation for future success.

## CONTINUOUS MONITORING OF INSTRUCTIONAL EFFECTIVENESS

Successful instruction must be flexible and adaptable to meet students' dynamic learning needs. To achieve this, teachers must continuously monitor the effectiveness of their instruction to determine if their teaching strategies, activities, and communication are effective. Frequent evaluation of instructional effectiveness is necessary to ensure that students understand **foundational concepts**

Copyright © Mometrix Media. You have been licensed one copy of this document for personal use only. Any other reproduction or redistribution is strictly prohibited. All rights reserved. This content is provided for test preparation purposes only and does not imply an endorsement by Mometrix of any particular political, scientific, or religious point of view.

before moving on to more advanced concepts. **Adaptations** to instruction, communication, or assessment may be necessary to ensure students are able to comprehend and retain concepts before moving on to more advanced topics. **Remediation** of missed concepts is often much more challenging and less successful than checking for comprehension within context and providing more detailed instruction. This ultimately fosters long-term achievement, as the teacher can identify and address student needs as they arise and prevent compounding issues. Continuous monitoring enables the teacher to ensure that learning opportunities are engaging, relevant, and challenging based on students' ability levels, as it provides immediate feedback on the effectiveness of instruction, which allows the teacher to make necessary changes. This ultimately enhances instruction by establishing a student-centered learning environment that is tailored to individual needs, interests, and abilities.

## PRE-INSTRUCTIONAL, PERI-INSTRUCTIONAL, AND POST-INSTRUCTIONAL STRATEGIES

Instructional effectiveness must be monitored on a whole-class and individual level throughout all stages of teaching. Prior to instruction, administering **pre-tests** provides the teacher with insight regarding whole-class and individual understanding. This enables them to select effective and appropriate instructional strategies that can be differentiated to meet individual needs. Pre-tests allow the teacher to identify and clarify misunderstandings before instruction to ensure effectiveness. During instruction, **observation** of students' participation in instruction during independent and group activities enables the teacher to evaluate overall and individual understanding and engagement. Frequent checks for understanding and **formative assessments** throughout instruction provide feedback on whole-group and individual learning, as the teacher can assess understanding and participation to adapt teaching strategies or individualize instruction. Leading student discussions allows the teacher to identify areas of misunderstanding among the class or individuals that may need reteaching through a different approach. Closure and reflection activities after instruction are valuable in monitoring effectiveness, as they indicate both whole-class and individual comprehension and retainment of new concepts. Likewise, incorporating **summative assessments** and analyzing the results provides the teacher with information regarding the overall effectiveness of their teaching process, as well as students' individual strengths and weaknesses to consider for future instruction.

## APPLYING FEEDBACK TO MAKE NECESSARY CHANGES TO INSTRUCTION

Continuous monitoring of instruction indicates the instruction's effectiveness on a **whole-class** and **individual** level, as it provides the teacher with immediate insight on student understanding, progress, and areas for improvement. Monitoring instructional effectiveness enables the teacher to evaluate students' **pace** in achieving learning goals and adjust the rate of instruction as necessary. Additionally, it allows the teacher to identify whole-class and individual **misconceptions** that require correction to ensure students do not fall behind schedule in meeting academic benchmarks. If monitoring reveals misunderstanding among the whole class, the teacher must alter their overall instructional approach and teaching strategies to clarify and regain understanding. Individual misconceptions indicate the need to differentiate instruction, adjust groupings, and provide supports and remediation as necessary to ensure the student progresses at the same rate as the rest of the class. By identifying student strengths and weaknesses through consistent monitoring of instructional effectiveness, the teacher can effectively make instructional decisions that are attuned to whole-class and individual student needs to maximize learning.

Copyright © Mometrix Media. You have been licensed one copy of this document for personal use only. Any other reproduction or redistribution is strictly prohibited. All rights reserved. This content is provided for test preparation purposes only and does not imply an endorsement by Mometrix of any particular political, scientific, or religious point of view.

## CHAPTER QUIZ

**1. Which of the following would be considered a post-instructional strategy?**

    a. Pre-test
    b. Observation
    c. Formative assessment
    d. Summative assessment

**2. All of the following are true EXCEPT:**

    a. Continuous monitoring lets the teacher ensure that learning opportunities are engaging, relevant, and challenging.
    b. Continuous monitoring provides immediate feedback on the effectiveness of instruction.
    c. Remediation of missed concepts is often much less challenging and more successful than checking for comprehension within context and providing more detailed instruction.
    d. Adaptations to instruction, communication, or assessment may be necessary to ensure students can comprehend and retain concepts before moving on to more advanced topics.

**3. Giving students a sense of agency over their own learning by letting them devise their own conclusions or solutions to problems is known as:**

    a. Inquiry-based learning
    b. Deductive learning
    c. Inductive learning
    d. Open-ended learning

**4. Which of the following puts the components of a daily lesson plan structure in chronological order?**

    a. Academic standard, learning objectives, learning goals, warm-up activity
    b. Learning objectives, warm-up activity, directed instruction, active learning activity
    c. Learning goals, learning objectives, directed instruction, warm-up activity
    d. Warm-up activity, active learning activity, directed instruction, closure activity

## CHAPTER QUIZ ANSWER KEY

**1. D:** Closure and reflection activities after instruction are valuable in monitoring effectiveness, as they indicate both whole-class and individual comprehension and retainment of new concepts. Likewise, incorporating summative assessments and analyzing the results provides the teacher with information regarding the overall effectiveness of their teaching process, as well as students' individual strengths and weaknesses to consider for future instruction.

**2. C:** Frequent evaluation of instructional effectiveness is necessary to ensure that students understand foundational concepts before moving on to more advanced concepts. Adaptations to instruction, communication, or assessment may be necessary to ensure students are able to comprehend and retain concepts before moving on to more advanced topics. Remediation of missed concepts is often much more challenging and less successful than checking for comprehension within context and providing more detailed instruction. This latter approach ultimately fosters long-term achievement, as the teacher can identify and address student needs as they arise and prevent compounding issues. Continuous monitoring enables the teacher to ensure that learning opportunities are engaging, relevant, and challenging based on students' ability levels, as it provides immediate feedback on the effectiveness of instruction, which allows the teacher to make necessary changes.

Copyright © Mometrix Media. You have been licensed one copy of this document for personal use only. Any other reproduction or redistribution is strictly prohibited. All rights reserved.
This content is provided for test preparation purposes only and does not imply an endorsement by Mometrix of any particular political, scientific, or religious point of view.

**3. A:** The promotion of inquiry is a valuable instructional technique in enhancing student engagement and intellectual involvement. In an inquiry-based learning environment, students are encouraged to explore instructional material and devise their own conclusions or solutions to problems. This increases the effectiveness of the learning process by giving students a sense of agency over their own learning.

**4. B:** Example of a daily lesson plan structure:

Copyright © Mometrix Media. You have been licensed one copy of this document for personal use only. Any other reproduction or redistribution is strictly prohibited. All rights reserved.
This content is provided for test preparation purposes only and does not imply an endorsement by Mometrix of any particular political, scientific, or religious point of view.

# Assessment Methodology

## ASSESSMENT METHODS

Effective teaching requires multiple methods of assessment to evaluate student comprehension and instructional effectiveness. Assessments are typically categorized as diagnostic, formative, summative, and benchmark, and are applicable at varying stages of instruction. **Diagnostic** assessments are administered before instruction and indicate students' prior knowledge and areas of misunderstanding to determine the path of instruction. **Formative** assessments occur continuously to measure student engagement, comprehension, and instructional effectiveness. These assessments indicate instructional strategies that require adjustment to meet students' needs in facilitating successful learning, and include such strategies as checking for understanding, observations, total participation activities, and exit tickets. **Summative** assessments are given at the end of a lesson or unit to evaluate student progress in reaching learning targets and identify areas of misconception for reteaching. Such assessments can be given in the form of exams and quizzes, or project-based activities in which students demonstrate their learning through hands-on, personalized methods. Additionally, portfolios serve as valuable summative assessments in allowing students to demonstrate their progress over time and provide insight regarding individual achievement. **Benchmark** assessments occur less frequently and encompass large portions of curriculum. These assessments are intended to evaluate the progress of groups of students in achieving state and district academic standards.

## ASSESSMENT TYPES

- **Diagnostic:** These assessments can either be formal or informal and are intended to provide teachers with information regarding students' level of understanding prior to beginning a unit of instruction. Examples include pretests, KWL charts, anticipation guides, and brainstorming activities. Digital resources, such as online polls, surveys, and quizzes are also valuable resources for gathering diagnostic feedback.
- **Formative:** These assessments occur throughout instruction to provide the teacher with feedback regarding student understanding. Examples include warm-up and closure activities, checking frequently for understanding, student reflection activities, and providing students with color-coded cards to indicate their level of understanding. Short quizzes and total participation activities, such as four corners, are also valuable formative assessments. Numerous digital resources, including polls, surveys, and review games, are also beneficial in providing teachers with formative feedback to indicate instructional effectiveness.
- **Summative:** Summative assessments are intended to indicate students' level of mastery and progress toward reaching academic learning standards. These assessments may take the form of written or digital exams and include multiple choice, short answer, or long answer questions. Examples also include projects, final essays, presentations, or portfolios to demonstrate student progress over time.
- **Benchmark:** Benchmark assessments measure students' progress in achieving academic standards. These assessments are typically standardized to ensure uniformity, objectivity, and accuracy. Benchmark assessments are typically given as a written multiple choice or short answer exam, or as a digital exam in which students answer questions on the computer.

> **Review Video: <u>Formative and Summative Assessments</u>**
> Visit mometrix.com/academy and enter code: 804991

Copyright © Mometrix Media. You have been licensed one copy of this document for personal use only. Any other reproduction or redistribution is strictly prohibited. All rights reserved. This content is provided for test preparation purposes only and does not imply an endorsement by Mometrix of any particular political, scientific, or religious point of view.

## DETERMINING APPROPRIATE ASSESSMENT STRATEGIES

As varying assessment methods provide different information regarding student performance and achievement, the teacher must consider the most applicable and effective assessment strategy in each stage of instruction. This includes determining the **desired outcomes** of assessment, as well as the information the teacher intends to ascertain and how they will apply the results to further instruction. **Age** and **grade level** appropriateness must be considered when selecting which assessment strategies will enable students to successfully demonstrate their learning. Additionally, the teacher must be cognizant of students' individual differences and learning needs to determine which assessment model is most **accommodating** and reflective of their progress. It is also important that the teacher consider the practicality of assessment strategies, as well as methods they will use to implement the assessment for maximized feedback regarding individual and whole-class progress in achieving learning goals.

## TECHNOLOGY-BASED ASSESSMENTS

**Technology-based assessments** provide teachers with multiple resources for evaluating student progress to guide instruction. They are applicable in most formal and informal instructional settings and can be utilized for formative and summative assessments. Technology-based assessments simplify and enhance the efficiency of determining comprehension and instructional effectiveness, as they quickly present the teacher with information regarding student progress. This data enables the teacher to make necessary adjustments to facilitate student learning and growth. Implementing this assessment format simplifies the process of aligning them to school and district academic standards. This establishes objectivity and uniformity for comparing results and progress among students, as well as ensures that all students are held to the same academic expectations. While technology-based assessments are beneficial, there are some shortcomings to consider. This format may not be entirely effective for all learning styles in demonstrating understanding, as individualization in technology-based assessment can be limited. These assessments may not illustrate individual students' growth over time, but rather their mastery of an academic standard, thus hindering the ability to evaluate overall achievement. As technology-based evaluation limits hands-on opportunities, the real-world application and relevancy of the assessment may be unapparent to students.

## ASSESSMENTS THAT REFLECT REAL-WORLD APPLICATIONS

Assessments that reflect **real-world applications** enhance relevancy and students' ability to establish personal connections to learning that deepen understanding. Implementing such assessments provides authenticity and enhances engagement by defining a clear and practical purpose for learning. These assessments often allow for hands-on opportunities for demonstrating learning and can be adjusted to accommodate students' varying learning styles and needs while measuring individual progress. However, assessments that focus on real-world applications can be subjective, thus making it difficult to extract concrete data and quantify student progress to guide future instructional decisions. In addition, teachers may have difficulty analyzing assessment results on a large scale and comparing student performance with other schools and districts, as individual assessments may vary.

## FORMATIVE ASSESSMENT

**Formative assessment** refers to any evaluation of a student's knowledge while they are still in the process of learning the content. The general purpose of formative assessment is to provide both the teacher and the student with an idea of comprehension throughout a unit. This allows for the teacher to make adjustments to instruction to meet the needs of the student or whole class, and it may help the student recognize deficiencies in understanding that they can improve on. Formative assessments can be formal or informal, including classroom discussion, checks for comprehension,

Copyright © Mometrix Media. You have been licensed one copy of this document for personal use only. Any other reproduction or redistribution is strictly prohibited. All rights reserved.
This content is provided for test preparation purposes only and does not imply an endorsement by Mometrix of any particular political, scientific, or religious point of view.

homework, quizzes, or portfolio assessments, as these all demonstrate the students' understanding during the course of the unit. Formative assessments can be focused on students as individuals or on the whole-class, as both help to shape future instruction. In addition, **total participation activities** such as response cards, surveys, games, or digital response activities enable the entire class to indicate their level of engagement and understanding. Formative assessment allows for more successful teaching and learning, as it enables the teacher to make informed present and future educational decisions that meet the needs of all students.

## SUMMATIVE ASSESSMENTS

**Summative assessment** refers to an evaluation at the end of a discrete unit of instruction, such as the end of a course, end of a unit, or end of a semester. Classic examples of summative assessments include end of course assessments, final exams, or even qualifying standardized tests such as the SAT or ACT. Most summative assessments are created to measure student mastery of particular **academic standards**. Whereas formative assessment generally informs current instruction, summative assessments are used to objectively demonstrate that each individual has achieved adequate mastery of the standards in question. If a student has not met the benchmark, they may need extra instruction or to repeat the course. These assessments usually take the form of **tests** or formal portfolios with rubrics and clearly defined goals. **Project-based** assessments are beneficial in evaluating achievement, as they incorporate several elements of instruction and highlight real-world applications of learning. This allows students to demonstrate understanding through a hands-on, individualized approach that reinforces connections to learning and increases retainment. **Portfolios** of student work over time serve as a valuable method for assessing individual progress toward reaching learning targets. Summative assessments provide insight regarding overall instructional effectiveness and are necessary for guiding future instruction in subsequent years but are not usually used to modify current instruction.

## DIAGNOSTIC TESTS

**Diagnostic tests** are integral to planning and delivering effective instruction. These tests are typically administered prior to beginning a unit or lesson and provide valuable feedback for guiding and planning instruction. Diagnostic tests provide **preliminary information** regarding students' level of understanding and prior knowledge. This serves as a baseline for instructional planning that connects and builds upon students' background knowledge and experiences to enhance success in learning. Diagnostic tests allow the teacher to identify and clarify areas of student misconception prior to engaging in instruction to ensure continued comprehension and avoid the need for remediation. They indicate areas of student strength and need, as well as individual instructional aids that may need to be incorporated into lessons to support student achievement. In addition, these tests enable the teacher to determine which instructional strategies, activities, groupings, and materials will be most valuable in maximizing engagement and learning. Diagnostic tests can be **formal** or **informal**, and include such formats as pre-tests, pre-reading activities, surveys, vocabulary inventories, and graphic organizers such as KWL charts to assess student understanding prior to engaging in learning. Diagnostic tests are generally not graded as there is little expectation that all students in a class possess the same baseline of proficiency at the start of a unit.

## BENCHMARK ASSESSMENTS

**Benchmark assessments** are intended to quantify, evaluate, and compare individual and groups of students' achievement of school-wide, district, and state **academic standards.** They are typically administered in specific intervals throughout the school year and encompass entire or large units of curriculum to determine student mastery and readiness for academic advancement. Benchmark assessments provide data that enable the teacher to determine students' progress toward reaching

Copyright © Mometrix Media. You have been licensed one copy of this document for personal use only. Any other reproduction or redistribution is strictly prohibited. All rights reserved. This content is provided for test preparation purposes only and does not imply an endorsement by Mometrix of any particular political, scientific, or religious point of view.

academic goals to guide current and continued instruction. This data can be utilized by the school and individual teachers to create learning goals and objectives aligned with academic standards, as well as plan instructional strategies, activities, and assessments to support students in achieving them. In addition, benchmark assessments provide feedback regarding understanding and the potential need for remediation to allow the teacher to instill necessary supports in future instruction that prepare students for success in achieving learning targets.

## ALIGNMENT OF ASSESSMENTS WITH INSTRUCTIONAL GOALS AND OBJECTIVES

To effectively monitor student progress, assessments must align with **instructional goals** and **objectives**. This allows the teacher to determine whether students are advancing at an appropriate pace to achieve state and district academic standards. When assessments are aligned with specific learning targets, the teacher ensures that students are learning relevant material to establish a foundation of knowledge necessary for growth and academic achievement. To achieve this, the teacher must determine which instructional goals and objectives their students must achieve and derive instruction, content, and activities from these specifications. Instruction must reflect and reinforce learning targets, and the teacher must select the most effective strategies for addressing students' needs as they work to achieve them. Assessments must be reflective of content instruction to ensure they are aligned with learning goals and objectives, as well as to enable the teacher to evaluate student progress in mastering them. The teacher must clearly communicate learning goals and objectives throughout all stages of instruction to provide students with clarity on expectations. This establishes a clear purpose and focus for learning that enhances relevancy and strengthens connections to support student achievement.

## CLEARLY COMMUNICATING ASSESSMENT CRITERIA AND STANDARDS

Students must be clear on the purpose of learning throughout all stages of instruction to enhance understanding and facilitate success. When assessment **criteria** and **standards** are clearly communicated, the purpose of learning is established, and students are able to effectively connect instructional activities to learning goals and criteria for assessment. Communicating assessment criteria and standards provides students with clarity on tasks and learning goals they are expected to accomplish as they prepare themselves for assessment. This allows for more **focused instruction** and engagement in learning, as it enhances relevancy and student motivation. Utilizing appropriate forms of **rubrics** is an effective strategy in specifying assessment criteria and standards, as it informs students about learning goals they are working toward, the quality of work they are expected to achieve, and skills they must master to succeed on the assessment. Rubrics indicate to students exactly how they will be evaluated, thus supporting their understanding and focus as they engage in learning to promote academic success.

The following are varying styles of rubrics that can be used to communicate criteria and standards:

- **Analytic:** Analytic rubrics break down criteria for an assignment into several categories and provide an explanation of the varying levels of performance in each one. This style of rubric is beneficial for detailing the characteristics of quality work, as well as providing students with feedback regarding specific components of their performance. Analytic rubrics are most effective when used for summative assessments, such as long-term projects or essays.
- **Holistic:** Holistic rubrics evaluate the quality of the student's assignment as a whole, rather than scoring individual components. Students' score is determined based upon their performance across multiple performance indicators. This style of rubric is beneficial for providing a comprehensive evaluation but limits the amount of feedback that students receive regarding their performance in specific areas.

Copyright © Mometrix Media. You have been licensed one copy of this document for personal use only. Any other reproduction or redistribution is strictly prohibited. All rights reserved.
This content is provided for test preparation purposes only and does not imply an endorsement by Mometrix of any particular political, scientific, or religious point of view.

- **Single-Point:** Single point rubrics outline criteria for assignments into several categories. Rather than providing a numeric score to each category, however, the teacher provides written feedback regarding the students' strengths and ways in which they can improve their performance. This style of rubric is beneficial in providing student-centered feedback that focuses on their overall progress.
- **Checklist:** Checklists typically outline a set of criteria that is scored using a binary approach based upon completion of each component. This style increases the efficiency of grading assignments and is often easy for students to comprehend but does not provide detailed feedback. This method of grading should generally be reserved for shorter assignments.

## COMMUNICATION OF HIGH ACADEMIC EXPECTATIONS
### ASSESSMENT CRITERIA AND STANDARDS

The attitudes and behaviors exhibited by the teacher are highly influential on students' attitudes toward learning. Teachers demonstrate belief in students' abilities to be successful in learning when they communicate **high academic expectations**. This promotes students' **self-concept** and establishes a **growth mindset** to create confident, empowered learners that are motivated to achieve. High expectations for assessments and reaching academic standards communicates to students the quality of work that is expected of them and encourages them to overcome obstacles as they engage in learning. When communicating expectations for student achievement, it is important that the teacher is aware of students' individual learning needs to provide the necessary support that establishes equitable opportunities for success in meeting assessment criteria and standards. Setting high expectations through assessment criteria and standards while supporting students in their learning enhances overall achievement and establishes a foundation for continuous academic success.

### EFFECTIVE COMMUNICATION AND IMPACT ON STUDENT LEARNING

Communicating high academic expectations enhances students' self-concept and increases personal motivation for success in learning. To maximize student achievement, it is important that the teacher set high academic expectations that are **clearly** communicated through **age-appropriate** terms and consistently reinforced. Expectations must be reflected through learning goals and objectives, and **visible** at all times to ensure student awareness. The teacher must be **specific** in communicating what they want students to accomplish and clearly detail necessary steps for achievement while assuming the role of facilitator to guide learning and provide support. Providing constructive **feedback** throughout instruction is integral in reminding students of academic expectations and ensuring they are making adequate progress toward reaching learning goals. When high academic expectations are communicated and reinforced, students are empowered with a sense of confidence and self-responsibility for their own learning that promotes their desire to learn. This ultimately enhances achievement and equips them with the tools necessary for future academic success.

## ENSURING ASSESSMENTS ARE CONGRUENT WITH INSTRUCTIONAL GOALS AND OBJECTIVES

Assessments that are congruent to instructional goals and objectives provide a **clear purpose** for learning that enhances student understanding and motivation. When learning targets are reflected in assessments, instructional activities and materials become more **relevant**, as they are derived from these specifications. Such clarity in purpose allows for more focus and productivity as students engage in instruction and fosters connections that strengthen overall understanding for maximized success in learning. Aligning assessments with instructional goals and objectives ensures that students are learning material that is relevant to the curriculum and academic standards to ensure **preparedness** as they advance in their academic careers. In addition, it

Copyright © Mometrix Media. You have been licensed one copy of this document for personal use only. Any other reproduction or redistribution is strictly prohibited. All rights reserved.
This content is provided for test preparation purposes only and does not imply an endorsement by Mometrix of any particular political, scientific, or religious point of view.

enables the teacher to evaluate and monitor student progress to determine whether they are progressing at an ideal pace for achieving academic standards. With this information, the teacher can effectively modify instruction as necessary to support students' needs in reaching desired learning outcomes.

## ASSESSMENT RELIABILITY

**Assessment reliability** refers to how well an assessment is constructed and is made up of a variety of measures. A test should perform similarly with different test administrators, graders, and test-takers and perform consistently over multiple iterations.

- **Test-retest reliability** refers to an assessment's consistency of results with the same test-taker over multiple retests. If one student shows inconsistent results over time, the test is not considered to have test-retest reliability.
- **Intertester reliability** refers to an assessment's consistency of results between multiple test-takers at the same level. Students at similar levels of proficiency should show similar results.
- **Interrater reliability** refers to an assessment's consistency of results between different administrators of the test. This plays an especially critical role in tests with interactive or subjective responses, such as Likert-scales, cloze tests, and short answer tests. Different raters of the same test need to have a consistent means of evaluating the test-takers' performance. Clear rubrics can help keep two or more raters consistent in scoring.
- **Intra-rater reliability** refers to an assessment's consistency of results with one rater over time. One test rater should be able to score different students objectively to rate subjective test formats fairly.
- **Parallel-forms reliability** refers to an assessment's consistency between multiple different forms. For instance, end-of-course assessments may have many distinctive test forms, with different questions or question orders. If the different forms of a test do not provide the same results, it is said to be lacking in parallel-forms reliability.
- **Internal consistency reliability** refers to the consistency of results of similar questions on a particular assessment. If there are two or more questions targeted at the same standard and at the same level, they should show the same results across each question.

## ASSESSMENT VALIDITY

**Assessment validity** is a measure of the relevancy that an assessment has to the skill or ability being evaluated, and the degree to which students' performance is representative of their mastery of the topic of assessment. In other words, how well does an assessment correlate to what it is looking to assess. Assessments should be evaluated for validity on both the individual question level and as a test overall. This can be especially helpful in refining tests for future classes. The overall validity of an assessment is determined by several types of validity measures.

- **Face validity** refers to the initial impression of whether an assessment seems to be fit for the task. As this method is subjective to interpretation and unquantifiable, it should not be used singularly as a measurement of validity.
- **Construct validity** asks if an assessment actually assesses what it is intended to assess. Some topics are more straightforward, such as assessing if a student can perform two-digit multiplication. This can be directly tested, which gives the assessment a strong content validity. Other measures, such as a person's overall happiness, must be measured indirectly. If an assessment asserted that a person is generally happy if they smile frequently, it would be fair to question the construct validity of that assessment because smiling is unlikely to be a consistent measure of all peoples' general happiness.

298

Copyright © Mometrix Media. You have been licensed one copy of this document for personal use only. Any other reproduction or redistribution is strictly prohibited. All rights reserved. This content is provided for test preparation purposes only and does not imply an endorsement by Mometrix of any particular political, scientific, or religious point of view.

- **Content validity** indicates whether the assessment is comprehensive of all aspects of the content being assessed. If a test leaves out an important topic, then the teacher will not have a full picture as a result of the assessment.
- **Criterion validity** refers to whether the results of an assessment can be used to **predict** a related value, known as **criterion**. An example of this is the hypothesis that IQ tests would predict a person's success later in life, but many critics believe that IQ tests are not valid predictors of success because intelligence is not the only predictor of success in life. IQ tests have shown validity toward predicting academic success, however. The measure of an assessment's criterion validity depends on how closely related the criterion is.
- **Discriminant validity** refers to how well an assessment tests only that which it is intended to test and successfully discriminates one piece of information from another. For instance, a student who is exceptional in mathematics should not be able to put that information into use on a science test and gain an unfair advantage. If they are able to score well due to their mathematics knowledge, the science test did not adequately discriminate science knowledge from mathematics knowledge.
- **Convergent validity** is related to discriminant validity, but takes into account that two measures may be distinct, but can be correlated. For instance, a personality test should distinguish self-esteem from extraversion so that they can be measured independently, but if an assessment has convergent validity, it should show a correlation between related measures.

Copyright © Mometrix Media. You have been licensed one copy of this document for personal use only. Any other reproduction or redistribution is strictly prohibited. All rights reserved.
This content is provided for test preparation purposes only and does not imply an endorsement by Mometrix of any particular political, scientific, or religious point of view.

## CHAPTER QUIZ

**1. Which of the following is NOT one of the assessment types?**

- a. Normative
- b. Summative
- c. Benchmark
- d. Diagnostic

**2. Which type of rubric evaluates the quality of the assignment as a whole rather than scoring individual components?**

- a. Analytic
- b. Holistic
- c. Single-point
- d. Checklist

**3. Which type of assessment reliability plays an especially critical role in tests with interactive or subjective responses, such as Likert-scales, cloze tests, and short-answer tests?**

- a. Test-retest reliability
- b. Interrater reliability
- c. Parallel-forms reliability
- d. Internal consistency reliability

**4. Which type of validity determines if an assessment actually assesses what it is intended to assess?**

- a. Construct validity
- b. Content validity
- c. Criterion validity
- d. Discriminant validity

## CHAPTER QUIZ ANSWER KEY

**1. A:** Assessments are typically categorized as diagnostic, formative, summative, and benchmark, and are applicable at varying stages of instruction.

**2. B:** With holistic rubrics, students' scores are based on their performance across multiple performance indicators. This style of rubric is beneficial for providing a comprehensive evaluation but limits the amount of feedback that students receive regarding their performance in specific areas.

**3. B:** Interrater reliability refers to an assessment's consistency of results between different administrators of the test. This plays an especially critical role in tests with interactive or subjective responses, such as Likert scales, cloze tests, and short-answer tests. Different raters of the same test need to have a consistent means of evaluating the test-takers' performance. Clear rubrics can help keep two or more raters consistent in scoring.

**4. A:** Construct validity asks if an assessment actually assesses what it is intended to assess. Content validity indicates whether the assessment is comprehensive of all aspects of the content being assessed. Criterion validity refers to whether the results of an assessment can be used to predict a related value, known as a criterion. Discriminant validity refers to how well an assessment tests only that which it is intended to test and successfully discriminates one piece of information from another.

Copyright © Mometrix Media. You have been licensed one copy of this document for personal use only. Any other reproduction or redistribution is strictly prohibited. All rights reserved. This content is provided for test preparation purposes only and does not imply an endorsement by Mometrix of any particular political, scientific, or religious point of view.

# Effective Feedback and Responsive Teaching

## TIMELY FEEDBACK

**Timely feedback** improves the effectiveness of teaching and learning for enhanced student achievement. When the teacher consistently provides feedback on students' progress throughout all stages of instruction, it is more relevant, thus enabling students to effectively connect it to the context of their learning. Providing timely feedback also ensures that instructional content is at the forefront of students' minds, thus increasing the likelihood that students will effectively apply it for enhanced learning. Immediate feedback increases student motivation and allows for more focused instruction, as students are continuously aware of their strengths and areas for improvement. In addition, efficient feedback enables the teacher to quickly identify areas of misconception before advancing in instruction, thus ensuring student understanding before moving forward and avoiding the need for remediation. This allows the teacher to progress smoothly through instruction while ensuring comprehension to enhance student achievement.

## APPROPRIATE LANGUAGE FOR PROVIDING FEEDBACK

The language of feedback influences its effectiveness in fostering student achievement. When providing students with feedback regarding their progress, the teacher must be mindful of their approach to ensure that it is properly received. It is important that the teacher consider students' **age** and **grade level** to tailor language accordingly and present feedback in a relevant and meaningful way. When the language of feedback is comprehensible to students, they are more effectively able to apply it to the context of their learning. The teacher's language must be **respectful, positive**, and **encouraging** while constructively suggesting areas for improvement so as to support students' self-concept and positive attitudes toward learning. This includes framing feedback with remarks that identify and reinforce students' **strengths** while offering support and guidance to enhance development. Language must be **direct** and **specific** to ensure understanding and that necessary changes are made as students progress through instruction. The teacher must also be attuned to students' individual characteristics in order to address them with language that is responsive and considerate of their needs. When the appropriate language is applied in presenting feedback, it increases student motivation, engagement, and ability to make improvements that enhance their learning experience.

## EFFECTIVE FORMATS FOR FEEDBACK

Successful instruction is reliant on continuous feedback through a variety of **formats** to ensure that the teacher's guidance is accurate, constructive, substantive, and specific. Varying formats for providing formative and summative feedback are applicable and effective in different stages of the learning process. **Formative feedback** is often informal and occurs throughout instruction to guide student learning. Some methods include oral feedback in the form of asking students open-ended questions and providing suggestions for improvement, written comments on assignments, and peer-to-peer feedback in which students can offer one another support to build understanding. **Summative feedback** is often formal and occurs at the end of a lesson or unit to evaluate students' progress in achieving learning goals. **Rubrics** are a versatile tool for providing summative feedback, as they vary in complexity and the criteria within them can be tailored to specific learning objectives. This format is valuable for communicating expectations and clearly demonstrating the characteristics of quality work. In utilizing rubrics to provide feedback, the teacher can outline specific areas for evaluation, assign point values, and explicitly specify areas of strength and skills that need improvement.

Copyright © Mometrix Media. You have been licensed one copy of this document for personal use only. Any other reproduction or redistribution is strictly prohibited. All rights reserved. This content is provided for test preparation purposes only and does not imply an endorsement by Mometrix of any particular political, scientific, or religious point of view.

## SUBSTANTIVE FEEDBACK

When teachers provide **substantive feedback**, they ensure that students are given focused, useful, and relevant direction regarding their progress throughout the learning process. With such feedback, students receive **concrete information** regarding ways in which they can improve their performance in a given area that enables them to apply it to the context of their learning in a meaningful way. This ultimately strengthens students' connections between the teacher's substantive feedback and their work, thus enhancing understanding and success in learning. In addition, the nature of substantive feedback facilitates **personalized learning**, as it is tailored to address individual student progress and areas for improvement. This allows for student-centered instruction that enhances learning by addressing the needs of all students.

## CONSTRUCTIVE FEEDBACK

Feedback on students' progress must always be **constructive** in nature to facilitate successful learning and development. Constructive feedback ensures students maintain a positive **self-concept** and attitude toward learning, which is integral to increasing self-motivation and engagement. When students are motivated and engaged, they are more likely to apply the teacher's suggestions to enhance their learning and understanding. When providing constructive feedback, it is important that the teacher consider the specific area in which the student needs improvement in order to provide effective guidance for enhancing comprehension and progress. In addition, the teacher must consider their approach to providing feedback to ensure that all suggestions are productive, encouraging, and helpful to the student. This includes presenting feedback through **positive** and **supportive language** that is free of negative connotations or inferences. The teacher should accompany feedback with comments that highlight students' **strengths** while offering **suggestions** and **guidance** on specific areas in which they can improve. Constructive feedback must include clear explanations on ways in which students can improve their performance, as well as establish how the teacher's suggestions will enhance their overall learning and growth.

## SPECIFIC FEEDBACK

**Specific feedback** provides students with clarity regarding how to effectively improve their progress as they work toward achieving learning targets. When the teacher consistently delivers specific feedback, students are clear on expectations, can identify areas for improvement within their performance, and make necessary changes. Students are more likely to effectively apply feedback that specifies areas for development as they progress toward learning goals. If feedback is too vague, students may either disregard it or make incorrect, uninformed changes that hinder understanding and progress. Providing detailed suggestions and guidance enhances student engagement and motivation, as it increases their focus on particular areas for improvement to allow for success in learning. In addition, highlighting students' strengths through specific feedback encourages them to apply their abilities to other areas of instruction, thus enhancing student productivity and success in achieving learning targets.

## STUDENTS' USE OF FEEDBACK AND SELF-ASSESSMENT TO ENHANCE LEARNING
### STRATEGIES TO PROMOTE UTILIZATION OF FEEDBACK

Students' ability to utilize feedback is a valuable tool in enhancing their own learning for increased achievement. To develop this skill among students, the teacher must emphasize the value of feedback, demonstrate its applications in specific learning situations, and explain how implementing it is beneficial in improving academic performance. This notion can be reinforced by effectively **modeling** how to receive and apply feedback to enhance student understanding of the process. Feedback must always be constructive and highlight students' strengths to help them identify specific areas for improvement. By **checking** students' understanding of feedback

Copyright © Mometrix Media. You have been licensed one copy of this document for personal use only. Any other reproduction or redistribution is strictly prohibited. All rights reserved.
This content is provided for test preparation purposes only and does not imply an endorsement by Mometrix of any particular political, scientific, or religious point of view.

frequently, the teacher ensures they know how to productively apply it for enhanced learning. This includes encouraging students to **respond** to given feedback by contributing their thoughts and asking for clarification as necessary. In addition, students are more likely to internalize and effectively apply feedback that is **timely** and provided throughout instruction, rather than at the end, thus fostering their ability to utilize it in guiding their own learning. This allows students to establish personal connections between feedback and their learning that strengthen their understanding and promote their academic success.

## STRATEGIES TO FACILITATE USE OF SELF-ASSESSMENT

Developing students' **self-assessment** capabilities provides them with a sense of self-sufficiency for guiding and enhancing their own learning. To facilitate this, the teacher must establish a supportive **classroom environment** in which students feel comfortable and empowered to take risks and objectively evaluate their own progress as they seek areas for improvement. **Modeling** strategies for utilizing self-assessment to enhance learning and explaining its significance in supporting continued success are valuable strategies in enabling students to assess their own progress to guide and improve their learning. By guiding students with **open-ended questions** as they engage in learning, the teacher encourages students to assess their own progress and demonstrates how to implement effective questioning to seek areas for improvement within their own work. The teacher should include multiple outlets for self-assessment to facilitate the development of this skill, including **reflection** opportunities that enable students to evaluate their own understanding and guide their development as they engage in learning.

## SIGNIFICANCE OF SELF-ASSESSMENT IN FACILITATING GROWTH AND ACHIEVEMENT

When students are able to objectively assess their own progress, they are equipped with the tools necessary to continuously seek areas for improvement that guide and enhance their learning. This empowers students with a sense of **ownership** and responsibility over their learning as they monitor their own performance to refine their skills for enhanced growth and achievement. Self-assessment and monitoring strengthen students' **personal connections** to their work, as they are able to relate their learning to their own prior knowledge and frames of reference. This ultimately makes learning more relevant, thus increasing motivation, productivity, and achievement. Students who regularly self-assess their work develop the independence necessary for engaging in **self-directed** learning, thus establishing a foundation for continued growth and success. In addition, continuously seeking areas for improvement allows students to develop a sense of confidence to take risks in their learning, as they understand how to overcome obstacles as they progress.

## DEVELOPMENT OF REAL-WORLD LIFE SKILLS FOR FUTURE SUCCESS

The ability to effectively apply feedback and self-assessment for enhanced learning prepares students with the life skills necessary for future success in academic and real-world situations. Developing this skill instills within students the notion that there is always room for improvement in their performance. In addition, it develops their understanding of the characteristics of quality overcoming learning obstacles and the **self-motivation** required to take initiative that is integral to success. Students that frequently employ feedback and self-assessment have a strong sense of **independence** for and enhancing their own learning. In addition, this skill provides students with the **self-awareness** necessary to recognize their strengths and weaknesses, thus making them more inclined to continuously seek areas for increased understanding and improvement for maximized achievement. Students' communication and cooperation skills are enhanced when they learn to properly use feedback and self-assessment, as it develops their ability to appreciate constructive criticism and internalize multiple perspectives as they work to improve their performance.

Copyright © Mometrix Media. You have been licensed one copy of this document for personal use only. Any other reproduction or redistribution is strictly prohibited. All rights reserved. This content is provided for test preparation purposes only and does not imply an endorsement by Mometrix of any particular political, scientific, or religious point of view.

### SELF-ASSESSMENT THAT ENCOURAGES EVALUATION OF LEARNING AND CONTINUOUS IMPROVEMENT

Providing multiple strategies for self-assessment throughout instruction develops students' ability to monitor and evaluate their performance for continuous improvement. Self-assessment strategies can be formal or informal and can occur on an individual or whole-class basis. Teaching students how to set **SMART goals** (specific, measurable, attainable, relevant, time-bound) enables them to set learning goals, determine a path to achieve them, and reflect upon their performance to seek areas for improvement as they progress. Implementing strategies for students to indicate their level of comprehension is valuable in encouraging reflection on their own understanding and areas for improvement as they progress through the learning process. Such strategies include open-ended **questioning** to encourage reflection, color-coded **response cards** to signify understanding, or **whole-class activities** such as four corners. Graphic organizer activities such as **KWL charts** are beneficial in prompting students to consider prior knowledge and reflect on their progress after a lesson. This facilitates students in forming personal connections and determining areas in which they can extend and improve upon their learning. **Reflection** opportunities, such as exit tickets or learning logs, are also valuable for encouraging self-assessment, as they prompt students to consider areas in which they excelled, as well as potential room for improvement.

### Characteristics of SMART Goals

| S | Specific | The goal is clearly stated and narrowed down in scope. Details of the goal, including who, what, where, when, why, and how much, are explicitly outlined. |
|---|---|---|
| M | Measurable | The goal includes a quantifiable method of measuring progress toward achievement, such as reading twenty-five books in a year. |
| A | Attainable | The goal is challenging, yet realistic and within the realm of the individual's current abilities and skills. |
| R | Relevant | The goal is meaningful to the individual and contributes toward personal improvement and the long-term goals. |
| T | Time-Bound | The goal sets a specific timeline for achievement. This helps the individual monitor progress and hold personal accountability. |

## FLEXIBILITY IN INSTRUCTION
### SITUATIONS REQUIRING FLEXIBILITY

The classroom environment is dynamic in nature. Teachers will inevitably encounter situations throughout instruction and assessment in which **flexibility** is integral to successful teaching and learning. As students have varying learning styles, needs, and interests, teachers may find that their instructional approaches are ineffective in maintaining engagement and may need to adjust strategies, activities, or assessments to better meet learning needs. Students may have difficulty grasping new material, which could result in a lack of engagement in instructional activities and, potentially, disruptive behavior. Teachers must consistently be attuned to students' level of comprehension and allow flexibility with their lesson plans to modify strategies, activities, or pacing as necessary to facilitate engagement and understanding before advancing in instruction. Students may also progress more quickly than others through instructional activities or assessments. **Scaffolding** activities to include opportunities for extension and enrichment allows for flexibility within instruction to ensure that all students are adequately challenged and engaged in learning. Throughout instruction and assessments, teachers may find valuable, unexpected learning opportunities. By remaining open and flexible to these instances, teachers can enhance the learning process by incorporating them into instruction to strengthen student understanding.

Copyright © Mometrix Media. You have been licensed one copy of this document for personal use only. Any other reproduction or redistribution is strictly prohibited. All rights reserved. This content is provided for test preparation purposes only and does not imply an endorsement by Mometrix of any particular political, scientific, or religious point of view.

### ENHANCING THE OVERALL LEARNING EXPERIENCE

**Flexibility** is an integral component of effective instruction, as it enables the teacher to adequately address and accommodate students' individual needs and interests for maximized success in learning. When the teacher considers their lesson plan as a **framework** while allowing for flexibility, they demonstrate an awareness of their students' individual differences and the potential for deviation from original instruction. This enables them to more effectively modify instructional and assessment strategies, activities, and approaches to create a **responsive, student-centered** environment that enhances the overall learning experience and promotes achievement. When instructional activities and assessments are adaptable to accommodate students' needs and interests, learning becomes more personalized and relevant, thus strengthening understanding and increasing motivation to engage in active learning. A flexible approach to instruction and assessment also provides students with the ability to explore content of interest on a deeper level and potentially encounter unanticipated learning opportunities that foster personal connections and enhance learning. In addition, this approach allows for **versatility** in assessment, as flexibility enables the teacher to modify assessments by providing necessary support to meet students' individual needs and supports students' choice in demonstrating learning.

### POOR STUDENT COMPREHENSION

Throughout instruction and assessments, students may have difficulty **comprehending** new or difficult material, despite being engaged in instruction. This may lead to confusion that can cause students to become discouraged and disengaged in learning, as well as have continued and compounded difficulty in grasping increasingly complex concepts. Difficulties with comprehension hinders academic success, as students that struggle face challenges in building the foundation of understanding necessary for advancing through curriculum. To ensure student comprehension throughout all stages of learning, the teacher must be aware of students' individual learning styles and needs and be able to respond flexibly to obstacles they may encounter. **Formative assessments** during instruction enable the teacher to evaluate the level of student comprehension and identify areas of need for flexible **adjustment** or additional support. This includes modifying **pacing** and allowing additional time for student processing to ensure understanding. In addition, the original lesson plan may require **chunking** into smaller, more manageable parts to allow students to internalize new concepts before moving on. The teacher may also need to respond flexibly to students' needs during instruction by **differentiating** teaching strategies, activities, groupings, or assessments to ensure that material is accessible and comprehensible to all students for enhanced success.

### UNANTICIPATED LEARNING OPPORTUNITIES

**Unanticipated learning opportunities**, when embraced by the teacher, are often highly valuable in establishing a classroom environment that promotes student engagement, motivation, and success. These instances often divert from the original lesson plan, but when utilized effectively, serve to strengthen student understanding and foster **personal connections** for an enhanced learning experience. Facilitating such opportunities allows students to investigate topics of interest and relevancy to them on a deeper level, thus increasing active engagement and promoting **self-directed** learning. This ultimately supports students in forming connections and recognizing the real-world applications of their learning, which increases the likelihood that they will internalize and **retain** new information. Responding flexibly to unanticipated learning opportunities includes acknowledging students' questions and comments, as well as demonstrating an awareness of their individual differences and learning needs. This enables the teacher to maximize the effectiveness of these opportunities by facilitating student-led instruction that is attuned to their learning styles, interests, and preferences for enhanced engagement and achievement.

Copyright © Mometrix Media. You have been licensed one copy of this document for personal use only. Any other reproduction or redistribution is strictly prohibited. All rights reserved. This content is provided for test preparation purposes only and does not imply an endorsement by Mometrix of any particular political, scientific, or religious point of view.

## CONDUCTING ONGOING ASSESSMENTS AND MAKING ADJUSTMENTS

Conducting **ongoing assessments** throughout instruction provides the teacher with continuous feedback regarding student comprehension, engagement, and performance. When practiced consistently, the teacher is more attuned and responsive to students' individual learning needs. This enables them to effectively modify instructional strategies, activities, and assessments accordingly for a **student-centered** learning environment that provides the support necessary for enhanced engagement, comprehension, and achievement. It allows the teacher to identify and address areas of **misconception** and student need to ensure understanding prior to progressing through the curriculum. Feedback from ongoing evaluation of student performance indicates to the teacher areas of instruction in which adjustment is necessary to effectively support students in achieving learning goals. The teacher may need to adjust their pacing to ensure comprehension and engagement, as well as differentiate instruction based on feedback regarding individual progress to ensure all students are adequately challenged and supported based on their ability levels. Student groupings may need to be adjusted to scaffold instruction and facilitate increased comprehension. When the teacher effectively applies feedback from ongoing assessments of student engagement and performance, they can tailor instruction to accommodate their individual needs and interests to enhance success in learning.

## PROGRESSING AHEAD OF SCHEDULE

Throughout instruction, the teacher will encounter instances in which individual students or the whole class progresses **faster than anticipated**. When this arises, the teacher must be prepared to respond flexibly to ensure that all students are engaged, on task, and challenged based on their ability level. Lesson plans should be **scaffolded** to include opportunities for enrichment and extended learning for students that finish before others. This includes incorporating such material as increasingly complex texts, practice activities, and project opportunities. The teacher can also establish a designated area in the classroom in which individuals or small groups that finish early can participate in **extended learning** or **review** activities that reinforce learning objectives. Such activities allow students to explore instructional topics on a deeper level for strengthened understanding and ensure they are engaging productively in meaningful activities that are relevant to instruction. When the whole class progresses faster than expected, the teacher can respond flexibly by incorporating **total participation** activities to reinforce instructional material. Such activities as review games, class discussions, and digital resources for extra practice ensure that the class remains engaged in instruction when they finish a lesson early.

Copyright © Mometrix Media. You have been licensed one copy of this document for personal use only. Any other reproduction or redistribution is strictly prohibited. All rights reserved. This content is provided for test preparation purposes only and does not imply an endorsement by Mometrix of any particular political, scientific, or religious point of view.

## CHAPTER QUIZ

**1. Which type of feedback is often formal and occurs at the end of a lesson or unit?**

    a. Formative
    b. Summative
    c. Substantive
    d. Constructive

**2. All of the following are true concerning specific feedback EXCEPT:**

    a. Highlighting students' strengths through specific feedback encourages them to apply their abilities to other areas of instruction.
    b. Providing detailed suggestions and guidance enhances student engagement and motivation.
    c. Students are more likely to effectively apply feedback that specifies areas for development as they progress toward learning goals.
    d. If feedback is too specific, students may either disregard it or make incorrect, uninformed changes that hinder understanding and progress.

**3. Teaching students how to set SMART goals enables them to set learning goals, determine a path to achieve them, and reflect upon their performance to seek areas for improvement as they progress. What does the M in "SMART goals" stand for?**

    a. Methodical
    b. Meaningful
    c. Manageable
    d. Measurable

**4. What does the R in "SMART goals" stand for?**

    a. Reasonable
    b. Reusable
    c. Relevant
    d. Rigid

## CHAPTER QUIZ ANSWER KEY

**1. B:** Summative feedback is often formal and occurs at the end of a lesson or unit to evaluate students' progress in achieving learning goals.

**2. D:** If feedback is too vague, students may either disregard it or make incorrect, uninformed changes that hinder understanding and progress.

**3. D:** Teaching students how to set SMART goals (specific, measurable, attainable, relevant, time-bound) enables them to set learning goals, determine a path to achieve them, and reflect upon their performance to seek areas for improvement as they progress.

**4. C:** Teaching students how to set SMART goals (specific, measurable, attainable, relevant, time-bound) enables them to set learning goals, determine a path to achieve them, and reflect upon their performance to seek areas for improvement as they progress.

Copyright © Mometrix Media. You have been licensed one copy of this document for personal use only. Any other reproduction or redistribution is strictly prohibited. All rights reserved.
This content is provided for test preparation purposes only and does not imply an endorsement by Mometrix of any particular political, scientific, or religious point of view.

# Professional Interaction and Collaboration

## VERTICAL TEAMING

Communication and collaboration among teachers of varying grade levels is integral to effective instruction that supports students' learning and development. Through **vertical teaming**, content specific teachers **across grade levels** have the opportunity to work together in discussing and planning curriculum, instruction, assessments, and strategies that prepare students for achievement. Teachers of lower grade levels are often unsure of what students in upper grade levels are learning. As a result, these teachers may be uncertain of the skills and abilities their students need to be adequately prepared for success as they transition through grade levels. Likewise, teachers of upper grade levels are often unsure of what students have learned in previous grades, thus hindering their ability to adequately plan instruction and implement necessary learning supports. Vertical teaming facilitates the communication necessary for teachers across grade levels to collaborate in **establishing expectations for preparedness** at each grade level and developing a common curriculum path. This enhances teaching and learning, in that teachers are more effectively able to plan instruction that is aligned with learning targets and prepare students with the necessary knowledge, tools, and supports for continued academic success.

## HORIZONTAL TEAMING

**Horizontal teaming** refers to the collaboration of **same-grade level** teachers and staff that work with a common group of students. These teams may comprise teachers within a **single subject area** or **across disciplines** and may also include special education workers, grade-level administrators, paraprofessionals, and guidance counselors. Horizontal teaming is beneficial in facilitating the **coordinated planning** of curriculum, instruction, and assessments, as well as discussion regarding students' progress in the educational program. In addition, this method of teaming provides teachers and staff the opportunity to work together in developing educational goals, addressing areas of need, and implementing strategies to support students' success in learning. Horizontal teaming is also beneficial in encouraging teachers and staff to cooperate with one another in alignment with the goals and mission of the school to create a positive learning community focused on promoting student achievement.

## TEAM TEACHING

**Team teaching** refers to the collaboration of two or more teachers, paraprofessionals, instructional aides, or special education workers in planning and delivering instruction and assessments. There are **several structures** to this approach to accommodate varying teaching styles and student needs. One teacher may provide direct instruction while another engages in lesson activities or monitors student progress. Similarly, one teacher may instruct while another observes and collects information to improve future planning. Students may be grouped with teachers according to their needs to provide differentiation, or teachers may participate simultaneously and equally in all aspects of the learning process. The intention of this approach is to create a **student-centered environment** focused on enhancing and deepening the learning experience. Team teaching is beneficial in allowing increased **individualized instruction** that more effectively meets students' learning needs. Additionally, when multiple teachers are present, students have access to varying **ideas** and **perspectives** that strengthen their understanding. Team teaching also benefits teachers, as it enables them to utilize one another's strengths for improved instruction. There are, however, limitations to this approach. Differences in **classroom management** styles, **teaching practices**, and **personalities**, when not addressed properly through respectful communication and flexibility, hinder the effectiveness of team teaching.

Copyright © Mometrix Media. You have been licensed one copy of this document for personal use only. Any other reproduction or redistribution is strictly prohibited. All rights reserved. This content is provided for test preparation purposes only and does not imply an endorsement by Mometrix of any particular political, scientific, or religious point of view.

## BENEFITS OF MENTORS IN ENHANCING PROFESSIONAL KNOWLEDGE AND SKILLS

**Mentors** within the school community are typically experienced teachers that are available to offer support, guidance, and expertise to new teachers. As these individuals typically have a great deal of experience as educators, they are highly valuable resources in increasing professional knowledge and improving teaching skills. Mentors can provide **strategies, tools**, and **advice** for planning and delivering instruction, classroom management, and meeting students' learning needs to promote achievement. This includes suggesting ideas and resources for lesson activities and assessments, as well as techniques for differentiating instruction, enhancing student engagement, and promoting positive behavior. In addition, mentors can offer insight on how to effectively **navigate the school community**, including how to interact appropriately with colleagues and superiors, complete administrative duties, and communicate effectively with students' families. Regularly working with mentors in the school building ensures that new teachers are supported in developing the knowledge and skills necessary to become effective educators.

## INTERACTION WITH PROFESSIONALS IN THE SCHOOL COMMUNITY

In order for an educational community to function effectively, professionals in the building must work together cohesively on a daily basis to support the school's mission and student learning. The nature of these interactions significantly determines the climate and culture of the school environment. Appropriate, professional interactions are important in facilitating the productive collaboration necessary to create a positive school community that promotes student success in learning. All interactions must therefore be **respectful**, **constructive**, and **sensitive** to the varying backgrounds, cultures, and beliefs among professionals in the school community. This includes using **appropriate language**, practicing **active listening**, and ensuring that discussions regarding colleagues, superiors, students, and other individuals in the building remain positive. When interacting in a team setting, it is important to maintain open dialogue and support one another's contributions to the educational program. All professionals in the school building must understand one another's roles and appreciate how these roles function together to support the educational program. Doing so ensures that collaboration is productive, purposeful, and aligned with enhancing students' learning experience.

## SUPPORTIVE AND COOPERATIVE RELATIONSHIPS WITH PROFESSIONAL COLLEAGUES
### SUPPORTS LEARNING AND ACHIEVEMENT OF CAMPUS AND DISTRICT GOALS

Effective collaboration among school staff and faculty members is reliant on establishing and maintaining supportive, cooperative professional relationships. Doing so facilitates a sense of **mutual respect** and **open communication** that allows colleagues to work together constructively in developing educational goals, plans to support students in achieving them, and strategies to address areas of need within the educational program. Mutual support and cooperation are also beneficial in fostering the **coordinated planning** of curriculum, learning activities, assessments, and accommodations to meet students' individual needs for academic achievement. Such professional relationships allow for more effective teaching and learning, as students are supported by a school community that works together cohesively to promote learning and the achievement of campus and district academic goals.

### STRATEGIES FOR ESTABLISHING AND MAINTAINING RELATIONSHIPS

Building and maintaining professional relationships founded on mutual support and cooperation is integral in creating a positive, productive school community focused on student achievement. **Frequent communication** with colleagues in a variety of settings is an important factor in establishing and sustaining such professional relationships. Maintaining continuous and open communication allows professional colleagues in the school building to develop the respect for and

Copyright © Mometrix Media. You have been licensed one copy of this document for personal use only. Any other reproduction or redistribution is strictly prohibited. All rights reserved.
This content is provided for test preparation purposes only and does not imply an endorsement by Mometrix of any particular political, scientific, or religious point of view.

understanding of one another necessary to establish a strong rapport. By participating together in **school activities**, **events**, and **programs**, teachers and staff members can build connections while contributing to enhancing the school community and climate. **Community building** strategies, such as participating in activities or games that require teamwork, are also valuable opportunities for developing supportive and cooperative professional relationships among colleagues. In addition, **collaborating** with one another in regard to curriculum, lesson planning, and promoting student achievement, contributes significantly to developing positive professional relationships. There are multiple avenues for such collaboration, including participating in professional learning communities (PLC's), department meetings, vertical or horizontal teaming, or engaging in team teaching. Doing so provides teachers and staff the opportunity to communicate and develop mutual goals that support the educational program and student learning.

## ROLES AND RESPONSIBILITIES OF BUILDING AND DISTRICT LEVEL PROFESSIONALS

### DEPARTMENT CHAIRPERSONS

**Department chairpersons** are appointed to act as **leaders** within their subject area. These individuals are responsible for a variety of instructional and administrative duties to ensure the **efficacy** of their academic department in supporting the goals and mission of the school. This includes contributing to curriculum development, communicating instructional expectations from administration to their colleagues, and ensuring that daily instruction within the department aligns with campus and district academic standards. Department chairpersons also serve as **resources** for their team, including collaborating with them to design instructional activities and assessments, offering support, and facilitating positive communication with administration. When working with administration, department chairpersons discuss the progress of their department in meeting academic goals, collaborate to develop strategies for assisting faculty in supporting student learning, and ensure their colleagues have the support, materials, and resources necessary for effective instruction. In addition, department chairpersons are often responsible for coordinating department activities and programs that promote student achievement and contribute to creating a positive school community.

### SCHOOL PRINCIPAL

The primary role of the **principal** is establishing and maintaining a **school culture** that supports students, teachers, staff, and families in the educational program. This role comprises a multifaceted array of responsibilities that extend to nearly every aspect of the school. The principal is responsible for supervising the **daily operations** of the school to ensure a safe, orderly environment in which teachers, staff, and students are working in alignment with the school's mission. To achieve this, the principal must communicate expectations for a positive, productive school community, ensure academic and behavioral policies are followed by staff and students, and assign staff members specific duties to facilitate an organized, efficient learning environment. In addition, it is important that the principal support staff, students, and families by engaging in frequent, open communication, addressing concerns, and providing resources necessary to promote growth and achievement. The principal is also responsible for ensuring that the school's educational program is effective in supporting teachers, staff, and students in the achievement of academic standards. This includes overseeing curriculum, monitoring instructional practices, measuring their school's performance in relation to district academic standards, as well as communicating the progress and needs of the school to the board of education.

### BOARD OF TRUSTEES

Each school within a district is overseen by a **board of trustees** responsible for making decisions to ensure that the educational program supports students' learning needs for academic achievement. The board of trustees is comprised of a group of **elected individuals** that are typically members of

Copyright © Mometrix Media. You have been licensed one copy of this document for personal use only. Any other reproduction or redistribution is strictly prohibited. All rights reserved.
This content is provided for test preparation purposes only and does not imply an endorsement by Mometrix of any particular political, scientific, or religious point of view.

the community in which they serve. As such, they have an understanding of the educational needs of the students within the community and can apply this knowledge to make effective decisions regarding the learning program. Members within a board of trustees are responsible for creating an educational program in alignment with students' needs, as well as setting goals and developing strategies that support students in achieving them. This includes determining a **budget plan, allocating resources**, and making **administrative decisions** that benefit the school. In addition, board members are responsible for analyzing assessment data to make informed decisions regarding strategies to best support individual schools within the district and ensuring that measures are being implemented to effectively meet students' learning needs.

## CURRICULUM COORDINATORS

**Curriculum coordinators** are responsible for the **development** and **implementation** of curriculum that is aligned with campus and district academic goals. These individuals work closely with teachers and administrators to analyze student progress in relation to the educational program, primarily through **assessment scores**, to determine the overall effectiveness of the curriculum in supporting students' achievement. Analyzing student progress enables curriculum coordinators to identify strengths and areas for improvement within the curriculum to make adjustments that best meet students' learning needs as they work to achieve learning targets. Ensuring that curriculum aligns with academic standards and students' learning needs facilitates more effective teaching and learning. Doing so provides teachers with a clear understanding of how to adequately prepare students for success, thus allowing them to design focused instruction and implement necessary supports to promote the achievement of campus and district academic standards.

## SCHOOL TECHNOLOGY COORDINATORS

Incorporating technology into the classroom is highly valuable in diversifying instructional strategies to promote student learning and engagement. School **technology coordinators** facilitate this integration to enhance teaching and learning, as they are responsible for the **organization, maintenance**, and **allocation** of available technology resources within the school building. This includes ensuring that all technology is functional, updated, properly stored, and accessible to teachers. These individuals are also responsible for **staying current** on developing digital resources that could be implemented to improve the learning experience, as well as communicating with the board of education regarding **acquiring** technology resources for their school. Doing so ensures that teachers have the materials necessary to best support students' learning. In addition, technology coordinators **educate** teachers and staff on the uses of technology resources, as well as strategies to implement them in the classroom for more effective instruction.

## SPECIAL EDUCATION PROFESSIONALS

Special education professionals work with students of various disabilities, their teachers, and families to provide an equitable, inclusive environment that supports learning and development. These individuals are responsible for creating an educational plan that is tailored to support the unique needs of disabled students and ensuring that this plan is followed in all areas of the school. Special educators develop **individualized education programs** (IEPs) according to students' areas of need, develop academic and behavioral goals, as well as provide supports and modifications to accommodate students in achieving them. Special education professionals work with teachers to educate them on the proper implementation of individualized accommodations to ensure all students have the support necessary to successfully engage in learning. This includes collaborating with teachers to adapt and modify curriculum, instructional activities, and assessments to meet the individual needs of students with disabilities. In addition, special educators may work alongside classroom teachers in a team-teaching setting or provide individualized instruction as necessary.

311

Copyright © Mometrix Media. You have been licensed one copy of this document for personal use only. Any other reproduction or redistribution is strictly prohibited. All rights reserved. This content is provided for test preparation purposes only and does not imply an endorsement by Mometrix of any particular political, scientific, or religious point of view.

Students' academic and behavioral progress is monitored over time, and special educators communicate this information to families in order to collaborate in developing future goals and strategies to support achievement.

## ROLES AND RESPONSIBILITIES OF PROFESSIONALS WITHIN THE EDUCATION PROGRAM

The roles and responsibilities of various professionals within the educational program are described as follows:

- **Principal**—The principal is responsible for ensuring that the daily operations of the school function in a safe, orderly manner that aligns with the goals of the educational program. This includes delegating tasks to staff, enforcing academic and behavioral policies, ensuring instructional practices support student achievement, and communicating with students, staff, and families to establish a positive learning environment.

- **Vice Principal**—The vice principal's role is to assist the principal in supervising the daily operations of the school to create a safe, orderly, and productive learning environment. They are responsible for working with teachers, staff, students, and families to support them in the educational program. This includes enforcing academic and behavioral policies, addressing concerns, facilitating communication, and ensuring instructional practices support student achievement of campus and district academic goals.

- **Board of Trustees**—The board of trustees is responsible for developing an educational program that reflects the learning needs of students within the community. This includes developing educational goals, strategies to support students in achieving them, and ensuring that schools within the district are in alignment with the educational program. The board of trustees is also responsible for such administrative decisions as developing a budget plan and allocating resources to schools within the district according to students' needs.

- **Curriculum Coordinator**—Curriculum coordinators are responsible for developing a curriculum that aligns with campus and district academic goals, and ensuring it is implemented properly to support student achievement. This includes working with teachers and administrators to measure student progress within the curriculum and adjusting instructional strategies as necessary to support student success.

- **Assessment Coordinator**—Assessment coordinators schedule, disperse, and collect standardized assessments and testing materials within the school building. They are responsible for educating teachers on proper assessment protocols to ensure that all practices align with district policies, collaborating with them to develop strategies that support student achievement, and ensuring all students are provided with necessary accommodations according to individual need.

- **Technology Coordinator**—Technology coordinators facilitate the integration of digital resources into the curriculum. They are responsible for acquiring, organizing, maintaining, and allocating technology within the school. These individuals also work with teachers and staff to educate them on ways to utilize technology resources to enhance instruction.

- **Department Chair**—Department chairpersons act as leaders among the teachers within their content area. Their responsibilities include contributing to curriculum development, facilitating communication between administration and their colleagues, and ensuring instructional practices align with the educational program. They also collaborate with members of their team to develop instructional practices that best support student achievement of campus and district academic goals.

Copyright © Mometrix Media. You have been licensed one copy of this document for personal use only. Any other reproduction or redistribution is strictly prohibited. All rights reserved. This content is provided for test preparation purposes only and does not imply an endorsement by Mometrix of any particular political, scientific, or religious point of view.

- **Teacher Assistant**—The teacher assistant's role is to support the classroom teacher in both instructional and non-instructional duties. This includes assisting with the preparation, organization, and cleanup of lesson materials, working with small groups of students, managing student behavior, and ensuring the classroom functions in a safe, orderly manner.

- **Paraprofessional**—Paraprofessionals are licensed within the field of education and are responsible for assisting the teacher with daily classroom operations. This includes working with individual or small groups of students to provide instructional support, assisting with the preparation of lesson plans and materials, managing student behavior, and completing administrative duties.

- **Speech-Language Pathologist**—Speech-Language pathologists are special education professionals that work with students that have varying degrees of language and communication difficulties. They are responsible for evaluating and diagnosing disabilities related to speech and language, as well as developing individualized treatment programs. Speech-language pathologists then work with these students to remedy language and communication disabilities, as well as collaborate with teachers, staff, and families regarding ways to support their progress.

- **ESL Specialist**—ESL (English as a second language) specialists work with students for whom English is not their native language. They are responsible for evaluating students' levels of English language proficiency across the domains of reading, writing, speaking, and listening, determining necessary linguistic supports, and working with teachers to develop strategies that support English language acquisition. ESL specialists also work with individual or small groups of students to monitor progress and develop English language proficiency skills.

- **Guidance Counselor**—The role of guidance counselors is to support students' social, emotional, academic, and behavioral needs. This includes providing counseling services, mediation, and for upper grade level students, advice regarding course selection and career choices. These individuals communicate with teachers, staff, and families to develop and implement plans to support students' personal growth and academic achievement.

- **School Nurse**—The school nurse is responsible for providing a range of healthcare to students and staff in the school building. This includes evaluating the physical, mental, and emotional health of students and staff, as well as delivering general first-aid treatments. School nurses are also responsible for organizing and dispersing prescribed medications to students in accordance with their healthcare plan and educating teachers and staff regarding best practices for ensuring students' health and safety. School nurses may work with special education professionals to assess students' needs in the development of an individualized education program.

- **Building Service Worker**—Building service workers are responsible for the general maintenance of the school building and outside campus. This includes ensuring that all areas, equipment, and furniture are clean, functional, and safe for student and staff use. These individuals are also responsible for transporting heavy equipment and furniture throughout the school building.

- **Secretary**—The school secretary is responsible for assisting the principal, vice principal, and other office personnel in daily administrative duties. This individual assumes a variety of responsibilities to ensure the efficient function of daily operations within the school. Their responsibilities include communicating with students, families, and other office visitors, directing phone calls to the appropriate location, handling financial matters, and coordinating the school calendar.

Copyright © Mometrix Media. You have been licensed one copy of this document for personal use only. Any other reproduction or redistribution is strictly prohibited. All rights reserved.
This content is provided for test preparation purposes only and does not imply an endorsement by Mometrix of any particular political, scientific, or religious point of view.

- **Library/Media Specialist**—Library and media specialists coordinate the organization, maintenance, and allocation of all library and media resources within the school building. They are responsible for educating students regarding the proper use of library and media resources to locate information, including how to navigate the internet safely and appropriately for educational purposes. Library and media specialists also direct students toward reading material aligned with their literacy skills and provide teachers with learning materials to incorporate into instruction.
- **Instructional Leadership Team (ILT)**—An instructional leadership team is comprised of individuals responsible for educating teachers regarding current and relevant instructional philosophies and practices to enhance student learning. These individuals collaborate with teachers to educate them regarding how to implement instructional strategies, activities, and assessments to effectively meet students' learning needs and support their achievement of campus and district academic goals.
- **School Resource Officer**—The role of the school resource officer is to maintain a safe, orderly environment for teachers, staff, and students. They are responsible for ensuring the physical security of the school, handling legal infractions within the school, and addressing conflicts among students. The school resource officer also works with administration and staff to develop emergency drill procedures.
- **Pupil Personnel Worker (PPW)**—Pupil personnel workers are responsible for addressing issues that hinder the academic achievement of at-risk students. These individuals communicate with teachers, administration, staff, and families to ensure these students are supported both within and outside of the school building. This includes addressing issues related to behavior, crisis intervention, attendance, and home lives. Pupil personnel workers direct families toward school and community support resources and collaborate with teachers to implement supports that facilitate success in learning.

## PARTICIPATING IN SCHOOL AND DISTRICT ACTIVITIES
### IMPACT OF VOLUNTEERING ON POSITIVE EDUCATIONAL COMMUNITY

Participating in school activities, events, and projects positively impacts the nature of the school community and culture. When teachers and staff members volunteer their time to contribute in such a way, it strengthens **connections** to the school community that foster positive attitudes toward it. By actively engaging in activities, events, and projects, teachers and staff have the opportunity to collaborate in making **positive contributions** to the school community. This facilitates the development of relationships among colleagues that enhance their ability to work cooperatively in creating a positive learning atmosphere that benefits students and the educational program. Students are more supported in such an environment, and therefore, develop positive attitudes toward learning and strong relationships with their teachers that enhance the overall school **climate**. In addition, as students are influenced by the behaviors, actions, and attitudes modeled by adults in the building, contributing positively to the school community encourages them to do the same.

### PARTICIPATION OPPORTUNITIES

Participating in school activities, events, and projects is valuable in integrating oneself into the school community while making positive contributions. Such participation can occur through a variety of avenues, both within and outside of the school campus. Teachers can assist in school fundraisers, food and clothing drives, or field trips, as well as serve as tutors, lead school clubs or other extracurricular activities. By attending school sporting events, recitals, concerts, or plays, teachers can participate in the school community while supporting students. Events such as open-

Copyright © Mometrix Media. You have been licensed one copy of this document for personal use only. Any other reproduction or redistribution is strictly prohibited. All rights reserved. This content is provided for test preparation purposes only and does not imply an endorsement by Mometrix of any particular political, scientific, or religious point of view.

house and parent teacher nights, as well as public forum meetings, are also valuable opportunities to participate in the school community in a way that positively contributes to students' learning.

## ENHANCING THE EDUCATIONAL COMMUNITY

As teachers work closely with students, colleagues, and administration, their contributions to the school and district are integral in enhancing the school community. Teachers provide valuable insight regarding the needs of the educational program and ways to improve the school environment. As such, their participation in the school and district is beneficial in helping to ensure the needs of staff and students are adequately met to create a positive educational community. In addition, active participation in the school and district facilitates the collaboration necessary for establishing relationships among colleagues that contribute to a positive school culture and climate. Teachers can contribute to building such an educational community in a variety of ways. By participating in **school activities**, **events**, and **projects**, teachers can work cooperatively to create a positive learning atmosphere. Teachers can also attend **school meetings** and serve on focused **committees** to solve problems and influence decisions that improve the nature of the school environment. At the district level, teachers can communicate with members of the board of education and participate in **public forums** to express ideas, discuss concerns, and offer input regarding ways to enhance the educational community.

Copyright © Mometrix Media. You have been licensed one copy of this document for personal use only. Any other reproduction or redistribution is strictly prohibited. All rights reserved. This content is provided for test preparation purposes only and does not imply an endorsement by Mometrix of any particular political, scientific, or religious point of view.

## CHAPTER QUIZ

**1. Which of the following describes a situation involving vertical teaming?**

    a.  Administration working with a teacher to help get a student necessary accommodations

    b.  Sixth-, seventh-, and eighth-grade English teachers meeting to plan curriculum

    c.  All third-grade math teachers meeting to discuss student assessment results

    d.  A family member volunteering to serve in a classroom with their child

**2. What does PLC stand for?**

    a.  Professional Liability Committee

    b.  Professional Listening Center

    c.  Professional Learning Community

    d.  Professional Lesson Collaboration

**3. Each school within a district is overseen by:**

    a.  Education liaison

    b.  Class president

    c.  Board of trustees

    d.  Curriculum committee

**4. The principal is responsible for all of the following EXCEPT:**

    a.  Supervising the daily operations of the school

    b.  Ensuring academic and behavioral policies are followed by staff and students

    c.  Communicating the progress and needs of the school to the board of education

    d.  Ensuring that no student falls behind academically

**5. Who has the responsibility of addressing issues that hinder the academic achievement of at-risk students?**

    a.  School resource officer

    b.  Guidance counselor

    c.  Paraprofessional

    d.  Pupil personnel worker

## CHAPTER QUIZ ANSWER KEY

**1. B:** Vertical teaming facilitates the communication necessary for teachers across grade levels to collaborate in establishing expectations for preparedness at each grade level and developing a common curriculum path. This enhances teaching and learning, in that teachers can more effectively plan instruction that is aligned with learning targets and prepare students with the necessary knowledge, tools, and supports for continued academic success.

**2. C:** Community-building strategies, such as participating in activities or games that require teamwork, are valuable opportunities for developing supportive and cooperative professional relationships among colleagues. In addition, colleagues collaborating with one another in regard to curriculum, lesson planning, and promoting student achievement, contributes significantly to developing positive professional relationships. There are multiple avenues for such collaboration, including participating in professional learning communities (PLCs), department meetings, vertical or horizontal teaming, or team teaching. Such collaboration lets teachers and staff communicate and develop mutual goals that support the educational program and student learning.

**3. C:** Each school within a district is overseen by a board of trustees, which is responsible for making decisions to ensure that the educational program supports students' learning needs for

Copyright © Mometrix Media. You have been licensed one copy of this document for personal use only. Any other reproduction or redistribution is strictly prohibited. All rights reserved. This content is provided for test preparation purposes only and does not imply an endorsement by Mometrix of any particular political, scientific, or religious point of view.

academic achievement. The board of trustees is composed of a group of elected individuals who are typically members of the community in which they serve. As such, they understand the educational needs of students in the community and can apply this knowledge to make effective decisions regarding the learning program.

**4. D:** The principal is responsible for supervising the daily operations of the school to ensure a safe, orderly environment in which teachers, staff, and students are working in alignment with the school's mission. To achieve this, the principal must communicate expectations for a positive, productive school community, ensure academic and behavioral policies are followed by staff and students, and assign staff members specific duties to facilitate an organized, efficient learning environment. In addition, it is important that the principal support staff, students, and families by engaging in frequent, open communication, addressing concerns, and providing resources necessary to promote growth and achievement. The principal is also responsible for ensuring that the school's educational program is effective in supporting teachers, staff, and students in the achievement of academic standards. This includes overseeing curriculum, monitoring instructional practices, measuring their school's performance in relation to district academic standards, and communicating the progress and needs of the school to the board of education.

**5. D:** Pupil personnel workers are responsible for addressing issues that hinder the academic achievement of at-risk students. These individuals communicate with teachers, administration, staff, and families to ensure that at-risk students are supported both within and outside the school building. This includes addressing issues related to behavior, crisis intervention, attendance, and home lives. Pupil personnel workers direct families toward school and community support resources and collaborate with teachers to implement supports that facilitate success in learning.

Copyright © Mometrix Media. You have been licensed one copy of this document for personal use only. Any other reproduction or redistribution is strictly prohibited. All rights reserved. This content is provided for test preparation purposes only and does not imply an endorsement by Mometrix of any particular political, scientific, or religious point of view.

# Legal and Ethical Roles and Responsibilities

## LEGAL REQUIREMENTS FOR EDUCATORS

### SPECIAL EDUCATION SERVICES

Establishing an inclusive, equitable learning environment for students with disabilities requires educators to adhere to strict legal guidelines regarding special education services. According to **IDEA (Individuals with Disabilities Education Act)**, educators must provide students with disabilities a **free and appropriate public education (FAPE)** in the **least restrictive environment (LRE)**. To do this effectively, educators are required to fully comply with students' **IEP (Individual Education Plan)** at all times. This includes providing students requiring special education services with the necessary supports, accommodations, and modifications according to their IEP throughout all stages of instruction. Educators must also document the academic and behavioral progress of these students in relation to the goals outlined in their IEP to report to the designated case manager. In addition, the specifics of students' special education services must be kept confidential in order to protect their privacy. Adhering to these legal requirements promotes equity in the classroom by ensuring that the unique needs of students with disabilities are met, thus allowing them to effectively participate and engage in learning.

### FERPA

Understanding and observing the legal requirements related to students' and families' rights is integral to maintaining their confidentiality and establishing a safe, secure learning environment. Educators are required to follow the guidelines of **FERPA (Family Educational Rights and Privacy Act)** regarding students' education records and personally identifiable information. According to FERPA, educators may not release students' education records or personally identifiable information except in authorized situations, such as when the student enrolls in another school, or the information is requested by a financial aid institution in which the student has applied. In all other instances, the educator must have written permission to disclose this information. FERPA also provides students' parents or legal guardians the right to access their child's education records and request that the education records be amended. While educators may not disclose personally identifiable information, they are permitted to release directory information regarding the student, including their name, phone number, or student identification number. However, educators must provide an appropriate amount of time to allow for the refusal of such disclosure. It is also important to note that the rights guaranteed under FERPA become applicable only to the student once they have turned 18 or begun postsecondary education.

### DISCIPLINE PROCEDURES AND STUDENT CODE OF CONDUCT

Adhering to legal requirements regarding student discipline procedures is necessary to ensure a safe, orderly, and unbiased learning environment. School districts are responsible for developing a **student code of conduct** to distribute among teachers, staff, students, and families. This document outlines expectations for student behavior, as well as specific consequences for varying degrees of infractions that may occur on school grounds. Educators must strictly adhere to the guidelines stated in the student code of conduct when enacting disciplinary measures. This includes ensuring that consequences for student misbehavior align with the nature of the action and do not interfere with the student's right to a free public education. Disciplinary actions must be free of bias, and must not endanger the student's physical, mental, or emotional health. In addition, the educator must document instances of student discipline, and keep these records confidential to protect the student's right to privacy. Extended suspensions and expulsions must be reserved for instances in which all other disciplinary measures have been exhausted. In such cases, the student is entitled to

Copyright © Mometrix Media. You have been licensed one copy of this document for personal use only. Any other reproduction or redistribution is strictly prohibited. All rights reserved. This content is provided for test preparation purposes only and does not imply an endorsement by Mometrix of any particular political, scientific, or religious point of view.

a hearing at the board of education, and teachers must provide adequate instructional materials for the time that the student is out of the classroom.

Guidelines for acceptable student behavior on school property are outlined in a student code of conduct. Providing students with this reference helps to ensure that the school functions in a safe, orderly, and productive manner so as to create and maintain an environment focused on learning. This document typically addresses a number of topics related to **daily school procedures**, including student dress code standards, acceptable use policies for the internet and digital devices, attendance, grading policies, and academic integrity. Student codes of conduct also address **potential behavioral issues**, such as acceptable conduct while riding school buses, the use of illegal substances on school property, and harmful or disruptive behavior, including bullying, harassment, or fighting. The expectations iterated in student codes of conduct are typically accompanied by an ascending matrix of classroom, administrative, and district-level **consequences** that coincide with the severity and frequency of student infractions.

## ESTABLISHING AN EQUITABLE LEARNING ENVIRONMENT FOR ALL STUDENTS

An **equitable environment** is one in which students receive the individual support necessary to facilitate their success in learning. Establishing such an environment requires educators to adhere to several legal guidelines to ensure all students are provided with fair access to learning opportunities. Educators must be sure that all students are included in the educational program, and therefore, may not discriminate based upon students' race, religion, gender, background, disability, or any other differentiating characteristics. All students must be provided with equal access to learning materials, resources, technologies, and supports. In addition, educators must fully comply with all accommodations outlined in students' **IEPs**, **504 plans**, and **Behavior Intervention Plans (BIP)**, and implement all required supports to provide them with equitable access to learning.

## CHILD ABUSE

One of the primary responsibilities of an educator is to ensure the safety of all students. In order to do so, it is important that educators understand and follow all legal requirements related to child abuse. Within the classroom, educators are responsible for establishing a safe, secure learning environment. All interactions with students must be appropriate and refrain from harming students' **physical**, **mental**, or **emotional health**. Educators must also recognize the signs of potential **child abuse** or **neglect** among their students. If any abuse or neglect is suspected, educators are legally required to report it immediately to the proper agency according to their state and local laws, regardless of whether there is concrete evidence, as waiting to report it may place the student in continued danger. Reports of potential child abuse or neglect must be **confidential** so as to protect the students' privacy. Depending on the protocols established by individual school districts, educators may be required to notify their school's administration and resource officer of the report.

## SIGNIFICANCE OF UNDERSTANDING AND ADHERING TO LEGAL REQUIREMENTS

Understanding the legal requirements for educators ensures that teachers know what is expected of them to maintain professionalism and establish a safe, secure learning environment. This avoids misconception regarding the teacher's **roles** and **responsibilities** within the educational program so teachers understand how to adhere to legal guidelines properly. When teachers are aware of the legal requirements they must follow, they are more effectively able to implement the appropriate protocols for addressing specific education-related situations. This includes instances related to establishing an equitable learning environment, providing special education services, interacting appropriately with students, colleagues, and families, as well as protecting students' privacy. In

Copyright © Mometrix Media. You have been licensed one copy of this document for personal use only. Any other reproduction or redistribution is strictly prohibited. All rights reserved.
This content is provided for test preparation purposes only and does not imply an endorsement by Mometrix of any particular political, scientific, or religious point of view.

addition, understanding the legal requirements for educators ensures that they are aware of their own professional rights and how to protect themselves in various education-related situations.

## LEGAL AND ETHICAL REQUIREMENTS FOR USING RESOURCES AND TECHNOLOGIES

The legal and ethical requirements regarding the use of educational resources and technologies serves as an important frame of reference for teachers when selecting learning materials. Understanding these guidelines is beneficial in effectively determining which resources and technologies are **safe**, **secure**, **appropriate**, and **legal** for classroom use. This helps to protect the data and privacy of both teachers and students when interacting with instructional materials. In addition, this ensures that teachers and students are aware of what constitutes acceptable use of technology resources to protect their safety when engaging online. It is also important to be cognizant of legal and ethical standards in relation to the **reproduction** and **redistribution** of learning materials and technologies. Doing so ensures teachers understand how to properly adhere to copyright laws so as not to infringe upon the original creator's ability to profit from their work.

### COPYRIGHT ACT

When selecting educational resources and technologies to implement in the classroom, it is important that teachers consider the guidelines of the **Copyright Act**. The Copyright Act protects creators by prohibiting the unauthorized use, reproduction, or redistribution of their original works. This extends to digital resources as well, including photographs, video clips, website articles, or online learning materials. While the **Fair Use Doctrine** permits teachers to utilize copyrighted materials for educational purposes, they must be mindful of its restrictions and take the proper precautions to avoid **copyright infringement**. When using copyrighted resources or technologies, teachers can obtain permission directly from the creator, purchase the materials or licenses for use themselves, or ask their school, district, or students to purchase them. In addition, when using, reproducing, or distributing lesson materials, teachers should always cite the appropriate source in order to give credit to the original creator.

### FAIR USE DOCTRINE

Under the **Fair Use Doctrine**, teachers are permitted to utilize, reproduce, and redistribute copyrighted materials for educational purposes. However, this doctrine includes limitations that teachers must adhere to when selecting educational resources and technologies to implement in the classroom. The **purpose** of utilizing copyrighted materials must be strictly educational and intended to achieve specific objectives. Teachers must also consider the **nature** of all copyrighted resources and technologies to determine whether they meet the requirements of the Fair Use Doctrine. All copyrighted materials must be used for informational purposes, and typically should be limited to published, nonfiction works. The **amount** of copyrighted material that is reproduced or redistributed must be limited to small excerpts rather than the entire work, and teachers must appropriately cite the original source. In addition, teachers must consider the effect of their use of copyrighted resources and technologies on the future **potential market**. Use of copyrighted materials must not interfere with the creator's ability to profit from their work.

### DATA SECURITY

Teachers, staff, and students engage with numerous digital resources for a variety of administrative and educational purposes. As such, protecting **data security** when interacting with these materials is increasingly important in establishing a safe, secure learning environment. When selecting educational technologies, such as student information systems (SIS) or digital learning tools, it is imperative that teachers ensure they are aligned with legal and ethical standards regarding data security. All resources must adhere to the requirements outlined by the **Family Educational Rights and Privacy Act (FERPA)** regarding the disclosure of students' sensitive or personally

Copyright © Mometrix Media. You have been licensed one copy of this document for personal use only. Any other reproduction or redistribution is strictly prohibited. All rights reserved. This content is provided for test preparation purposes only and does not imply an endorsement by Mometrix of any particular political, scientific, or religious point of view.

identifiable information. Teachers must also observe their **district and school's policies** regarding the implementation of educational technologies to ensure they are approved for use. In addition, many education technology companies collect students' data as they interact with digital resources with the intention of utilizing it to inform future educational decisions. It is therefore important that teachers consider the nature of the technology they are implementing to ensure that the data collected from students is used strictly for educational purposes. Taking measures to protect students' data when interacting with educational technology resources ensures their safety both within and outside of the classroom.

## PRIVACY

Protecting students' privacy when interacting with educational resources and technologies is paramount to ensuring their safety both within and outside of the classroom. Prior to selecting learning materials, teachers must ensure that they follow all legal and ethical requirements regarding student privacy. This includes determining whether the resources and technologies in question follow the standards outlined by the **Family Educational Rights and Privacy Act (FERPA)** and the **Children's Online Privacy Protection Act (COPPA)**. In doing so, teachers ensure that students' sensitive and personally identifiable information, such as academic, behavioral, or medical records, are secure when interacting with instructional materials. This is necessary to protecting students from encountering potentially harmful situations or individuals that could compromise their privacy and cause long-term negative impacts.

## ACCEPTABLE USE POLICIES

**Acceptable use policies** to govern the use of educational technologies are integral to ensuring a safe, secure learning environment. These documents give guidelines for **acceptable behavior** when interacting with digital resources under the school network, as well as outline **consequences** for violating the terms. Acceptable use policies also inform teachers, staff, students, and families of the measures in place to protect **data security** and **privacy** within the school, such as only allowing individuals with the proper credentials to access the network. Acceptable use policies are beneficial in discouraging users from engaging in inappropriate behavior by outlining standards for responsible use to ensure that sensitive information remains secure. This helps to prevent interaction with potentially harmful individuals or situations that could threaten the safety and privacy of students, teachers, staff, or families, as well as the security of the school network.

## ETHICAL GUIDELINES
### CONFIDENTIALITY

Adhering to ethical guidelines in relation to confidentiality is an important part of demonstrating professionalism as well as protecting the privacy of students, their families, and others in the school building. Teachers are required to follow all standards outlined by **FERPA** regarding student and family privacy. This includes preserving the confidentiality of all **personally identifiable information** about students, such as grades, medical history, discipline records, or special education services, except in authorized situations. By following these guidelines, teachers ensure that they do not release any information that may compromise the safety of students or their families. In addition, when students and families feel their personal information is kept confidential, they are more likely to seek necessary supports from the educational program without the fear of being stigmatized. Similarly, teachers must follow ethical guidelines to protect the privacy of their colleagues. Any knowledge about a colleague's personal information must be kept confidential so as to establish positive, professional relationships founded on mutual trust. Doing so facilitates productive collaboration among colleagues to benefit student success in learning.

Copyright © Mometrix Media. You have been licensed one copy of this document for personal use only. Any other reproduction or redistribution is strictly prohibited. All rights reserved. This content is provided for test preparation purposes only and does not imply an endorsement by Mometrix of any particular political, scientific, or religious point of view.

## INTERACTIONS WITH STUDENTS AND OTHERS IN THE SCHOOL COMMUNITY

The daily interactions among students, teachers, staff, and administration largely determine the quality of the school environment. A positive, safe, and professional school community is one in which educators adhere to ethical guidelines regarding interactions with one another and students. Communication with colleagues must be respectful of one another's privacy and confidentiality. This includes avoiding gossiping situations and ensuring that all discussions about colleagues are factual, neutral, and professional in nature. In addition, interactions with members of the school community must **avoid discrimination** of any sort. Similarly, all interactions with students must be inclusive, accepting, and respectful of differences. In addition, educators must maintain proper **boundaries** when communicating with students. This includes avoiding communication outside of the school setting except in authorized situations and ensuring that all interactions maintain professionalism. Any interactions with students must avoid compromising their **physical or mental health**, **safety**, or **ability to learn**. By adhering to these ethical guidelines, educators can ensure that all communication with students and members of the school community contribute to establishing and maintaining a safe, appropriate, and professional learning environment.

Copyright © Mometrix Media. You have been licensed one copy of this document for personal use only. Any other reproduction or redistribution is strictly prohibited. All rights reserved.
This content is provided for test preparation purposes only and does not imply an endorsement by Mometrix of any particular political, scientific, or religious point of view.

## CHAPTER QUIZ

**1. In accordance with the Family Educational Rights and Privacy Act (FERPA), which of the following is true?**

    a. If an adult calls the school and claims they are the guardian of a student, the school is allowed to release that student's information to them over the phone.

    b. A school may release education records when requested by a financial aid institution to which the student has applied.

    c. The school is allowed to deny a student over the age of 18 access to their own educational records.

    d. A school should discard old education records directly into the trash.

**2. What determines how disciplinary measures are enacted by a teacher?**

    a. The teacher's personal convictions

    b. Directives given by the student's guardians

    c. The student code of conduct

    d. The disciplinary measures experienced by the teacher when they were going through school

**3. When teachers are determining whether resources and technology are fully protecting students' online privacy, they must follow both the Family Educational Rights and Privacy Act (FERPA) and which of the following?**

    a. COBRA

    b. HIPAA

    c. DACA

    d. COPPA

## CHAPTER QUIZ ANSWER KEY

**1. B:** Understanding and observing the legal requirements related to students' and families' rights is integral to maintaining confidentiality and establishing a safe, secure learning environment. Educators are required to follow the guidelines of the Family Educational Rights and Privacy Act (FERPA) regarding students' education records and personally identifiable information. According to FERPA, educators may not release students' education records or personally identifiable information except in authorized situations, such as when the student enrolls in another school, or the information is requested by a financial aid institution to which the student has applied. In all other instances, the educator must have written permission to disclose this information.

**2. C:** School districts are responsible for developing a student code of conduct to distribute among teachers, staff, students, and families. This document outlines expectations for student behavior, as well as specific consequences for varying degrees of infractions that may occur on school grounds. Educators must strictly adhere to the guidelines stated in the student code of conduct when enacting disciplinary measures. This includes ensuring that consequences for student misbehavior align with the nature of the action and do not interfere with the student's right to a free public education. Disciplinary actions must be free of bias, and must not endanger the student's physical, mental, or emotional health. In addition, the educator must document instances of student discipline, and keep these records confidential to protect the student's right to privacy.

**3. D:** *Protecting students' privacy when they interact with educational resources and technologies is paramount to ensuring their safety both within and outside the classroom. Prior to selecting learning materials, teachers must ensure that they follow all legal and ethical requirements regarding student privacy. This includes determining whether the resources and technologies in question follow the*

Copyright © Mometrix Media. You have been licensed one copy of this document for personal use only. Any other reproduction or redistribution is strictly prohibited. All rights reserved. This content is provided for test preparation purposes only and does not imply an endorsement by Mometrix of any particular political, scientific, or religious point of view.

*standards outlined by the Family Educational Rights and Privacy Act (FERPA) and the Children's Online Privacy Protection Act (COPPA).*

Copyright © Mometrix Media. You have been licensed one copy of this document for personal use only. Any other reproduction or redistribution is strictly prohibited. All rights reserved.
This content is provided for test preparation purposes only and does not imply an endorsement by Mometrix of any particular political, scientific, or religious point of view.

# Paraprofessional Practice Test #1

## Reading

*Refer to the following for questions 1 - 2:*

Physically, at least, Hal seemed a most unlikely burglar. He looked more suited to the life of a professional athlete, the practitioner of some brutal contact sport. His legs were the trunks of ancient trees and his white shirts – he always wore white shirts – spread across is belly like the winter snow on an Alberta meadow. And yet, at night, he moved across the glistening rooftops on cat's feet, a passing shadow, dropping unseen to the topmost landing of fire escape or outside stairway. There, by starlight, his soft hands found whatever open window had been left unguarded and, in a matter of seconds, he would disappear inside.

**1. The reference to tree trunks shows that**

a. Hal's legs were brown
b. Hal's wore pants the color of bark
c. Hal's legs were very large
d. Hal's skin was wrinkled

**2. The passage describes Hal as moving on cat's feet. This means that**

a. he had fur-lined shoes
b. he moved very quietly
c. he was disguised
d. he moved on all fours

*Refer to the following for questions 3 - 7:*

Global warming and the depletion of natural resources are constant threats to the future of our planet. All people have a responsibility to be proactive participants in the fight to save Earth by working now to conserve resources for later. Participation begins with our everyday choices. From what you buy to what you do to how much you use, your decisions affect the planet and everyone around you. Now is the time to take action.

When choosing what to buy, look for sustainable products made from renewable or recycled resources. The packaging of the products you buy is just as important as the products themselves. Is the item minimally packaged in a recycled container? How did the product reach the store? Locally grown food and other products manufactured within your community are the best choices. The fewer miles a product traveled to reach you, the fewer resources it required.

You can continue to make a difference for the planet in how you use what you bought and the resources you have available. Remember the locally grown food you purchased? Don't pile it on your plate at dinner. Food that remains on your plate is a wasted resource, and you can always go back for seconds. You should try to be aware of your consumption of water and energy. Turn off the water when you brush your teeth, and limit your showers to

325

Copyright © Mometrix Media. You have been licensed one copy of this document for personal use only. Any other reproduction or redistribution is strictly prohibited. All rights reserved.
This content is provided for test preparation purposes only and does not imply an endorsement by Mometrix of any particular political, scientific, or religious point of view.

five minutes. Turn off the lights, and don't leave appliances or chargers plugged in when not in use.

Together, we can use less, waste less, recycle more, and make the right choices. It may be the only chance we have.

**3. What is the author's tone?**
   a. The author's tone is optimistic.
   b. The author's tone is pessimistic.
   c. The author's tone is matter-of-fact.
   d. The author's tone is angry.

**4. Why does the author say it is important to buy locally grown food?**
   a. Buying locally grown food supports people in your community.
   b. Locally grown food travels the least distance to reach you and therefore uses fewer resources.
   c. Locally grown food uses less packaging.
   d. Locally grown food is healthier for you because it has been exposed to fewer pesticides.

**5. What does the author imply will happen if people do not follow his suggestions?**
   a. The author implies we will run out of resources in the next 10 years.
   b. The author implies water and energy prices will rise sharply in the near future.
   c. The author implies global warming and the depletion of natural resources will continue.
   d. The author implies local farmers will lose their farms.

**6. What is the best definition of the underlined word in the selection below, taken from the third paragraph of the passage?**

   You should try to be aware of your consumption of water and energy.
   a. Using the greatest amount
   b. Illness of the lungs
   c. Using the least amount
   d. Depletion of goods

**7. Which of the following is one way the author specifies that a person can try to be aware of their consumption of water and energy?**
   a. Food that remains on your plate is a wasted resource, and you can always go back for a second helping.
   b. Locally grown food and other products manufactured within your community are the best choices.
   c. Don't leave appliances or chargers plugged in when not in use.
   d. Participation begins with our everyday choices.

Copyright © Mometrix Media. You have been licensed one copy of this document for personal use only. Any other reproduction or redistribution is strictly prohibited. All rights reserved.
This content is provided for test preparation purposes only and does not imply an endorsement by Mometrix of any particular political, scientific, or religious point of view.

*Refer to the following for questions 8 - 11:*

It was the best of times, it was the worst of times, it was the age of wisdom, it was the age of foolishness, it was the epoch of belief, it was the epoch of incredulity, it was the season of Light, it was the season of Darkness, it was the spring of hope, it was the winter of despair, we had everything before us, we had nothing before us, we were all going direct to heaven, we were all going direct the other way – in short, the period was so far like the present period, that some of its noisiest authorities insisted on its being received, for good or for evil, in the superlative degree of comparison only.

From *A Tale of Two Cities* by Charles Dickens (1859)

**8. Which best expresses one main idea that Dickens wanted readers to realize from this introduction?**

   a.  That everything could seem to be best or worst according to individual perceptions
   b.  That the past described was so identical to the present they were indistinguishable
   c.  That the past and present both had equal balances of good/light and evil/darkness
   d.  That the extremities of good and bad described were imagined by the "authorities"

**9. Of the following statements, which accurately describe(s) textual evidence of Dickens's techniques and their effects?**

   a.  The even rhythm and use of anaphora reinforce the ideas of equal and opposing forces.
   b.  The presentation of multiple opposites introduces a main "doubles" motif and structure.
   c.  The author's use of anastrophe together with rhythm emphasizes contrasting opposites.
   d.  The statements in (a) and (b) are both accurate, but the statement in (c) makes an error.

**10. Among the following, which pair most represents the use of figurative meanings?**

   a.  Wisdom and foolishness
   b.  Belief and incredulity
   c.  Light and darkness
   d.  Hope and despair

**11. From reading only this introductory paragraph, what can readers infer about this novel overall?**

   a.  That the story may include equal proportions of positives and negatives
   b.  That the story may include a greater proportion of negatives than positives
   c.  That the story may include a greater proportion of positives than negatives
   d.  That the story may include nothing readers can infer from just this beginning

*Refer to the following for questions 12 - 13:*

Educators began applying behavioral techniques to education as early as the nineteenth century. It was the theories of B.F. Skinner in the mid-twentieth century, though, that sealed the influence of behaviorism in the American education system. Skinner argued against moral training and instead claimed that human behavior is simply a function of reinforcement. He also suggested that instruction is most effective when students do not fear failure and resulting punishment. Skinner recommended the use of positive reinforcement, with information provided in small but useful steps, as well as frequent praise to remove fear from students and provide as welcoming a learning environment as possible. However interesting

Copyright © Mometrix Media. You have been licensed one copy of this document for personal use only. Any other reproduction or redistribution is strictly prohibited. All rights reserved.
This content is provided for test preparation purposes only and does not imply an endorsement by Mometrix of any particular political, scientific, or religious point of view.

Skinner's theories were, his claims about human behavior seem to make human beings a little less human.

**12. According to the author, what did Skinner see as a major hindrance to effective learning in students?**
a. Need for useful behavioral training
b. Anxiety about the penalties for being wrong
c. Lack of constant praise during the learning process
d. A welcoming learning environment for all students

**13. Which sentence in the passage indicates a suggestion of bias on the author's part?**
a. "Educators began...nineteenth century"
b. "It was...education system"
c. "Skinner recommended...as possible"
d. "However interesting...less human"

*Refer to the following for questions 14 - 17:*

Journalists often use a recording device to capture the audio transcript of an interview with a subject. The recording device is thought of as a reliable and efficient way to ensure that all important parts of the interview have been archived, which is something that may be complicated for a journalist to do by hand. Besides being difficult to execute quickly, legibly, and efficiently, taking notes by hand can distract the journalist from the interview subject's body language, verbal cues, or other subtle information that can go unnoticed when the journalist is not fully concentrating on the person talking. These missed cues, for example, noticing that the tough-guy interview subject closed his eyes and trembled slightly when he talked about his recently departed mother, could add an interesting perspective to the article.

Relying on a recording device is not without troubles; however, most journalists can quickly relate stories of disappointments they or co-workers have endured due to problems with equipment. For instance, a journalist may not notice low batteries until it is too late. As a result, a portion of an interview can be lost without any way to reclaim it. The machine's volume can be accidentally left too low to hear the subject on later playback, the recorder may be accidentally switched off during the interview, and any number of other unplanned and unexpected electronic malfunctions can occur to sabotage the recording. While recording device problems may not occur often, even a rate of once a year can be extremely problematic for a writer. Some glitches may be unrealized until hours later when the journalist is prepared to work with the recording.

Most experienced journalists do not rely solely on technology when they are interviewing a subject for an article. Instead, as the recording device creates an audio record of the interview, journalists will simultaneously record their own notes

Copyright © Mometrix Media. You have been licensed one copy of this document for personal use only. Any other reproduction or redistribution is strictly prohibited. All rights reserved. This content is provided for test preparation purposes only and does not imply an endorsement by Mometrix of any particular political, scientific, or religious point of view.

by hand. This dual-note method means that most of the time, a wise journalist has two good resources to use as he or she writes the article draft.

**14. According to the passage, which of the following are reasons an audio recording device can be superior to taking notes by hand during an interview? (Select all that apply.)**

a. A recording device may be low on batteries without the journalist noticing.
b. Efficient, legible note-taking is a difficult skill to master.
c. The journalist has to look away from the interview subject to write notes.
d. Recording devices capture only what is said, ignoring non-verbal cues.
e. Taking notes by hand does not require any advanced technology.

**15. Which of the following are examples of body language or non-verbal cues as described in the passage? (Select all that apply.)**

a. A surprised look
b. Rubbing hands together
c. A quiet answer
d. An angry expression
e. A trembling voice
f. A nodding head

**16. Which statement from the passage best supports the conclusion that taking notes and recording audio during an interview is a good practice for journalists?**

a. Journalists often use a recording device to capture the audio transcript of an interview with a subject.
b. Relying on a recording device is not without troubles, however.
c. As a result, a portion of an interview can be lost without any way to reclaim it.
d. This dual-note method means that most of the time, a wise journalist has two good resources to use as he or she writes the article draft.

**17. Which title is the best choice for this passage?**

a. "The Art of Writing Notes"
b. "Conducting an Interview"
c. "Recording an Interview"
d. "Problems with Interviews"

Copyright © Mometrix Media. You have been licensed one copy of this document for personal use only. Any other reproduction or redistribution is strictly prohibited. All rights reserved.
This content is provided for test preparation purposes only and does not imply an endorsement by Mometrix of any particular political, scientific, or religious point of view.

*Refer to the following for question 18:*

NOTE: The year listed with each country is when the nation gained independence.

## 18. Which of the following generalizations is valid?
a. The nations of North America were also fighting for independence at the same time as those nations in South America listed above.
b. France lost most of its possessions in the New World as a result of these revolutions.
c. Nations on the west coast received independence first.
d. South America experienced multiple revolutions during the first three decades of the nineteenth century.

*Refer to the following for questions 19 - 22:*

"His pride," said Miss Lucas, "does not offend me so much as pride often does, because there is an excuse for it. One cannot wonder that so very fine a young man,

Copyright © Mometrix Media. You have been licensed one copy of this document for personal use only. Any other reproduction or redistribution is strictly prohibited. All rights reserved.
This content is provided for test preparation purposes only and does not imply an endorsement by Mometrix of any particular political, scientific, or religious point of view.

with family, fortune, everything in his favour, should think highly of himself. If I may so express it, he has a right to be proud."

"That is very true," replied Elizabeth, "and I could easily forgive his pride, if he had not mortified mine."

"Pride," observed Mary, who piqued herself upon the solidity of her reflections, "is a very common failing I believe. By all that I have ever read, I am convinced that it is very common indeed, that human nature is particularly prone to it, and that there are very few of us who do not cherish a feeling of self-complacency on the score of some quality or other, real or imaginary. Vanity and pride are different things, though the words are often used synonymously. A person may be proud without being vain. Pride relates more to our opinion of ourselves, vanity to what we would have others think of us."

**19. Why doesn't the gentleman's pride offend Miss Lucas?**

a. She admires his vanity.
b. It is human nature to be proud.
c. He is poor and homeless.
d. He is handsome and rich.

**20. What are Elizabeth's feelings towards the gentleman?**

a. She is offended by him.
b. She is proud of him.
c. She wants to get to know him better.
d. She is glad he is rich.

**21. Which sentence best states the theme of this passage?**

a. Pride and vanity are offensive.
b. Fame and fortune can make a person proud.
c. Every person is proud in one way or another.
d. If you have a fortune, you deserve to be proud.

**22. According to the passage, what is the difference between pride and vanity?**

a. Pride relates to a person's abilities; vanity relates to a person's looks.
b. Men are proud; women are vain.
c. Pride is what you think of yourself; vanity is what you want others to think of you.
d. Pride is part of human nature; vanity is not.

*Refer to the following for questions 23 - 25:*

Photosynthesis is the process that occurs when plants use sunlight to convert carbon dioxide into energy. When humans exhale, they release carbon dioxide into the atmosphere, and the plants then take this in and use it for food. Photosynthesis allows plants to use what is in the air to make their own food for survival. As plants begin to create energy from the carbon dioxide, they release oxygen back into the atmosphere. Humans then use this oxygen when they inhale. As a result, photosynthesis is a vital process that keeps the delicate balance between carbon dioxide and oxygen and allows both plants and animals to survive.

Copyright © Mometrix Media. You have been licensed one copy of this document for personal use only. Any other reproduction or redistribution is strictly prohibited. All rights reserved. This content is provided for test preparation purposes only and does not imply an endorsement by Mometrix of any particular political, scientific, or religious point of view.

**23. The teacher asks students to discuss this passage in groups. The groups are to consider the main point of the passage. Which of the following answers is most correct?**

  a. Photosynthesis is the process that plants use to turn carbon dioxide into food, with the help of sunlight

  b. Without photosynthesis, humans could not survive on the earth, because photosynthesis creates oxygen

  c. Photosynthesis allows plants to make their own food and keeps them alive without the help of humans

  d. Photosynthesis is an important process that provides plants with food and helps keep a balance in the atmosphere

**24. The teacher wants to make sure that students understand the importance of the balance of carbon dioxide and oxygen that occurs with photosynthesis. What question might the teacher ask about the passage to ensure that students appreciate this point?**

  a. How can we define photosynthesis, based on the passage that I have just read?

  b. In addition to sunlight, what else do plants use to make their own food?

  c. How do humans and plants work together to ensure a healthy atmosphere?

  d. Why do plants need carbon dioxide from humans in order to survive?

**25. The teacher wants to encourage students to think beyond the passage and consider how essential photosynthesis is for the survival of all life forms on earth. How might the teacher prompt students to get them to use the information from the passage and analyze beyond it?**

  a. Ask students what might happen if there were not enough plants to release oxygen

  b. Develop a tree-planting project and encourage each student to plant a tree to improve the environment

  c. Have students draw a picture showing how photosynthesis works

  d. Tell students a story that shows how photosynthesis improves the life of both plants and humans

**26. Which of these is an indication that a child has problems with reading comprehension?**

  a. The child wonders about why the characters in a story did some things.

  b. The child can tell how a story s/he read ended, but cannot explain why.

  c. The child makes predictions about what will happen next in a narrative.

  d. The child associates things in the reading with things in his/her own life.

**27. What is the best way for teachers to help students develop larger reading and writing vocabularies?**

  a. Give students weekly vocabulary lists to memorize for tests.

  b. Assign students to search texts for new vocabulary words.

  c. Give students many opportunities for reading and writing.

  d. Assign students new-word quotas to include in writing.

Copyright © Mometrix Media. You have been licensed one copy of this document for personal use only. Any other reproduction or redistribution is strictly prohibited. All rights reserved.
This content is provided for test preparation purposes only and does not imply an endorsement by Mometrix of any particular political, scientific, or religious point of view.

**28. Which of the following is true about how teachers can cultivate print awareness in young children?**

   a. It is effective to have children narrate picture books and give them matching reinforcements.
   b. It is superfluous to use large-print texts for reading to younger children who cannot read yet.
   c. Teachers should label things/areas in classrooms using either pictures or words, but not both.
   d. When reading storybooks to young children, the texts should use novel, unpredictable words.

**29. Which of the following best explains the information presented in the chart below?**

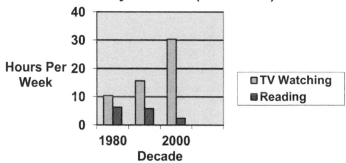

**TV Watching & Reading Among Elementary Children (1980-2000)**

   a. The variety of educational material on video has contributed to increased TV viewing among elementary children
   b. Reading has decreased dramatically over the course of three decades
   c. While reading has decreased over the last two decades, TV watching among elementary children has more than doubled
   d. Publishers of children's books have failed to provide reading material that captures the interest of children like TV programs do

**30. The teacher provides students with a more advanced passage of reading, in which there are a variety of new words that many of the students do not know how to pronounce. How might the teacher go about helping the students in pronouncing the new words?**

   a. Hint at the correct pronunciation with a variety of different rhyming words
   b. Assist the students in sounding out the words phonetically, by recognizing rules for vowels and consonants
   c. Have the students look up the words in a dictionary to review the pronunciation information that is provided there
   d. Ask students who are already familiar with the words to a help their classmates in pronouncing the new words

Copyright © Mometrix Media. You have been licensed one copy of this document for personal use only. Any other reproduction or redistribution is strictly prohibited. All rights reserved.
This content is provided for test preparation purposes only and does not imply an endorsement by Mometrix of any particular political, scientific, or religious point of view.

## Mathematics

**31.** In a graduating high school class of 532, 15% of the students will receive As and 55% of the students will receive Bs. If 53 students receive Ds and no one failed, what approximate percentage of the students received Cs?

    a. 10%
    b. 20%
    c. 30%
    d. 40%

**32.** 37% of 461 can be rounded to which of the following?

    a. 168
    b. 169
    c. 171
    d. 172

**33.** $3\frac{2}{3} \div 5\frac{1}{3} =$

    a. 3/11
    b. 7/11
    c. 11/16
    d. 15/16

**34.** $5/6 \div 3/7 \times 5/9 =$

    a. 6/5
    b. 11/6
    c. 135/129
    d. 175/162

**35.** Don is planning to buy a new computer that costs $700. A local store has marked the computer he would like to buy down by 15%. Additionally, Don has a coupon for a further 10% off. How much will Don save off the original list price?

    a. $140.75
    b. $157.00
    c. $164.50
    d. $175.00

**36.** 19% =

    a. 0.19
    b. 1.9
    c. 0.019
    d. 1.09

**37.** Anne is two inches taller than Morris, who is 1 inch shorter than Aiden. If Anne $= x$, Morris $= y$, and Aiden $= z$, which inequality best describes their heights?

    a. $y > x > z$
    b. $z > y > x$
    c. $x > y > z$
    d. $x > z > y$

Copyright © Mometrix Media. You have been licensed one copy of this document for personal use only. Any other reproduction or redistribution is strictly prohibited. All rights reserved. This content is provided for test preparation purposes only and does not imply an endorsement by Mometrix of any particular political, scientific, or religious point of view.

**38.** $f(x) = x^4 + 2x^3 + 4x - 1$, when $x = -3$

    a.  12
    b.  14
    c.  23
    d.  26

**39.** In the number 1,492.738, what is the place value of the number 3?

    a.  Tenths
    b.  Hundredths
    c.  Thousandths
    d.  Ten-thousandths

**40.** Due to the outbreak of illness, only 75% of the students were in class at Monroe Middle School on Thursday. If there were 834 students who attended class on Thursday, how many students total are there in the school?

    a.  1,004
    b.  1,008
    c.  1,110
    d.  1,112

**41.** $(4 + 6)^3 =$

    a.  10
    b.  100
    c.  1000
    d.  10000

**42.** Identify the missing term from the following series: 1/6, 1/12, 1/18, 1/24, ____, 1/36

    a.  1/27
    b.  1/30
    c.  1/33
    d.  1/42

**43.** $(-0.19) \times (0.23) =$

    a.  -0.0437
    b.  -0.0439
    c.  -0.0521
    d.  -0.0547

**44.** 2/3 __ 5/6

    a.  >
    b.  =
    c.  <
    d.  Impossible to determine

**45.** $(4x + 3)(4x - 3) =$

    a.  $16x^2 - 9$
    b.  $16x^2 + 9$
    c.  $16x^2 + 12x - 9$
    d.  $16x^2 - 12x + 9$

Copyright © Mometrix Media. You have been licensed one copy of this document for personal use only. Any other reproduction or redistribution is strictly prohibited. All rights reserved.
This content is provided for test preparation purposes only and does not imply an endorsement by Mometrix of any particular political, scientific, or religious point of view.

**46. It usually takes 7 workers a total of 10 hours to clean the stately home Duncombe Park in North Yorkshire. Illness has caused several of the workers to be unavailable, so now the cleaning of Duncombe Park takes 14 hours. How many people are now available to clean the house?**

    a. 3
    b. 4
    c. 5
    d. 6

**47. Ariadne drives 456 miles in 9 hours. Using the formula $d = rt$, which of the following best represents her approximate speed as she drives?**

    a. 45 mi/hr
    b. 50 mi/hr
    c. 55 mi/hr
    d. 60 mi/hr

**48. If the area of a right triangle is 20 ft$^2$, which of the following represent the possible measurements for the base and height of the triangle?**

    a. base = 4 ft; height = 5 ft
    b. base = 10 ft; height = 2 ft
    c. base = 8 ft; height = 5 ft
    d. base = 15 ft; height = 3 ft

**49. A yoga facility has four studios, labeled A, B, C, and D, where the studio can hold classes concurrently. At 5 PM, the facility has four classes, with the following number of students in each class: Studio A,15 students; Studio B, 23 students; Studio C, 8 students; and Studio D, 14 students. What is the mean class size for students attending yoga classes at 5 PM?**

    a. 18
    b. 21
    c. 10
    d. 15

**50. Perdita is planning to prepare a recipe for a traditional English trifle. While reviewing the recipe, she notices that it calls for 350 grams of fruit. If one ounce is equal to about 28 grams, which of the following is the approximate amount of fruit in ounces that Perdita will need?**

    a. 9 ounces
    b. 11 ounces
    c. 12 ounces
    d. 15 ounces

Copyright © Mometrix Media. You have been licensed one copy of this document for personal use only. Any other reproduction or redistribution is strictly prohibited. All rights reserved.
This content is provided for test preparation purposes only and does not imply an endorsement by Mometrix of any particular political, scientific, or religious point of view.

*Refer to the following for questions 51 - 52:*

> The instructor is helping students find the perimeter of a rectangle, where the width is 10 feet and the height is 15 feet.

**51. Which of the following equations is correct for finding the perimeter of the rectangle?**

    a. $10 \times 15$
    b. $10 \times 10 \times 15 \times 15$
    c. $(10 + 10)(15 + 15)$
    d. $2(10) + 2(15)$

**52. The students arrive at a variety of answers for the perimeter of the rectangle. Which of the following is correct?**

    a. 40 feet
    b. 50 feet
    c. 60 feet
    d. 65 feet

**53. Which of the following is true if $x = -\frac{2}{3}$?**

    I. $-3x > -2 + \frac{5}{6x}$
    II. $3x^2 - 3 \leq 12x + 4$
    III. $|x| > 1$

    a. I only
    b. I and III
    c. II and III
    d. I, II, and III

**54. For two points $(4, 2)$ and $(3, 5)$, what is the slope of a line going through both?**

    a. $-1$
    b. $4$
    c. $-3$
    d. $5$

**55. Mrs. Vories, a fifth-grade teacher, asks her class to use compatible numbers to help her determine approximately how many chicken nuggets she needs to buy for a school-wide party. The school has 589 students and each student will be served nine nuggets. Which student correctly applied the concept of compatible numbers?**

    a. Madison estimates: $500 \times 10 = 5,000$ nuggets
    b. Audrey estimates: $600 \times 5 = 3,000$ nuggets
    c. Ian estimates: $600 \times 10 = 6,000$ nuggets
    d. Andrew estimates: $500 \times 5 = 2,500$ nuggets

Copyright © Mometrix Media. You have been licensed one copy of this document for personal use only. Any other reproduction or redistribution is strictly prohibited. All rights reserved.
This content is provided for test preparation purposes only and does not imply an endorsement by Mometrix of any particular political, scientific, or religious point of view.

Refer to the following for questions 56 - 57:

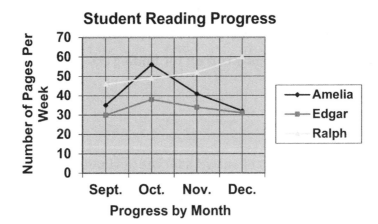

**56.** Due to concerns about the reading progress among several students, the instructor began charting the average number of pages that the students were reading on a weekly basis. The chart above shows the results over a four-month period, from September through December. Which of the following can be deduced from the information provided in the chart?

    a.  Amelia gradually improved in her reading progress from September through December

    b.  The improvement in Edgar's reading was clearly halted by a personal situation in November

    c.  Ralph is the only student that consistently increased his reading from September through December

    d.  This chart does not provide enough detail to show the reading progress of all three students from September through December

**57.** According to the chart, approximately how many pages per week did Amelia read during the month of December?

    a.  25

    b.  30

    c.  40

    d.  45

**58.** Students are given the following word problem and are asked to convert it to numbers and symbols: divide the product of seven and six by the sum of three and four. What is the correct way to write this with numbers and symbols?

    a.  $(7 \times 6) \div (3 + 4)$

    b.  $(3 + 4) \div (7 + 6)$

    c.  $(7 + 6) \div (3 + 4)$

    d.  $(7 \times 6) \div (3 \times 4)$

Copyright © Mometrix Media. You have been licensed one copy of this document for personal use only. Any other reproduction or redistribution is strictly prohibited. All rights reserved.
This content is provided for test preparation purposes only and does not imply an endorsement by Mometrix of any particular political, scientific, or religious point of view.

**59. Which formula shown below is the correct formula for finding the area of the following polygon?**

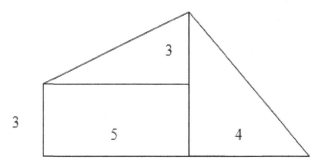

a. $(3 \times 5)/2 + (3 \times 5) + (4 \times 6)/2$
b. $2(3 \times 5) + (4 \times 6)/2$
c. $(3 \times 5) + (3 \times 6)/2 + (4 \times 6)$
d. $(5 \times 6) + (4 \times 6)/2$

**60. The instructor gives students the following word problem:**

According to legend, when Queen Dido first arrived in the place that would become the city of Carthage, she requested the land to build the city. She was told that she could have as much land as could fit within the area of a small piece of animal skin. Not to be outdone, Dido then proceeded to cut the piece of animal skin into tiny pieces and outline the perimeter of the city that she would build – thus making the city considerably larger than the area of animal skin that she was given! If the animal skin was in the shape of a rectangle and measured 3 feet by 4 feet, and if Dido cut the tiny pieces into equal strips of 1 inch along the shorter side by two inches along the longer side, how many would she have for the perimeter of the city that she built?

a. 120
b. 365
c. 578
d. 864

Copyright © Mometrix Media. You have been licensed one copy of this document for personal use only. Any other reproduction or redistribution is strictly prohibited. All rights reserved.
This content is provided for test preparation purposes only and does not imply an endorsement by Mometrix of any particular political, scientific, or religious point of view.

# Writing

*Refer to the following for questions 61 - 65:*

This passage contains a variety of errors. Read carefully, and then review the questions that follow. Each of the questions reproduces a sentence or sentences from the passage with a selection of underlined words. Identify the <u>error</u> that is underlined, or select the answer choice for "The sentence is correct."

> Although the story of Robin Hood is often considered to be legend, many scholars argue that the legend has some fact to it. Thirteenth-century legal documents refers to a "Robinhood" who is described as something of a common, and very successful, thief. After this, the ballads of the thirteenth and fourteenth centuries provide something of a legendery story for him. It is in these ballads that Robin Hood and his Merry Men of Sherwood Forest begin to make an appearance. Over time, the story came to take on other characters as well. Maid Marian and Friar Tuck would became part of the story in the fifteenth century and beyond.
>
> Despite the historical confidence from some scholars, others disagree about the validity of the story. Those who study mythology tend to argue that the story, itself is just a part of myth and cannot be assumed to be anything but pure fantasy. Some concede that the legend might have the more vague of historical origins, but those who oppose a root in reality tend to believe that the story is purely mythology and should be enjoyed as such.

**61. Thirteenth-century legal documents <u>refers</u> to a "Robinhood" <u>who</u> is described as <u>something</u> of a common, and very successful, thief.**

    a. refer
    b. whom
    c. somewhat
    d. The sentence is correct

**62. After this, the ballads of the thirteenth and fourteenth centuries <u>provide</u> something of a <u>legendery</u> story for <u>him</u>.**

    a. provides
    b. legendary
    c. he
    d. The sentence is correct

**63. Over time, the story came <u>to take on</u> other characters as well. Maid Marian and Friar Tuck <u>would became</u> part of the story in the <u>fifteenth century</u> and beyond.**

    a. took on
    b. would become
    c. fifteenth-century
    d. The sentence is correct

Copyright © Mometrix Media. You have been licensed one copy of this document for personal use only. Any other reproduction or redistribution is strictly prohibited. All rights reserved. This content is provided for test preparation purposes only and does not imply an endorsement by Mometrix of any particular political, scientific, or religious point of view.

**64.** Those who study mythology <u>tend to argue</u> that the <u>story, itself</u> is just a part of <u>myth and</u> cannot be assumed to be anything but pure fantasy.

    a. tends to argue
    b. story itself
    c. myth, and
    d. The sentence is correct

**65.** <u>Some concede</u> that the legend might have the <u>most vague</u> of historical origins, but those <u>who</u> oppose a root in reality tend to believe that the story is purely mythology and should be enjoyed as such.

    a. Some conceded
    b. more vague
    c. whom
    d. The sentence is correct

**66.** A word's part of speech can be recognizable, even if it's meaning is unknown. In the sentence above, what is the part of speech of the word *trouvère,* based on its context in the following sentence?

    Many of the Arthurian legends are believed to have come from the writings of twelfth-century *trouvère* Chretien de Troyes.

    a. noun
    b. verb
    c. adjective
    d. adverb

**67.** The statements below exhibit which of the following grammatical errors?

    Many literary scholars also point to the traditions of the Welsh story collection known as the *Mabinogion* for the origins. And even the name of the legendary King Arthur.

    a. Incorrectly placed comma
    b. Incorrect use of capitalization
    c. Incomplete sentence
    d. There is no error

**68.** The sentence below exhibits which of the following grammatical errors?

    For modern readers, the stories contained within the Arthurian legends are often most familiar because of English poet Alfred, Lord Tennyson, his *Idylls of the King* focuses largely on the romantic triangle of Arthur, Guinevere, and Lancelot.

    a. Comma splice
    b. Incorrect verb tense
    c. Incorrect use of parallelism
    d. There is no error

Copyright © Mometrix Media. You have been licensed one copy of this document for personal use only. Any other reproduction or redistribution is strictly prohibited. All rights reserved. This content is provided for test preparation purposes only and does not imply an endorsement by Mometrix of any particular political, scientific, or religious point of view.

**69. In the sentence below, the expressions "to reflect" and "to enlighten" are examples of which of the following types of verbals?**

> While set in the ancient and mythical world of Camelot, Tennyson's *Idylls of the King* often do more to reflect the Victorian issues of his day than to enlighten the reader about the world of King Arthur.

a. adverb
b. gerund
c. participle
d. infinitive

**70. Which of the following words is <u>not</u> spelled correctly?**

a. liaison
b. definitely
c. relevant
d. accomodate

*Refer to the following for questions 71 - 78:*

This passage contains a variety of errors. Read carefully, and then review the questions that follow. Each of the questions reproduces a sentence or sentences from the passage with a selection of underlined words. Identify the error that is underlined, or select the answer choice for "The sentence is correct."

> Today, history remembers Tsar Ivan IV of Russia as "Ivan Grozny," or "Ivan the Terrible." Scholars are in disagreement about just *how* terrible Ivan was but they do agree that his reign is one of the most significant in Russian history. Ivan was born into a tumultuous period. On the night of his birth, soothsayers prophesy that his life and reign will bring darkness upon Russia. When Ivan was only three years old, his father Grand Prince Vasili III died, leaving the Russian nobles to vie for power in the Russian court. Ivan's mother Yelena was poisoned when he was only eight years old, and when Ivan was fourteen he finally through off the authority of the nobles, called *boyars*, and took power for himself.
>
> Many of Ivan the Terribles reforms brought positive change to Russia. Ivan attempted to modernize sixteenth-century Russia and improve its legal code, as well as increase building projects that would place Russia firm in the position of a world power. With the greater power for Russia, though, also came greater power for the ruler, Ivan was the first to take the official and permanent title of "tsar." (Which his grandfather, Ivan III, had first used intermittently.) Historian argue that over time the increased power began to influence Ivan's behavior to the point that he became paranoid, and unstable. One night, he attacked his pregnant daughter in law, causing her to lose her child, and when his son confronted him, Ivan attacked and killed his son. After Ivan's death in 1584, the Russian throne would pass to at least seven

Copyright © Mometrix Media. You have been licensed one copy of this document for personal use only. Any other reproduction or redistribution is strictly prohibited. All rights reserved.
This content is provided for test preparation purposes only and does not imply an endorsement by Mometrix of any particular political, scientific, or religious point of view.

different rulers in less than fifteen years, and it would not be until the accession of Mikhail Romanov in 1596, that Russia would regain stability.

**71. Scholars <u>are in disagreement</u> about just how terrible Ivan <u>was but</u> they do agree that his reign is one of the most significant in <u>Russian history</u>.**

    a.  is in disagreement

    b.  was, but

    c.  Russian History

    d.  There is no error

**72. On the night of his <u>birth</u>, soothsayers <u>prophesy</u> that his life and reign <u>would bring</u> darkness upon Russia.**

    a.  birth

    b.  prophesied

    c.  will bring

    d.  There is no error.

**73. Ivan's mother Yelena was poisoned when <u>he was</u> only eight years old, and when Ivan was fourteen he finally <u>through off</u> the authority of the nobles, called *boyars*, and took power for <u>himself</u>.**

    a.  he is

    b.  threw off

    c.  him

    d.  There is no error

**74. Many of Ivan the <u>Terribles reforms</u> brought positive <u>change</u> to Russia.**

    a.  Terrible's

    b.  reform

    c.  changes

    d.  There is no error

**75. Ivan attempted to modernize <u>sixteenth-century Russia</u> and improve its legal <u>code, as well</u> as increase building projects that would <u>place Russia firm</u> in the position of a world power.**

    a.  sixteenth century Russia

    b.  code as well as

    c.  place Russia firmly

    d.  There is no error

**76. (Which his grandfather Ivan III had first used intermittently.)**

**The sentence above exhibits which of the following grammatical errors?**

    a.  Incorrectly used adverb

    b.  Incomplete sentence

    c.  Incorrect capitalization

    d.  There is no error

Copyright © Mometrix Media. You have been licensed one copy of this document for personal use only. Any other reproduction or redistribution is strictly prohibited. All rights reserved. This content is provided for test preparation purposes only and does not imply an endorsement by Mometrix of any particular political, scientific, or religious point of view.

**77.** <u>Historians</u> argue <u>that over time</u> the increased power began to influence Ivan's behavior to the point that he became <u>paranoid, and</u> unstable.

    a. Historian
    b. that, over time,
    c. paranoid and
    d. There is no error

**78.** <u>One night</u>, he attacked his pregnant <u>daughter in law</u>, causing her to lose her child, and when his son confronted him, Ivan <u>attacked and</u> killed his son.

    a. One night
    b. daughter-in-law
    c. attacked, and
    d. There is no error

**79.** One of Mikhail Romanov's most famous heirs is Peter the Great. Who is renowned for the enormous modernization that he brought to Russia and for the construction of the city of Saint Petersburg.

**Which of the following changes will best correct the grammatical error in the sentence above?**

    a. ...Peter the Great who is renowned...
    b. ...to Russia, and for the construction...
    c. ...the city of St. Petersburg
    d. The sentence needs no correction

**80.** The Romanov dynasty ended in 1917 when the last tsar, Nicholas II, was forced to abdicate. Nicholas, his wife Alexandra, and their five children were then placed in captivity, and in 1918, they were brutally murdered by Bolshevik revolutionaries.

**Which of the following changes will best correct the grammatical error in the sentences above?**

    a. ...ended in 1917, when the last tsar...
    b. ...his wife Alexandra and their five children...
    c. ...murdered by bolshevik revolutionaries
    d. The sentences need no correction

*Refer to the following for questions 81 - 85:*

In the following section, there are underlined parts to each sentence. One of the underlined parts is incorrectly written. Choose the letter that corresponds with the incorrect underlined part of the sentence. If the entire sentence is correct, choose D for NO ERROR.

**81.** <u>Nobody</u> could have anticipated <u>the extent</u> of the <u>storm's damage.</u>
      A                 B               C

    a. Nobody
    b. the extent
    c. storm's damage
    d. No error

Copyright © Mometrix Media. You have been licensed one copy of this document for personal use only. Any other reproduction or redistribution is strictly prohibited. All rights reserved.
This content is provided for test preparation purposes only and does not imply an endorsement by Mometrix of any particular political, scientific, or religious point of view.

82. **Most people <u>believed</u> that the game would <u>end up</u> being cancelled.**
          A       B                                 C
   a. Most people
   b. believed
   c. end up
   d. No error

83. **We <u>gawked at</u> him as he <u>drug</u> the picnic table <u>closer to</u> the grill area.**
          A                B                  C
   a. gawked at
   b. drug
   c. closer to
   d. No error

84. **Her <u>bicycle basket</u> was <u>loaded down</u> with books and materials <u>to return</u> to the library.**
          A                  B                          C
   a. Her bicycle basket
   b. loaded down
   c. to return
   d. No error

85. **Her <u>Grandmother</u> ordered <u>monogrammed towels</u> as a gift for the <u>upcoming</u>**
          A                         B                          C
**bridal shower.**
   a. Her Grandmother
   b. monogrammed towels
   c. upcoming
   d. No error

*Refer to the following for questions 86 - 90:*

The upcoming sentences are given to measure your ability to correctly and efficiently convey meaning. When you are choosing your answer, remember that the sentences should utilize conventional written English, including grammar, word selection, conventional sentence structure, and punctuation.

There will be either a section or a complete sentence underlined. Beneath the sentence there are different choices. The first choice (A) will be the same as the underlined section. The remaining choices give different substitutions that could replace the underlined section.

Choose the letter that corresponds with the choice that best conveys the meaning of the original sentence. If the original wording is the best, select answer choice A. If not, choose one of the other choices. The correct answer is the one that keeps the original meaning and makes the sentence the

Copyright © Mometrix Media. You have been licensed one copy of this document for personal use only. Any other reproduction or redistribution is strictly prohibited. All rights reserved.
This content is provided for test preparation purposes only and does not imply an endorsement by Mometrix of any particular political, scientific, or religious point of view.

most effective. Make sure your choice makes the sentence understandable without being cumbersome or unclear.

**86. When he accepted the award, Mr. Stewart <u>said "that he had never been so wonderfully honored in his life."</u>**

    a. said "that he had never been so wonderfully honored in my life."
    b. said that he had never been so wonderfully honored in his life.
    c. said that "he had never been so wonderfully honored in my life."
    d. said that he had "never been so wonderfully honored in my life."

**87. Jake <u>borrowed his parents</u> car without permission so they had no way to get to work.**

    a. borrowed his parents car
    b. borrowed his parent's car
    c. borrowed his parents' car
    d. borrowed his Parents car

**88. <u>Irregardless of the weather</u>, we will still hold the picnic at the park.**

    a. Irregardless of the weather,
    b. Irregardless because of the weather,
    c. Irregardless of weather
    d. Regardless of the weather,

**89. <u>George sounded excited as he tells his mother</u> about the trip to the factory.**

    a. George sounded excited as he tells his mother
    b. George sounded excited and he tells his mother
    c. George sounds excited as he told his mother
    d. George sounded excited as he told his mother

**90. <u>Feeling weak after running in the long race.</u>**

    a. Feeling weak after running in the long race.
    b. Feeling weak since she had been running in the long race.
    c. Feeling weak on account of running in the long race.
    d. She was feeling weak after running in the long race.

Copyright © Mometrix Media. You have been licensed one copy of this document for personal use only. Any other reproduction or redistribution is strictly prohibited. All rights reserved. This content is provided for test preparation purposes only and does not imply an endorsement by Mometrix of any particular political, scientific, or religious point of view.

# Answer Key and Explanations

## Reading

**1. C:** The passage describes Hal as a very large man suited to contact sports, and this metaphor indicates that he had massive legs the size of tree trunks.

**2. B:** Cats are known to move very quietly. Here, Hal's massive size is being contrasted with his ability to move as quietly as a cat.

**3. C:** The author states what he believes to be the current state of the planet's environment and makes practical suggestions for making better use of its resources in the future, so choice C is correct. The author does not express expectations for improvement or regression, nor does the author condemn, complain, or make accusations in his descriptions.

**4. B:** As the passage states: "Locally grown food and other products manufactured within your community are the best choices. The fewer miles a product traveled to reach you, the fewer resources it required." This is summarized by choice B. The passage does not mention whether buying locally grown food supports community members, uses less packaging, or is healthier to eat, so choices A, C, and D are incorrect.

**5. C:** The author describes global warming and the depletion of natural resources as constant threats and makes suggestions that can slow or prevent the effects of these threats. This implies that if the author's suggestions are not followed, then these threats will continue. The author does not mention running out of resources in a specific time period, the cost of water and energy, or the possibility of hardship for local farmers.

**6. D:** The passage states: "You should try to be aware of your consumption of water and energy." The passage then gives examples for decreasing one's use of water and energy. The contexts of these sentences indicate that consumption means the depletion of goods. The passage instructs readers to be aware of their consumption of water and energy, but it does not suggest anything about using the greatest or least amount of water and energy. There also is no information about an illness of the lungs in the passage, so consumption does not refer to lung disease in this context.

**7. C:** To reduce water and energy, the author suggests that the reader turn off the water when brushing his or her teeth, limit showers to five minutes, turn off lights, and unplug appliances and chargers that are not being used. Choice C includes an item from this list, so it is correct. Choices A and B are statements related to conserving other types of resources, and choice D is a statement that applies to general conservation practices.

**8. C:** Charles Dickens used a series of opposites to convey the idea that the period described involved conflicts between extremes of positive and negative, matched so equally that neither could win. He also introduced the tension of such conflicts around which the novel revolves—of love vs. hate and family vs. oppression. He was not ascribing all the contrasts to personal subjectivity (a), saying in comparing the past and present that they could not be separated (b), or attributing the extremes to the imagination of its most vocal experts (d).

**9. D:** The even rhythm, plus ample use of anaphora—repeating the same phrase starting contiguous clauses ("it was the age... it was the age... it was the epoch... it was the epoch... it was the season... it was the season... we had... we had... we were all... we were all...")—introduce and emphasize the

347

Copyright © Mometrix Media. You have been licensed one copy of this document for personal use only. Any other reproduction or redistribution is strictly prohibited. All rights reserved. This content is provided for test preparation purposes only and does not imply an endorsement by Mometrix of any particular political, scientific, or religious point of view.

concept of equal, opposing forces; AND all the opposites introduce a pivotal "doubles" motif and structure—Sydney Carton and Charles Darnay, London and Paris, Miss Pross and Mme. Defarge, etc. This introduction uses anaphora, NOT anastrophe (c), which reverses adjective-noun order to noun-adjective (e.g., "ocean blue," "time immemorial," "trials unending," etc.).

**10. C:** In the sense that Charles Dickens uses them here, light and darkness do not literally mean physical illumination or its absence, but figuratively symbolize good and evil, knowledge and ignorance, happiness and unhappiness, hope and despair, etc. The other three choices all represent the use of words chosen for their literal meanings.

**11. A:** Because of the balancing of opposites in the introduction, readers can infer that the story may more likely achieve a similar balance than that it will present a greater proportion of either one (b), (c). Therefore, choice (d) is incorrect in that readers can infer nothing the story may include after the introduction.

**12. B:** The author notes in the passage: "He also suggested that instruction is most effective when students do not fear failure and resulting punishment." In other words, effective learning can be hindered by anxiety about the penalties for being wrong.

**13. D:** At the end of the passage, the author states, "However interesting Skinner's theories were, his claims about human behavior seem to make human beings a little less human." The wording of this statement indicates bias on the author's part.

**14. B, C:** The passage mentions advantages and disadvantages to both processes. Note-taking is described as being difficult to do efficiently and legibly, and it carries with it the necessity for frequently looking away from the interview subject. Choices A and E, on the other hand, are reasons that note-taking may be superior to audio recording. Technology can fail unexpectedly, causing information to be lost. Choice D alludes to a potential drawback of both methods, namely that non-verbal cues may be missed.

**15. A, B, D, F:** In the passage, the first paragraph gives two examples of body language when it describes an interview subject closing his eyes and trembling slightly. A surprised look, rubbing hands together, an angry expression, and a nodding head are all examples of body language or non-verbal cues that could be missed if the journalist is looking down to take notes instead of looking at the interview subject. A quiet answer would be heard rather than seen, as would a trembling voice.

**16. D:** Choice D states that wise journalists both record audio and take hand-written notes during interviews so that they have a backup resource in case the recording or notes are not reliable. Choice A simply states the purpose of recording devices but does not give enough information to support the conclusion that journalists should both record audio and take notes. Choices B and C show that recording audio is not always reliable, but neither of these choices shows why it is a good practice.

**17. C:** "Recording an Interview" is relevant to each section of the passage. The passage includes details related to writing notes, but since this is not the main idea, choice A is not the best choice. Recording an interview is only one part of interviewing, so choice B is too broad for this passage. The passage also only talks about problems that occur when taking notes, not problems with interviews in general, so choice D is also not the best title.

**18. D:** Ten nations received independence during the first thirty years of the nineteenth century. A is incorrect; the American Revolution was fought during the latter 1770s and early 1780s, some decades before independence movements in South America. In fact, the American Revolution

Copyright © Mometrix Media. You have been licensed one copy of this document for personal use only. Any other reproduction or redistribution is strictly prohibited. All rights reserved. This content is provided for test preparation purposes only and does not imply an endorsement by Mometrix of any particular political, scientific, or religious point of view.

inspired some of the movements. France did not have significant possessions in South America, so B is wrong. Nations on the west coast were among the last to receive independence, making C incorrect. The landlocked countries of Bolivia and Uruguay were among the last to receive their independence.

**19. D:** In the first paragraph, Miss Lucas states that "so very fine a young man, with family, fortune, every thing in his favour, should think highly of himself. If I may so express it, he has a *right* to be proud." Basically, she feels he deserves to be proud because he is physically attractive, comes from a good family, has money, and is successful. The best choice is (E).

**20. A:** This question is asking you to make an inference about Elizabeth's feeling towards the gentleman. In paragraph 2, Elizabeth is "mortified" by the gentleman's actions towards her. From this statement, you can make the inference that she was offended by his actions.

**21. C:** Theme is a message or lesson conveyed by a written text. The message is usually about life, society or human nature. This particular excerpt is exploring pride as it relates to human nature. Mary's observations on pride are the best summary of the theme of this passage. "By all that I have ever read, I am convinced that it is very common indeed, that human nature is particularly prone to it." The best answer choice is (C).

**22. C:** Paragraph 3 gives the answer to this question. According to Mary, pride is an opinion of yourself, and vanity is what we want others to think of us.

**23. D:** The main point of the passage is to show that photosynthesis is necessary to provide plants with food and to create a balance in the atmosphere between oxygen and carbon dioxide.

**24. C:** If the teacher wants students to understand the significance of the balance that photosynthesis helps to maintain, the best question to ask students would be how humans and plants work together. This will require that students consider the symbiotic relationship that occurs during and as a result of photosynthesis.

**25. A:** By asking the students what would happen if there were not enough plants, the teacher is encouraging the students to think beyond the information and infer consequences based on information in the passage. The teacher can then point out that a shortage of plants results in a potential for a shortage of oxygen and a surplus of carbon dioxide, which leaves the atmosphere imbalanced.

**26. B:** If a child can repeat the factual elements of how a story ended, but cannot explain why this ending occurred, this may show that the child cannot reason about cause and effect, logic, and sequencing in the material s/he has read; and/or lacks the expressive language skills to explain. Wondering about characters' reasons for their actions (A) indicates comprehension, not its lack: readers with good comprehension will speculate about character motivations, and will also try to predict future events in a book (C) before reading of them. Relating reading matter to one's own life (D) and pre-existing knowledge also does not indicate comprehension problems, but rather good reading comprehension.

**27. C:** The best way for teachers to help students develop larger reading and writing vocabularies is simply to provide them with as many opportunities as possible for reading and writing. The more they read and write, the bigger their reading and writing vocabularies will grow, more effectively than from having to memorize vocabulary lists and being tested on them weekly (A). Having students search for new vocabulary words in texts (B) does not let them actually read, which is superior for learning new words within meaningful contexts as well as developing all other reading

Copyright © Mometrix Media. You have been licensed one copy of this document for personal use only. Any other reproduction or redistribution is strictly prohibited. All rights reserved. This content is provided for test preparation purposes only and does not imply an endorsement by Mometrix of any particular political, scientific, or religious point of view.

skills. Students learning new words in isolation will not learn their appropriate use. Rather than assigning minimum numbers of new words to include in their writing (D), teachers should give students actual opportunities to write, which both develops all writing skills and increases writing vocabulary. Also, choice B involves reading vocabulary but not writing vocabulary, and choice D involves writing vocabulary but not reading vocabulary, in addition to the fact that neither one involves actual reading and writing.

**28. A:** One teaching technique that is effective for promoting print awareness in young children is to have them narrate books that contain only pictures. This is even more effective when teachers reinforce the activity by providing a directly related reward, such as having them eat pancakes after they narrate the picture book *Pancakes*. Even with young children who cannot read yet, it is good to read to them from large-print books (B) that they can more easily view, facilitating their beginning to learn to read sooner. Teachers should label objects and areas in their classrooms using both pictures and words together (C) to teach and reinforce correspondences between spoken and written words. Storybooks teachers read to preschoolers should use predictable, familiar words (D).

**29. C:** The graph indicates that reading has decreased to a degree, but at the same time the graph suggests that weekly television viewing has increased considerably among elementary children. The graph shows that television watching in 1980 was around ten hours per week, while viewing jumps to around thirty hours per week in 2000.

**30. B:** Among the answer choices provided, the best option for helping students pronounce new words is to encourage students to sound out the words slowly, keeping the rules of vowels and consonants in mind. This is not, of course, the only option for assisting students with word pronunciation, but it is the best option among the available choices for this question.

# Mathematics

**31. B:** The students making As and Bs represent 70% of the student body. If 53 students make Ds, that is approximately 10% of the student body, leaving the remaining 20% to make Cs.

**32. C:** First find 37% of 461, which is 170.57. The rules of rounding require that the number be rounded up, so the approximate answer is 171.

**33. C:** Remember that to divide fractions, the second fraction must be reversed and then multiplied by the other fraction. This means multiplying 11/3 (or $3\frac{2}{3}$) by 3/16 (or the reverse of 16/3, which is $5\frac{1}{3}$). The 3 on the top and the 3 on the bottom cancel each other out, leaving the product 11/16.

**34. D:** Follow the order of operations, which in this case is simply left to right with multiplication and division. $\frac{5}{6} \times \frac{7}{3} \times \frac{5}{9} = \frac{35}{18} \times \frac{5}{9} = \frac{175}{162}$.

**35. C:** Taking 15% off the original price, the computer comes down $105 in value to be $595. Taking 10% off this price (and not the original price of $700), the computer comes down another $59.50. This in addition to the $105 makes for a savings in $164.50.

**36. A:** When converted to a decimal, 19% is equivalent to 0.19. The other answer choices place the decimal point in the wrong place and create different percentages than 19%.

**37. D:** The order of heights, from tallest to shortest, is Anne, Aiden, and Morris. So, $x > z > y$.

Copyright © Mometrix Media. You have been licensed one copy of this document for personal use only. Any other reproduction or redistribution is strictly prohibited. All rights reserved. This content is provided for test preparation purposes only and does not imply an endorsement by Mometrix of any particular political, scientific, or religious point of view.

**38. B:** When the number (-3) is filled into the equation $f(x) = x^4 + 2x^3 + 4x - 1$, the equation becomes $81 - 54 - 12 - 1$, which equals 14.

**39. B:** To the right of a decimal point, the first number is in the tenths position, and the second number is in the hundredths position. This means that the number 3, which is the second number to the right of the decimal point, is in the hundredths position.

**40. D:** To determine the total number of students, the test-taker should divide the number that is given (834) by the percentage that is represents (75% or 0.75). The result is 1,112 students total in the school.

**41. C:** The expression $(4 + 6)^3$ is equal to $10^3$ or 1000.

**42. B:** The series is arranged in multiples of 6 in the denominator, with the fraction 1/6 multiplied by 1/2, 1/3, 1/4, 1/5, and so forth. The missing expression is $1/6 \times 1/5$, which equals 1/30.

**43. A:** This is a simple multiplication question, with the product of the two expressions being equal to exactly -0.0437.

**44. C:** The fraction 2/3 may be multiplied by 2/2 to get the denominators equal on both sides of the equation. From here, it is easy to see the 4/6 is less than 5/6.

**45. A:** When multiplied out, the product equals $16x^2 - 12x + 12x - 9$. The two middle expressions cancel each other, leaving a product of $16x^2 - 9$.

**46. C:** The original number of workers (7) multiplied by the original number of hours to clean Duncombe Park (10) equals 70. By dividing 70 by 14 – the number of hours with the reduced number of workers – the result is a new number of workers: 5.

**47. B:** With the formula $d = rt$, the correct answer is largely a matter is filling in the numbers that are provided. Ariadne travels 456 miles ($d$) in 9 hours ($t$). By dividing 456 by 9, the rate or speed of her driving may be found. It is important to note that the actual answer is 50.667, which is approximately 50 mi/hr.

**48. C:** The formula for the area of a triangle is (½)bh, or one-half the base times the height. This means that the product of the two sides will actually be twice the number that is provided as the area, i.e., $20 \times 2$ or 40. Although the actual base and height aren't provided, only one answer choice offers two numbers that equal a product of 40, 8 and 5.

**49. D:** The mean or average of a set of numbers is the sum of the numbers divided by the count. In this case, $(15 + 23 + 8 + 14) \div 4 = 60 \div 4 = 15$ students.

**50. C:** The total of 350 grams should be divided by the rate of grams per ounce (or 28) to acquire the number of ounces, in this case 12.5, or just 12.

**51. D:** The perimeter is found by adding all sides of a figure. In the case of a rectangle, two of the sides are going to be equal in length, so if the width is 10 feet and the height 15 feet, formula would be $10 + 10 + 15 + 15$, or $2(10) + 2(15)$.

**52. B:** The perimeter of the rectangle is $2(10) + 2(15) = 50$ feet.

Copyright © Mometrix Media. You have been licensed one copy of this document for personal use only. Any other reproduction or redistribution is strictly prohibited. All rights reserved.
This content is provided for test preparation purposes only and does not imply an endorsement by Mometrix of any particular political, scientific, or religious point of view.

**53. A:** Substitute the value (-2/3) for $x$ in each equation and evaluate each one.

For *I*,

$$-3\left(-\frac{2}{3}\right) > -2 + \frac{5}{6\left(-\frac{2}{3}\right)}$$

$$\frac{6}{3} > -2 + \frac{5}{-\frac{12}{3}}$$

$$2 > -2 + \frac{5}{-4}$$

$$2 > -3\frac{1}{4}$$

True

For *II*,

$$3\left(-\frac{2}{3}\right)^2 - 3 \le 12\left(-\frac{2}{3}\right) + 4$$

$$3\left(\frac{4}{9}\right) - 3 \le -\frac{24}{3} + 4$$

$$\frac{12}{9} - 3 \le -8 + 4$$

$$1\frac{1}{3} - 3 \le -4$$

$$-1\frac{2}{3} \le -4$$

False

For *III*,

$$\left|-\frac{2}{3}\right| > 1$$

$$\frac{2}{3} > 1$$

False

**54. C:** The equation for finding the slope is $\frac{y_2 - y_1}{x_2 - x_1}$. With the points provided, the equation becomes $\frac{5-2}{3-4}$, or $\frac{3}{-1} = -3$.

**55. C:** The number 589 can be estimated to be 600. The number 9 can be estimated to be 10. The number of chicken nuggets is approximately $600 \times 10$, which is 6,000 nuggets. Therefore, the correct choice is C.

**56. C:** Reviewing the chart carefully, the only answer choice that may be deduced is that the student Ralph consistently increased his reading from September through December. The chart indicates that Amelia's reading increased during September and October but then decreased in November and December. Likewise Edgar's reading increased during the first two months but showed little improvement during the last two months. (What is more, the chart provides no reason behind the students' improvement or lack thereof, so it is impossible to deduce that Ralph's reading progress was hindered by personal reasons.)

**57. B:** For the month of December, Amelia's reading is just above 30 pages per week. Of the answer choices provided, 30 is the best approximation.

**58. A:** The word problem says that the product of 7 and 6, or $7 \times 6$, is divided by the sum of 3 and 4, or $3 + 4$. This is $(7 \times 6) \div (3 + 4)$.

**59. A:** To find the area of the parallelogram, the area of each shape must be determined and then added together. The area of the smaller triangle is $(3 \times 5)/2$. The area of the rectangle is $3 \times 5$, and the area of the larger triangle is $(4 \times 6)/2$. The sum of these is $(3 \times 5)/2 + (3 \times 5) + (4 \times 6)/2$.

**60. D:** The animal skin is said to be 3 feet by 4 feet. In inches, this is 36 inches by 48 inches. This leaves the size to be 36 inches by 48 inches. The area then is $36 \times 48 = 1,728$. By dividing this by the area of each smaller strip ($1 \times 2 = 2$), the answer is 864.

# Writing

**61. A:** Because of the plural subject *documents* the word *refers* should be *refer*. "Thirteenth-century legal documents refer…"

**62. B:** The word *legendary* is spelled incorrectly in the passage and needs to be changed.

Copyright © Mometrix Media. You have been licensed one copy of this document for personal use only. Any other reproduction or redistribution is strictly prohibited. All rights reserved. This content is provided for test preparation purposes only and does not imply an endorsement by Mometrix of any particular political, scientific, or religious point of view.

**63. B:** For correct tense, the verb should be *would become*: "Maid Marian and Friar Tuck would become..."

**64. B:** No comma is necessary between *story* and *itself*: "...the story itself is just a part..."

**65. D:** There is no error in this sentence.

**66. A:** In this sentence, the word *trouvère* functions as the object of the preposition, which can be either a noun or a pronoun Because pronoun is not an option, the only choice is noun.

**67. C:** The statement "And even the name of the legendary King Arthur" is not a complete sentence and thus cannot stand on its own. The period that is placed before the word *And* should be removed and the two statements combined.

**68. A:** The comma that is located before "his Idylls of the King" represents a comma splice and should be replaced with a period, a semicolon, or a comma and a coordinating conjunction. The two statements before and after the comma represent individual sentences and cannot be joined with a comma alone.

**69. D:** The clue for identifying infinitives is the word *to* before a verb. In this case, *to reflect* and *to enlighten* are excellent examples of infinitives, which are a type of verbal, or a verb form that actually function as a different part of speech. Infinitives (and gerunds) function as nouns.

**70. D:** The word *accommodate* needs two c's as well as two m's.

**71. B:** Because the word *but* represents a coordinating conjunction that joins two independent clauses, it should have a comma just before it.

**72. B:** The sentence is in the past tense, so the verb should also be in the past tense: "On the night of his birth, soothsayers prophesied..."

**73. B:** The phrase "through off" is incorrect (even if it sounds correct). The correct expression should be "threw off."

**74. A:** To demonstrate possession, there should be an apostrophe in the name: "Ivan the Terrible's reforms."

**75. C:** To modify the verb correctly, the word *firm* should be converted into the adverb form *firmly*: "...that would place Russia firmly in the position of a world power."

**76. B:** The statement in parentheses is an incomplete sentence. In fact, this statement functions as a dependent clause that modifies the word *tsar* just before it in the sentence. The sentence should read: "...and permanent title of 'tsar' (which his grandfather, Ivan III, had first used intermittently)."

**77. C:** No comma is necessary before the conjunction *and*, which simply joins two items in a series: "...paranoid and unstable."

**78. B:** The phrase *daughter-in-law* should be hyphenated so that it represents a single expression, instead of three separate words.

**79. A:** The statement beginning "Who is renowned..." is a dependent clause and should be combined with the sentence just before it: "...heirs is Peter the Great who is renowned for..." Note that no comma is necessary before the word who.

Copyright © Mometrix Media. You have been licensed one copy of this document for personal use only. Any other reproduction or redistribution is strictly prohibited. All rights reserved.
This content is provided for test preparation purposes only and does not imply an endorsement by Mometrix of any particular political, scientific, or religious point of view.

**80. A:** Due to the wording of the sentence, a comma should fall after the date 1917: "The Romanov dynasty ended in 1917, when the last tsar…"

**81. D:** The sentence is correct as it is written.

**82. D:** The sentence is correct as it is written.

**83. B:** The past tense of *drag* is *dragged*, not *drug*.

**84. D:** The sentence is correct as it is written.

**85. A:** Nouns that name family members are capitalized only when used as a proper noun:

Her grandmother ordered <u>dinner</u>.

I asked Grandmother if she <u>had</u> ordered <u>dinner</u>.

**86. B:** Quotation marks should enclose only those words that a speaker says. Here, the speaker is not directly quoted.

**87. C:** Since "they" indicates more than one parent, the plural possessive form of parent should be used here.

**88. D:** *Irregardless* is not considered to be a conventional English word. *Regardless* is the correct word to use in this sentence.

**89. D:** Since the sentence begins in the past tense, the rest of the sentence must be in the past tense as well.

**90. D:** As presented, the original words form a fragment, not a complete sentence with a subject and a verb. The correct response is a sentence and demonstrates better usage than the answer choice before it.

Copyright © Mometrix Media. You have been licensed one copy of this document for personal use only. Any other reproduction or redistribution is strictly prohibited. All rights reserved. This content is provided for test preparation purposes only and does not imply an endorsement by Mometrix of any particular political, scientific, or religious point of view.

# Paraprofessional Practice Test #2

## Reading

*Refer to the following for questions 1 - 4:*

### The Bermuda Triangle

The area known as the Bermuda Triangle has become such a part of popular culture that it can be difficult to separate fact from fiction. The interest first began when five Navy planes vanished in 1945, officially resulting from "causes or reasons unknown." The explanations about other accidents in the Triangle range from the scientific to the supernatural. Researchers have never been able to find anything truly mysterious about what happens in the Bermuda Triangle, if there even is a Bermuda Triangle. What is more, one of the biggest challenges in considering the phenomenon is deciding how much area actually represents the Bermuda Triangle. Most consider the Triangle to stretch from Miami out to Puerto Rico and to include the island of Bermuda. Others expand the area to include all of the Caribbean islands and to extend eastward as far as the Azores, which are closer to Europe than they are to North America.

The problem with having a larger Bermuda Triangle is that it increases the odds of accidents. There is near-constant travel, by ship and by plane, across the Atlantic, and accidents are expected to occur. In fact, the Bermuda Triangle happens to fall within one of the busiest navigational regions in the world, and the reality of greater activity creates the possibility for more to go wrong. Shipping records suggest that there is not a greater than average loss of vessels within the Bermuda Triangle, and many researchers have argued that the reputation of the Triangle makes any accident seem out of the ordinary. In fact, most accidents fall within the expected margin of error. The increase in ships from East Asia no doubt contributes to an increase in accidents. And as for the story of the Navy planes that disappeared within the Triangle, many researchers now conclude that it was the result of mistakes on the part of the pilots who were flying into storm clouds and simply got lost.

**1. Which of the following describes this type of writing?**
a. Narrative
b. Persuasive
c. Expository
d. Technical

**2. Which of the following sentences is most representative of a summary sentence for this passage?**
a. The problem with having a larger Bermuda Triangle is that it increases the odds of accidents.
b. The area that is called the Bermuda Triangle happens to fall within one of the busiest navigational regions in the world, and the reality of greater activity creates the possibility for more to go wrong.
c. One of the biggest challenges in considering the phenomenon is deciding how much area actually represents the Bermuda Triangle.
d. Researchers have never been able to find anything truly mysterious about what happens in the Bermuda Triangle, if there even is a Bermuda Triangle.

355

Copyright © Mometrix Media. You have been licensed one copy of this document for personal use only. Any other reproduction or redistribution is strictly prohibited. All rights reserved. This content is provided for test preparation purposes only and does not imply an endorsement by Mometrix of any particular political, scientific, or religious point of view.

## 3. With which of the following statements would the author most likely agree?

   a. There is no real mystery about the Bermuda Triangle because most events have reasonable explanations.
   b. Researchers are wrong to expand the focus of the Triangle to the Azores, because this increases the likelihood of accidents.
   c. The official statement of "causes or reasons unknown" in the loss of the Navy planes was a deliberate concealment from the Navy.
   d. Reducing the legends about the mysteries of the Bermuda Triangle will help to reduce the number of reported accidents or shipping losses in that region.

## 4. Which of the following should the writer consult for more detailed information about the Bermuda Triangle?

   a. An encyclopedia entry about the Bermuda Triangle
   b. Travel journal entries from a ship captain who sailed the area frequently
   c. A brochure for a resort located in the Bermuda Triangle
   d. A biography of someone who disappeared in the Bermuda Triangle

Copyright © Mometrix Media. You have been licensed one copy of this document for personal use only. Any other reproduction or redistribution is strictly prohibited. All rights reserved. This content is provided for test preparation purposes only and does not imply an endorsement by Mometrix of any particular political, scientific, or religious point of view.

*Refer to the following for questions 5 - 8:*

**Table 1. Consumer Price Index for All Urban Consumers (CPI-U): U.S. city average, by expenditure category and commodity and service group**

(1982-84=100, unless otherwise noted)

| Item and group | Relative importance, December 2008 | Unadjusted indexes | | Unadjusted percent change to June 2009 from— | | Seasonally adjusted percent change from— | | |
|---|---|---|---|---|---|---|---|---|
| | | May 2009 | June 2009 | June 2008 | May 2009 | Mar. to Apr. | Apr. to May | May to June |
| **Expenditure category** | | | | | | | | |
| All items | 100.000 | 213.856 | 215.693 | -1.4 | 0.9 | 0.0 | 0.1 | 0.7 |
| All items (1967=100) | - | 640.616 | 646.121 | - | - | - | - | - |
| Food and beverages | 15.757 | 218.076 | 218.030 | 2.2 | .0 | -.2 | -.2 | .1 |
| Food | 14.629 | 217.826 | 217.740 | 2.1 | .0 | -.2 | -.2 | .0 |
| Food at home | 8.156 | 215.088 | 214.824 | .8 | -.1 | -.6 | -.5 | .0 |
| Cereals and bakery products | 1.150 | 252.714 | 253.008 | 3.0 | .1 | -.7 | -.2 | .0 |
| Meats, poultry, fish, and eggs | 1.898 | 203.789 | 204.031 | .6 | .1 | .0 | -.9 | -.2 |
| Dairy and related products [1] | .910 | 196.055 | 194.197 | -7.1 | -.9 | -1.3 | -.5 | -.9 |
| Fruits and vegetables | 1.194 | 274.006 | 272.608 | -1.9 | -.5 | .0 | -1.0 | 1.1 |
| Nonalcoholic beverages and beverage materials | .982 | 162.803 | 162.571 | 2.7 | -.1 | -1.0 | -.1 | .1 |
| Other food at home | 2.022 | 191.144 | 191.328 | 4.1 | .1 | -.8 | -.1 | .0 |
| Sugar and sweets | .300 | 196.403 | 197.009 | 6.2 | .3 | -.5 | .0 | .2 |
| Fats and oils | .241 | 200.679 | 201.127 | 2.5 | .2 | -1.4 | -.7 | .6 |
| Other foods | 1.481 | 205.587 | 205.654 | 3.9 | .0 | -.8 | .0 | -.2 |
| Other miscellaneous foods [1][2] | .433 | 122.838 | 122.224 | 3.2 | -.5 | .4 | .0 | -.5 |
| Food away from home [1] | 6.474 | 223.023 | 223.163 | 3.8 | .1 | .3 | .1 | .1 |
| Other food away from home [1][2] | .314 | 155.099 | 155.841 | 4.0 | .5 | .4 | .0 | .5 |
| Alcoholic beverages | 1.127 | 220.005 | 220.477 | 3.1 | .2 | -.1 | .3 | .2 |
| Housing | 43.421 | 216.971 | 218.071 | .1 | .5 | -.1 | -.1 | .0 |
| Shelter | 33.200 | 249.779 | 250.243 | 1.3 | .2 | .2 | .1 | .1 |
| Rent of primary residence [3] | 5.957 | 249.069 | 249.092 | 2.7 | .0 | .2 | .1 | .1 |
| Lodging away from home [2] | 2.478 | 135.680 | 138.318 | -6.9 | 1.9 | .5 | .1 | .3 |
| Owners' equivalent rent of primary residence [3][4] | 24.433 | 256.875 | 256.981 | 1.9 | .0 | .1 | .1 | .1 |
| Tenants' and household insurance [1][2] | .333 | 120.728 | 121.083 | 1.7 | .3 | -.1 | .0 | .3 |
| Fuels and utilities | 5.431 | 206.358 | 212.677 | -8.1 | 3.1 | -1.7 | -1.3 | -.8 |
| Household energy | 4.460 | 183.783 | 190.647 | -10.8 | 3.7 | -2.2 | -1.8 | -1.0 |
| Fuel oil and other fuels | .301 | 225.164 | 232.638 | -40.3 | 3.3 | -2.1 | -3.1 | 2.0 |
| Gas (piped) and electricity [3] | 4.159 | 189.619 | 196.754 | -7.8 | 3.8 | -2.2 | -1.7 | -1.2 |
| Water and sewer and trash collection services [2] | .971 | 159.517 | 159.831 | 6.2 | .2 | .6 | .6 | .4 |
| Household furnishings and operations | 4.790 | 129.644 | 129.623 | 1.6 | .0 | .0 | .0 | .0 |
| Household operations [1][2] | .781 | 149.468 | 149.995 | 1.3 | .4 | -.1 | -.9 | .4 |
| Apparel | 3.691 | 121.751 | 118.799 | 1.5 | -2.4 | -.2 | -.2 | .7 |
| Men's and boys' apparel | .923 | 117.146 | 112.849 | .7 | -3.7 | -1.7 | .4 | -.5 |
| Women's and girls' apparel | 1.541 | 109.460 | 106.455 | 2.1 | -2.7 | .2 | -.1 | 1.6 |
| Infants' and toddlers' apparel | .183 | 114.142 | 113.915 | 2.1 | -.2 | 1.3 | -1.6 | 2.2 |
| Footwear | .688 | 127.519 | 125.515 | 1.6 | -1.6 | .4 | .1 | .2 |
| Transportation | 15.314 | 175.997 | 183.735 | -13.2 | 4.4 | -.4 | .8 | 4.2 |
| Private transportation | 14.189 | 171.757 | 179.649 | -13.3 | 4.6 | -.3 | .9 | 4.5 |
| New and used motor vehicles [2] | 6.931 | 92.701 | 93.020 | -.6 | .3 | .4 | .5 | .4 |
| New vehicles | 4.480 | 135.162 | 135.719 | .9 | .4 | .4 | .5 | .7 |
| Used cars and trucks | 1.628 | 122.650 | 124.323 | -8.6 | 1.4 | -.1 | 1.0 | .9 |
| Motor fuel | 3.164 | 193.609 | 225.021 | -35.2 | 16.2 | -2.6 | 2.7 | 17.2 |
| Gasoline (all types) | 2.964 | 193.727 | 225.526 | -34.6 | 16.4 | -2.8 | 3.1 | 17.3 |
| Motor vehicle parts and equipment [1] | .382 | 134.347 | 134.270 | 5.0 | -.1 | .1 | -.2 | -.1 |
| Motor vehicle maintenance and repair [1] | 1.188 | 242.488 | 242.683 | 4.1 | .1 | .2 | -.1 | .1 |
| Public transportation | 1.125 | 228.878 | 232.540 | -12.1 | 1.6 | -.8 | -1.0 | -.5 |

## 5. Which expenditure category was the most important in December of 2008?

a. Housing
b. Food and beverages
c. Apparel
d. Transportation

Copyright © Mometrix Media. You have been licensed one copy of this document for personal use only. Any other reproduction or redistribution is strictly prohibited. All rights reserved. This content is provided for test preparation purposes only and does not imply an endorsement by Mometrix of any particular political, scientific, or religious point of view.

**6. On a seasonally adjusted basis, which of the following decreased by the greatest percentage between April and May of 2009?**

    a.  Gasoline
    b.  Fuel oil and other fuels
    c.  Infants' and toddlers' apparel
    d.  Fruits and vegetables

**7. According to the organization of the table, which of the following expense categories is not considered to be a component of the "Food at Home" category?**

    a.  Cereals and bakery products
    b.  Fats and oils
    c.  Other miscellaneous foods
    d.  Alcoholic beverages

**8. Which apparel category increased by the greatest percentage between May and June of 2009?**

    a.  Men's and boy's apparel
    b.  Women's and girls' apparel
    c.  Infants' and toddlers' apparel
    d.  Footwear

*Refer to the following for question 9:*

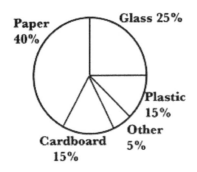

**9. A recycling company collects sorted materials from its clients. The materials are weighed and processed for re-use. The chart shows the weights of different classes of materials that were collected by the company in one month. Which of the following statements is NOT supported by the data in the chart?**

    a.  Paper products and cardboard make up a majority of the collected materials.
    b.  One quarter of the materials collected are made of glass.
    c.  More plastic is collected than cardboard.
    d.  The largest category of collected materials includes newspapers.

*Refer to the following for questions 10 - 16:*

In the United States, where we have more land than people, it is not at all difficult for persons in good health to make money. In this comparatively new field there are so many avenues of success open, so many vocations which are not crowded, that any person of

Copyright © Mometrix Media. You have been licensed one copy of this document for personal use only. Any other reproduction or redistribution is strictly prohibited. All rights reserved.
This content is provided for test preparation purposes only and does not imply an endorsement by Mometrix of any particular political, scientific, or religious point of view.

either sex who is willing, at least for the time being, to engage in any respectable occupation that offers, may find lucrative employment.

Those who really desire to attain an independence, have only to set their minds upon it, and adopt the proper means, as they do in regard to any other object which they wish to accomplish, and the thing is easily done. But however easy it may be found to make money, I have no doubt many of my hearers will agree it is the most difficult thing in the world to keep it. The road to wealth is, as Dr. Franklin truly says, "as plain as the road to the mill." It consists simply in expending less than we earn; that seems to be a very simple problem. Mr. Micawber, one of those happy creations of the genial Dickens, puts the case in a strong light when he says that to have annual income of twenty pounds, per annum, and spend twenty pounds and sixpence, is to be the most miserable of men; whereas, to have an income of only twenty pounds, and spend but nineteen pounds and sixpence, is to be the happiest of mortals.

Many of my hearers may say, "we understand this; this is economy, and we know economy is wealth; we know we can't eat our cake and keep it also." Yet I beg to say that perhaps more cases of failure arise from mistakes on this point than almost any other. The fact is, many people think they understand economy when they really do not.

—Excerpted from *The Art of Money-Getting* by P.T. Barnum

**10. Who is the most likely audience for this passage?**

   a. economists
   b. general readers
   c. teachers
   d. philanthropists

**11. Which word best describes the author's attitude towards those who believe they understand money?**

   a. supportive
   b. incriminating
   c. excessive
   d. patronizing

**12. This passage is most likely taken from a(n) ____.**

   a. self-help manual
   b. autobiography
   c. epistle
   d. novel

**13. According to the author, what is more difficult than making money?**

   a. managing money
   b. traveling to a mill
   c. reading Dickens
   d. understanding the economy

Copyright © Mometrix Media. You have been licensed one copy of this document for personal use only. Any other reproduction or redistribution is strictly prohibited. All rights reserved. This content is provided for test preparation purposes only and does not imply an endorsement by Mometrix of any particular political, scientific, or religious point of view.

**14. Which of the following statements best expresses the main idea of the passage?**
 a. Getting a job is easier now than it ever has been before.
 b. Earning money is much less difficult than managing it properly.
 c. Dr. Franklin advocated getting a job in a mill.
 d. Spending money is the greatest temptation in the world.

**15. What would this author's attitude likely be to a person unable to find employment?**
 a. Descriptive
 b. Conciliatory
 c. Ingenuous
 d. Incredulous

**16. What is the best definition of *economy* as it is used in this passage?**
 a. Exchange of money, goods, and services
 b. Delegation of household affairs
 c. Efficient money management
 d. Less expensive

*Refer to the following for questions 17 - 20:*

In the United States, the foreign language requirement for high school graduation is decided at the state level. This means the requirement varies, with some states deciding to forego a foreign language requirement altogether (www.ncssfl.org). It is necessary that these states reconsider their position and amend their requirements to reflect compulsory completion of a course of one or more foreign languages. Studying a foreign language has become increasingly important for the global economy. As technology continues to make international business relations increasingly easy, people need to keep up by increasing their communication capabilities. High school graduates with foreign language credits have been shown to have an increased college acceptance rate. In addition, students who have mastered more than one language typically find themselves in greater demand when they reach the job market. Students who did not study a foreign language often find themselves unable to obtain a job at all.

**17. What is the main idea of this passage?**
 a. Studying a foreign language will help graduating students find jobs after high school.
 b. Studying a foreign language should be a mandatory requirement for high school graduation.
 c. Studying a foreign language helps students gain an understanding of other cultures.
 d. Studying a foreign language is essential if a student hopes to get into college.

**18. Which of the following statements represents the best summary of the claims made in this passage?**
 a. Studying a foreign language is important if you want to graduate from high school and get a job.
 b. Studying a foreign language is important for the global economy because of the technological advances that have been made in international communications.
 c. Studying a foreign language is important for the global economy, college acceptance rates, and becoming a sought-after candidate in the job market.
 d. Studying a foreign language is important for college acceptance rates and obtaining a job after college.

Copyright © Mometrix Media. You have been licensed one copy of this document for personal use only. Any other reproduction or redistribution is strictly prohibited. All rights reserved. This content is provided for test preparation purposes only and does not imply an endorsement by Mometrix of any particular political, scientific, or religious point of view.

**19. Which of the following statements represents an exaggerated claim in support of the argument presented in this passage?**

a. In the United States, the foreign language requirement for high school graduation is decided at the state level.
b. Studying a foreign language has become increasingly important for the global economy.
c. High school graduates with foreign language credits have been shown to have an increased college acceptance rate.
d. Students who did not study a foreign language often find themselves unable to obtain a job at all.

**20. Which of the following would be a useful source of information to determine the validity of the argument presented in this passage?**

a. A survey of high school students' preferences with regard to foreign language requirements
b. A comparison of the correlation between a second language introduced at home and subsequent college acceptance rates
c. A survey that asks parents to select the foreign language they would like their children to study in high school
d. A comparison of the correlation between high school students' study of a foreign language and subsequent college acceptance rates

*Refer to the following for questions 21 - 22:*

The classic opera *Madame Butterfly* was written by Giacomo Puccini. In the opus, an American naval officer stationed in Japan falls in love with Butterfly, a Japanese woman. He returns to America but promises to come back to marry her. When the soldier does return to Japan three years later, he is accompanied by his American wife. Shocked and humiliated, Butterfly stabs herself. She dies in the soldier's arms as he begs her to forgive him.

**21. This passage describes characters' feelings in *Madame Butterfly* as all of the following EXCEPT:**

a. Romantic
b. Poignant
c. Tragic
d. Musical

**22. What is the purpose of the italicized text in the passage?**

a. To show Madame Butterfly's thoughts
b. To emphasize an idea
c. To format a heading
d. To indicate the title of the opera

*Refer to the following for questions 23 - 25:*

Akhenaten was a powerful pharaoh, or king, of Egypt. He was born with the name Amenhotep, but he changed his name to Akhenaten to reflect his favorite god Aten, who was connected to the worship of the sun. Akhenaten was so devoted to Aten that he decided to change the religious system within Egypt, and during his reign Egypt became a monotheistic society; in other words, Egyptians began to worship the one god Aten. Akhenaten's queen was the beautiful Nefertiti, and he thought so

Copyright © Mometrix Media. You have been licensed one copy of this document for personal use only. Any other reproduction or redistribution is strictly prohibited. All rights reserved. This content is provided for test preparation purposes only and does not imply an endorsement by Mometrix of any particular political, scientific, or religious point of view.

highly of her that he built monuments showing her alongside him in power. At a time when pharaohs were revered as gods in their own right, this was unusual. Akhenaten is the only pharaoh known to have placed his queen beside him as an equal. As a result of his choices and the changes that he made, Akhenaten remains one of Egypt's most unique and memorable pharaohs.

**23. The teacher wants the students to be able to apply basic reading skills to the passage they are studying, so the teacher quizzes the students on the word "monotheistic". Breaking this word down, the teacher asks students to identify how "mono" functions in this word:**

    a.  Root word
    b.  Prefix
    c.  Suffix
    d.  Syllable

**24. The teacher also wants the students to be able to make accurate inferences based on information they are studying. Considering this passage carefully, which of the following inferences can students make regarding the monotheism that Akhenaten brought to Egypt during his reign?**

    a.  Egypt was the only monotheistic society in the world
    b.  Before Akhenaten, monotheism did not exist among ancient societies
    c.  The monotheism that Akhenaten introduced was popular among the Egyptian people
    d.  Before Akhenaten, the Egyptians had worshipped many gods

**25. To explain the distinction between the monotheistic system that Akhenaten introduced and the previous religious system in Egypt, the teacher explains to students that Egypt had been polytheistic, or had worshipped many gods. The teacher then explains that these words are opposites. Which concept is the teacher describing to students?**

    a.  Synonyms
    b.  Homonyms
    c.  Antonyms
    d.  Consonants

**26. After students have read the first chapter of a book, their teacher asks them to speculate on what the main character is going to do next. The students are being asked to use a comprehension strategy called:**

    a.  summarizing.
    b.  monitoring and correcting.
    c.  making predictions.
    d.  drawing conclusions.

Copyright © Mometrix Media. You have been licensed one copy of this document for personal use only. Any other reproduction or redistribution is strictly prohibited. All rights reserved. This content is provided for test preparation purposes only and does not imply an endorsement by Mometrix of any particular political, scientific, or religious point of view.

**27. A teacher is working with a student who is struggling with reading. The teacher gives him a story with key words missing:**

> The boy wanted to take the dog for a walk. The boy opened the door. The ____ ran out. The ____ looked for the dog. When he found the dog, he was very _____.

**The student is able to fill in the blanks by considering:**

a. Syntax. Often, word order gives enough clues that a reader can predict what happens next.
b. Pretext. By previewing the story, the student can deduce the missing words.
c. Context. By considering the other words in the story, the student can determine the missing words.
d. Fallacies. By checking for common errors of thought, the student can determine the missing words.

**28. A teacher is working with a group of third graders at the same reading level. Her goal is to improve reading fluency. She asks each child in turn to read a page from a book about mammal young. She asks the children to read with expression. She also reminds them they don't need to stop between each word; they should read as quickly as they comfortably can. She cautions them, however, not to read so quickly that they leave out or misread a word. The teacher knows the components of reading fluency are:**

a. Speed, drama, and comprehension
b. Cohesion, rate, and prosody
c. Understanding, rate, and prosody
d. Rate, accuracy, and prosody

**29. A high school English teacher asked the students to read a magazine article about the Uffizi Gallery in Florence, Italy, and its collection of Italian Renaissance paintings. The teacher advised the students to annotate the text with comments and questions. Later the students would discuss their respective annotations. What does Jason's comment indicate about what he learned?**

> Jason's annotation: The Italian Renaissance produced some of the world's greatest masterpieces from the thirteenth to the sixteenth centuries.

a. He understands the timeline of the historical period of the collection.
b. He knows about the content of the paintings in the collection.
c. He recognizes the names of the artists who did these paintings.
d. He knows about the architecture of this museum.

**30. A third-grade teacher has several students reading above grade level. Most of the remaining students are reading at grade level. There are also a few students reading below grade level. She decides to experiment. Her hypothesis is that by giving the entire class a chapter book above grade level, high-level readers will be satisfied, grade-level readers will be challenged in a positive way, and students reading below grade level will be inspired to improve. Her method is most likely to:**

a. Succeed, producing students reading at an Instructional reading level.
b. Succeed, producing students reading at an Independent reading level.
c. Fail, producing students at a Frustration reading level.
d. Fail, producing students reading at a Chaotic reading level.

Copyright © Mometrix Media. You have been licensed one copy of this document for personal use only. Any other reproduction or redistribution is strictly prohibited. All rights reserved. This content is provided for test preparation purposes only and does not imply an endorsement by Mometrix of any particular political, scientific, or religious point of view.

## Mathematics

**31. Given this stem and leaf plot, what are the mean and median?**

| Stem | Leaf |
|------|------|
| 1 | 6  8 |
| 2 | 0  1 |
| 3 | 4 |
| 4 | 5  9 |

  a.  Mean = 28 and median = 20
  b.  Mean = 29 and median = 20
  c.  Mean = 29 and median = 21
  d.  Mean = 28 and median = 21

**32. Everyone in a class has blue, green, or brown eyes. 40% of the students have brown eyes and 90% of the other students have blue eyes. What can we infer from this information?**

  a.  We can infer that there is a majority of students with brown eyes.
  b.  We can infer that there is a majority of students with blue eyes.
  c.  We can infer that there is a majority of students with green eyes.
  d.  We can infer that there is an equal number of students with each eye color.

**33. What is the probability of spinning a D on the spinner below?**

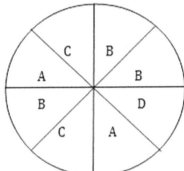

  a.  $\dfrac{1}{8}$
  b.  $\dfrac{1}{7}$
  c.  $\dfrac{3}{8}$
  d.  $\dfrac{6}{7}$

**34. What is the value of the expression -3 x 5² + 2(4-18) + 33?**

  a.  -130
  b.  -70
  c.  -20
  d.  74

Copyright © Mometrix Media. You have been licensed one copy of this document for personal use only. Any other reproduction or redistribution is strictly prohibited. All rights reserved.
This content is provided for test preparation purposes only and does not imply an endorsement by Mometrix of any particular political, scientific, or religious point of view.

35. What is the value of $x$ in the following equation?

$$15 - x = 78$$

    a. 5.2
    b. 63
    c. -63
    d. -93

36. Find the area of the rectangle.

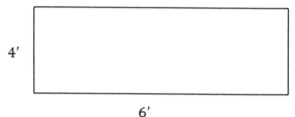

    a. 10 ft$^2$
    b. 12 ft$^2$
    c. 20 ft$^2$
    d. 24 ft$^2$

37. A $1,000 lottery winner had 35% deducted for taxes. How much was the winning check?

    a. $300
    b. $350
    c. $650
    d. $965

38. What is the percent increase in cars sold in 2005 when compared to those sold in 2004?

| Year | Cars Sold |
|------|-----------|
| 2002 | 1,430 |
| 2003 | 1,300 |
| 2004 | 1,580 |
| 2005 | 1,817 |
| 2006 | 1,900 |

    a. 15%
    b. 18%
    c. 25%
    d. 32%

39. Which of these would best illustrate the percentage of a budget allocated to various departments?

    a. Pie chart
    b. Line graph
    c. Box-and-whisker plot
    d. Venn diagram

Copyright © Mometrix Media. You have been licensed one copy of this document for personal use only. Any other reproduction or redistribution is strictly prohibited. All rights reserved. This content is provided for test preparation purposes only and does not imply an endorsement by Mometrix of any particular political, scientific, or religious point of view.

**40. Which of the following statements is true?**

    a.  -6 is to the right of -5 on the number line
    b.  -7 is to the left of -2 on the number line
    c.  0 is to the left of -1 on the number line
    d.  7 is to the left of -2 on the number line

**41. A woman wants to park her 15-foot-long car in a garage that is 19 feet long. How far from the front of the garage will the front of her car need to be so that the car is centered on the floor of the garage?**

    a.  2 feet
    b.  $2\frac{1}{2}$ feet
    c.  3 feet
    d.  $3\frac{1}{2}$ feet

**42. The average highway speed of a charter bus is 65 miles per hour, while a car's average highway speed is 70 miles per hour. If the bus and car both depart from the same place at the same time today, how much farther ahead of the bus is the car after eight hours?**

    a.  5 miles
    b.  15 miles
    c.  22 miles
    d.  40 miles

**43. A man loans his friend $10,000 at 7% simple interest. The friend repays $5,035. How much money does she still owe the man?**

    a.  $5,665
    b.  $5,465
    c.  $5,035
    d.  $4,965

**44. Solve for $y$ in the following equation, if $x = -\frac{1}{3}$.**

$$y = x + 3$$

    a.  $y = 2\frac{1}{3}$
    b.  $y = 2\frac{2}{3}$
    c.  $y = -2\frac{2}{3}$
    d.  $y = -3\frac{1}{3}$

**45. Arrange the following numbers in order from least to greatest:**

    0.083      0.017      −0.18      0      1.03      −2.8

    a.  $-2.8, -0.18, 0, 0.017, 0.083, 1.03$
    b.  $1.03, 0, 0.017, 0.083, -0.18, -2.8$
    c.  $0, -2.8, -0.18, 0.083, 0.017, 1.03$
    d.  $0.017, 0.083, 0, 1.03, -0.18, -2.8$

Copyright © Mometrix Media. You have been licensed one copy of this document for personal use only. Any other reproduction or redistribution is strictly prohibited. All rights reserved.
This content is provided for test preparation purposes only and does not imply an endorsement by Mometrix of any particular political, scientific, or religious point of view.

**46. Solve for $x$:**

$$4x + 4 = 36$$

   a.  5
   b.  -8
   c.  8
   d.  11

**47. Simplify $8(x + 2) - 7 + 4(x - 7)$.**

   a.  $5x + 23$
   b.  $5x - 23$
   c.  $12x - 19$
   d.  $12x + 37$

**48. What is 40% of 360?**

   a.  90
   b.  120
   c.  144
   d.  270

**49. Write $\frac{4}{5}$ as a percentage.**

   a.  40%
   b.  45%
   c.  60%
   d.  80%

**50. Solve for $x$:**

$$\frac{1}{6} \div \frac{3}{8} = x$$

   a.  $x = \frac{1}{16}$
   b.  $x = \frac{4}{9}$
   c.  $x = 2\frac{3}{8}$
   d.  $x = 2\frac{1}{3}$

**51. A six-sided die is thrown one time. What is the probability of the throw yielding an odd number?**

   a.  60%
   b.  50%
   c.  25%
   d.  10%

**52. Solve for $x$:**

$$(2x - 3) + 2x = 9$$

   a.  1
   b.  -2
   c.  3
   d.  -3

367

Copyright © Mometrix Media. You have been licensed one copy of this document for personal use only. Any other reproduction or redistribution is strictly prohibited. All rights reserved.
This content is provided for test preparation purposes only and does not imply an endorsement by Mometrix of any particular political, scientific, or religious point of view.

**53. Express 18% as a decimal.**

    a.  0.018
    b.  0.18
    c.  1.8
    d.  0.108

**54. Three rectangular gardens, each with an area of 48 square feet, are created on a tract of land. Garden A measures 6 feet by 8 feet; Garden B measures 12 feet by 4 feet; Garden C measures 16 feet by 3 feet. Which garden will require the least amount of fencing to surround it?**

    a.  Garden A
    b.  Garden B
    c.  Garden C
    d.  All gardens will require the same amount of fencing

**55. In the mathematical order of operations, which of these is true?**

    a.  Exponents are done before adding, subtracting, multiplying, or dividing.
    b.  Calculations outside parentheses are done before those inside of them.
    c.  Addition and subtraction are done before multiplication and division are.
    d.  Multiplication is done before division and addition is before subtraction.

**56. Triangle ABC below is a scalene triangle, not drawn to scale. Which statement is true about side BC?**

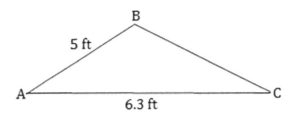

    a.  It measures 5 ft.
    b.  It measures 6.3 ft.
    c.  It does not measure 5 ft or 6.3 ft.
    d.  It measures either 5 ft or 6.3 ft.

**57. Find the value of $100 \div (9 + 1) \times 2$.**

    a.  20
    b.  5
    c.  15
    d.  80
    e.  76

**58. Simplify the expression $(10 + 4 \times 3) \div 2$.**

    a.  22
    b.  21
    c.  6
    d.  20
    e.  11

Copyright © Mometrix Media. You have been licensed one copy of this document for personal use only. Any other reproduction or redistribution is strictly prohibited. All rights reserved. This content is provided for test preparation purposes only and does not imply an endorsement by Mometrix of any particular political, scientific, or religious point of view.

**59. One inch is equivalent to 2.54 centimeters. How long, in centimeters, is a stick measuring 9.5 inches?**

   a.  241.3 centimeters
   b.  24.13 centimeters
   c.  12.70 centimeters
   d.  18.55 centimeters
   e.  3.7 centimeters

**60. Sean and Hillary are baking cookies for a bake sale. Sean baked 48 chocolate chip cookies, and Hillary baked 36 sugar cookies. If 50 cookies were sold altogether, how many were left over at the end of the bake sale?**

   a.  43 cookies
   b.  33 cookies
   c.  34 cookies
   d.  44 cookies

Copyright © Mometrix Media. You have been licensed one copy of this document for personal use only. Any other reproduction or redistribution is strictly prohibited. All rights reserved.
This content is provided for test preparation purposes only and does not imply an endorsement by Mometrix of any particular political, scientific, or religious point of view.

# Writing

*Refer to the following for questions 61 - 70:*

In the following section, there are underlined parts to each sentence. One of the underlined parts is incorrectly written. Choose the letter that corresponds with the incorrect underlined part of the sentence. If the entire sentence is correct, choose D for NO ERROR.

**61.** Let's write the <u>entire sign</u> in <u>capitol</u> letters so that it <u>can be seen</u> by people who
$\qquad$ A $\qquad$ B $\qquad$ C
are driving by.

    a. entire sign
    b. capitol
    c. can be seen
    d. No error

**62.** All of the <u>students</u> <u>except</u> Marcus for the <u>free-spirited</u> boy that he is.
$\qquad$ A $\qquad$ B $\qquad$ C

    a. students
    b. except
    c. free spirited
    d. No error

**63.** <u>One flu patient</u> had an <u>averse</u> reaction to the drug and <u>had to</u> be hospitalized
$\qquad$ A $\qquad$ B $\qquad$ C
for a week.

    a. One flu patient
    b. averse
    c. had to
    d. No error

**64.** Grandfather said that when <u>he died</u> he wanted <u>his assets</u> divided <u>among</u> his two sons.
$\qquad$ A $\qquad$ B $\qquad$ C

    a. he died
    b. his assets
    c. among
    d. No error

**65.** <u>"I</u> hope Mrs. Johnson <u>lets</u> us swim in her <u>pool."</u> Pam said.
A $\qquad$ B $\qquad$ C

    a. "I
    b. lets
    c. pool." Pam
    d. No error

**66.** We must <u>ensure that</u> Mike <u>proceeds</u> Ann when the students <u>line up</u>
$\qquad$ A $\qquad$ B $\qquad$ C
for the graduation ceremony.

    a. ensure that
    b. proceeds
    c. line up
    d. No error

Copyright © Mometrix Media. You have been licensed one copy of this document for personal use only. Any other reproduction or redistribution is strictly prohibited. All rights reserved.
This content is provided for test preparation purposes only and does not imply an endorsement by Mometrix of any particular political, scientific, or religious point of view.

**67.** He was <u>discrete</u> in what he <u>said and wrote</u> since he was <u>not yet sure</u> of his role.
<br>              A                       B                           C

    a. discrete
    b. said and wrote
    c. not yet sure
    d. No error

**68.** When <u>funding</u> becomes available, we anticipate receiving a new <u>dual-control</u>
<br>          A                                           B

car for our <u>driver training program</u>.
<br>                 C

    a. funding
    b. dual control
    c. driver training program
    d. No error

**69.** Many students <u>yawned, dozed,</u> or talked during the assembly <u>because they were</u>
<br>                     A                                                  B

<u>disinterested in the speaker's message</u>.
<br>                   C

    a. yawned, dozed,
    b. because they were
    c. disinterested in the speaker' s message
    d. No error

**70.** Since school vacation is <u>eminent, teachers have</u> difficulty <u>getting students to pay</u>
<br>                               A                                         B

<u>attention to their lessons</u> during the last few weeks of school. <u>No error</u>
<br>              C                                                   D

    A. eminent, teachers have
    b. getting students to
    c. attention to their lessons
    d. No error

**71.** Select the word or phrase that corrects an error in the underlined portion of the text. If no correction is needed, select "no correction needed."

    In 2010, an oil spill occurred in the Gulf of Mexico. Today, the effects of that spill still <u>alter</u> the nesting habits of pelicans native to the area.

    a. altered
    b. altering
    c. have altered
    d. no correction needed

**72.** Identify the synonym for the underlined word.

    Stacey <u>abhorred</u> cooking, but loved to eat.

    a. enjoyed
    b. laborious
    c. cuisine
    d. detested

Copyright © Mometrix Media. You have been licensed one copy of this document for personal use only. Any other reproduction or redistribution is strictly prohibited. All rights reserved.
This content is provided for test preparation purposes only and does not imply an endorsement by Mometrix of any particular political, scientific, or religious point of view.

**73. Identify the synonym for the underlined word.**

Fiona's smirk showed her <u>content</u> with the outcome of the election.

a. Subject matter
b. Disapproval
c. Satisfaction
d. Condemnation

**74. Identify the word that best completes the sentence.**

The football player blasted _____ the defense and scored his first touchdown.

a. threw
b. through
c. passed
d. huddled

**75. Choose the word that best completes the sentence.**

_____ going to wash the dishes after they clear the table.

a. There
b. Their
c. They're
d. We'll

*Refer to the following for questions 76 - 80:*

The upcoming sentences are given to measure your ability to correctly and efficiently convey meaning. When you are choosing your answer, remember that the sentences should utilize conventional written English, including grammar, word selection, conventional sentence structure, and punctuation.

There will be either a section or a complete sentence underlined. Beneath the sentence there are different choices. The first choice (A) will be the same as the underlined section. The remaining choices give different substitutions that could replace the underlined section.

Choose the letter that corresponds with the choice that best conveys the meaning of the original sentence. If the original wording is the best, select answer choice A. If not, choose one of the other choices. The correct answer is the one that keeps the original meaning and makes the sentence the most effective. Make sure your choice makes the sentence understandable without being cumbersome or unclear.

**76. <u>The leaves were raked all day by Sergio and Gina.</u>**
a. The leaves were raked all day by Sergio and Gina.
b. The leaves were being raked all day by Sergio and Gina.
c. Sergio and Gina raked leaves all day.
d. Leaves were raked all day by Sergio and Gina.

**77. <u>Her hand-sewn dress was beautiful she was proud to wear it to the dinner party.</u>**
a. Her hand-sewn dress was beautiful she was proud to wear it to the dinner party.
b. Her hand-sewn dress was beautiful, she was proud to wear it to the dinner party.
c. Her hand-sewn dress was beautiful; she was proud to wear it to the dinner party.
d. Her hand-sewn dress was beautiful but she was proud to wear it to the dinner party.

Copyright © Mometrix Media. You have been licensed one copy of this document for personal use only. Any other reproduction or redistribution is strictly prohibited. All rights reserved. This content is provided for test preparation purposes only and does not imply an endorsement by Mometrix of any particular political, scientific, or religious point of view.

**78. "I hope we find Boots." "He'll be a hungry and tired cat if he spends the night out here,"**

a.  "I hope we find Boots." "He'll be a hungry and tired cat if he spends the night out here,"
b.  "I hope we find Boots." He'll be a hungry and tired cat if he spends the night out here,"
c.  "I hope we find Boots. "He'll be a hungry and tired cat if he spends the night out here,"
d.  "I hope we find Boots. He'll be a hungry and tired cat if he spends the night out here,"

**79. Two of our dogs like to bark at the vacuum cleaner.**

a.  Two of our dogs like to bark
b.  Two of our dog's like to bark
c.  Two of our dogs' like to bark
d.  Two of our dog's like to "bark"

**80. Driving past the park, the new swimming pool was seen.**

a.  the new swimming pool was seen.
b.  he is seeing the new swimming pool.
c.  the new swimming pool was shown.
d.  he saw the new swimming pool.

**81. Which of the following contains a comma splice?**

a.  Many athletes have personal trainers, trainers help them stay fit in the off-season.
b.  The child didn't finish his dinner, so his mother would not allow him to have dessert.
c.  We were able to attend the dinner; however, we were not able to attend the after-party.
d.  Tom enjoys fiction, while Jack prefers autobiographies.

**82. Identify the run-on sentence.**

a.  We loved climbing the mountain and enjoying the beautiful view.
b.  Jonathan lived in Utah, but now he lives in Nebraska with his entire extended family.
c.  I learned what marine biologists do I think I would like to pursue that career.
d.  She is beautiful, but her manners are atrocious.

**83. Select the word or phrase that corrects an error in one of the underlined portions of the text. If no correction is needed, select "no correction needed."**

"I am definately sleeping in tomorrow."

a.  definitely
b.  tommorrow
c.  tomorow
d.  no correction needed

**84. Identify the correction needed in the sentence.**

"The season finale is fast approaching; and I still don't know which singer I'm rooting for."

a.  Add a hyphen: "fast-approaching"
b.  Omit the semicolon
c.  The word "rooting" should be "routing"
d.  The period should be replaced with a question mark

Copyright © Mometrix Media. You have been licensed one copy of this document for personal use only. Any other reproduction or redistribution is strictly prohibited. All rights reserved.
This content is provided for test preparation purposes only and does not imply an endorsement by Mometrix of any particular political, scientific, or religious point of view.

**85. Select the word or phrase that corrects an error in one of the underlined portions of the text. If no correction is needed, select "no correction needed."**

The <u>Museum</u> of Natural History has a new <u>dinosaur</u>, the <u>titanosaur</u>.

   a. museum
   b. Dinosaur
   c. Titanosaur
   d. no correction needed

*Refer to the following for questions 86 - 90:*

> Some camels have two humps on their backs, but the dromedary only has one. Dromedaries are popular for carrying things on their backs. They are known to be stubborn and kick people. Dromedaries are very useful to many people in Africa and Saudi Arabia. The dromedary hair is often used by people in these places for tents and clothing. Dromedaries are also eaten. In Egypt, guards use dromedaries instead of horses to keep an eye on the borders.

**86. The student is working on primary paragraph elements, including a strong topic sentence. Which of the following would make a good topic sentence for the paragraph that the student has written?**

   a. The dromedary is a part of the camel family
   b. Dromedaries are very interesting
   c. The dromedary is not as friendly as the camel
   d. The dromedary is a very useful animal

**87. Which of the sentences in the paragraph above does not fit with the primary topic of the paragraph?**

   a. Dromedaries are popular for carrying things on their backs
   b. They are known to be stubborn and kick people
   c. Dromedaries are also eaten
   d. In Egypt, guards use dromedaries instead of horses to keep an eye on the borders

**88. In order to improve the flow of the paragraph, the instructor recommends that the student incorporate a transitional word or phrase. Which of the following transitional expressions is most appropriate before this sentence: "Dromedaries are very useful to many people in Africa and Saudi Arabia."**

   a. As a result
   b. In addition
   c. Although
   d. Perhaps

**89. The student is also working on using strong, descriptive language instead of simple words. Which of the following phrase might be a good alternative to the phrase "people in these places"?**

   a. Many who live in Africa and Saudi Arabia
   b. The people that dwell in these places
   c. Bedouins living in this part of the world
   d. The inhabitants here

Copyright © Mometrix Media. You have been licensed one copy of this document for personal use only. Any other reproduction or redistribution is strictly prohibited. All rights reserved.
This content is provided for test preparation purposes only and does not imply an endorsement by Mometrix of any particular political, scientific, or religious point of view.

**90. The instructor is concerned about the use of the passive tense in one of the sentences. Which of the following sentences exhibits the use of the passive tense?**

    a.  Some camels have two humps on their backs, but the dromedary only has one

    b.  Dromedaries are popular for carrying things on their backs

    c.  Dromedaries are very useful to many people in Africa and Saudi Arabia

    d.  The dromedary hair is often used by people in these places for tents and clothing

Copyright © Mometrix Media. You have been licensed one copy of this document for personal use only. Any other reproduction or redistribution is strictly prohibited. All rights reserved.
This content is provided for test preparation purposes only and does not imply an endorsement by Mometrix of any particular political, scientific, or religious point of view.

# Answer Key and Explanations

## Reading

**1. C:** The passage is expository because it communicates information about the mysteries of the Bermuda Triangle and what researchers have studied and now believe. The author includes facts to inform the reader, which is the goal of expository writing. The passage does not tell a story or describe one event, so it is not a narrative. The passage also does not seek to lead the reader to take action or accept a particular conclusion, so this passage is not persuasive. The passage also does not give technical information and does not aim to help the reader understand a technical concept, so this passage is not technical.

**2. D:** This sentence is the best summary statement for the entire passage because it clearly describes what the author is saying about the results of studies on the Bermuda Triangle. Each paragraph in the passage includes details that support the statement that researchers have never found anything truly mysterious about the Bermuda Triangle. Choices A, B, and C are all details found in the passage, but none of these answer choices give a summary of the whole passage. Each of these answer choices support the statement in choice D, as do the rest of the details in the passage. Choice D is the best summary of these choices.

**3. A:** Of all the sentences provided, this is the one with which the author would most likely agree. The passage suggests that most of the "mysteries" of the Bermuda Triangle can be explained in a reasonable way. The passage mentions that some expand the Triangle to the Azores, but this is a point of fact, and the author makes no mention of whether or not this is in error. The author quotes the Navy's response to the disappearance of the planes, but there is no reason to believe the author questions this response. The author raises questions about the many myths surrounding the Triangle, but at no point does the author claim that these myths are to blame for the accidents that fall "within the expected margin of error."

**4. B:** A collection of travel journal entries from someone who frequently traveled the Bermuda Triangle is the most likely of these choices to provide detailed information. Choice A would provide useful information, but this information is not likely to go into much detail. Choice C would likely include many details, but it would only contain information about a very small section of the Bermuda Triangle. Choice D could include details about the Bermuda Triangle, but these details would also only describe a limited section of the area and would be given through a narrow perspective.

**5. A:** This answer can be found in the second column of the table, "Relative Importance December 2008." These numbers represent the average percentage of household budgets that are spent on the expenditure category. The greatest number, 43.421%, is on the row corresponding to housing.

**6. B:** This information can be found in the second column from the right. Fuel oil and other fuels decreased by 3.1% during this period. Gasoline increased by 3.1%. The other commodities decreased, but by lesser amounts.

**7. D:** In the table, components of each category are shown by indentation under the name of the category itself. There may be sub-categories within each category that are further indented. All of the choices are indented under "Food at Home" except for "Alcoholic Beverages," which is a separate category.

Copyright © Mometrix Media. You have been licensed one copy of this document for personal use only. Any other reproduction or redistribution is strictly prohibited. All rights reserved. This content is provided for test preparation purposes only and does not imply an endorsement by Mometrix of any particular political, scientific, or religious point of view.

**8. C:** The column showing seasonally adjusted percent changes from May to June shows that infants' and toddlers' apparel increased by 2.2%. Women's and girls' apparel and footwear also increased, but they increased by smaller percentages. Men's and boys' apparel decreased from May to June.

**9. C:** The chart shows that plastic and cardboard materials are made of 15% of the collected materials. So, it is incorrect to say that there is more plastic than cardboard. They are present in equal amounts.

**10. B:** This passage is clearly intended for a non-expert adult readership.

**11. D:** The author suggests that many people who believe they understand economy in fact do not.

**12. A:** It seems clear that the author is about to describe the correct means of personal economy.

**13. A:** The author insists that many people who have no trouble earning money waste it through lavish spending, along with several other statements that show the reader that the author believes managing money is more challenging than making it.

**14. B:** The author asserts that earning money is easy, but what often challenges people is managing money. This is the main idea of the passage. Choice B says that earning money is less difficult than managing money, so it is correct. Getting a job and the temptation to spend money are both mentioned in the passage as details. However, neither of these are the main idea, so choices A and D are both incorrect. The quote from Franklin does not advocate for working at a mill and does not summarize the main idea, so choice C is also incorrect.

**15. D:** The author seems to believe that there are plenty of lucrative jobs for everyone, so he or she would doubt that a person really could not find employment. This makes choice D the best choice, as *incredulous* means to struggle to believe something. *Descriptive* means describing, *conciliatory* means satisfying or appeasing, and *ingenuous* means innocent. None of these terms describe the attitude of the author, so choices A, B, and C are incorrect.

**16. C:** In this passage, the author is speaking of money management on a personal or household level. In this context, economy refers to efficient money management, so choice C is correct. While this definition of economy is relevant to households, it is not related to delegation within a household, making choice B incorrect. Economy in the context of the exchange of money, goods, and services is more applicable beyond personal or household finances, so choice A is incorrect. This passage uses economy to describe wise money management, not simply goods that are less expensive than others, so choice D is incorrect.

**17. B:** The passage argues that high schools should require that students study a foreign language and gives reasons to support this argument. Choice B accurately describes the main idea of the passage. The passage does say that studying a foreign language is helpful for college acceptance and finding a job, but neither of these points are the main idea of the passage. They are both supporting details. The passage does not say that studying a foreign language will help students gain an understanding of other cultures.

**18. C:** The passage includes claims that studying a foreign language is helpful for participating in the global economy, being accepted into college, and being a desirable candidate for various jobs. These points are summarized in choice C, making it the best summary of the passage. The passage argues that studying a foreign language should be mandatory, but it does not claim that studying a

Copyright © Mometrix Media. You have been licensed one copy of this document for personal use only. Any other reproduction or redistribution is strictly prohibited. All rights reserved.
This content is provided for test preparation purposes only and does not imply an endorsement by Mometrix of any particular political, scientific, or religious point of view.

foreign language is currently essential to high school graduation, so choice A is incorrect. Choices B and D represent claims made in the passage, but do not include all of the claims made.

**19. D:** Although students may find knowledge of a foreign language helpful for obtaining a job, it is clearly an exaggeration to claim that students who did not study a foreign language are unemployable. Choice A simply lists a fact that can be verified, so it cannot be an exaggeration. Choices B and C include statements that the importance of knowing a foreign language and the acceptance rates for students who have studied a foreign language have increased. These statements simply describe the direction of a trend, so while they can be incorrect, they cannot be exaggerations.

**20. D:** Choice D can confirm the author's claim that high school graduates who studied a foreign language are more likely to be accepted to college, so it is correct. Choices A and C would provide information regarding the opinions of students and parents, but not actual evidence regarding the influence of studying a foreign language on future success. Choice B specifies a second language taught at home, whereas the passage focuses specifically on a foreign language taught in high school.

**21. D:** Although this passage describes an opera, the feelings experienced by the characters would not be considered musical. The passage does mention that the American officer falls in love with Butterfly, so it is reasonable to describe the characters' feelings as romantic. *Poignant* and *tragic* both refer to feelings of intense emotional distress, which are expressed through both Butterfly and the officer's reactions at the end of the passage. These terms clearly describe the characters' feelings, making *musical* the correct answer.

**22. D:** The passage is describing the events of an opera titled *Madame Butterfly*. The opera title is given in the first sentence of the passage, and since an opera is a major work, its title should be italicized in typed text. The first sentence simply gives the name of the opera and the writer, it does not introduce an important idea or a section heading, so choices B and C are incorrect. None of the character's thoughts or dialogue are quoted in the passage, so choice A is also incorrect.

**23. B:** An affix that is placed at the beginning of a word and alters the inflection of that word is considered a prefix. In this case, "mono" is a prefix that indicates "one" or "alone."

**24. D:** Reading the sentence carefully, the student should see that the author says, "Akhenaten was so devoted to Aten that he decided to change the religious system within Egypt, and during his reign Egypt became a monotheistic society; in other words, Egyptians began to worship the one god Aten." The only answer choice that can be accurately inferred is that Egyptian society before Akhenaten had involved the worship of many gods.

**25. C:** An antonym is a word that expresses the opposite of another word. Groupings such as "yes" and "no" represent antonyms, as do groupings such as "remain" and "leave." If the teacher is introducing the concept of antonyms to students, the words "monotheism" and "polytheism" – while not exactly perfect antonyms – can be represented as opposites to elementary students.

**26. C:** Predicting events in a story builds anticipation and helps propel the reading forward. Students activate prior knowledge from life and literature to understand characters and anticipate their thoughts and actions.

**27. C:** Context. By considering the other words in the story, the student can determine the missing words. The student is depending on the information supplied by the rest of the story. This information puts the story into context.

Copyright © Mometrix Media. You have been licensed one copy of this document for personal use only. Any other reproduction or redistribution is strictly prohibited. All rights reserved.
This content is provided for test preparation purposes only and does not imply an endorsement by Mometrix of any particular political, scientific, or religious point of view.

**28. D:** Rate, accuracy, and prosody are the components of reading fluency. Fluent readers are able to read smoothly and comfortably at a steady pace (rate). The more quickly a child reads, the greater the chance of leaving out a word or substituting one word for another (for example, *sink* instead of *shrink*). Fluent readers are able to maintain accuracy without sacrificing rate. Fluent readers also stress important words in a text, group words into rhythmic phrases, and read with intonation (prosody).

**29. A:** Jason comments on the time in which the masterpieces were painted. B is incorrect because the contents of the paintings are not described. C is incorrect because he does not mention the artists. D is incorrect because the architecture of the Uffizi Gallery is not mentioned.

**30. C:** Fail, producing students at a Frustration reading level. Those reading below grade level are likely to give up entirely. Those reading at grade level are likely to get frustrated and form habits that will actually slow down their development. Giving students texts that are too far beyond their reach produces frustrated readers. In an effort to succeed, frustrated readers are likely to apply strategies that have worked for them in the past but cannot work in this case because the text is simply beyond them. Looking for contextual clues to understand the meaning of unfamiliar words requires that most of the words in the passage are familiar. Breaking unfamiliar words into individual phonemes or syllables can be effective, but not if the number of such words is excessive. In this case, students below reading level and students at reading level will become frustrated when the skills that have worked for them in the past now fail.

# Mathematics

**31. C:** The mean is the average of the data and can be found by dividing the sum of the data by the number of data: $\frac{16+18+20+21+34+45+49}{7} = 29$. The median is the middle data point when the data are ranked numerically. The median is 21.

**32. B:** Regardless of the exact number of students, we can determine the relative percentages of each eye color. We are given that 40% of the total have brown eyes, which means that 100% − 40% or 60% of the students have either blue or green eyes. Since 90% of those have blue eyes, we know that 10% have green eyes. Now, 90% of 60% can be found by converting both percentages to decimals and multiplying them: $(0.9) \times (0.6) = 0.54$ or 54%. So, in total, 40% have brown eyes, 54% have blue eyes, and 6% have green eyes and we can definitively say that blue eyed students are the majority.

**33. A:** Experimental probability is a ratio of how many times the spinner will land on the specific letter to the total number of places the spinner can land. In this case, there are eight possible places where the spinner may land. The D is present only in one space, so the probability of landing there is 1 to 8 or $\frac{1}{8}$.

**34. B:** Use the order of operations to find the value for this expression: parentheses, exponents, multiplication and division, addition and subtraction:

$$-3 \times 5^2 + 2(4-18) + 33$$
$$= -3 \times 5^2 + 2(-14) + 33$$
$$= -3 \times 25 + 2(-14) + 33$$
$$= -75 + (-28) + 33$$
$$= -70$$

Copyright © Mometrix Media. You have been licensed one copy of this document for personal use only. Any other reproduction or redistribution is strictly prohibited. All rights reserved.
This content is provided for test preparation purposes only and does not imply an endorsement by Mometrix of any particular political, scientific, or religious point of view.

**35. C:** The equation can be rearranged and simplified as follows:

$$15 - x = 78$$
$$15 - 78 = x$$
$$-63 = x$$

**36. D:** Recall that area ($A$) is length ($l$) times width ($w$):

$$A = l \times w$$
$$A = 4 \text{ ft} \times 6 \text{ ft}$$
$$A = 24 \text{ ft}^2$$

**37. C:** Multiply $1,000 by 35% to get the amount deducted: $1,000 \times 35\% = \$350.00$. Subtract this value from the original amount: $1000 - \$350 = \$650$.

**38. A:** Use the formula for percent change to solve this problem.

$$\% \text{ change} = \frac{new - old}{old} \times 100\%$$

The "new" value is the number of cars sold in 2005 (1,817). The "old" value is the number of cars sold in 2004 (1,580). Plug these values into the formula and solve:

$$\% \text{ change} = \frac{1,817 - 1,580}{1,580} \times 100\%$$
$$= \frac{237}{1,580} \times 100\%$$
$$= 15\%$$

Because this number is positive, it shows a percent increase of 15%.

**39. A:** A pie chart shows the relationship of parts to a whole. A line graph is often used to show change over time. A box-and-whisker plot displays how numeric data are distributed throughout the range. A Venn diagram shows the relationships among sets.

**40. B:** The number line orders numbers from least to greatest. When comparing any two numbers, the smaller value will always be to the left of the greater value. Because -7 is *less than* -2, -7 will always be to the *left* of -2 on the number line. All of the other options have greater values placed to the left of smaller values. This can never be true on any number line.

**41. A:** To solve, first figure out how much room is left when her car and the garage are taken into account: 19 feet − 15 feet = 4 feet. To center the car, it would have to be parked 2 feet from the front of the garage.

**42. D:** Subtract 65 from 70 to find out how much faster the bus is going:

$$70 - 65 = 5 \text{ miles per hour}$$

If the bus is traveling five miles each hour faster than the car, in eight hours it will be 40 miles ahead of the car:

$$5 \frac{\text{miles}}{\text{hr}} \times 8 \text{ hr} = 40 \text{ miles}$$

Copyright © Mometrix Media. You have been licensed one copy of this document for personal use only. Any other reproduction or redistribution is strictly prohibited. All rights reserved. This content is provided for test preparation purposes only and does not imply an endorsement by Mometrix of any particular political, scientific, or religious point of view.

**43. A:** To begin, calculate the amount of interest: $10,000 \times 7\% = \$700$. Add this to the original amount to find out what she owes in total: $\$10,000 + \$700 = \$10,700$. Subtract what she has paid to find what she still owes: $\$10,700 - \$5,035 = \$5,665$.

**44. B:** To solve, place the value of $x$ into the equation:

$$y = -\frac{1}{3} + 3$$
$$y = 2\frac{2}{3}$$

**45. A:** Think of the numbers as they would appear on a number line to place them in the correct order, from the greatest negative number to the greatest positive number.

**46. C:** To solve, isolate the $x$ on one side of the equation.

$$4x = 36 - 4$$
$$4x = 32$$
$$x = 8$$

**47. C:** To solve, first multiply through the parentheses and then combine like terms:

$$8(x + 2) - 7 + 4(x - 7) = 8x + 16 - 7 + 4x - 28$$
$$= 12x - 19$$

**48. C:** Multiply 360 by 0.40 to get 144.

**49. D:** To solve, divide the numerator by the denominator and multiply by 100:

$$\frac{4}{5} = 0.8 \times 100\% = 80\%$$

**50. B:** To divide fractions, multiply the dividend (the first fraction) by the reciprocal (turn it upside down) of the divisor (the second fraction):

$$\frac{1}{6} \div \frac{3}{8} = \frac{1}{6} \times \frac{8}{3}$$
$$= \frac{8}{18}$$
$$= \frac{4}{9}$$

**51. B:** A die has a total of six sides, with a different number on each side. Three of these numbers are odd, and three are even. When throwing a die, the probability of rolling an odd number is 3 out of 6 or $\frac{3}{6}$. Reducing the fraction, yields a $\frac{1}{2}$ or 50% chance an odd number will be rolled.

**52. C:** To solve, rearrange the equation and simplify by combining like terms:

$$(2x - 3) + 2x = 9$$
$$2x - 3 + 2x = 9$$
$$4x - 3 = 9$$
$$4x = 12$$
$$x = 3$$

Copyright © Mometrix Media. You have been licensed one copy of this document for personal use only. Any other reproduction or redistribution is strictly prohibited. All rights reserved.
This content is provided for test preparation purposes only and does not imply an endorsement by Mometrix of any particular political, scientific, or religious point of view.

**53. B:** To convert a percent into a decimal, move the decimal two places to the left (or divide by 100).

**54. A:** To solve, find the perimeter (sum of all sides) of each garden:

Garden A: 6 ft by 8 ft rectangle, 6 ft + 8 ft + 6 ft + 8 ft = 28 ft

Garden B: 12 ft by 4 ft rectangle, 12 ft + 4 ft + 12 ft + 4 ft = 32 ft

Garden C: 16 ft by 3 ft rectangle, 16 ft + 3 ft + 16 ft + 3 ft = 38 ft

The smallest perimeter, Garden A, will require the least amount of fencing.

**55. A:** Exponents like square roots and powers of numbers come before addition, subtraction, multiplication, and division in the mathematical order of operations. Calculations inside of parentheses are done before those outside of them, not vice versa. Multiplication and division are done before addition and subtraction, not vice versa. Multiplication and division have the same rank in the order; and addition and subtraction have the same rank. With operations having the same rank, the rule is to go from left to right in the calculation. (A mnemonic for this order is PEMDAS, i.e., Parentheses, Exponents, Multiplication and Division, Addition and Subtraction. Various phrases have been invented as acrostics for these initials, e.g., "People Everywhere Made Decisions About Sums.")

**56. C:** A scalene triangle has three sides of different lengths, so side BC could not have a length of 5 feet or 6.3 feet.

**57. A:** Parentheses must be completed first. Here, $9 + 1 = 10$, so we can rewrite our expression as $100 \div 10 \times 2$. When dealing with multiplication and division, we must solve the operations in the order in which they appear, from left to right. Because division appears *before* multiplication, we must divide 100 by 10 before we multiply by 2. The quotient of 100 and 10 is 10, simplifying our expression to $10 \times 2$, or 20. Our final answer is 20.

**58. E:** When there are two operations within our parentheses, we must follow the order of operations *within* the parentheses as well. Because multiplication comes before addition, we must start by finding the product of 4 and 3, which is 12. Next, we add 10 and 12 to get 22. Finally, we can divide 22 by 2 to arrive at our final answer, 11.

**59. B:** If one inch is equal to 2.54 centimeters, then we can multiply any measurement in inches by 2.54 to convert it to centimeters. To multiply decimals, we simply ignore the decimal points and multiply using the traditional algorithm. When finished, we count the total number of digits after the decimal point in each of the factors. The total number of digits after the decimal points in the factors should match the number of digits after the decimal point in the product. Here, $254 \times 95 = 24130$. There are two digits after the decimal point in 2.54 and one digit after the decimal point in 9.5, for a total of three digits after the decimal points in the factors. That means we must insert a decimal point in our product so that there are three digits after the decimal point, like this: 24.130. The final zero does not affect the value of our answer so we can drop it and conclude that 9.5 inches is equivalent to 24.13 centimeters.

**60. C:** First, write an equation to represent the word problem. This scenario can be represented by the equation $48 + 36 - 50 = \_\_$. First, add the first two integers in the problem, 48 and 36. Write the problem vertically, making sure to line up the numbers according to place value. Start by adding the ones column to the right. Since $8 + 6 = 14$, write 4 in the ones place as part of the answer and

Copyright © Mometrix Media. You have been licensed one copy of this document for personal use only. Any other reproduction or redistribution is strictly prohibited. All rights reserved. This content is provided for test preparation purposes only and does not imply an endorsement by Mometrix of any particular political, scientific, or religious point of view.

carry the 1 over to the tens place column. Next, add the tens column. Since $1 + 4 + 3 = 8$, write 8 in the tens place as part of the answer. Therefore, $48 + 36 = 84$.

$$
\begin{array}{r} 48 \\ +36 \\ \hline \end{array}
\qquad
\begin{array}{r} {}^{1}\phantom{0} \\ 48 \\ +36 \\ \hline 4 \end{array}
\qquad
\begin{array}{r} {}^{1}\phantom{0} \\ 48 \\ +36 \\ \hline 84 \end{array}
$$

From here, subtract the next integer from the original problem, 50, from 84. Write the problem vertically, making sure to line up the numbers according to place value. Start by subtracting the ones column on the right. Since $4 - 0 = 4$, write 4 in the ones column as part of the answer. From here, move to the tens column and subtract. Since $8 - 5 = 3$, write 3 in the tens place as part of the answer. $48 + 36 - 50 = 34$. There were 34 cookies left over after the bake sale. Therefore, the correct answer is C.

$$
\begin{array}{r} 84 \\ -50 \\ \hline \end{array}
\qquad
\begin{array}{r} 84 \\ -50 \\ \hline 4 \end{array}
\qquad
\begin{array}{r} 84 \\ -50 \\ \hline 34 \end{array}
$$

# Writing

**61. B:** "Capitol" refers to the capitol building. The correct word here is "capital," which means an uppercase letter.

**62. B:** "Except" means "instead of." Here, the word should be "accept."

**63. B:** To be averse to something is to be reluctant to take part in it or to loath it:

*She was averse to going to the beach since she was afraid of the big waves.*

The word here should be "adverse," which means to have a bad reaction or the opposite reaction that was expected.

**64. C:** With two people, "between" is used. When speaking of more than two people, "among" is used.

**65. C:** The sentence is not complete until *said.* Instead of a period after *pool*, a comma should be used.

**66. B:** *Precedes* means "to come before" and is the appropriate choice in this sentence. *Proceeds* means "to carry on."

**67. A:** *Discrete* means "separate" or "disconnected." *Discreet* means "careful to avoid mistakes" and should be used in this sentence.

**68. D:** The sentence is correct as it is written.

**69. C:** *Disinterested* means that a person is impartial or shows no preference. *Uninterested* means "bored" or "showing no interest." *Uninterested* is the appropriate word to use in this sentence.

**70. A:** *Eminent* means "famous." *Imminent* means "soon." *Imminent* should be used here.

Copyright © Mometrix Media. You have been licensed one copy of this document for personal use only. Any other reproduction or redistribution is strictly prohibited. All rights reserved. This content is provided for test preparation purposes only and does not imply an endorsement by Mometrix of any particular political, scientific, or religious point of view.

**71. D:** The sentence has a change of time, offering information from 2010 and relating it to today. The time change necessitates a shift to present tense. The verb "alter" is in present tense, therefore no change is needed.

**72. D:** The conjunction, "but" is used to show a contrast in something that has already been stated. Here, we know that Stacey's feelings about eating differ from her feelings about cooking. If she enjoys eating, then she must detest cooking.

**73. C:** Fiona's smirk insinuates that she was pleased with the election results. This leads us to determine that the word "content," as used in this sentence, most closely illustrates Fiona's satisfaction.

**74. B:** Our answer has to be "through" as it is the only choice that provides the correct spelling and meaning for running past the defense.

**75. C:** "They're" is a contraction used in place of "they are." Because reading the sentence as "They are going to wash the dishes after they clear the table" makes sense, we can choose C as our answer.

**76. C:** This sentence is in passive voice. The subject of the sentence should be performing the action rather than having the action done to him/her/it.

**77. C:** The original sentence is a run-on sentence—two sentences joined together with no punctuation to separate them. A semi-colon must be added after "beautiful."

**78. D:** Quotation marks are closed when a speaker has finished what he or she is saying, not between sentences of dialogue.

**79. A:** The sentence is correct as it is written.

**80. D:** The original sentence is in passive voice and does not provide a subject. Answer choice D provides the best sentence structure.

**81. A:** A comma splice occurs when only a comma connects two independent clauses. Choice C can eliminate the comma splice by separating the thoughts into two complete sentences, by using a semicolon to separate the thoughts, or by rewriting the sentence as "Many athletes have personal trainers, because trainers help them stay fit in the off-season."

**82. C:** A run-on sentence contains two complete thoughts without appropriate punctuation separating them. Choice C contains two complete thoughts without any separation. We can rewrite it as, "I learned what marine biologists do, and I think I would like to pursue that career."

**83. A:** The word "definitely" is misspelled in this sentence as "definately."

**84. B:** Semicolons are used to separate two independent clauses in an effort to avoid run-on sentences. Here, the second clause depends on the first clause, making the semicolon incorrect.

**85. C:** The first part of a dinosaur name, known as the genus, must always be capitalized. We can correct this sentence by capitalizing "Titanosaur."

**86. A:** Among the options provided, only answer choice A provides a broad enough scope for the information that is provided in the paragraph, ranging from a discussion of dromedaries and camels to the qualities of the dromedary that make it popular. Answer choice B is just an opinion statement and does not necessarily introduce the topic of the paragraph. Answer choice C has little

Copyright © Mometrix Media. You have been licensed one copy of this document for personal use only. Any other reproduction or redistribution is strictly prohibited. All rights reserved.
This content is provided for test preparation purposes only and does not imply an endorsement by Mometrix of any particular political, scientific, or religious point of view.

relevance to the information in the paragraph, and answer choice D limits the scope only to the information about the usefulness of the animal. More importantly, though, answer choice D would make no sense when placed at the beginning of the sentence.

**87. B:** However interesting this information might be, it has no immediate relevance to the details of the paragraph. Had the student explained that dromedaries kick, while camels do not, this information might have gained context. As it is, it is largely superfluous to the topic of the paragraph.

**88. A:** Question 28 assumes that the test-taker has answer question 27 correctly. With the sentence "They are known to be stubborn and kick people" out of the way, it is easier to see the flow of the paragraph and the value of a transitional expression. In this case, "As a result" best fits the direction that the sentence takes in the paragraph: "Dromedaries are popular for carrying things on their backs. As a result, dromedaries are very useful to many people in Africa and Saudi Arabia."

**89. C:** The word Bedouin is very specific and also provides some idea of the people group for whom dromedary hair is useful. The other answer choices, while slightly better than the statement in the sentence (with the possible exception of answer choice D) are not as strong and descriptive as answer choice C.

**90. D:** A sentence in the passive tense reverses the subject and object roles, so that the subject of the sentence becomes the object or recipient of the action: "The book was given to Harold by Hanna," instead of "Hanna gave the book to Harold." Writing instructors strongly recommend avoiding the passive tense and utilizing the active tense instead. In the paragraph provided, the sentence would more comfortably read: "People in these places [or Bedouins living in this part of the world] often use the dromedary hair for tents and clothing."

Copyright © Mometrix Media. You have been licensed one copy of this document for personal use only. Any other reproduction or redistribution is strictly prohibited. All rights reserved. This content is provided for test preparation purposes only and does not imply an endorsement by Mometrix of any particular political, scientific, or religious point of view.

# Paraprofessional Practice Test #3

## Reading

*Refer to the following for questions 1 - 6:*

*Selection of* "The Gettysburg Address" *by Abraham Lincoln*

Four score and seven years ago our fathers brought forth, upon this continent, a new nation, conceived in Liberty, and dedicated to the proposition that all men are created equal.

Now we are engaged in a great civil war, testing whether that nation, or any nation so conceived, and so dedicated, can long endure. We are met here on a great battlefield of that war. We have come to dedicate a portion of it as a final resting place for those who here gave their lives that that nation might live. It is altogether fitting and proper that we should do this.

But in a larger sense we cannot dedicate - we cannot consecrate - we cannot hallow this ground. The brave men, living and dead, who struggled here, have consecrated it far above our poor power to add or detract. The world will little note, nor long remember, what we say here, but can never forget what they did here.

It is for us, the living, rather to be dedicated here to the unfinished work which they have, thus far, so nobly carried on. It is rather for us to be here dedicated to the great task remaining before us - that from these honored dead we take increased devotion to that cause for which they here gave the last full measure of devotion - that we here highly resolve that these dead shall not have died in vain; that this nation shall have a new birth of freedom; and that this government of the people, by the people, for the people, shall not perish from the earth.

**1. What is the main message of this speech?**
   a. Those who died in this battle honor this land we are dedicating today better than anyone else.
   b. As we honor those who died in this battle, we should move forward with renewed dedication to ensuring the nation our founding fathers created continues to function the way they intended.
   c. We need to put the regrets of the past aside, without remembering the sacrifices of those who gave their lives for our country.
   d. The war we are fighting is far from over, as evidenced by the number of lives lost in this battle.

**2. The phrase "the world will little note" means what?**
   a. The world will not soon forget.
   b. The world will record what we say here.
   c. The world will not pay much attention.
   d. The world will recall what we do with perfect accuracy.

Copyright © Mometrix Media. You have been licensed one copy of this document for personal use only. Any other reproduction or redistribution is strictly prohibited. All rights reserved. This content is provided for test preparation purposes only and does not imply an endorsement by Mometrix of any particular political, scientific, or religious point of view.

**3. There were nearly 100 years between the American Revolution and the Civil War. The speech connects ideas about these two conflicts by saying that the ideas of the Civil War**

    a. threaten those of the Revolution.

    b. are similar to those of the Revolution.

    c. are newer than those of the Revolution.

    d. are better than those of the Revolution.

**4. Why does Lincoln most likely talk about the past before he talks about the present?**

    a. to incite listeners of his message to protest

    b. to remember what has been lost in the past

    c. to establish context for his main message

    d. to try to get listeners to side with his position

**5. What is the following sentence addressing?**

*Now we are engaged in a great civil war, testing whether that nation, or any nation so conceived, and so dedicated, can long endure.*

    a. whether or not a nation based on ideas of freedom and equality can survive for any significant length of time

    b. whether or not the Union will be able to preserve the existing structure of the United States by preventing the Confederacy from seceding

    c. whether or not the Confederacy will be successful in seceding from the United States and surviving on its own

    d. whether or not Lincoln should continue dedicating troops to the war

**6. In paragraph 4, the word "vain" most nearly means:**

    a. decisive

    b. frivolous

    c. momentous

    d. practical

*Refer to the following for questions 7 - 12:*

George Washington Carver was always interested in plants. When he was a child, he was known as the "plant doctor." He had a secret garden where he grew all kinds of plants. People would ask him for advice when they had sick plants. Sometimes he'd take their plants to his garden and nurse them back to health.

Later, when he was teaching at Tuskegee Institute, he put his plant skills to good use. Many people in the South had been growing only cotton on their land. Cotton plants use most of the nutrients in the soil. (Nutrients provide nourishment

Copyright © Mometrix Media. You have been licensed one copy of this document for personal use only. Any other reproduction or redistribution is strictly prohibited. All rights reserved.
This content is provided for test preparation purposes only and does not imply an endorsement by Mometrix of any particular political, scientific, or religious point of view.

to plants.) So the soil becomes "worn out" after a few years. Eventually, cotton will no longer grow on this land.

This was especially bad for poor African American farmers, who relied on selling cotton to support themselves. Carver was dedicated to helping those farmers, so he came up with a plan.

Carver knew that certain plants put nutrients back into the soil. One of those plants is the peanut! Peanuts are also a source of protein.

Carver thought that if those farmers planted peanuts, the plants would help restore their soil, provide food for their animals, and provide protein for their families--quite a plant! In 1896 peanuts were not even recognized as a crop in the United States, but Carver would help change that.

Carver told farmers to rotate their crops: plant cotton one year, then the next year plant peanuts and other soil-restoring plants, like peas and sweet potatoes. It worked! The peanut plants grew and produced lots of peanuts. The plants added enough nutrients to the soil so cotton grew the next year.

**7. Why was George Washington Carver known as the "plant doctor"?**
a. He grew peanuts on sick soil.
b. He was a plant pathologist.
c. He could nurse sick plants back to health.
d. He knew plants could put nutrients back into the soil.

**8. How is this passage structured?**
a. cause and effect
b. problem and solution
c. chronological order
d. proposition and support

**9. According to the passage, what problem were cotton farmers facing?**
a. They needed food for their animals.
b. Peanuts were not recognized as a crop in the United States.
c. They were growing too much cotton.
d. The cotton had stripped the land of its nutrients.

**10. How did Carver resolve the farmers' problem?**
a. He told the farmers to rotate their crops.
b. He came up with a plan.
c. He invented the peanut.
d. He gave advice to farmers with sick plants.

**11. This passage is mainly about**
a. how George Washington Carver became a teacher at the Tuskegee Institute.
b. how George Washington Carver helped farmers improve their crop production.
c. why George Washington Carver studied plants.
d. how George Washington Carver made peanuts a recognized crop in the United States.

Copyright © Mometrix Media. You have been licensed one copy of this document for personal use only. Any other reproduction or redistribution is strictly prohibited. All rights reserved.
This content is provided for test preparation purposes only and does not imply an endorsement by Mometrix of any particular political, scientific, or religious point of view.

**12. According to this passage, "crop rotation" can be described as**

a. planting a soil depleting crop like cotton one year, and then planting a soil restoring plant like peanuts, the next year.
b. growing only one crop on the land year after year.
c. nursing sick plants back to health
d. studying plants at an institute.

*Refer to the following for questions 13 - 15:*

For lunch, she likes ham and cheese (torn into bites), yogurt, raisins, applesauce, peanut butter sandwiches in the fridge drawer, or any combo of these. She's not a huge eater. Help yourself too. Bread is on counter if you want to make a sandwich.

It's fine if you want to go somewhere, just leave us a note of where you are. Make sure she's buckled and drive carefully! Certain fast-food places are fun if they have playgrounds and are indoors. It's probably too hot for the playground, but whatever you want to do is fine. Take a sippy cup of water and a diaper wherever you go. There's some money here for you in case you decide to go out for lunch with her.

As for nap, try after lunch. She may not sleep, but try anyway. Read her a couple of books first, put cream on her mosquito bites (it's in the den on the buffet), then maybe rock in her chair. Give her a bottle of milk, and refill as needed, but don't let her drink more than $2\frac{1}{2}$ bottles of milk or she'll throw up. Turn on music in her room, leave her in her crib with a dry diaper and bottle to try to sleep. She likes a stuffed animal too. Try for 30–45 minutes. You may have to start the tape again. If she won't sleep, that's fine. We just call it "rest time" on those days that naps won't happen.

**13. To whom is this passage probably being written?**

a. A mother
b. A father
c. A babysitter
d. A nurse

**14. Which of the following details from the passage best supports the conclusion that the little girl is no older than three years old?**

a. For lunch, she likes ham and cheese (torn into bites), yogurt, raisins, applesauce, peanut butter sandwiches in the fridge drawer, or any combo of these.
b. It's fine if you want to go somewhere, just leave us a note of where you are.
c. As for nap, try after lunch. She may not sleep, but try anyway.
d. Turn on music in her room, leave her in her crib with a dry diaper and bottle to try to sleep.

**15. What is the first thing the instruction say to do to get the young girl to sleep?**

a. Give her a stuffed animal.
b. Read her a couple of books.
c. Rock her in her chair.
d. Play music in her room.

Copyright © Mometrix Media. You have been licensed one copy of this document for personal use only. Any other reproduction or redistribution is strictly prohibited. All rights reserved. This content is provided for test preparation purposes only and does not imply an endorsement by Mometrix of any particular political, scientific, or religious point of view.

*Refer to the following for question 16:*

One component of good story writing is showing and not telling. Showing can be achieved through descriptions of settings, events, and characters' appearances, words, and actions to show what is happening in the story rather than directly telling information as though the story is being narrated by the writer:

*It was a cold and rainy morning. The first track meet of the season was scheduled for that day.*

Instead of telling the reader information this way, it's often better to show the information. For example, the characters can show information through their words and actions:

*Marissa shivered as she stood next to Jessica on the side walk. "Why didn't I bring my coat?" Marissa whined. "It's going to feel like this on the bus, too! And why does it have to rain the morning of our first track meet?"*

*"I know. I hope it isn't cancelled. I really wanted to see how my meet times were looking. I want to move up to a varsity slot so bad." Jessica huddled close to Marissa and craned her neck to look down the street. She glanced at her watch and frowned.*

By having the two characters show the information, the reader has jumped right into the story and learned about the characters in the first few sentences.

**16. What is the purpose of the italicized text in the passage?**
   a.  To distinguish dialogue from the rest of the passage
   b.  To distinguish the examples of narrative writing from the rest of the passage
   c.  To format a title of a major work
   d.  To show the characters' inner thoughts

*Refer to the following for questions 17 - 22:*

*Forest Manager:* Salvage logging is removing dead or dying forest stands that are left behind by a fire or disease. This practice has been used for several decades. These dead or dying trees become fuel that feeds future fires. The best way to lower the risk of forest fires is to remove the dead timber from the forest floor. Salvage logging followed by replanting ensures the reestablishment of desirable tree species.

For example, planting conifers accelerates the return of fire resistant forests. Harvesting timber helps forests by reducing fuel load, thinning the forest stands, and relieving competition between trees. Burned landscapes leave black surfaces and ash layers that have very high soil temperatures. These high soil temperatures can kill many plant species. Logging mixes the soil. So, this lowers surface temperatures to more normal levels. The shade from material that is left behind by logging also helps to lower surface temperatures. After an area has been salvage logged, seedlings in the area start to grow almost immediately. However, this regrowth can take several years in areas that are not managed well.

*Ecology professor:* Salvage logging moves material like small, broken branches to the forest floor. These pieces can become fuel for more fires. The removal of larger, less flammable

Copyright © Mometrix Media. You have been licensed one copy of this document for personal use only. Any other reproduction or redistribution is strictly prohibited. All rights reserved. This content is provided for test preparation purposes only and does not imply an endorsement by Mometrix of any particular political, scientific, or religious point of view.

trees leaves behind small limbs and increases the risk of forest fires. In unmanaged areas, these pieces are found more commonly on the tops of trees where they are unavailable to fires. Logging destroys old forests that are more resistant to wildfires. So, this creates younger forests that are more open to fires. In old forests, branches of bigger trees are higher above the floor where fires may not reach.

Replanting after wildfires creates monoculture plantations where only a single crop is planted. This monoculture allows less biological diversity. Also, it allows plants to be less resistant to disease. So, this increases the chance of fire. Salvage logging also upsets natural forest regrowth by killing most of the seedlings that grow after a wildfire. It breaks up the soil and increases erosion. Also, it removes most of the shade that is needed for young seedlings to grow.

**17. According to the professor, why are the broken branches in unmanaged forests preferable to those in logged areas for wildfire resistance?**
   a. They are left on the forest floor and bring nutrients to the soil.
   b. They are left on the forest floor and serve as fuel for fires.
   c. They are left on the tops of trees where fires cannot reach.
   d. They are spread more evenly across the forest floor.

**18. Which of the following is NOT a supporting detail for the forest manager's argument?**
   a. "This practice has been used for decades."
   b. "Logging mixes the soil. So, this lowers surface temperatures to more normal levels."
   c. "After an area has been salvage logged, seedlings in the area start to grow almost immediately."
   d. "Salvage logging is removing dead or dying forest stands that are left behind by a fire or disease."

**19. A study compared two plots of land that were managed differently after a fire. Plot A was salvage logged. Plot B was left unmanaged. After a second fire, they compared two plant groups between Plots A and B. They found that both plant groups burned worse in Plot A than in Plot B. Whose viewpoint do these results support?**
   a. only the manager
   b. only the professor
   c. both the manager and professor
   d. neither the manager nor the professor

**20. What is the main idea of the forest manager's argument?**
   a. Salvage logging is helpful because it removes dead or dying timber from the forest floor. So, this lowers the risk of future fires.
   b. Salvage logging is helpful because it has been practiced for many decades.
   c. Salvage logging is harmful because it raises soil temperatures above normal levels. So, this threatens the health of plant species.
   d. Salvage logging is helpful because it gives shade for seedlings to grow after a wildfire.

**21. Which of the following statements does NOT agree with the professor?**
   a. In younger forests, small branches are closer to the forest floor and more available for fires.
   b. Old growth forests have taller trees, so branches are high up and fires cannot reach them.
   c. Monoculture forests have less biological diversity and fewer disease-resistant trees.
   d. Larger trees are common in old growth forests and serve as the main fuel source for fires.

Copyright © Mometrix Media. You have been licensed one copy of this document for personal use only. Any other reproduction or redistribution is strictly prohibited. All rights reserved.
This content is provided for test preparation purposes only and does not imply an endorsement by Mometrix of any particular political, scientific, or religious point of view.

**22. Whose viewpoints would be proven by a future study looking at the spreading out and regrowth of seedlings for many years after a wildfire in managed and unmanaged forests?**

    a.  only the manager
    b.  only the professor
    c.  both the manager and professor
    d.  neither the manager nor professor

*Refer to the following for questions 23 - 24:*

> The earliest form of the alphabet that we use today is usually attributed to the Phoenician people. The Phoenicians were ancient traders who lived and worked along the Mediterranean Sea. Their extensive connections with people outside Phoenicia, and particularly in Greece, led them to standardize their writing with an alphabet.
>
> Many historians know, however, that the Phoenicians were not necessarily the first to develop the idea of an alphabet. The people of ancient Egypt created hieroglyphics, or pictures that represented different letters in their language. Additionally, writing has been found in the areas of Palestine and Sinai, and it indicates another early script that pre-dates the Phoenicians that might have influenced their alphabet.

**23. The teacher asks the students to describe the main point of the passage they have just read. Assuming the following answer choices come from the students, which is most correct?**

    a.  To explain that people before the Phoenicians had been using alphabets
    b.  To show that the Phoenicians stole their alphabet from earlier people
    c.  To describe the way that the alphabet has developed over the years
    d.  To explain that the trading the Phoenicians did affected their need for an alphabet

**24. The teacher wants students to be able to understand the meaning of words based on the context of the passage. How might the teacher ask for students to deduce the meaning of the word "script"?**

    a.  Ask students to consider words that have a similar structure
    b.  Ask students to think about the main topic of the passage and how this word might relate to it
    c.  Ask students to focus on the shift in thought that occurs between the first paragraph and the second
    d.  Ask students to split the word into individual sounds and deduce its meaning phonetically

*Refer to the following for question 25:*

> A teacher is concerned about three of her students. While they are enthusiastic about writing, they do not always recognize letters, confusing b, d, and p, or e and o. They do, however, know which sounds go with certain letters when they are orally drilled. When they write, they appear to be attempting letter–sound associations.
>
> "Now I'm writing *M*," the teacher heard one boy say as he scripted a large *N* in the upper right corner of his paper. He studied it for a moment and added, "Nope, it needs another leg." The student then wrote an *I* beside the *N*. "There," he said. "Now you are an *M*. I can write the word, 'man,' because now I have *M*." The child then moved to the lower left corner of the paper. "M-A-N," he said to himself, slowly pronouncing each

Copyright © Mometrix Media. You have been licensed one copy of this document for personal use only. Any other reproduction or redistribution is strictly prohibited. All rights reserved.
This content is provided for test preparation purposes only and does not imply an endorsement by Mometrix of any particular political, scientific, or religious point of view.

sound. "I already have that *M*. Here is where the rest of the word goes." He turned the paper sideways and wrote *N*.

The second child sang to herself as she gripped the crayon and scribbled lines here and there on her paper. Some of the lines resembled letters, but few actually were. Others were scribbles. As she "wrote," she seemed to be making up a story and seemed to believe she was writing the story down.

The third child didn't vocalize at all while he worked. He gripped the paper and carefully wrote the same letter over and over and over. Sometimes the letter was large, sometimes tiny. He turned the paper in every direction so that sometimes the letter was sideways or upside down. Sometimes he flipped it backward. "What are you writing?" the teacher asked him. "My name," the child told her. The teacher then realized the letter was, indeed, the first letter of his name. She gently told him he had done a fine job of writing the first letter of his name. Did he want her to help him write the rest of it? "Nope," he cheerfully told her, "it's all here." He pointed at one of the letters and "read" his full name. He pointed at another letter and again seemed to believe it represented all the sounds of his name.

**25. The kindergarten teacher isn't certain if these children are exhibiting signs of a reading disability or other special needs. What should the teacher do?**
   a. Nothing. These children are simply at an early stage in the reading/writing process.
   b. Nothing. She doesn't want to have to tell the parents that their children are sub-par in terms of intelligence. They are perfectly nice children and can contribute to society in other ways. She resolves to give them extra attention in other areas to help them build confidence.
   c. She should recommend that the parents take the children to be tested for a number of reading disorders, including dyslexia.
   d. She should arrange a meeting between herself, the school psychologist, and the reading specialist to discuss the matter and resolve it using a three-pronged approach.

**26. The purpose of corrective feedback is:**
   a. To provide students with methods for explaining to the teacher or classmates what a passage was about
   b. To correct an error in reading a student has made, specifically clarifying where and how the error was made so that the student can avoid similar errors in the future
   c. To provide a mental framework that will help the student correctly organize new information
   d. To remind students that error is essential in order to truly understand and that it is not something to be ashamed of

**27. Dr. Jenks is working with a group of high school students. They are about to read a science book about fossils. Before they begin, she writes the words stromatolites, fossiliferous, and Eocene on the board. She explains the meaning of each word. These words are examples of:**
   a. Academic words
   b. Alliteration
   c. Content-specific words
   d. Ionization

Copyright © Mometrix Media. You have been licensed one copy of this document for personal use only. Any other reproduction or redistribution is strictly prohibited. All rights reserved. This content is provided for test preparation purposes only and does not imply an endorsement by Mometrix of any particular political, scientific, or religious point of view.

**28. Which of the following BEST explains the importance prior knowledge brings to the act of reading?**

    a. Prior knowledge is information the student gets through researching a topic prior to reading the text. A student who is well-prepared through such research is better able to decode a text and retain its meaning.

    b. Prior knowledge is knowledge the student brings from previous life or learning experiences to the act of reading. It is not possible for a student to fully comprehend new knowledge without first integrating it with prior knowledge.

    c. Prior knowledge is predictive. It motivates the student to look for contextual clues in the reading and predict what is likely to happen next.

    d. Prior knowledge is not important to any degree to the act of reading, because every text is self-contained and therefore seamless. Prior knowledge is irrelevant in this application.

**29. Of the three tiers of words, the MOST important words for direct instruction are:**

    a. Tier-one words

    b. Common words

    c. Tier-two words

    d. Words with Latin roots

**30. A reading teacher is assessing a fifth grader to determine her reading level. Timed at a minute, the student reads with 93% accuracy. She misreads an average of seven words out of 100. What is her reading level?**

    a. She is reading at a Frustration level

    b. She is reading at an Excellence level

    c. She is reading at an Instructional level

    d. She is reading at an Independent level

Copyright © Mometrix Media. You have been licensed one copy of this document for personal use only. Any other reproduction or redistribution is strictly prohibited. All rights reserved.
This content is provided for test preparation purposes only and does not imply an endorsement by Mometrix of any particular political, scientific, or religious point of view.

# Mathematics

*Refer to the following for question 31:*

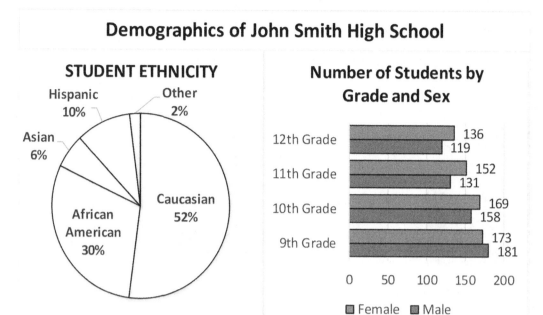

**Demographics of John Smith High School**

**STUDENT ETHNICITY**

Hispanic 10%
Other 2%
Asian 6%
Caucasian 52%
African American 30%

**Number of Students by Grade and Sex**

12th Grade — 136 / 119
11th Grade — 152 / 131
10th Grade — 169 / 158
9th Grade — 173 / 181

0   50   100   150   200

■ Female   ■ Male

**31. Which of these is the greatest quantity?**

   a. The average number of male students in the 11th and 12th grades
   b. The number of Hispanic students at the school
   c. The difference in the number of male and female students at the school
   d. The difference in the number of 9th and 12th grade students at the school

**32. Jerry and his four friends step onto an elevator with a weight limit of 900 pounds. Jerry weighs 256 pounds. What would the average weight of each of his friends have to be so that the elevator's weight limit is not exceeded?**

   a. 128 pounds
   b. 161 pounds
   c. 175 pounds
   d. 200 pounds

Copyright © Mometrix Media. You have been licensed one copy of this document for personal use only. Any other reproduction or redistribution is strictly prohibited. All rights reserved.
This content is provided for test preparation purposes only and does not imply an endorsement by Mometrix of any particular political, scientific, or religious point of view.

33. Two piano instructors compared notes on how long their students had been taking lessons. The charts below compare the two sets of data. Note: the instructors did not count the students who had been taking lessons for less than a year.

Which of the following is a true statement for these data?

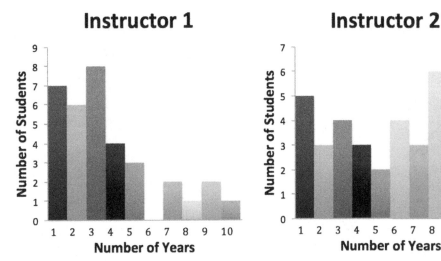

a. The median number of years a student has been taking lessons from Instructor 1 is five less than the median number for Instructor 2.

b. On average, students of Instructor 2 have been taking lessons for two years longer than students of Instructor 1 (round to the nearest whole number).

c. The mode number of years is higher for Instructor 1 than for Instructor 2.

d. The median number of years for Instructor 1 is greater than the mean.

34. A television that regularly costs $400 is offered today at a price reflecting 20% off. When a customer shows a Super Saver card, another 5% is deducted at the register. What does a customer with a Super Saver card pay for the television today?

a. $380

b. $375

c. $300

d. $304

35. What is the simplest form of $\frac{3}{8} \times \frac{3}{8}$?

a. $\frac{3}{4}$

b. $\frac{6}{8}$

c. $\frac{9}{64}$

d. $1\frac{1}{8}$

Copyright © Mometrix Media. You have been licensed one copy of this document for personal use only. Any other reproduction or redistribution is strictly prohibited. All rights reserved. This content is provided for test preparation purposes only and does not imply an endorsement by Mometrix of any particular political, scientific, or religious point of view.

36. Most students can expect to see their grade point averages increase by 8.2% after taking Mrs. Wilson's review class. George's average prior to the class is a 72. What can he expect it to be after taking the class?

    a.  74
    b.  75
    c.  78
    d.  80

37. Which of the following values is closest to the diameter of a circle with an area of 314 square inches?

    a.  20 inches
    b.  10 inches
    c.  100 inches
    d.  31.4 inches

38. Mary's basketball team is losing tonight's game 42-15. Mary scores a three-point shot. How many more three-point shots will someone on her team have to score in order to tie the game?

    a.  5
    b.  6
    c.  7
    d.  8

39. Which of the following fractions is $0.18$ expressed in its lowest terms?

    a.  $\frac{9}{50}$
    b.  $\frac{18}{100}$
    c.  $\frac{9}{5}$
    d.  $\frac{18}{10}$

40. A can of soda costs 89 cents. A six-pack of the same soda costs $4.50. What is the savings per can when a person buys a six-pack instead of a single can?

    a.  5 cents
    b.  14 cents
    c.  28 cents
    d.  84 cents

41. Which of the following is the largest number?

    a.  0.004
    b.  0.03
    c.  0.2
    d.  0.400

42. If 1" on a map represents 25 ft, how many yards apart are two points if the distance between the points on the map is 12"?

    a.  600
    b.  300
    c.  100
    d.  12

Copyright © Mometrix Media. You have been licensed one copy of this document for personal use only. Any other reproduction or redistribution is strictly prohibited. All rights reserved.
This content is provided for test preparation purposes only and does not imply an endorsement by Mometrix of any particular political, scientific, or religious point of view.

**43.** What is the probability of spinning a 2 on the first try on the spinner below?

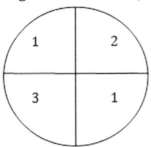

a. $\frac{1}{2}$

b. $\frac{1}{3}$

c. $\frac{1}{4}$

d. $\frac{2}{4}$

**44.** Which of the following best describes an isosceles triangle?

    a. A triangle with no sides of equal measurement and one obtuse angle

    b. A triangle with three sides of equal measurement

    c. A triangle with two sides of equal measurement and at least two acute angles

    d. A triangle with one right angle and two non-congruent acute angles

**45.** Molly borrows $12,000 from a friend. She agrees to make monthly payments to repay the loan in two years along with an additional 10% for interest. What are her monthly payments?

    a. $465

    b. $550

    c. $650

    d. $1,010

**46.** Calculate the value of $x$ in the following equation: $13 + x = 130$.

    a. 10

    b. 117

    c. 143

    d. $\frac{13}{130}$

**47.** Find the area of the rectangle.

    a. 50 ft$^2$

    b. 75 ft$^2$

    c. 100 ft$^2$

    d. 150 ft$^2$

Copyright © Mometrix Media. You have been licensed one copy of this document for personal use only. Any other reproduction or redistribution is strictly prohibited. All rights reserved.
This content is provided for test preparation purposes only and does not imply an endorsement by Mometrix of any particular political, scientific, or religious point of view.

48. 30% of a woman's paycheck goes to health insurance, 15% goes to savings, and 32% goes to taxes. After these deductions, what percentage of the check is remaining?

    a. 19%
    b. 23%
    c. 38%
    d. It cannot be determined from the information given.

49. Which of the following choices expresses $\frac{17}{20}$ as a percentage?

    a. 85%
    b. 80%
    c. 63%
    d. 32%

50. Simplify $(8 \times 10^3) + (1 \times 10^3)$.

    a. $8 \times 10^3$
    b. $8 \times 10^6$
    c. $9 \times 10^3$
    d. $9 \times 10^6$

51. Solve for $x$: $(2x - 6) + 4x = 24$

    a. 0
    b. -3
    c. 5
    d. 3

52. A father measures his daughter's height regularly. She is presently 3'8" tall. If she grows 5" in the next year, how much more will she need to grow to be as tall as her 5'1" mother?

    a. 8 inches
    b. 10 inches
    c. 11 inches
    d. 12 inches

53. On Day 1, a driver averages 60 miles per hour for 15 hours of a 2,000-mile car trip. If he maintains this average speed and duration on Day 2, how far will he be from his destination at the end of the day?

    a. 200 miles
    b. 400 miles
    c. 500 miles
    d. 900 miles

54. A woman buys a $125,000 home by putting down 22% of the price and financing the rest. How much of the price has she financed?

    a. $103,000
    b. $97,500
    c. $78,000
    d. $47,500

Copyright © Mometrix Media. You have been licensed one copy of this document for personal use only. Any other reproduction or redistribution is strictly prohibited. All rights reserved.
This content is provided for test preparation purposes only and does not imply an endorsement by Mometrix of any particular political, scientific, or religious point of view.

55. Solve for $y$ in the following equation if $x = -\frac{1}{2}$

$$y = x + 4$$

a. $y = 2$
b. $y = 3\frac{1}{2}$
c. $y = -3\frac{1}{2}$
d. $y = -4\frac{1}{2}$

56. It costs Jack $7/month for 50 incoming or outgoing text messages and $0.15 for each text message over that. Jack sent 35 text messages this month and received 48. What will his bill be for this month?

a. $4.20
b. $4.95
c. $11.95
d. $14.20

57. Put the following decimal numbers in order from least to greatest:

$$-1.32 \qquad 0.014 \qquad 0.31 \qquad 0.308 \qquad -0.42 \qquad 0$$

a. $-0.42, -1.32, 0.31, 0.308, 0, 0.014$
b. $0.014, 0, 0.308, 0.31, -1.32, -0.42$
c. $-1.32, -0.42, 0, 0.014, 0.308, 0.31$
d. $0, -1.32, -0.42, 0.31, 0.308, 0.014$

58. You are putting a new rug in your bedroom. The length of the rug can be no longer than 15 feet. When you are purchasing the rug at the store, the measure on it states that it is 5 meters long. Will the length of the rug fit in your bedroom? Why or why not?

a. No, because the length of the rug is 5 yd, and the length of the bedroom is 4.57 yd
b. Yes, because the length of the rug is 4.57 yd, and the length of the bedroom is 5 yd
c. No, because the length of the rug is 5.47 yd, and the length of the bedroom is 5 yd
d. Yes, because the length of the rug is 5 yd, and the length of the bedroom is 5 yd

59. What is the value of $y$ in the following equation?

$$4y + 16 = 60$$

a. 4
b. 11
c. 12
d. 19

60. Simplify: $3(x - 12) - 11 - 3(x - 4)$.

a. $6x - 35$
b. $6x + 35$
c. $6x + 37$
d. $-35$

Copyright © Mometrix Media. You have been licensed one copy of this document for personal use only. Any other reproduction or redistribution is strictly prohibited. All rights reserved.
This content is provided for test preparation purposes only and does not imply an endorsement by Mometrix of any particular political, scientific, or religious point of view.

## Writing

*Refer to the following for questions 61 - 70:*

In the following section, there are underlined parts to each sentence. One of the underlined parts is incorrectly written. Choose the letter that corresponds with the incorrect underlined part of the sentence. If the entire sentence is correct, choose D for NO ERROR.

61. Marcy <u>believed</u> her parents <u>had ought</u> to have told her she was still <u>grounded</u>
    A                              B                                                        C
for the weekend.
    a. believed
    b. had ought
    c. grounded
    d. No error

62. Fourteen people <u>hanged</u> <u>seven heavy pictures</u> on the <u>interior walls</u>
    A                    B                              C
of the lecture room.
    a. hanged
    b. seven heavy pictures
    c. interior walls
    d. No error

63. The <u>entire class</u> <u>disagrees with</u> <u>Dr. Olson's views about</u>
    A                  B                    C
the future of the mining industry in our area.
    a. entire class
    b. disagrees with
    c. Dr. Olson' s views about
    d. No error

64. I <u>was shocked</u> to realize I <u>had run</u> much <u>further than</u> my two running buddies. <u>No error</u>
    A                          B              C                                      D
    a. was shocked
    b. had run
    c. further than
    d. No error

65. Brianna <u>says</u> <u>less children</u> enrolled in our camp program this summer <u>than</u>
    A              B                                                      C
last summer.
    a. Brianna says
    b. less children
    c. than
    d. No error

Copyright © Mometrix Media. You have been licensed one copy of this document for personal use only. Any other reproduction or redistribution is strictly prohibited. All rights reserved.
This content is provided for test preparation purposes only and does not imply an endorsement by Mometrix of any particular political, scientific, or religious point of view.

**66. The mayor** <u>stopped by</u> **and gave** <u>our principal</u> **a compliment** <u>about the</u>
<br>              A                          B                                   C
**interesting landscaping in front of the school.**

    a. stopped by
    b. our principal
    c. about the
    d. No error

**67.** <u>Our itinerary</u> **shows that we will be at the** <u>capitol building</u> **all day** <u>on Thursday.</u>
<br>              A                                         B                    C

    a. Our itinerary
    b. capitol building
    c. on Thursday
    d. No error

**68.** <u>That area</u> **with the** <u>huge sign</u> **will be** <u>the sight</u> **of our new cultural center.**
<br>          A                        B               C

    a. That area
    b. huge sign
    c. the sight
    d. No error

**69. The** <u>teaching staff</u> **included** <u>two aids</u> **who helped out in any classroom** <u>whenever</u>
<br>               A                     B                         C
**they were needed.**

    a. teaching staff
    b. two aids
    c. whenever
    d. No error

**70. If you** <u>put</u> **your backpack by the door, you will** <u>insure</u> **you won't forget to** <u>take it</u> **home.**
<br>             A                                        B                     C

    a. put
    b. insure
    c. take it
    d. No error

*Refer to the following for questions 71 - 80:*

The upcoming sentences are given to measure your ability to correctly and efficiently convey meaning. When you are choosing your answer, remember that the sentences should utilize conventional written English, including grammar, word selection, conventional sentence structure, and punctuation.

There will be either a section or a complete sentence underlined. Beneath the sentence there are different choices. The first choice (A) will be the same as the underlined section. The remaining choices give different substitutions that could replace the underlined section.

Choose the letter that corresponds with the choice that best conveys the meaning of the original sentence. If the original wording is the best, select answer choice A. If not, choose one of the other choices. The correct answer is the one that keeps the original meaning and makes the sentence the

Copyright © Mometrix Media. You have been licensed one copy of this document for personal use only. Any other reproduction or redistribution is strictly prohibited. All rights reserved.
This content is provided for test preparation purposes only and does not imply an endorsement by Mometrix of any particular political, scientific, or religious point of view.

most effective. Make sure your choice makes the sentence understandable without being cumbersome or unclear.

**71. All of the revisions need to be <u>approved by Ellen Jackson and I.</u>**
a. approved by Ellen Jackson and I.
b. approved by Ellen Jackson and myself.
c. approved by myself and Ellen Jackson.
d. approved by Ellen Jackson and me.

**72. <u>It was he who wrote the email.</u>**
a. It was he who wrote the email.
b. It was him who wrote the email.
c. It was himself who wrote the email.
d. It was he who had written the email.

**73. The <u>scout leader, who had been standing in the road, were</u> hurt in the collision.**
a. scout leader. who had been standing in the road, were
b. scout leader who had been standing in the road were
c. scout leader who had been standing in the road were
d. scout leader, who had been standing in the road, was

**74. <u>Using foreign coins is not permitted in our store.</u>**
a. Using foreign coins is not permitted in our store.
b. Using foreign coins are not permitted in our store.
c. To be using foreign coins is not permitted in our store.
d. Using foreign coins, they are not permitted in our store.

**75. <u>The turtle trapped himself inside our screened-in porch.</u>**
a. The turtle trapped himself inside our screened-in porch.
b. The turtle had trapped himself inside our screened-in porch.
c. The turtle trapped him- or herself inside our screened-in porch.
d. The turtle trapped itself inside our screened-in porch.

**76. <u>"Does your salad taste okay," she asked?</u>**
a. "Does your salad taste okay," she asked?
b. "Does your salad taste okay," She asked?
c. "Does your salad taste okay?" she asked.
d. "Does your salad taste okay." She asked.

**77. Most students missed <u>Spanish, Math, and Science today.</u>**
a. Spanish, Math, and Science today.
b. Spanish, math, and Science today.
c. Spanish, Math, and science today.
d. Spanish, math, and science today.

**78. She passed <u>the salt and pepper, the butter, and the ketchup to</u> the other table.**
a. the salt and pepper, the butter, and the ketchup to
b. the salt, and pepper, the butter, and the ketchup to
c. the salt and pepper, the butter and the ketchup to
d. the salt and pepper, the butter, and the ketchup, to

403

Copyright © Mometrix Media. You have been licensed one copy of this document for personal use only. Any other reproduction or redistribution is strictly prohibited. All rights reserved. This content is provided for test preparation purposes only and does not imply an endorsement by Mometrix of any particular political, scientific, or religious point of view.

79. **Now that both of my brothers are married, I have <u>two sister's-in-law.</u>**

    a. two sister's-in-law.
    b. two sisters-in-law.
    c. two sisters-in-laws.
    d. two sister-in-laws.

80. **When questioned, most students <u>said the Math test</u> was too difficult.**

    a. said the Math test
    b. say the Math test
    c. said the math test
    d. said that the Math test

81. **"The forecast called for rain, so James packed his umbrella" is an example of which type of organizational writing?**

    a. Compare and contrast
    b. Sequential
    c. Spatial
    d. Problem and solution

82. **"We adopted a dog. A giant Rhodesian Ridgeback." This contains _____.**

    a. a fragment
    b. a capitalization error
    c. an error in word usage
    d. a spelling error

83. **Select the word or phrase that corrects an error in the underlined portion of the text. If no correction is needed, select "no correction needed."**

    The game was <u>canceled</u> and removed from the <u>calendar</u>.

    a. cancilled
    b. calender
    c. calandar
    d. no correction needed

84. **Identify the correction needed in the sentence.**

    The lotion worked so well, it left my skin feeling like a childs.

    a. "worked" should be "work"
    b. omit the comma
    c. "feeling" should be "feel"
    d. "childs" should be "child's"

85. **Select the word or phrase that corrects an error in one of the underlined portions of the text. If no correction is needed, select "no correction needed."**

    In the <u>Spring</u>, we plan to visit the <u>Midwest</u>, most specifically <u>South Dakota</u>.

    a. spring
    b. midwest
    c. south dakota
    d. no correction needed

Copyright © Mometrix Media. You have been licensed one copy of this document for personal use only. Any other reproduction or redistribution is strictly prohibited. All rights reserved.
This content is provided for test preparation purposes only and does not imply an endorsement by Mometrix of any particular political, scientific, or religious point of view.

*Refer to the following for questions 86 - 90:*

*In each of the questions below, there are four underlined selections. Next to each underlined portion is a letter that corresponds to an answer choice on the answer sheet, (A), (B), (C), or (D). Select the letter that is next to the error. This may be an error in spelling, punctuation, word choice, and grammatical construction. Note that each sentence contains only one error.*

**86. Although William Wordsworth is usually <u>remember</u> [A] as the first major Romantic poet, some <u>scholars</u> [B] look to William Blake as one of the <u>most</u> [C] important early figures in <u>Romanticism</u> [D].**

    a. remember
    b. scholars
    c. most
    d. Romanticism

**87. William Blake <u>was</u> [A] certainly unique for his time; an engraver by trade, Blake <u>is</u> [B] known for having <u>illustrated</u> [C] a number of different copies for <u>much</u> [D] of his poems.**

    a. was
    b. is
    c. illustrated
    d. much

**88. <u>One</u> [A] of Blake's most creative works is the <u>collection</u> [B] of poetry known as *Visions of the Daughters of Albion*, which still <u>mystify</u> [C] literary <u>scholars</u> [D] to this day.**

    a. One
    b. collection
    c. mystify
    d. scholars

**89. <u>More</u> [A] famous, perhaps, is Blake's popular poem *"The Tiger."* While often <u>anthologized</u> [B] among children's poetry, *"The Tiger"* <u>contained</u> [C] fairly complex <u>themes</u> [D].**

    a. More
    b. anthologized
    c. contained
    d. themes

**90. Though often viewed as highly <u>abstruse</u> [A] in his own time, William Blake has <u>became</u> [B] increasingly popular during the twentieth century and was <u>particularly</u> [C] popular with poets and musicians of the <u>1950s and 1960s</u> [D].**

    a. abstruse
    b. became
    c. particularly
    d. 1950s and 1960s

Copyright © Mometrix Media. You have been licensed one copy of this document for personal use only. Any other reproduction or redistribution is strictly prohibited. All rights reserved.
This content is provided for test preparation purposes only and does not imply an endorsement by Mometrix of any particular political, scientific, or religious point of view.

# Answer Key and Explanations

## Reading

**1. B:** Lincoln begins this speech by discussing the founding of the U.S. and what the original purpose of the U.S. was. Then, he goes on to talk about how the U.S. is currently engaged in a war intended to fracture the nation, and he states that the battle being discussed was one large tragedy that came out of the war. Next, Lincoln says that his speech and even the memorial itself can't truly honor those who died, and that it's up to those who survived to continue the fight to ensure the nation does not break apart. Answer B best communicates this message.

**2. C:** The sentence in which this phrase is found is: The world will little note, nor long remember, what we say here, but can never forget what they did here. In this context, the phrase "the world will little note" means that no one outside of those in attendance or possibly those outside the country will pay attention to the speech or the ceremony. This eliminates all of the answer choices except C.

**3. A:** The ideals of the revolution are addressed in the first paragraph: Four score and seven years ago our fathers brought forth, upon this continent, a new nation, conceived in Liberty, and dedicated to the proposition that all men are created equal. This introduces the point that Lincoln is trying to make about the battle at hand and the war as a whole: the Civil War is threatening the ideas upon which the nation was created.

**4. C:** There is a comparison between the ideas of the Revolution and the Civil War in this speech. To facilitate understanding of this comparison, Lincoln has to set the stage by telling his audience about the past event he is referencing. This establishes the context of his message.

**5. A:** This line directly references the idea in the previous paragraph, which is that the U.S. is a nation that was created to ensure liberty and equality. This sentence talks about how the Civil War is testing whether or not a nation that was created to ensure liberty and equality can really survive.

**6. B:** When President Lincoln argues that the people who died at Gettysburg did not die in vain, he asserts that their passing was not frivolous or unimportant or meaningless.

**7. C:** The first paragraph gives the information to correctly answer this question.

**8. B:** This passage in arranged by problem and solution. The author states a problem that the cotton farmers were having: "Eventually, cotton will no longer grow on this land." The author then presents a solution: "Carver told farmers to rotate their crops: plant cotton one year, then the next year plant peanuts and other soil-restoring plants, like peas and sweet potatoes. It worked! The peanut plants grew and produced lots of peanuts."

**9. D:** The second paragraph discusses the problem the cotton farmers were facing. The cotton crops had depleted the nutrients from the soil.

**10. A:** The last paragraph answers this question. "Carver told farmers to rotate their crops: plant cotton one year, then the next year plant peanuts and other soil-restoring plants, like peas and sweet potatoes. It worked! The peanut plants grew and produced lots of peanuts."

Copyright © Mometrix Media. You have been licensed one copy of this document for personal use only. Any other reproduction or redistribution is strictly prohibited. All rights reserved. This content is provided for test preparation purposes only and does not imply an endorsement by Mometrix of any particular political, scientific, or religious point of view.

**11. B:** Answer choice (B) best summarizes what this passage is mainly about. Choices (A), and (C) are not even discussed in this passage. Paragraph 5 does discuss choice (D), but it is not the main focus of the passage.

**12. A:** Answer choice (A) best defines "crop rotation." The passage gives the definition in the last paragraph.

**13. C:** The directions in the passage are clearly instructions for how to take care of a little girl, so this is probably written for a babysitter. A mother or father would most likely not need this information written down in such detail. A nurse would need more information about how to medically care for the child, rather than information about how to entertain the child or settle her down for a nap.

**14. D:** The need for a dry diaper and a bottle are the best indications that the child is no older than three years old. Many children, but by no means all, are potty trained by the time they are four years old. Also, most children no longer drink from bottles by the age of four. Of the details presented, this makes choice D the best answer to the question. Choice A does not necessarily support the conclusion that the little girl is no older than three years old; children of any age could enjoy the foods that are listed. Choice B does not support the conclusion either, as the babysitter would still probably need to leave a note regardless of the child's age. Children of any age may also nap, so choice C is not the best answer.

**15. B:** The first instruction for getting the young girl to take a nap is to read her a couple of books. The passage says "read her a couple of books first." The signal word *first* shows that reading is the first thing the babysitter should try. After this instruction, the passage says "then maybe rock her in her chair," so choice C is the second thing the babysitter should try. Choice D is a later step in these instructions. Choice A is not an instruction given in the passage, as the passage simply states that the girl "likes a stuffed animal."

**16. B:** The italicized paragraphs are examples of narrative writing used to exemplify the difference between showing and telling. There is description and dialogue included in the italicized paragraphs, so choice A is incorrect. No major works are named in this passage, and the characters' inner thoughts are not explicitly narrated, so choices C and D are incorrect.

**17. C:** The professor argues that small, woody material is left on the tops of trees and is less likely to be reached by fire.

**18. D:** Choice D is not a supporting detail because it is a definition of salvage logging. The other choices are supporting details of the Forest Manager's argument.

**19. B:** Plot A was salvage logged and burned worse than the unmanaged plot (Plot B). This study supports the professor's view that salvage logging increases the risk and severity of fire.

**20. A:** The question asks which option is the chief argument regarding fire prevention. Choices B and D are not helpful for fire prevention. Choice C is incorrect because logging decreases soil temperature.

**21. D:** The professor says the larger trees in old growth forests are more resistant to fire than smaller, younger trees. Answers A, B, and C all agree with the professor.

Copyright © Mometrix Media. You have been licensed one copy of this document for personal use only. Any other reproduction or redistribution is strictly prohibited. All rights reserved. This content is provided for test preparation purposes only and does not imply an endorsement by Mometrix of any particular political, scientific, or religious point of view.

**22. C:** A study looking at the regrowth of seedlings in logged and unmanaged forests would help to explain and/or prove both arguments. The reason is that the manager and the professor talk on the importance of seedling growth after a fire.

**23. A:** At the beginning of the second paragraph, the authors says, "Many historians know, however, that the Phoenicians were not necessarily the first to develop the idea of an alphabet." This would indicate that the author is using a compare-and-contrast method of organization by introducing the idea of the Phoenician alphabet but then explaining that the Phoenicians were not necessary the first to use the alphabet.

**24. B:** In this case, the best way to assist students in understanding the meaning of the word "script" is to consider the context of the word. In the last sentence, the author states, "Additionally, writing has been found in the areas of Palestine and Sinai, and it indicates another early script that pre-dates the Phoenicians that might have influenced their alphabet." The teacher can remind students that the topic of the passage is alphabets and also point the students' attention to the use of the word "writing" early in this sentence. This should help students in deciphering the meaning of the word "script."

**25. A:** The teacher should not do anything because these children are simply at an early stage in the reading/writing process. When emergent readers become aware of the connections between letters and sounds, and between reading and writing, they want to practice the skills they see proficient readers use. While a proficient writer knows that letters are grouped into words and that words are constructed into sentences that move from left to right and from the top of the page to the bottom, an emergent reader/writer knows only that letters contain sounds that other people can read. It is necessary for children to pass through early stages in which they scribble-write and pretend they are scripting letters, which leads to a stage in which they actually do write the initial letter of a word all over the page. Next, the emergent reader/writer will write the initial letter of many of the words that belong in the sentence and will write them sequentially.

**26. B:** To correct an error in reading a student has made, specifically clarifying where and how the error was made so that the student can avoid similar errors in the future. A reading teacher offers corrective feedback to a student in order to explain why a particular error in reading is, in fact, an error. Corrective feedback is specific; it locates where and how the student went astray so that similar errors can be avoided in future reading.

**27. C:** Content-specific words. Because these words are specific to paleontology, it's unlikely the students know their meanings. Without understanding what these words mean, the students would not be able to understand the content of the passage they were about to read.

**28. B:** Prior knowledge is knowledge the student brings from previous life or learning experiences to the act of reading. It is not possible for a student to fully comprehend new knowledge without first integrating it with prior knowledge. Prior knowledge, which rises from experience and previous learning, provides a framework by which new knowledge gained from the act of reading can be integrated. Every act of reading enriches a student's well of prior knowledge and increases that student's future ability to comprehend more fully any new knowledge acquired through reading.

**29. C:** Tier-two words. Tier-two words are words that are used with high frequency across a variety of disciplines or words with multiple meanings. They are characteristic of mature language users. Knowing these words is crucial to attaining an acceptable level of reading comprehension and communication skills.

Copyright © Mometrix Media. You have been licensed one copy of this document for personal use only. Any other reproduction or redistribution is strictly prohibited. All rights reserved. This content is provided for test preparation purposes only and does not imply an endorsement by Mometrix of any particular political, scientific, or religious point of view.

**30. C:** She is reading at an Instructional level. In one minute, a student who misreads one or less than one word per twenty words, or with 95%–100% accuracy, is at an Independent reading level. A student who misreads one or less than one word per ten words, or with 90%–95% accuracy, is at an Instructional level. A student misreading more than one word out of ten, or with less than 90% accuracy, is at a Frustration level.

# Mathematics

**31. A:** The average number of male students in the 11th and 12th grades is 125 (calculated as $\frac{131 + 119}{2}$). The number of Hispanic students at the school is 10% of 1219, which is 122 students (rounded up from 121.9). The difference in the number of male and female students at the school is $630 - 589 = 41$, and the difference in the number of 9th and 12th grade students at the school is $354 - 255 = 99$.

**32. B:** To solve, first subtract Jerry's weight from the total permitted: $900 \text{ lb} - 256 \text{ lb} = 644 \text{ lb}$. Divide this by 4 to get the average weight: $\frac{644 \text{ lb}}{4} = 166 \text{ lb}$

**33. B:** Instructor 1 has 34 students, so the median number of years is the average of the 17th and 18th student. These students have both been taking lessons for 3 years, so the median is 3. Instructor 2 has 38 students, so the median number of years is the average of the 19th and 20th student. These students have both been taking lessons for 6 years, so the median is 6. Since $6 - 3 = 3$, the median number of years a student has been taking lessons from Instructor 1 is three less than the median number for Instructor 2.

To find the mean, find the sum of the number of years and divide by the number of students. If the frequency of students who have been taking lessons for one year is 7, the number 1 is added seven times ($1 \times 7$), if frequency for two years is 6, the number 2 is added six times ($2 \times 6$), and so on. Divide the sum of these products by the number of students to find the mean. For Instructor 1, the mean is 3.65 years, which rounds up to 4 years. For Instructor 2, the mean is 5.63, which rounds up to 6 years. So, the students of Instructor 2 have been taking lessons for two years longer than the students of Instructor 1, on average.

The mode is the number of years for which the frequency is the highest. For Instructor 1, the mode is 3 years, and for Instructor 2, the mode is 8 years.

As seen above, the median for Instructor 1 is 3 and the mean is 3.65, so the median is less than the mean.

**34. D:** To solve, first subtract the 20% discount ($\$400 \times 0.20 = \$80$) from the original price:

$$\$400 - \$80 = \$320$$

Then take the 5% discount ($\$320 \times 0.05 = \$16$) from the total:

$$\$320 - \$16 = \$304$$

**35. C:** Multiply the numerators by one another to get the new numerator ($3 \times 3 = 9$), and the denominators by one another to get the new denominator ($8 \times 8 = 64$). The result ($\frac{9}{16}$) is in simplest form.

Copyright © Mometrix Media. You have been licensed one copy of this document for personal use only. Any other reproduction or redistribution is strictly prohibited. All rights reserved. This content is provided for test preparation purposes only and does not imply an endorsement by Mometrix of any particular political, scientific, or religious point of view.

**36. C:** Multiply George's grade (72) by 8.2% to get 5.904. Add 5.904 to 72 to get 77.904, which rounds to 78.

**37. A:** The area $A$ of a circle is given by $A = \pi \times r^2$, where $r$ is the radius. Since $\pi$ is approximately 3.14, we can solve for $r = \sqrt{\dfrac{A}{\pi}} = \sqrt{\dfrac{314 \text{ inches}^2}{3.14}} = \sqrt{100 \text{ inches}^2} = 10$ inches. Now, the diameter $d$ is twice the radius, or $2 \times 10$ inches $= 20$ inches.

**38. D:** To solve, first add Mary's shot to the score: 42-18. Subtract the figures to see how many points still need to be scored: $42 - 18 = 24$. Divide by three, since three points are attained with each shot: $24 \div 3 = 8$.

**39. A:** The number 0.18 as a fraction is $\dfrac{18}{100}$. This can be reduced, by dividing the numerator and denominator by two, to get $\dfrac{9}{50}$.

**40. B:** To solve, divide the 6-pack price by 6 to get the single can price: $\dfrac{\$4.50}{6} = \$0.75$. Subtract $0.75 from $0.89 to find the difference between the prices: $\$0.89 - \$0.75 = \$0.14$

**41. D:** A is a number in the thousandths; B is a number in the hundredths; C, D, and E are in tenths. Four-tenths is the largest of these choices.

**42. C:** If 1" represents 25 feet, 12" represents 300 ft, which is the same as 100 yards.

**43. C:** There are four, equally possible places the spinner may land. The digit 2 is only present in one space, so the probability of landing there is 1 out of 4 or $\dfrac{1}{4}$.

**44. C:** Triangles can be classified as scalene, isosceles, or equilateral. Scalene triangles have no equal side measurements and no equal angle measurements. Isosceles triangles have two sides of equal measurement and two angles of equal measurement. Equilateral triangles have three sides of equal measurement and three angles of equal measurement. A right triangle is isosceles only if its two acute angles are congruent.

**45. B:** Multiply $12,000 by 10% to get $1,200. Add these figures together to find out the total amount. Molly will repay $13,200. Divide this by 24 months to find out the monthly payments:

$$\frac{\$13,200}{24} = \$550$$

**46. B:** Rearrange the equation to isolate the variable:

$$13 + x = 130$$
$$x = 130 - 13$$
$$x = 117$$

**47. D:** Recall that, for a rectangle, area ($A$) is length ($l$) times width ($w$):

$$A = l \times w$$
$$= 10 \text{ ft} \times 15 \text{ ft}$$
$$= 150 \text{ ft}^2$$

Copyright © Mometrix Media. You have been licensed one copy of this document for personal use only. Any other reproduction or redistribution is strictly prohibited. All rights reserved. This content is provided for test preparation purposes only and does not imply an endorsement by Mometrix of any particular political, scientific, or religious point of view.

**48. B:** To solve, first find what percent of the paycheck is taken out: 30% + 15% + 32% = 77%. Subtract this number from 100% to find out the amount of her paycheck that is remaining: 23%.

**49. A:** Divide 17 by 20 to get 0.85. Convert 0.85 into a percentage by multiplying by 100%, essentially moving the decimal two places to the right.

**50. C:** Because both expressions share the factor $10^3$, we can simply factor and add the ones places. $(8 \times 10^3) + (1 \times 10^3) = (1 + 8)(10^3) = 9 \times 10^3$.

**51. C:** To solve, isolate $x$ by rearranging the equation:

$$
\begin{aligned}
2x - 6 + 4x &= 24 \\
6x - 6 &= 24 \\
6x &= 30 \\
x &= 5
\end{aligned}
$$

**52. D:** To solve, add the increase in her measurement to her present height:

$$3' \, 8'' + 5'' = 4' \, 1''$$

Now subtract that new height from her mother's height to find out how much more she will have to grow:

$$5' \, 1'' - 4' \, 1'' = 1' = 12''$$

**53. A:** Multiply 60 mph by 15 hours to find out how far he drove on Day 1:

$$60 \text{ mph} \times 15 \text{ hr} = 900 \text{ mi}$$

If he does the same on Day 2, he will have driven a total of 1,800 miles. He will have 200 miles left to go on a 2,000-mile trip.

**54. B:** To solve, first figure out how much money she put down:

$$\$125,000 \times 22\% = \$27,500$$

Subtract the down payment from the original price:

$$\$125,000 - \$27,500 = \$97,500$$

**55. B:** To solve, place the value of $x$ into the equation:

$$
\begin{aligned}
y &= -\frac{1}{2} + 4 \\
y &= 3\frac{1}{2}
\end{aligned}
$$

**56. C:** To solve, first figure out how many messages he had this month: 35 + 48 = 83. Subtract this from the amount he gets each month: 83 − 50 = 33. Multiply these extra messages by 15 cents: 33 × $0.15 = $4.95. Add the monthly fee: $4.95 + $7.00 = $11.95.

Copyright © Mometrix Media. You have been licensed one copy of this document for personal use only. Any other reproduction or redistribution is strictly prohibited. All rights reserved.
This content is provided for test preparation purposes only and does not imply an endorsement by Mometrix of any particular political, scientific, or religious point of view.

**57. C:** To order these numbers, first order the negative numbers from least to greatest. Remember, the largest negative number is the smallest.

$$-1.32, -0.42$$

Then, 0 will separate the negative numbers from the positive numbers.

Finally, order the positive numbers from least to greatest.

$$0.014, 0.308, 0.31$$

The numbers ordered from least to greatest are: $-1.32, -0.42, 0, 0.014, 0.308, 0.31$.

**58. C:** A meter is a metric unit of measure. A yard is a standard unit of measure. We can convert the given length of the rug to a standard unit of measure to see if its length will fit in the bedroom. Use the unit conversion factor of 1 yd $\approx$ 0.914 m to convert meters to yards.

To begin, convert the length of the rug given in meters to yards by multiplying it by the conversion factor.

$$\frac{5\,\cancel{m}}{1} \times \frac{1\text{ yd}}{0.914\,\cancel{m}} = 5.47 \text{ yd}$$

So, the rug is 5.47 yards.

Now, convert the length of the bedroom from feet to yards. There are 3 feet in 1 yard, so:

$$\frac{15\,\cancel{ft}}{1} \times \frac{1\text{ yd}}{3\,\cancel{ft}} = 5 \text{ yd}$$

Therefore, the length of the bedroom is 5 yards. Since the length of the rug is greater than the length of the bedroom, it will not fit in the bedroom.

**59. B:** To solve, isolate $y$ on one side of the equation:

$$4y = 60 - 16$$
$$4y = 44$$
$$y = 11$$

**60. D:** To solve, first multiply it out:

$$3(x - 12) - 11 - 3(x - 4) = 3x - 36 - 11 - 3x + 12$$

Positive and negative $3x$ cancel each other out, leaving:

$$-36 - 11 + 12 = -35$$

# Writing

**61. B:** *Had ought* is considered to be bad grammar. *Ought* should be used alone in this sentence.

**62. A:** *Hanged* is a word used to describe a method of execution. *Hung* is the past tense of *hang* and should be used here.

Copyright © Mometrix Media. You have been licensed one copy of this document for personal use only. Any other reproduction or redistribution is strictly prohibited. All rights reserved.
This content is provided for test preparation purposes only and does not imply an endorsement by Mometrix of any particular political, scientific, or religious point of view.

**63. D:** The sentence is correct as written.

**64. C:** *Further* refers to the degree or extent of something, while *farther* refers to physical distance.

**65. B:** *Less* is a comparative adjective used with things that cannot be counted or are talked about as a single unit, as in *less afraid* or *less gasoline*. *Fewer* is used when talking about people or about objects and things that are considered in units, as in *fewer students* or *fewer apples*.

**66. D:** The sentence is correct as it is written.

**67. D:** The sentence is correct as it is written.

**68. C:** *Sight* may mean "something that is seen." *Site* refers to a location and is the correct word to use in this sentence.

**69. B:** *Aid* is a verb meaning "to help." *Aide* means "assistant" and is the appropriate answer choice.

**70. B:** The correct word is *ensure*—to make certain by stressing an action taken beforehand.

**71. D:** The objective case, Ellen Jackson and me, is used here. To test whether *I* or *me* is the correct form to use, remove Ellen Jackson: "All of the revisions need to be approved by *me*."

**72. A:** The sentence is correct as it is written.

**73. D:** The subject of the sentence is one person. The singular verb was must be used in order for the subject to agree with the verb.

**74. A:** The sentence is correct as it is written.

**75. D:** The gender of most animals in the wild is not known, so *it* is used.

**76. C:** The question is this part of the sentence: "Does your salad taste okay?" The question mark is laced at the end after "okay." A comma is not added after a question mark that is part of dialogue.

**77. D:** When written in a sentence, only school subjects that are proper nouns are capitalized.

**78. A:** The items are part of a list, with salt and pepper considered to be one unit and the other two items as separate units.

**79. B:** *Sisters-in-law* is the plural of *sister-in-law*.

**80. C:** Only those subjects that are proper nouns (e.g., English, Spanish) are capitalized.

**81. D:** The sentence explains that James packed an umbrella to solve the problem of getting wet in the rain. This type of organizational structure is known as problem and solution.

**82. A:** A sentence must contain a subject and a predicate (or verb). "A giant Rhodesian Ridgeback" is a fragment because it is missing a verb.

**83. D:** The sentence contains no errors, so no correction is needed.

**84. D:** In this sentence, "child's" is being used to show possession of the skin, necessitating the need for an apostrophe.

**85. A:** Seasons are never capitalized, so we can correct this sentence by *not* capitalizing "spring."

Copyright © Mometrix Media. You have been licensed one copy of this document for personal use only. Any other reproduction or redistribution is strictly prohibited. All rights reserved.
This content is provided for test preparation purposes only and does not imply an endorsement by Mometrix of any particular political, scientific, or religious point of view.

**86. A:** The wording should be: "Although William Wordsworth is usually remembered as the first major Romantic poet…"

**87. D:** The use of much is awkward with of his poems and should be revised to read: "…different copies for many of his poems."

**88. C:** Due to the use of the singular form which the correct verb should be mystifies: "…which still mystifies literary scholars to this day."

**89. C:** The verb form is inaccurate within the context of the sentence. Because the rest of the sentence indicates a present tense – and because the qualities of the poem remain current – the verb contained should also be adjusted to present tense: "While often anthologized among children's poetry, 'The Tiger' contains fairly complex themes."

**90. B:** The correct verb form with the word has (or have) is become: "…William Blake has become increasingly popular…"

Copyright © Mometrix Media. You have been licensed one copy of this document for personal use only. Any other reproduction or redistribution is strictly prohibited. All rights reserved. This content is provided for test preparation purposes only and does not imply an endorsement by Mometrix of any particular political, scientific, or religious point of view.

# How to Overcome Test Anxiety

Just the thought of taking a test is enough to make most people a little nervous. A test is an important event that can have a long-term impact on your future, so it's important to take it seriously and it's natural to feel anxious about performing well. But just because anxiety is normal, that doesn't mean that it's helpful in test taking, or that you should simply accept it as part of your life. Anxiety can have a variety of effects. These effects can be mild, like making you feel slightly nervous, or severe, like blocking your ability to focus or remember even a simple detail.

If you experience test anxiety—whether severe or mild—it's important to know how to beat it. To discover this, first you need to understand what causes test anxiety.

## Causes of Test Anxiety

While we often think of anxiety as an uncontrollable emotional state, it can actually be caused by simple, practical things. One of the most common causes of test anxiety is that a person does not feel adequately prepared for their test. This feeling can be the result of many different issues such as poor study habits or lack of organization, but the most common culprit is time management. Starting to study too late, failing to organize your study time to cover all of the material, or being distracted while you study will mean that you're not well prepared for the test. This may lead to cramming the night before, which will cause you to be physically and mentally exhausted for the test. Poor time management also contributes to feelings of stress, fear, and hopelessness as you realize you are not well prepared but don't know what to do about it.

Other times, test anxiety is not related to your preparation for the test but comes from unresolved fear. This may be a past failure on a test, or poor performance on tests in general. It may come from comparing yourself to others who seem to be performing better or from the stress of living up to expectations. Anxiety may be driven by fears of the future—how failure on this test would affect your educational and career goals. These fears are often completely irrational, but they can still negatively impact your test performance.

> **Review Video: <u>3 Reasons You Have Test Anxiety</u>**
> Visit mometrix.com/academy and enter code: 428468

Copyright © Mometrix Media. You have been licensed one copy of this document for personal use only. Any other reproduction or redistribution is strictly prohibited. All rights reserved.
This content is provided for test preparation purposes only and does not imply an endorsement by Mometrix of any particular political, scientific, or religious point of view.

# Elements of Test Anxiety

As mentioned earlier, test anxiety is considered to be an emotional state, but it has physical and mental components as well. Sometimes you may not even realize that you are suffering from test anxiety until you notice the physical symptoms. These can include trembling hands, rapid heartbeat, sweating, nausea, and tense muscles. Extreme anxiety may lead to fainting or vomiting. Obviously, any of these symptoms can have a negative impact on testing. It is important to recognize them as soon as they begin to occur so that you can address the problem before it damages your performance.

**Review Video: 3 Ways to Tell You Have Test Anxiety**
Visit mometrix.com/academy and enter code: 927847

The mental components of test anxiety include trouble focusing and inability to remember learned information. During a test, your mind is on high alert, which can help you recall information and stay focused for an extended period of time. However, anxiety interferes with your mind's natural processes, causing you to blank out, even on the questions you know well. The strain of testing during anxiety makes it difficult to stay focused, especially on a test that may take several hours. Extreme anxiety can take a huge mental toll, making it difficult not only to recall test information but even to understand the test questions or pull your thoughts together.

**Review Video: How Test Anxiety Affects Memory**
Visit mometrix.com/academy and enter code: 609003

# Effects of Test Anxiety

Test anxiety is like a disease—if left untreated, it will get progressively worse. Anxiety leads to poor performance, and this reinforces the feelings of fear and failure, which in turn lead to poor performances on subsequent tests. It can grow from a mild nervousness to a crippling condition. If allowed to progress, test anxiety can have a big impact on your schooling, and consequently on your future.

Test anxiety can spread to other parts of your life. Anxiety on tests can become anxiety in any stressful situation, and blanking on a test can turn into panicking in a job situation. But fortunately, you don't have to let anxiety rule your testing and determine your grades. There are a number of relatively simple steps you can take to move past anxiety and function normally on a test and in the rest of life.

**Review Video: How Test Anxiety Impacts Your Grades**
Visit mometrix.com/academy and enter code: 939819

Copyright © Mometrix Media. You have been licensed one copy of this document for personal use only. Any other reproduction or redistribution is strictly prohibited. All rights reserved. This content is provided for test preparation purposes only and does not imply an endorsement by Mometrix of any particular political, scientific, or religious point of view.

# Physical Steps for Beating Test Anxiety

While test anxiety is a serious problem, the good news is that it can be overcome. It doesn't have to control your ability to think and remember information. While it may take time, you can begin taking steps today to beat anxiety.

Just as your first hint that you may be struggling with anxiety comes from the physical symptoms, the first step to treating it is also physical. Rest is crucial for having a clear, strong mind. If you are tired, it is much easier to give in to anxiety. But if you establish good sleep habits, your body and mind will be ready to perform optimally, without the strain of exhaustion. Additionally, sleeping well helps you to retain information better, so you're more likely to recall the answers when you see the test questions.

Getting good sleep means more than going to bed on time. It's important to allow your brain time to relax. Take study breaks from time to time so it doesn't get overworked, and don't study right before bed. Take time to rest your mind before trying to rest your body, or you may find it difficult to fall asleep.

> **Review Video: The Importance of Sleep for Your Brain**
> Visit mometrix.com/academy and enter code: 319338

Along with sleep, other aspects of physical health are important in preparing for a test. Good nutrition is vital for good brain function. Sugary foods and drinks may give a burst of energy but this burst is followed by a crash, both physically and emotionally. Instead, fuel your body with protein and vitamin-rich foods.

Also, drink plenty of water. Dehydration can lead to headaches and exhaustion, especially if your brain is already under stress from the rigors of the test. Particularly if your test is a long one, drink water during the breaks. And if possible, take an energy-boosting snack to eat between sections.

> **Review Video: How Diet Can Affect your Mood**
> Visit mometrix.com/academy and enter code: 624317

Along with sleep and diet, a third important part of physical health is exercise. Maintaining a steady workout schedule is helpful, but even taking 5-minute study breaks to walk can help get your blood pumping faster and clear your head. Exercise also releases endorphins, which contribute to a positive feeling and can help combat test anxiety.

When you nurture your physical health, you are also contributing to your mental health. If your body is healthy, your mind is much more likely to be healthy as well. So take time to rest, nourish your body with healthy food and water, and get moving as much as possible. Taking these physical steps will make you stronger and more able to take the mental steps necessary to overcome test anxiety.

Copyright © Mometrix Media. You have been licensed one copy of this document for personal use only. Any other reproduction or redistribution is strictly prohibited. All rights reserved. This content is provided for test preparation purposes only and does not imply an endorsement by Mometrix of any particular political, scientific, or religious point of view.

# Mental Steps for Beating Test Anxiety

Working on the mental side of test anxiety can be more challenging, but as with the physical side, there are clear steps you can take to overcome it. As mentioned earlier, test anxiety often stems from lack of preparation, so the obvious solution is to prepare for the test. Effective studying may be the most important weapon you have for beating test anxiety, but you can and should employ several other mental tools to combat fear.

First, boost your confidence by reminding yourself of past success—tests or projects that you aced. If you're putting as much effort into preparing for this test as you did for those, there's no reason you should expect to fail here. Work hard to prepare; then trust your preparation.

Second, surround yourself with encouraging people. It can be helpful to find a study group, but be sure that the people you're around will encourage a positive attitude. If you spend time with others who are anxious or cynical, this will only contribute to your own anxiety. Look for others who are motivated to study hard from a desire to succeed, not from a fear of failure.

Third, reward yourself. A test is physically and mentally tiring, even without anxiety, and it can be helpful to have something to look forward to. Plan an activity following the test, regardless of the outcome, such as going to a movie or getting ice cream.

When you are taking the test, if you find yourself beginning to feel anxious, remind yourself that you know the material. Visualize successfully completing the test. Then take a few deep, relaxing breaths and return to it. Work through the questions carefully but with confidence, knowing that you are capable of succeeding.

Developing a healthy mental approach to test taking will also aid in other areas of life. Test anxiety affects more than just the actual test—it can be damaging to your mental health and even contribute to depression. It's important to beat test anxiety before it becomes a problem for more than testing.

> **Review Video: <u>Test Anxiety and Depression</u>**
> Visit mometrix.com/academy and enter code: 904704

Copyright © Mometrix Media. You have been licensed one copy of this document for personal use only. Any other reproduction or redistribution is strictly prohibited. All rights reserved. This content is provided for test preparation purposes only and does not imply an endorsement by Mometrix of any particular political, scientific, or religious point of view.

# Study Strategy

Being prepared for the test is necessary to combat anxiety, but what does being prepared look like? You may study for hours on end and still not feel prepared. What you need is a strategy for test prep. The next few pages outline our recommended steps to help you plan out and conquer the challenge of preparation.

## STEP 1: SCOPE OUT THE TEST

Learn everything you can about the format (multiple choice, essay, etc.) and what will be on the test. Gather any study materials, course outlines, or sample exams that may be available. Not only will this help you to prepare, but knowing what to expect can help to alleviate test anxiety.

## STEP 2: MAP OUT THE MATERIAL

Look through the textbook or study guide and make note of how many chapters or sections it has. Then divide these over the time you have. For example, if a book has 15 chapters and you have five days to study, you need to cover three chapters each day. Even better, if you have the time, leave an extra day at the end for overall review after you have gone through the material in depth.

If time is limited, you may need to prioritize the material. Look through it and make note of which sections you think you already have a good grasp on, and which need review. While you are studying, skim quickly through the familiar sections and take more time on the challenging parts. Write out your plan so you don't get lost as you go. Having a written plan also helps you feel more in control of the study, so anxiety is less likely to arise from feeling overwhelmed at the amount to cover.

## STEP 3: GATHER YOUR TOOLS

Decide what study method works best for you. Do you prefer to highlight in the book as you study and then go back over the highlighted portions? Or do you type out notes of the important information? Or is it helpful to make flashcards that you can carry with you? Assemble the pens, index cards, highlighters, post-it notes, and any other materials you may need so you won't be distracted by getting up to find things while you study.

If you're having a hard time retaining the information or organizing your notes, experiment with different methods. For example, try color-coding by subject with colored pens, highlighters, or post-it notes. If you learn better by hearing, try recording yourself reading your notes so you can listen while in the car, working out, or simply sitting at your desk. Ask a friend to quiz you from your flashcards, or try teaching someone the material to solidify it in your mind.

## STEP 4: CREATE YOUR ENVIRONMENT

It's important to avoid distractions while you study. This includes both the obvious distractions like visitors and the subtle distractions like an uncomfortable chair (or a too-comfortable couch that makes you want to fall asleep). Set up the best study environment possible: good lighting and a comfortable work area. If background music helps you focus, you may want to turn it on, but otherwise keep the room quiet. If you are using a computer to take notes, be sure you don't have any other windows open, especially applications like social media, games, or anything else that could distract you. Silence your phone and turn off notifications. Be sure to keep water close by so you stay hydrated while you study (but avoid unhealthy drinks and snacks).

Also, take into account the best time of day to study. Are you freshest first thing in the morning? Try to set aside some time then to work through the material. Is your mind clearer in the afternoon or evening? Schedule your study session then. Another method is to study at the same time of day that

Copyright © Mometrix Media. You have been licensed one copy of this document for personal use only. Any other reproduction or redistribution is strictly prohibited. All rights reserved. This content is provided for test preparation purposes only and does not imply an endorsement by Mometrix of any particular political, scientific, or religious point of view.

you will take the test, so that your brain gets used to working on the material at that time and will be ready to focus at test time.

## STEP 5: STUDY!

Once you have done all the study preparation, it's time to settle into the actual studying. Sit down, take a few moments to settle your mind so you can focus, and begin to follow your study plan. Don't give in to distractions or let yourself procrastinate. This is your time to prepare so you'll be ready to fearlessly approach the test. Make the most of the time and stay focused.

Of course, you don't want to burn out. If you study too long you may find that you're not retaining the information very well. Take regular study breaks. For example, taking five minutes out of every hour to walk briskly, breathing deeply and swinging your arms, can help your mind stay fresh.

As you get to the end of each chapter or section, it's a good idea to do a quick review. Remind yourself of what you learned and work on any difficult parts. When you feel that you've mastered the material, move on to the next part. At the end of your study session, briefly skim through your notes again.

But while review is helpful, cramming last minute is NOT. If at all possible, work ahead so that you won't need to fit all your study into the last day. Cramming overloads your brain with more information than it can process and retain, and your tired mind may struggle to recall even previously learned information when it is overwhelmed with last-minute study. Also, the urgent nature of cramming and the stress placed on your brain contribute to anxiety. You'll be more likely to go to the test feeling unprepared and having trouble thinking clearly.

So don't cram, and don't stay up late before the test, even just to review your notes at a leisurely pace. Your brain needs rest more than it needs to go over the information again. In fact, plan to finish your studies by noon or early afternoon the day before the test. Give your brain the rest of the day to relax or focus on other things, and get a good night's sleep. Then you will be fresh for the test and better able to recall what you've studied.

## STEP 6: TAKE A PRACTICE TEST

Many courses offer sample tests, either online or in the study materials. This is an excellent resource to check whether you have mastered the material, as well as to prepare for the test format and environment.

Check the test format ahead of time: the number of questions, the type (multiple choice, free response, etc.), and the time limit. Then create a plan for working through them. For example, if you have 30 minutes to take a 60-question test, your limit is 30 seconds per question. Spend less time on the questions you know well so that you can take more time on the difficult ones.

If you have time to take several practice tests, take the first one open book, with no time limit. Work through the questions at your own pace and make sure you fully understand them. Gradually work up to taking a test under test conditions: sit at a desk with all study materials put away and set a timer. Pace yourself to make sure you finish the test with time to spare and go back to check your answers if you have time.

After each test, check your answers. On the questions you missed, be sure you understand why you missed them. Did you misread the question (tests can use tricky wording)? Did you forget the information? Or was it something you hadn't learned? Go back and study any shaky areas that the practice tests reveal.

Copyright © Mometrix Media. You have been licensed one copy of this document for personal use only. Any other reproduction or redistribution is strictly prohibited. All rights reserved.
This content is provided for test preparation purposes only and does not imply an endorsement by Mometrix of any particular political, scientific, or religious point of view.

Taking these tests not only helps with your grade, but also aids in combating test anxiety. If you're already used to the test conditions, you're less likely to worry about it, and working through tests until you're scoring well gives you a confidence boost. Go through the practice tests until you feel comfortable, and then you can go into the test knowing that you're ready for it.

## Test Tips

On test day, you should be confident, knowing that you've prepared well and are ready to answer the questions. But aside from preparation, there are several test day strategies you can employ to maximize your performance.

First, as stated before, get a good night's sleep the night before the test (and for several nights before that, if possible). Go into the test with a fresh, alert mind rather than staying up late to study.

Try not to change too much about your normal routine on the day of the test. It's important to eat a nutritious breakfast, but if you normally don't eat breakfast at all, consider eating just a protein bar. If you're a coffee drinker, go ahead and have your normal coffee. Just make sure you time it so that the caffeine doesn't wear off right in the middle of your test. Avoid sugary beverages, and drink enough water to stay hydrated but not so much that you need a restroom break 10 minutes into the test. If your test isn't first thing in the morning, consider going for a walk or doing a light workout before the test to get your blood flowing.

Allow yourself enough time to get ready, and leave for the test with plenty of time to spare so you won't have the anxiety of scrambling to arrive in time. Another reason to be early is to select a good seat. It's helpful to sit away from doors and windows, which can be distracting. Find a good seat, get out your supplies, and settle your mind before the test begins.

When the test begins, start by going over the instructions carefully, even if you already know what to expect. Make sure you avoid any careless mistakes by following the directions.

Then begin working through the questions, pacing yourself as you've practiced. If you're not sure on an answer, don't spend too much time on it, and don't let it shake your confidence. Either skip it and come back later, or eliminate as many wrong answers as possible and guess among the remaining ones. Don't dwell on these questions as you continue—put them out of your mind and focus on what lies ahead.

Be sure to read all of the answer choices, even if you're sure the first one is the right answer. Sometimes you'll find a better one if you keep reading. But don't second-guess yourself if you do immediately know the answer. Your gut instinct is usually right. Don't let test anxiety rob you of the information you know.

If you have time at the end of the test (and if the test format allows), go back and review your answers. Be cautious about changing any, since your first instinct tends to be correct, but make sure you didn't misread any of the questions or accidentally mark the wrong answer choice. Look over any you skipped and make an educated guess.

At the end, leave the test feeling confident. You've done your best, so don't waste time worrying about your performance or wishing you could change anything. Instead, celebrate the successful

Copyright © Mometrix Media. You have been licensed one copy of this document for personal use only. Any other reproduction or redistribution is strictly prohibited. All rights reserved.
This content is provided for test preparation purposes only and does not imply an endorsement by Mometrix of any particular political, scientific, or religious point of view.

# Mometrix

completion of this test. And finally, use this test to learn how to deal with anxiety even better next time.

**Review Video: 5 Tips to Beat Test Anxiety**
Visit mometrix.com/academy and enter code: 570656

## Important Qualification

Not all anxiety is created equal. If your test anxiety is causing major issues in your life beyond the classroom or testing center, or if you are experiencing troubling physical symptoms related to your anxiety, it may be a sign of a serious physiological or psychological condition. If this sounds like your situation, we strongly encourage you to seek professional help.

Copyright © Mometrix Media. You have been licensed one copy of this document for personal use only. Any other reproduction or redistribution is strictly prohibited. All rights reserved.
This content is provided for test preparation purposes only and does not imply an endorsement by Mometrix of any particular political, scientific, or religious point of view.

# How to Overcome Your Fear of Math

Not again. You're sitting in math class, look down at your test, and immediately start to panic. Your stomach is in knots, your heart is racing, and you break out in a cold sweat. You're staring at the paper, but everything looks like it's written in a foreign language. Even though you studied, you're blanking out on how to begin solving these problems.

Does this sound familiar? If so, then you're not alone! You may be like millions of other people who experience math anxiety. Anxiety about performing well in math is a common experience for students of all ages. In this article, we'll discuss what math anxiety is, common misconceptions about learning math, and tips and strategies for overcoming math anxiety.

## What Is Math Anxiety?

Psychologist Mark H. Ashcraft explains math anxiety as a feeling of tension, apprehension, or fear that interferes with math performance. Having math anxiety negatively impacts people's beliefs about themselves and what they can achieve. It hinders achievement within the math classroom and affects the successful application of mathematics in the real world.

### SYMPTOMS AND SIGNS OF MATH ANXIETY

To overcome math anxiety, you must recognize its symptoms. Becoming aware of the signs of math anxiety is the first step in addressing and resolving these fears.

### NEGATIVE SELF-TALK

If you have math anxiety, you've most likely said at least one of these statements to yourself:

- "I hate math."
- "I'm not good at math."
- "I'm not a math person."

The way we speak to ourselves and think about ourselves matters. Our thoughts become our words, our words become our actions, and our actions become our habits. Thinking negatively about math creates a self-fulfilling prophecy. In other words, if you take an idea as a fact, then it will come true because your behaviors will align to match it.

### AVOIDANCE

Some people who are fearful or anxious about math will tend to avoid it altogether. Avoidance can manifest in the following ways:

- Lack of engagement with math content
- Not completing homework and other assignments
- Not asking for help when needed
- Skipping class
- Avoiding math-related courses and activities

Avoidance is one of the most harmful impacts of math anxiety. If you steer clear of math at all costs, then you can't set yourself up for the success you deserve.

Copyright © Mometrix Media. You have been licensed one copy of this document for personal use only. Any other reproduction or redistribution is strictly prohibited. All rights reserved. This content is provided for test preparation purposes only and does not imply an endorsement by Mometrix of any particular political, scientific, or religious point of view.

## LACK OF MOTIVATION

Students with math anxiety may experience a lack of motivation. They may struggle to find the incentive to get engaged with what they view as a frightening subject. These students are often overwhelmed, making it difficult for them to complete or even start math assignments.

## PROCRASTINATION

Another symptom of math anxiety is procrastination. Students may voluntarily delay or postpone their classwork and assignments, even if they know there will be a negative consequence for doing so. Additionally, they may choose to wait until the last minute to start projects and homework, even when they know they need more time to put forth their best effort.

## PHYSIOLOGICAL REACTIONS

Many people with a fear of math experience physiological side effects. These may include an increase in heart rate, sweatiness, shakiness, nausea, and irregular breathing. These symptoms make it difficult to focus on the math content, causing the student even more stress and fear.

## STRONG EMOTIONAL RESPONSES

Math anxiety also affects people on an emotional level. Responding to math content with strong emotions such as panic, anger, or despair can be a sign of math anxiety.

## LOW TEST SCORES AND PERFORMANCE

Low achievement can be both a symptom and a cause of math anxiety. When someone does not take the steps needed to perform well on tests and assessments, they are less likely to pass. The more they perform poorly, the more they accept this poor performance as a fact that can't be changed.

## FEELING ALONE

People who experience math anxiety feel like they are the only ones struggling, even if the math they are working on is challenging to many people. Feeling isolated in what they perceive as failure can trigger tension or nervousness.

## FEELING OF PERMANENCY

Math anxiety can feel very permanent. You may assume that you are naturally bad at math and always will be. Viewing math as a natural ability rather than a skill that can be learned causes people to believe that nothing will help them improve. They take their current math abilities as fact and assume that they can't be changed. As a result, they give up, stop trying to improve, and avoid engaging with math altogether.

## LACK OF CONFIDENCE

People with low self-confidence in math tend to feel awkward and incompetent when asked to solve a math problem. They don't feel comfortable taking chances or risks when problem-solving because they second-guess themselves and assume they are incorrect. They don't trust in their ability to learn the content and solve problems correctly.

## PANIC

A general sense of unexplained panic is also a sign of math anxiety. You may feel a sudden sense of fear that triggers physical reactions, even when there is no apparent reason for such a response.

Copyright © Mometrix Media. You have been licensed one copy of this document for personal use only. Any other reproduction or redistribution is strictly prohibited. All rights reserved. This content is provided for test preparation purposes only and does not imply an endorsement by Mometrix of any particular political, scientific, or religious point of view.

## CAUSES OF MATH ANXIETY

Math anxiety can start at a young age and may have one or more underlying causes. Common causes of math anxiety include the following:

### THE ATTITUDE OF PARENTS OR GUARDIANS

Parents often put pressure on their children to perform well in school. Although their intentions are usually good, this pressure can lead to anxiety, especially if the student is struggling with a subject or class.

Perhaps your parents or others in your life hold negative predispositions about math based on their own experiences. For instance, if your mother once claimed she was not good at math, then you might have incorrectly interpreted this as a predisposed trait that was passed down to you.

### TEACHER INFLUENCE

Students often pick up on their teachers' attitudes about the content being taught. If a teacher is happy and excited about math, students are more likely to mirror these emotions. However, if a teacher lacks enthusiasm or genuine interest, then students are more inclined to disengage.

Teachers have a responsibility to cultivate a welcoming classroom culture that is accepting of mistakes. When teachers blame students for not understanding a concept, they create a hostile classroom environment where mistakes are not tolerated. This tension increases student stress and anxiety, creating conditions that are not conducive to inquiry and learning. Instead, when teachers normalize mistakes as a natural part of the problem-solving process, they give their students the freedom to explore and grapple with the math content. In such an environment, students feel comfortable taking chances because they are not afraid of being wrong.

Students need teachers that can help when they're having problems understanding difficult concepts. In doing so, educators may need to change how they teach the content. Since different people have unique learning styles, it's the job of the teacher to adapt to the needs of each student. Additionally, teachers should encourage students to explore alternate problem-solving strategies, even if it's not the preferred method of the educator.

### FEAR OF BEING WRONG

Embarrassing situations can be traumatic, especially for young children and adolescents. These experiences can stay with people through their adult lives. Those with math anxiety may experience a fear of being wrong, especially in front of a group of peers. This fear can be paralyzing, interfering with the student's concentration and ability to focus on the problem at hand.

### TIMED ASSESSMENTS

Timed assessments can help improve math fluency, but they often create unnecessary pressure for students to complete an unrealistic number of problems within a specified timeframe. Many studies have shown that timed assessments often result in increased levels of anxiety, reducing a student's overall competence and ability to problem-solve.

Copyright © Mometrix Media. You have been licensed one copy of this document for personal use only. Any other reproduction or redistribution is strictly prohibited. All rights reserved.
This content is provided for test preparation purposes only and does not imply an endorsement by Mometrix of any particular political, scientific, or religious point of view.

# Debunking Math Myths

There are lots of myths about math that are related to the causes and development of math-related anxiety. Although these myths have been proven to be false, many people take them as fact. Let's go over a few of the most common myths about learning math.

## MYTH: MEN ARE BETTER AT MATH THAN WOMEN

Math has a reputation for being a male-dominant subject, but this doesn't mean that men are inherently better at math than women. Many famous mathematical discoveries have been made by women. Katherine Johnson, Dame Mary Lucy Cartwright, and Marjorie Lee Brown are just a few of the many famous women mathematicians. Expecting to be good or bad at math because of your gender sets you up for stress and confusion. Math is a skill that can be learned, just like cooking or riding a bike.

## MYTH: THERE IS ONLY ONE GOOD WAY TO SOLVE MATH PROBLEMS

There are many ways to get the correct answer when it comes to math. No two people have the same brain, so everyone takes a slightly different approach to problem-solving. Moreover, there isn't one way of problem-solving that's superior to another. Your way of working through a problem might differ from someone else's, and that is okay. Math can be a highly individualized process, so the best method for you should be the one that makes you feel the most comfortable and makes the most sense to you.

## MYTH: MATH REQUIRES A GOOD MEMORY

For many years, mathematics was taught through memorization. However, learning in such a way hinders the development of critical thinking and conceptual understanding. These skill sets are much more valuable than basic memorization. For instance, you might be great at memorizing mathematical formulas, but if you don't understand what they mean, then you can't apply them to different scenarios in the real world. When a student is working from memory, they are limited in the strategies available to them to problem-solve. In other words, they assume there is only one correct way to do the math, which is the method they memorized. Having a variety of problem-solving options can help students figure out which method works best for them. Additionally, it provides students with a better understanding of how and why certain mathematical strategies work. While memorization can be helpful in some instances, it is not an absolute requirement for mathematicians.

## MYTH: MATH IS NOT CREATIVE

Math requires imagination and intuition. Contrary to popular belief, it is a highly creative field. Mathematical creativity can help in developing new ways to think about and solve problems. Many people incorrectly assume that all things are either creative or analytical. However, this black-and-white view is limiting because the field of mathematics involves both creativity and logic.

## MYTH: MATH ISN'T SUPPOSED TO BE FUN

Whoever told you that math isn't supposed to be fun is a liar. There are tons of math-based activities and games that foster friendly competition and engagement. Math is often best learned through play, and lots of mobile apps and computer games exemplify this.

Additionally, math can be an exceptionally collaborative and social experience. Studying or working through problems with a friend often makes the process a lot more fun. The excitement and satisfaction of solving a difficult problem with others is quite rewarding. Math can be fun if you look for ways to make it more collaborative and enjoyable.

Copyright © Mometrix Media. You have been licensed one copy of this document for personal use only. Any other reproduction or redistribution is strictly prohibited. All rights reserved. This content is provided for test preparation purposes only and does not imply an endorsement by Mometrix of any particular political, scientific, or religious point of view.

## MYTH: NOT EVERYONE IS CAPABLE OF LEARNING MATH

There's no such thing as a "math person." Although many people think that you're either good at math or you're not, this is simply not true. Everyone is capable of learning and applying mathematics. However, not everyone learns the same way. Since each person has a different learning style, the trick is to find the strategies and learning tools that work best for you. Some people learn best through hands-on experiences, and others find success through the use of visual aids. Others are auditory learners and learn best by hearing and listening. When people are overwhelmed or feel that math is too hard, it's often because they haven't found the learning strategy that works best for them.

## MYTH: GOOD MATHEMATICIANS WORK QUICKLY AND NEVER MAKE MISTAKES

There is no prize for finishing first in math. It's not a race, and speed isn't a measure of your ability. Good mathematicians take their time to ensure their work is accurate. As you gain more experience and practice, you will naturally become faster and more confident.

Additionally, everyone makes mistakes, including good mathematicians. Mistakes are a normal part of the problem-solving process, and they're not a bad thing. The important thing is that we take the time to learn from our mistakes, understand where our misconceptions are, and move forward.

## MYTH: YOU DON'T NEED MATH IN THE REAL WORLD

Our day-to-day lives are so infused with mathematical concepts that we often don't even realize when we're using math in the real world. In fact, most people tend to underestimate how much we do math in our everyday lives. It's involved in an enormous variety of daily activities such as shopping, baking, finances, and gardening, as well as in many careers, including architecture, nursing, design, and sales.

# Tips and Strategies for Overcoming Math Anxiety

If your anxiety is getting in the way of your level of mathematical engagement, then there are lots of steps you can take. Check out the strategies below to start building confidence in math today.

## FOCUS ON UNDERSTANDING, NOT MEMORIZATION

Don't drive yourself crazy trying to memorize every single formula or mathematical process. Instead, shift your attention to understanding concepts. Those who prioritize memorization over conceptual understanding tend to have lower achievement levels in math. Students who memorize may be able to complete some math, but they don't understand the process well enough to apply it to different situations. Memorization comes with time and practice, but it won't help alleviate math anxiety. On the other hand, conceptual understanding will give you the building blocks of knowledge you need to build up your confidence.

Copyright © Mometrix Media. You have been licensed one copy of this document for personal use only. Any other reproduction or redistribution is strictly prohibited. All rights reserved.
This content is provided for test preparation purposes only and does not imply an endorsement by Mometrix of any particular political, scientific, or religious point of view.

## REPLACE NEGATIVE SELF-TALK WITH POSITIVE SELF-TALK

Start to notice how you think about yourself. Whenever you catch yourself thinking something negative, try replacing that thought with a positive affirmation. Instead of continuing the negative thought, pause to reframe the situation. For ideas on how to get started, take a look at the table below:

| Instead of thinking... | Try thinking... |
| --- | --- |
| "I can't do this math." "I'm not a math person." | "I'm up for the challenge, and I'm training my brain in math." |
| "This problem is too hard." | "This problem is hard, so this might take some time and effort. I know I can do this." |
| "I give up." | "What strategies can help me solve this problem?" |
| "I made a mistake, so I'm not good at this." | "Everyone makes mistakes. Mistakes help me to grow and understand." |
| "I'll never be smart enough." | "I can figure this out, and I am smart enough." |

## PRACTICE MINDFULNESS

Practicing mindfulness and focusing on your breathing can help alleviate some of the physical symptoms of math anxiety. By taking deep breaths, you can remind your nervous system that you are not in immediate danger. Doing so will reduce your heart rate and help with any irregular breathing or shakiness. Taking the edge off of the physiological effects of anxiety will clear your mind, allowing your brain to focus its energy on problem-solving.

## DO SOME MATH EVERY DAY

Think about learning math as if you were learning a foreign language. If you don't use it, you lose it. If you don't practice your math skills regularly, you'll have a harder time achieving comprehension and fluency. Set some amount of time aside each day, even if it's just for a few minutes, to practice. It might take some discipline to build a habit around this, but doing so will help increase your mathematical self-assurance.

## USE ALL OF YOUR RESOURCES

Everyone has a different learning style, and there are plenty of resources out there to support all learners. When you get stuck on a math problem, think about the tools you have access to, and use them when applicable. Such resources may include flashcards, graphic organizers, study guides, interactive notebooks, and peer study groups. All of these are great tools to accommodate your individual learning style. Finding the tools and resources that work for your learning style will give you the confidence you need to succeed.

## REALIZE THAT YOU AREN'T ALONE

Remind yourself that lots of other people struggle with math anxiety, including teachers, nurses, and even successful mathematicians. You aren't the only one who panics when faced with a new or challenging problem. It's probably much more common than you think. Realizing that you aren't alone in your experience can help put some distance between yourself and the emotions you feel about math. It also helps to normalize the anxiety and shift your perspective.

Copyright © Mometrix Media. You have been licensed one copy of this document for personal use only. Any other reproduction or redistribution is strictly prohibited. All rights reserved. This content is provided for test preparation purposes only and does not imply an endorsement by Mometrix of any particular political, scientific, or religious point of view.

## ASK QUESTIONS

If there's a concept you don't understand and you've tried everything you can, then it's okay to ask for help! You can always ask your teacher or professor for help. If you're not learning math in a traditional classroom, you may want to join a study group, work with a tutor, or talk to your friends. More often than not, you aren't the only one of your peers who needs clarity on a mathematical concept. Seeking understanding is a great way to increase self-confidence in math.

## REMEMBER THAT THERE'S MORE THAN ONE WAY TO SOLVE A PROBLEM

Since everyone learns differently, it's best to focus on understanding a math problem with an approach that makes sense to you. If the way it's being taught is confusing to you, don't give up. Instead, work to understand the problem using a different technique. There's almost always more than one problem-solving method when it comes to math. Don't get stressed if one of them doesn't make sense to you. Instead, shift your focus to what does make sense. Chances are high that you know more than you think you do.

## VISUALIZATION

Visualization is the process of creating images in your mind's eye. Picture yourself as a successful, confident mathematician. Think about how you would feel and how you would behave. What would your work area look like? How would you organize your belongings? The more you focus on something, the more likely you are to achieve it. Visualizing teaches your brain that you can achieve whatever it is that you want. Thinking about success in mathematics will lead to acting like a successful mathematician. This, in turn, leads to actual success.

## FOCUS ON THE EASIEST PROBLEMS FIRST

To increase your confidence when working on a math test or assignment, try solving the easiest problems first. Doing so will remind you that you are successful in math and that you do have what it takes. This process will increase your belief in yourself, giving you the confidence you need to tackle more complex problems.

## FIND A SUPPORT GROUP

A study buddy, tutor, or peer group can go a long way in decreasing math-related anxiety. Such support systems offer lots of benefits, including a safe place to ask questions, additional practice with mathematical concepts, and an understanding of other problem-solving explanations that may work better for you. Equipping yourself with a support group is one of the fastest ways to eliminate math anxiety.

## REWARD YOURSELF FOR WORKING HARD

Recognize the amount of effort you're putting in to overcome your math anxiety. It's not an easy task, so you deserve acknowledgement. Surround yourself with people who will provide you with the positive reinforcement you deserve.

# Remember, You Can Do This!

Conquering a fear of math can be challenging, but there are lots of strategies that can help you out. Your own beliefs about your mathematical capabilities can limit your potential. Working toward a growth mindset can have a tremendous impact on decreasing math-related anxiety and building confidence. By knowing the symptoms of math anxiety and recognizing common misconceptions about learning math, you can develop a plan to address your fear of math. Utilizing the strategies discussed can help you overcome this anxiety and build the confidence you need to succeed.

Copyright © Mometrix Media. You have been licensed one copy of this document for personal use only. Any other reproduction or redistribution is strictly prohibited. All rights reserved.
This content is provided for test preparation purposes only and does not imply an endorsement by Mometrix of any particular political, scientific, or religious point of view.

# Tell Us Your Story

We at Mometrix would like to extend our heartfelt thanks to you for letting us be a part of your journey. It is an honor to serve people from all walks of life, people like you, who are committed to building the best future they can for themselves.

We know that each person's situation is unique. But we also know that, whether you are a young student or a mother of four, you care about working to make your own life and the lives of those around you better.

**That's why we want to hear your story.**

We want to know why you're taking this test. We want to know about the trials you've gone through to get here. And we want to know about the successes you've experienced after taking and passing your test.

In addition to your story, which can be an inspiration both to us and to others, we value your feedback. We want to know both what you loved about our book and what you think we can improve on.

**The team at Mometrix would be absolutely thrilled to hear from you!** So please, send us an email at tellusyourstory@mometrix.com or visit us at mometrix.com/tellusyourstory.php and let's stay in touch.

Copyright © Mometrix Media. You have been licensed one copy of this document for personal use only. Any other reproduction or redistribution is strictly prohibited. All rights reserved. This content is provided for test preparation purposes only and does not imply an endorsement by Mometrix of any particular political, scientific, or religious point of view.

# Additional Bonus Material

Due to our efforts to try to keep this book to a manageable length, we've created a link that will give you access to all of your additional bonus material:

**mometrix.com/bonus948/parapro**

Copyright © Mometrix Media. You have been licensed one copy of this document for personal use only. Any other reproduction or redistribution is strictly prohibited. All rights reserved. This content is provided for test preparation purposes only and does not imply an endorsement by Mometrix of any particular political, scientific, or religious point of view.

Made in United States
Orlando, FL
06 March 2023

30781317R00241